Chevrolet Corsica & Beretta Automotive Repair Manual

**by Jon LaCourse
and John H Haynes**
Member of the Guild of Motoring Writers

Models covered:
Chevrolet Corsica and Beretta – all models
1987 through 1995

(10W6 – 1628)   ABCDE

Haynes Publishing Group
Sparkford Nr Yeovil
Somerset BA22 7JJ England

Haynes North America, Inc
861 Lawrence Drive
Newbury Park
California 91320 USA

Acknowledgements

We are grateful for the help and cooperation of the Chevrolet Motor Division of General Motors Corporation for assistance with technical information, certain illustrations and vehicle photos. The Champion Spark Plug Company supplied the illustrations of various spark plug conditions. Technical writers who contributed to this project include Larry Warren, Mike Stubblefield, Robert Maddox and Ken Freund. Special thanks to Jim Feuling of Feuling Engineering, Inc. of Ventura, California, for supplying the Quad-4 engine used for the photographs in Chapter 2.

© **Haynes North America, Inc. 1990, 1992, 1994**

With permission from J. H. Haynes & Co. Ltd.

A book in the **Haynes Automotive Repair Manual Series**

Printed in the USA

ISBN 1 56392 133 2

Library of Congress Catalog Card Number 94-073118

While every attempt is made to ensure that the information in this manual is correct, no liability can be accepted by the authors or publishers for loss, damage or injury caused by any errors in, or omissions from, the information given.

Contents

Chevrolet Corsica

Chevrolet Beretta GTU

About this manual

Its purpose

The purpose of this manual is to help you get the best value from your vehicle. It can do so in several ways. It can help you decide what work must be done, even if you choose to have it done by a dealer service department or a repair shop; it provides information and procedures for routine maintenance and servicing; and it offers diagnostic and repair procedures to follow when trouble occurs.

We hope you use the manual to tackle the work yourself. For many simpler jobs, doing it yourself may be quicker than arranging an appointment to get the vehicle into a shop and making the trips to leave it and pick it up. More importantly, a lot of money can be saved by avoiding the expense the shop must pass on to you to cover its labor and overhead costs. An added benefit is the sense of satisfaction and accomplishment that you feel after doing the job yourself.

Using the manual

The manual is divided into Chapters. Each Chapter is divided into numbered Sections, which are headed in bold type between horizontal lines. Each Section consists of consecutively numbered paragraphs.

At the beginning of each numbered section you will be referred to any illustrations which apply to the procedures in that section. The reference numbers used in illustration captions pinpoint the pertinent Section and the Step within that section. That is, illustration 3.2 means the illustration refers to Section 3 and Step (or paragraph) 2 within that Section.

Procedures, once described in the text, are not normally repeated. When it's necessary to refer to another Chapter, the reference will be given as Chapter and Section number. Cross references given without use of the word "Chapter" apply to Sections and/or paragraphs in the same Chapter. For example, "see Section 8" means in the same Chapter.

References to the left or right side of the vehicle assume you are sitting in the driver's seat, facing forward.

Even though we have prepared this manual with extreme care, neither the publisher nor the author can accept responsibility for any errors in, or omissions from, the information given.

NOTE

A **Note** provides information necessary to properly complete a procedure or information which will make the procedure easier to understand.

CAUTION

A **Caution** provides a special procedure or special steps which must be taken while completing the procedure where the **Caution** is found. Not heeding a **Caution** can result in damage to the assembly being worked on.

WARNING

A **Warning** provides a special procedure or special steps which must be taken while completing the procedure where the **Warning** is found. Not heeding a **Warning** can result in personal injury.

Introduction to the Chevrolet Corsica and Beretta

The Chevrolet Corsica four-door sedan and Beretta two-door coupe are popular mid-size, front wheel drive vehicles first introduced for the 1987 model year.

Engines used in these vehicles include the 2.0 and 2.2 liter overhead valve (OHV) four-cylinder, the 2.3 liter overhead cam (OHC) Quad-4 four-cylinder (later years only), the 2.8 liter V6 and the 3.1 liter V6, which is an enlarged version of the 2.8 liter engine.

Throttle body injection (TBI) is used on the overhead valve four-cylinder engines through 1991, while multi-port fuel injection is standard on the Quad-4, 1992 and later 2.2L four-cylinder engines and all V6 engines.

The engine drives the front wheels through either a manual or automatic transaxle via unequal length driveaxles. The power assisted rack and pinion steering is mounted behind the engine.

The front suspension is composed of MacPherson struts, three-point control arms and a stabilizer bar. The rear suspension is semi-independent, made up of a solid axle with trailing arms, a stabilizer bar, coil springs and shock absorbers.

The brakes are disc at the front and drum at the rear with power assist as standard equipment. An Anti-lock Brake System (ABS) is available as an option on some models.

Vehicle identification numbers

Modifications are a continuing and unpublicized part of vehicle manufacturing. Since spare parts manuals and lists are compiled on a numerical basis, the individual vehicle numbers are essential to correctly identify the component required.

Vehicle Identification Number (VIN)

This very important identification number is stamped on a plate attached to the left side of the dashboard and is visible through the driver's side of the windshield (see illustration). The VIN also appears on the Vehicle Certificate of Title and Registration. It contains valuable information such as where and when the vehicle was manufactured, the model year and the body style.

Body identification plate

This metal plate is located on the top side of the radiator support. Like the VIN, it contains important information concerning the production of the vehicle as well as information about how the vehicle came equipped from the factory. It's especially useful for matching the color and type of paint during repair work.

Service parts identification label

This label is located in the trunk (see illustration). It lists the VIN number, wheelbase, paint number, options and other information specific to the vehicle it's attached to. Always refer to this label when ordering parts.

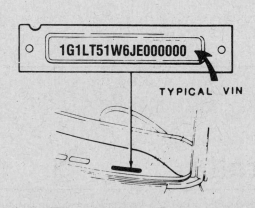

TYPICAL VIN

The Vehicle Identification Number (VIN) is on a plate attached to the top of the dashboard on the driver's side of the vehicle – it can be seen through the windshield

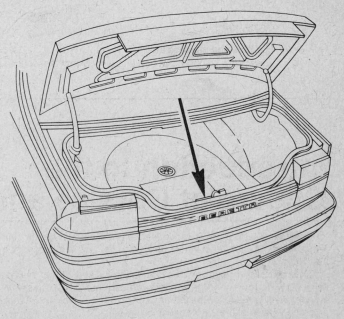

The Service parts identification label is located in the trunk (arrow)

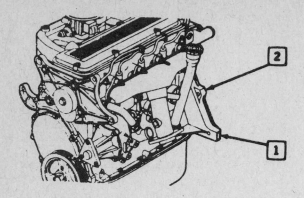

2.0/2.2 liter four-cylinder engine number locations

1   VIN number   2   Engine code

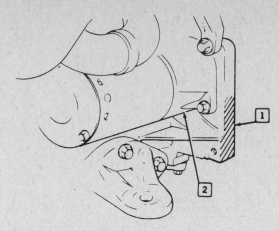

2.3 liter four-cylinder (Quad-4) engine number location

1   Partial VIN number   2   Starter motor

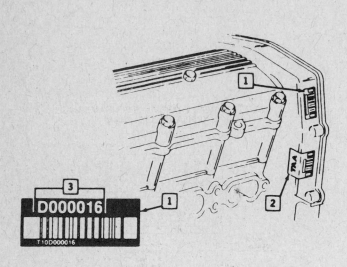

2.3 liter four-cylinder (Quad-4) engine code label location

1   Traceability label   3   Unit number
2   Verification label

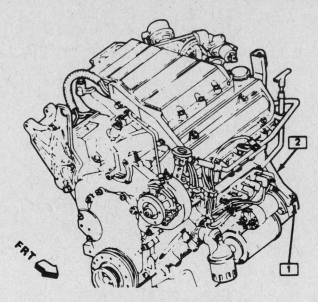

V6 engine number locations

1   VIN number   2   Engine code

Engine identification numbers

The engine code number on 2.0/2.2 liter four-cylinder engines is stamped on a pad on the radiator side, at the rear of the block **(see illustration)**. The 2.3 liter OHC (Quad-4) engine VIN number is stamped into the rear of the block, near the starter motor **(see illustration)**. The Quad-4 engine also has a code label attached to the rear edge of the timing belt housing **(see illustration)**. On V6 engines, the code number is found on a pad on the rear of the block, just above the starter motor **(see illustration)**.

Manual transaxle number

The VIN number on the Isuzu 76 mm five-speed transaxle is stamped into either the front edge or the upper edge of the case, where it joins the bellhousing **(see illustration)**. The Muncie transaxle has an adhesive-backed identification label attached to the rear of the case and an ID

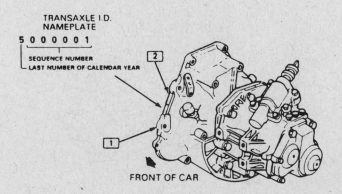

Isuzu transaxle number locations

1   VIN number   2   Optional VIN location

MODEL YEAR
(9 = 1989)

BUILD DAY OF MONTH
01 = 1ST DAY
15 = 15TH DAY

P 9 B 17

HM-282

BUILD MONTH
A = JANUARY
B = FEBRUARY
C = MARCH
D = APRIL
E = MAY
H = JUNE
K = JULY
M = AUGUST
P = SEPTEMBER
R = OCTOBER
S = NOVEMBER
T = DECEMBER

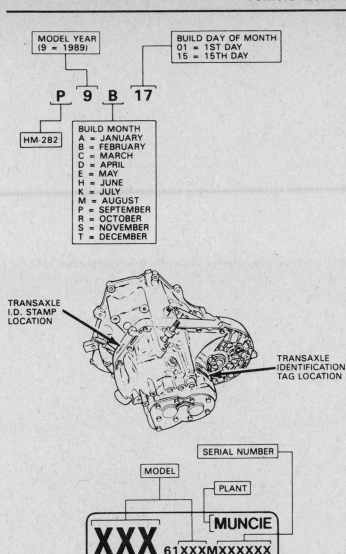

TRANSAXLE
I.D. STAMP
LOCATION

TRANSAXLE
IDENTIFICATION
TAG LOCATION

SERIAL NUMBER

MODEL

PLANT

MUNCIE

XXX 61XXXMXXXXXX

Muncie transaxle number locations

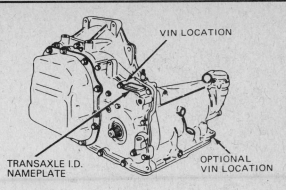

VIN LOCATION

TRANSAXLE I.D.
NAMEPLATE

OPTIONAL
VIN LOCATION

THM 125/125-C TRANSAXLE I.D. NAMEPLATE LOCATION

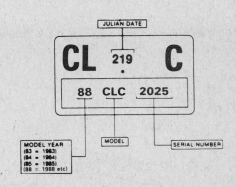

JULIAN DATE

CL 219 **C**

88 CLC 2025

MODEL YEAR
(83 = 1983)
(84 = 1984)
(85 = 1985)
(88 = 1988 etc)

MODEL

SERIAL NUMBER

**THM 125/125-C TRANSAXLE I.D. NAMEPLATE
YPSILANTI, MICHIGAN**

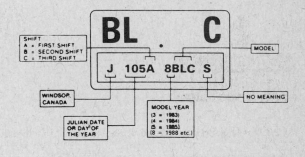

SHIFT
A = FIRST SHIFT
B = SECOND SHIFT
C = THIRD SHIFT

BL . **C**

J 105A 8BLC S

MODEL

WINDSOR,
CANADA

NO MEANING

JULIAN DATE
OR DAY OF
THE YEAR

MODEL YEAR
(3 = 1983)
(4 = 1984)
(5 = 1985)
(8 = 1988 etc.)

**THM 125/125-C TRANSAXLE I.D. NAMEPLATE
WINDSOR, CANADA**

Automatic transaxle number locations

Getrag transaxle number locations

1   VIN number   2   Optional VIN location

number stamped into the front **(see illustration)**. On the Getrag five-speed transaxle, the VIN is on a pad at the front (radiator) side of the case edge, near the bellhousing **(see illustration)**. If the transaxle label is missing or unreadable, use the Service parts identification label to determine which transaxle was installed at the factory.

Automatic transaxle number

The automatic transaxle nameplate/VIN number is attached to the upper surface of the case, near the rear **(see illustration)**.

Vehicle Emissions Control Information label

This label is found in the engine compartment, usually on the air cleaner intake (see Chapter 6 for an illustration of the label).

Buying parts

Replacement parts are available from many sources, which generally fall into one of two categories – authorized dealer parts departments and independent retail auto parts stores. Our advice concerning these parts is as follows:

Retail auto parts stores: Good auto parts stores will stock frequently needed components which wear out relatively fast, such as clutch components, exhaust systems, brake parts, tune-up parts, etc. These stores often supply new or reconditioned parts on an exchange basis, which can save a considerable amount of money. Discount auto parts stores are often very good places to buy materials and parts needed for general vehicle maintenance such as oil, grease, filters, spark plugs, belts, touch-up paint, bulbs, etc. They also usually sell tools and general accessories, have con-venient hours, charge lower prices and can often be found not far from home.

Authorized dealer parts department: This is the best source for parts which are unique to the vehicle and not generally available else-where (such as major engine parts, transmission parts, trim pieces, etc.).

Warranty information: If the vehicle is still covered under warranty, be sure that any replacement parts purchased – regardless of the source – do not invalidate the warranty!

To be sure of obtaining the correct parts, have engine and chassis numbers available and, if possible, take the old parts along for positive identification.

Maintenance techniques, tools and working facilities

Maintenance techniques

There are a number of techniques involved in maintenance and repair that will be referred to throughout this manual. Application of these tech-niques will enable the home mechanic to be more efficient, better orga-nized and capable of performing the various tasks properly, which will ensure that the repair job is thorough and complete.

Fasteners

Fasteners are nuts, bolts, studs and screws used to hold two or more parts together. There are a few things to keep in mind when working with fasteners. Almost all of them use a locking device of some type, either a lockwasher, locknut, locking tab or thread adhesive. All threaded fasten-ers should be clean and straight, with undamaged threads and undam-aged corners on the hex head where the wrench fits. Develop the habit of replacing all damaged nuts and bolts with new ones. Special locknuts with nylon or fiber inserts can only be used once. If they are removed, they lose their locking ability and must be replaced with new ones.

Rusted nuts and bolts should be treated with a penetrating fluid to ease removal and prevent breakage. Some mechanics use turpentine in a spout-type oil can, which works quite well. After applying the rust pene-trant, let it work for a few minutes before trying to loosen the nut or bolt. Badly rusted fasteners may have to be chiseled or sawed off or removed with a special nut breaker, available at tool stores.

If a bolt or stud breaks off in an assembly, it can be drilled and removed with a special tool commonly available for this purpose. Most automotive machine shops can perform this task, as well as other repair procedures, such as the repair of threaded holes that have been stripped out.

Flat washers and lockwashers, when removed from an assembly, should always be replaced exactly as removed. Replace any damaged washers with new ones. Never use a lockwasher on any soft metal surface (such as aluminum), thin sheet metal or plastic.

Fastener sizes

For a number of reasons, automobile manufacturers are making wider and wider use of metric fasteners. Therefore, it is important to be able to tell the difference between standard (sometimes called U.S. or SAE) and metric hardware, since they cannot be interchanged.

All bolts, whether standard or metric, are sized according to diameter, thread pitch and length. For example, a standard 1/2 – 13 x 1 bolt is 1/2 inch in diameter, has 13 threads per inch and is 1 inch long. An M12 – 1.75 x 25 metric bolt is 12 mm in diameter, has a thread pitch of 1.75 mm (the distance between threads) and is 25 mm long. The two bolts are nearly identical, and easily confused, but they are not interchangeable.

In addition to the differences in diameter, thread pitch and length, metric and standard bolts can also be distinguished by examining the bolt heads. To begin with, the distance across the flats on a standard bolt head is measured in inches, while the same dimension on a metric bolt is sized in millimeters (the same is true for nuts). As a result, a standard wrench should not be used on a metric bolt and a metric wrench should not be

used on a standard bolt. Also, most standard bolts have slashes radiating out from the center of the head to denote the grade or strength of the bolt, which is an indication of the amount of torque that can be applied to it. The greater the number of slashes, the greater the strength of the bolt. Grades 0 through 5 are commonly used on automobiles. Metric bolts have a property class (grade) number, rather than a slash, molded into their heads to indicate bolt strength. In this case, the higher the number, the stronger the bolt. Property class numbers 8.8, 9.8 and 10.9 are commonly used on automobiles.

Strength markings can also be used to distinguish standard hex nuts from metric hex nuts. Many standard nuts have dots stamped into one side, while metric nuts are marked with a number. The greater the number of dots, or the higher the number, the greater the strength of the nut.

Metric studs are also marked on their ends according to property class (grade). Larger studs are numbered (the same as metric bolts), while smaller studs carry a geometric code to denote grade.

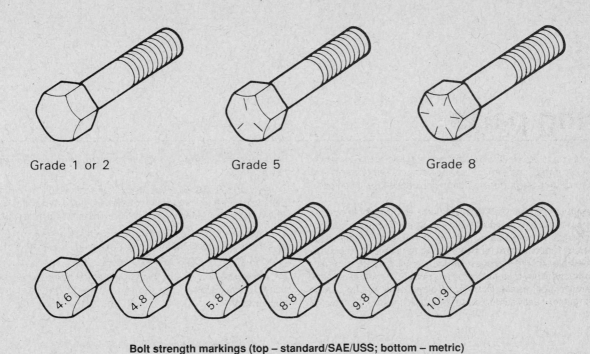

Grade 1 or 2　　　Grade 5　　　Grade 8

Bolt strength markings (top – standard/SAE/USS; bottom – metric)

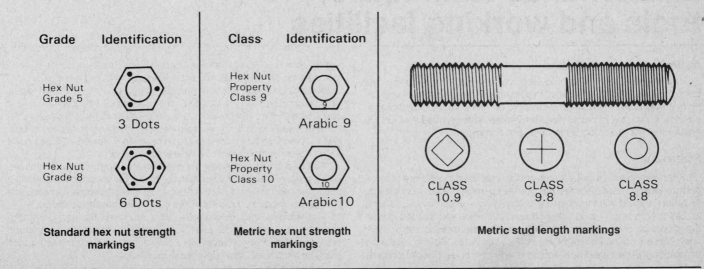

Grade	Identification	Class	Identification
Hex Nut Grade 5	3 Dots	Hex Nut Property Class 9	Arabic 9
Hex Nut Grade 8	6 Dots	Hex Nut Property Class 10	Arabic 10

Standard hex nut strength markings

Metric hex nut strength markings

CLASS 10.9　　　CLASS 9.8　　　CLASS 8.8

Metric stud length markings

It should be noted that many fasteners, especially Grades 0 through 2, have no distinguishing marks on them. When such is the case, the only way to determine whether it is standard or metric is to measure the thread pitch or compare it to a known fastener of the same size.

Standard fasteners are often referred to as SAE, as opposed to metric. However, it should be noted that SAE technically refers to a non-metric *fine thread* fastener only. Coarse thread non-metric fasteners are referred to as USS sizes.

Since fasteners of the same size (both standard and metric) may have different strength ratings, be sure to reinstall any bolts, studs or nuts removed from your vehicle in their original locations. Also, when replacing a fastener with a new one, make sure that the new one has a strength rating equal to or greater than the original.

Tightening sequences and procedures

Most threaded fasteners should be tightened to a specific torque value (torque is the twisting force applied to a threaded component such as a nut or bolt). Overtightening the fastener can weaken it and cause it to break, while undertightening can cause it to eventually come loose. Bolts, screws and studs, depending on the material they are made of and their thread diameters, have specific torque values, many of which are noted in the Specifications at the beginning of each Chapter. Be sure to follow the torque recommendations closely. For fasteners not assigned a specific torque, a general torque value chart is presented here as a guide. These torque values are for dry (unlubricated) fasteners threaded into steel or cast iron (not aluminum). As was previously mentioned, the size and grade of a fastener determine the amount of torque that can safely be

Metric thread sizes	Ft-lbs	Nm
M-6	6 to 9	9 to 12
M-8	14 to 21	19 to 28
M-10	28 to 40	38 to 54
M-12	50 to 71	68 to 96
M-14	80 to 140	109 to 154
Pipe thread sizes		
1/8	5 to 8	7 to 10
1/4	12 to 18	17 to 24
3/8	22 to 33	30 to 44
1/2	25 to 35	34 to 47
U.S. thread sizes		
1/4 – 20	6 to 9	9 to 12
5/16 – 18	12 to 18	17 to 24
5/16 – 24	14 to 20	19 to 27
3/8 – 16	22 to 32	30 to 43
3/8 – 24	27 to 38	37 to 51
7/16 – 14	40 to 55	55 to 74
7/16 – 20	40 to 60	55 to 81
1/2 – 13	55 to 80	75 to 108

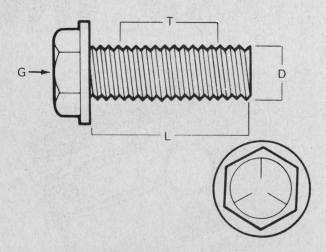

Standard (SAE and USS) bolt dimensions/grade marks

G   Grade marks (bolt length)
L   Length (in inches)
T   Thread pitch (number of threads per inch)
D   Nominal diameter (in inches)

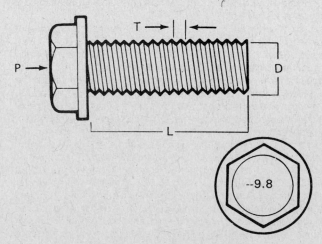

Metric bolt dimensions/grade marks

P   Property class (bolt strength)
L   Length (in millimeters)
T   Thread pitch (distance between threads in millimeters)
D   Diameter

applied to it. The figures listed here are approximate for Grade 2 and Grade 3 fasteners. Higher grades can tolerate higher torque values.

Fasteners laid out in a pattern, such as cylinder head bolts, oil pan bolts, differential cover bolts, etc., must be loosened or tightened in sequence to avoid warping the component. This sequence will normally be shown in the appropriate Chapter. If a specific pattern is not given, the following procedures can be used to prevent warping.

Initially, the bolts or nuts should be assembled finger-tight only. Next, they should be tightened one full turn each, in a criss-cross or diagonal pattern. After each one has been tightened one full turn, return to the first one and tighten them all one-half turn, following the same pattern. Finally, tighten each of them one-quarter turn at a time until each fastener has been tightened to the proper torque. To loosen and remove the fasteners, the procedure would be reversed.

Component disassembly

Component disassembly should be done with care and purpose to help ensure that the parts go back together properly. Always keep track of the sequence in which parts are removed. Make note of special characteristics or marks on parts that can be installed more than one way, such as a grooved thrust washer on a shaft. It is a good idea to lay the disassembled parts out on a clean surface in the order that they were removed. It may also be helpful to make sketches or take instant photos of components before removal.

When removing fasteners from a component, keep track of their locations. Sometimes threading a bolt back in a part, or putting the washers and nut back on a stud, can prevent mix-ups later. If nuts and bolts cannot be returned to their original locations, they should be kept in a compartmented box or a series of small boxes. A cupcake or muffin tin is ideal for this purpose, since each cavity can hold the bolts and nuts from a particular area (i.e. oil pan bolts, valve cover bolts, engine mount bolts, etc.). A pan of this type is especially helpful when working on assemblies with very small parts, such as the carburetor, alternator, valve train or interior dash and trim pieces. The cavities can be marked with paint or tape to identify the contents.

Whenever wiring looms, harnesses or connectors are separated, it is a good idea to identify the two halves with numbered pieces of masking tape so they can be easily reconnected.

Gasket sealing surfaces

Throughout any vehicle, gaskets are used to seal the mating surfaces between two parts and keep lubricants, fluids, vacuum or pressure contained in an assembly.

Many times these gaskets are coated with a liquid or paste-type gasket sealing compound before assembly. Age, heat and pressure can sometimes cause the two parts to stick together so tightly that they are very difficult to separate. Often, the assembly can be loosened by striking it with a soft-face hammer near the mating surfaces. A regular hammer can be used if a block of wood is placed between the hammer and the part. Do not hammer on cast parts or parts that could be easily damaged. With any particularly stubborn part, always recheck to make sure that every fastener has been removed.

Avoid using a screwdriver or bar to pry apart an assembly, as they can easily mar the gasket sealing surfaces of the parts, which must remain smooth. If prying is absolutely necessary, use an old broom handle, but keep in mind that extra clean up will be necessary if the wood splinters.

After the parts are separated, the old gasket must be carefully scraped off and the gasket surfaces cleaned. Stubborn gasket material can be soaked with rust penetrant or treated with a special chemical to soften it so it can be easily scraped off. A scraper can be fashioned from a piece of copper tubing by flattening and sharpening one end. Copper is recommended because it is usually softer than the surfaces to be scraped, which reduces the chance of gouging the part. Some gaskets can be removed with a wire brush, but regardless of the method used, the mating surfaces must be left clean and smooth. If for some reason the gasket surface is gouged, then a gasket sealer thick enough to fill scratches will have to be used during reassembly of the components. For most applications, a non-drying (or semi-drying) gasket sealer should be used.

Hose removal tips

Warning: *If the vehicle is equipped with air conditioning, do not disconnect any of the A/C hoses without first having the system depressurized by a dealer service department or a service station.*

Hose removal precautions closely parallel gasket removal precautions. Avoid scratching or gouging the surface that the hose mates against or the connection may leak. This is especially true for radiator hoses. Because of various chemical reactions, the rubber in hoses can bond itself to the metal spigot that the hose fits over. To remove a hose, first loosen the hose clamps that secure it to the spigot. Then, with slip-joint pliers, grab the hose at the clamp and rotate it around the spigot. Work it back and forth until it is completely free, then pull it off. Silicone or other lubricants will ease removal if they can be applied between the hose and the outside of the spigot. Apply the same lubricant to the inside of the hose and the outside of the spigot to simplify installation.

As a last resort (and if the hose is to be replaced with a new one anyway), the rubber can be slit with a knife and the hose peeled from the spigot. If this must be done, be careful that the metal connection is not damaged.

If a hose clamp is broken or damaged, do not reuse it. Wire-type clamps usually weaken with age, so it is a good idea to replace them with screw-type clamps whenever a hose is removed.

Tools

A selection of good tools is a basic requirement for anyone who plans to maintain and repair his or her own vehicle. For the owner who has few tools, the initial investment might seem high, but when compared to the spiraling costs of professional auto maintenance and repair, it is a wise one.

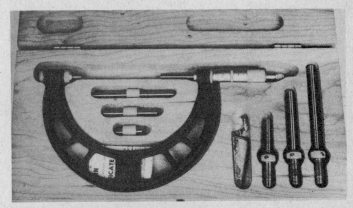

Micrometer set

Dial indicator set

Dial caliper

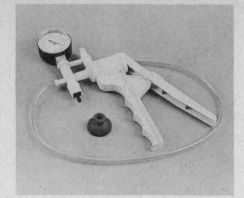

Hand-operated vacuum pump

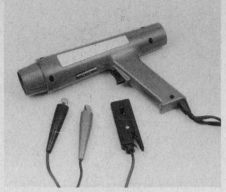

Timing light

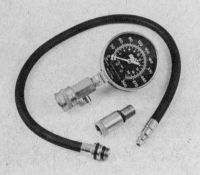

Compression gauge with spark plug hole adapter

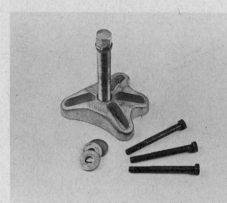

Damper/steering wheel puller

General purpose puller

Hydraulic lifter removal tool

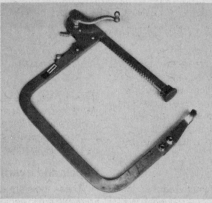

Valve spring compressor

Valve spring compressor

Ridge reamer

Piston ring groove cleaning tool

Ring removal/installation tool

Ring compressor

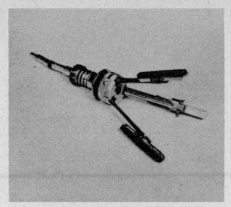

Cylinder hone

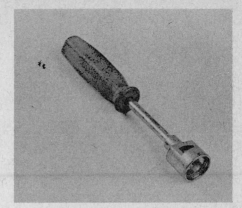

Brake hold-down spring tool

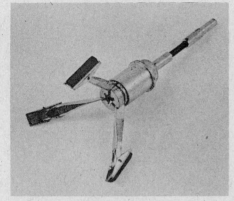

Brake cylinder hone

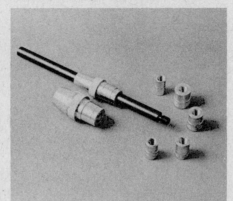

Clutch plate alignment tool

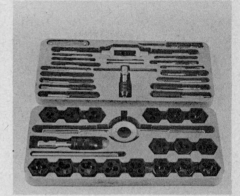

Tap and die set

To help the owner decide which tools are needed to perform the tasks detailed in this manual, the following tool lists are offered: *Maintenance and minor repair, Repair/overhaul* and *Special.*

The newcomer to practical mechanics should start off with the maintenance and minor repair tool kit, which is adequate for the simpler jobs performed on a vehicle. Then, as confidence and experience grow, the owner can tackle more difficult tasks, buying additional tools as they are needed. Eventually the basic kit will be expanded into the repair and overhaul tool set. Over a period of time, the experienced do-it-yourselfer will assemble a tool set complete enough for most repair and overhaul procedures and will add tools from the special category when it is felt that the expense is justified by the frequency of use.

Maintenance and minor repair tool kit

The tools in this list should be considered the minimum required for performance of routine maintenance, servicing and minor repair work. We recommend the purchase of combination wrenches (box-end and open-end combined in one wrench). While more expensive than open end wrenches, they offer the advantages of both types of wrench.

Combination wrench set (1/4-inch to 1 inch or 6 mm to 19 mm)
Adjustable wrench, 8 inch
Spark plug wrench with rubber insert
Spark plug gap adjusting tool
Feeler gauge set
Brake bleeder wrench
Standard screwdriver (5/16-inch x 6 inch)
Phillips screwdriver (No. 2 x 6 inch)
Combination pliers – 6 inch
Hacksaw and assortment of blades
Tire pressure gauge
Grease gun
Oil can
Fine emery cloth
Wire brush

Battery post and cable cleaning tool
Oil filter wrench
Funnel (medium size)
Safety goggles
Jackstands(2)
Drain pan

Note: *If basic tune-ups are going to be part of routine maintenance, it will be necessary to purchase a good quality stroboscopic timing light and combination tachometer/dwell meter. Although they are included in the list of special tools, it is mentioned here because they are absolutely necessary for tuning most vehicles properly.*

Repair and overhaul tool set

These tools are essential for anyone who plans to perform major repairs and are in addition to those in the maintenance and minor repair tool kit. Included is a comprehensive set of sockets which, though expensive, are invaluable because of their versatility, especially when various extensions and drives are available. We recommend the 1/2-inch drive over the 3/8-inch drive. Although the larger drive is bulky and more expensive, it has the capacity of accepting a very wide range of large sockets. Ideally, however, the mechanic should have a 3/8-inch drive set and a 1/2-inch drive set.

Socket set(s)
Reversible ratchet
Extension – 10 inch
Universal joint
Torque wrench (same size drive as sockets)
Ball peen hammer – 8 ounce
Soft-face hammer (plastic/rubber)
Standard screwdriver (1/4-inch x 6 inch)
Standard screwdriver (stubby – 5/16-inch)
Phillips screwdriver (No. 3 x 8 inch)
Phillips screwdriver (stubby – No. 2)

Pliers – vise grip
Pliers – lineman's
Pliers – needle nose
Pliers – snap-ring (internal and external)
Cold chisel – 1/2-inch
Scribe
Scraper (made from flattened copper tubing)
Centerpunch
Pin punches (1/16,.1/8, 3/16-inch)
Steel rule/straightedge – 12 inch
Allen wrench set (1/8 to 3/8-inch or 4 mm to 10 mm)
A selection of files
Wire brush (large)
Jackstands (second set)
Jack (scissor or hydraulic type)

Note: *Another tool which is often useful is an electric drill motor with a chuck capacity of 3/8-inch and a set of good quality drill bits.*

Special tools

The tools in this list include those which are not used regularly, are expensive to buy, or which need to be used in accordance with their manufacturer's instructions. Unless these tools will be used frequently, it is not very economical to purchase many of them. A consideration would be to split the cost and use between yourself and a friend or friends. In addition, most of these tools can be obtained from a tool rental shop on a temporary basis.

This list primarily contains only those tools and instruments widely available to the public, and not those special tools produced by the vehicle manufacturer for distribution to dealer service departments. Occasionally, references to the manufacturer's special tools are included in the text of this manual. Generally, an alternative method of doing the job without the special tool is offered. However, sometimes there is no alternative to their use. Where this is the case, and the tool cannot be purchased or borrowed, the work should be turned over to the dealer service department or an automotive repair shop.

Valve spring compressor
Piston ring groove cleaning tool
Piston ring compressor
Piston ring installation tool
Cylinder compression gauge
Cylinder ridge reamer
Cylinder surfacing hone
Cylinder bore gauge
Micrometers and/or dial calipers
Hydraulic lifter removal tool
Balljoint separator
Universal-type puller
Impact screwdriver
Dial indicator set
Stroboscopic timing light (inductive pick-up)
Hand operated vacuum/pressure pump
Tachometer/dwell meter
Universal electrical multimeter
Cable hoist
Brake spring removal and installation tools
Floor jack

Buying tools

For the do-it-yourselfer who is just starting to get involved in vehicle maintenance and repair, there are a number of options available when purchasing tools. If maintenance and minor repair is the extent of the work to be done, the purchase of individual tools is satisfactory. If, on the other hand, extensive work is planned, it would be a good idea to purchase a modest tool set from one of the large retail chain stores. A set can usually be bought at a substantial savings over the individual tool prices, and they often come with a tool box. As additional tools are needed, add–on sets, individual tools and a larger tool box can be purchased to expand the tool selection. Building a tool set gradually allows the cost of the tools to be spread over a longer period of time and gives the mechanic the freedom to choose only those tools that will actually be used.

Tool stores will often be the only source of some of the special tools that are needed, but regardless of where tools are bought, try to avoid cheap ones, especially when buying screwdrivers and sockets, because they won't last very long. The expense involved in replacing cheap tools will eventually be greater than the initial cost of quality tools.

Care and maintenance of tools

Good tools are expensive, so it makes sense to treat them with respect. Keep them clean and in usable condition and store them properly when not in use. Always wipe off any dirt, grease or metal chips before putting them away. Never leave tools lying around in the work area. Upon completion of a job, always check closely under the hood for tools that may have been left there so they won't get lost during a test drive.

Some tools, such as screwdrivers, pliers, wrenches and sockets, can be hung on a panel mounted on the garage or workshop wall, while others should be kept in a tool box or tray. Measuring instruments, gauges, meters, etc. must be carefully stored where they cannot be damaged by weather or impact from other tools.

When tools are used with care and stored properly, they will last a very long time. Even with the best of care, though, tools will wear out if used frequently. When a tool is damaged or worn out, replace it. Subsequent jobs will be safer and more enjoyable if you do.

Working facilities

Not to be overlooked when discussing tools is the workshop. If anything more than routine maintenance is to be carried out, some sort of suitable work area is essential.

It is understood, and appreciated, that many home mechanics do not have a good workshop or garage available, and end up removing an engine or doing major repairs outside. It is recommended, however, that the overhaul or repair be completed under the cover of a roof.

A clean, flat workbench or table of comfortable working height is an absolute necessity. The workbench should be equipped with a vise that has a jaw opening of at least four inches.

As mentioned previously, some clean, dry storage space is also required for tools, as well as the lubricants, fluids, cleaning solvents, etc. which soon become necessary.

Sometimes waste oil and fluids, drained from the engine or cooling system during normal maintenance or repairs, present a disposal problem. To avoid pouring them on the ground or into a sewage system, pour the used fluids into large containers, seal them with caps and take them to an authorized disposal site or recycling center. Plastic jugs, such as old antifreeze containers, are ideal for this purpose.

Always keep a supply of old newspapers and clean rags available. Old towels are excellent for mopping up spills. Many mechanics use rolls of paper towels for most work because they are readily available and disposable. To help keep the area under the vehicle clean, a large cardboard box can be cut open and flattened to protect the garage or shop floor.

Whenever working over a painted surface, such as when leaning over a fender to service something under the hood, always cover it with an old blanket or bedspread to protect the finish. Vinyl covered pads, made especially for this purpose, are available at auto parts stores.

Booster battery (jump) starting

Observe these precautions when using a booster battery to start a vehicle:

a) Before connecting the booster battery, make sure the ignition switch is in the Off position.
b) Turn off the lights, heater and other electrical loads.
c) Your eyes should be shielded. Safety goggles are a good idea.
d) Make sure the booster battery is the same voltage as the dead one in the vehicle.
e) The two vehicles MUST NOT TOUCH each other!
f) Make sure the transmission is in Neutral (manual) or Park (automatic).
g) If the booster battery is not a maintenance-free type, remove the vent caps and lay a cloth over the vent holes.

Connect the red jumper cable to the positive (+) terminals of each battery.

Connect one end of the black jumper cable to the negative (–) terminal of the booster battery. The other end of this cable should be connected to a good ground on the vehicle to be started, such as a bolt or bracket on the engine block **(see illustrations)**. Make sure the cable will not come into contact with the fan, drivebelts or other moving parts of the engine.

Start the engine using the booster battery, then, with the engine running at idle speed, disconnect the jumper cables in the reverse order of connection.

Adapters designed to make jumper cable connections to side terminal batteries safer and easier are available at auto parts stores

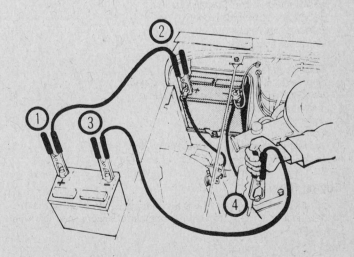

Make the booster battery cable connections in the numerical order shown (note that the negative cable of the booster battery is NOT attached to the negative terminal of the dead battery)

Jacking and towing

Jacking

Warning: *The jack supplied with the vehicle should only be used for raising the vehicle when changing a tire or placing jackstands under the frame. Never work under the vehicle or start the engine while the jack is being used as the only means of support.*

The vehicle must be on a level surface with the wheels blocked and the transaxle in Park (automatic) or Reverse (manual). Apply the parking brake if the front of the vehicle must be raised. Make sure no one is in the vehicle as it's being raised with the jack.

Remove the jack, lug nut wrench and spare tire (if needed) from the trunk. If a tire is being replaced, use the lug wrench to remove the wheel cover. **Warning:** *Wheel covers may have sharp edges – be very careful not to cut yourself.* Loosen the lug nuts one-half turn, but leave them in place until the tire is raised off the ground. **Note:** *Some models have nylon lug nut caps. Loosen them very carefully with the wrench, then remove them by hand before loosening the lug nuts. Also, some vehicles have one locking lug nut that must be loosened with a special anti-theft wrench adapter.*

Position the jack under the side of the vehicle at the indicated jacking point. There's a front and rear jacking point on each side of the vehicle **(see illustration)**.

Turn the jack handle clockwise until the tire clears the ground. Remove the lug nuts and pull the tire off. Clean the mating surfaces of the hub and wheel, then install the spare. Replace the lug nuts with the bevelled edges facing in and tighten them snugly. Don't attempt to tighten them completely until the vehicle is lowered or it could slip off the jack.

Turn the jack handle counterclockwise to lower the vehicle. Remove the jack and tighten the lug nuts in a criss-cross pattern. If possible, tighten the nuts with a torque wrench (see Chapter 1 for the torque figures). If you don't have access to a torque wrench, have the nuts checked by a service station or repair shop as soon as possible. **Caution:** *The compact spare included with these vehicles is intended for temporary use only. Have the tire repaired and reinstall it on the vehicle at the earliest opportunity and don't exceed 50 mph with the spare tire on the car.*

Install the wheel cover or nylon lug nut caps, then stow the tire, jack and wrench and unblock the wheels.

Towing

These vehicles can be towed with all four wheels on the ground, provided that speeds don't exceed 35 mph and the distance is less than 50 miles, otherwise transaxle damage can result.

Equipment specifically designed for towing should be used. It must be attached to the main structural members of the vehicle, not the bumpers or brackets.

Safety is a major consideration when towing and all applicable state and local laws must be obeyed. A safety chain must be used at all times. The parking brake must be released and the transaxle must be in Neutral. The steering must be unlocked (ignition switch in the Off position). Remember that power steering and power brakes won't work with the engine off.

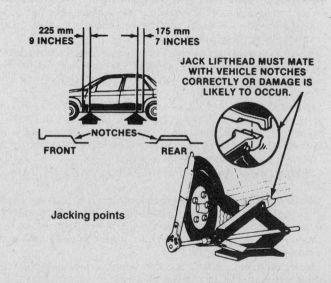

225 mm 9 INCHES   175 mm 7 INCHES

JACK LIFTHEAD MUST MATE WITH VEHICLE NOTCHES CORRECTLY OR DAMAGE IS LIKELY TO OCCUR.

NOTCHES

FRONT   REAR

Jacking points

Automotive chemicals and lubricants

A number of automotive chemicals and lubricants are available for use during vehicle maintenance and repair. They include a wide variety of products ranging from cleaning solvents and degreasers to lubricants and protective sprays for rubber, plastic and vinyl.

Cleaners

Carburetor cleaner and choke cleaner is a strong solvent for gum, varnish and carbon. Most carburetor cleaners leave a dry-type lubricant film which will not harden or gum up. Because of this film it is not recommended for use on electrical components.

Brake system cleaner is used to remove grease and brake fluid from the brake system, where clean surfaces are absolutely necessary. It leaves no residue and often eliminates brake squeal caused by contaminants.

Electrical cleaner removes oxidation, corrosion and carbon deposits from electrical contacts, restoring full current flow. It can also be used to clean spark plugs, carburetor jets, voltage regulators and other parts where an oil-free surface is desired.

Demoisturants remove water and moisture from electrical components such as alternators, voltage regulators, electrical connectors and fuse blocks. They are non-conductive, non-corrosive and non-flammable.

Degreasers are heavy-duty solvents used to remove grease from the outside of the engine and from chassis components. They can be sprayed or brushed on and, depending on the type, are rinsed off either with water or solvent.

Lubricants

Motor oil is the lubricant formulated for use in engines. It normally contains a wide variety of additives to prevent corrosion and reduce foaming and wear. Motor oil comes in various weights (viscosity ratings) from 5 to 80. The recommended weight of the oil depends on the season, temperature and the demands on the engine. Light oil is used in cold climates and under light load conditions. Heavy oil is used in hot climates and where high loads are encountered. Multi-viscosity oils are designed to have characteristics of both light and heavy oils and are available in a number of weights from 5W-20 to 20W-50.

Gear oil is designed to be used in differentials, manual transmissions and other areas where high-temperature lubrication is required.

Chassis and wheel bearing grease is a heavy grease used where increased loads and friction are encountered, such as for wheel bearings, balljoints, tie-rod ends and universal joints.

High-temperature wheel bearing grease is designed to withstand the extreme temperatures encountered by wheel bearings in disc brake equipped vehicles. It usually contains molybdenum disulfide (moly), which is a dry-type lubricant.

White grease is a heavy grease for metal-to-metal applications where water is a problem. White grease stays soft under both low and high temperatures (usually from −100 to +190-degrees F), and will not wash off or dilute in the presence of water.

Assembly lube is a special extreme pressure lubricant, usually containing moly, used to lubricate high-load parts (such as main and rod bearings and cam lobes) for initial start-up of a new engine. The assembly lube lubricates the parts without being squeezed out or washed away until the engine oiling system begins to function.

Silicone lubricants are used to protect rubber, plastic, vinyl and nylon parts.

Graphite lubricants are used where oils cannot be used due to contamination problems, such as in locks. The dry graphite will lubricate metal parts while remaining uncontaminated by dirt, water, oil or acids. It is electrically conductive and will not foul electrical contacts in locks such as the ignition switch.

Moly penetrants loosen and lubricate frozen, rusted and corroded fasteners and prevent future rusting or freezing.

Heat-sink grease is a special electrically non-conductive grease that is used for mounting electronic ignition modules where it is essential that heat is transferred away from the module.

Sealants

RTV sealant is one of the most widely used gasket compounds. Made from silicone, RTV is air curing, it seals, bonds, waterproofs, fills surface irregularities, remains flexible, doesn't shrink, is relatively easy to remove, and is used as a supplementary sealer with almost all low and medium temperature gaskets.

Anaerobic sealant is much like RTV in that it can be used either to seal gaskets or to form gaskets by itself. It remains flexible, is solvent resistant and fills surface imperfections. The difference between an anaerobic sealant and an RTV-type sealant is in the curing. RTV cures when exposed to air, while an anaerobic sealant cures only in the absence of air. This means that an anaerobic sealant cures only after the assembly of parts, sealing them together.

Thread and pipe sealant is used for sealing hydraulic and pneumatic fittings and vacuum lines. It is usually made from a teflon compound, and comes in a spray, a paint-on liquid and as a wrap-around tape.

Chemicals

Anti-seize compound prevents seizing, galling, cold welding, rust and corrosion in fasteners. High-temperature anti-seize, usually made with copper and graphite lubricants, is used for exhaust system and exhaust manifold bolts.

Anaerobic locking compounds are used to keep fasteners from vibrating or working loose and cure only after installation, in the absence of air. Medium strength locking compound is used for small nuts, bolts and screws that may be removed later. High-strength locking compound is for large nuts, bolts and studs which aren't removed on a regular basis.

Oil additives range from viscosity index improvers to chemical treatments that claim to reduce internal engine friction. It should be noted that most oil manufacturers caution against using additives with their oils.

Gas additives perform several functions, depending on their chemical makeup. They usually contain solvents that help dissolve gum and varnish that build up on carburetor, fuel injection and intake parts. They also serve to break down carbon deposits that form on the inside surfaces of the combustion chambers. Some additives contain upper cylinder lubricants for valves and piston rings, and others contain chemicals to remove condensation from the gas tank.

Miscellaneous

Brake fluid is specially formulated hydraulic fluid that can withstand the heat and pressure encountered in brake systems. Care must be taken so this fluid does not come in contact with painted surfaces or plastics. An opened container should always be resealed to prevent contamination by water or dirt.

Weatherstrip adhesive is used to bond weatherstripping around doors, windows and trunk lids. It is sometimes used to attach trim pieces.

Undercoating is a petroleum-based, tar-like substance that is designed to protect metal surfaces on the underside of the vehicle from corrosion. It also acts as a sound-deadening agent by insulating the bottom of the vehicle.

Waxes and polishes are used to help protect painted and plated surfaces from the weather. Different types of paint may require the use of different types of wax and polish. Some polishes utilize a chemical or abrasive cleaner to help remove the top layer of oxidized (dull) paint on older vehicles. In recent years many non-wax polishes that contain a wide variety of chemicals such as polymers and silicones have been introduced. These non-wax polishes are usually easier to apply and last longer than conventional waxes and polishes.

Safety first!

Regardless of how enthusiastic you may be about getting on with the job at hand, take the time to ensure that your safety is not jeopardized. A moment's lack of attention can result in an accident, as can failure to observe certain simple safety precautions. The possibility of an accident will always exist, and the following points should not be considered a comprehensive list of all dangers. Rather, they are intended to make you aware of the risks and to encourage a safety conscious approach to all work you carry out on your vehicle.

Essential DOs and DON'Ts

DON'T rely on a jack when working under the vehicle. Always use approved jackstands to support the weight of the vehicle and place them under the recommended lift or support points.

DON'T attempt to loosen extremely tight fasteners (i.e. wheel lug nuts) while the vehicle is on a jack – it may fall.

DON'T start the engine without first making sure that the transmission is in Neutral (or Park where applicable) and the parking brake is set.

DON'T remove the radiator cap from a hot cooling system – let it cool or cover it with a cloth and release the pressure gradually.

DON'T attempt to drain the engine oil until you are sure it has cooled to the point that it will not burn you.

DON'T touch any part of the engine or exhaust system until it has cooled sufficiently to avoid burns.

DON'T siphon toxic liquids such as gasoline, antifreeze and brake fluid by mouth, or allow them to remain on your skin.

DON'T inhale brake lining dust – it is potentially hazardous (see Asbestos below)

DON'T allow spilled oil or grease to remain on the floor – wipe it up before someone slips on it.

DON'T use loose fitting wrenches or other tools which may slip and cause injury.

DON'T push on wrenches when loosening or tightening nuts or bolts. Always try to pull the wrench toward you. If the situation calls for pushing the wrench away, push with an open hand to avoid scraped knuckles if the wrench should slip.

DON'T attempt to lift a heavy component alone – get someone to help you.

DON'T rush or take unsafe shortcuts to finish a job.

DON'T allow children or animals in or around the vehicle while you are working on it.

DO wear eye protection when using power tools such as a drill, sander, bench grinder, etc. and when working under a vehicle.

DO keep loose clothing and long hair well out of the way of moving parts.

DO make sure that any hoist used has a safe working load rating adequate for the job.

DO get someone to check on you periodically when working alone on a vehicle.

DO carry out work in a logical sequence and make sure that everything is correctly assembled and tightened.

DO keep chemicals and fluids tightly capped and out of the reach of children and pets.

DO remember that your vehicle's safety affects that of yourself and others. If in doubt on any point, get professional advice.

Asbestos

Certain friction, insulating, sealing, and other products – such as brake linings, brake bands, clutch linings, torque converters, gaskets, etc. – contain asbestos. *Extreme care must be taken to avoid inhalation of dust from such products since it is hazardous to health.* If in doubt, assume that they *do* contain asbestos.

Fire

Remember at all times that gasoline is highly flammable. Never smoke or have any kind of open flame around when working on a vehicle. But the risk does not end there. A spark caused by an electrical short circuit, by two metal surfaces contacting each other, or even by static electricity built up in your body under certain conditions, can ignite gasoline vapors, which in a confined space are highly explosive. Do not, under any circumstances, use gasoline for cleaning parts. Use an approved safety solvent.

Always disconnect the battery ground (–) cable *at the battery* before working on any part of the fuel system or electrical system. Never risk spilling fuel on a hot engine or exhaust component.

It is strongly recommended that a fire extinguisher suitable for use on fuel and electrical fires be kept handy in the garage or workshop at all times. Never try to extinguish a fuel or electrical fire with water.

Fumes

Certain fumes are highly toxic and can quickly cause unconsciousness and even death if inhaled to any extent. Gasoline vapor falls into this category, as do the vapors from some cleaning solvents. Any draining or pouring of such volatile fluids should be done in a well ventilated area.

When using cleaning fluids and solvents, read the instructions on the container carefully. Never use materials from unmarked containers.

Never run the engine in an enclosed space, such as a garage. Exhaust fumes contain carbon monoxide, which is extremely poisonous. If you need to run the engine, always do so in the open air, or at least have the rear of the vehicle outside the work area.

If you are fortunate enough to have the use of an inspection pit, never drain or pour gasoline and never run the engine while the vehicle is over the pit. The fumes, being heavier than air, will concentrate in the pit with possibly lethal results.

The battery

Never create a spark or allow a bare light bulb near a battery. They normally give off a certain amount of hydrogen gas, which is highly explosive.

Always disconnect the battery ground (–) cable *at the battery* before working on the fuel or electrical systems.

If possible, loosen the filler caps or cover when charging the battery from an external source (this does not apply to sealed or maintenancefree batteries). Do not charge at an excessive rate or the battery may burst.

Take care when adding water to a non maintenance–free battery and when carrying a battery. The electrolyte, even when diluted, is very corrosive and should not be allowed to contact clothing or skin.

Always wear eye protection when cleaning the battery to prevent the caustic deposits from entering your eyes.

Household current

When using an electric power tool, inspection light, etc., which operates on household current, always make sure that the tool is correctly connected to its plug and that, where necessary, it is properly grounded. Do not use such items in damp conditions and, again, do not create a spark or apply excessive heat in the vicinity of fuel or fuel vapor.

Secondary ignition system voltage

A severe electric shock can result from touching certain parts of the ignition system (such as the spark plug wires) when the engine is running or being cranked, particularly if components are damp or the insulation is defective. In the case of an electronic ignition system, the secondary system voltage is much higher and could prove fatal.

Conversion factors

Length (distance)

Inches (in)	X 25.4	= Millimetres (mm)	X 0.0394	= Inches (in)
Feet (ft)	X 0.305	= Metres (m)	X 3.281	= Feet (ft)
Miles	X 1.609	= Kilometres (km)	X 0.621	= Miles

Volume (capacity)

Cubic inches (cu in; in³)	X 16.387	= Cubic centimetres (cc; cm³)	X 0.061	= Cubic inches (cu in; in³)
Imperial pints (Imp pt)	X 0.568	= Litres (l)	X 1.76	= Imperial pints (Imp pt)
Imperial quarts (Imp qt)	X 1.137	= Litres (l)	X 0.88	= Imperial quarts (Imp qt)
Imperial quarts (Imp qt)	X 1.201	= US quarts (US qt)	X 0.833	= Imperial quarts (Imp qt)
US quarts (US qt)	X 0.946	= Litres (l)	X 1.057	= US quarts (US qt)
Imperial gallons (Imp gal)	X 4.546	= Litres (l)	X 0.22	= Imperial gallons (Imp gal)
Imperial gallons (Imp gal)	X 1.201	= US gallons (US gal)	X 0.833	= Imperial gallons (Imp gal)
US gallons (US gal)	X 3.785	= Litres (l)	X 0.264	= US gallons (US gal)

Mass (weight)

Ounces (oz)	X 28.35	= Grams (g)	X 0.035	= Ounces (oz)
Pounds (lb)	X 0.454	= Kilograms (kg)	X 2.205	= Pounds (lb)

Force

Ounces-force (ozf; oz)	X 0.278	= Newtons (N)	X 3.6	= Ounces-force (ozf; oz)
Pounds-force (lbf; lb)	X 4.448	= Newtons (N)	X 0.225	= Pounds-force (lbf; lb)
Newtons (N)	X 0.1	= Kilograms-force (kgf; kg)	X 9.81	= Newtons (N)

Pressure

Pounds-force per square inch (psi; lbf/in²; lb/in²)	X 0.070	= Kilograms-force per square centimetre (kgf/cm²; kg/cm²)	X 14.223	= Pounds-force per square inch (psi; lbf/in²; lb/in²)
Pounds-force per square inch (psi; lbf/in²; lb/in²)	X 0.068	= Atmospheres (atm)	X 14.696	= Pounds-force per square inch (psi; lbf/in²; lb/in²)
Pounds-force per square inch (psi; lbf/in²; lb/in²)	X 0.069	= Bars	X 14.5	= Pounds-force per square inch (psi; lbf/in²; lb/in²)
Pounds-force per square inch (psi; lbf/in²; lb/in²)	X 6.895	= Kilopascals (kPa)	X 0.145	= Pounds-force per square inch (psi; lbf/in²; lb/in²)
Kilopascals (kPa)	X 0.01	= Kilograms-force per square centimetre (kgf/cm²; kg/cm²)	X 98.1	= Kilopascals (kPa)

Torque (moment of force)

Pounds-force inches (lbf in; lb in)	X 1.152	= Kilograms-force centimetre (kgf cm; kg cm)	X 0.868	= Pounds-force inches (lbf in; lb in)
Pounds-force inches (lbf in; lb in)	X 0.113	= Newton metres (Nm)	X 8.85	= Pounds-force inches (lbf in; lb in)
Pounds-force inches (lbf in; lb in)	X 0.083	= Pounds-force feet (lbf ft; lb ft)	X 12	= Pounds-force inches (lbf in; lb in)
Pounds-force feet (lbf ft; lb ft)	X 0.138	= Kilograms-force metres (kgf m; kg m)	X 7.233	= Pounds-force feet (lbf ft; lb ft)
Pounds-force feet (lbf ft; lb ft)	X 1.356	= Newton metres (Nm)	X 0.738	= Pounds-force feet (lbf ft; lb ft)
Newton metres (Nm)	X 0.102	= Kilograms-force metres (kgf m; kg m)	X 9.804	= Newton metres (Nm)

Power

Horsepower (hp)	X 745.7	= Watts (W)	X 0.0013	= Horsepower (hp)

Velocity (speed)

Miles per hour (miles/hr; mph)	X 1.609	= Kilometres per hour (km/hr; kph)	X 0.621	= Miles per hour (miles/hr; mph)

Fuel consumption*

Miles per gallon, Imperial (mpg)	X 0.354	= Kilometres per litre (km/l)	X 2.825	= Miles per gallon, Imperial (mpg)
Miles per gallon, US (mpg)	X 0.425	= Kilometres per litre (km/l)	X 2.352	= Miles per gallon, US (mpg)

Temperature

Degrees Fahrenheit = (°C x 1.8) + 32   Degrees Celsius (Degrees Centigrade; °C) = (°F - 32) x 0.56

*It is common practice to convert from miles per gallon (mpg) to litres/100 kilometres (l/100km), where mpg (Imperial) x l/100 km = 282 and mpg (US) x l/100 km = 235

Troubleshooting

Contents

This section provides an easy reference guide to the more common problems which may occur during the operation of your vehicle. Various symptoms and their possible causes are grouped under headings denoting components or systems, such as *Engine, Cooling system,* etc. They also refer to the Chapter and/or Section that deals with the problem.

Remember that successful troubleshooting isn't a mysterious "black art" practiced only by professional mechanics. It's simply the result of knowledge combined with an intelligent, systematic approach to a problem. Always use a process of elimination, starting with the simplest solution and working through to the most complex – and never overlook the obvious. Anyone can run the gas tank dry or leave the lights on overnight, so don't assume that you're exempt from such oversights.

Finally, always establish a clear idea why a problem has occurred and take steps to ensure that it doesn't happen again. If the electrical system fails because of a poor connection, check all other connections in the system to make sure they don't fail as well. If a particular fuse continues to blow, find out why – don't just go on replacing fuses. Remember, failure of a small component can often be indicative of potential failure or incorrect functioning of a more important component or system.

Engine and performance

1 Engine will not rotate when attempting to start

1 Battery terminal connections loose or corroded (Chapter 1).
2 Battery discharged or faulty (Chapter 1).
3 Automatic transaxle not completely engaged in Park (Chapter 7) or clutch not completely depressed (Chapter 8).
4 Broken, loose or disconnected wiring in the starting circuit (Chapters 5 and 12).
5 Starter motor pinion jammed in flywheel ring gear (Chapter 5).
6 Starter solenoid faulty (Chapter 5).
7 Starter motor faulty (Chapter 5).
8 Ignition switch faulty (Chapter 12).
9 Starter pinion or flywheel teeth worn or broken (Chapter 5).

2 Engine rotates but will not start

1 Fuel tank empty.
2 Battery discharged (engine rotates slowly) (Chapter 5).
3 Battery terminal connections loose or corroded (Chapter 1).
4 Leaking fuel injector(s), fuel pump, pressure regulator, etc. (Chapter 4).
5 Fuel not reaching fuel injection system (Chapter 4).
6 Ignition components damp or damaged (Chapter 5).
7 Worn, faulty or incorrectly gapped spark plugs (Chapter 1).
8 Broken, loose or disconnected wiring in the starting circuit (Chapter 5).
9 Broken, loose or disconnected wires at the ignition coil(s) or faulty coil(s) (Chapter 5).

3 Engine hard to start when cold

1 Battery discharged or low (Chapter 1).
2 Fuel system malfunctioning (Chapter 4).
3 Injector(s) leaking (Chapter 4).

4 Engine hard to start when hot

1 Air filter clogged (Chapter 1).
2 Fuel not reaching the fuel injection system (Chapter 4).
3 Corroded battery connections, especially ground (Chapter 1).

5 Starter motor noisy or excessively rough in engagement

1 Pinion or flywheel gear teeth worn or broken (Chapter 5).
2 Starter motor mounting bolts loose or missing (Chapter 5).

6 Engine starts but stops immediately

1 Loose or faulty electrical connections at coil pack or alternator (Chapter 5).
2 Insufficient fuel reaching the fuel injectors (Chapter 4).
3 Vacuum leak at the gasket between the intake manifold/plenum and throttle body (Chapters 1 and 4).

7 Oil puddle under engine

1 Oil pan gasket and/or oil pan drain bolt seal leaking (Chapters 1 and 2).
2 Oil pressure sending unit leaking (Chapter 2).
3 Rocker arm cover gaskets leaking (Chapter 2).
4 Engine oil seals leaking (Chapter 2).
5 Timing cover sealant or sealing flange leaking (Chapter 2).

8 Engine lopes while idling or idles erratically

1 Vacuum leakage (Chapter 4).
2 Leaking EGR valve or plugged PCV valve (Chapters 1 and 6).
3 Air filter clogged (Chapter 1).
4 Fuel pump not delivering sufficient fuel to the fuel injection system (Chapter 4).
5 Leaking head gasket (Chapter 2).
6 Timing chain and/or gears worn (Chapter 2).
7 Camshaft lobes worn (Chapter 2).

9 Engine misses at idle speed

1 Spark plugs worn or not gapped properly (Chapter 1).
2 Faulty spark plug wires (Chapter 1).
3 Vacuum leaks (Chapters 1 and 4).
4 Incorrect ignition timing (Chapter 5).
5 Uneven or low compression (Chapter 2).

10 Engine misses throughout driving speed range

1 Fuel filter clogged and/or impurities in the fuel system (Chapters 1 and 4).
2 Low fuel output at the injector (Chapter 4).
3 Faulty or incorrectly gapped spark plugs (Chapter 1).
4 Incorrect ignition timing (Chapter 5).
5 Leaking spark plug wires (Chapter 1).
6 Faulty emission system components (Chapter 6).
7 Low or uneven cylinder compression pressures (Chapter 2).
8 Weak or faulty ignition system (Chapter 5).
9 Vacuum leak in fuel injection system, intake manifold or vacuum hoses (Chapter 4).

11 Engine stumbles on acceleration

1 Spark plugs fouled (Chapter 1).
2 Fuel injection system needs adjustment or repair (Chapter 4).
3 Fuel filter clogged (Chapter 1).

4   Incorrect ignition timing (Chapter 5).
5   Intake manifold air leak (Chapter 4).

12   Engine surges while holding accelerator steady

1   Intake air leak (Chapter 4).
2   Fuel pump faulty (Chapter 4).
3   Loose fuel injector harness connections (Chapter 4)..
4   Defective ECM (Chapter 6).

13   Engine stalls

1   Idle speed incorrect (Chapters 1 and 4).
2   Fuel filter clogged and/or water and impurities in the fuel system (Chapters 1 and 4).
3   Ignition components damp or damaged (Chapter 5).
4   Faulty emissions system components (Chapter 6).
5   Faulty or incorrectly gapped spark plugs (Chapter 1).
6   Faulty spark plug wires (Chapter 1).
7   Vacuum leak in the fuel injection system, intake manifold or vacuum hoses (Chapter 4).

14   Engine lacks power

1   Incorrect ignition timing (Chapter 5).
2   Faulty or incorrectly gapped spark plugs (Chapter 1).
3   Fuel injection system out of adjustment or malfunctioning (Chapter 4).
4   Faulty coil(s) (Chapter 5).
5   Brakes binding (Chapter 1).
6   Automatic transaxle fluid level incorrect (Chapter 1).
7   Clutch slipping (Chapter 8).
8   Fuel filter clogged and/or impurities in the fuel system (Chapter 1).
9   Emission control system not functioning properly (Chapter 6).
10 Low or uneven cylinder compression pressures (Chapter 2).

15   Engine backfires

1   Emissions system not functioning properly (Chapter 6).
2   Ignition timing incorrect (Chapter 5).
3   Faulty secondary ignition system (Chapter 5).
4   Fuel injection system in need of adjustment or worn excessively (Chapter 4).
5   Vacuum leak at fuel injectors, intake manifold or vacuum hoses (Chapter 4).
6   Valves sticking (Chapter 2).

16   Pinging or knocking engine sounds during acceleration or uphill

1   Incorrect grade of fuel.
2   Ignition timing incorrect (Chapter 5).
3   Fuel injection system in need of adjustment (Chapter 4).
4   Improper or damaged spark plugs or wires (Chapter 1).
5   Worn or damaged ignition components (Chapter 5).
6   Faulty emissions system (Chapter 6).
7   Vacuum leak (Chapter 4).

17   Engine runs with oil pressure light on

1   Low oil level (Chapter 1).

2   Idle rpm below specification (Chapter 1).
3   Short in wiring circuit (Chapter 12).
4   Faulty oil pressure sender (Chapter 2).
5   Worn engine bearings and/or oil pump (Chapter 2).

18   Engine diesels (continues to run) after switching off

1   Idle speed too high (Chapters 1 and 4).
2   Thermo-controlled air cleaner heat valve not operating properly (TBI equipped engines only) (Chapter 6).
3   Excessive engine operating temperature (Chapter 3).

Engine electrical system

19   Battery will not hold a charge

1   Alternator drivebelt defective or not adjusted properly (Chapter 1).
2   Battery terminals loose or corroded (Chapter 1).
3   Alternator not charging properly (Chapter 5).
4   Loose, broken or faulty wiring in the charging circuit (Chapter 5).
5   Short in vehicle wiring (Chapters 5 and 12).
6   Internally defective battery (Chapters 1 and 5).

20   Voltage warning light fails to go out

1   Faulty alternator or charging circuit (Chapter 5).
2   Alternator drivebelt defective or out of adjustment (Chapter 1).
3   Alternator voltage regulator inoperative (Chapter 5).

21   Voltage warning light fails to come on when key is turned on

1   Warning light bulb defective (Chapter 12).
2   Fault in the printed circuit, dash wiring or bulb holder (Chapter 12).

Fuel system

22   Excessive fuel consumption

1   Dirty or clogged air filter element (Chapter 1).
2   Incorrectly set ignition timing (Chapter 5).
3   Emissions system not functioning properly (Chapter 6).
4   Fuel injection internal parts worn or damaged (Chapter 4).
5   Low tire pressure or incorrect tire size (Chapter 1).

23   Fuel leakage and/or fuel odor

1   Leak in a fuel feed or vent line (Chapter 4).
2   Tank overfilled.
3   Evaporative canister filter clogged (Chapters 1 and 6).
4   Fuel injector internal parts excessively worn (Chapter 4).

Cooling system

24   Overheating

1   Insufficient coolant in system (Chapter 1).
2   Water pump drivebelt defective or out of adjustment (Chapter 1).
3   Radiator core blocked or grille restricted (Chapter 3).

4   Thermostat faulty (Chapter 3).
5   Electric cooling fan blades broken or cracked (Chapter 3).
6   Radiator cap not maintaining proper pressure (Chapter 3).
7   Ignition timing incorrect (Chapter 5).

25   Overcooling

Faulty thermostat (Chapter 3).

26   External coolant leakage

1   Deteriorated/damaged hoses or loose clamps (Chapters 1 and 3).
2   Water pump seal defective (Chapters 1 and 3).
3   Leakage from radiator core or header tank (Chapter 3).
4   Engine drain or water jacket core plugs leaking (Chapter 2).

27   Internal coolant leakage

1   Leaking cylinder head gasket (Chapter 2).
2   Cracked cylinder bore or cylinder head (Chapter 2).

28   Coolant loss

1   Too much coolant in system (Chapter 1).
2   Coolant boiling away because of overheating (Chapter 3).
3   Internal or external leakage (Chapter 3).
4   Faulty radiator cap (Chapter 3).

29   Poor coolant circulation

1   Inoperative water pump (Chapter 3).
2   Restriction in cooling system (Chapters 1 and 3).
3   Water pump drivebelt defective or out of adjustment (Chapter 1).
4   Thermostat sticking (Chapter 3).

Clutch

30   Pedal travels to floor – no pressure or very little resistance

1   Master or slave cylinder faulty (Chapter 8).
2   Hose/pipe burst or leaking (Chapter 8).
3   Connections leaking (Chapter 8).
4   No fluid in reservoir (Chapter 8).
5   If fluid is present in master cylinder dust cover, rear master cylinder seal has failed (Chapter 8).
6   If fluid level in reservoir rises as pedal is depressed, master cylinder center valve seal is faulty (Chapter 8).
7   Broken release bearing or fork (Chapter 8).

31   Fluid in area of master cylinder dust cover and on pedal

Rear seal failure in master cylinder (Chapter 8).

32   Fluid on slave cylinder

Slave cylinder seal faulty (Chapter 8).

33   Pedal feels spongy when depressed

Air in system (Chapter 8).

34   Unable to select gears

1   Faulty transaxle (Chapter 7).
2   Faulty clutch disc (Chapter 8).
3   Fork and bearing not assembled properly (Chapter 8).
4   Faulty pressure plate (Chapter 8).
5   Pressure plate-to-flywheel bolts loose (Chapter 8).

35   Clutch slips (engine speed increases with no increase in vehicle speed)

1   Clutch plate worn (Chapter 8).
2   Clutch plate is oil soaked by leaking rear main seal (Chapter 8).
3   Clutch plate not seated. It may take 30 or 40 normal starts for a new one to seat.
4   Warped pressure plate or flywheel (Chapter 8).
5   Weak diaphragm spring (Chapter 8).
6   Clutch plate overheated. Allow to cool.

36   Grabbing (chattering) as clutch is engaged

1   Oil soaked, burned or glazed linings (Chapter 8).
2   Worn or loose engine or transaxle mounts (Chapters 2 and 7).
3   Worn splines on clutch plate hub (Chapter 8).
4   Warped pressure plate or flywheel (Chapter 8).

37   Noise in clutch area

1   Fork shaft improperly installed (Chapter 8).
2   Faulty release bearing (Chapter 8).

38   Clutch pedal stays on floor

1   Fork shaft binding in housing (Chapter 8).
2   Broken release bearing or fork (Chapter 8).

39   High pedal effort

1   Fork shaft binding in housing (Chapter 8).
2   Pressure plate faulty (Chapter 8).

Manual transaxle

40   Vibration

1   Rough wheel bearing (Chapter 10).
2   Damaged driveaxle (Chapter 8).
3   Out-of-round tires (Chapter 1).

4   Tire out-of-balance (Chapter 10).
5   Worn or damaged CV joint (Chapter 8).

41   Noisy in Neutral with engine running

. Damaged clutch release bearing (Chapter 8).

42   Noisy in one particular gear

1   Damaged or worn constant mesh gears (Chapter 7).
2   Damaged or worn synchronizers (Chapter 7).

43   Noisy in all gears

1   Insufficient lubricant (Chapter 1).
2   Damaged or worn bearings (Chapter 7).
3   Worn or damaged input gear shaft and/or output gear shaft (Chapter 7).

44   Slips out of gear

1   Worn or improperly adjusted linkage (Chapter 7).
2   Transaxle loose on engine (Chapter 7).
3   Shift linkage does not work freely, binds (Chapter 7).
4   Input shaft bearing retainer broken or loose (Chapter 7).
5   Dirt between clutch cover and engine housing (Chapter 7).
6   Worn shift fork (Chapter 7).

45   Leaks lubricant

1   Excessive amount of lubricant in transaxle (Chapter 1).
2   Loose or broken input shaft bearing retainer (Chapter 7).
3   Input shaft bearing retainer O-ring and/or lip seal damaged (Chapter 7).

Automatic transaxle

Note: *Due to the complexity of the automatic transaxle, it's difficult for the home mechanic to properly diagnose and service this component. For problems other than the following, the vehicle should be taken to a dealer service department or a transmission shop.*

46   Fluid leakage

1   Automatic transmission fluid is a deep red color. Fluid leaks should not be confused with engine oil, which can easily be blown by air flow to the transaxle.
2   To pinpoint a leak, first remove all built-up dirt and grime from the transaxle housing with degreasing agents and/or steam cleaning. Drive the vehicle at low speeds so air flow will not blow the leak far from its source. Raise the vehicle and determine where the leak is coming from. Common areas of leakage are:
   a) Pan (Chapters 1 and 7)
   b) Filler pipe (Chapter 7)
   c) Fluid cooler lines (Chapter 7)
   d) Speedometer gear or sensor (Chapter 7)

47   Transaxle fluid brown or has a burned smell

Transaxle overheated. Change fluid (Chapter 1).

48   General shift mechanism problems

1   Chapter 7 Part B deals with checking and adjusting the shift linkage on automatic transaxles. Common problems which may be attributed to poorly adjusted linkage are:
   a) Engine starting in gears other than Park or Neutral.
   b) Indicator on shifter pointing to a gear other than the one actually being used.
   c) Vehicle moves when in Park.
2   Refer to Chapter 7 Part B for the shift linkage adjustment procedure.

49   Transaxle will not downshift with accelerator pedal pressed to the floor

Throttle valve (TV) cable out of adjustment (Chapter 7).

50   Engine will start in gears other than Park or Neutral

Starter safety switch malfunctioning (Chapter 7).

51   Transaxle slips, shifts roughly, is noisy or has no drive in forward or reverse gears

There are many probable causes for the above problems, but the home mechanic should be concerned with only one possibility – fluid level. Before taking the vehicle to a repair shop, check the level and condition of the fluid as described in Chapter 1.
Correct the fluid level as necessary or change the fluid and filter if needed. If the problem persists, have a professional diagnose the probable cause.

Driveaxles

52   Clicking noise in turns

Worn or damaged outer CV joint. Check for cut or damaged boots (Chapter 1). Repair as necessary (Chapter 8).

53   Knock or clunk when accelerating after coasting

Worn or damaged outer CV joint. Check for cut or damaged boots (Chapter 1). Repair as necessary (Chapter 8).

54   Shudder or vibration during acceleration

1   Excessive inner CV joint angle. Check and correct as necessary (Chapter 8).
2   Worn or damaged CV joints. Repair or replace as necessary (Chapter 8).
3   Sticking inner joint assembly. Correct or replace as necessary (Chapter 8).

Brakes

Note: *Before assuming that a brake problem exists, make sure . . .*
- a) The tires are in good condition and properly inflated (Chapter 1).
- b) The front end alignment is correct (Chapter 10).
- c) The vehicle isn't loaded with weight in an unequal manner.

55   Vehicle pulls to one side during braking

1   Incorrect tire pressures (Chapter 1).
2   Front end out of line (have the front end aligned).
3   Unmatched tires on same axle.
4   Restricted brake lines or hoses (Chapter 9).
5   Malfunctioning brake assembly (Chapter 9).
6   Loose suspension parts (Chapter 10).
7   Loose brake calipers (Chapter 9).

56   Noise (high-pitched squeal when the brakes are applied)

Front disc brake pads worn out. The noise comes from the wear sensor rubbing against the disc. Replace pads with new ones immediately (Chapter 9).

57   Brake roughness or chatter (pedal pulsates)

1   Excessive front brake disc lateral runout (Chapter 9).
2   Parallelism not within specifications (Chapter 9).
3   Uneven pad wear caused by caliper not sliding due to improper clearance or dirt (Chapter 9).
4   Defective brake disc (Chapter 9).
5   Rear brake drum out-of-round.

58   Excessive pedal effort required to stop vehicle

1   Malfunctioning power brake booster (Chapter 9).
2   Partial system failure (Chapter 9).
3   Excessively worn pads or shoes (Chapter 9).
4   One or more caliper pistons or wheel cylinders seized or sticking (Chapter 9).
5   Brake pads or shoes contaminated with oil or grease (Chapter 9).
6   New pads or shoes installed and not yet seated. It will take a while for the new material to seat.

59   Excessive brake pedal travel

1   Partial brake system failure (Chapter 9).
2   Insufficient fluid in master cylinder (Chapters 1 and 9).
3   Air trapped in system (Chapters 1 and 9).

60   Dragging brakes

1   Master cylinder pistons not returning correctly (Chapter 9).
2   Restricted brakes lines or hoses (Chapters 1 and 9).
3   Incorrect parking brake adjustment (Chapter 9).

61   Grabbing or uneven braking action

1   Malfunction of proportioner valves (Chapter 9).
2   Malfunction of power brake booster unit (Chapter 9).
3   Binding brake pedal mechanism (Chapter 9).

62   Brake pedal feels spongy when depressed

1   Air in hydraulic lines (Chapter 9).
2   Master cylinder mounting bolts loose (Chapter 9).
3   Master cylinder defective (Chapter 9).

63   Brake pedal travels to the floor with little resistance

Little or no fluid in the master cylinder reservoir caused by leaking caliper or wheel cylinder pistons, loose, damaged or disconnected brake lines (Chapter 9).

64   Parking brake does not hold

Parking brake linkage improperly adjusted (Chapter 9).

Suspension and steering systems

Note: *Before attempting to diagnose the suspension and steering systems, perform the following preliminary checks:*
- a) Check the tire pressures and look for uneven wear.
- b) Check the steering universal joints or coupling from the column to the steering gear for loose fasteners and wear.
- c) Check the front and rear suspension and the steering gear assembly for loose and damaged parts.
- d) Look for out-of-round or out-of-balance tires, bent rims and loose and/or rough wheel bearings.

65   Vehicle pulls to one side

1   Mismatched or uneven tires (Chapter 10).
2   Broken or sagging springs (Chapter 10).
3   Front wheel alignment incorrect (Chapter 10).
4   Front brakes dragging (Chapter 9).

66   Abnormal or excessive tire wear

1   Front wheel alignment incorrect (Chapter 10).
2   Sagging or broken springs (Chapter 10).
3   Tire out-of-balance (Chapter 10).
4   Worn shock absorber (Chapter 10).
5   Overloaded vehicle.
6   Tires not rotated regularly.

67   Wheel makes a "thumping" noise

1   Blister or bump on tire (Chapter 1).
2   Improper shock absorber action (Chapter 10).

68   Shimmy, shake or vibration

1   Tire or wheel out-of-balance or out-of-round (Chapter 10).
2   Loose or worn wheel bearings (Chapter 10).
3   Worn tie-rod ends (Chapter 10).
4   Worn balljoints (Chapter 10).
5   Excessive wheel runout (Chapter 10).
6   Blister or bump on tire (Chapter 1).

69   Hard steering

1   Lack of lubrication at balljoints, tie-rod ends and steering gear assembly (Chapter 10).

2   Front wheel alignment incorrect (Chapter 10).
3   Low tire pressure (Chapter 1).

70   Steering wheel does not return to center position correctly

1   Lack of lubrication at balljoints and tie-rod ends (Chapter 10).
2   Binding in steering column (Chapter 10).
3   Defective rack-and-pinion assembly (Chapter 10).
4   Front wheel alignment problem (Chapter 10).

71   Abnormal noise at the front end

1   Lack of lubrication at balljoints and tie-rod ends (Chapter 1).
2   Loose upper strut mount (Chapter 10).
3   Worn tie-rod ends (Chapter 10).
4   Loose stabilizer bar (Chapter 10).
5   Loose wheel lug nuts (Chapter 1).
6   Loose suspension bolts (Chapter 10).

72   Wander or poor steering stability

1   Mismatched or uneven tires (Chapter 10).
2   Lack of lubrication at balljoints or tie-rod ends (Chapters 1 and 10).
3   Worn shock absorbers (Chapter 10).
4   Loose stabilizer bar (Chapter 10).
5   Broken or sagging springs (Chapter 10).
6   Front wheel alignment incorrect (Chapter 10).
7   Worn steering gear clamp bushings (Chapter 10).

73   Erratic steering when braking

1   Wheel bearings worn (Chapters 8 and 10).
2   Broken or sagging springs (Chapter 10).
3   Leaking wheel cylinder or caliper (Chapter 9).
4   Warped rotors or brake drums (Chapter 9).
5   Worn steering gear clamp bushings (Chapter 10).

74   Excessive pitching and/or rolling around corners or during braking

1   Loose stabilizer bar (Chapter 10).
2   Worn shock absorbers or mounts (Chapter 10).
3   Broken or sagging springs (Chapter 10).
4   Overloaded vehicle.

75   Suspension bottoms

1   Overloaded vehicle.
2   Worn shock absorbers (Chapter 10).
3   Incorrect, broken or sagging springs (Chapter 10).

76   Cupped tires

1   Front wheel alignment incorrect (Chapter 10).
2   Worn shock absorbers (Chapter 10).
3   Wheel bearings worn (Chapters 8 and 10).
4   Excessive tire or wheel runout (Chapter 10).
5   Worn balljoints (Chapter 10).

77   Excessive tire wear on outside edge

1   Inflation pressures incorrect (Chapter 1).
2   Excessive speed in turns.
3   Front end alignment incorrect (excessive toe-in or positive camber). Have professionally aligned.
4   Suspension arm bent or twisted (Chapter 10).

78   Excessive tire wear on inside edge

1   Inflation pressures incorrect (Chapter 1).
2   Front end alignment incorrect (toe-out or excessive negative camber). Have professionally aligned.
3   Loose or damaged steering components (Chapter 10).

79   Tire tread worn in one place

1   Tires out-of-balance.
2   Damaged or buckled wheel. Inspect and replace if necessary.
3   Defective tire (Chapter 1).

80   Excessive play or looseness in steering system

1   Wheel bearings worn (Chapter 10).
2   Tie-rod end loose or worn (Chapter 10).
3   Steering gear loose (Chapter 10).

81   Rattling or clicking noise in rack and pinion

Steering gear clamps loose (Chapter 10).

Chapter 1   Tune-up and routine maintenance

Contents

1

Specifications

Recommended lubricants and fluids

Engine oil
  Type .... SG/CC or SG/CD
  Viscosity .... See accompanying chart
Automatic transaxle fluid .... **Dexron II**
Manual transaxle lubricant .... See your owner's manual or consult a dealer service department
Engine coolant .... Mixture of water and ethylene glycol-based antifreeze
Brake fluid .... Delco Supreme II or DOT 3 fluid
Clutch fluid .... Delco Supreme II or DOT 3 fluid
Power steering fluid .... GM power steering fluid or equivalent
Chassis lubrication .... Multi-purpose, lithium-base chassis grease (meeting specification GM-6031M)

Capacities

Engine oil (approximate)
  2.0/2.2 liter four-cylinder engines .... 3.0 qts (2.8 liters)
  2.3 liter four-cylinder (Quad-4) engine .... 4.0 qts (3.8 liters)
  V6 engine .... 4.0 qts (3.8 liters)
Fuel tank .... 13.6 gals (51.5 liters)
Cooling system .... 8.0 qts (7.5 liters)
Automatic transaxle .... 8.0 pts (3.8 liters)
Manual transaxle
  Muncie .... 5.3 pts (2.5 liters)
  Isuzu .... 4.1 pts (1.9 liters)
  Getrag .... Consult a dealer service department

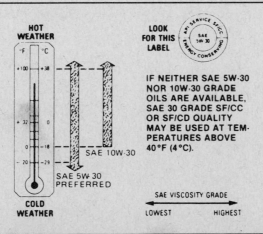

ENGINE OIL
VISCOSITY CHART

Ignition system

Spark plug type and gap
1989 and earlier
    2.0L . . . . AC R44LTSM or equivalent @ 0.035 inch
    2.8L . . . . AC R43LTSE or equivalent @ 0.045 inch
1990
    2.2L . . . . AC R44LTSM or equivalent @ 0.035 inch
    2.3L . . . . AC FR3L3 or equivalent @ 0.035 inch
    3.1L . . . . AC R43LTSE or equivalent @ 0.045 inch
1991
    2.2L . . . . AC R44LTSM or equivalent @ 0.035 inch
    2.3L . . . . AC FR3LS or equivalent @ 0.035 inch
    3.1L . . . . AC R44LTSM or equivalent @ 0.045 inch
1992
    2.2L . . . . AC R44LTSMA or equivalent @ 0.045 inch
    2.3L . . . . AC FR3LSK or equivalent @ 0.035 inch
    3.1L . . . . AC R44LTSM or equivalent @ 0.045 inch
1993
    2.2L . . . . AC R44LTSM or equivalent @ 0.035 inch
    2.3L . . . . AC FR2LSK or equivalent @ 0.035 inch
    3.1L . . . . AC R44LTSM or equivalent @ 0.045 inch
1994
    2.2L . . . . AC 41–908 or equivalent @ 0.060 inch
    2.3L . . . . AC 41–602 or equivalent @ 0.035 inch
    3.1L . . . . AC R44LTSM or equivalent @ 0.045 inch
1995
    2.2L . . . . AC 41–908 or equivalent @ 0.060 inch
    3.1L . . . . AC R44LTSM6 or equivalent @ 0.060 inch
Ignition timing . . . . Refer to *Vehicle Emission Control Information label* in the engine compartment
Firing order
    Four-cylinder engines 1-3-4-2
    V6 engine 1-2-3-4-5-6
Cylinder locations . . . . See Chapter 2

Drivebelt tension . . . . Automatically adjusted

Radiator cap pressure rating . . . . 15 psi

Brakes

Brake pad wear limit . . . . 1/8 in
Brake shoe wear limit . . . . 1/16 in

Torque specifications   **Ft-lbs (unless otherwise indicated)**

Throttle body bolts 12
Spark plugs
    2.2/2.0 liter four-cylinder engines . . . . 120 to 180 in-lbs
    2.3 liter four-cylinder (Quad-4) engine . . . . 84 to 120 in-lbs
    V6 engine
        1991 and earlier 18
        1992 on . . . . 132 in-lbs
Engine oil drain plug . . . . 15 to 20
Automatic transaxle oil pan bolts . . . . 96 to 120 in-lbs
Wheel lug nuts 100

V6 engine

0754H

2.3L (Quad-4)

Front

0758H

2.0/2.2 Liter

Cylinder and coil terminal location diagram

---

1   Introduction

This Chapter is designed to help the home mechanic maintain the Chevrolet Corsica and Beretta with the goals of maximum performance, economy, safety and reliability in mind.

Included is a master maintenance schedule (page 34), followed by procedures dealing specifically with each item on the schedule. Visual checks, adjustments, component replacement and other helpful items are included. Refer to the accompanying illustrations of the engine compartment and the underside of the vehicle for the locations of various components.

Servicing your vehicle in accordance with the mileage/time maintenance schedule and the step-by-step procedures will result in a planned maintenance program that should produce a long and reliable service life. Keep in mind that it's a comprehensive plan, so maintaining some items but not others at the specified intervals will not produce the same results.

As you service your vehicle, you'll discover that many of the procedures can – and should – be grouped together because of the nature of the particular procedure you're performing or because of the close proximity of two otherwise unrelated components to one another.

For example, if the vehicle is raised, you should inspect the exhaust, suspension, steering and fuel systems while you're under the vehicle. When you're rotating the tires, it makes good sense to check the brakes since the wheels are already removed. Finally, let's suppose you have to borrow or rent a torque wrench. Even if you only need it to tighten the spark plugs, you might as well check the torque of as many critical fasteners as time allows.

The first step in this maintenance program is to prepare yourself before the actual work begins. Read through all the procedures you're planning to do, then gather up all the parts and tools needed. If it looks like you might run into problems during a particular job, seek advice from a mechanic or an experienced do-it-yourselfer.

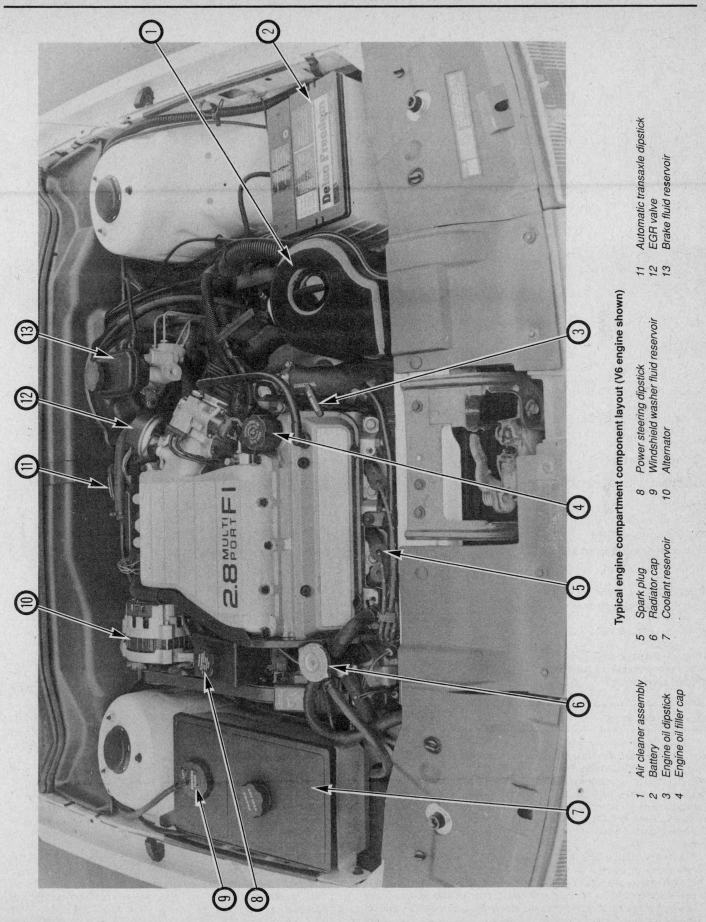

Typical engine compartment component layout (V6 engine shown)

1	Air cleaner assembly	
2	Battery	
3	Engine oil dipstick	
4	Engine oil filler cap	
5	Spark plug	
6	Radiator cap	
7	Coolant reservoir	
8	Power steering dipstick	
9	Windshield washer fluid reservoir	
10	Alternator	
11	Automatic transaxle dipstick	
12	EGR valve	
13	Brake fluid reservoir	

1

Underside view of engine/transaxle

1 CV joint boot	3 Engine oil drain plug	5 Disc brake caliper
2 Automatic transaxle	4 Engine oil filter	6 Exhaust pipe

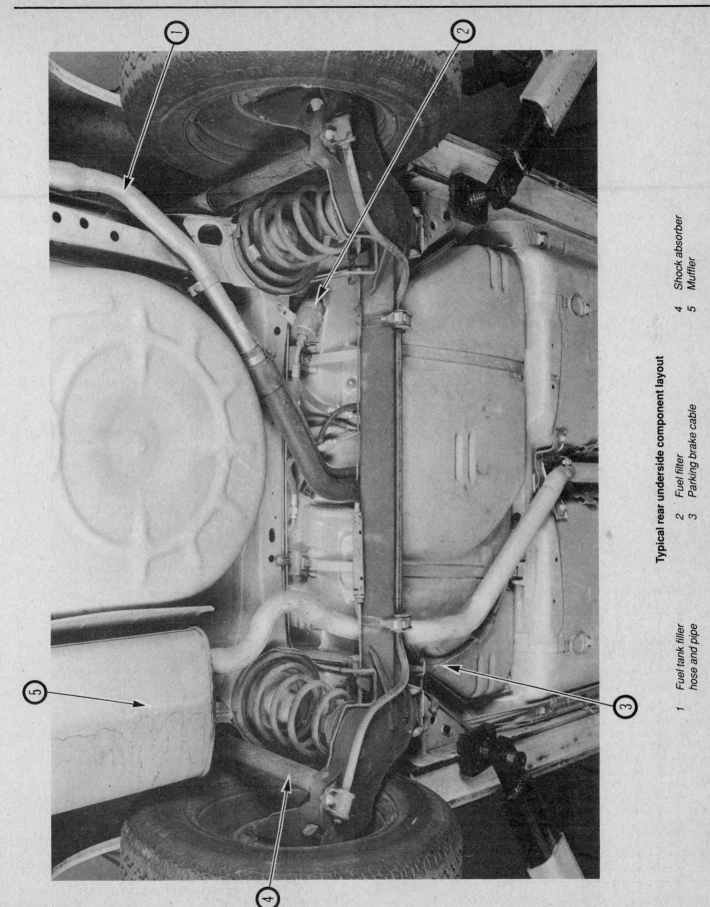

Typical rear underside component layout

1	Fuel tank filler hose and pipe	4	Shock absorber
2	Fuel filter	5	Muffler
3	Parking brake cable		

Chevrolet Corsica and Beretta Maintenance schedule

The following maintenance intervals are based on the assumption that the vehicle owner will be doing the maintenance or service work, as opposed to having a dealer service department do the work. Although the time/mileage intervals are loosely based on factory recommendations, most have been shortened to ensure, for example, that such items as lubricants and fluids are checked/changed at intervals that promote maximum engine/driveline service life. Also, subject to the preference of the individual owner interested in keeping his or her vehicle in peak condition at all times, and with the vehicle's ultimate resale in mind, many of the maintenance procedures may be performed more often than recommended in the following schedule. We encourage such owner initiative.

When the vehicle is new it should be serviced initially by a factory authorized dealer service department to protect the factory warranty. In many cases the initial maintenance check is done at no cost to the owner (check with your dealer service department for more information).

Every 250 miles or weekly, whichever comes first

Check the engine oil level (Section 4)
Check the engine coolant level (Section 4)
Check the windshield washer fluid level (Section 4)
Check the brake and clutch fluid levels (Section 4)
Check the tires and tire pressures (Section 5)

Every 3000 miles or 3 months, whichever comes first

All items listed above plus:
Check the automatic transaxle fluid level (Section 6)*
Check the power steering fluid level (Section 7)*
Check and service the battery (Section 8)
Check the cooling system (Section 9)
Inspect and replace, if necessary, all underhood hoses (Section 10)
Inspect and replace, if necessary, the windshield wiper blades (Section 11)

Every 7500 miles or 12 months, whichever comes first

All items listed above plus:
Change the engine oil and filter (Section 12)*
Lubricate the chassis components (Section 13)

Check the driveaxle boots (Section 14)
Inspect the suspension and steering components (Section 15)*
Inspect the exhaust system (Section 16)*
Check the manual transaxle lubricant level (Section 17)*
Rotate the tires (Section 18)
Check the brakes (Section 19)*
Inspect the fuel system (Section 20)
Replace the air filter and PCV filter (Section 21)
Check the throttle body mounting bolt torque (Section 22)
Check the engine drivebelts (Section 23)
Check the seat belts (Section 24)
Check the starter safety switch (Section 25)
Check the seatback latch (Section 26)
Check the spare tire and jack (Section 27)

Every 30,000 miles or 24 months, whichever comes first

All items listed above plus:
Replace the fuel filter (Section 28)
Change the automatic transaxle fluid (Section 29)**
Change the manual transaxle lubricant (Section 30)
Service the cooling system (drain, flush and refill) (Section 31)
Inspect and replace, if necessary, the PCV valve (Section 32)
Inspect the evaporative emissions control system (Section 33)
Check the EGR system (Section 34)
Replace the spark plugs (Section 35)
Inspect the spark plug/coil wires (Section 36)

This item is affected by "severe" operating conditions as described below. If the vehicle is operated under severe conditions, perform all maintenance indicated with an asterisk (*) at 3000 mile/3 month intervals. Severe conditions are indicated if the vehicle is operated mainly . . .

in dusty areas
while towing a trailer
when allowed to idle for extended periods and/or at low speeds when outside temperatures remain below freezing and most trips are less than four miles long

**If operated under one or more of the following conditions, change the automatic transaxle fluid every 15,000 miles:*

In heavy city traffic where the outside temperature regularly reaches 90-degrees F or higher
In hilly or mountainous terrain
Frequent trailer pulling

3 Tune-up general information

The term tune-up is used in this manual to represent a combination of individual operations rather than one specific procedure.

If, from the time the vehicle is new, the routine maintenance schedule is followed closely and frequent checks are made of fluid levels and high wear items, as suggested throughout this manual, the engine will be kept in relatively good running condition and the need for additional work will be minimized.

More likely than not, however, there will be times when the engine is running poorly due to lack of regular maintenance. This is even more likely if a used vehicle, which has not received regular and frequent maintenance checks, is purchased. In such cases, an engine tune-up will be needed outside of the regular routine maintenance intervals.

The first step in any tune-up or diagnostic procedure to help correct a poor running engine is a cylinder compression check. A compression check (see Chapter 2, Part D) will help determine the condition of internal engine components and should be used as a guide for tune-up and repair procedures. If, for instance, a compression check indicates serious internal engine wear, a conventional tune-up won't improve the performance of the engine and would be a waste of time and money. Because of its importance, the compression check should be done by someone with the right equipment and the knowledge to use it properly.

The following procedures are those most often needed to bring a generally poor running engine back into a proper state of tune.

Minor tune-up

Check all engine related fluids (Section 4)
Clean, inspect and test the battery (Section 8)
Check the cooling system (Section 9)
Check all underhood hoses (Section 10)
Check the air and PCV filters (Section 21)
Check and adjust the drivebelts (Section 23)
Check the PCV valve (Section 32)
Replace the spark plugs (Section 35)
Inspect the spark plug and coil wires (Section 36)

Major tune-up

All items listed under Minor tune-up plus . . .
Check the fuel system (Section 20)
Replace the air and PCV filters (Section 21)
Check the EGR system (Section 33)

Check the ignition system (Section 36 and Chapter 5)
Check the charging system (Chapter 5)
Replace the spark plug and coil wires (Section 36)

4 Fluid level checks

Note: *The following are fluid level checks to be done on a 250 mile or weekly basis. Additional fluid level checks can be found in specific maintenance procedures which follow. Regardless of intervals, be alert to fluid leaks under the vehicle which would indicate a problem to be corrected immediately.*

1   Fluids are an essential part of the lubrication, cooling, brake and windshield washer systems. Because the fluids gradually become depleted and/or contaminated during normal operation of the vehicle, they must be periodically replenished. See *Recommended lubricants and fluids* at the beginning of this Chapter before adding fluid to any of the following components. **Note:** *The vehicle must be on level ground when fluid levels are checked.*

Engine oil

Refer to illustrations 4.2 and 4.4

2   The engine oil level is checked with a dipstick **(see illustration)**. The dipstick extends through a metal tube down into the oil pan.
3   The oil level should be checked before the vehicle has been driven, or about 15 minutes after the engine has been shut off. If the oil is checked immediately after driving the vehicle, some of the oil will remain in the upper part of the engine, resulting in an inaccurate reading on the dipstick.
4   Pull the dipstick from the tube and wipe all the oil from the end with a clean rag or paper towel. Insert the clean dipstick all the way back into the tube and pull it out again. Note the oil at the end of the dipstick. Add oil as necessary to keep the level above the ADD mark in the cross-hatched area of the dipstick **(see illustration)**.
5   Do not overfill the engine by adding too much oil since this may result in oil fouled spark plugs, oil leaks or oil seal failures.
6   Oil is added to the engine after removing a twist off cap located on the rocker arm or camshaft cover **(see illustration 4.2)**. An oil can spout or funnel may help to reduce spills.
7   Checking the oil level is an important preventive maintenance step. A consistently low oil level indicates oil leakage through damaged seals, defective gaskets or past worn rings or valve guides. If the oil looks milky in color or has water droplets in it, the cylinder head gasket may be blown or the head or block may be cracked. The engine should be checked immediately. The condition of the oil should also be checked. Whenever you check the oil level, slide your thumb and index finger up the dipstick before wiping off the oil. If you see small dirt or metal particles clinging to the dipstick, the oil should be changed (Section 12).

4.2   The engine oil dipstick is clearly marked "ENGINE OIL" (arrow), as is the oil filler cap, which threads into the rocker arm cover (arrow) (V6 engine shown)

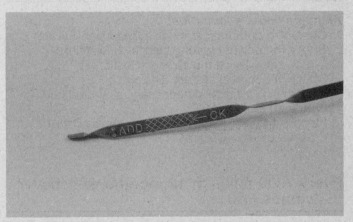

4.4   The oil level should be in the cross-hatched area – if it's below the ADD line, add enough oil to bring the level into the cross-hatched area

4.9a   The coolant level must be maintained between the FULL HOT and FULL COLD marks on the reservoir

4.9b   The coolant and windshield washer reservoirs are located in the same housing and use different fluids – even though the caps are clearly marked, don't mix them up!

Engine coolant

Refer to illustrations 4.9a and 4.9b

Warning: *Do not allow antifreeze to come in contact with your skin or painted surfaces of the vehicle. Flush contaminated areas immediately with plenty of water. Do not store new coolant or leave old coolant lying around where it's accessible to children or pets – they're attracted by its sweet taste. Ingestion of even a small amount of coolant can be fatal! Wipe up garage floor and drip pan coolant spills immediately. Keep antifreeze containers covered and repair leaks in the cooling system immediately.*

8   All vehicles covered by this manual are equipped with a pressurized coolant recovery system. A black plastic coolant reservoir located in the right front corner of the engine compartment is connected by a hose to the radiator filler neck. If the engine overheats, coolant escapes through a valve in the radiator cap and travels through the hose into the reservoir. As the engine cools, the coolant is automatically drawn back into the cooling system to maintain the correct level.

9   The coolant level in the reservoir should be checked regularly. **Warning:** *Do not remove the radiator cap to check the coolant level when the engine is warm.* The level in the reservoir varies with the temperature of the engine. When the engine is cold, the coolant level should be at or slightly above the FULL COLD mark on the reservoir. Once the engine has warmed up, the level should be at or near the FULL HOT mark **(see illustration)**. If it isn't, allow the engine to cool, then unscrew the cap from the reservoir and add a 50/50 mixture of ethylene glycol based antifreeze and water. The coolant and windshield washer reservoirs are located in the same housing, so be sure to add the correct fluids; the caps are clearly marked **(see illustration)**.

10   Drive the vehicle and recheck the coolant level. If only a small amount of coolant is required to bring the system up to the proper level, water can be used. However, repeated additions of water will dilute the antifreeze and water solution. In order to maintain the proper ratio of antifreeze and water, always top up the coolant level with the correct mixture. An empty plastic milk jug or bleach bottle makes an excellent container for mixing coolant. Do not use rust inhibitors or additives.

11   If the coolant level drops consistently, there may be a leak in the system. Inspect the radiator, hoses, filler cap, drain plugs and water pump (see Section 9). If no leaks are noted, have the radiator cap pressure tested by a service station.

12   If you have to remove the radiator cap, wait until the engine has cooled completely, then wrap a thick cloth around the cap and turn it to the first stop. If coolant or steam escapes, let the engine cool down longer, then remove the cap.

13   Check the condition of the coolant as well. It should be relatively clear. If it is brown or rust colored, the system should be drained, flushed and refilled. Even if the coolant appears to be normal, the corrosion inhibitors wear out, so it must be replaced at the specified intervals.

Windshield washer fluid

Refer to illustration 4.14

14   Fluid for the windshield washer system is located in a plastic reservoir in the same housing with the coolant reservoir on the right side of the engine compartment **(see illustration)**. In milder climates, plain water can be used in the reservoir, but it should be kept no more than two-thirds full to allow for expansion if the water freezes. In colder climates, use windshield washer system antifreeze, available at any auto parts store, to lower the freezing point of the fluid. Mix the antifreeze with water in accordance with the manufacturer's directions on the container. **Caution:** *Do not use cooling system antifreeze – it will damage the vehicle's paint.*

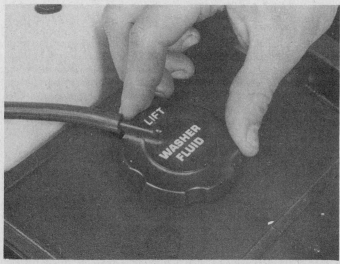

4.14   The reservoir for the windshield washer is located on the right side of the engine compartment (fluid is added after removing the top – how often you use the washers will dictate how often you need to check the reservoir)

4.18a On black plastic reservoirs, unscrew the cap . . .

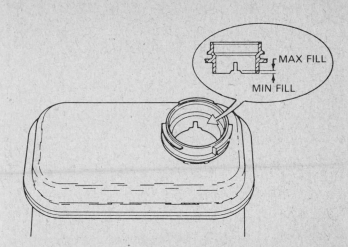

MAX FILL

MIN FILL

4.18b . . . and make sure the brake fluid level is up to the bottom of the slot in the neck

15 To help prevent icing in cold weather, warm the windshield with the defroster before using the washer.

Battery electrolyte

16 All vehicles covered by this manual are equipped with a battery which is permanently sealed (except for vent holes) and has no filler caps. Water does not have to be added to these batteries at any time.

Brake and clutch fluid

Refer to illustrations 4.18a and 4.18b

17 The brake master cylinder is mounted on the front of the power booster unit in the engine compartment. The clutch master cylinder used with manual transaxles is mounted adjacent to it on the firewall.

18 On black plastic reservoirs, unscrew the cap and make sure the fluid level is even with the bottom of the filler neck slot **(see illustrations)**. On translucent white plastic reservoirs, the fluid inside is readily visible. If a low level is indicated, be sure to clean the reservoir cap, to prevent contamination of the brake and/or clutch system, before removing it.

19 When adding fluid, pour it carefully into the reservoir to avoid spilling it on surrounding painted surfaces. Be sure the specified fluid is used, since mixing different types of brake fluid can cause damage to the system. See *Recommended lubricants and fluids* at the front of this Chapter or your owner's manual. **Warning:** *Brake fluid can harm your eyes and damage painted surfaces, so use extreme caution when handling or pouring it. Do not use brake fluid that has been standing open or is more than one year old. Brake fluid absorbs moisture from the air. Excess moisture can cause a dangerous loss of braking effectiveness.*

20 At this time the fluid and master cylinder can be inspected for contamination. The system should be drained and refilled if deposits, dirt particles or water droplets are seen in the fluid.

21 After filling the reservoir to the proper level, make sure the cap is on tight to prevent fluid leakage.

22 The brake fluid level in the master cylinder will drop slightly as the pads and the brake shoes at each wheel wear down during normal operation. If the master cylinder requires repeated replenishing to keep it at the proper level, this is an indication of leakage in the brake system, which should be corrected immediately. Check all brake lines and connections (see Section 19 for more information).

23 If, when checking the master cylinder fluid level, you discover one or both reservoirs empty or nearly empty, the brake system should be bled (Chapter 9).

5 Tire and tire pressure checks

Refer to illustrations 5.2, 5.3, 5.4a, 5.4b and 5.8

1 Periodic inspection of the tires may spare you the inconvenience of being stranded with a flat tire. It can also provide you with vital information regarding possible problems in the steering and suspension systems before major damage occurs.

2 The original tires on this vehicle are equipped with 1/2-inch side bands that appear when tread depth reaches 1/16-inch, but they don't appear until the tires are worn out. Tread wear can be monitored with a simple, inexpensive device known as a tread depth indicator **(see illustration)**.

3 Note any abnormal tread wear **(see illustration on next page)**. Tread pattern irregularities such as cupping, flat spots and more wear on one side than the other are indications of front end alignment and/or balance problems. If any of these conditions are noted, take the vehicle to a tire shop or service station to correct the problem.

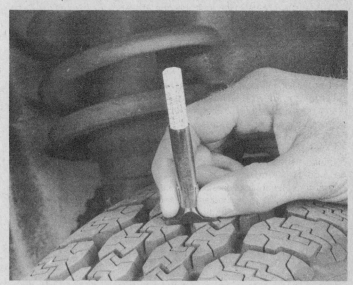

5.2 Use a tire tread depth indicator to monitor tire wear – they are available at auto parts stores and service stations and cost very little

Condition	Probable cause	Corrective action	Condition	Probable cause	Corrective action
Shoulder wear	• Underinflation (both sides wear) • Incorrect wheel camber (one side wear) • Hard cornering • Lack of rotation	• Measure and adjust pressure. • Repair or replace axle and suspension parts. • Reduce speed. • Rotate tires.	Feathered edge Toe wear	• Incorrect toe	• Adjust toe-in.
Center wear	• Overinflation • Lack of rotation	• Measure and adjust pressure. • Rotate tires.	Uneven wear	• Incorrect camber or caster • Malfunctioning suspension • Unbalanced wheel • Out-of-round brake drum • Lack of rotation	• Repair or replace axle and suspension parts. • Repair or replace suspension parts. • Balance or replace. • Turn or replace. • Rotate tires.

5.3   This chart will help you determine the condition of the tires, the probable cause(s) of abnormal wear and the corrective action necessary

4   Look closely for cuts, punctures and embedded nails or tacks. Sometimes a tire will hold air pressure for short time or leak down very slowly after a nail has embedded itself in the tread. If a slow leak persists, check the valve stem core to make sure it's tight **(see illustration)**. Examine the tread for an object that may have embedded itself in the tire or for a "plug" that may have begun to leak (radial tire punctures are repaired with a plug that's installed in a puncture). If a puncture is suspected, it can be easily verified by spraying a solution of soapy water onto the suspected area **(see illustration)**. The soapy solution will bubble if there's a leak. Unless the puncture is unusually large, a tire shop or service station can usually repair the tire.

5   Carefully inspect the inner sidewall of each tire for evidence of brake fluid. If you see any, inspect the brakes immediately.

6   Correct air pressure adds miles to the lifespan of the tires, improves mileage and enhances overall ride quality. Tire pressure cannot be accurately estimated by looking at a tire, especially if it's a radial. A tire pressure gauge is essential. Keep an accurate gauge in the vehicle. The pressure gauges attached to the nozzles of air hoses at gas stations are often inac-

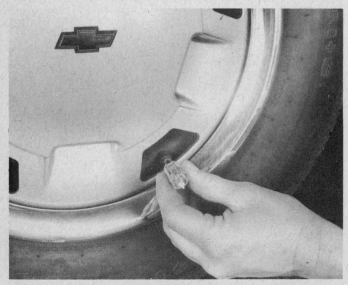

5.4a   If a tire loses air on a steady basis, check the valve core first to make sure it's snug (special inexpensive wrenches are commonly available at hardware and auto parts stores)

5.4b   If the valve core is tight, raise the corner of the vehicle with the low tire and spray a soapy water solution onto the tread as the tire is turned slowly – leaks will cause small bubbles to appear

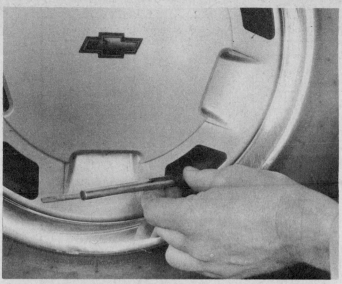

5.8 To extend the life of the tires, check the air pressure at least once a week with an accurate gauge (don't forget the spare!)

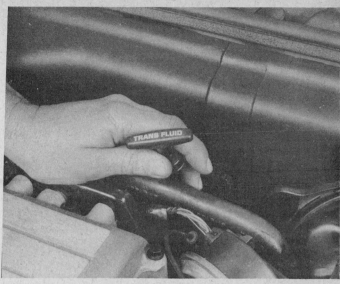

6.3 The automatic transaxle fluid dipstick is clearly marked ("TRANS FLUID") and is located at the rear of the engine compartment (V6 engine shown)

curate.

7   Always check tire pressure when the tires are cold. Cold, in this case, means the vehicle has not been driven over a mile in the three hours preceding a tire pressure check. A pressure rise of four to eight pounds is not uncommon once the tires are warm.

8   Unscrew the valve cap protruding from the wheel or hubcap and push the gauge firmly onto the valve stem **(see illustration)**. Note the reading on the gauge and compare the figure to the recommended tire pressure shown on the label attached to the inside of the glove compartment door. Be sure to reinstall the valve cap to keep dirt and moisture out of the valve stem mechanism. Check all four tires and, if necessary, add enough air to bring them up to the recommended pressure.

9   Don't forget to keep the spare tire inflated to the specified pressure (refer to your owner's manual or the tire sidewall).

6   Automatic transaxle fluid level check

Refer to illustrations 6.3 and 6.6

1   The automatic transaxle fluid level should be carefully maintained. Low fluid level can lead to slipping or loss of drive, while overfilling can cause foaming and loss of fluid.

2   With the parking brake set, start the engine, then move the shift lever through all the gear ranges, ending in Park. The fluid level must be checked with the vehicle level and the engine running at idle. **Note:** *Incorrect fluid level readings will result if the vehicle has just been driven at high speeds for an extended period, in hot weather in city traffic, or if it has been pulling a trailer. If any of these conditions apply, wait until the fluid has cooled (about 30 minutes).*

3   With the transaxle at normal operating temperature, remove the dipstick from the filler tube. The dipstick is located at the rear of the engine compartment **(see illustration)**.

4   Carefully touch the fluid at the end of the dipstick to determine if the fluid is cool, warm or hot. Wipe the fluid from the dipstick with a clean rag and push it back into the filler tube until the cap seats.

5   Pull the dipstick out again and note the fluid level.

6   If the fluid felt cool, the level should be about 1/8-to-3/8 inch below the "ADD 1 PT" mark **(see illustration)**. If it felt warm, the level should be close to the "ADD 1 PT" mark. If the fluid was hot, the level should be within the cross-hatched area. If additional fluid is required, pour it directly into

the tube using a funnel. It takes about one pint to raise the level from the ADD mark to the upper edge of the cross-hatched area with a hot transaxle, so add the fluid a little at a time and keep checking the level until it's correct.

7   The condition of the fluid should also be checked along with the level. If the fluid at the end of the dipstick is a dark reddish-brown color, or if the fluid has a burned smell, the fluid should be changed. If you're in doubt about the condition of the fluid, purchase some new fluid and compare the two for color and smell.

7   Power steering fluid level check

Refer to illustrations 7.2 and 7.6

1   Unlike manual steering, the power steering system relies on fluid which may, over a period of time, require replenishing.

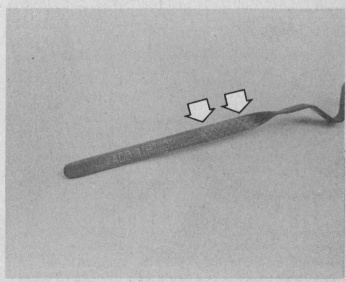

6.6 The automatic transaxle fluid level must be maintained within the cross-hatched area on the dipstick

7.2   The power steering fluid reservoir is located near the front (drivebelt end) of the engine; turn the cap clockwise for removal (V6 engine shown)

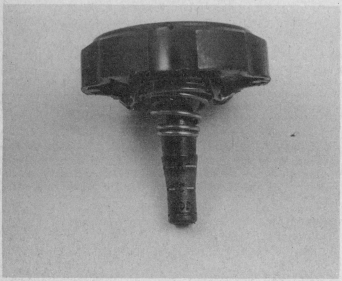

7.6   The marks on the power steering fluid dipstick indicate the safe fluid level range

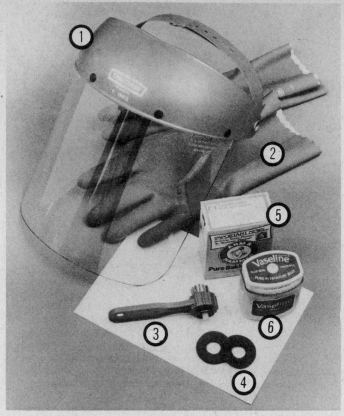

8.1   Tools and materials required for battery maintenance

1 **Face shield/safety goggles** – *When removing corrosion with a brush, the acidic particles can easily fly up into your eyes*
2 **Rubber gloves** – *Another safety item to consider when servicing the battery; remember that's acid inside the battery!*
3 **Battery terminal cable cleaner** – *This wire brush cleaning tool will remove all traces of corrosion from the battery and cable*
4 **Treated felt washers** – *Placing one of these on each terminal, directly under the cable end, will help prevent corrosion (be sure to get the correct type for side terminal batteries)*
5 **Baking soda** – *A solution of baking soda and water can be used to neutralize corrosion*
6 **Petroleum jelly** – *A layer of this on the battery terminal bolts will help prevent corrosion*

2   The fluid reservoir for the power steering pump is located behind the radiator near the front (drivebelt end) of the engine **(see illustration)**.
3   For the check, the front wheels should be pointed straight ahead and the engine should be off.
4   Use a clean rag to wipe off the reservoir cap and the area around the cap. This will help prevent any foreign matter from entering the reservoir during the check.
5   Twist off the cap and check the temperature of the fluid at the end of the dipstick with your finger.
6   Wipe off the fluid with a clean rag, reinsert it, then withdraw it and read the fluid level. The level should be at the HOT mark if the fluid was hot to the touch **(see illustration)**. It should be at the COLD mark if the fluid was cool to the touch. Note that on some models the marks (FULL HOT and COLD) are on opposite sides of the dipstick. At no time should the fluid level drop below the ADD mark.
7   If additional fluid is required, pour the specified type directly into the reservoir, using a funnel to prevent spills.

8   If the reservoir requires frequent fluid additions, all power steering hoses, hose connections, the power steering pump and the rack and pinion assembly should be carefully checked for leaks.

---

8   Battery check and maintenance

Refer to illustration 8.1
Warning: *Certain precautions must be followed when checking and servicing the battery. Hydrogen gas, which is highly flammable, is always present in the battery cells, so keep lighted tobacco and all other open flames and sparks away from the battery. The electrolyte inside the battery is actually dilute sulfuric acid, which will cause injury if splashed on your skin or in your eyes. It will also ruin clothes and painted surfaces. When removing the battery cables, always detach the negative cable first and hook it up last!*

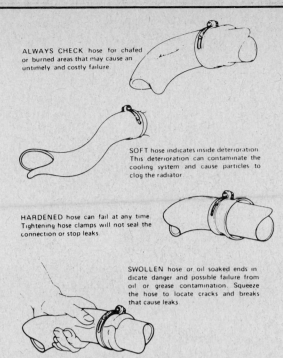

ALWAYS CHECK hose for chafed or burned areas that may cause an untimely and costly failure

SOFT hose indicates inside deterioration This deterioration can contaminate the cooling system and cause particles to clog the radiator

HARDENED hose can fail at any time. Tightening hose clamps will not seal the connection or stop leaks

SWOLLEN hose or oil soaked ends indicate danger and possible failure from oil or grease contamination. Squeeze the hose to locate cracks and breaks that cause leaks

9.4   Hoses, like drivebelts, have a habit of failing at the worst possible time – to prevent the inconvenience of a blown radiator or heater hose, inspect them carefully as shown here

1   Battery maintenance is an important procedure which will help ensure you aren't stranded because of a dead battery. Several tools are required for this procedure **(see illustration)**.

2   A sealed battery is standard equipment on all vehicles covered by this manual. Although this type of battery has many advantages over the older, capped cell type, and never requires the addition of water, it should still be routinely maintained according to the procedure which follows.

3   The battery is located on the left side of the engine compartment. The exterior of the battery should be inspected periodically for damage such as a cracked case or cover.

4   Check the tightness of the battery cable bolts to ensure good electrical connections and check the entire length of each cable for cracks and frayed conductors.

5   If corrosion (visible as white, fluffy deposits) is evident, remove the cables from the terminals, clean them with a battery brush and reinstall the cables. Corrosion can be kept to a minimum by using special treated fiber washers available at auto parts stores or by applying a layer of petroleum jelly to the terminals and cables after they are assembled.

6   Make sure that the battery tray is in good condition and the hold-down clamp bolt is tight. If the battery is removed from the tray, make sure no parts remain in the bottom of the tray when the battery is reinstalled. When reinstalling the hold-down clamp bolt, do not overtighten it.

7   Corrosion on the hold-down components, battery case and surrounding areas can be removed with a solution of water and baking soda. Thoroughly rinse all cleaned areas with plain water.

8   Any metal parts of the vehicle damaged by corrosion should be covered with a zinc-based primer then painted.

9   Further information on the battery, charging and jump starting can be found in Chapter 5 and at the front of this manual.

9   Cooling system check

Refer to illustration 9.4

1   Many major engine failures can be attributed to a faulty cooling system. If the vehicle is equipped with an automatic transaxle, the cooling system also cools the transaxle fluid and plays an important role in prolonging transaxle life.

2   The cooling system should be checked with the engine cold. Do this before the vehicle is driven for the day or after the engine has been shut off for at least three hours.

3   Remove the radiator cap by turning it to the left until it reaches a stop. If you hear any hissing sounds (indicating there is still pressure in the system), wait until it stops. Now press down on the cap with the palm of your hand and continue turning to the left until the cap can be removed. Thoroughly clean the cap, inside and out, with clean water. Also clean the filler neck on the radiator. All traces of corrosion should be removed. The coolant inside the radiator should be relatively transparent. If it is rust colored, the system should be drained and refilled (Section 30). If the ooolant level Is not up to the top, add additional antifreeze/coolant mixture (Section 4).

4   Carefully check the large upper and lower radiator hoses along with any smaller diameter heater hoses which run from the engine to the firewall. Inspect each hose along its entire length, replacing any hose which is cracked, swollen or shows signs of deterioration. Cracks may become more apparent if the hose is squeezed **(see illustration)**.

5   Make sure all hose connections are tight. A leak in the cooling system will usually show up as white or rust colored deposits on the areas adjoining the leak. If wire-type clamps are used at the ends of the hoses, it may be wise to replace them with more secure screw-type clamps.

6   Use compressed air or a soft brush to remove bugs, leaves, etc. from the front of the radiator or air conditioning condenser. Be careful not to damage the delicate cooling fins or cut yourself on them.

7   Every other inspection, or at the first indication of cooling system problems, have the cap and system pressure tested. If you don't have a pressure tester, most gas stations and repair shops will do this for a minimal charge.

10   Underhood hose check and replacement

General

Refer to illustration 10.1

1   **Caution:** *Replacement of air conditioning hoses must be left to a dealer service department or air conditioning shop that has the equipment to depressurize the system safely. Never remove air conditioning components or hoses* **(see illustration)** *until the system has been depressurized.*

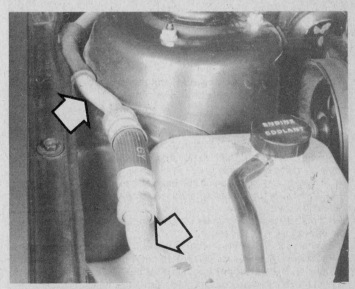

10.1   Air conditioning hoses are easily identified by the metal tubes used at all bends (arrows) – DO NOT disconnect or accidentally damage the air conditioning hoses (the system is under high pressure)

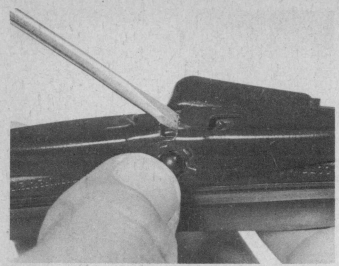

11.5a   Using a small screwdriver, gently pry on the spring at the center of the windshield wiper arm . . .

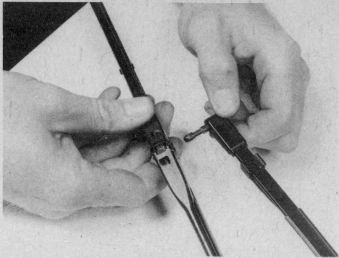

11.5b   . . . while pulling the blade assembly away from the arm

2   High temperatures under the hood can cause the deterioration of the rubber and plastic hoses used for engine, accessory and emission systems operation. Periodic inspection should be made for cracks, loose clamps, material hardening and leaks. Information specific to the cooling system hoses can be found in Section 9.

3   Some, but not all, hoses are secured to the fittings with clamps. Where clamps are used, check to be sure they haven't lost their tension, allowing the hose to leak. If clamps aren't used, make sure the hose hasn't expanded and/or hardened where it slips over the fitting, allowing it to leak.

Vacuum hoses

4   It's quite common for vacuum hoses, especially those in the emissions system, to be color coded or identified by colored stripes molded into each hose. Various systems require hoses with different wall thicknesses, collapse resistance and temperature resistance. When replacing hoses, be sure the new ones are made of the same material.

5   Often the only effective way to check a hose is to remove it completely from the vehicle. If more than one hose is removed, be sure to label the hoses and fittings to ensure correct installation.

6   When checking vacuum hoses, be sure to include any plastic T-fittings in the check. Inspect the fittings for cracks and the hose where it fits over the fitting for distortion, which could cause leakage.

7   A small piece of vacuum hose (1/4-inch inside diameter) can be used as a stethoscope to detect vacuum leaks. Hold one end of the hose to your ear and probe around vacuum hoses and fittings, listening for the "hissing" sound characteristic of a vacuum leak. **Warning:** *When probing with the vacuum hose stethoscope, be careful not to allow your body or the hose to come into contact with moving engine components such as the drivebelt, cooling fan, etc.*

Fuel hose

Warning: *There are certain precautions which must be taken when inspecting or servicing fuel system components. Work in a well ventilated area and do not allow open flames (cigarettes, appliance pilot lights, etc.) or bare light bulbs near the work area. Mop up any spills immediately and do not store fuel soaked rags where they could ignite. The fuel system is under pressure, so if any fuel lines must be disconnected, the pressure in the system must be relieved first (see Chapter 4 for more information).*

8   Check all rubber fuel lines for deterioration and chafing. Check especially for cracks in areas where the hose bends and just before fittings, such as where a hose attaches to the fuel filter and fuel injection unit.

9   High quality fuel line, usually identified by the word Fluroelastomer printed on the hose, should be used for fuel line replacement. Never, under any circumstances, use unreinforced vacuum line, clear plastic tubing or water hose for fuel lines.

10   Spring-type clamps are commonly used on fuel lines. These clamps often lose their tension over a period of time, and can be "sprung" during the removal process. As a result spring-type clamps be replaced with screw-type clamps whenever a hose is replaced.

Metal lines

11   Sections of steel tubing often used for fuel line between the fuel pump and fuel injection unit. Check carefully for cracks, kinks and flat spots in the line.

12   If a section of metal fuel line must be replaced, only seamless steel tubing should be used, since copper and aluminum tubing do not have the strength necessary to withstand normal engine vibration.

13   Check the metal brake lines where they enter the master cylinder and brake proportioning unit (if used) for cracks in the lines and loose fittings. Any sign of brake fluid leakage calls for an immediate thorough inspection of the brake system.

---

11   Windshield wiper blade inspection and replacement

Refer to illustrations 11.5a, 11.5b and 11.7

1   The windshield wiper and blade assembly should be inspected periodically for damage, loose components and cracked or worn blade elements.

2   Road film can build up on the wiper blades and affect their efficiency, so they should be washed regularly with a mild detergent solution.

3   The action of the wiping mechanism can loosen the bolts, nuts and fasteners, so they should be checked and tightened, as necessary, at the same time the wiper blades are checked.

4   If the wiper blade elements (sometimes called inserts) are cracked, worn or warped, they should be replaced with new ones.

5   Remove the wiper blade assembly from the wiper arm by inserting a small screwdriver into the opening and gently prying on the spring while pulling on the blade to release it **(see illustrations)**.

6   With the blade removed from the vehicle, you can remove the rubber element from the blade.

7   Using pliers, pinch the metal backing of the element **(see illustration)**, then slide the element out of the blade assembly.

8   Compare the new element with the old for length, design, etc.

9   Slide the new element into place. It will automatically lock at the correct location.

10   Reinstall the blade assembly on the arm, wet the windshield glass and test for proper operation.

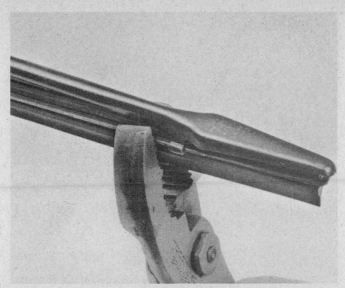

**11.7   The rubber element is retained in the blade by small clips –
the metal backing of the rubber element can be compressed at
one end with pliers, allowing the element to slide out
of the clips**

12   Engine oil and filter change

Refer to illustrations 12.3, 12.9, 12.14 and 12.18

1   Frequent oil changes are the most important preventive maintenance procedures that can be done by the home mechanic. As engine oil ages, it becomes diluted and contaminated, which leads to premature engine wear.

2   Although some sources recommend oil filter changes every other oil change, we feel that the minimal cost of an oil filter and the relative ease with which it is installed dictate that a new filter be used every time the oil is changed.

3   Gather together all necessary tools and materials before beginning the procedure **(see illustration)**.

4   In addition, you should have plenty of clean rags and newspapers handy to mop up any spills. Access to the underside of the vehicle is greatly improved if the vehicle can be lifted on a hoist, driven onto ramps or supported by jackstands. **Warning:** *Do not work under a vehicle which is supported only by a bumper, hydraulic or scissors-type jack.*

5   If this is your first oil change, get under the vehicle and familiarize yourself with the locations of the oil drain plug and the oil filter. The engine and exhaust components will be warm during the actual work, so note how they are situated to avoid touching them when working under the vehicle.

6   Warm the engine to normal operating temperature. If the new oil or any tools are needed, use this warm-up time to gather everything necessary for the job. The correct type of oil for your application can be found in *Recommended lubricants and fluids* at the beginning of this Chapter.

7   With the engine oil warm (warm engine oil will drain better and more built-up sludge will be removed with the oil), raise and support the vehicle. Make sure it's safely supported.

8   Move all necessary tools, rags and newspapers under the vehicle. Position the drain pan under the drain plug. Keep in mind that the oil will initially flow from the pan with some force, so place the pan accordingly.

9   Being careful not to touch any of the hot exhaust components, remove the drain plug at the bottom of the oil pan **(see illustration)**. Depending on how hot the oil is, you may want to wear gloves while unscrewing the plug the final few turns.

10   Allow the old oil to drain into the pan. It may be necessary to move the pan farther under the engine as the oil flow slows to a trickle.

11   After all the oil has drained, wipe off the drain plug with a clean rag. Small metal particles may cling to the plug which would immediately contaminate the new oil.

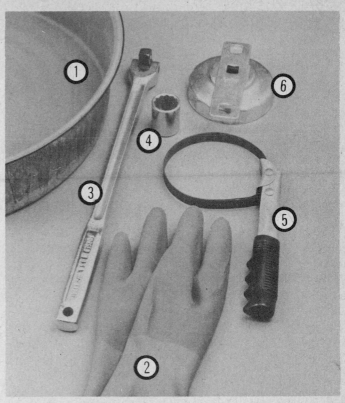

**12.3   These tools are required when changing the
engine oil and filter**

1   *Drain pan – It should be fairly shallow in depth, but wide to prevent spills*

2   *Rubber gloves – When removing the drain plug and filter, you will get oil on your hands (the gloves will prevent burns)*

3   *Breaker bar – Sometimes the oil drain plug is tight and a long breaker bar is needed to loosen it*

4   *Socket – To be used with the breaker bar or a ratchet (must be the correct size to fit the drain plug – 6-point preferred)*

5   *Filter wrench – This is a metal band-type wrench, which requires clearance around the filter to be effective*

6   *Filter wrench – This type fits on the bottom of the filter and can be turned with a ratchet or breaker bar (different size wrenches are available for different types of filters)*

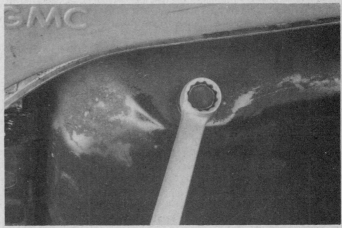

**12.9   The engine oil drain plug is located at the rear of the oil pan
(V6 engine shown) – it's usually very tight, so use a box-end
wrench to avoid rounding off the hex**

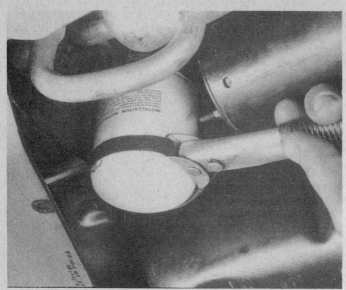

12.14   The oil filter is usually on very tight as well and will require a special wrench for removal – DO NOT use the wrench to tighten the new filter!

12.18   Lubricate the oil filter gasket with clean engine oil before installing the filter on the engine

12   Clean the area around the drain plug opening and reinstall the plug. Tighten the plug securely with the wrench. If a torque wrench is available, use it to tighten the plug.

13   Move the drain pan into position under the oil filter.

14   Use the filter wrench to loosen the oil filter **(see illustration)**. Chain or metal band filter wrenches may distort the filter canister, but this is of no concern as the filter will be discarded anyway.

15   Completely unscrew the old filter. Be careful – it's full of oil. Empty the oil inside the filter into the drain pan.

16   Compare the old filter with the new one to make sure they are the same type.

17   Use a clean rag to remove all oil, dirt and sludge from the area where the oil filter mounts on the engine. Check the old filter to make sure the rubber gasket isn't stuck to the engine. If the gasket is stuck to the engine (use a flashlight if necessary), remove it.

18   Apply a light coat of oil to the rubber gasket on the new oil filter **(see illustration)**. Open a container of oil and partially fill the oil filter with fresh oil. Oil pressure will not build in the engine until the oil pump has filled the filter with oil, so partially filling it at this time will reduce the amount of time the engine runs with no oil pressure.

19   Attach the new filter to the engine, following the tightening directions printed on the filter canister or box. Most filter manufacturers recommend against using a filter wrench due to the possibility of overtightening and damage to the seal.

20   Remove all tools, rags, etc. from under the vehicle, being careful not to spill the oil in the drain pan, then lower the vehicle.

21   Move to the engine compartment and locate the oil filler cap.

22   Pour the fresh oil through the filler opening. A funnel can be used.

23   Pour three quarts of fresh oil into the engine. Wait a few minutes to allow the oil to drain into the pan, then check the level on the dipstick (see Section 4 if necessary). If the oil level is above the ADD mark, start the engine and allow the new oil to circulate.

24   Run the engine for only about a minute and then shut it off. Immediately look under the vehicle and check for leaks at the oil pan drain plug and around the oil filter. If either is leaking, tighten with a bit more force.

25   With the new oil circulated and the filter now completely full, recheck the level on the dipstick and add more oil as necessary.

26   During the first few trips after an oil change, make it a point to check frequently for leaks and proper oil level.

27   The old oil drained from the engine cannot be reused in its present state and should be disposed of. Oil reclamation centers, auto repair shops and gas stations will normally accept the oil, which can be refined and used again. After the oil has cooled it can be drained into a container (capped plastic jugs, topped bottles, milk cartons, etc.) for transport to a disposal site.

---

13   Chassis lubrication

Refer to illustrations 13.1 and 13.6

1   Refer to *Recommended lubricants and fluids* at the front of this Chapter to obtain the necessary lubricants. You'll also need a grease gun **(see illustration)**. Occasionally plugs will be installed rather than grease fittings. If so, grease fittings will have to be purchased and installed.

2   Look under the vehicle and see if grease fittings or plugs are installed in the balljoints and tie-rod ends. If there are plugs, remove them and buy grease fittings, which will thread into the component. A dealer or auto parts store will be able to supply the correct fittings. Straight, as well as angled, fittings are available.

3   For easier access under the vehicle, raise it with a jack and place jackstands under the frame. Make sure it's securely supported by the stands. If the wheels are being removed at this interval for rotation or brake inspection, loosen the lug nuts slightly while the vehicle is still on the ground.

4   Before beginning, force a little grease out of the nozzle to remove any dirt from the end of the gun. Wipe the nozzle clean with a rag.

5   With the grease gun and plenty of clean rags, crawl under the vehicle and begin lubricating the components.

6   Wipe off the grease fitting and push the nozzle firmly over it **(see illustration)**. Squeeze the trigger on the grease gun to force grease into the component. The balljoints and tie-rod ends should be lubricated until each rubber seal is firm to the touch. Do not pump too much grease into the fitting or it could rupture the seal. If the grease escapes around the grease gun nozzle, the fitting is clogged or the nozzle isn't completely seated on the fitting. Resecure the gun nozzle to the fitting and try again. If necessary, replace the fitting with a new one.

7   Wipe the excess grease off the components and the grease fitting. Repeat the procedure for the remaining fittings.

8   If the vehicle is equipped with a manual transaxle, lubricate the shift linkage with a little multi-purpose grease. While you are under the vehicle, clean and lubricate the parking brake cable along with the cable guides and levers. This can be done by smearing some of the chassis grease onto the cable and its related parts with your fingers.

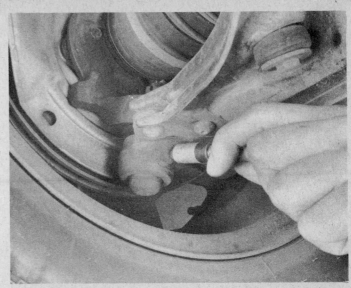

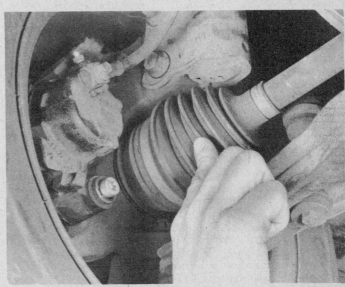

13.6   After cleaning the grease fitting, push the gun nozzle firmly into place and pump the grease into the component (usually about two pumps will be sufficient)

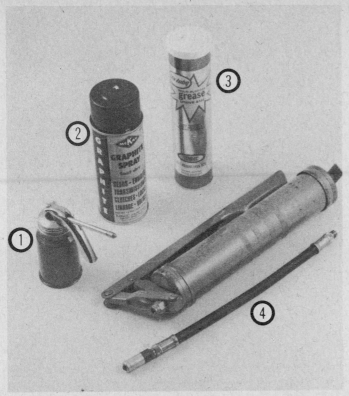

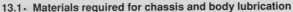

13.1   Materials required for chassis and body lubrication

1   *Engine oil – Light engine oil in a can like this can be used for door and hood hinges*
2   *Graphite spray – Used to lubricate lock cylinders*
3   *Grease – Grease, in a variety of types and weights, is available for use in a grease gun. Check the Specifications for your requirements.*
4   *Grease gun – A common grease gun, shown here with a detachable hose and nozzle, is needed for chassis lubrication. After use, clean it thoroughly!*

9   Open the hood and smear a little chassis grease on the hood latch mechanism. Have an assistant pull the hood release lever from inside the vehicle as you lubricate the cable at the latch.
10   Lubricate all the hinges (door, hood, etc.) with engine oil.
11   The key lock cylinders can be lubricated with spray-on graphite or silicone lubricant, which is available at auto parts stores. **Caution:** *The manufacturer doesn't recommend using oil in black plastic lock cylinders – it could damage them by washing out the factory-applied lubricant.*
12   Lubricate the door weatherstripping with silicone spray. This will reduce chafing and retard wear.

---

14   Driveaxle boot check

Refer to illustration 14.2

1   The driveaxle boots are very important because they prevent dirt, water and foreign material from entering and damaging the constant velocity (CV) joints.
2   Inspect the boots for tears and cracks as well as loose clamps **(see illustration)**. If there is any evidence of cracks or leaking lubricant, they must be replaced as described in Chapter 8.

---

15   Suspension and steering check

1   Raise the front of the vehicle periodically and visually check the suspension and steering components for wear.

14.2   Push on the driveaxle boots to check for cracks

2   Be alert for excessive play in the steering wheel before the front wheels react, excessive sway around corners, body movement over rough roads and binding at some point as the steering wheel is turned. If you notice any of the above symptoms, the steering and suspension systems should be checked.
3   Support the vehicle on jackstands placed under the frame rails. Because of the work to be done, make sure the vehicle cannot fall off the stands.
4   Check the front wheel hub nuts and make sure they are securely locked in place.
5   Working under the vehicle, check for loose bolts, broken or disconnected parts and deteriorated rubber bushings on all suspension and steering components. Look for grease or fluid leaking from the steering assembly. Check the power steering hoses and connections for leaks.
6   Have an assistant turn the steering wheel from side-to-side and check the steering components for free movement, chafing and binding. If the steering doesn't react with the movement of the steering wheel, try to determine where the slack is located.

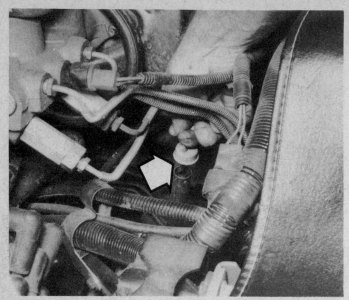

17.2   The manual transaxle dipstick (arrow) is located adjacent to the brake master cylinder

17.3   Follow the manual transaxle lubricant level checking procedure printed on the dipstick

16   Exhaust system check

1   With the engine cold (at least three hours after the vehicle has been driven), check the complete exhaust system from the engine to the end of the tailpipe. Ideally, the inspection should be done with the vehicle on a hoist to permit unrestricted access. If a hoist is not available, raise the vehicle and support it securely on jackstands.
2   Check the exhaust pipes and connections for evidence of leaks, severe corrosion and damage. Make sure that all brackets and hangers are in good condition and tight.
3   At the same time, inspect the underside of the body for holes, corrosion, open seams, etc. which may allow exhaust gases to enter the interior. Seal all body openings with silicone or body putty.
4   Rattles and other noises can often be traced to the exhaust system, especially the mounts and hangers. Try to move the pipes, muffler and catalytic converter. If the components can come in contact with the body or suspension parts, secure the exhaust system with new mounts.
5   Check the running condition of the engine by inspecting inside the end of the tailpipe. The exhaust deposits here are an indication of engine state-of-tune. If the pipe is black and sooty or coated with white deposits, the engine is in need of a tune-up, including a thorough fuel system inspection and adjustment.

17   Manual transaxle lubricant level check

Refer to illustrations 17.2 and 17.3
1   A dipstick is used for checking the lubricant level in the manual transaxles used on these models.
2   With the transaxle cold (cool to the touch) and the vehicle parked on a level surface, remove the dipstick from the filler tube located at the left rear side of the engine compartment, adjacent to the brake master cylinder **(see illustration)**.
3   The level must be even with our slightly above the FULL COLD mark on the dipstick **(see illustration)**. Make sure the level is at the FULL COLD mark because lubricant may appear on the end of the dipstick even when the transaxle is several pints low.
4   If the level is low, add the specified lubricant through the filler tube, using a funnel.
5   Insert the dipstick into the filler tube and seat it securely.

18   Tire rotation

Refer to illustration 18.2
1   The tires should be rotated at the specified intervals and whenever uneven wear is noticed.
2   Front wheel drive vehicles require a special tire rotation pattern **(see illustration)**.

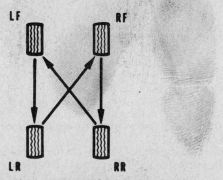

DO NOT INCLUDE "TEMPORARY USE ONLY" SPARE TIRE IN ROTATION

18.2   Tire rotation diagram

3   Refer to the information in *Jacking and towing* at the front of this manual for the proper procedures to follow when raising the vehicle and changing a tire. If the brakes are going to be checked, don't apply the parking brake as stated. Make sure the tires are blocked to prevent the vehicle from rolling as it's raised.
4   The entire vehicle should be raised at the same time. This can be done on a hoist or by jacking up each corner and then lowering the vehicle onto jackstands placed under the frame rails. Always use four jackstands and make sure the vehicle is safely supported.
5   After rotation, check and adjust the tire pressures as necessary and be sure to check the lug nut tightness.

19.3   The brake pad wear indicator (arrow) will contact the disc and make a squealing noise when the pad is worn

19.5   Look through the opening in the front of the caliper to check the brake pads (arrow) – the pad lining, which rubs against the disc, can also be inspected by looking through each end of the caliper

19   Brake check

Note: *For detailed photographs of the brake system, refer to Chapter 9.*
Warning: *Brake system dust contains asbestos, which is hazardous to your health. DO NOT blow it out with compressed air or inhale it. DO NOT use gasoline or solvents to remove the dust. Use brake system cleaner or denatured alcohol only.*

1   In addition to the specified intervals, the brakes should be inspected every time the wheels are removed or whenever a defect is suspected. Raise the vehicle and place it securely on jackstands. Remove the wheels (see Jacking and towing at the front of this manual, if necessary).

Disc brakes
Refer to illustrations 19.3 and 19.5

2   Disc brakes are used on the front of this vehicle. Extensive rotor damage can occur if the pads are not replaced when needed.
3   The disc brake pads have built-in wear indicators which make a high-pitched squealing or cricket-like warning sound when the pads are worn **(see illustration)**. **Caution:** *Expensive rotor damage can result if the pads are not replaced soon after the wear indicators start squealing.*
4   The disc brake calipers, which contain the pads, are now visible. There is an outer pad and an inner pad in each caliper. All pads should be inspected.
5   Each caliper has a "window" to inspect the pads **(see illustration)**. If the pad material has worn to about 1/8-inch thick or less, the pads should be replaced.
6   If you're unsure about the exact thickness of the remaining lining material, remove the pads for further inspection or replacement (refer to Chapter 9).
7   Before installing the wheels, check for leakage and/or damage at the brake hoses and connections. Replace the hose or fittings as necessary, referring to Chapter 9.
8   Check the condition of the brake rotor. Look for score marks, deep scratches and overheated areas (they will appear blue or discolored). If damage or wear is noted, the rotor can be removed and resurfaced by an automotive machine shop or replaced with a new one. Refer to Chapter 9 for more detailed inspection and repair procedures.

Drum brakes
Refer to illustrations 19.11a, 19.11b and 19.12

9   Using a scribe or chalk, mark the drum and hub so the drum can be reinstalled in the same position on the hub.

10   Remove and discard the retaining clip and pull the brake drum off the hub and brake assembly. If this proves difficult, make sure the parking brake is released, then squirt some penetrating oil around the center hub area. Allow the oil to soak in and try to pull the drum off again.
11   If the drum still cannot be pulled off, the brake shoes will have to be adjusted in. This is done by first removing the plug in the backing plate. If the plug is located at the bottom edge of the backing plate, pull the self-adjusting lever off the star wheel and use a small screwdriver to turn the wheel, which will move the shoes away from the drum **(see illustration)**. If

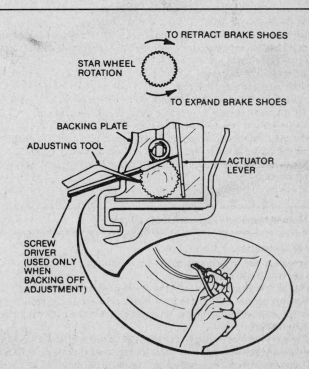

19.11a   On models with the adjustment hole at the bottom of the backing plate, use a screwdriver and adjusting tool to back off the rear brake shoes so the brake drum can be removed

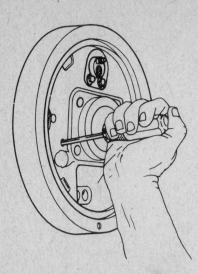

19.11b   Insert a screwdriver through the hole in the backing plate and push the parking brake lever off the stop to release the shoes from the drum

19.12   Measure the depth of the rivet hole (arrow) to determine the thickness of remaining brake shoe material

the plug is located higher up on the backing plate, insert a screwdriver and push the parking brake lever off the stop, releasing the shoes from the brake drum **(see illustration)**. With the drum removed, carefully brush away the accumulations of dirt and dust (see **Warning** above).

12   Note the thickness of the lining material on the brake shoes. If the material is worn to within 1/16-inch of the recessed rivets or metal backing, the shoes should be replaced **(see illustration)**. The shoes should also be replaced if they are cracked, glazed, (shiny surface) or contaminated with brake fluid.

13   Check to make sure all the brake assembly springs are connected and in good condition.

14   Check the brake components for signs of fluid leakage. Carefully pry back the rubber cups on the wheel cylinder, located at the top of the backing plate. Any leakage is an indication that the wheel cylinders should be replaced or overhauled immediately (Chapter 9). Also check the hoses and connections for signs of leakage.

15   Wipe the inside of the drum with a clean rag and brake cleaner or denatured alcohol.

16   Check the inside of the drum for cracks, scoring, deep scratches and hard spots, which will appear as small discolored areas. If imperfections cannot be removed with fine emery cloth, the drum must be taken to a machine shop for resurfacing.

17   After the inspection process is complete, and if all the components are in good condition, reinstall the brake drums. Install the wheels and lower the vehicle to the ground.

Parking brake

18   The parking brake is operated by a hand lever and locks the rear drum brake system. The easiest, and perhaps most obvious, method of periodically checking the operation of the parking brake assembly is to park the vehicle on a steep hill with the parking brake set and the transaxle in Neutral. If the parking brake cannot prevent the vehicle from rolling, it is in need of adjustment (see Chapter 9).

20   Fuel system check

Warning: *Certain precautions must be taken when inspecting or servicing fuel system components. Work in a well ventilated area and don't allow open flames (cigarettes, appliance pilot lights, etc.) near the work area. Mop up spills immediately and do not store fuel soaked rags where they could ignite. The fuel system is under pressure – nothing should be disconnected until the pressure is relieved (see Chapter 4).*

1   The fuel system is most easily checked with the vehicle raised on a hoist so the components underneath the vehicle are readily visible and accessible.

2   If the smell of gasoline is noticed while driving or after the vehicle has been in the sun, the system should be thoroughly inspected immediately.

3   Remove the gas tank cap and check for damage, corrosion and an unbroken sealing imprint on the gasket. Replace the cap with a new one if necessary.

4   With the vehicle raised, inspect the gas tank and filler neck for punctures, cracks and other damage. The connection between the filler neck and tank is especially critical. Sometimes a rubber filler neck will leak due to loose clamps or deteriorated rubber, problems a home mechanic can usually rectify. **Warning:** *Do not, under any circumstances, try to repair a fuel tank yourself (except rubber components). A welding torch or any open flame can easily cause the fuel vapors to explode if the proper precautions are not taken.*

5   Carefully check all rubber hoses and metal lines leading away from the fuel tank. Check for loose connections, deteriorated hoses, crimped lines and other damage. Follow the lines to the front of the vehicle, carefully inspecting them all the way. Repair or replace damaged sections as necessary.

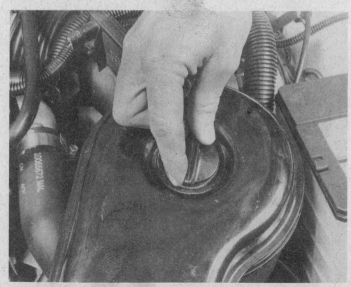

21.2a   On 2.8 liter V6 engines, remove the wing nut, . . .

21.2b ... lift off the spark arrester ...

21.2c ... and pull the air filter element out of the housing

21   Air filter and PCV filter replacement

1   At the specified intervals, the air filter and PCV filter (if equipped) should be replaced with new ones. Both filters should be inspected between changes. **Note:** *The MFI fuel injection system used on the V6 and 2.3 liter Quad-4 engines doesn't have an individual PCV filter. The engine air cleaner supplies filtered air to the PCV system.*

Air filter replacement
Multi-Port Fuel Injection (MFI) models

2.8 liter V6 engine
Refer to illustrations 21.2a, 21.2b and 21.2c

2   The air filter is located inside the air cleaner housing located at the front of the engine, near the battery. Remove the wing nut, lift off the cover and spark arrestor, then lift the filter out **(see illustrations)**.

3.1 liter V6 engine and 1992 and later 2.2L four-cylinder engine
Refer to illustration 21.3

3   Remove the bolts, lift the upper air cleaner housing off, then lift the filter element out **(see illustration)**.

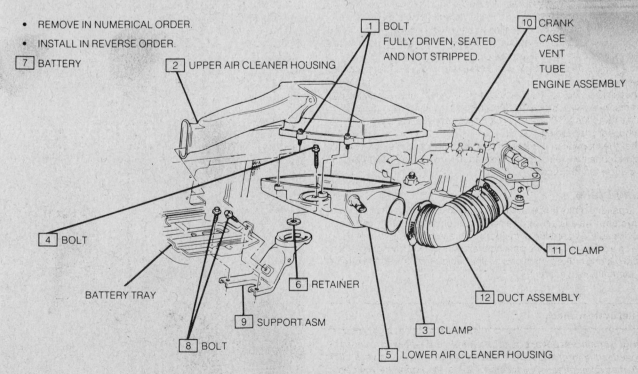

- REMOVE IN NUMERICAL ORDER.
- INSTALL IN REVERSE ORDER.

7 BATTERY

2 UPPER AIR CLEANER HOUSING

1 BOLT
FULLY DRIVEN, SEATED AND NOT STRIPPED.

10 CRANK CASE VENT TUBE ENGINE ASSEMBLY

4 BOLT

BATTERY TRAY

6 RETAINER

9 SUPPORT ASM

8 BOLT

3 CLAMP

5 LOWER AIR CLEANER HOUSING

11 CLAMP

12 DUCT ASSEMBLY

21.3   3.1 liter V6 engine air cleaner (1992 and later 2.2L four-cylinder engine similar)

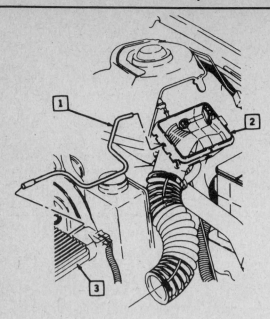

21.4   2.3 liter Quad-4 engine air cleaner

1   Inlet tube   3   Engine
2   Air cleaner assembly cover

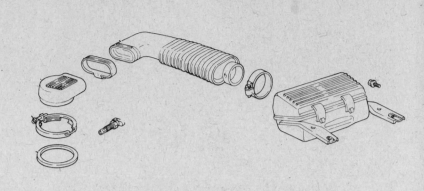

21.5   2.0 liter four-cylinder engine TBI air cleaner

2.3 liter four-cylinder (Quad-4) engine
Refer to illustration 21.4

4   The air cleaner housing is located on the left (driver's) side of the engine compartment. Remove the wing nut, lift the top cover off and withdraw the filter **(see illustration)**.

Throttle Body Injection (TBI) models

2.0 liter four-cylinder engine
Refer to illustration 21.5

5   Release the clips, lift the air cleaner housing cover up and pull the filter element out **(see illustration)**.

2.2 liter four-cylinder engine (1991 and earlier models)
Refer to illustration 21.6

6   The air filter element is located on top of the throttle body. Unscrew the nuts or bolts from the top of the filter housing, lift off the cover and remove the the filter element **(see illustration)**.

All models

7   While the filter housing cover is off, be careful not to drop anything down into the throttle body or air cleaner assembly.
8   Wipe out the inside of the air cleaner housing with a clean rag.
9   Except on TBI models with a PCV filter, place the new filter in the air cleaner housing. Make sure it seats properly in the bottom of the housing. Install the top plate or cover.

PCV filter replacement
Refer to illustrations 21.10 and 21.11

10   The PCV filter is usually located in a holder in the side of the filter housing and can be removed after disconnecting the hose and removing a clip **(see illustration)**.
11   Pull the PCV filter out of the holder **(see illustration)**.
12   Install a new PCV filter in the holder and attach it to the air cleaner housing. Install the air filter.

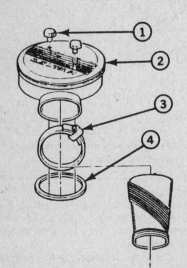

21.6   2.2 liter four-cylinder engine TBI air cleaner (1991 and earlier models)

1   Nuts
2   Housing
3   Clamp
4   Gasket

21.10   Remove the clip and withdraw the PCV filter housing from the air cleaner (TBI equipped engine)

21.11   Pull the PCV filter element out of the holder (TBI equipped engine)

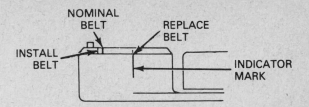

23.4   The drivebelt tensioner automatically keeps proper tension on the drivebelt, but does have limits – the indicator mark should remain in the nominal range, between the "INSTALL" and "REPLACE BELT" marks

22   Throttle Body Injection (TBI) mounting bolt torque check (2.0/2.2 liter four-cylinder engines only)

1   The TBI throttle body is attached to the top of the intake manifold by two bolts. They can sometimes work loose from vibration and temperature changes during normal engine operation and cause a vacuum leak.
2   If you suspect a vacuum leak exists at the bottom of the throttle body, use a rubber hose as a stethoscope. Start the engine and place one end of the hose next to your ear as you probe around the base of the throttle body with the other end. You will hear a hissing sound if a leak exists (be careful of hot and moving engine components).
3   Remove the air cleaner assembly (see Chapter 4).
4   Locate the throttle body mounting bolts. Decide what special tools or adapters will be necessary, if any, to tighten them.
5   Tighten the bolts securely and evenly. Do not overtighten them, as the manifold threads could strip.
6   If, after the bolts are properly tightened, a vacuum leak still exists, the throttle body must be removed and a new gasket installed. See Chapter 4 for more information.
7   After tightening the fasteners, reinstall the air cleaner and return all hoses to their original positions.

23   Drivebelt check, adjustment and replacement

Refer to illustrations 23.4, 23.5a, 23.5b, 23.5c and 23.7
1   A single serpentine drivebelt is located at the front of the engine and plays an important role in the overall operation of the engine and its components. Due to its function and material make up, the belt is prone to wear and should be periodically inspected. The serpentine belt drives the alternator, power steering pump, water pump and air conditioning compressor.
2   With the engine off, open the hood and use your fingers (and a flashlight, if necessary), to move along the belt checking for cracks and separation of the belt plies. Also check for fraying and glazing, which gives the belt a shiny appearance. Both sides of the belt should be inspected, which means you will have to twist the belt to check the underside.
3   Check the ribs on the underside of the belt. They should all be the same depth, with none of the surface uneven.
4   The tension of the belt is checked visually. Locate the belt tensioner at the front of the engine under the air conditioning compressor on the right (passenger) side, then find the tensioner operating marks (**see illustration**) located on the side of the tensioner. If the indicator mark is outside of the operating range, the belt should be replaced.

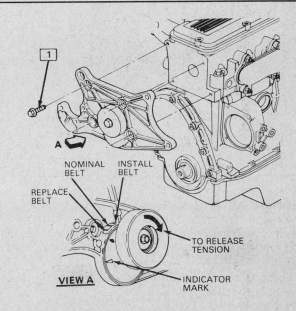

23.5a   2.0/2.2 liter four-cylinder engine serpentine drivebelt tensioner

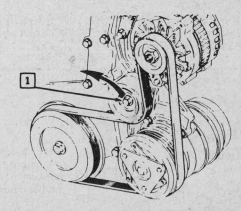

23.5b   2.3 liter four-cylinder (Quad-4) engine drivebelt tensioner (lift the tensioner [1] in the direction shown to release it)

5   To replace the belt, rotate the tensioner (clockwise on 2.0/2.2 liter four-cylinder engines/counterclockwise on V6 and 2.3 liter Quad-4 engines) to release belt tension (**see illustrations**). The tensioner will swing down once the tension of the belt is released.
6   Remove the belt from the auxiliary components and carefully release the tensioner.

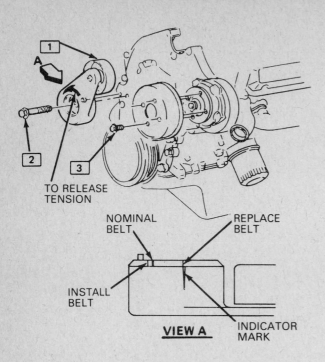

TO RELEASE
TENSION

NOMINAL
BELT

REPLACE
BELT

INSTALL
BELT

INDICATOR
MARK

VIEW A

23.5c   V6 engine drivebelt tensioner

7   Route the new belt over the various pulleys, again rotating the tensioner to allow the belt to be installed, then release the belt tensioner. **Note:** *Most models have a drivebelt routing decal on the belt guard to help during drivebelt installation* (**see illustration**).

24   Seat belt check

1   Check the seat belts, buckles, latch plates and guide loops for obvious damage and signs of wear.
2   See if the seat belt reminder light comes on when the key is turned to the Run or Start position. A chime should also sound.
3   The seat belts are designed to lock up during a sudden stop or impact, yet allow free movement during normal driving. Make sure the retractors return the belt against your chest while driving and rewind the belt fully when the buckle is unlatched.
4   If any of the above checks reveal problems with the seat belt system, replace parts as necessary.

25   Starter safety switch check

Warning: *During the following checks there's a chance the vehicle could lunge forward, possibly causing damage or injuries. Allow plenty of room around the vehicle, apply the parking brake and hold down the regular brake pedal during the checks.*

1   On automatic transaxle equipped vehicles, try to start the engine in each gear. The engine should crank only in Park or Neutral.
2   If equipped with a manual transaxle, place the shift lever in Neutral and push the clutch pedal down about halfway. The engine should crank only with the clutch pedal fully depressed.
3   Make sure the steering column lock allows the key to go into the Lock position only when the shift lever is in Park (automatic transaxle) or Reverse (manual transaxle).
4   The ignition key should come out only in the Lock position.

23.7   The serpentine drivebelt routing diagram is located on the belt guard

26   Seatback latch check

1   It's important to periodically check the seatback latch mechanism to prevent the seatback from moving forward during a sudden stop or an accident.
2   Grasping the top of the seat, attempt to tilt it forward. It should tilt only when the latch on the rear of the seat is pulled up. Note that there is a certain amount of free play built into the latch mechanism.
3   When returned to the upright position, the seatback should latch securely.

27   Spare tire and jack check

1   Periodically checking the security and condition of the spare tire and jack will help to familiarize you with the procedures necessary for emergency tire replacement and also ensure that no components work loose during normal vehicle operation.
2   Following the instructions in your owner's manual or under Jacking and towing near the front of this manual, remove the spare tire and jack.
3   Using a reliable air pressure gauge, check the pressure in the spare tire. It should be kept at the pressure marked on the tire sidewall.
4   Make sure the jack operates freely and all components are undamaged.
5   When finished, make sure the wing nuts hold the jack and tire securely in place.

28   Fuel filter replacement

Warning: *Gasoline is extremely flammable, so extra precautions must be taken when working on any part of the fuel system. Don't smoke or allow open flames or unshielded light bulbs in or near the work area. Also, don't work in a garage where a natural gas appliance (clothes dryer or water heater) with a pilot light is present. Have a fire extinguisher rated for gasoline fires handy and know how to use it!*

1   Relieve the fuel system pressure (see Chapter 4).
2   Raise the vehicle and support it securely on jackstands.

1987 and 1988 models
Refer to illustration 28.3

3   Unscrew the fuel line-to-fuel filter fittings (**see illustration**). Use a back-up wrench to keep from twisting the line.

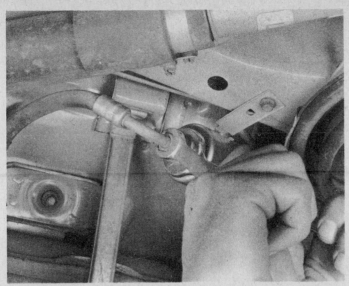

28.3   To remove the fuel filter on 1987 and 1988 models, use two wrenches to unscrew the fuel line fittings from both ends of the filter

1989 and later models

Refer to illustration 28.5

4   Grasp the filter and one of the nylon quick-connect fittings and turn the fitting 1/4-turn in each direction to loosen any dirt in it. Repeat the procedure for the other fitting. Use compressed air or carburetor cleaner to blow or wash the dirt out of the fitting.

5   Squeeze the tabs and disconnect the fuel lines from the filter **(see illustration)**.

All models

6   Remove the filter from the clip. Later model fuel filters are mounted with bolts.

7   Snap the new filter securely into the clip or install the filter mounting bolts. Make sure the arrow on the filter points toward the engine.

8   Reattach the fuel lines to the filter. **Note:** *On 1989 and later models, lubricate the fittings on the filter with clean engine oil before pushing the quick-connect fittings onto them. Make sure the tabs snap into place. Also, the fuel line and/or filter must be replaced with new ones if they are scratched or damaged during installation.*

---

29   Automatic transaxle fluid and filter change

Refer to illustration 29.11

1   At the specified time intervals, the transaxle fluid should be drained and replaced. Since the fluid will remain hot long after driving, perform this procedure only after everything has cooled down completely.

2   Before beginning work, purchase the specified transaxle fluid (see *Recommended lubricants and fluids* at the front of this Chapter) and a new filter.

3   Other tools necessary for this job include jackstands to support the vehicle in a raised position, a drain pan capable of holding several quarts, newspapers and clean rags.

4   Raise and support the vehicle on jackstands.

5   With a drain pan in place, remove the front and side oil pan mounting bolts.

6   Loosen the rear pan bolts approximately four turns.

7   Carefully pry the transaxle oil pan loose with a screwdriver, allowing the fluid to drain.

8   Remove the remaining bolts, pan and gasket. Carefully clean the gasket surface of the transaxle to remove all traces of the old gasket and sealant.

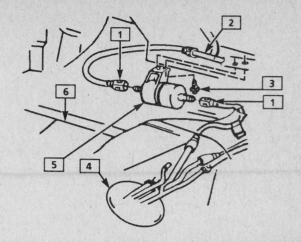

28.5   1989 and later model fuel filter

1	Nylon quick-connect fittings	4	Sending unit
2	Fuel line	5	Fuel filter
3	Filter mounting bolt	6	Fuel tank

---

9   Drain the fluid from the transaxle oil pan, clean the pan with solvent and dry it with compressed air. Be careful not to lose the magnet.

10   Remove the filter from the mount inside the transaxle.

11   Install a new filter and seal **(see illustration)**.

12   Make sure the gasket surface on the transaxle oil pan is clean, then install a new gasket. Put the pan in place against the transaxle and install the bolts. Working around the pan, tighten each bolt a little at a time until the final torque figure is reached.

13   Lower the vehicle and add the specified amount of automatic transaxle fluid through the filler tube (see Section 6).

14   With the shift lever in Park and the parking brake set, run the engine at a fast idle, but don't race it.

15   Move the shift lever through each gear and back to Park. Check the fluid level.

16   Check under the vehicle for leaks during the first few trips.

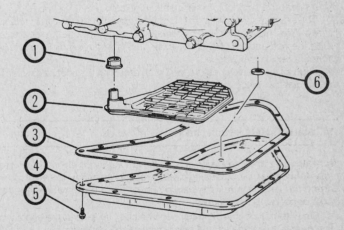

29.11   Automatic transaxle filter installation details

1	Seal	4	Pan
2	Filter	5	Bolt
3	Pan gasket	6	Magnet

30.3   Manual transaxle drain plug location (arrow)

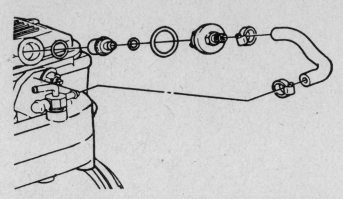

32.1a   Typical four-cylinder engine PCV system components

30   Manual transaxle lubricant change

Refer to illustration 30.3

1   Raise the vehicle and support it securely on jackstands.
2   Move a drain pan, rags, newspapers and wrenches under the transaxle.
3   Remove the transaxle drain plug and allow the oil to drain into the pan **(see illustration)**.
4   After the oil has drained completely, reinstall the plug and tighten it securely.
5   Remove the transaxle dipstick. Using a hand pump, syringe or funnel, fill the transaxle with the correct amount of specified lubricant.
6   Lower the vehicle. Check the lubricant level as described in Section 17. Add more lubricant as necessary

31   Cooling system servicing (draining, flushing and refilling)

1   Periodically, the cooling system should be drained, flushed and refilled to replenish the antifreeze mixture and prevent formation of rust and corrosion, which can impair the performance of the cooling system and cause engine damage.
2   At the same time the cooling system is serviced, all hoses and the radiator cap should be inspected and replaced if defective (see Section 9).
3   Since antifreeze is a corrosive and poisonous solution, be careful not to spill any of the coolant mixture on the vehicle's paint or your skin. If this happens, rinse it off immediately with plenty of clean water. Consult local authorities about the dumping of antifreeze before draining the cooling system. In many areas, reclamation centers have been set up to collect automobile oil and drained antifreeze/water mixtures, rather than allowing them to be added to the sewage system.
4   With the engine cold, remove the radiator cap. On 2.8 liter V6 engines, remove the vent plug in the thermostat housing.
5   Move a large container under the radiator to catch the coolant as it's drained.
6   Drain the radiator by removing the plug at the bottom on the left side. If the plug is corroded and can't be turned easily, or if the radiator isn't equipped with a plug, disconnect the lower radiator hose to allow the coolant to drain. Be careful not to get antifreeze on your skin or in your eyes.
7   Disconnect the hose from the coolant reservoir and remove the reservoir. Flush it out with clean water.
8   Place a garden hose in the radiator filler neck and flush the system until the water runs clear at all drain points.

9   In severe cases of contamination or clogging of the radiator, remove it (see Chapter 3) and reverse flush it. This involves inserting the hose in the bottom radiator outlet to allow the water to run against the normal flow, draining through the top. A radiator repair shop should be consulted if further cleaning or repair is necessary.
10   When the coolant is regularly drained and the system refilled with the correct antifreeze/water mixture, there should be no need to use chemical cleaners or descalers.
11   To refill the system, reconnect the radiator hoses and install the reservoir and the overflow hose.
12   Fill the radiator with the recommended mixture of antifreeze and water (see Section 4) to the base of the filler neck and then add more coolant to the reservoir until it reaches the lower mark.
13   With the radiator cap still removed, start the engine and run it until normal operating temperature is reached. With the engine idling, add additional coolant to the radiator and the reservoir. Install the radiator and reservoir caps. On 2.8L V6 engines, install the vent plug.
14   Keep a close watch on the coolant level and the cooling system hoses during the first few miles of driving. Tighten the hose clamps and/or add more coolant as necessary. The coolant level should be at the FULL HOT mark on 2.0/2.2 liter four-cylinder engines and V6 engines and about one-inch above the FULL HOT mark on Quad-4 engines with the engine at normal operating temperature.

32   Positive Crankcase Ventilation (PCV) valve check and replacement

Refer to illustrations 32.1a and 32.1b

1   With the engine idling at normal operating temperature, pull the valve (with hose attached) out of the rubber grommet in the rocker arm cover or camshaft cover **(see illustrations)**.
2   Place your finger over the end of the valve. If there is no vacuum at the valve, check for a plugged hose, manifold port, or the valve itself. Replace any plugged or deteriorated hoses.
3   Turn off the engine and shake the PCV valve, listening for a rattle. If the valve doesn't rattle, replace it with a new one.
4   To replace the valve, pull it out of the end of the hose, noting its installed position and direction.
5   When purchasing a replacement PCV valve, make sure it's for your particular vehicle, model year and engine size. Compare the old valve with the new one to make sure they are the same.
6   Push the valve into the end of the hose until it's seated.
7   Inspect the rubber grommet for damage and replace it with a new one if necessary.
8   Push the PCV valve and hose securely into position in the rocker arm cover or camshaft cover.

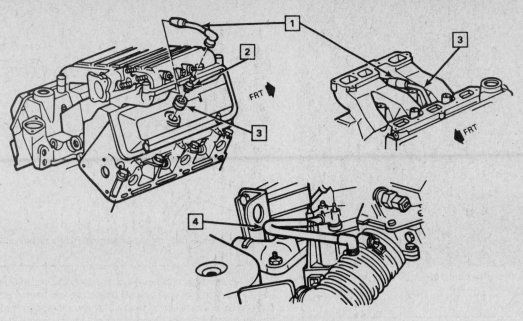

32.1b V6 engine PCV system

1 Tube
2 PCV valve
3 Manifold
4 Air vent tube

33 Evaporative emissions control system check

Refer to illustration 33.2

1   The function of the evaporative emissions control system is to draw fuel vapors from the gas tank and fuel system, store them in a charcoal canister and then burn them during normal engine operation.

2   The most common symptom of a fault in the evaporative emissions system is a strong fuel odor in the engine compartment. If a fuel odor is detected, inspect the charcoal canister, located at the front of the engine compartment **(see illustration)**. Check the canister and all hoses for damage and deterioration.

3   The evaporative emissions control system is explained in more detail in Chapter 6.

34 Exhaust Gas Recirculation (EGR) system check

Refer to illustration 34.2

1   The EGR valve is located on the intake manifold. Most of the time, when a problem develops in the emissions system, it's due to a stuck or corroded EGR valve.

2   With the engine cold to prevent burns, reach under the valve and push on the diaphragm **(see illustration)**. Using moderate pressure, you should be able to move the diaphragm.

3   If the diaphragm doesn't move or moves only with much effort, replace the EGR valve with a new one. If in doubt about the condition of the valve, compare the free movement with a new valve.

4   Refer to Chapter 6 for more information on the EGR system.

33.2   The evaporative emissions system canister is located at the right front corner of the engine compartment (arrow) – inspect the hoses attached to it and the canister itself for damage

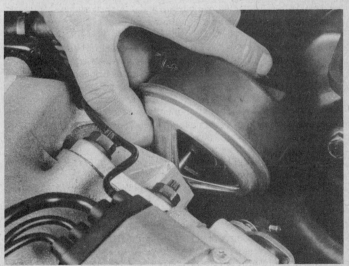

34.2   The diaphragm, reached from under the EGR valve, should move easily with finger pressure

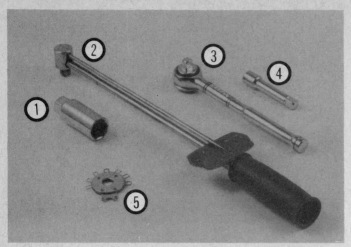

35.2   Tools required for changing spark plugs

1 **Spark plug socket** – *This will have special padding inside to protect the spark plug's porcelain insulator*
2 **Torque wrench** – *Although not mandatory, using this tool is the best way to ensure the plugs are tightened properly*
3 **Ratchet** – *Standard hand tool to fit the spark plug socket*
4 **Extension** – *Depending on model and accessories, you may need special extensions and universal joints to reach one or more of the plugs*
5 **Spark plug gap gauge** – *This gauge for checking the gap comes in a variety of styles. Make sure the gap for your engine is included.*

---

35   Spark plug replacement

Refer to illustrations 35.2, 35.5a, 35.5b, 35.6 and 35.10

1   The spark plugs are located on the front (radiator) side of the engine on four-cylinder models. On V6 engines, three plugs are located at the front and three at the rear (firewall) side of the engine.

2   In most cases, the tools necessary for spark plug replacement included a spark plug socket which fits onto a ratchet (spark plug sockets are padded inside to prevent damage to the porcelain insulators on the new plugs), various extensions and a gap gauge to check and adjust the gaps on the new plugs **(see illustration)**. A special plug wire removal tool is available for separating the wire boots from the spark plugs, but it isn't absolutely necessary. A torque wrench should be used to tighten the new plugs. Because the aluminum cylinder heads used on these models are easily damaged, allow the engine to cool before removing or installing the spark plugs.

3   The best approach when replacing the spark plugs is to purchase the new ones in advance, adjust them to the proper gap and replace the plugs one at a time. When buying the new spark plugs, be sure to obtain the correct plug type for your particular engine. The plug type can be found on the Emission Control Information label located under the hood and on the reference chart at the store where you buy the plugs. If differences exist between the plug specified on the emissions label and other sources, assume the emissions label is correct.

4   Allow the engine to cool completely before attempting to remove any of the plugs. While you are waiting for the engine to cool, check the new plugs for defects and adjust the gaps.

5   The gap is checked by inserting the proper thickness gauge between the electrodes at the tip of the plug **(see illustration)**. The gap between the electrodes should be the same as the one specified on the Emissions Control Information label. The wire should just slide between the electrodes with a slight amount of drag. If the gap is incorrect, use the adjuster on the gauge body to bend the curved side electrode slightly until the proper gap is obtained **(see illustration)**. If the side electrode is not exactly

35.5a   Spark plug manufacturers recommend using a wire type gauge when checking the gap – if the wire does not slide between the electrodes with a slight drag, adjustment is required

35.5b   To change the gap, bend the side electrode only, as indicated by the arrows, and be very careful not to crack or chip the porcelain insulator surrounding the center electrode

over the center electrode, bend it with the adjuster until it is. Check for cracks in the porcelain insulator (if any are found, the plug should not be used).

6   With the engine cool, remove the spark plug wire from one spark plug. Pull only on the boot at the end of the wire – do not pull on the wire **(see illustration on page 58)**. A plug wire removal tool should be used if available.

7   If compressed air is available, use it to blow any dirt or foreign material away from the spark plug hole. A common bicycle pump will also work. The idea here is to eliminate the possibility of debris falling into the cylinder as the spark plug is removed.

8   Place the spark plug socket over the plug and remove it from the engine by turning it in a counterclockwise direction.

9   Compare the spark plug to those shown in the accompanying photos to get an indication of the general running condition of the engine.

CARBON DEPOSITS

Symptoms: Dry sooty deposits indicate a rich mixture or weak ignition. Causes misfiring, hard starting and hesitation.

Recommendation: Check for a clogged air cleaner, high float level, sticky choke and worn ignition points. Use a spark plug with a longer core nose for greater anti-fouling protection.

OIL DEPOSITS

Symptoms: Oily coating caused by poor oil control. Oil is leaking past worn valve guides or piston rings into the combustion chamber. Causes hard starting, misfiring and hesition.

Recommendation: Correct the mechanical condition with necessary repairs and install new plugs.

TOO HOT

Symptoms: Blistered, white insulator, eroded electrode and absence of deposits. Results in shortened plug life.

Recommendation: Check for the correct plug heat range, over-advanced ignition timing, lean fuel mixture, intake manifold vacuum leaks and sticking valves. Check the coolant level and make sure the radiator is not clogged.

PREIGNITION

Symptoms: Melted electrodes. Insulators are white, but may be dirty due to misfiring or flying debris in the combustion chamber. Can lead to engine damage.

Recommendation: Check for the correct plug heat range, over-advanced ignition timing, lean fuel mixture, clogged cooling system and lack of lubrication.

HIGH SPEED GLAZING

Symptoms: Insulator has yellowish, glazed appearance. Indicates that combustion chamber temperatures have risen suddenly during hard acceleration. Normal deposits melt to form a conductive coating. Causes misfiring at high speeds.

Recommendation: Install new plugs. Consider using a colder plug if driving habits warrant.

GAP BRIDGING

Symptoms: Combustion deposits lodge between the electrodes. Heavy deposits accumulate and bridge the electrode gap. The plug ceases to fire, resulting in a dead cylinder.

Recommendation: Locate the faulty plug and remove the deposits from between the electrodes.

NORMAL

Symptoms: Brown to grayish-tan color and slight electrode wear. Correct heat range for engine and operating conditions.

Recommendation: When new spark plugs are installed, replace with plugs of the same heat range.

ASH DEPOSITS

Symptoms: Light brown deposits encrusted on the side or center electrodes or both. Derived from oil and/or fuel additives. Excessive amounts may mask the spark, causing misfiring and hesitation during acceleration.

Recommendation: If excessive deposits accumulate over a short time or low mileage, install new valve guide seals to prevent seepage of oil into the combustion chambers. Also try changing gasoline brands.

WORN

Symptoms: Rounded electrodes with a small amount of deposits on the firing end. Normal color. Causes hard starting in damp or cold weather and poor fuel economy.

Recommendation: Replace with new plugs of the same heat range.

DETONATION

Symptoms: Insulators may be cracked or chipped. Improper gap setting techniques can also result in a fractured insulator tip. Can lead to piston damage.

Recommendation: Make sure the fuel anti-knock values meet engine requirements. Use care when setting the gaps on new plugs. Avoid lugging the engine.

SPLASHED DEPOSITS

Symptoms: After long periods of misfiring, deposits can loosen when normal combustion temperature is restored by an overdue tune-up. At high speeds, deposits flake off the piston and are thrown against the hot insulator, causing misfiring.

Recommendation: Replace the plugs with new ones or clean and reinstall the originals.

MECHANICAL DAMAGE

Symptoms: May be caused by a foreign object in the combustion chamber or the piston striking an incorrect reach (too long) plug. Causes a dead cylinder and could result in piston damage.

Recommendation: Remove the foreign object from the engine and/or install the correct reach plug.

1

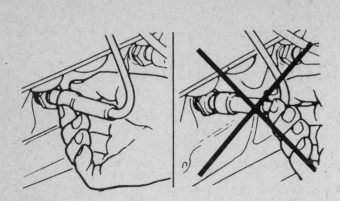

35.6   When removing a spark plug wire from a spark plug, pull only on the boot (left) and twist it back-and-forth – don't pull on the wire (as shown at the right)

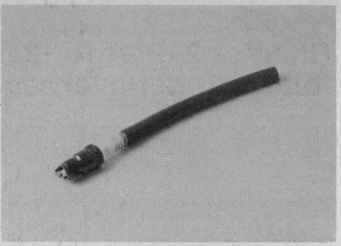

35.10   A short length of 3/16-inch ID rubber hose will prevent damaged threads when installing the spark plugs

10   Thread one of the new plugs into the hole until you can no longer turn it with your fingers, then tighten it with a torque wrench (if available) or the ratchet. It might be a good idea to slip a short length of rubber hose over the end of the plug to use as a tool to thread it into place **(see illustration)**. The hose will grip the plug well enough to turn it, but will start to slip if the plug begins to cross-thread in the hole – this will prevent damaged threads and the accompanying repair costs.

11   Before pushing the spark plug wire onto the end of the plug, inspect it following the procedures outlined in Section 36.

12   Attach the plug wire to the new spark plug, again using a twisting motion on the boot until it's seated on the spark plug.

13   Repeat the procedure for the remaining spark plugs, replacing them one at a time to prevent mixing up the spark plug wires.

36   Spark plug coil wire check and replacement

Note: *These models are equipped with distributorless ignition systems. The spark plug wires are connected directly to the ignition coils.*

1   The spark plug wires should be checked at the recommended intervals and whenever new spark plugs are installed in the engine.

2   The wires should be inspected one at a time to prevent mixing up the order, which is essential for proper engine operation.

3   Disconnect the plug wire from the spark plug. To do this, grab the rubber boot, twist slightly and pull the wire off. Do not pull on the wire itself, only on the rubber boot.

4   Check inside the boot for corrosion, which will look like a white crusty powder. Push the wire and boot back onto the end of the spark plug. It should be a tight fit on the plug. If it isn't, remove the wire and use pliers to carefully crimp the metal connector inside the boot until it fits securely on the end of the spark plug.

5   Using a clean rag, wipe the entire length of the wire to remove any built-up dirt and grease. Once the wire is clean, check for burns, cracks and other damage. Do not bend the wire excessively or pull the wire lengthwise – the conductor inside might break.

6   Disconnect the wire from the coil. Again, pull only on the rubber boot. Check for corrosion and a tight fit in the same manner as the spark plug end. Replace the wire at the coil.

7   Check the remaining spark plug wires one at a time, making sure they are securely fastened at the ignition coil and the spark plug when the check is complete.

8   If new spark plug wires are required, purchase a set for your specific engine model. Wire sets are available pre-cut, with the rubber boots already installed. Remove and replace the wires one at a time to avoid mix-ups in the firing order.

Chapter 2 Part A 2.0/2.2 liter four-cylinder overhead valve engines

Contents

2A

Specifications

General

Cylinder numbers (drivebelt end-to-transaxle end) 1-2-3-4
Firing order 1-3-4-2

Torque specifications

Ft-lbs (unless otherwise indicated)

Camshaft sprocket bolts
  1987 through 1989 .... 66 to 89
  1990 and later 77
Crankshaft pulley-to-hub bolts
  1989 .... 29 to 44
  1990 and later models 37
Crankshaft pulley center bolt
  1987 through 1989 .... 66 to 89
  1990 85
  1991 and later 77
Cylinder head bolts
  1987 through 1989
    Short bolts .... 62 to 70
    Long bolts .... 73 to 83
  1990
    First step 41
    Second step .... Rotate an additional 45-degrees (1/8-turn)
    Third step .... Rotate an additional 45-degrees
    Fourth step
      Short bolts .... Rotate an additional 10-degrees
      Long bolts .... Rotate an additional 20-degrees
  1991 and later
    First step
      Short bolts 43
      Long bolts 46
    Second step .... Rotate all bolts an additional 90-degrees
Exhaust manifold fasteners
  1987 through 1989 .... 72 to 156 in-lbs
  1990 and later .... 115 in-lbs
Flywheel bolts 55
Driveplate bolts
  1992 and earlier 52
  1993 and later 55
Intake manifold fasteners
  1987 through 1991 18
  1992 22

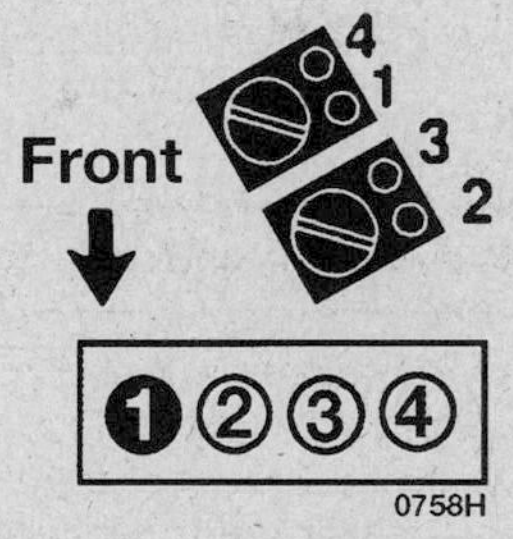

2.0/2.2 Liter

Cylinder and coil terminal location diagram

0758H

Front

Torque specifications (continued)

Ft-lbs (unless otherwise indicated)

Oil pan bolts
    1987 through 1990 .... 84 in-lbs
    1991 and 1992 .... 71 in-lbs
    1993 and later .... 89 in-lbs
Oil pump mounting bolt 32
Rocker arm cover bolts
    1992 and earlier .... 84 in-lbs
    1993 and later .... 89 in-lbs
Rocker arm nut
    1987 through 1989 .... 11 to 18
    1990 and later 22
Timing chain cover bolts .... 96 in-lbs
Timing chain tensioner 18

1   General information

Note: *On models equipped with the Delco Loc II audio system, be sure the lockout feature is turned off before performing any procedure which requires disconnecting the battery.*

    This Part of Chapter 2 is devoted to in-vehicle repair procedures for the 2.0/2.2 liter four-cylinder overhead valve engines. These engines have cast iron blocks and cast aluminum pistons. The aluminum cylinder head has replaceable valve seats and guides. Stamped steel rocker arms and tubular pushrods actuate the valves.

    All information concerning engine removal and installation and engine block and cylinder head overhaul can be found in Part D of this Chapter.

    The following repair procedures are based on the assumption the engine is in the vehicle. If the engine has been removed from the vehicle and mounted on a stand, many of the steps outlined in this Part of Chapter 2 will not apply.

    The Specifications included in this Part of Chapter 2 apply only to the procedures contained in this Part. Part D of Chapter 2 contains the Specifications necessary for cylinder head and engine block rebuilding.

2   Repair operations possible with the engine in the vehicle

    Many major repair operations can be accomplished without removing the engine from the vehicle.

    Clean the engine compartment and the exterior of the engine with some type of degreaser before any work is done. It'll make the job easier and help keep dirt out of the internal areas of the engine.

    Depending on the components involved, it may be helpful to remove the hood to improve access to the engine as repairs are performed (refer to Chapter 11 if necessary). Cover the fenders to prevent damage to the paint. Special pads are available, but an old bedspread or blanket will also work.

    If vacuum, exhaust, oil or coolant leaks develop, indicating a need for gasket or seal replacement, the repairs can generally be made with the engine in the vehicle. The intake and exhaust manifold gaskets, timing chain cover gasket, oil pan gasket, crankshaft oil seals and cylinder head gasket are all accessible with the engine in place.

    Exterior engine components, such as the intake and exhaust manifolds, the oil pan (and the oil pump), the water pump, the starter motor, the alternator and the fuel system components can be removed for repair with the engine in place.

    Since the cylinder head can be removed without pulling the engine, valve component servicing can also be accomplished with the engine in the vehicle. Replacement of the timing chain and sprockets is also possible with the engine in the vehicle.

    In extreme cases caused by a lack of necessary equipment, repair or replacement of piston rings, pistons, connecting rods and rod bearings is possible with the engine in the vehicle. However, this practice is not recommended because of the cleaning and preparation work that must be done to the components involved.

3   Rocker arm cover – removal and installation

Refer to illustration 3.4

Removal

1   Remove the air cleaner assembly, tagging each hose to be disconnected with a piece of numbered tape to simplify installation.
2   Disconnect the air hose at the throttle body and air cleaner.
3   Remove the breather hose from the rocker arm cover.
4   Remove the rocker arm cover bolts **(see illustration)**.
5   Detach the rocker arm cover from the head. **Note:** *If the cover is stuck to the cylinder head, use a block of wood and hammer to dislodge it. If that doesn't work, try to slip a flexible putty knife between the head and cover to break the gasket seal. Don't pry at the cover-to-head joint or damage to the sealing surfaces may occur (leading to oil leaks in the future).*

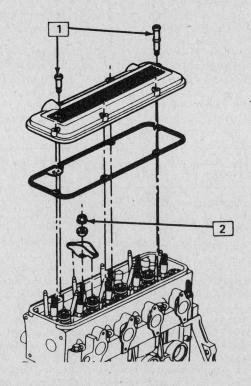

3.4 Rocker arms and related components – exploded view

1   Rocker arm cover bolts   *2   Rocker arm nuts*

2A

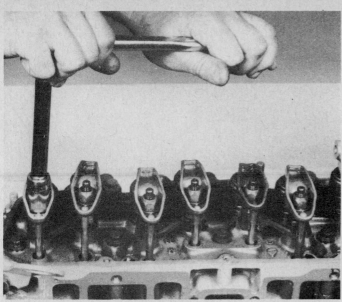

4.2   Loosen the nuts and pivot the rocker arms to one side if just the pushrods are being removed (otherwise, remove the nuts and lift off the pivot balls and rocker arms)

4.4a   The pushrods can be lifted straight out

Installation

6   The mating surfaces of the cylinder head and rocker arm cover must be perfectly clean when the cover is installed. Use a gasket scraper to remove all traces of sealant or old gasket, then clean the mating surfaces with lacquer thinner or acetone (if there's sealant or oil on the mating surfaces when the cover is installed, oil leaks may develop). The head and cover are made of aluminum, so be extra careful not to nick or gouge the mating surfaces with the scraper.

7   Clean the mounting bolt threads with a die if necessary to remove any corrosion and restore damaged threads. Make sure the threaded holes in the head are clean – run a tap into them if necessary to remove corrosion and restore damaged threads.

8   Apply a thin coat of RTV-type sealant to the sealing flange on the cover and install a new gasket.

9   Place the rocker arm cover on the cylinder head and install the mounting bolts. Tighten the bolts a little at a time to the torque listed in this Chapter's Specifications. Work from the center out in a spiral pattern.

10   Complete the installation by reversing the removal procedure.

---

4   Rocker arms and pushrods – removal, inspection and installation

---

Refer to illustrations 4.2, 4.4a and 4.4b

Removal

1   Refer to Section 3 and detach the rocker arm cover from the cylinder head.

2   Beginning at the front of the cylinder head, loosen the rocker arm nuts **(see illustration)**. **Note:** *If the pushrods are the only items being removed, rotate the rocker arms to one side so the pushrods can be lifted out.*

3   Remove the nuts, the rocker arms and the pivot balls and store them in marked containers (they must be reinstalled in their original locations).

4   Remove the pushrods and store them separately to make sure they don't get mixed up during installation **(see illustrations)**.

5   If the pushrod guides must be removed for any reason, make sure they're marked so they can be reinstalled in their original locations.

Inspection

6   Check each rocker arm for wear, cracks and other damage, especially where the pushrods and valve stems contact the rocker arm faces.

4.4b   A perforated cardboard box can be used to store the pushrods to ensure they're reinstalled in their original locations – note the label indicating the front (drivebelt end) of the engine

7   Make sure the hole at the pushrod end of each rocker arm is open.

8   Check each rocker arm pivot area for wear, cracks and galling. If the rocker arms are worn or damaged, replace them with new ones and use new pivot balls as well.

9   Inspect the pushrods for cracks and excessive wear at the ends. Roll each pushrod across a piece of plate glass to see if it's bent (if it wobbles, it's bent).

Installation

10   Lubricate the lower ends of the pushrods with clean engine oil or moly-base grease and install them in their original locations. Make sure each pushrod seats completely in the lifter socket.

11   Apply moly-base grease to the ends of the valve stems and the upper ends of the pushrods before positioning the rocker arms and installing the nuts.

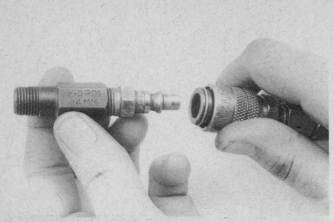

5.4   This is what the air hose adapter that threads into the spark plug hole looks like – they're commonly available at auto parts stores

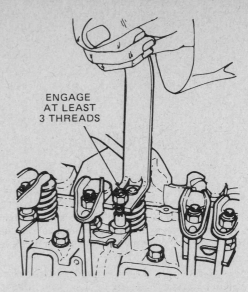

ENGAGE
AT LEAST
3 THREADS

5.9a   A special tool can be used to compress the valve springs and remove the spring keepers

5.9b   The stamped steel lever-type valve spring compressor is usually less expensive than the type that grips the spring coils

12   Set the rocker arms in place, then install the pivot balls and nuts. Apply moly-base grease to the pivot balls to prevent damage to the mating surfaces before engine oil pressure builds up. Tighten the nuts to the torque listed in this Chapter's Specifications.

5   Valve springs, retainers and seals – replacement

Refer to illustrations 5.4, 5.9a, 5.9b and 5.17
Note: *Broken valve springs and defective valve stem seals can be replaced without removing the cylinder head. Two special tools and a compressed air source are normally required to perform this operation, so read through this Section carefully and rent or buy the tools before beginning the job. If compressed air isn't available, a length of nylon rope can be used to keep the valves from falling into the cylinder during this procedure.*

1   Refer to Section 3 and remove the rocker arm cover.
2   Remove the spark plug from the cylinder which has the defective component. If all of the valve stem seals are being replaced, all of the spark plugs should be removed.
3   Turn the crankshaft until the piston in the affected cylinder is at top dead center on the compression stroke (refer to Chapter 2, Part D, for instructions). If you're replacing all of the valve stem seals, begin with cylinder number one and work on the valves for one cylinder at a time. Move

from cylinder-to-cylinder following the firing order sequence (see this Chapter's Specifications).
4   Thread an adapter into the spark plug hole **(see illustration)** and connect an air hose from a compressed air source to it. Most auto parts stores can supply the air hose adapter. **Note:** *Many cylinder compression gauges utilize a screw-in fitting that may work with your air hose quick-disconnect fitting.*
5   Remove the nut, pivot ball and rocker arm for the valve with the defective part and pull out the pushrod. If all of the valve stem seals are being replaced, all of the rocker arms and pushrods should be removed (refer to Section 4).
6   Apply compressed air to the cylinder. **Warning:** *The piston may be forced down by compressed air, causing the crankshaft to turn suddenly. If the wrench used when positioning the number one piston at TDC is still attached to the bolt in the crankshaft nose, it could cause damage or injury when the crankshaft moves.*
7   The valves should be held in place by the air pressure. If the valve faces or seats are in poor condition, leaks may prevent air pressure from retaining the valves – a "valve job" is necessary to correct this problem.
8   If you don't have access to compressed air, an alternative method can be used. Position the piston at a point just before TDC on the compression stroke, then feed a long piece of nylon rope through the spark plug hole until it fills the combustion chamber. Be sure to leave the end of the rope hanging out of the engine so it can be removed easily. Use a large ratchet and socket to rotate the crankshaft in the normal direction of rotation (clockwise) until slight resistance is felt.
9   Stuff shop rags into the cylinder head holes above and below the valves to prevent parts and tools from falling into the engine, then use a valve spring compressor to compress the spring. Remove the keepers with small needle-nose pliers or a magnet **(see illustrations)**. **Note:** *A couple of different types of tools are available for compressing the valve springs with the head in place. One type, shown here (GM no. J5892-B or equivalent) utilizes the rocker arm stud and nut for leverage, while the other type grips the lower spring coils and presses on the retainer as the knob is turned. Both types work very well, although the lever type is usually less expensive.*
10   Remove the spring retainer and valve spring, then remove the valve guide seal. **Note:** *If air pressure fails to hold the valve in the closed position during this operation, the valve face or seat is probably damaged. If so, the cylinder head will have to be removed for additional repair operations.*
11   Wrap a rubber band or tape around the top of the valve stem so the valve won't fall into the combustion chamber, then release the air pressure. **Note:** *If a rope was used instead of air pressure, turn the crankshaft slightly in the direction opposite normal rotation.*

5.17 Keepers don't always stay in place, so apply a small dab of grease to each one as shown here before installation – it'll hold them in place on the valve stem as the spring is released

12 Inspect the valve stem for damage. Rotate the valve in the guide and check the end for eccentric movement, which would indicate the valve stem is bent.

13 Move the valve up-and-down in the guide and make sure it doesn't bind. If the valve stem binds, either the valve is bent or the guide is damaged. In either case, the head will have to be removed for repair.

14 Reapply air pressure to the cylinder to retain the valve in the closed position, then remove the tape or rubber band from the valve stem. If a rope was used instead of air pressure, rotate the crankshaft in the normal direction of rotation until slight resistance is felt.

15 Lubricate the valve stem with engine oil and install a new valve guide seal. **Note:** *Intake and exhaust valve seals are different.*

16 Install the spring in position over the valve.

17 Install the valve spring retainer. Compress the valve spring and carefully install the keepers in the groove. Apply a small dab of grease to the inside of each keeper to hold it in place if necessary **(see illustration)**. Remove the pressure from the spring tool and make sure the keepers are seated.

18 Disconnect the air hose and remove the adapter from the spark plug hole. If a rope was used in place of air pressure, pull it out of the cylinder.

19 Refer to Section 4 and install the rocker arm(s) and pushrod(s).

20 Install the spark plug(s) and hook up the wire(s).

21 Refer to Section 3 and install the rocker arm cover.

22 Start and run the engine, then check for oil leaks and unusual sounds coming from the rocker arm cover area.

---

6   Intake manifold – removal and installation

Refer to illustration 6.11

1 Relieve the fuel pressure (see Chapter 4), then disconnect the negative battery cable from the battery.

2 Remove the TBI cover/air cleaner assembly (see Chapter 4).

3 Raise the front of the vehicle and support it securely on jackstands. Drain the coolant (refer to Chapter 1).

4 Label and disconnect any wires and vacuum hoses which will interfere with manifold removal.

5 Remove the throttle and TV cables and brackets (Chapter 4).

6 Remove the TBI assembly and fuel lines (see Chapter 4).

7 Remove the power steering pump (if equipped) and tie it aside in an upright position (see Chapter 10).

8 Remove the heater hose and coolant line retaining nut near the bottom of the intake manifold.

9 Remove the mounting nuts from the intake manifold.

10 Separate the intake manifold and gasket from the engine. Scrape all traces of gasket material off the intake manifold and head gasket mating surfaces.

11 Installation is the reverse of removal. Be sure to use a new gasket. Tighten the nuts/bolts to the torque listed in this Chapter's Specifications.

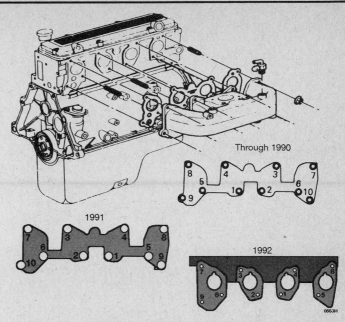

Through 1990

1991

1992

6.11   Intake manifold nut/bolt tightening sequence

Work in a spiral pattern from the center out **(see illustration)**.

12 Add coolant, run the engine and check for leaks and proper operation.

---

7   Exhaust manifold – removal and installation

Refer to illustration 7.5

1 Disconnect the negative cable from the battery.

2 Unplug the oxygen sensor lead.

3 Remove the drivebelt and the alternator (Chapters 1 and 5).

4 Raise the front of the vehicle, support it securely on jackstands and apply the parking brake. Block the rear wheels to keep the vehicle from rolling off the jackstands. Unbolt the exhaust pipe from the manifold. Lower the vehicle.

5 Remove the exhaust manifold-to-cylinder head nuts/bolts **(see illustration)**, pull the manifold off the engine and lift it out of the exhaust pipe flange. Remove and discard the gasket.

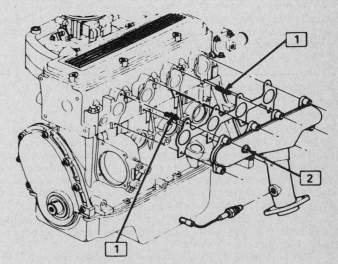

7.5   Exhaust manifold mounting details

1   Stud   2   Nut

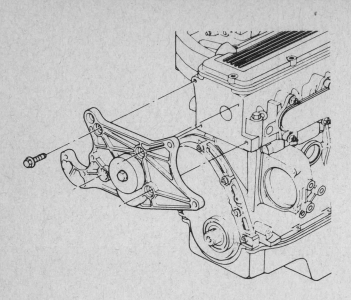

8.5   Drivebelt tensioner bracket

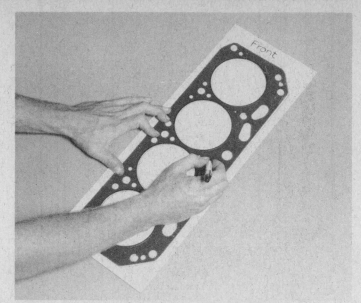

8.11a   To avoid mixing up the head bolts, use the new gasket to transfer the bolt hole pattern to a piece of cardboard, then punch holes in the cardboard to accept the bolts

Note: *On vehicles with high mileage and during an engine overhaul, camshaft lobe height should be checked prior to cylinder head removal (see Chapter 2, Part D, Section 13 for instructions).*

Removal

Refer to illustrations 8.5, 8.11a and 8.11b

1   Relieve the fuel pressure and remove the TBI cover (see Chapter 4). Disconnect the cable from the negative battery terminal.
2   Remove the alternator and brackets as described in Chapter 5.
3   Remove the intake manifold as described in Section 6.
4   Remove the exhaust manifold as described in Section 7.
5   Unbolt the drivebelt tensioner bracket **(see illustration)**.
6   Unbolt the power steering pump (if equipped) and set it aside without disconnecting the hoses (see Chapter 10).
7   Disconnect any remaining wires, hoses, fuel and vacuum lines from the cylinder head. Be sure to label them to simplify reinstallation.
8   Disconnect the spark plug wires and remove the spark plugs. Be sure the plug wires are labeled to simplify reinstallation.
9   Remove the rocker arm cover (see Section 3).
10   Remove the rocker arms and pushrods (see Section 4).
11   Using the new head gasket, outline the cylinders and bolt pattern on a piece of cardboard **(see illustration)**. Be sure to indicate the front of the engine for reference. Punch holes at the bolt locations. Loosen each of the cylinder head mounting bolts 1/4-turn at a time until they can be removed by hand **(see illustration)**. Store the bolts in the cardboard holder as they're removed – this will ensure they are reinstalled in their original locations, which is absolutely essential.
12   Lift the head off the engine. If it's stuck, don't attempt to pry it off – you could damage the sealing surfaces. Instead, use a hammer and block of wood to tap the head and break the gasket seal. Place the head on a block of wood to prevent damage to the gasket surface.
13   Remove the cylinder head gasket.
14   Refer to Chapter 2, Part D, for cylinder head disassembly and valve service procedures.

Installation

Refer to illustrations 8.17, 8.21a and 8.21b

15   If a new cylinder head is being installed, transfer all external parts from the old cylinder head to the new one.
16   If not already done, thoroughly clean the gasket surfaces on the cylinder head and the engine block. Do not gouge or otherwise damage the soft aluminum gasket surfaces.

8.11b   Loosen the cylinder head bolts in 1/4-turn increments to avoid warping the head

6   Scrape all traces of gasket material off the exhaust manifold and cylinder head mating surfaces.
7   Clean all bolt and stud threads before installation. A wire brush can be used on the manifold mounting studs, while a tap works well when cleaning the cylinder head bolt holes.
8   If a new manifold is being installed, transfer the oxygen sensor from the old manifold to the new one.
9   Installation is the reverse of removal. Be sure to use a new gasket and tighten the nuts/bolts to the torque listed in this Chapter's Specifications. Work in a spiral pattern from the center out.

---

8   Cylinder head – removal and installation

Caution: *Allow the engine to cool completely before loosening the cylinder head bolts.*

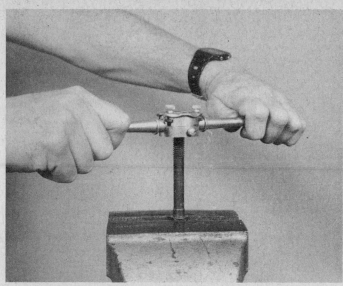

8.17   A die should be used to remove corrosion and sealant from the head bolt threads prior to installation

17   To get the proper torque readings, the threads of the head bolts must be clean **(see illustration)**. This also applies to the threaded holes in the engine block. Run a tap through the holes to ensure they are clean.

18   On 1987 through 1989 models, apply a thin coat of GM 1050026 (or equivalent) gasket sealant to both sides of the new gasket. Place the gasket in position over the engine block dowel pins. Note any marks like "THIS SIDE UP" and install the gasket accordingly.

19   Carefully lower the cylinder head onto the engine, over the dowel pins and the gasket.

20   Install the bolts finger tight. Don't tighten any of the bolts at this time.

21   Tighten each of the bolts in 1/4-turn increments in the recommended sequence **(see illustration)**. Beginning with 1990 models, a special tool (GM no. J-36660, or equivalent) must be used on the head bolts. Note that early and late models have different procedures and the rear bolts have a different torque specification than the front bolts **(see illustration)**. Continue tightening in the recommended sequence until the torque (and angle of rotation on later models) specified in this Chapter is reached. Mark each bolt with a felt-tip marker each time you tighten it to make sure none of the bolts have been left out of the sequence.

22   The remaining installation steps are the reverse of removal.

23   Be sure to refill the cooling system and change the oil and filter (see Chapter 1).

9   Hydraulic lifters – removal, inspection and installation

Refer to illustrations 9.6, 9.7, 9.9a, 9.9b and 9.9c

1   A noisy valve lifter can be isolated when the engine is idling. Place a length of hose near the location of each valve while listening at the other end of the hose. Another method is to remove the rocker arm cover and, with the engine idling, place a finger on each of the valve spring retainers, one at a time. If a valve lifter is defective it will be evident from the shock felt at the retainer as the valve seats. The most likely cause of a noisy valve lifter is a piece of dirt trapped inside the lifter.

2   Disconnect the cable from the negative battery terminal.

3   Remove the rocker arm cover as described in Section 3.

4   Loosen the rocker arm nut and rotate the rocker arm away from the pushrod (see Section 4).

5   Remove the pushrod.

6   A magnetic pick-up tool or scribe can be positioned at the top of the lifter and used to raise it up and out of the bore. To remove a stuck lifter, a special hydraulic lifter removal tool may be used **(see illustration)**. Do not use pliers or other tools on the outside of the lifter body – they will damage the machined surface and render the lifter useless.

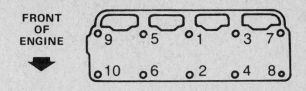

8.21a   Cylinder head bolt tightening sequence

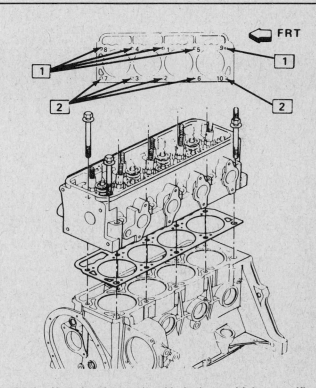

8.21b   Note that the rear head bolts have a higher specified torque than the front bolts

1   Rear (long) bolts   *2   Front (short) bolts*

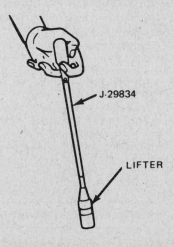

9.6   Special tools are available for removing stuck lifters

2A

9.7   If you're removing more than one lifter, keep them in order in a clearly labelled box

9.9a   The foot of each lifter should be slightly convex – the side of another lifter can be used as a straightedge to check it; if it appears flat, it's worn and must not be reused

7   If you're removing more than one lifter at a time, store them in a marked container **(see illustration)**. They must be returned to the same locations. **Note:** *Refer to Chapter 2, Part D, for camshaft removal and inspection procedures.*

8   Clean the lifters with solvent and dry them thoroughly without mixing them up.

9   Check each lifter wall, pushrod seat and foot for scuffing, score marks and uneven wear. Each lifter foot (the surface that rides on the cam lobe) must be slightly convex, although this can be difficult to determine by eye. If the base of the lifter is concave **(see illustrations)**, the lifters and camshaft must be replaced. If the lifter walls are damaged or worn (which isn't very likely), inspect the lifter bores in the engine block as well. If the pushrod seats **(see illustration)** are worn, check the pushrod ends.

10   On the roller lifters, check the rollers carefully for wear and damage and make sure they turn freely without excessive play.

11   If new lifters are being installed, a new camshaft must also be installed. If the camshaft is replaced, then install new lifters as well (see Chapter 2, Part D). Never install used lifters unless the original camshaft is

used and the lifters can be installed in their original locations! When installing lifters, make sure they're coated with moly-base grease or engine assembly lube.

12   The remaining installation steps are the reverse of removal.

---

10   Crankshaft pulley – removal and installation

Refer to illustrations 10.4a, 10.4b, 10.4c and 10.5

Removal

1   Remove the cable from the negative battery terminal.

2   Remove the drivebelt (see Chapter 1).

3   With the parking brake applied and the shifter in Park (automatic) or in gear (manual), raise the front of the vehicle and support it securely on jackstands. Remove the right front tire and the inner fender splash shield.

4   On 1989 and later models, remove the pulley-to-hub bolts. Then, on all models, remove the crankshaft pulley-to-crankshaft bolt **(see illustra-**

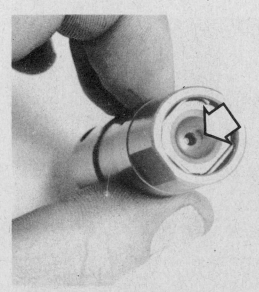

9.9b   If the bottom of any lifter is worn concave, scratched or galled, replace the entire set with new lifters

9.9c   Check the pushrod seat (arrow) in the top of each lifter for wear

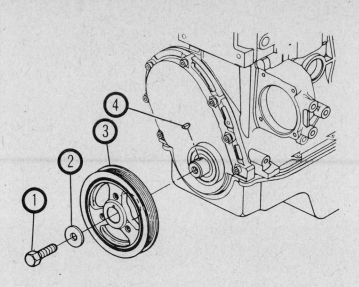

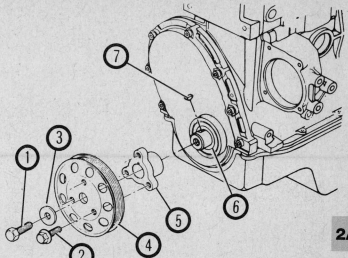

10.4a   Crankshaft pulley – 1987 and 1988 models

1	Crankshaft pulley-to-crankshaft bolt	3	Vibration damper
2	Washer	4	Woodruff key

10.4b   Crankshaft pulley – 1989 and later models

1	Pulley-to-crankshaft bolt (1)	4	Pulley
2	Pulley-to-hub bolt (3)	5	Hub
3	Washer	6	Seal
		7	Woodruff key

2A

tions). A breaker bar will probably be needed, since the bolt is very tight. If necessary, remove the lower bellhousing cover and insert a large screwdriver into the teeth of the flywheel/driveplate ring gear to prevent the crankshaft from turning **(see illustration)**.

5   Using a puller, remove the crankshaft pulley or hub from the crankshaft **(see illustration)**.

Installation

6   Refer to Section 11 for the oil seal replacement procedure.

7   Apply a thin layer of clean multi-purpose grease to the seal contact surface of the hub.

8   Position the hub on the crankshaft and slide it through the seal until it bottoms against the crankshaft gear. Note that the slot (keyway) in the hub must be aligned with the Woodruff key in the end of the crankshaft. The pulley-to-crankshaft bolt can be used to press the hub into position.

9   Tighten the pulley-to-crankshaft bolt to the torque listed in this Chapter's specifications.

10   The remaining installation steps are the reverse of removal.

11   Crankshaft front oil seal – replacement

1   Remove the crankshaft pulley (see Section 10).

2   Pry the old oil seal out with a seal removal tool or a screwdriver. Be very careful not to nick or otherwise damage the crankshaft in the process.

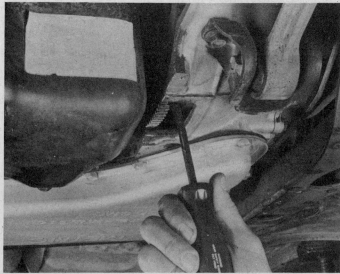

10.4c   Have an assistant hold the ring gear with a large screwdriver as the pulley-to-crankshaft bolt is loosened/tightened

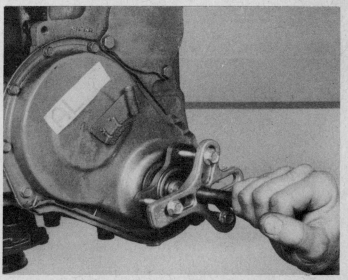

10.5   Use a puller to remove the crankshaft pulley or hub

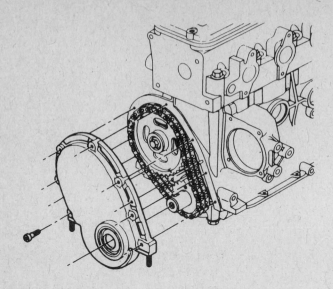

12.3 The timing chain cover is bolted to the front of the engine block and the oil pan

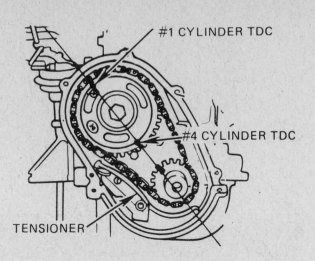

13.9 Align the camshaft and crankshaft sprocket marks as shown here – note that the marks will be positioned differently depending on which piston (number 1 or number 4) is at TDC on the compression stroke

Wrap the screwdriver tip with vinyl tape to protect the crankshaft.

3   Apply a thin coat of RTV-type sealant to the outer edge of the new seal. Lubricate the seal lip with moly-base grease or clean engine oil.

4   Place the seal squarely in position in the bore and drive it into place with special tool J 35468 (or equivalent).

5   If you don't have the special, carefully tap the seal into place with a large socket or piece of pipe and a hammer. The outer diameter of the socket or pipe should be the same size as the seal outer diameter. Make sure the seal is seated completely in the bore.

6   Install the crankshaft pulley (see Section 10).

7   Reinstall the remaining parts in the reverse order of removal.

8   Start the engine and check for oil leaks at the seal.

12 Timing chain cover – removal and installation

Refer to illustration 12.3

1   Remove the crankshaft pulley (and hub, if equipped) as described in Section 10.

2   Remove the oil pan (see Section 15).

3   Remove the drivebelt tensioner **(see illustration 8.5)** and the timing chain cover-to-block bolts, then detach the cover **(see illustration)**.

4   Using a scraper and degreaser, remove all old gasket material from the sealing surfaces of the timing chain cover, engine block and oil pan.

5   If necessary, replace the front oil seal by carefully prying it out of the cover with a large screwdriver. Don't distort the cover.

6   Install the new seal with the spring side toward the inside of the cover. Drive the seal into place using a seal installation tool or a large socket and hammer. A block of wood will also work.

7   Use a thin coat of RTV-type sealant to position a new gasket on the timing chain cover.

8   Place the cover in position over the dowel pins on the block.

9   Install the bolts that secure the cover to the block, then tighten all of them to the torque listed in this Chapter's Specifications. Follow a criss-cross pattern to avoid distorting the cover.

10 Install the oil pan (see Section 15).

11 Complete the installation by reversing the removal procedure.

13 Timing chain and sprockets – inspection, removal and installation

Refer to illustrations 13.9, 13.10 and 13.18

Inspection

1   Disconnect the cable from the negative battery terminal.

2   Remove the crankshaft pulley (see Section 10).

3   Remove the timing chain cover (see Section 12).

4   Before removing the chain and sprockets, visually inspect the teeth on the sprockets for wear and the chain for excessive slack. Also check the condition of the timing chain tensioner.

5   If either or both sprockets show any signs of wear (edges on the teeth of the camshaft sprocket not "square," bright or blue areas on the teeth of either sprocket, chipping, pitting, etc.), they should be replaced with new ones. Wear in these areas is very common.

6   Failure to replace a worn timing chain may result in erratic engine performance, loss of power and lowered fuel mileage.

7   If any one component requires replacement, all related components, including the tensioner, should be replaced as well.

8   If the chain and sprockets must be replaced, proceed as follows.

Removal

9   Temporarily install the bolt in the end of the crankshaft. Turn the engine over using the bolt until the marks on the camshaft and crankshaft line up **(see illustration)**. **Note:** *Do not attempt to remove the timing chain until this is done and do not turn the crankshaft or camshaft while the sprockets/chain are off.*

10 Remove the timing chain tensioner upper bolt **(see illustration)**. Loosen the timing chain tensioner Torx bolt as far as possible but don't remove it.

11 Remove the camshaft sprocket retaining bolt and detach the camshaft sprocket and timing chain. It may be necessary to tap the sprocket with a soft-face hammer to dislodge it.

12 If the crankshaft sprocket must be removed, it can be drawn off the crankshaft with a puller (GM no. J 22888 or equivalent).

Installation

13 Lubricate the thrust side with moly-base grease and install the crankshaft sprocket (if removed) on the crankshaft using GM tool J 5590 (or

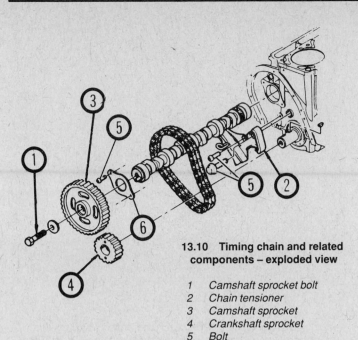

13.10   Timing chain and related components – exploded view

1   *Camshaft sprocket bolt*
2   *Chain tensioner*
3   *Camshaft sprocket*
4   *Crankshaft sprocket*
5   *Bolt*
6   *Thrust plate*

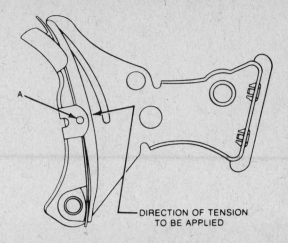

DIRECTION OF TENSION
TO BE APPLIED

13.18   Compress the timing chain tensioner and insert a pin or nail into hole "A"

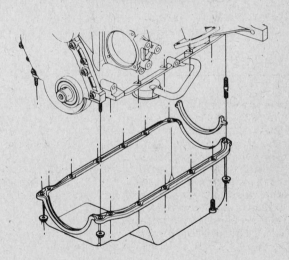

15.16   Oil pan mounting details

2A

equivalent). Be sure the Woodruff key is aligned with the keyway as the sprocket is installed. If the special tool is unavailable, drive the sprocket into place using a section of pipe just large enough to fit over the nose of the crankshaft.

14   Slip the timing chain onto the camshaft sprocket.

15   With the timing marks aligned, slip the chain over the crankshaft sprocket. Align the dowel in the camshaft with the dowel hole in the camshaft sprocket and install the sprocket on the camshaft. Draw the camshaft sprocket into place with the retaining bolt and tighten it to the torque specified in this Chapter. **Caution:** *Do not hammer or attempt to drive the camshaft sprocket into place – it could dislodge the welch plug at the rear of the engine.*

16   With the chain and both sprockets in place, check again to make sure the timing marks on the two sprockets are properly aligned **(see illustration 13.9)**. If not, remove the camshaft sprocket and move the chain until they are.

17   Lubricate the chain with clean engine oil.

18   The timing chain tensioner spring must be compressed using a special tool (GM no. J-33875 or equivalent), prior to installation. Insert a nail or cotter pin into hole A **(see illustration)** to hold the spring in place during installation. Remove the nail or pin after installation.

19   Install the remaining components in the reverse order of removal.

---

14   Camshaft and bearings – removal, inspection and installation

Due to the fact the engine is mounted transversely in the vehicle, there isn't enough room to remove the camshaft with the engine in place. Therefore, the procedure is covered in Chapter 2, Part D.

---

15   Oil pan – removal and installation

Refer to illustration 15.16

1   Warm up the engine, then drain the oil and remove the oil filter (see Chapter 1).

2   Detach the cable from the negative battery terminal.

3   Raise the vehicle and support it securely on jackstands.

4   Remove the exhaust pipe shield.

5   On air conditioned models, remove the air conditioner brace at the starter and compressor bracket.

6   Remove the starter and bracket (see Chapter 5).

7   Remove the lower bellhousing cover.

8   On air conditioned models, remove the air conditioner brace.

9   Remove the four right support bolts. Lower the support slightly to gain clearance for oil pan removal.

10   Remove the oil filter extension (automatic transaxle equipped models only).

11   Remove the bolts and nuts securing the oil pan to the engine block.

12   Tap on the pan with a soft-face hammer to break the gasket seal, then detach the oil pan from the engine.

13   Using a gasket scraper, remove all traces of old gasket and/or sealant from the engine block and oil pan. Make sure the threaded bolt holes in the block are clean. Wash the oil pan with solvent and dry it thoroughly.

14   Check the gasket flanges for distortion, particularly around the bolt holes. If necessary, place the pan on a block of wood and use a hammer to flatten and restore the gasket surfaces. Clean the mating surfaces with lacquer thinner or acetone.

15   Place a 2 mm diameter bead of RTV sealant (GM no. 1052914 or equivalent) on the oil pan-to-block sealing flanges and the oil pan-to-front cover surface.

16   Apply a thin coat of RTV sealant to the ends of the rear oil pan seal down to the ears. Press the oil pan seal into position **(see illustration)**.

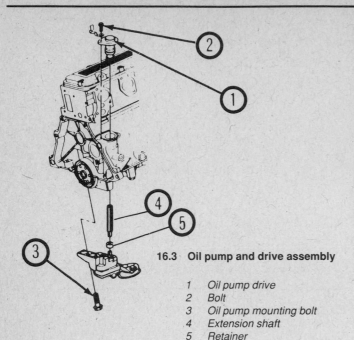

16.3 Oil pump and drive assembly

1   *Oil pump drive*
2   *Bolt*
3   *Oil pump mounting bolt*
4   *Extension shaft*
5   *Retainer*

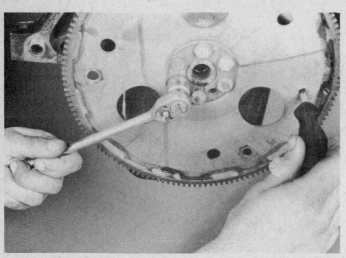

17.4 A large screwdriver wedged in the starter ring gear teeth or one of the holes in the driveplate can be used to keep the flywheel/driveplate from turning as the mounting bolts are removed

17   Carefully place the oil pan against the block.
18   Install the bolts/nuts and tighten them in 1/4-turn increments to the torque listed in this Chapter's Specifications. Start with the bolts closest to the center of the pan and work out in a spiral pattern. Don't overtighten them or leakage may occur.
19   Reinstall components removed for access to the oil pan.
20   Add oil and install a new filter, run the engine and check for oil leaks.

16   Oil pump – removal and installation

Refer to illustration 16.3

1   Remove the oil pan (see Section 15).
2   Place a large drain pan under the engine.
3   Unbolt the pump from the rear main bearing cap **(see illustration)**.
4   Lower the pump and extension shaft from the engine.

17.3 Most flywheels and driveplates have locating dowels (arrow) – if the one you're working on doesn't, make some marks to ensure correct installation

5   Before installation, prime the pump with engine oil. Pour oil into the pick-up while the pump extension shaft is turned.
6   Attach the pump, extension shaft and retainer to the main bearing cap. While aligning the pump with the dowel pins at the bottom of the main bearing cap, align the top end of the extension shaft with the lower end of the oil pump drive. When aligned properly, it should slip into place easily.
7   Install the pump mounting bolt and tighten it to the torque specified in this Chapter.
8   Install the oil pan and add oil (see Section 15).

17   Flywheel/driveplate – removal and installation

Refer to illustrations 17.3 and 17.4

1   Raise the vehicle and support it securely on jackstands, then refer to Chapter 7 and remove the transaxle. If it's leaking, now would be a very good time to replace the front pump seal/O-ring (automatic transaxle only).
2   Remove the pressure plate and clutch disc (Chapter 8 – manual transaxle equipped vehicles). Now is a good time to check/replace the clutch components and pilot bearing.
3   If there is no dowel pin, make some marks on the flywheel/driveplate and crankshaft to ensure correct alignment during reinstallation **(see illustration)**.
4   Remove the bolts that secure the flywheel/driveplate to the crankshaft **(see illustration)**. If the crankshaft turns, wedge a screwdriver through the openings in the driveplate (automatic transaxle) or against the flywheel ring gear teeth (manual transaxle). Since the flywheel is fairly heavy, be sure to support it while removing the last bolt.
5   Remove the flywheel/driveplate from the crankshaft.
6   Clean the flywheel to remove grease and oil. Inspect the friction surface for cracks, rivet grooves, burned areas and score marks. Light scoring can be removed with emery cloth. Check for cracked and broken ring gear teeth. Lay the flywheel on a flat surface and use a straightedge to check for warpage.
7   Clean and inspect the mating surfaces of the flywheel/driveplate and the crankshaft. If the crankshaft rear seal is leaking, replace it before reinstalling the flywheel/driveplate.
8   Position the flywheel/driveplate against the crankshaft. Be sure to align the dowel or marks made during removal. Before installing the bolts, apply thread locking compound to the threads.
9   Keep the flywheel/driveplate from turning as described above while you tighten the bolts to the torque listed in this Chapter's Specifications.
10   The remainder of installation is the reverse of the removal procedure.

18.2   Carefully pry the old oil seal out (V6 engine shown; four-cylinder similar)

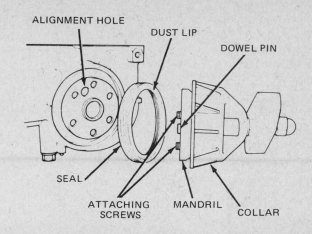

18.4   GM special tool J-34686 is needed to install the seal

2A

18   Rear main oil seal – replacement

Refer to illustrations 18.2 and 18.4
1   Remove the flywheel/driveplate (see Section 17).
2   Using a thin screwdriver or seal removal tool, carefully remove the oil seal from the engine block **(see illustration)**. Be very careful not to damage the crankshaft surface while prying the seal out.
3   Clean the bore in the block and the seal contact surface on the crankshaft. Check the seal contact surface on the crankshaft for scratches and nicks that could damage the new seal lip and cause oil leaks – if the crankshaft is damaged, the only alternative is a new or different crankshaft. Inspect the seal bore for nicks and scratches. Carefully smooth it with a fine file if necessary, but don't nick the crankshaft in the process.
4   A special tool is recommended to install the new oil seal **(see illustration)**. Lubricate the oil seal lips. Slide the seal onto the mandril until the dust lip bottoms squarely against the collar of the tool. **Note:** *If the special tool isn't available, carefully work the seal lip over the crankshaft and tap it into place with a hammer and punch.*
5   Align the dowel pin on the tool with the dowel pin hole in the crankshaft and attach the tool to the crankshaft by hand-tightening the bolts.
6   Turn the tool handle until the collar bottoms against the case, seating the seal.
7   Loosen the tool handle and remove the bolts. Remove the tool.
8   Check the seal and make sure it's seated squarely in the bore.
9   Install the flywheel/driveplate (see Section 17).
10   Install the transaxle.

19   Engine mounts – check and replacement

Refer to illustrations 19.8a, 19.8b and 19.8c
1   Engine mounts seldom require attention, but broken or deteriorated mounts should be replaced immediately or the added strain placed on the driveline components may cause damage or wear.

Check

2   During the check, the engine must be raised slightly to remove the weight from the mounts.
3   Raise the vehicle and support it securely on jackstands, then position a jack under the engine oil pan. Place a large block of wood between the jack head and the oil pan, then carefully raise the engine just enough to

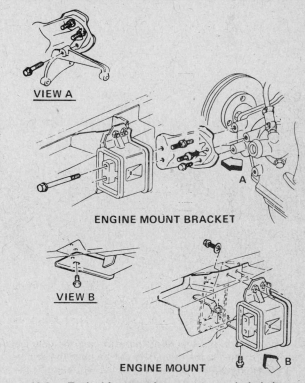

19.8a   Typical front engine mount – exploded view (1992 models use a strut-type mount)

take the weight off the mounts. **Warning:** *DO NOT place any part of your body under the engine when it's supported only by a jack!*
4   Check the mounts to see if the rubber is cracked, hardened or separated from the metal plates. Sometimes the rubber will split right down the center.
5   Check for relative movement between the mount plates and the engine or frame (use a large screwdriver or pry bar to attempt to move the mounts). If movement is noted, lower the engine and tighten the mount fasteners.
6   Rubber preservative should be applied to the mounts to slow deterioration.

Replacement

7   Disconnect the negative battery cable from the battery, then raise the vehicle and support it securely on jackstands (if not already done).

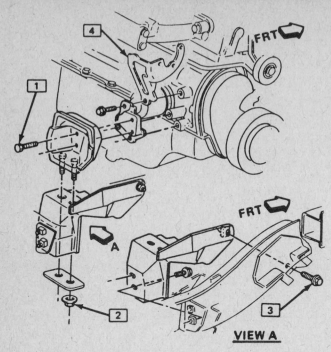

19.8b   Typical rear engine mount – exploded view

1	Bolt	3	Bolt
2	Nut	4	Power steering bracket

8   Raise the engine slightly with a jack or hoist. Remove the fasteners and detach the mount from the frame bracket **(see illustrations)**.
9   Remove the mount-to-block bracket bolts/nuts and detach the mount.
10   Installation is the reverse of removal. Use thread locking compound on the threads and be sure to tighten everything securely.

19.8c   Remove the mount-to-frame bracket nuts (arrows) – V6 engine shown; four-cylinder similar

Chapter 2 Part B
2.3 liter four-cylinder (Quad-4) engine

Contents

2B

Specifications

General

Cylinder numbers (drivebelt end-to-transaxle end)	1-2-3-4
Firing order	1-3-4-2

Camshafts and housings

Lobe lift (intake and exhaust)	0.4100 in (10.414 mm)
Lobe taper limit	0.0018 to 0.0033 inch per 0.5512 in (0.046 to 0.083 mm per 14.0 mm)
Endplay	0.0009 to 0.0088 in (0.025 to 0.225 mm)
Journal diameter	
No. 1	1.5728 to 1.5720 in (39.95 to 39.93 mm)
All others	1.3751 to 1.3760 in (34.93 to 34.95 mm)
Bearing oil clearance	0.0019 to 0.0043 in (0.050 to 0.110 mm)
Lifters	
Bore diameter	1.3775 to 1.3787 in (34.989 to 34.019 mm)
Outside diameter	1.3763 to 1.3770 in (34.959 to 34.975 mm)
Lifter-to-bore clearance	0.0006 to 0.0024 in (0.014 to 0.060 mm)
Camshaft housing warpage limit	0.001 inch per 3.937 in (0.025 mm per 100 mm)

Oil pump gear backlash

....	0.0091 to 0.0201 in (0.23 to 0.51 mm)

Torque specifications

Ft-lbs (unless otherwise indicated)

Camshaft housing-to-cylinder head bolts	
Step 1	11
Step 2	
1992 and earlier	Rotate an additional 75-degrees
1993 and later	Rotate an additional 90-degrees
Camshaft sprocket-to-camshaft bolt	
1992 and earlier	40
1993 and later	52
Vibration damper-to-crankshaft bolt	
Step 1	
1992 and earlier	74
1993	110
1994	129
Step 2	Rotate an additional 90-degrees
Cylinder head bolts	
1987 through 1991 **(see illustration 11.15a)**	
Step 1	26
Step 2	
Short bolts	Rotate an additional 100-degrees
Long bolts	Rotate an additional 110-degrees
1992 (see illustration 11.15b)	
Step 1	
Bolts 1 through 6	26
Bolts 7 & 8	15
Bolts 9 & 10	22

❶ ② ③ ④
0754H

2.3L (Quad-4)

Front
↓

Cylinder location diagram

Torque specifications (continued)

Cylinder head bolts, 1992 (continued)

	Ft-lbs (unless otherwise indicated)
Step 2	Rotate an additional 90-degrees in sequence
Step 3	Loosen each bolt 1 turn in sequence and immediately re-tighten to the torque in Step 1
Step 4	Rotate an additional 90-degrees in sequence
1993 (see illustration 11.15c)	
Step 1	
Bolts 1 through 6	18
Bolts 7 and 8	22
Bolts 9 and 10	26
Step 2	
Bolts 1 through 6	Rotate an additional 90-degrees in sequence
Bolts 7 through 10	Rotate an additional 60-degrees in sequence
Step 3	Loosen each bolt one turn (one at a time) and immediately tighten it to the Step 1 specification
Step 4	Repeat Step 2
1994 (see illustration 11.15b)	
Step 1	
Bolts 1 through 8	30
Bolts 9 and 10	26
Step 2	Rotate an additional 90-degrees in sequence
Exhaust manifold-to-cylinder head nuts	
1987 through 1990	27
1991 and later	31
Exhaust manifold-to-cylinder head studs	106 in-lbs
Flywheel-to-crankshaft bolts	
Step 1	22
Step 2	Rotate an additional 45-degrees
Intake manifold-to-cylinder head nuts/bolts	18
Oil pan baffle studs/bolts	30
Oil pan bolts	
6 mm	106 in-lbs
8 mm	17
Oil pump-to-block bolts	
1987 through 1990	33
1991 and later	40
Oil pump cover-to-oil pump body bolts	106 in-lbs
Oil pump screen assembly-to-pump bolts	
1987 through 1990	22
1991 and later	30
Oil pump screen assemby-to-brace bolts	106 in-lbs
Crankshaft rear main oil seal housing bolts	106 in-lbs
Timing chain cover-to-housing bolts	106 in-lbs
Timing chain housing bolts	19
Timing chain housing-to-block stud	
1992 and earlier	19
1993 and later	21
Timing chain tensioner	
1987 through 1991	115 in-lbs
1992	84 in-lbs
1993 and later	89 in-lbs

1   General information

Note: *On models equipped with the Delco Loc II audio system, be sure the lockout feature is turned off before performing any procedure which requires disconnecting the battery.*

This Part of Chapter 2 is devoted to in-vehicle repair procedures for the 2.3 liter four-cylinder (Quad-4) engine. All information concerning engine removal and installation and engine block and cylinder head overhaul can be found in Part D of this Chapter.

The following repair procedures are based on the assumption the engine is installed in the vehicle. If the engine has been removed from the vehicle and mounted on a stand, many of the steps outlined in this Part of Chapter 2 will not apply.

The Specifications included in this Part of Chapter 2 apply only to the procedures contained in this Part. Part D of Chapter 2 contains the Specifications necessary for cylinder head and engine block rebuilding.

The Quad-4 engine utilizes a number of advanced design features to increase power output and improve durability. The aluminum cylinder head contains four valves per cylinder. A double-row timing chain drives two overhead camshafts – one for intake and one for exhaust. Lightweight bucket-type hydraulic lifters actuate the valves. Rotators are used on all valves for extended service life.

2   Repair operations possible with the engine in the vehicle

Many major repair operations can be accomplished without removing the engine from the vehicle.

Clean the engine compartment and the exterior of the engine with some type of degreaser before any work is done. It'll make the job easier and help keep dirt out of the internal areas of the engine.

Depending on the components involved, it may be helpful to remove the hood to improve access to the engine as repairs are performed (refer

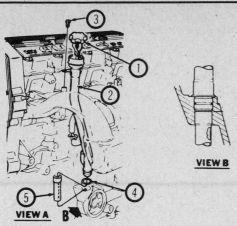

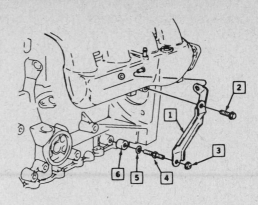

3.6 Oil fill tube components – exploded view

1	Oil fill cap and dipstick		
2	Oil fill tube	4	O-ring
3	Bolt	5	Guide

3.8 Intake manifold brace mounting details

1	Intake manifold brace	4	Stud
2	Bolt	5	Washer
3	Nut	6	Spacer

2B

to Chapter 11 if necessary). Cover the fenders to prevent damage to the paint. Special pads are available, but an old bedspread or blanket will also work.

If vacuum, exhaust, oil or coolant leaks develop, indicating a need for gasket or seal replacement, the repairs can generally be made with the engine in the vehicle. The intake and exhaust manifold gaskets, timing chain housing gasket, oil pan gasket, crankshaft oil seals and cylinder head gasket are all accessible with the engine in place.

Exterior engine components, such as the intake and exhaust manifolds, the oil pan (and the oil pump), the water pump, the starter motor, the alternator and the fuel system components can be removed for repair with the engine in place.

Since the cylinder head can be removed without pulling the engine, camshaft and valve component servicing can also be accomplished with the engine in the vehicle. Replacement of the timing chain and sprockets is also possible with the engine in the vehicle.

In extreme cases caused by a lack of necessary equipment, repair or replacement of piston rings, pistons, connecting rods and rod bearings is possible with the engine in the vehicle. However, this practice is not recommended because of the cleaning and preparation work that must be done to the components involved.

---

3   Intake manifold – removal and installation

Removal

Refer to illustrations 3.6 and 3.8

1   Relieve the fuel system pressure as described in Chapter 4.
2   Disconnect the negative battery cable from the battery, then refer to Chapter 1 and drain the cooling system.
3   Remove the throttle body (see Chapter 4).
4   Label and disconnect the vacuum and breather hoses and electrical wires.
5   Remove the oil/air separator (see Chapter 6).
6   Remove the oil fill cap and dipstick assembly **(see illustration)**.
7   Unbolt the oil fill tube and detach it from the engine block, rotating it as necessary to gain clearance between the intake tubes.
8   Remove the intake manifold brace **(see illustration)**.
9   Loosen the manifold mounting nuts/bolts in 1/4-turn increments until they can be removed by hand.
10   The manifold will probably be stuck to the cylinder head and force may be required to break the gasket seal. If necessary, dislodge the manifold with a soft-face hammer. **Caution:** *Don't pry between the head and manifold or damage to the gasket sealing surfaces will result and vacuum leaks could develop.*

Installation

Refer to illustration 3.16

Note: *The mating surfaces of the cylinder head and manifold must be perfectly clean when the manifold is installed. Gasket removal solvents in aerosol cans are available at most auto parts stores and may be helpful when removing old gasket material stuck to the head and manifold (since the components are made of aluminum, aggressive scraping can cause damage). Be sure to follow the directions printed on the container.*

11   Use a gasket scraper to remove all traces of sealant and old gasket material, then clean the mating surfaces with lacquer thinner or acetone. If there's old sealant or oil on the mating surfaces when the manifold is reinstalled, vacuum leaks may develop.
12   Use a tap of the correct size to chase the threads in the bolt holes, then use compressed air (if available) to remove the debris from the holes. **Warning:** *Wear safety glasses or a face shield to protect your eyes when using compressed air.* Use a die to clean and restore the stud threads.
13   Position the gasket on the cylinder head. Make sure all intake port openings, coolant passage holes and bolt holes are aligned correctly.
14   Install the manifold, taking care to avoid damaging the gasket.
15   Thread the nuts/bolts into place by hand.
16   Tighten the nuts/bolts to the torque listed in this Chapter's Specifications following the recommended sequence **(see illustration)**. Work up to the final torque in three steps.
17   The remaining installation steps are the reverse of removal. Start the engine and check carefully for leaks at the intake manifold joints.

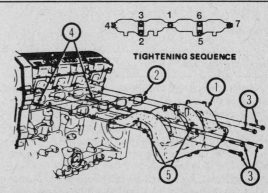

3.16 Intake manifold bolt/nut tightening sequence

1	Intake manifold	4	Studs
2	Gasket	5	Nuts
3	Bolts		

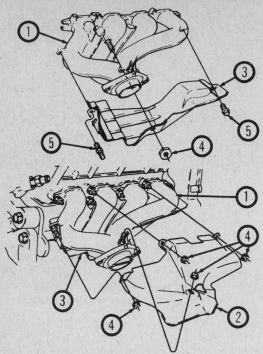

4.3   Exhaust manifold heat shields – exploded view

1   Exhaust manifold   4   Nut
2   Upper heat shield   5   Bolt
3   Lower heat shield

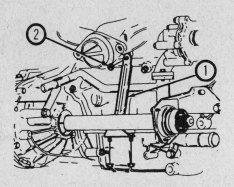

4.5   Exhaust manifold brace mounting details

1   Brace   2   Mounting nut

4   Exhaust manifold – removal and installation

Refer to illustrations 4.3, 4.4, 4.5 and 4.10

Removal

Warning: Allow the engine to cool completely before performing this procedure.

1   Disconnect the negative battery cable from the battery.
2   Unplug the oxygen sensor (see Chapter 6).
3   Remove the manifold heat shields **(see illustration)**.
4   Raise the vehicle and support it securely on jackstands, then remove the exhaust pipe-to-manifold nuts. The nuts are usually rusted in place, so penetrating oil should be applied to the stud threads before attempting to remove them. Loosen them a little at a time, working from side-to-side to prevent the flange from jamming **(see illustration)**.

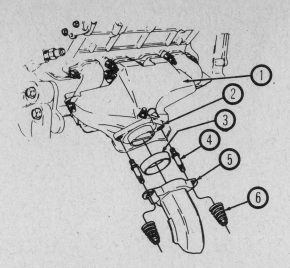

4.4   Exhaust pipe-to-manifold mounting details

1   Heat shield   4   Stud (2)
2   Exhaust manifold   5   Exhaust pipe flange
3   Seal   6   Spring nut (2)

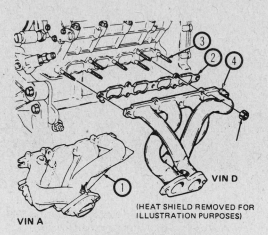

TIGHTENING SEQUENCE

4.10   Exhaust manifold nut tightening sequence

1   Exhaust manifold   3   Stud (7)
2   Gasket   4   Nut (7)

5   Remove the exhaust manifold brace **(see illustration)**.
6   Separate the exhaust pipe flange from the manifold studs, then pull the pipe down slightly to break the seal at the manifold joint.
7   Loosen the exhaust manifold mounting nuts 1/4-turn at a time each, working from the inside out, until they can be removed by hand.
8   Separate the manifold from the head and remove it.

Installation

9   The manifold and cylinder head mating surfaces must be clean when the manifold is reinstalled. Use a gasket scraper to remove all traces of old gasket material and carbon deposits.

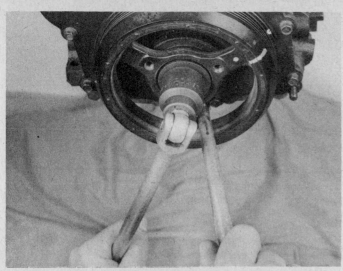

5.4   The Vibration damper can be kept from turning with a bar while the bolt is loosened/tightened

5.5   Use a bolt-type puller that applies force to the damper hub as shown here – if a jaw-type puller that applies force to the outer edge is used, the damper will be damaged

2B

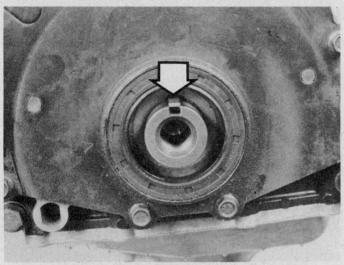

5.8   Align the keyway in the vibration damper hub with the Woodruff key in the crankshaft (arrow)

6.2   Pry the old seal out with a seal removal tool (shown here) or a screwdriver

10   Using a new gasket, install the manifold and hand tighten the fasteners. Working from the center out following the recommended sequence **(see illustration)**, tighten the bolts/nuts to the torque listed in this Chapter's Specifications.
11   The remaining installation steps are the reverse of removal.

5   Vibration damper – removal and installation

Refer to illustrations 5.4, 5.5 and 5.8
1   Remove the cable from the negative battery terminal.
2   Remove the drivebelt (see Chapter 1).
3   With the parking brake applied and the shifter in Park (automatic) or in gear (manual), raise the front of the vehicle and support it securely on jackstands.
4   Remove the bolt from the front of the crankshaft. A breaker bar will probably be necessary, since the bolt is very tight. Use GM special tool J-38122 (or equivalent) to keep the crankshaft from turning. If the special tool isn't available, insert a bar through a hole in the damper to prevent the crankshaft from turning **(see illustration)**.
5   Using a puller (tool J-24420-B or equivalent), remove the vibration

damper from the crankshaft **(see illustration)**.
6   Check the oil seal and replace it if necessary. Refer to Section 8.
7   Apply a thin layer of clean multi-purpose grease to the seal contact surface of the vibration damper hub.
8   Position the damper on the crankshaft and slide it through the seal until it bottoms against the crankshaft sprocket. Note that the slot (keyway) in the hub must be aligned with the Woodruff key in the end of the crankshaft **(see illustration)**. The crankshaft bolt can also be used to press the damper into position.
9   Tighten the crankshaft bolt to the torque and angle of rotation listed in this Chapter's Specifications.
10   The remaining installation steps are the reverse of removal.

6   Crankshaft front oil seal – replacement

Refer to illustrations 6.2 and 6.5
1   Remove the vibration damper (see Section 5).
2   Pry the old oil seal out with a seal removal tool **(see illustration)** or a screwdriver. Be very careful not to nick or otherwise damage the crank-

6.5   Install the new seal with a large socket or piece of pipe and a hammer

7.3   Remove the vent hose and engine lifting bracket bolts

1   Vent hose fitting   2   Engine lifting bracket bolts

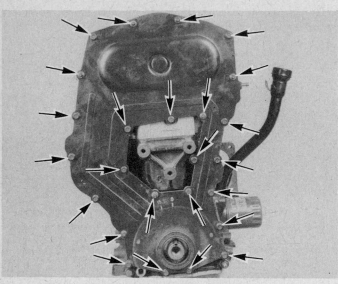

7.5   Timing chain cover fastener locations (arrows)

7.8   Note how it's installed, then remove the oil slinger (arrow) from the crankshaft

shaft in the process and don't distort the timing chain cover.

3   Apply a thin coat of RTV-type sealant to the outer edge of the new seal. Lubricate the seal lip with moly-base grease or clean engine oil.

4   Place the seal squarely in position in the bore with the spring side facing in.

5   Carefully tap the seal into place with a large socket or section of pipe and a hammer **(see illustration)**. The outer diameter of the socket or pipe should be the same size as the seal outer diameter.

6   Install the vibration damper (see Section 5).

7   Start the engine and check for oil leaks at the seal.

---

7   Timing chain and sprockets – removal, inspection and installation

---

Note: *Special tools are required for this procedure, so read through it before beginning work.*

Removal

Refer to illustrations 7.3, 7.5, 7.8, 7.10, 7.11, 7.12, 7.13, 7.14, 7.15, 7.17, 7.18 and 7.20

1   Disconnect the negative battery cable from the battery.

2   Remove the coolant reservoir (see Chapter 3).

3   Detach the timing chain cover vent hose and unbolt the engine lifting bracket at the drivebelt end of the engine **(see illustration)**.

4   Remove the vibration damper (see Section 5).

5   Working from above, remove the upper timing chain cover fasteners **(see illustration)**.

6   Working from below, remove the lower timing chain cover fasteners.

7   Detach the cover and gaskets from the housing.

8   Slide the oil slinger off the crankshaft **(see illustration)**.

9   Temporarily reinstall the vibration damper bolt to use when turning the crankshaft.

10   Turn the crankshaft clockwise until the camshaft sprocket's timing pin holes line up with the holes in the timing chain housing. Insert 8 mm pins or bolts into the holes to maintain alignment **(see illustration)**.

7.10   Insert 8 mm (5/16-inch) bolts (arrows) or pins to hold the camshaft sprockets

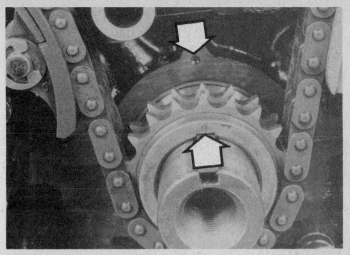

7.11   The mark on the crankshaft sprocket must align with the mark on the block (arrows)

2B

7.12   The timing chain guides are wedged into the housing at four points (arrows) – just pull them out

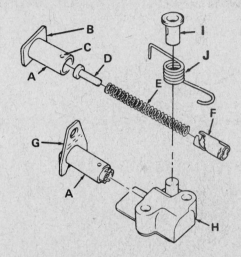

7.13   Timing chain tensioner components – exploded view

A	Plunger assembly	F	Restraint cylinder
B	Long end	G	J-36589 (anti-release device)
C	Peg	H	Tensioner body
D	Nylon plug	I	Sleeve
E	Spring	J	Spring

11   The mark on the crankshaft sprocket should line up with the mark on the engine block **(see illustration)**. The crankshaft sprocket keyway should point up and line up with the centerline of the cylinder bores.
12   Remove the three timing chain guides **(see illustration)**.
13   On models through 1991, detach the timing chain tensioner sleeve and spring **(see illustration)**.
14   On models through 1991, make sure all the slack in the timing chain is above the tensioner assembly, then remove the chain tensioner shoe **(see illustration)**. The timing chain must be disengaged from the wear grooves in the tensioner shoe in order to remove the shoe. Slide a screwdriver blade under the timing chain while pulling the shoe out. **Note:** *If difficulty is encountered when removing the chain tensioner shoe, proceed as follows:*

  a)   Hold the intake camshaft sprocket with tool J-36013 (or equivalent) and remove the sprocket bolt and washer.
  b)   Remove the washer from the bolt and thread the bolt back into the camshaft by hand.
  c)   Remove the intake camshaft sprocket, using a three-jaw puller in the three relief holes in the sprocket, if necessary. **Caution:** *Don't try to pry the sprocket off the camshaft or damage to the sprocket could occur.*

7.14   The timing chain tensioner shoe is held in place by an E-clip (1991 and earlier models)

1   *Tensioner mounting bolts*   2   *E-clip*

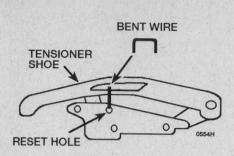

7.15   On 1992 models, after retracting the tensioner shoe, insert a piece of wire bent into a "U" shape between the tensioner shoe and reset hole

7.17   Begin removing the chain at the exhaust camshaft sprocket

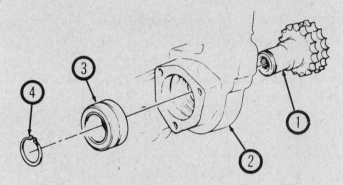

7.20   Timing chain idler sprocket, bearing and retainer

1   Idler sprocket
2   Timing chain housing
3   Bearing
4   Snap-ring

7.18   Mark the sprockets, then remove the bolts and pull the sprockets off

15   On 1992 models, bend a piece of heavy wire into a "U", then apply light force to the tensioner shoe. While applying force, insert a small screwdriver into the reset hole **(see illustration)** and pry the ratchet pawl away from the ratchet teeth. When the shoe is fully retracted, insert the piece of bent wire as shown to hold the shoe in place.

16   On all models, remove the tensioner assembly retaining bolts and tensioner. On models through 1991, the spring can be caged with GM tool J-36589, or equivalent. **Warning:** *The tensioner plunger is spring loaded and could come out with great force, causing personal injury.* Remove the chain housing-to-block stud (timing chain tensioner shoe pivot).

17   Slip the timing chain off the sprockets **(see illustration)**.

18   To remove the camshaft sprockets (if not already done), loosen the bolts while the pins are still in place. Mark the sprockets for identification **(see illustration)**, remove the bolts and pins, then pull on the sprockets by hand until they slip off the dowels.

19   The crankshaft sprocket will slip off the crankshaft by hand.

20   The idler sprocket and bearing **(see illustration)** are pressed into place. If replacement is necessary, remove the timing chain housing (see Section 8) and take it to a dealer service department or automotive machine shop. Special tools are required and the bearing must be replaced each time it's pressed out.

Inspection

21   Visually inspect all parts for wear and damage. Look for loose pins, cracks, worn rollers and side plates. Check the sprockets for hook-shaped, chipped and broken teeth. **Note:** *Some scoring of the timing chain shoe and guides is normal. Replace the timing chain, sprockets, chain shoe and guides as a set if the engine has high mileage or fails the visual parts inspection.*

Installation

Refer to illustrations 7.22, 7.23 and 7.31

22   Turn the camshafts until the dowel pins are at the top **(see illustration)**. Install both camshaft sprockets (if removed). Apply GM sealant 12345493 (or equivalent) to the camshaft sprocket bolt threads and make sure the washers are in place. Keep the camshaft from turning with tool J-36013 (or equivalent, such as 8 mm bolts). Tighten the bolts to the torque listed in this Chapter's Specifications.

23   Recheck the positions of the camshaft and crankshaft sprockets for correct valve timing **(see illustration)**. **Note:** *If the camshafts are out of*

7.22   **The camshaft sprocket locating dowels should be near the top (arrows) prior to sprocket installation**

24   Slip the timing chain over the exhaust camshaft sprocket, then around the idler and crankshaft sprockets.

25   Remove the alignment dowel pin from the intake camshaft. Using tool J-36013 (or equivalent), rotate the intake camshaft sprocket counter-clockwise enough to mesh the timing chain with it. Release the special tool. The chain run between the two camshaft sprockets will tighten. If the valve timing is correct, the intake cam alignment dowel pin should slide in easily. If it doesn't index, the camshafts aren't timed correctly; repeat the procedure.

26   Leave the dowel pins installed for now. Working under the vehicle, check the timing marks. With slack removed from the timing chain between the intake cam sprocket and the crankshaft sprocket, the timing marks on the crankshaft sprocket and the engine block should be aligned. If the marks aren't aligned, move the chain one tooth forward or backward, remove the slack and recheck the marks.

27   Install the chain housing-to-block stud (timing chain tensioner shoe pivot), and tighten it to the torque specified in this Chapter.

28   On models through 1991, reload the timing chain tensioner assembly to its "zero" position as follows:

   a)   Assemble the restraint cylinder, spring and nylon plug in the plunger. While rotating the restraint cylinder clockwise, push it into the plunger until it bottoms. Keep rotating the restraint cylinder clockwise, but allow the spring to push it out of the plunger. The pin in the plunger will lock the restraint cylinder in the loaded position.

   b)   Position tool J-36589 on the plunger assembly.

   c)   Install the plunger assembly in the tensioner body with the long end toward the crankshaft when installed.

29   Install the tensioner assembly in the chain housing. Tighten the bolts to the torque specified in this Chapter. **Note:** *Recheck the plunger assembly installation – it's correctly installed when the long end is toward the crankshaft.*

30   Install the tensioner shoe, spring and sleeve.

31   Remove tool J-36589 or the bent piece of wire and squeeze the plunger assembly into the tensioner body to unload the plunger assembly **(see illustration)**.

position and must be rotated more than 1/8-turn in order to install the alignment dowel pins:

   a)   The crankshaft must be rotated 90-degrees clockwise past Top Dead Center to give the valves adequate clearance to open.

   b)   Once the camshafts are in position and the dowels installed, rotate the crankshaft counterclockwise back to Top Dead Center. **Caution:** *Do not rotate the crankshaft clockwise to TDC (valve or piston damage could occur).*

2B

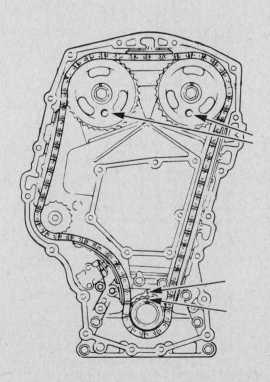

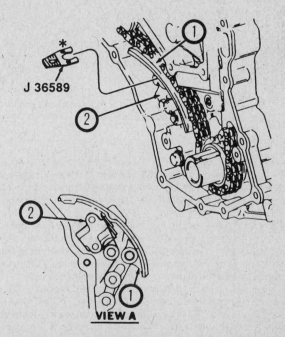

7.31   **Remove the anti-release device from the tensioner and depress the shoe once to release the tensioner (1991 and earlier models)**

7.23   **Recheck the timing mark alignment (arrows)**

1   *Timing chain tensioner shoe*   2   *Tensioner*

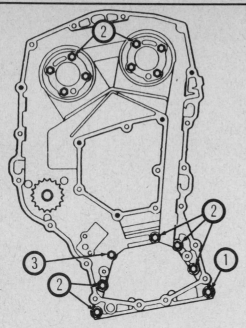

8.6   Timing chain housing mounting details

1   Bolt
2   Bolt (chain housing-to-block
*   and camshaft housings) (13)*
3   Stud (timing chain tensioner
*   shoe pivot)*

32   Remove the alignment pins.
33   Slowly rotate the crankshaft clockwise two full turns (720-degrees). Do not force it; if resistance is felt, back up and recheck the installation procedure. Align the crankshaft timing mark with the mark on the engine block and temporarily reinstall the 8 mm alignment pins. The pins should slide in easily if the valve timing is correct. **Caution:** *If the valve timing is incorrect, severe engine damage could occur.*
34   Install the remaining components in the reverse order of removal. Check fluid levels, start the engine and check for proper operation and coolant/oil leaks.

---

8   Timing chain housing – removal and installation

Refer to illustrations 8.6 and 8.14
1   Remove the timing chain and sprockets (see Section 7).
2   Remove the exhaust manifold (see Section 4).
3   If you're installing a replacement timing chain housing, remove the water pump (see Chapter 3).
4   Remove the timing chain housing-to-belt tensioner bracket brace.
5   Remove the four oil pan-to-timing chain housing bolts.
6   Remove the timing chain housing-to-block lower fasteners **(see illustration)**.
7   Remove the lowest cover retaining stud from the timing chain housing.
8   Remove the rear engine mount nut (see Section 16).
9   Loosen the front engine mount nut, leaving about three threads remaining in contact.
10   Remove the eight chain housing-to-camshaft housing bolts.
11   Position a floor jack under the oil pan, using an 18-inch long piece of wood (2x4) on the jack pad to distribute the weight.
12   Raise the engine off the front and rear mounts until the front mount bracket contacts the nut.
13   Remove the timing chain housing and gaskets. Thoroughly clean the mating surfaces to remove any traces of old sealant or gasket material.

8.14   Position a new gasket over the dowel pins (arrows)

14   Install the timing chain housing with new gaskets **(see illustration).** Tighten the bolts to the torque listed in this Chapter's Specifications.
15   The remaining steps are the reverse of removal.

---

9   Camshaft, lifters and housing – removal, inspection and installation

Note: *Special tools are required for this procedure, so read through it before beginning work.*

Removal

Intake (front)
Refer to illustrations 9.7a, 9.7b, 9.10, 9.11, 9.12 and 9.14,
1   Disconnect the cable from the negative battery terminal.
2   Remove the timing chain and sprockets (see Section 7).
3   Remove the timing chain housing-to-camshaft housing bolts (see Section 8).
4   Remove the ignition coil and module assembly (see Chapter 5).
5   Disconnect the idle speed power steering pressure switch.
6   Remove the power steering pump and brackets (see Chapter 10).
7   Remove the power steering pump drive pulley **(see illustrations).**
Caution: *The power steering pump drive pulley must be removed following this procedure or damage to the pulley will result. If any other removal procedure is used, a new pulley must be installed.*

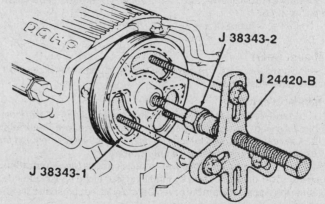

9.7a   The power steering pump drive pulley must be removed with a puller like this one . . .

9.7b   . . . or an aftermarket tool like this one – don't use any other tools

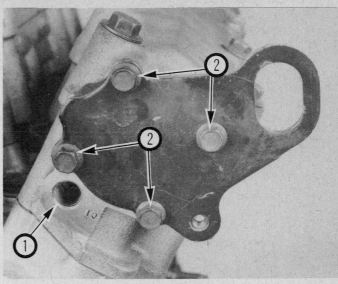

9.10   Oil pressure sending unit mounting hole (1) and engine lifting bracket bolts (2)

2B

9.11   Gently lift the camshaft housing off the cylinder head and turn it over so the lifters won't fall out

8   Remove the oil/air separator as an assembly, with the hoses attached (see Chapter 6).
9   Remove the fuel rail from the cylinder head and set it aside (see Chapter 4).

Exhaust (rear)
10   Unplug the oil pressure sending unit wire and unbolt the engine lifting bracket **(see illustration)**.

Intake and exhaust
11   Loosen the camshaft housing-to-cylinder head bolts in 1/4-turn increments, following the tightening sequence in reverse **(see illustration 9.28)**. Leave the two cover-to-housing bolts in place temporarily. Lift the housing off the cylinder head **(see illustration)**.
12   Remove the two camshaft cover-to-housing bolts **(see illustration)**. Push the cover off the housing by threading four of the housing-to-head bolts into the tapped holes in the cover. Carefully lift the camshaft out of the housing.
13   Remove all traces of old gasket material from the mating surfaces and clean them with lacquer thinner or acetone to remove any traces of oil.

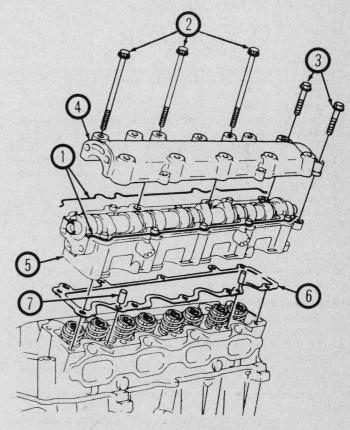

9.12   Camshaft, housing and related components – exploded view

1   *Side seal*
2   *Camshaft housing-to-cylinder head bolts*
3   *Camshaft cover-to-housing bolts*
4   *Camshaft cover*
5   *Camshaft housing*
6   *Gasket*
7   *Dowel pin*

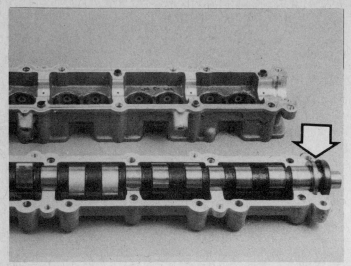

9.14   Remove the oil seal (arrow) from the intake camshaft

9.17a   Check the camshaft lobe surfaces and the bore surfaces (arrows) of the lifters for wear

9.17b   Check the valve-side of the lifters too

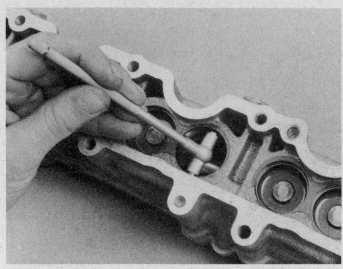

9.18   Use a telescoping gauge and micrometer to measure the lifter bores, . . .

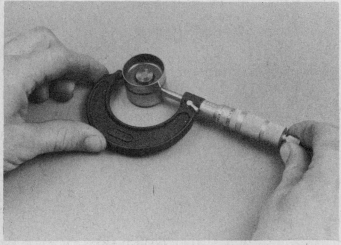

9.19   . . . then measure the lifters with a micrometer – subtract each lifter diameter from the corresponding bore diameter to obtain the lifter-to-bore clearances

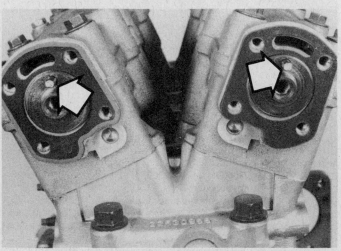

9.24   The dowel pins (arrows) should be at the top (12 o'clock position)

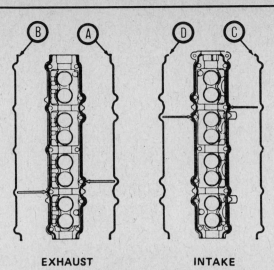

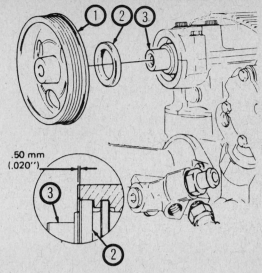

EXHAUST   **INTAKE**

9.26 Each housing side seal is different

| A | Inner exhaust (red) | C | Outer intake (blue) |
| B | Outer exhaust (red) | D | Inner intake (blue) |

9.27 Intake camshaft pulley and seal mounting details

| 1 | Power steering pulley | 3 | Intake camshaft |
| 2 | Seal | | |

2B

14   Remove the oil seal from the intake camshaft **(see illustration)** and discard it.

15   Remove the lifters and store them in order so they can be reinstalled in their original locations. To minimize lifter bleed-down, store the lifters valve-side up, submerged in clean engine oil.

Inspection

Refer to illustrations 9.17a, 9.17b, 9.18 and 9.19

16   Refer to Chapter 2, Part D, for camshaft inspection procedures, but use this Chapter's Specifications. Do not attempt to salvage camshafts. Whenever a camshaft is replaced, replace all the lifters actuated by the camshaft as well.

17   Visually inspect the lifters for wear, galling, score marks and discoloration from overheating **(see illustrations)**.

18   Measure each lifter bore inside diameter and record the results **(see illustration)**.

19   Measure each lifter outside diameter and record the results **(see illustration)**.

20   Subtract the lifter outside diameter from the corresponding bore inside diameter to determine the clearance. Compare the results to this Chapter's specifications and replace parts as necessary.

Installation

Refer to illustrations 9.24, 9.26, 9.27, 9.28 and 9.29

21   Using a new gasket, position the camshaft housing on the cylinder head and temporarily hold it in place with one bolt.

22   Coat the camshaft journals and lobes and the lifters with GM Camshaft and Lifter Prelube (no. 12345501) or equivalent and install them in their original locations.

23   On the intake camshaft only, lubricate the lip of the oil seal, then position the seal on the camshaft journal with the spring side facing in.

24   Install the camshaft in the housing with the sprocket dowel pin UP (12 o'clock position) **(see illustration)**. Position the cover on the housing, holding it in place with the two bolts, as described above.

25   Apply Pipe Sealant (GM no. 1052080) or equivalent to the threads of the camshaft housing and cover bolts.

26   Install new housing seals **(see illustration)**.

27   Install the camshaft cover and bolts while positioning the oil seal (intake side only). Be sure the seal is installed to the depth shown **(see illustration)**.

28   Tighten the bolts in the sequence shown **(see illustration)** to the torque and angle of rotation listed in this Chapter's Specifications.

29   Install the power steering pump pulley with GM tool no. J-36015 or equivalent **(see illustration)**.

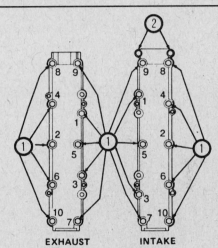

EXHAUST   INTAKE

9.28 Camshaft housing-to-cylinder head bolt tightening sequence

| 1 | Housing-to-cylinder head bolts |
| 2 | Cover-to-housing bolts |

9.29 The power steering pump drive pulley must be pressed on with a special tool

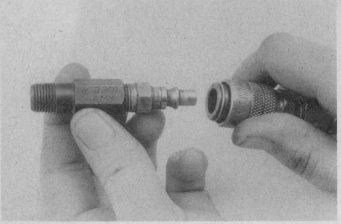

10.5   This is what the air hose adapter that threads into the spark plug hole looks like – they're commonly available from auto parts stores

10.18   Apply a small dab of grease to each keeper before installation to hold it in place on the valve stem until the spring is released

30   Install the remaining parts in the reverse order of removal.

31   Change the oil and filter (see Chapter 1). Add GM engine oil supplement 1052367 (or equivalent). **Note:** *If new lifters have been installed or the lifters bled down while the engine was disassembled, excessive lifter noise may be experienced after startup – this is normal. Use the following procedure to purge the lifters of air:*

   a) Start the engine and allow it to warm up for five minutes.
   b) Increase engine speed to 2000 rpm until the lifter noise is gone.

32   Road test the vehicle and check for oil and coolant leaks.

10   Valve springs, retainers and seals – replacement

Refer to illustrations 10.5 and 10.18

Note: *Broken valve springs and defective valve stem seals can be replaced without removing the cylinder head. Two special tools and a compressed air source are normally required to perform this operation, so read through this Section carefully and rent or buy the tools before beginning the job. If compressed air isn't available, a length of nylon rope can be used to keep the valves from falling into the cylinder during this procedure.*

1   Remove the spark plug from the cylinder which has the defective part. Due to the design of this engine, the intake and exhaust camshaft housings can be removed separately to service their respective components. If all of the valve stem seals are being replaced, all of the spark plugs and both camshaft housings should be removed.

2   Refer to Chapter 5 and remove the ignition coil assembly.

3   Remove the camshaft(s), lifters and housing(s) as described in Section 9.

4   Turn the crankshaft until the piston in the affected cylinder is at top dead center on the compression stroke (refer to Chapter 2, Part D, for instructions). If you're replacing all of the valve stem seals, begin with cylinder number one and work on the valves for one cylinder at a time. Move from cylinder-to-cylinder following the firing order sequence (see this Chapter's Specifications).

5   Thread an adapter into the spark plug hole **(see illustration)** and connect an air hose from a compressed air source to it. Most auto parts stores can supply the air hose adapter. **Note:** *Many cylinder compression gauges utilize a screw-in fitting that may work with your air hose quick-disconnect fitting.*

6   Apply compressed air to the cylinder. **Warning:** *The piston may be forced down by compressed air, causing the crankshaft to turn suddenly. If the wrench used when positioning the number one piston at TDC is still attached to the bolt in the crankshaft nose, it could cause damage or injury when the crankshaft moves.*

7   The valves should be held in place by the air pressure. If the valve faces or seats are in poor condition, leaks may prevent air pressure from retaining the valves – in this case a "valve job" is needed.

8   If you don't have access to compressed air, an alternative method can be used. Position the piston at a point just before TDC on the compression stroke, then feed a long piece of nylon rope through the spark plug hole until it fills the combustion chamber. Be sure to leave the end of the rope hanging out of the engine so it can be removed easily. Use a large ratchet and socket to rotate the crankshaft in the normal direction of rotation (clockwise) until slight resistance is felt.

9   Stuff shop rags into the cylinder head holes adjacent to the valves to prevent parts and tools from falling into the engine, then use a valve spring compressor to compress the spring. Remove the keepers with small needle-nose pliers or a magnet.

10   Remove the retainer and valve spring, then remove the valve guide seal and rotator. **Note:** *If air pressure fails to hold the valve in the closed position during this operation, the valve face or seat is probably damaged. If so, the cylinder head will have to be removed for additional repair operations.*

11   Wrap a rubber band or tape around the top of the valve stem so the valve won't fall into the combustion chamber, then release the air pressure. **Note:** *If a rope was used instead of air pressure, turn the crankshaft slightly in a counterclockwise direction (opposite normal rotation).*

12   Inspect the valve stem for damage. Rotate the valve in the guide and check the end for eccentric movement, which would indicate the valve stem is bent.

13   Move the valve up-and-down in the guide and make sure it doesn't bind. If the valve stem binds, either the valve is bent or the guide is damaged. In either case, the head will have to be removed for repair.

14   Reapply air pressure to the cylinder to retain the valve in the closed position, then remove the tape or rubber band from the valve stem. If a rope was used instead of air pressure, rotate the crankshaft in the normal direction of rotation until slight resistance is felt.

15   Reinstall the valve rotator.

16   Lubricate the valve stem with engine oil and install a new guide seal.

17   Install the spring in position over the valve.

18   Install the valve spring retainer. Compress the valve spring and carefully install the keepers in the groove. Apply a small dab of grease to the inside of each keeper to hold it in place if necessary **(see illustration)**. Remove the pressure from the spring tool and make sure the keepers are seated.

19   Disconnect the air hose and remove the adapter from the spark plug hole. If a rope was used in place of air pressure, pull it out of the cylinder.

20   Refer to Section 9 and install the camshaft(s), lifters and housing(s).

21   Install the spark plug(s) and coil assembly.

22   Start and run the engine, then check for oil leaks and unusual sounds coming from the camshaft housings.

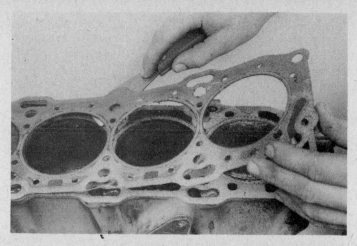

11.10   Remove the old gasket and clean the head thoroughly

11.15a   Cylinder head bolt TIGHTENING sequence
(1991 and earlier models)

2B

11   Cylinder head – removal and installation

Removal

1   Disconnect the negative cable from the battery.

2   Refer to Section 3 and remove the intake manifold. The cooling system must be drained to prevent coolant from getting into internal areas of the engine when the head is removed.

3   Refer to Section 4 and detach the exhaust manifold.

4   Remove the camshafts and housings as described in Section 9.

5   Make a holder for the head bolts. Using the new head gasket, outline the cylinders and bolt pattern on a piece of cardboard. Be sure to indicate the front of the engine for reference. Punch holes at the bolt locations **(see illustration 8.11a in Part A)**.

6   Loosen the head bolts in 1/4-turn increments until they can be removed by hand. Work from bolt-to-bolt in a pattern that's the reverse of the tightening sequence **(see illustration 11.15)**. Store the bolts in the cardboard holder as they're removed – this will ensure they are reinstalled in their original locations.

7   Lift the head off the engine. If resistance is felt, don't pry between the head and block as damage to the mating surfaces will result. To dislodge the head, place a block of wood against the end of it and strike the wood block with a hammer. Store the head on blocks of wood to prevent damage to the gasket sealing surfaces.

8   Cylinder head disassembly and inspection procedures are covered in detail in Chapter 2, Part D.

Installation

Refer to illustrations 11.10, 11.15a, 11.15b and 11.15c

9   The mating surfaces of the cylinder head and block must be perfectly clean when the head is installed.

10   Use a gasket scraper to remove all traces of carbon and old gasket material **(see illustration)**, then clean the mating surfaces with lacquer thinner or acetone. If there's oil on the mating surfaces when the head is installed, the gasket may not seal correctly and leaks could develop. **Note:** *Since the head is made of aluminum, aggressive scraping can cause damage. Be extra careful not to nick or gouge the mating surface with the scraper.* Use a vacuum cleaner to remove debris that falls into the cylinders.

11   Check the block and head mating surfaces for nicks, deep scratches and other damage. If damage is slight, it can be removed with a flat mill file; if it's excessive, machining may be the only alternative.

12   Use a tap of the correct size to chase the threads in the head bolt holes. Mount each bolt in a vise and run a die down the threads to remove corrosion and restore the threads. Dirt, corrosion, sealant and damaged threads will affect torque readings.

13   Position the new gasket over the dowel pins in the block.

14   Carefully position the head on the block without disturbing the gasket.

15   Install the bolts in their original locations and tighten them finger tight. Following the recommended sequence **(see illustrations)**, tighten the bolts in several steps to the torque and angle of rotation listed in this Chapter's Specifications.

16   The remaining installation steps are the reverse of removal.

17   Refill the cooling system and change the oil and filter (see Chapter 1, if necessary).

18   Run the engine and check for leaks and proper operation.

11.15b   Cylinder head bolt TIGHTENING sequence
(1992 and 1994 models)

11.15c   Cylinder head bolt TIGHTENING sequence
(1993 models)

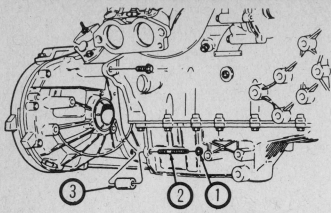

12.6   Remove the nut, stud and spacer

1	Nut	3 Spacer
2	Stud	

12.11   The oil pan baffle is held in place by four bolts (arrows)

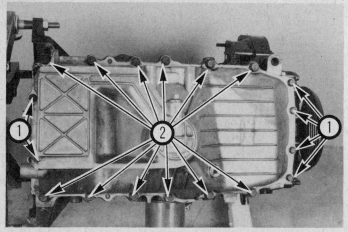

12.15   Oil pan bolt locations – viewed from below

1	6 mm bolts	2	8 mm bolts

12   Oil pan – removal and installation

Refer to illustrations 12.6, 12.11 and 12.15

Note: *The following procedure is based on the assumption the engine is in place in the vehicle. If its been removed, simply unbolt the oil pan and detach it from the block.*

Removal

1   Disconnect the negative battery cable from the battery, then refer to Chapter 1 and drain the oil.
2   Remove the lower splash shield.
3   Detach the lower bellhousing cover.
4   Unbolt the exhaust manifold brace (see Section 4).
5   Remove the radiator outlet pipe-to-oil pan bolt.
6   On manual transaxle equipped models, remove the transaxle-to-oil pan nut and stud with a 7 mm socket **(see illustration)**.
7   Gently pry the spacer out from between the oil pan and transaxle.
8   Remove the oil pan-to-transaxle bolt.
9   Remove the oil pan mounting bolts.
10   Carefully separate the pan from the block. Don't pry between the block and pan or damage to the sealing surfaces may result and oil leaks may develop. **Note:** *The Crankshaft may have to be rotated to gain clearance for oil pan removal.*
11   If you need to get at the crankshaft or other lower end components, remove the oil pan baffle **(see illustration)**.

Installation

12   Clean the sealing surfaces with lacquer thinner or acetone. Make sure the bolt holes in the block are clean.
13   The gasket should be checked carefully and replaced with a new one if damage is noted. Minor imperfections can be repaired with GM silicone sealant (no. 1052915) or equivalent. **Caution:** *Use only enough sealant to restore the gasket to its original size and shape. Excess sealant may cause part misalignment and oil leaks.*
14   Reinstall the oil pan baffle, if removed. With the gasket in position, carefully hold the pan against the block and install the bolts finger tight.
15   Tighten the bolts in three steps to the torque specified in this Chapter **(see illustration)**. Start at the center of the pan and work out toward the ends in a spiral pattern. Note that the bolts are not all tightened to the same torque figure.
16   The remaining steps are the reverse of removal. **Caution:** *Don't forget to refill the engine with oil before starting it (see Chapter 1).*
17   Start the engine and check carefully for oil leaks at the oil pan.

13   Oil pump – removal, inspection and installation

Refer to illustrations 13.2, 13.4, 13.5, 13.7a and 13.7b

Removal

1   Remove the oil pan as described in Section 12.
2   While supporting the oil pump, remove the mounting bolts **(see illustration)**.
3   Lower the pump from the engine.

Inspection

4   Clean all parts thoroughly and remove the cover **(see illustration)**.
5   Visually inspect all parts for wear, cracks and other damage **(see illustration)**. Replace the pump if it's defective, if the engine has high mileage or if the engine is being rebuilt.

Installation

6   Position the pump and shims on the engine and install the mounting bolts. Tighten them to the torque specified in this Chapter.
7   Oil pump drive gear backlash must be checked whenever the oil pump, crankshaft or engine block is replaced. Mount a dial indicator (GM tools J-26900 and J-8001, or equivalents) on the engine with the indicator stem touching the oil pump driven gear **(see illustration)**. Check the backlash and compare it to the Specifications in this Chapter. Add or subtract shims **(see illustration)** to obtain the desired backlash.
8   Install the oil pan (and baffle, if removed).
9   Add oil and run the engine. Check for oil pressure and leaks.

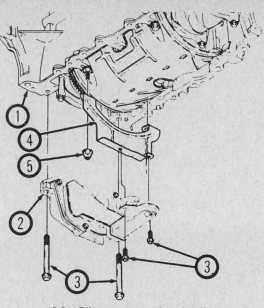

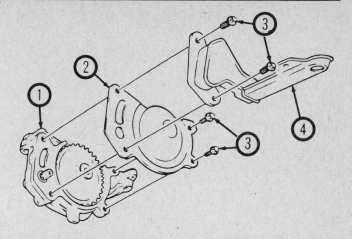

13.4   Oil pump components – exploded view

1   Oil pump   3   Bolt
2   Oil pump gear cover   4   Screen assembly

2B

13.2   Oil pump mounting details

1   Engine block   4   Brace
2   Oil pump   5   Nut
3   Bolt

13.5   Check the oil pump drive gear (arrow) and driven gear for wear and damage

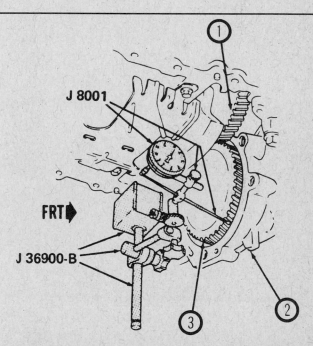

13.7a   Measuring oil pump driven gear backlash with a dial indicator

1   Oil pump drive gear
2   Oil pump (gear cover removed)
3   Oil pump driven gear

14   Flywheel – removal and installation

This procedure is essentially the same for all engines. Refer to Part A and follow the procedure outlined there. Be sure to use the bolt torque specified in this Chapter.

15   Rear main oil seal – replacement

Refer to illustrations 15.5, 15.6, 15.7 and 15.8
Note: The rear main (crankshaft) oil seal is a one-piece unit that can be replaced without removing the engine. However, the transaxle must be removed and the engine must be supported as this procedure is done. GM

special tool no. J-36005 is available for seal installation, but the procedure outlined here was devised to avoid having to use the tool.
Warning: A special tool (GM no. J-28467-A) is available to support the engine during repair operations. Similar fixtures are available from rental yards. Improper lifting methods or devices are hazardous and could result in severe injury or death. DO NOT place any part of your body under the engine/transaxle when it's supported only by a jack. Failure of the lifting device could result in serious injury or death.

1   Remove the transaxle (see Chapter 7).
2   Remove the pressure plate and clutch disc (see Chapter 8).

13.7b   Shims between the oil pump and engine block allow for adjustment of gear backlash

15.5   Remove the seal housing bolts (arrows)

15.6   After removing the housing from the engine, support it on wood blocks and drive out the old seal with a punch and hammer

15.7   Drive the new seal into the housing with a block of wood or a section of pipe, if you have one large enough – don't cock the seal in the housing bore

15.8   Lubricate the seal journal and lip, then position a new gasket over the dowel pins (arrows)

3   Remove the flywheel (see Section 14).
4   Remove the oil pan (see Section 12).
5   After the oil pan has been removed, remove the bolts (see illustration), detach the seal housing and peel off all the old gasket material.
6   Position the seal housing on a couple of wooden blocks on a workbench and drive the old seal out from the back side with a punch and hammer (see illustration).
7   Drive the new seal into the housing with a block of wood (see illustration).
8   Lubricate the crankshaft seal journal and the lip of the new seal with moly-base grease. Position a new gasket on the engine block (see illustration).
9   Slowly and carefully push the new seal onto the crankshaft. The seal lip is stiff, so work it onto the crankshaft with a smooth object such as the end of an extension as you push the housing against the block.
10   Install and tighten the housing bolts to the torque listed in this Chapter's specifications.
11   Install the flywheel and clutch components.
12   Reinstall the transaxle.

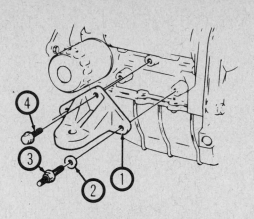

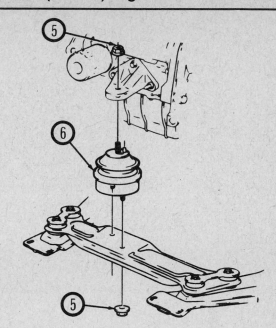

16.7   Typical front engine mount – exploded view (1992 models use a strut-type mount)

1	Bracket	4	Bolt
2	Washer	5	Nut
3	Stud	6	Mount

2B

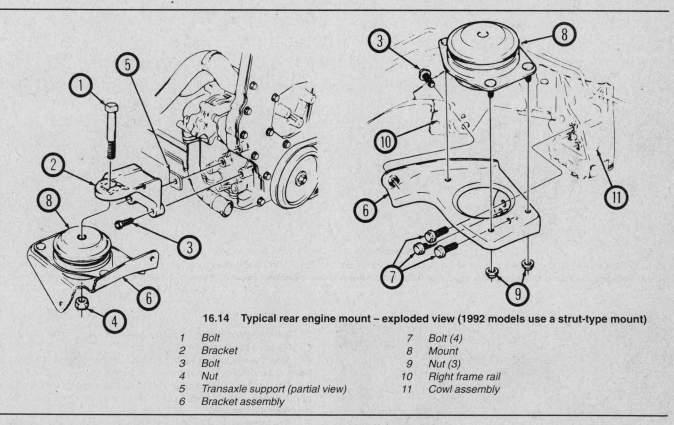

16.14   Typical rear engine mount – exploded view (1992 models use a strut-type mount)

1	Bolt	7	Bolt (4)
2	Bracket	8	Mount
3	Bolt	9	Nut (3)
4	Nut	10	Right frame rail
5	Transaxle support (partial view)	11	Cowl assembly
6	Bracket assembly		

16   Engine mounts – check and replacement

Refer to illustrations 16.7 and 16.14

Warning: *A special tool (GM no. J-28467-A) is available to support the engine during repair operations. Similar fixtures are available from rental yards. Improper lifting methods or devices are hazardous and could result in severe injury or death. DO NOT place any part of your body under the engine/transaxle when it's supported only by a jack. Failure of the lifting device could result in serious injury or death.*

1   Engine mounts seldom require attention, but broken or deteriorated mounts should be replaced immediately or the added strain placed on the driveline components may cause damage or wear.

Check

2   During the check, the engine must be raised slightly to remove the weight from the mounts.
3   Raise the vehicle and support it securely on jackstands. Support the engine as described above. If the special support fixture is unavailable, position a jack under the engine oil pan. Place a large block of wood between the jack head and the oil pan, then carefully raise the engine just enough to take the weight off the mounts. **Warning:** *DO NOT place any part of your body under the engine when it's supported only by a jack!*

4   Check the mounts to see if the rubber is cracked, hardened or separated from the metal plates. Sometimes the rubber will split right down the center.

5   Check for relative movement between the mount plates and the engine or frame (use a large screwdriver or pry bar to attempt to move the mounts). If movement is noted, lower the engine and tighten the mount fasteners.

6   Rubber preservative should be applied to the mounts to slow deterioration.

Replacement

Front mount

7   Detach the negative battery cable from the battery. Remove the upper mount nut **(see illustration)**.

8   Raise the engine off the mount.

9   Remove the two lower mount nuts.

10   Remove the mount.

11   Place the new mount in position and install the nuts. Gently lower the engine and tighten the nuts securely.

12   Reconnect the negative battery cable.

Rear mount

13   Detach the negative battery cable from the battery. Remove the right lower splash shield.

14   Working under the mount, remove the nut from the through-bolt **(see illustration)**.

15   Raise the engine off the mount.

16   Remove the four mount-to-bracket nuts.

17   Remove the mount from the vehicle.

18   Installation is the reverse of removal.

19   Gently lower the engine.

20   Tighten the nuts securely.

21   Reconnect the negative battery cable.

Chapter 2 Part C V6 Engines

Contents

Specifications

General

Cylinder numbers (drivebelt end-to-transaxle end)	
Front bank (radiator side)	2-4-6
Rear bank	1-3-5
Firing order	1-2-3-4-5-6

Torque specifications

Ft-lbs (unless otherwise indicated)

Cylinder head bolts	
First step	33
Second step	Rotate an additional 1/4-turn (90-degrees)
Exhaust manifold-to-cylinder head bolts	
1992 and earlier	18
1993	21
1994 on	144 in-lbs
Flywheel/driveplate-to-crankshaft bolts	
1992 and earlier	52
1993 on	61
Intake manifold-to-cylinder head bolts/nuts	
1987 and 1988	18
1989 to 1993	
Step one	15
Step two	23
1994 on	115 in-lbs
Lifter guide bolts	89 in-lbs
Oil pan bolts/nuts	
1987 through 1990	
6 mm	84 in-lbs
8 mm	18
1991 and 1992	
All except rear bolts	71 in-lbs
Rear bolts	18

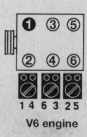

V6 engine

Front
↓

Cylinder and coil terminal location diagram

Torque specifications (continued)

Ft-lbs (unless otherwise indicated)

Oil pan bolts/nuts (continued)
  1993
    All except rear bolts . . . .   89 in-lbs
    Rear bolts   18
  1994 on
    All except rear bolts   18
    Rear bolts   37
Oil pump mounting bolts   30
Rocker arm cover bolts
  1992 and earlier . . . .   84 in-lbs
  1993 and later . . . .   89 in-lbs
Rocker arm nuts   18
Timing chain cover bolts
  1992 and earlier
    Small bolts   20
    Large bolts   28
  1993 on
    Small bolts   15
    Large bolts   35
Timing chain sprocket-to-camshaft bolt(s)
  1987 through 1989   18
  1990 through 1992   21
  1993 and later   74
Vibration damper bolt   76

---

1   General information

Warning: *Later models are equipped with airbags. Impact sensors for the airbag system are located just above the radiator grille on the right side. The airbag(s) could accidentally deploy if these sensors are disturbed, so be extremely careful when working in this area. Airbag system components are also located in the steering wheel, steering column and base of the steering column, so be extremely careful when working in this area and don't disturb any airbag system components or wiring. You could easily be injured if an airbag accidently deploys, and the airbag might not deploy correctly in a collision if any components or wiring in the system have been disturbed.*

Note: *On models equipped with the Delco Loc II audio system, be sure the lockout feature is turned off before performing any procedure which requires disconnecting the battery.*

This Part of Chapter 2 is devoted to in-vehicle repair procedures for the V6 engines. These engines utilize cast-iron blocks with six cylinders arranged in a "V" shape at a 60-degree angle between the two banks. The overhead valve aluminum cylinder heads are equipped with replaceable valve guides and seats. Hydraulic lifters actuate the valves through tubular pushrods.

All information concerning engine removal and installation and engine block and cylinder head overhaul can be found in Part D of this Chapter. The following repair procedures are based on the assumption the engine is installed in the vehicle. If the engine has been removed from the vehicle and mounted on a stand, many of the steps outlined in this Part of Chapter 2 will not apply.

The Specifications included in this Part of Chapter 2 apply only to the procedures contained in this Part. Part D of Chapter 2 contains the Specifications necessary for cylinder head and engine block rebuilding.

---

2   Repair operations possible with the engine in the vehicle

Many major repair operations can be accomplished without removing the engine from the vehicle.

Clean the engine compartment and the exterior of the engine with some type of degreaser before any work is done. It'll make the job easier and help keep dirt out of the internal areas of the engine.

Depending on the components involved, it may be helpful to remove the hood to improve access to the engine as repairs are performed (refer to Chapter 11 if necessary). Cover the fenders to prevent damage to the paint. Special pads are available, but an old bedspread or blanket will also work.

If vacuum, exhaust, oil or coolant leaks develop, indicating a need for gasket or seal replacement, the repairs can generally be done with the engine in the vehicle. The intake and exhaust manifold gaskets, timing chain cover gasket, oil pan gasket, crankshaft oil seals and cylinder head gaskets are all accessible with the engine in place.

Exterior engine components, such as the intake and exhaust manifolds, the oil pan (and the oil pump), the water pump, the starter motor, the alternator and the fuel system components can be removed for repair with the engine in place.

Since the cylinder heads can be removed without pulling the engine, valve component servicing can also be accomplished with the engine in the vehicle. Replacement of the timing chain and sprockets is also possible with the engine in the vehicle.

In extreme cases caused by a lack of necessary equipment, repair or replacement of piston rings, pistons, connecting rods and rod bearings is possible with the engine in the vehicle. However, this practice is not recommended because of the cleaning and preparation work that must be done to the components involved.

---

3   Rocker arm covers – removal and installation

Refer to illustrations 3.3, 3.4 and 3.5

Removal

Front cover

1   Disconnect the negative battery cable from the battery.

2   Remove the spark plug wires from the spark plugs (see Chapter 1). Be sure each wire is labeled before removal to ensure correct reinstallation.

3   Detach the spark plug wire harness cover **(see illustration)**.

4   Remove the PCV tube from the rocker arm cover **(see illustration)**.

5   Remove the rocker arm cover mounting bolts with a T-30 Torx driver **(see illustration)**.

6   Detach the rocker arm cover. **Note:** *If the cover sticks to the cylinder head, use a block of wood and a hammer to dislodge it. If the cover still won't come loose, pry on it carefully, but don't distort the sealing flange.*

3.3 Remove the spark plug wire harness cover bolts (arrows)

Rear cover

7 Disconnect the negative battery cable from the battery.
8 Remove the brake booster vacuum line at the bracket.
9 Detach the vacuum line bracket and the cable bracket at the plenum.
10 Disconnect the lines at the alternator brace stud.
11 Remove the serpentine drivebelt (see Chapter 1).
12 Remove the alternator and rear brace and loosen the alternator bracket (see Chapter 5).
13 Detach the breather hose from the PCV valve.
14 Remove the spark plug wires from the spark plugs (see Chapter 1). Be sure each wire is labelled before removal to ensure correct reinstallation.
15 Remove the rocker arm cover mounting bolts with a T-30 Torx driver.
16 Detach the rocker arm cover. **Note:** *If the cover sticks to the cylinder head, use a block of wood and a hammer to dislodge it. If the cover still won't come loose, pry on it carefully, but don't distort the sealing flange.*

Installation

17 The mating surfaces of each cylinder head and rocker arm cover must be perfectly clean when the covers are installed. Use a gasket scraper to remove all traces of sealant or old gasket material, then clean the mating surfaces with lacquer thinner or acetone (if there's sealant or oil on the mating surfaces when the cover is installed, oil leaks may develop). The

3.4 Remove the PCV tube (arrow) from the rocker arm cover

rocker arm covers are made of aluminum, so be extra careful not to nick or gouge the mating surfaces with the scraper.
18 Clean the mounting bolt threads with a die if necessary to remove any corrosion and restore damaged threads. Use a tap to clean the threaded holes in the heads.
19 Place the rocker arm cover and new gasket in position, then install the bolts. Tighten the bolts in several steps to the torque listed in this Chapter's Specifications.
20 Complete the installation by reversing the removal procedure. Start the engine and check carefully for oil leaks at the rocker arm cover-to-head joints.

2C

---

4 Rocker arms and pushrods – removal, inspection and installation

---

Refer to illustrations 4.2 and 4.3

Removal

1 Refer to Section 3 and remove the rocker arm covers.

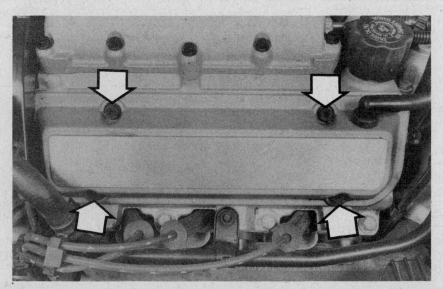

3.5 The rocker arm cover mounting bolts (arrows) require a Torx bit for removal and installation

4.2   Remove the rocker arm nuts (arrows)

**4.3   A perforated cardboard box can be used to store
the pushrods to ensure they are reinstalled in their
original locations – note the label indicating the
transaxle end of the engine**

2   Beginning at the drivebelt end of one cylinder head, remove the rocker arm mounting nuts one at a time and detach the rocker arms, nuts, and pivot balls **(see illustration)**. Store each set of rocker arm components separately in a marked plastic bag to ensure they're reinstalled in their original locations. **Note:** *If you only need to remove the pushrods, loosen the rocker arm nuts and turn the rocker arms to allow room for pushrod removal.*
3   Remove the pushrods and store them separately to make sure they don't get mixed up during installation **(see illustration)**. **Note:** *Intake and exhaust pushrods are different lengths. Intake pushrods are color-coded orange and exhaust pushrods are coded blue.*

Inspection

4   Inspect each rocker arm for wear, cracks and other damage, especially where the pushrods and valve stems make contact.
5   Check the pivot seat in each rocker arm and the pivot ball faces. Look for galling, stress cracks and unusual wear patterns. If the rocker arms are worn or damaged, replace them with new ones and install new pivot balls as well.
6   Make sure the hole at the pushrod end of each rocker arm is open.
7   Inspect the pushrods for cracks and excessive wear at the ends. Roll each pushrod across a piece of plate glass to see if it's bent (if it wobbles, it's bent).

Installation

8   Lubricate the lower end of each pushrod with clean engine oil or moly-base grease and install them in their original locations. Make sure each pushrod seats completely in the lifter socket.
9   Apply moly-base grease to the ends of the valve stems and the upper ends of the pushrods.
10   Apply moly-base grease to the pivot balls to prevent damage to the mating surfaces before engine oil pressure builds up. Install the rocker arms, pivot balls and nuts and tighten the nuts to the torque specified in this Chapter. As the nuts are tightened, make sure the pushrods engage properly in the rocker arms.
11   Install the rocker arm covers.

---

5   Valve springs, retainers and seals – replacement

This procedure is essentially the same for the V6 and 2.0/2.2 liter four-cylinder engines. Refer to Part A and follow the procedure outlined there.

---

6   Intake manifold – removal and installation

Removal

Refer to illustrations 6.8, 6.10a and 6.10b
1   Relieve the fuel system pressure (see Chapter 4).
2   Disconnect the negative battery cable from the battery.
3   Remove the plenum, fuel rail and injectors (see Chapter 4). When disconnecting fuel line fittings, be prepared to catch some fuel with a rag, then cap the fittings to prevent contamination.
4   Remove the serpentine drivebelt and drain the cooling system (see Chapter 1).
5   Remove the alternator and loosen the bracket (see Chapter 5).
6   Unbolt the power steering pump (if equipped) and set it aside without disconnecting the hoses.
7   Disconnect the coolant tubes and hoses as necessary.

6.8   Label (arrow) and disconnect all remaining hoses and lines

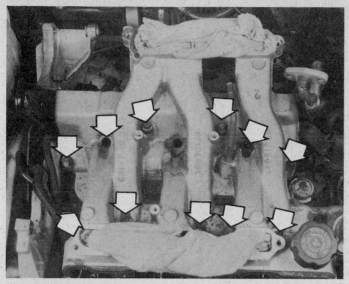

6.10a   Intake manifold mounting bolt/nut locations (arrows)

6.10b   Pry the manifold loose at a casting boss – don't pry between the gasket surfaces!

8   Label and disconnect any remaining fuel and vacuum lines **(see illustration)** and wires from the manifold.

9   Remove the rocker arm covers (see Section 3).

10   Remove the manifold mounting bolts and separate the manifold from the engine **(see illustrations)**. Don't pry between the manifold and heads, as damage to the soft aluminum gasket sealing surfaces may result. If you're installing a new manifold, transfer all fittings and sensors to the new manifold.

11   Loosen the rocker arm nuts, rotate the rocker arms out of the way and remove the pushrods that go through the manifold gasket (see Section 4).

Installation

Refer to illustrations 6.15 and 6.17

Note: *The mating surfaces of the cylinder heads, block and manifold must be perfectly clean when the manifold is installed. Gasket removal solvents in aerosol cans are available at most auto parts stores and may be helpful when removing old gasket material that's stuck to the heads and manifold*

(since the manifold is made of aluminum, aggressive scraping can cause damage). Be sure to follow the directions printed on the container.

12   Lift the old gasket off. Use a gasket scraper to remove all traces of sealant and old gasket material, then clean the mating surfaces with lacquer thinner or acetone. If there's old sealant or oil on the mating surfaces when the manifold is installed, oil or vacuum leaks may develop. Use a vacuum cleaner to remove any gasket material that falls into the intake ports or the lifter valley.

13   Use a tap of the correct size to chase the threads in the bolt holes, if necessary, then use compressed air (if available) to remove the debris from the holes. **Warning:** *Wear safety glasses or a face shield to protect your eyes when using compressed air!*

14   Apply a 3/16-inch (5 mm) bead of GM RTV sealant (no. 1052917) or equivalent to the front and rear ridges of the engine block between the heads. **Note:** *Some gasket sets include end seals.*

15   Install the intake manifold gasket **(see illustration)**.

16   Install the pushrods and rocker arms (see Section 4).

6.15   Apply a bead of sealant to or position an end seal on the ridges between the heads (arrows)

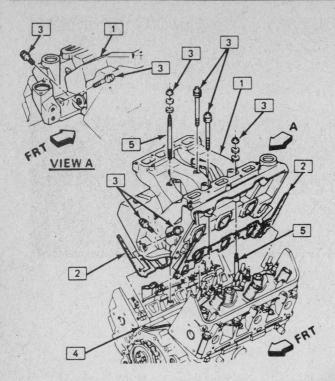

6.17   Intake manifold and related components – exploded view

1	Intake manifold	4	Sealant (GM no. 1052917
2	Gasket		or equivalent)
3	Fasteners	5	Stud

17   Carefully lower the manifold into place and install the mounting bolts/nuts **(see illustration)** finger tight.

18   Tighten the mounting bolts/nuts in three steps, working from the center out, in a criss-cross pattern, until they're all at the torque listed in this Chapter's Specifications.

19   Install the remaining components in the reverse order of removal.

20   Change the oil and filter and refill the cooling system (see Chapter 1). Start the engine and check for leaks.

7   Exhaust manifolds – removal and installation

Front manifold

Refer to illustrations 7.6a, 7.6b, 7.8, 7.9a and 7.9b

1   Disconnect the negative battery cable from the battery.

2   Remove the air cleaner assembly, inlet hose and mass air flow sensor (see Chapter 4).

3   Allow the engine to cool completely, then drain the coolant (see Chapter 1) and disconnect the coolant bypass tube, if necessary.

4   Remove the cooling fan assembly (see Chapter 3).

5   Remove the oil dipstick tube mounting bolt.

6   On early models with tubular steel manifolds, disconnect the front manifold extension pipe where it joins the rear manifold near the firewall **(see illustrations)**.

7   On later models with cast iron manifolds, unbolt the crossover pipe where it joins the front manifold.

8   Remove the manifold heat shield **(see illustration)**.

9   Remove the mounting bolts and detach the manifold from the cylinder head **(see illustrations)**.

10   Clean the mating surfaces to remove all traces of old gasket material, then inspect the manifold for distortion and cracks. Warpage can be checked with a precision straightedge held against the mating flange. If a feeler gauge thicker than 0.030-inch can be inserted between the straight-

7.6a   On models with tubular steel manifolds, the extension pipe is attached with two bolts at each end (arrows) . . .

7.6b   . . . that are reached as shown here (master cylinder removed for clarity)

edge and flange surface, take the manifold to an automotive machine shop for resurfacing.

11   Place the manifold in position with a new gasket and install the mounting bolts finger tight.

12   Starting in the middle and working out toward the ends, tighten the mounting bolts a little at a time until all of them are at the torque specified in this Chapter.

13   Install the remaining components in the reverse order of removal.

14   Start the engine and check for exhaust leaks between the manifold and cylinder head and between the manifold and exhaust pipe.

Rear manifold

Refer to illustrations 7.18, 7.22 and 7.23

15   Disconnect the negative battery cable from the battery.

16   Allow the engine to cool completely, then disconnect the EGR tube from the exhaust manifold (see Chapter 6).

17   On some models it may be necessary to remove the throttle and TV cables and brackets for clearance (see Chapters 4 and 7).

18   Remove the heat shield **(see illustration)**.

7.8 Tubular steel front exhaust manifold heat shield nuts (arrows)

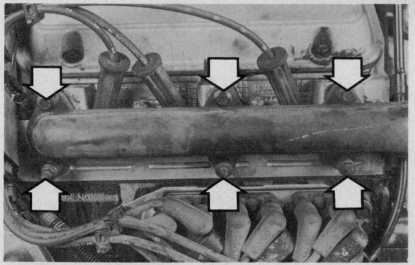

7.9a Tubular steel exhaust manifold fastener locations (arrows) – cast iron manifold similar

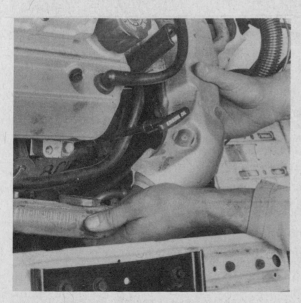

7.9b Detach the manifold and maneuver it away from the engine

7.18 Tubular steel exhaust manifold heat shield mounting nut locations (arrows)

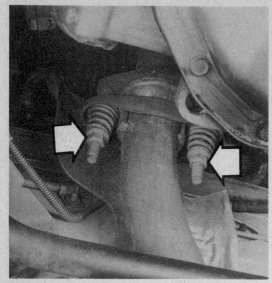

7.22   Exhaust pipe-to-rear manifold mounting nuts (arrows) – viewed from below

7.23   Tubular steel exhaust manifold mounting nut locations (arrows)

8.3   Remove the oil dipstick tube mounting bolt (arrow)

19   Unbolt the crossover pipe (or front manifold extension pipe) where it joins the rear manifold.

20   Disconnect the oxygen sensor wire. If you intend to replace the manifold, transfer the sensor to the replacement manifold.

21   Set the parking brake, block the rear wheels and raise the front of the vehicle, supporting it securely on jackstands.

22   Working under the vehicle, remove the two exhaust pipe-to-manifold bolts **(see illustration)**. You may have to apply penetrating oil to the fastener threads – they're usually corroded.

23   Unbolt and remove the exhaust manifold **(see illustration)**.

24   Clean the mating surfaces to remove all traces of old sealant, then check for warpage and cracks. Warpage can be checked with a precision straightedge held against the mating flange. If a feeler gauge thicker than 0.030-inch can be inserted between the straightedge and flange surface, take the manifold to an automotive machine shop for resurfacing.

25   Place the manifold in position with a new gasket and install the bolts finger tight.

26   Starting in the middle and working out toward the ends, tighten the mounting bolts a little at a time until all of them are at the torque specified in this Chapter.

27   Install the remaining components in the reverse order of removal.

28   Start the engine and check for exhaust leaks between the manifold and cylinder head and between the manifold and exhaust pipe.

---

8   Cylinder heads – removal and installation

Refer to illustrations 8.3, 8.13, 8.16a, 8.16b, 8.18 and 8.19

Note: *On engines with high mileage and during an overhaul, camshaft lobe height should be checked prior to cylinder head removal (see Chapter 2, Part D, Section 13 for instructions).*

Caution: *Allow the engine to cool completely before loosening the cylinder head bolts.*

Removal

1   Disconnect the negative battery cable from the battery.

2   Remove the intake manifold as described in Section 6.

3   If you're removing the front cylinder head, remove the oil dipstick tube mounting bolt **(see illustration)**.

4   Disconnect all wires and vacuum hoses from the cylinder head(s). Be sure to label them to simplify reinstallation.

5   Disconnect the spark plug wires and remove the spark plugs (see Chapter 1). Be sure the plug wires are labelled to simplify reinstallation.

6   Detach the exhaust manifold from the cylinder head being removed (see Section 7).

7   Remove the rocker arm cover(s) (see Section 3).

8   Remove the rocker arms and pushrods (see Section 4).

9   Using the new head gasket, outline the cylinders and bolt pattern on a piece of cardboard **(see illustration 8.11a in Part A)**. Be sure to indicate the front (drivebelt end) of the engine for reference. Punch holes at the bolt locations. Loosen each of the cylinder head mounting bolts 1/4-turn at a time until they can be removed by hand – work from bolt-to-bolt in a pattern that's the reverse of the tightening sequence **(see illustration 8.19)**. Store the bolts in the cardboard holder as they're removed – this will ensure they are reinstalled in their original locations, which is absolutely essential.

10   Lift the head(s) off the engine. If resistance is felt, don't pry between the head and block as damage to the mating surfaces will result. Recheck for head bolts that may have been overlooked, then use a hammer and

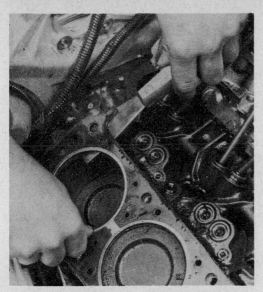

8.13 Remove the old gasket and carefully scrape off all old gasket material and sealant

8.16a Position the new gasket over the dowel pins (arrows) . . .

2C

block of wood to tap up on the head and break the gasket seal. Be careful because there are locating dowels in the block which position each head. As a last resort, pry each head up at the rear corner only and be careful not to damage anything. After removal, place the head on blocks of wood to prevent damage to the gasket surfaces.

11   Refer to Chapter 2, Part D, for cylinder head disassembly, inspection and valve service procedures.

Installation

12   The mating surfaces of each cylinder head and block must be perfectly clean when the head is installed.

13   Use a gasket scraper to remove all traces of carbon and old gasket material **(see illustration)**, then clean the mating surfaces with lacquer thinner or acetone. If there's oil on the mating surfaces when the head is installed, the gasket may not seal correctly and leaks may develop. When working on the block, it's a good idea to cover the lifter valley with shop

rags to keep debris out of the engine. Use a shop rag or vacuum cleaner to remove any debris that falls into the cylinders.

14   Check the block and head mating surfaces for nicks, deep scratches and other damage. If damage is slight, it can be removed with a file; if it's excessive, machining may be the only alternative.

15   Use a tap of the correct size to chase the threads in the head bolt holes. Dirt, corrosion, sealant and damaged threads will affect torque readings.

16   Position the new gasket over the dowel pins in the block. Some gaskets are marked TOP or THIS SIDE UP to ensure correct installation **(see illustrations)**.

17   Carefully position the head on the block without disturbing the gasket.

18   Apply GM sealant (no. 1052080) or equivalent to the threads and the under sides of the bolt heads. Install the bolts in the correct locations – two different lengths are used **(see illustration)**. Here's where the cardboard holder comes in handy.

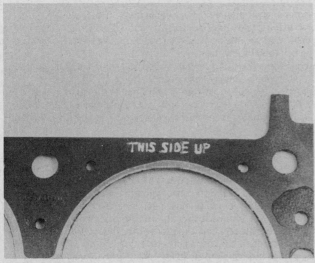

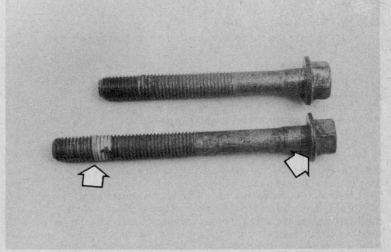

8.16b   . . . with the correct side facing up

8.18   Two different length cylinder head bolts are used – apply sealant to the threads and the under sides of the bolt heads (arrows)

8.19   Cylinder head bolt TIGHTENING SEQUENCE (reverse the sequence to loosen the bolts)

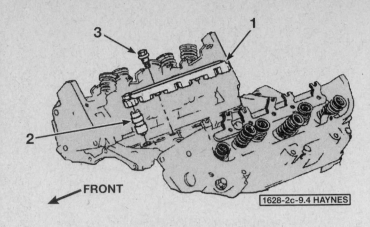

FRONT

9.4   Lifter guide and details

1   Lifter guide
2   Roller lifter
3   Bolt

19   Tighten the bolts to 33 ft-lbs in the recommended sequence **(see illustration)**. Tighten each bolt an additional 90-degrees (1/4-turn) following the same sequence.
20   The remaining installation steps are the reverse of removal.
21   Change the oil and filter (see Chapter 1).

9   Hydraulic lifters – removal, inspection and installation

Refer to illustrations 9.4, 9.5a, 9.5b, 9.6a and 9.6b

1   A noisy valve lifter can be isolated when the engine is idling. Hold a mechanic's stethoscope or a length of hose near the location of each valve while listening at the other end. Another method is to remove the rocker arm cover and, with the engine idling, touch each of the valve spring retainers, one at a time. If a valve lifter is defective, it'll be evident from the shock felt at the retainer each time the valve seats.
2   The most likely causes of noisy valve lifters are dirt trapped inside the lifter and lack of oil flow, viscosity or pressure. Before condemning the lifters, check the oil for fuel contamination, correct level, cleanliness and correct viscosity.

Removal

3   Remove the intake manifold and rocker arm cover(s) as described in Sections 3 and 6.
4   Remove the rocker arms and pushrods (see Section 4). If your engine is equipped with roller lifters (1994 and later models), remove the lifter guide **(see illustration).**
5   There are several ways to extract the lifters from the bores. A special tool designed to grip and remove lifters is manufactured by many tool companies and is widely available, but it may not be required in every case. On newer engines without a lot of varnish buildup, the lifters can often be removed with a small magnet or even with your fingers. A machinist's scribe with a bent end can be used to pull the lifters out by positioning the point under the retainer ring in the top of each lifter **(see illustrations)**. **Caution:** *Don't use pliers to remove the lifters unless you intend to replace them with new ones (along with the camshaft). The pliers may damage the precision machined and hardened lifters, rendering them useless.*
6   Before removing the lifters, arrange to store them in a clearly labelled box to ensure they're reinstalled in their original locations. Remove the lifters and store them where they won't get dirty **(see illustration)**. **Note:** *Some engines may have both standard and 0.010-inch oversize lifters installed at the factory. They are marked on the block* **(see illustration)**.

9.5a   A magnetic pick-up tool . . .

9.5b   . . . or a scribe can be used to remove the lifters

9.6a   Store the lifters in a box like this to ensure installation in their original locations

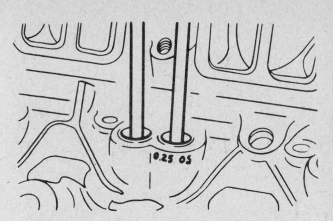

9.6b If the engine is factory equipped with oversize lifters, the lifter boss will be marked with a dab of white paint and will have 0.25 (mm) OS stamped on it

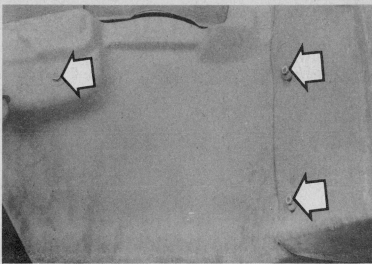

10.5 Remove the right front inner splash shield bolts (arrows) to gain access to the vibration damper

2C

Inspection and installation

7 Parts for valve lifters are not available separately. The work required to remove them from the engine again if cleaning is unsuccessful outweighs any potential savings from repairing them. Refer to Chapter 2, Part A, for lifter inspection procedures and Part D for camshaft inspection procedures. If the lifters are worn, they must be replaced with new ones and, if the engine is equipped with conventional lifters, the camshaft must be replaced as well – never install used conventional lifters with a new camshaft or new conventional lifters with a used camshaft. Used roller lifters can be reinstalled with a new camshaft and the original camshaft can be used if new roller lifters are installed (provided the used parts are in good condition).

8 When reinstalling used lifters, make sure they're replaced in their original bores. Soak new lifters in oil to remove trapped air. Coat all lifters with moly-base grease or engine assembly lube prior to installation.

9 The remaining installation steps are the reverse of removal. If you're installing roller lifters, be sure to tighten the lifter guide bolts to the torque listed in this Chapter's Specifications.

10 Run the engine and check for oil leaks.

10 Vibration damper – removal and installation

Refer to illustrations 10.5, 10.7, 10.8 and 10.9

1 Disconnect the negative battery cable from the battery.

2 Loosen the lug nuts on the right front wheel.

3 Raise the vehicle and support it securely on jackstands.

4 Remove the right front tire.

5 Remove the right front inner fender splash shield **(see illustration)**.

6 Remove the serpentine drivebelt (see Chapter 1).

7 On automatic transaxle equipped models, remove the driveplate cover and position a large screwdriver in the ring gear teeth to keep the crankshaft from turning while an assistant removes the vibration damper-to-crankshaft bolt **(see illustration)**. On manual transaxle equipped models, engage high gear and apply the brakes while an assistant removes the vibration damper bolt. The bolt is normally very tight, so use a large breaker bar and a six-point socket.

8 Pull the damper off the crankshaft with a bolt-type puller **(see illustration)**. Leave the Woodruff key in place in the end of the crankshaft.

10.7 Remove the vibration damper-to-crankshaft bolt (arrow) – it's very tight, so use a six-point socket and a breaker bar

10.8 Use a puller that bolts to the vibration damper hub; jaw-type pullers will damage the vibration damper

10.9   The damper keyway must be aligned with the woodruff key (arrow) in the crankshaft nose

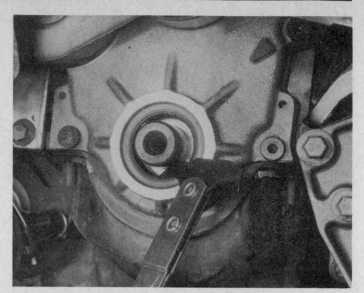

11.2   Carefully pry the old seal out of the timing chain cover – don't damage the crankshaft in the process

9   Installation is the reverse of removal. Be sure to apply moly-base grease to the seal contact surface of the damper hub (if it isn't lubricated, the seal lip could be damaged and oil leakage would result). Align the damper hub keyway with the Woodruff key **(see illustration)**.
10   Tighten the vibration damper-to-crankshaft bolt to the torque listed in this Chapter's Specifications.
11   Reinstall the remaining parts in the reverse order of removal.

11   Crankshaft front oil seal – replacement

Refer to illustrations 11.2 and 11.3
1   Remove the vibration damper (see Section 10).
2   Note how the seal is installed – the new one must be installed to the same depth and facing the same way. Carefully pry the oil seal out of the cover with a seal puller or a large screwdriver **(see illustration)**. Be very careful not to distort the cover or scratch the crankshaft! Wrap electricians tape around the tip of the screwdriver to avoid damage to the crankshaft.

3   Apply clean engine oil or multi-purpose grease to the outer edge of the new seal, then install it in the cover with the lip (spring side) facing IN. Drive the seal into place **(see illustration)** with a large socket and a hammer (if a large socket isn't available, a piece of pipe will also work). Make sure the seal enters the bore squarely and stop when the front face is at the proper depth.
4   Reinstall the vibration damper.

12   Timing chain cover – removal and installation

Refer to illustrations 12.5, 12.15 and 12.18
1   Disconnect the negative battery cable from the battery.
2   Loosen the water pump pulley bolts, then remove the serpentine drivebelt (see Chapter 1).
3   Remove the water pump pulley (see Chapter 3).
4   Remove the vibration damper (see Section 10).
5   Unbolt the drivebelt tensioner **(see illustration)** and idler, if equipped.

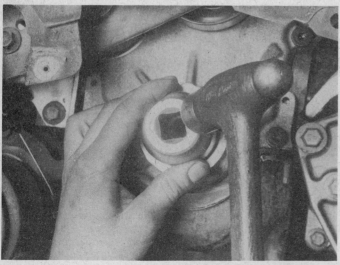

11.3   Drive the new seal into place with a large socket and hammer

12.5   The drivebelt tensioner is secured to the timing chain cover by a bolt (arrow)

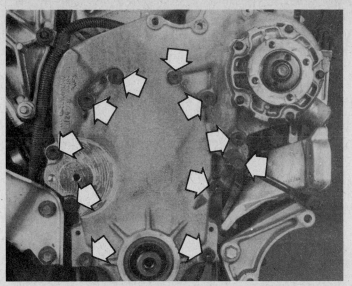

12.15 Timing chain cover bolt locations (arrows)

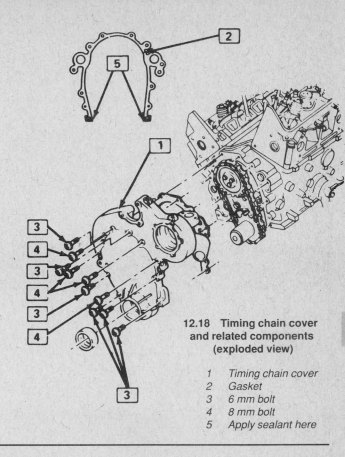

12.18 Timing chain cover and related components (exploded view)

1 Timing chain cover
2 Gasket
3 6 mm bolt
4 8 mm bolt
5 Apply sealant here

2C

6 Drain the coolant and engine oil (see Chapter 1).
7 Remove the alternator and loosen the mounting bracket (see Chapter 5).
8 Unbolt the power steering pump (if equipped) and tie it aside (see Chapter 10). Leave the hoses connected.
9 Unbolt the flywheel/driveplate cover below the transaxle.
10 Remove the starter (see Chapter 5).
11 Remove the oil pan (see Section 14).
12 Disconnect the coolant hoses from the fill pipe and water pump.
13 Unbolt the spark plug wire shield at the water pump.
14 Disconnect the canister purge hose and tie it aside.
15 Remove the timing chain cover-to-engine block bolts **(see illustration)**. Note that some of the bolts require T-40 or T-50 Torx bits for removal.
16 Separate the cover from the engine. If it's stuck, tap it with a soft-face hammer, but don't try to pry it off.
17 Use a gasket scraper to remove all traces of old gasket material and sealant from the cover and engine block. The cover is made of aluminum, so be careful not to nick or gouge it. Clean the gasket sealing surfaces with lacquer thinner or acetone.
18 Apply a thin layer of GM sealant (no. 1052080) or equivalent to both sides of the new gasket, then position the gasket on the engine block (the dowel pins should keep it in place). Attach the cover to the engine and install the bolts **(see illustration)**.
19 Apply sealant to the bottom of the gasket **(see illustration)**. Follow a criss-cross pattern when tightening the fasteners and work up to the torque specified in this Chapter in three steps.
20 The remainder of installation is the reverse of removal.
21 Add oil and coolant, start the engine and check for leaks.

13 Timing chain and sprockets – inspection, removal and installation

Refer to illustrations 13.3, 13.4 and 13.10

Inspection

1 The timing chain should be replaced with a new one if the engine has high mileage, the chain has visible damage, or total freeplay midway between the sprockets exceeds one-inch. Failure to replace a worn timing chain may result in erratic engine performance, loss of power and decreased fuel mileage. Loose chains can "jump" timing. In the worst case, chain "jumping" or breakage will result in severe engine damage.

Removal

2 Remove the timing chain cover (see Section 12).
3 Temporarily install the vibration damper bolt and turn the crankshaft with the bolt to align the timing marks on the crankshaft and camshaft sprockets. Both should be at the top (12 o'clock position) **(see illustration)**.

13.3 The timing marks (arrows) on the sprockets should be at the top (12 o'clock position) – a straight line should pass through the camshaft sprocket timing mark, the center of the camshaft, the crankshaft sprocket timing mark and the center of the crankshaft

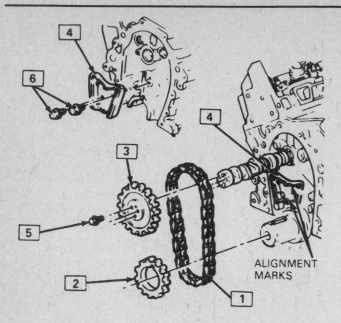

13.10   The camshaft is positioned correctly when the dowel pin (arrow) is in the 9 o'clock position

13.4   Timing chain and related components – exploded view

1	Timing chain	4	Timing chain dampener (guide)
2	Crankshaft sprocket	5	Camshaft sprocket bolts (3)
3	Camshaft sprocket	6	Timing chain dampener bolts (2)

4   Remove the camshaft sprocket bolts **(see illustration)**. Do not turn the camshaft in the process (if you do, realign the timing marks before the bolts are removed).

5   Use two large screwdrivers to carefully pry the camshaft sprocket off the camshaft dowel pin. Slip the timing chain and camshaft sprocket off the engine.

6   Timing chains and sprockets should be replaced in sets. If you intend to install a new timing chain, remove the crankshaft sprocket with a puller and install a new one. Be sure to align the key in the crankshaft with the keyway in the sprocket during installation.

7   Inspect the timing chain dampener (guide) for cracks and wear and replace it if necessary. The dampener is held to the engine block by two bolts.

8   Clean the timing chain and sprockets with solvent and dry them with compressed air (if available). **Warning:** *Wear eye protection when using compressed air.*

9   Inspect the components for wear and damage. Look for teeth that are deformed, chipped, pitted and cracked.

Installation

10   Turn the camshaft to position the dowel pin at 9 o'clock, if necessary **(see illustration)**. Mesh the timing chain with the camshaft sprocket, then engage it with the crankshaft sprocket. The timing marks should be aligned as shown in illustration 13.3. **Note:** *If the crankshaft has been disturbed, turn it until the "O" stamped on the crankshaft sprocket is exactly at the top. If the camshaft was turned, install the sprocket temporarily and turn the camshaft until the sprocket timing mark is at the top, opposite the mark on the crankshaft sprocket.*

11   Install the camshaft sprocket bolts and tighten them to the torque specified in this Chapter.

12   Lubricate the chain and sprocket with clean engine oil. Install the timing chain cover (see Section 12).

13   The remaining installation steps are the reverse of removal.

---

14   Oil pan – removal and installation

Refer to illustrations 14.5a, 14.5b and 14.8

Removal

1   Disconnect the cable from the negative battery terminal.

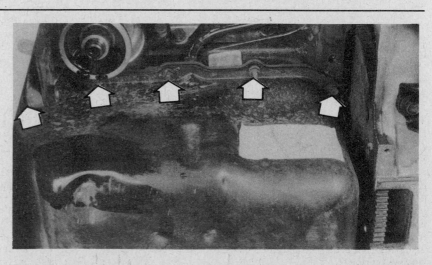

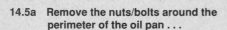

14.5a   Remove the nuts/bolts around the perimeter of the oil pan . . .

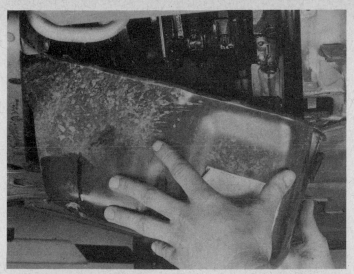

14.5b   . . . then lower the pan from the engine

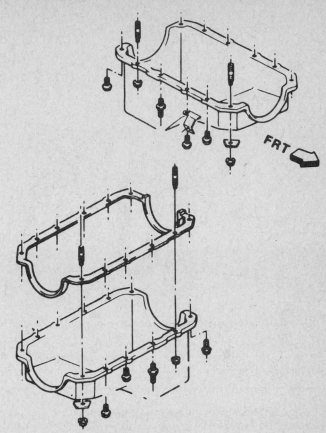

14.8   Oil pan mounting details

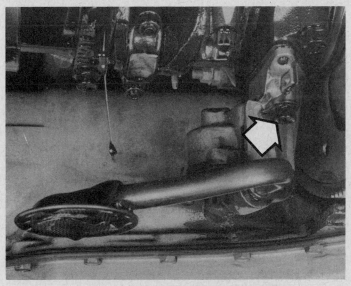

15.2   Oil pump mounting bolt location (arrow)

2   Raise the front of the vehicle and place it securely on jackstands. Apply the parking brake and block the rear wheels to keep it from rolling off the stands. Remove the lower splash pan and drain the engine oil (refer to Chapter 1 if necessary).
3   Remove the lower flywheel/driveplate cover.
4   Remove the starter (see Chapter 5).

1994 and later models only
5   Remove the serpentine drivebelt (see Chapter 1).
6   Loosen, but do not remove, the upper air conditioning compressor bolts (if equipped).
7   Remove the right front wheel. Also remove the right side splash shields.
8   Support the engine from above with a hoist, then detach the engine mount strut from the suspension support. If equipped, remove the right front ABS wheel speed sensor harness from the right suspension support.
9   Separate the right front balljoint from the steering knuckle, detach the right side stabilizer bar link from the control arm, then remove the right side suspension support.

10   Remove the air conditioning compressor bolts, position compressor aside and support with a piece of wire. **Warning:** *Don't disconnect the hoses!* Remove the engine mount strut bracket, the engine to transaxle brace and the oil filter.
11   Remove the bolts and nuts, then carefully separate the oil pan from the block **(see illustrations)**. Don't pry between the block and the pan or damage to the sealing surfaces could occur and oil leaks may develop. Instead, tap the pan with a soft-face hammer to break the gasket seal.

Installation
12   Clean the pan with solvent and remove all old sealant and gasket material from the block and pan mating surfaces. Clean the mating surfaces with lacquer thinner or acetone and make sure the bolt holes in the block are clear. Check the oil pan flange for distortion, particularly around the bolt holes. If necessary, place the pan on a block of wood and use a hammer to flatten and restore the gasket surface.
13   Always use a new gasket whenever the oil pan is installed.
14   Place the oil pan in position on the block and install the nuts/bolts **(see illustration)**.
15   After the fasteners are installed, tighten them to the torque listed in this Chapter's Specifications. Starting at the center, follow a criss-cross pattern and work up to the final torque in three steps.
16   The remaining steps are the reverse of the removal procedure.
17   Refill the engine with oil, run it until normal operating temperature is reached and check for leaks.

---

15   Oil pump – removal and installation

Refer to illustration 15.2
1   Remove the oil pan (see Section 14).
2   Unbolt the oil pump and lower it from the engine **(see illustration)**.
3   If the pump is defective, replace it with a new one – don't reuse the original or attempt to rebuild it.

4   Prime the pump by pouring motor oil into the pick-up screen while turning the pump driveshaft.
5   To install the pump, turn the hexagonal driveshaft so it mates with the oil pump drive.
6   Install the pump mounting bolt and tighten it to the torque listed in this Chapter's specifications.

16   Flywheel/driveplate – removal and installation

This procedure is essentially the same for all engines. Refer to Part A and follow the procedure outlined there. However, use the bolt torque listed in this Chapter.

17   Rear main oil seal – replacement

This procedure is essentially the same for all engines. Refer to Part A and follow the procedure outlined there.

18   Engine mounts – check and replacement

This procedure is essentially the same for all engines. Refer to Part A and follow the procedure outlined there.

Chapter 2 Part D
General engine overhaul procedures

Contents

Specifications

2.0/2.2 liter four-cylinder engines

General

RPO sales code
  2.0 liter LL8
  2.2 liter .... LM3 or LN2
VIN engine code
  2.0 liter 1
  2.2 liter .... G or 4
Displacement
  2.0 liter .... 122 cubic inches
  2.2 liter .... 134 cubic inches
Cylinder compression pressure
  Minimum .... 100 psi
  Maximum variation between cylinders 30-percent
Oil pressure (minimum) .... 15 psi at 1200 rpm

Cylinder head

Warpage limit .... 0.005 in (0.127 mm)

Valves and related components

Valve face angle 45-degrees
Valve seat
  Angle 46-degrees
  Width
    Intake .... 0.049 to 0.059 in (1.25 to 1.50 mm)
    Exhaust .... 0.063 to 0.075 in (1.60 to 1.90 mm)
  Runout .... 0.002 in (0.05 mm)
Margin width .... 1/32 in minimum
Valve stem-to-guide clearance
  Intake .... 0.0011 to 0.0026 in (0.028 to 0.066 mm)
  Exhaust .... 0.0014 to 0.003 in (0.035 to 0.078 mm)
Valve spring free length
  1987 and 1988 .... 1.91 in (48.5 mm)
  1989 through 1991 .... 2.06 in (52.3 mm)
  1992 .... 1.89 in (48 mm)
  1994 and later .... 1.95 in (49.5 mm)
Valve spring pressure and length (intake and exhaust)
  1987 and 1988
    Valve closed .... 73 to 81 lb @ 1.60 in (324 to 360 N @ 40.6 mm)
    Valve open .... 176 to 188 lb @ 1.33 in (783 to 837 N @ 33.9 mm)
  1989 through 1991
    Valve closed .... 100 to 110 lb @ 1.61 in (446 to 488 N @ 40.9 mm)
    Valve open .... 208 to 222 lb @ 1.22 in (925 to 987 N @ 30.9 mm)

2.0/2.2 liter four-cylinder engines (continued)

Valves and related components (valve spring pressure and length continued)

1992 and 1993	
Valve closed	79 to 85 lb @ 1.637 in (350 to 380 N @ 41.58 mm)
Valve open	225 to 233 lb @ 1.247 in (965 to 1036 N @ 31.67 mm)
1994 on	
Valve closed	75 to 81 lb @ 1.710 in (332 to 362 N @ 43.43 mm)
Valve open	220 to 236 lb @ 1.278 in (979 to 1049 N @ 32.47 mm)

Crankshaft and connecting rods

Crankshaft endplay	0.002 to 0.008 in (0.05 to 0.21 mm)
Connecting rod side clearance (endplay)	0.004 to 0.015 in (0.10 to 0.38 mm)
Main bearing journal	
Diameter	2.4945 to 2.4954 in (63.360 to 63.385 mm)
Taper/out-of-round limits	0.0002 in (0.005 mm)
Main bearing oil clearance	0.0006 to 0.0019 in (0.015 to 0.047 mm)
Connecting rod journal	
Diameter	1.9983 to 1.9994 in (50.758 to 50.784 mm)
Taper/out-of-round limits	0.0002 in (0.005 mm)
Connecting rod bearing oil clearance	0.001 to 0.0031 in (0.025 to 0.079 mm)

Engine block

Cylinder bore	
Diameter	
1987 and 1988	3.5036 to 3.5067 in (88.991 to 89.00 mm)
1989-on	3.5036 to 3.5043 in (88.991 to 89.009 mm)
Out-of-round limit	
1987 and 1988	0.001 in (0.025 mm)
1989-on	0.0005 in (0.013 mm)
Taper limit (thrust side)	
1991 and earlier	0.001 in (0.02 mm)
1992 on	0.0005 in (0.013 mm)
Block deck warpage limit	If more than 0.010 in (0.25 mm) must be removed, replace the block

Pistons and rings

Piston-to-bore clearance	
1987 through 1989	0.0010 to 0.0022 in (0.025 to 0.055 mm)
1990 on	0.0007 to 0.0017 in (0.015 to 0.045 mm)
Piston ring side clearance	
Top compression ring	
1987 and 1988	0.001 to 0.003 in (0.03 to 0.07 mm)
1989-on	0.0019 to 0.0027 in (0.05 to 0.07 mm)
Oil control ring	
1987 and 1988	0.0006 to 0.009 in (0.015 to 0.227 mm)
1989-on	0.0019 to 0.0082 in (0.05 to 0.21 mm)
Piston ring end gap	
Compression rings	0.010 to 0.020 in (0.25 to 0.50 mm)
Oil control ring	0.010 to 0.050 in (0.25 to 1.27 mm)

Camshaft

Lobe lift (intake and exhaust, unless indicated)	
1987 and 1988	0.260 in (6.67 mm)
1989 through 1991	0.259 in (6.60 mm)
1992	
Intake	0.259 in (6.60 mm)
Exhaust	0.250 in (6.35 mm)
1993 on	0.288 in (7.309 mm)
Bearing journal diameter	1.867 to 1.869 in (47.44 to 47.49 mm)
Bearing oil clearance	0.001 to 0.0039 in (0.026 to 0.101 mm)

Torque specifications*

	Ft-lbs (unless otherwise indicated)
Main bearing cap bolts	70
Connecting rod cap nuts	38
Camshaft thrust plate-to-block bolts	108 in-lbs

* **Note:** *Refer to Part A for additional torque specifications.*

2.3 liter four-cylinder (Quad-4) engine

General

RPO sales code	LGO
VIN engine code	A
Displacement	138 cubic inches
Cylinder compression pressure	
Minimum	100 psi
Maximum variation between cylinders	30-percent

Oil pressure
  At 900 rpm .... 15 psi minimum
  At 2000 rpm .... 30 psi minimum

Cylinder head
Warpage limit .... 0.008 in (0.203 mm)

Valves and related components
Valve face
  Angle
    Intake 44-degrees
    Exhaust
      1991 and earlier, 1993 on 44.5-degrees
      1992 .... 44-degrees
    Runout limit .... 0.0015 in (0.038 mm)
Valve seats
  Angle (intake and exhaust) 45-degrees
  Width
    Intake .... 0.0370 to 0.0748 in (0.94 to 1.90 mm)
    Exhaust .... 0.0037 to 0.0748 in (0.094 to 1.90 mm)
Valve margin width .... 1/32 in minimum
Valve stem diameter
  Intake .... 0.27512 to 0.27445 in (6,990 to 6.972 mm)
  Exhaust .... 0.2740 to 0.2747 in (6.959 to 6.977 mm)
Valve stem-to-guide clearance
  Intake .... 0.0010 to 0.0027 in (0.025 to 0.069 mm)
  Exhaust .... 0.0015 to 0.0032 in (0.038 to 0.081 mm)
Valves
  Length
    Intake .... 4.3300 in (109.984 mm)
    Exhaust .... 4.3103 in (109.482 mm)
  Installed height* .... 0.9840 to 1.0040 in (25.00 to 25.50 mm)
  Stem length exposed beyond retainer
    Through 1989 .... 0.1190 to 0.1367 in (3.023 to 3.473 mm)
    1990 and later .... 0.394 to 0.0787 in (1.00 to 2.00 mm)

* Measured from tip of stem to top of camshaft housing mounting surface

Crankshaft and connecting rods
Crankshaft
  Endplay .... 0.0034 to 0.0095 in (0.087 to 0.243 mm)
  Runout
    At center main journal .... 0.00098 in (0.025 mm)
    At flywheel flange .... 0.00098 in (0.025 mm)
Main bearing journal
  Diameter .... 2.0470 to 2.0480 in (51.996 to 52.020 mm)
  Out-of-round/taper limits .... 0.0005 in (0.0127 mm)
Main bearing oil clearance .... 0.0005 to 0.0023 in (0.013 to 0.058 mm)
Connecting rod bearing journal
  Diameter .... 1.8887 to 1.8897 in (47.975 to 48.00 mm)
  Out-of-round/taper limits .... 0.0005 in (0.0127 mm)
Connecting rod bearing oil clearance .... 0.0005 to 0.0020 in (0.013 to 0.053 mm)
Seal journal
  Diameter .... 3.2210 to 3.2299 in (81.96 to 82.04 mm)
  Runout limit .... 0.0012 in (0.03 mm)
Connecting rod side clearance (endplay) .... 0.0059 to 0.0177 in (0.150 to 0.450 mm)

Engine block
Cylinder bore
  Diameter .... 3.6217 to 3.6223 in (91.992 to 92.008 mm)
  Out-of-round limit .... 0.0004 in (0.010 mm)
  Taper limit (thrust side) .... 0.0003 in (0.008 mm) measured 4.173 in (106 mm) down the bore
Block deck warpage limit .... If more than 0.010 in (0.25 mm) must be removed, replace the block
Transaxle mounting bolt boss runout limit
  (rear face-to-crankshaft flange) .... 0.008 in (0.203 mm)

Pistons and rings
Piston diameter .... 3.6203 to 3.6210 in (91.957 to 91.973 mm) at 70-degrees F (21-degrees C)
Piston-to-bore clearance .... 0.0007 to 0.0020 in (0.019 to 0.051 mm)
Piston ring end gap
  Top compression ring .... 0.0138 to 0.0236 in (0.35 to 0.60 mm)
  Second compression ring .... 0.0157 to 0.0256 in (0.40 to 0.65 mm)
  Oil control ring .... 0.0157 to 0.0551 in (0.40 to 1.40 mm)

2D

2.3 liter four-cylinder (Quad-4) engine (continued)
Pistons and rings (continued)
Piston ring side clearance
    Top compression ring .... 0.0027 to 0.0047 in (0.070 to 0.120 mm)
    Second compression ring .... 0.00157 to 0.00315 in (0.040 to 0.080 mm)

Camshaft
Lobe lift (intake and exhaust) .... 0.410 in (10.414 mm)
Journal diameter
    Number 1 .... 1.5728 to 1.5720 in (39.95 to 39.93 mm)
    Numbers 2 through 5 .... 1.3751 to 1.3760 in (34.93 to 34.95 mm)
Endplay .... 0.0009 to 0.0088 in (0.025 to 0.225 mm)

Torque specifications**   **Ft-lbs**
Main bearing cap bolts
    Step 1 15
    Step 2 .... Rotate an additional 90-degrees
Connecting rod cap nuts
    Step 1 18
    Step 2 .... Rotate an additional 80-degrees

** **Note:** *Refer to Part B for additional torque specifications.*

V6 engines
General
RPO sales code
    2.8 liter LB6
    3.1 liter .... LHO
    3100 (1994 on) L82
VIN engine code
    2.8 liter .... W
    3.1 liter .... T
    3100 (1994 on) .... M
Displacement
    2.8 liter .... 173 cubic inches
    3.1 liter .... 192 cubic inches
    3100 (1994 on) .... 191 cubic inches
Cylinder compression pressure .... 100 psi minimum
Maximum variation between cylinders 30-percent
Oil pressure (minimum) .... 15 psi at 1100 rpm

Cylinder head
Warpage limit .... 0.005 in (0.127 mm)

Valves and related components
Valve margin width
    1993 and earlier .... 1/32 in minimum
    1994 on
        Intake .... 0.083 in (2.10 mm)
        Exhaust .... 0.106 in (2.70 mm)
Valve seat angle
    1993 and earlier 46-degrees
    1994 on 45-degrees
Valve stem-to-guide clearance .... 0.001 to 0.0027 in (0.026 to 0.068 mm)
Valve spring pressure
    1993 and earlier
        Closed .... 90 lbs @ 1.701 in (400 N @ 43 mm)
        Open .... 215 lbs @ 1.291 in (956 N @ 33 mm)
    1994 on
        closed .... 80 lbs @ 1.710 in (356 N @ 43 mm)
        open .... 250 lbs @ 1.239 in (1111 N @ 31.5 mm)

Crankshaft and connecting rods
Connecting rod journal
    Diameter ....
        1993 and earlier .... 1.9994 to 1.9983 in (50.784 to 50.758 mm)
        1994 on .... 1.9982 to 1.9984 in (50.768 to 50.784 mm)
Bearing oil clearance
    1987 and 1988 .... 0.0013 to 0.0026 in (0.030 to 0.066 mm)
    1989 .... 0.0014 to 0.0036 in (0.038 to 0.093 mm)
    1990 and later .... 0.0011 to 0.0037 in (0.028 to 0.086 mm)
Connecting rod side clearance (endplay)
    1992 and earlier .... 0.14 to 0.027 in (0.36 to 0.68 mm)
    1993 on .... 0.0071 to 0.0173 in (0.18 to 0.44 mm)

Main bearing journal
  Diameter . . . . 2.6473 to 2.6483 in (67.241 to 67.265 mm)
  Bearing oil clearance
    1987 and 1988 . . . . 0.0016 to 0.0032 in (0.041 to 0.081 mm)
    1989 . . . . 0.0012 to 0.0027 in (0.032 to 0.069 mm)
    1990 and later . . . . 0.0012 to 0.0030 in (0.032 to 0.077 mm)
Crankshaft endplay (at thrust bearing) . . . . 0.0024 to 0.0083 in (0.06 to 0.21 mm)
Journal taper/out of round limits . . . . 0.0002 in (0.005 mm)

Engine block
Cylinder bore
  Diameter
    2.8 liter engine . . . . 3.503 to 3.506 in (88.992 to 89.070 mm)
    3.1 liter (and 3100) engine . . . . 3.5046 to 3.5053 in (89.016 to 89.034 mm)
  Out-of-round limit . . . . 0.0005 in (0.013 mm)
  Taper limit (thrust side)
    1993 and earlier . . . . 0.0005 in (0.013 mm)
    1994 on . . . . 0.0008 in (0.020 mm)
Block deck warpage limit . . . . If more than 0.010 in (0.25 mm) must be removed, replace the block
Transaxle mounting bolt boss runout limit
  (rear face-to-crankshaft flange) . . . . 0.010 in (0.25 mm)

Pistons and rings
Piston-to-bore clearance
  1987 through 1989 . . . . 0.0020 to 0.0028 in (0.051 to 0.073 mm)
  1990 through 1993 . . . . 0.0009 to 0.0023 in (0.0235 to 0.0565 mm)
  1994 on . . . . 0.0013 to 0.0027 in (0.032 to 0.068 mm)
Piston ring end gap
  Top compression ring
    1992 and earlier . . . . 0.010 to 0.020 in (0.25 to 0.50 mm)
    1993 on . . . . 0.007 to 0.016 in (0.18 to 0.41 mm)
  Second compression ring
    1987 through 1989 . . . . 0.010 to 0.020 in (0.025 to 0.50 mm)
    1990 and later . . . . 0.020 to 0.028 in (0.050 to 0.71 mm)
  Oil control ring
    1987 through 1989 . . . . 0.020 to 0.055 in (0.51 to 1.40 mm)
    1990 and later . . . . 0.001 to 0.003 in (0.25 to 0.75 mm)
Piston ring side clearance
  Compression ring
    1987 through 1989 . . . . 0.0010 to 0.0030 in (0.03 to 0.08 mm)
    1990 and later . . . . 0.0020 to 0.0035 in (0.05 to 0.09 mm)
  Oil control ring . . . . 0.01 to 0.08 in (0.20 mm)

Camshaft
Bearing journal diameter (all)
  1993 and earlier . . . . 1.8678 to 1.8815 in (47.44 to 47.79 mm)
  1994 on . . . . 1.868 to 1.869 in (47.45 to 47.48 mm)
Bearing oil clearance . . . . 0.001 to 0.004 in (0.026 to 0.101 mm)

Torque specifications***   Ft-lbs
Main bearing cap bolts
  1992 and earlier 73
  1993 on . . . . 37, plus an additional 77-degrees rotation
Connecting rod cap nuts
  1993 and earlier 39
  1994 on . . . . 15, plus an additional 75-degrees rotation

*** **Note:** *Refer to Part C for additional torque specifications.*

1   General information

Included in this portion of Chapter 2 are the general overhaul procedures for the cylinder head(s) and internal engine components.

The information ranges from advice concerning preparation for an overhaul and the purchase of replacement parts to detailed, step-by-step procedures covering removal and installation of internal engine components and the inspection of parts.

The following Sections have been written based on the assumption the engine has been removed from the vehicle. For information concerning in-vehicle engine repair, as well as removal and installation of the external components necessary for the overhaul, see Part A, B or C of this Chapter and Section 8 of this Part.

The Specifications included in this Part are only those necessary for the inspection and overhaul procedures which follow. Refer to Parts A, B and C for additional Specifications.

2   Engine overhaul – general information

Refer to illustrations 2.4a, 2.4b, 2.4c and 2.4d

It's not always easy to determine when, or if, an engine should be completely overhauled, as a number of factors must be considered.

High mileage isn't necessarily an indication an overhaul is needed, while low mileage doesn't preclude the need for an overhaul. Frequency of servicing is probably the most important consideration. An engine that's had regular and frequent oil and filter changes, as well as other required maintenance, will most likely give many thousands of miles of reliable ser-

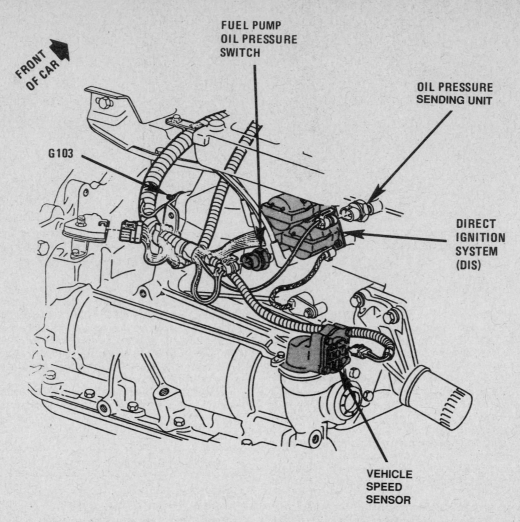

2.4a   On 2.0/2.2 liter four-cylinder engines, the oil pressure sending unit is located adjacent to the direct ignition system

2.4b   On the Quad-4 engine, the oil pressure sending unit is located in the transaxle end of the cylinder head

2.4c   On V6 engines, the oil pressure sending unit is located adjacent to the oil filter housing (arrow) – remove the sending unit . . .

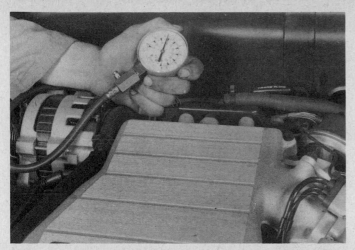

2.4d   . . . and install a gauge to check the engine oil pressure (2.8 liter V6 engine shown)

3.6   A compression gauge with a threaded fitting for the spark plug hole is preferred over the type that requires hand pressure to maintain the seal

vice. Conversely, a neglected engine may require an overhaul very early in its life.

Excessive oil consumption is an indication that piston rings, valve seals and/or valve guides are in need of attention. Make sure oil leaks aren't responsible before deciding the rings and/or guides are bad. Perform a cylinder compression check to determine the extent of the work required (see Section 3).

Remove the oil pressure sending unit and check the oil pressure with a gauge installed in its place **(see illustrations)**. Compare the results to this Chapter's Specifications. As a general rule, engines should have ten psi oil pressure for every 1,000 rpm's. If the pressure is extremely low, the bearings and/or oil pump are probably worn out.

Loss of power, rough running, knocking or metallic engine noises, excessive valve train noise and high fuel consumption rates may also point to the need for an overhaul, especially if they're all present at the same time. If a complete tune-up doesn't remedy the situation, major mechanical work is the only solution.

An engine overhaul involves restoring the internal parts to the specifications of a new engine. During an overhaul, the piston rings are replaced and the cylinder walls are reconditioned (rebored and/or honed). If a rebore is done by an automotive machine shop, new oversize pistons will also be installed. The main bearings, connecting rod bearings and camshaft bearings are generally replaced with new ones and, if necessary, the crankshaft may be reground to restore the journals. Generally, the valves are serviced as well, since they're usually in less-than-perfect condition at this point. While the engine is being overhauled, other components, such as the starter and alternator, can be rebuilt as well. The end result should be a like new engine that will give many trouble free miles. **Note:** *Critical cooling system components such as the hoses, drivebelts, thermostat and water pump MUST be replaced with new parts when an engine is overhauled. The radiator should be checked carefully to ensure it isn't clogged or leaking (see Chapter 3). Also, we don't recommend overhauling the oil pump – always install a new one when an engine is rebuilt.*

Before beginning the engine overhaul, read through the entire procedure to familiarize yourself with the scope and requirements of the job. Overhauling an engine isn't particularly difficult, if you follow all of the instructions carefully, have the necessary tools and equipment and pay close attention to all specifications; however, it can be time consuming. Plan on the vehicle being tied up for a minimum of two weeks, especially if parts must be taken to an automotive machine shop for repair or reconditioning. Check on availability of parts and make sure any necessary special tools and equipment are obtained in advance. Most work can be done with typical hand tools, although a number of precision measuring tools are required for inspecting parts to determine if they must be replaced. Often an automotive machine shop will handle the inspection of parts and offer advice concerning reconditioning and replacement. **Note:** *Always wait until the engine has been completely disassembled and all compo-*

nents, especially the engine block, have been inspected before deciding what service and repair operations must be performed by an automotive machine shop. Since the block's condition will be the major factor to consider when determining whether to overhaul the original engine or buy a rebuilt one, never purchase parts or have machine work done on other components until the block has been thoroughly inspected. As a general rule, time is the primary cost of an overhaul, so it doesn't pay to install worn or substandard parts.

As a final note, to ensure maximum life and minimum trouble from a rebuilt engine, everything must be assembled with care in a spotlessly clean environment.

2D

---

3   Cylinder compression check

Refer to illustration 3.6

1   A compression check will tell you what mechanical condition the upper end (pistons, rings, valves, head gaskets) of the engine is in. Specifically, it can tell you if the compression is down due to leakage caused by worn piston rings, defective valves and seats or a blown head gasket. **Note:** *The engine must be at normal operating temperature and the battery must be fully charged for this check.*

2   Begin by cleaning the area around the spark plugs before you remove them. Compressed air should be used, if available, otherwise a small brush or even a bicycle tire pump will work. The idea is to prevent dirt from getting into the cylinders as the compression check is being done.

3   Remove all of the spark plugs from the engine (see Chapter 1).

4   Block the throttle wide open.

5   Disable the fuel and ignition systems by removing the ECM fuse (see Chapter 6).

6   Install the compression gauge in the number one spark plug hole **(see illustration)**.

7   Crank the engine over at least seven compression strokes and watch the gauge. The compression should build up quickly in a healthy engine. Low compression on the first stroke, followed by gradually increasing pressure on successive strokes, indicates worn piston rings. A low compression reading on the first stroke, which doesn't build up during successive strokes, indicates leaking valves or a blown head gasket (a cracked head could also be the cause). Deposits on the undersides of the valve heads can also cause low compression. Record the highest gauge reading obtained.

8   Repeat the procedure for the remaining cylinders and compare the results to this Chapter's Specifications.

9   If the readings are below normal, add some engine oil (about three squirts from a plunger-type oil can) to each cylinder, through the spark plug hole, and repeat the test.

4.7a   The timing marks should be aligned as shown here (arrows) (V6 engine)

4.7b   Timing marks (arrows) on the Quad-4 engine

10   If the compression increases after the oil is added, the piston rings are definitely worn. If the compression doesn't increase significantly, the leakage is occurring at the valves or head gasket. Leakage past the valves may be caused by burned valve seats and/or faces or warped, cracked or bent valves.

11   If two adjacent cylinders have equally low compression, there's a strong possibility the head gasket between them is blown. The appearance of coolant in the combustion chambers or the crankcase would verify this condition.

12   If one cylinder is about 20 percent lower than the others, and the engine has a slightly rough idle, a worn exhaust lobe on the camshaft could be the cause.

13   If the compression is unusually high, the combustion chambers are probably coated with carbon deposits. If that's the case, the cylinder head(s) should be removed and decarbonized.

14   If compression is way down or varies greatly between cylinders, it would be a good idea to have a leak-down test performed by an automotive repair shop. This test will pinpoint exactly where the leakage is occurring and how severe it is.

15   Install the ECM fuse and drive the vehicle to restore the block learn memory.

4   Top Dead Center (TDC) for number one piston – locating

Refer to illustrations 4.7a and 4.7b

1   Top Dead Center (TDC) is the highest point in the cylinder each piston reaches as it travels up-and-down when the crankshaft turns. Each piston reaches TDC on the compression stroke and again on the exhaust stroke, but TDC generally refers to piston position on the compression stroke.

2   Positioning the piston(s) at TDC is an essential part of certain procedures such as camshaft removal and timing chain/sprocket removal.

3   Before beginning this procedure, be sure to place the transaxle in Neutral (or Park on automatic transaxle models), apply the parking brake and block the rear wheels.

4   Remove the spark plugs (see Chapter 1).

5   When looking at the drivebelt end of the engine, normal crankshaft rotation is clockwise. In order to bring any piston to TDC, the crankshaft must be turned with a socket and ratchet attached to the bolt threaded into the center of the lower drivebelt pulley (vibration damper) on the crankshaft.

6   Have an assistant turn the crankshaft with a socket and ratchet as described above while you hold a finger over the number one spark plug hole. **Note:** *See the Specifications for the engine you are working on for the*

number one cylinder location.

7   When the piston approaches TDC, pressure will be felt at the spark plug hole. Have your assistant stop turning the crankshaft when the timing marks are aligned **(see illustrations)**.

8   If the timing marks are bypassed, turn the crankshaft two complete revolutions clockwise until the timing marks are properly aligned.

9   After the number one piston has been positioned at TDC on the compression stroke, TDC for any of the remaining pistons can be located by turning the crankshaft one-half turn (180-degrees) on four-cylinder engines or one-third turn (120-degrees) on V6 engines to get to TDC for the next cylinder in the firing order.

5   Engine removal – methods and precautions

If you've decided the engine must be removed for overhaul or major repair work, several preliminary steps should be taken.

Locating a suitable place to work is extremely important. Adequate work space, along with storage space for the vehicle, will be needed. If a shop or garage isn't available, at the very least a flat, level, clean work surface made of concrete or asphalt is required.

Cleaning the engine compartment and engine before beginning the removal procedure will help keep tools clean and organized.

An engine hoist or A-frame will also be necessary. Make sure the equipment is rated in excess of the combined weight of the engine and transaxle. Safety is of primary importance, considering the potential hazards involved in lifting the engine out of the vehicle.

If the engine is being removed by a novice, a helper should be available. Advice and aid from someone more experienced would also be helpful. There are many instances when one person cannot simultaneously perform all of the operations required when lifting the engine out of the vehicle.

Plan the operation ahead of time. Arrange for or obtain all of the tools and equipment you'll need prior to beginning the job. Some of the equipment necessary to perform engine removal and installation safely and with relative ease are (in addition to an engine hoist) a heavy duty floor jack, complete sets of wrenches and sockets as described in the front of this manual, wooden blocks and plenty of rags and cleaning solvent for mopping up spilled oil, coolant and gasoline. If the hoist must be rented, be sure to arrange for it in advance and perform all of the operations possible without it beforehand. This will save you money and time.

Plan for the vehicle to be out of use for quite a while. A machine shop will be required to perform some of the work which the do-it-yourselfer can't accomplish without special equipment. These shops often have a busy schedule, so it would be a good idea to consult them before removing

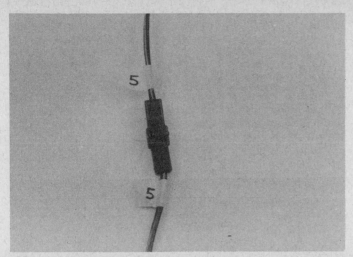

6.5   One way to ensure proper reattachment of wires and hoses is to fasten numbered pieces of masking tape to both sides of the connection as shown here

6.12   Unbolt the power steering pump and move it aside, then use wire or rope to hold it in place (V6 engine shown, others similar)

the engine in order to accurately estimate the amount of time required to rebuild or repair components that may need work.

Always be extremely careful when removing and installing the engine. Serious injury can result from careless actions. Plan ahead, take your time and a job of this nature, although major, can be accomplished successfully.

6   Engine – removal and installation

Refer to illustrations 6.5, 6.12, 6.21, 6.24a, 6.24b and 6.28

Note 1: *Read through the following steps carefully and familiarize yourself with the procedure before beginning work.*

Note 2: *On models equipped with the Delco Loc II audio system, be sure the lockout feature is turned to OFF before performing any procedure that requires disconnecting the battery.*

Warning 1: *Gasoline is extremely flammable, so take extra precautions when disconnecting any part of the fuel system. Don't smoke or allow open flames or bare light bulbs in or near the work area and don't work in a garage where a natural gas appliance (such as a clothes dryer or water heater) is installed. If you spill gasoline on your skin, rinse it off immediately. Have a fire extinguisher rated for gasoline fires handy and know how to use it! Also, the air conditioning system is under high pressure – have a dealer service department or service station discharge the system before disconnecting any of the hoses or fittings.*

Warning 2: *Later models are equipped with airbags. Impact sensors for the airbag system are located just above the radiator grille on the right side. The airbag(s) could accidently deploy if these sensors are disturbed, so be extremely careful when working in this area. Airbag system components are also located in the steering wheel, steering column and base of the steering column, so be extremely careful in these areas and don't disturb any airbag system components or wiring. You could easily be injured if an airbag accidently deploys, and the airbag might not deploy correctly in a collision if any components or wiring in the system have been disturbed.*

Removal

1   On air-conditioned Quad-4 models only, have the air conditioning system discharged by a dealer service department or service station.

All models

2   Refer to Chapter 4 and relieve the fuel system pressure, then disconnect the negative cable from the battery.

3   Cover the fenders and cowl and remove the hood (see Chapter 11). Special pads are available to protect the fenders, but an old bedspread or blanket will also work.

4   Remove the air cleaner assembly (and mass airflow sensor on V6

models so equipped) (see Chapter 4).

5   Remove the plastic firewall covers. Label the vacuum lines, emissions system hoses, wiring connectors, ground straps and fuel lines to ensure correct reinstallation, then detach them. The relay panel and bracket can be detached as an assembly. Pieces of masking tape with numbers or letters written on them work well **(see illustration)**. If there's any possibility of confusion, make a sketch of the engine compartment and clearly label the lines, hoses and wires. **Note:** *The ECM wiring can be unplugged and the harness pulled through the firewall. The engine harness plugs into the firewall connector.*

6   Raise the vehicle and support it securely on jackstands. Drain the cooling system (see Chapter 1).

7   Label and detach all coolant hoses from the engine.

8   Remove the coolant reservoir, cooling fan, shroud and radiator (see Chapter 3).

9   Remove the drivebelt and idler, if equipped (see Chapter 1). On 2.0 L and 2.2 liter four-cylinder and V6 models, remove the crankshaft pulley/vibration damper (see Part A or C).

10   Disconnect the fuel lines running from the engine to the chassis (see Chapter 4). Plug or cap all open fittings/lines.

11   Disconnect the throttle linkage (and TV linkage/speed control cable, if equipped) from the engine (see Chapters 4 and 7).

12   Unbolt the power steering pump and set it aside (see Chapter 10). Leave the lines/hoses attached and make sure the pump is kept in an upright position in the engine compartment **(see illustration)**. **Note:** *On some 2.0/2.2 liter four-cylinder engines, you have to detach the pump after the engine is lifted off the mounts.*

13   Unbolt the air conditioning compressor (see Chapter 3) and set it aside. On 2.0/2.2 liter four-cylinder and V6 models, do not disconnect the hoses.

14   Drain the engine oil and remove the filter (see Chapter 1).

15   Remove the starter and the alternator (see Chapter 5).

16   On Quad-4 models, remove the oil/air separator (Chapter 6).

17   Check for clearance and remove the brake master cylinder, if necessary, to allow clearance for the transaxle (see Chapter 9).

18   Disconnect the exhaust system from the engine (see Chapter 4). On Quad-4 models, remove the exhaust manifold (see Chapter 2B). **Note:** *On V6 and Quad-4 models, the engine and transaxle are removed from the vehicle as a unit. 2.0/2.2 liter four-cylinder engines should be removed from the vehicle after the transaxle has been removed.*

V6 and Quad-4 models only

19   Disconnect all the components attaching the transaxle to the vehicle (including driveaxles, intermediate shaft, cables, wiring, linkage, etc. – see Chapter 7).

20   Support the transaxle with a jack. Position a block of wood on the jack head to prevent damage to the transaxle.

2D

6.21   Attach the chain or hoist cable to the engine
brackets (arrows)

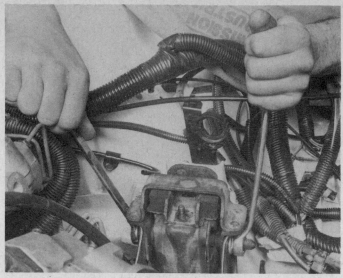

6.24a   Loosen the through-bolt . . .

All models

21   Attach an engine sling or a length of chain to the lifting brackets on the engine **(see illustration)**.

22   Roll the hoist into position and connect the sling to it. Take up the slack in the sling or chain, but don't lift the engine. **Warning:** *DO NOT place any part of your body under the engine when it's supported only by a hoist or other lifting device.*

23   If you're working on a vehicle with an automatic transaxle, refer to Chapter 7 and remove the torque converter-to-driveplate fasteners.

24   Remove the transaxle-to-body mount through-bolt and pry the mount out of the frame bracket **(see illustrations)**.

25   On 2.0/2.2 liter four-cylinder models, remove the transaxle (see Chapter 7).

26   Remove the engine mount-to-chassis bolts/nuts.

27   Recheck to be sure nothing is still connecting the engine to the vehicle (or transaxle, where applicable). Disconnect anything still remaining.

28   Raise the engine (or engine/transaxle assembly) slightly to disengage the mounts. Slowly raise the engine out of the vehicle **(see illustration)**. Check carefully to make sure nothing is hanging up as the hoist is raised.

29   On V6 and Quad-4 models, once the engine/transaxle assembly is out of the vehicle, remove the transaxle-to-engine block bolts. Carefully separate the engine from the transaxle. If you're working on a vehicle with an automatic transaxle, be sure the torque converter stays in place (clamp a pair of vise-grips to the housing to keep the converter from sliding out). If you're working on a vehicle with a manual transaxle, the input shaft must be completely disengaged from the clutch.

30   Remove the clutch and flywheel or driveplate and mount the engine on an engine stand.

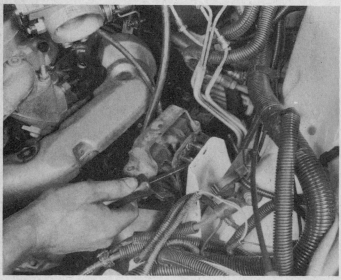

6.24b   . . . and pry the mount out of the frame bracket (V6
engine shown)

6.28   Lift the engine off the mounts and guide it carefully around
any obstacles as an assistant raises the hoist until it clears the
front of the vehicle

Installation

31   Check the engine and transaxle mounts. If they're worn or damaged, replace them.

32   If you're working on a manual transaxle equipped vehicle, install the clutch and pressure plate (see Chapter 7). Now is a good time to install a new clutch. Apply a dab of high-temperature grease to the input shaft.

33   **Caution:** *DO NOT use the transaxle-to-engine bolts to force the transaxle and engine together.* If you're working on an automatic transaxle equipped vehicle, take great care when installing the torque converter, following the procedure outlined in Chapter 7.

34   Carefully lower the engine into the engine compartment – make sure the mounts line up. Reinstall the remaining components in the reverse order of removal. Double-check to make sure everything is hooked up right.

35   Add coolant, oil, power steering and transmission fluid as needed. If the brake master cylinder was removed, bleed the brakes (see Chapter 9). Recheck the fluid level and test the brakes.

36   Run the engine and check for leaks and proper operation of all accessories, then install the hood and test drive the vehicle.

37   If the air conditioning system was discharged, have it evacuated, recharged and leak tested by the shop that discharged it.

---

7   Engine rebuilding alternatives

The home mechanic is faced with a number of options when performing an engine overhaul. The decision to replace the engine block, piston/connecting rod assemblies and crankshaft depends on a number of factors, with the number one consideration being the condition of the block. Other considerations are cost, access to machine shop facilities, parts availability, time required to complete the project and the extent of prior mechanical experience.

Some of the rebuilding alternatives include:

Individual parts – If the inspection procedures reveal the engine block and most engine components are in reusable condition, purchasing individual parts may be the most economical alternative. The block, crankshaft and piston/connecting rod assemblies should all be inspected carefully. Even if the block shows little wear, the cylinder bores should be surface honed.

Short block – A short block consists of an engine block with a crankshaft and piston/connecting rod assemblies already installed. All new bearings are incorporated and all clearances will be correct. The existing camshaft, valve train components, cylinder head(s) and external parts can be bolted to the short block with little or no machine shop work necessary.

Long block – A long block consists of a short block plus an oil pump, oil pan, cylinder head(s), rocker arm cover(s), camshaft and valve train components, timing sprockets and chain and timing chain cover. All components are installed with new bearings, seals and gaskets incorporated throughout. The installation of manifolds and external parts is all that's necessary.

Give careful thought to which alternative is best for you and discuss the situation with local automotive machine shops, auto parts dealers and experienced rebuilders before ordering or purchasing replacement parts.

---

8   Engine overhaul – disassembly sequence

Refer to illustrations 8.3a, 8.3b, 8.3c, 8.3d, 8.3e, 8.3f and 8.3g

1   It's much easier to disassemble and work on the engine if it's mounted on a portable engine stand. A stand can often be rented quite cheaply from an equipment rental yard. Before it's mounted on a stand, the flywheel/driveplate should be removed from the engine.

2   If a stand isn't available, it's possible to disassemble the engine with it blocked up on the floor. Be extra careful not to tip or drop the engine when working without a stand.

3   If you're going to obtain a rebuilt engine, all external components (**see**

illustrations) must come off first, to be transferred to the replacement engine, just as they will if you're doing a complete engine overhaul yourself. These include:

> Alternator and brackets
> Emissions control components
> Ignition coil/module assembly, spark plug wires and spark plugs
> Thermostat and housing cover
> Water pump
> EFI components
> Intake/exhaust manifolds
> Oil filter
> Engine mounts
> Clutch and flywheel/driveplate
> Engine rear plate (if equipped)

Note: *When removing the external components from the engine, pay close attention to details that may be helpful or important during installation. Note the installed position of gaskets, seals, spacers, pins, brackets, washers, bolts and other small items.*

4   If you're obtaining a short block, which consists of the engine block, crankshaft, pistons and connecting rods all assembled, then the cylinder head(s), oil pan and oil pump will have to be removed as well. See Engine rebuilding alternatives for additional information regarding the different possibilities to be considered.

5   If you're planning a complete overhaul, the engine must be disassembled and the internal components removed in the following general order:

2D

2.0/2.2 liter four-cylinder engines

> Rocker arm cover
> Intake and exhaust manifolds
> Rocker arms and pushrods
> Valve lifters
> Cylinder head
> Timing chain cover
> Timing chain and sprockets
> Camshaft
> Oil pan
> Oil pump
> Piston/connecting rod assemblies
> Crankshaft and main bearings

2.3 liter four-cylinder (Quad-4) engine

> Timing chain and sprockets
> Timing chain housing
> Cylinder head and camshafts
> Oil pan
> Oil pump
> Piston/connecting rod assemblies
> Rear main oil seal housing
> Crankshaft and main bearings

V6 engines

> Rocker arm covers
> Intake and exhaust manifolds
> Rocker arms and pushrods
> Valve lifters
> Cylinder heads
> Timing chain cover
> Timing chain and sprockets
> Camshaft
> Oil pan
> Oil pump
> Piston/connecting rod assemblies
> Rear main oil seal housing
> Crankshaft and main bearings

6   Before beginning the disassembly and overhaul procedures, make sure the following items are available. Also, refer to Engine overhaul – reassembly sequence for a list of tools and materials needed for engine reassembly.

    Common hand tools
    Small cardboard boxes or plastic bags for storing parts
    Gasket scraper
    Ridge reamer
    Vibration damper puller
    Micrometers
    Telescoping gauges
    Dial indicator set
    Valve spring compressor
    Cylinder surfacing hone
    Piston ring groove cleaning tool
    Electric drill motor
    Tap and die set
    Wire brushes
    Oil gallery brushes
    Cleaning solvent

8.3a   Typical 2.0/2.2 liter four-cylinder engine cylinder head and related components – exploded view

1	Air cleaner	45	Exhaust manifold
2	Screw	46	Nut
3	Washer	47	Exhaust valve
4	Front air intake duct	48	Intake valve
5	Bolt	49	Cylinder head gasket
6	Spark plug wire support	50	Cylinder head
7	Spark plug wire support	51	Bolt
8	Bolt	52	Bolt
9	Wire support	53	Coolant temperature sensor
10	Bolt	54	Drivebelt tensioner bracket
11	Crankcase vent tube	55	Bolt
12	Bolt	56	Stud
13	Rocker arm cover	57	Throttle cable bracket
14	Gasket	58	Stud
15	Nut	59	Nut
16	Rocker arm pivot ball	60	Stud
17	Rocker arm	61	Intake manifold stud
18	Stud	62	Intake manifold stud
19	Pushrod guide	63	Intake manifold gasket
20	Valve spring seat	64	Intake manifold
21	Heater coolant hose control	65	Power brake vacuum fitting
22	Valve stem oil seal	66	Intake manifold vacuum fitting
23	Valve spring	67	EGR vacuum and evaporator canister tube
24	Retainer	68	TBI gasket
25	Keepers	69	TBI unit
26	Spark plug	70	Bolt
27	Spark plug wire	71	Fuel return line
28	Nut	72	Fuel feed line
29	EGR valve	73	Crankcase vent valve
30	EGR valve gasket	74	Seal
31	Coolant outlet plug	75	Clamp
32	Coolant temperature sensor	76	Crankcase vent hose
33	Stud	77	Crankcase vent valve cap
34	Coolant outlet adapter	78	Crankcase vent valve (top) seal
35	Thermostat	79	Crankcase vent valve (bottom) seal
36	Coolant outlet	80	Manifold air temperature sensor
37	Stud	81	Seal
38	Nut	82	Clamp
39	Gasket	83	Adapter
40	Nut	84	Clamp
41	Engine lift bracket	85	Duct
42	Cylinder head stud	86	Clamp
43	Exhaust manifold stud		
44	Exhaust manifold gasket		

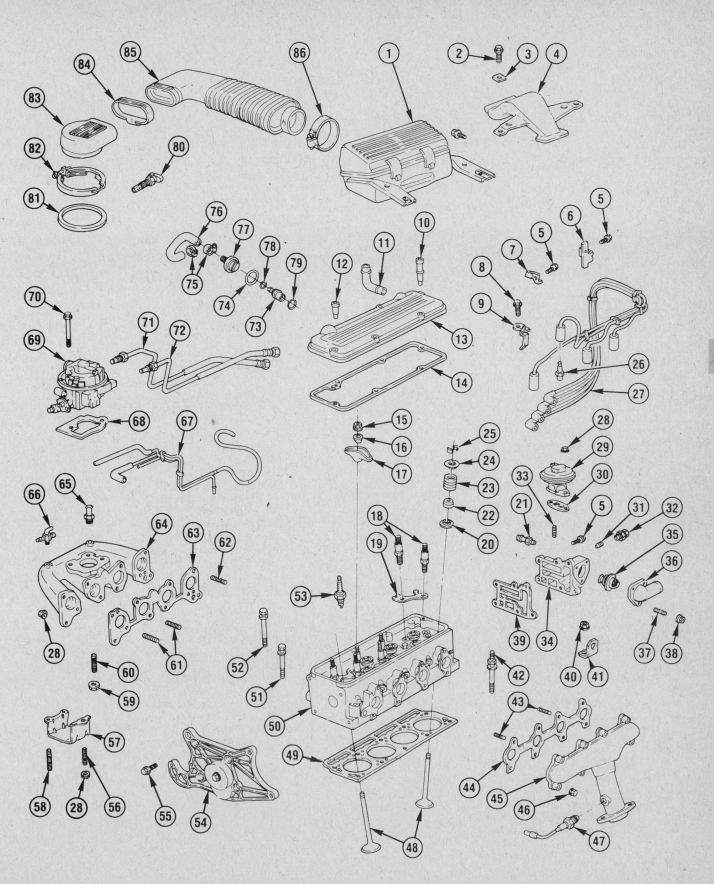

8.3b   2.0/2.2 liter four-cylinder engine block and related components – exploded view

1	Piston rings	50	Nut
2	Piston	51	Bolt
3	Connecting rod bolt	52	Gasket
4	Connecting rod bearing	53	Oil pan drain plug
5	Cylinder head dowel pin	54	Starter motor shim
6	Core plug	55	Starter motor
7	Bellhousing dowel pin	56	Bolt
8	Engine block heater cord	57	Bolt
9	Engine block heater	58	Bolt
10	Retainer	59	Nut
11	Dipstick	60	Washer
12	Bolt	61	Starter motor bracket
13	Oil fill tube	62	Bolt
14	Seal	63	Washer
15	Bolt	64	Vibration damper/crankshaft pulley
16	Plug	65	Crankshaft front oil seal
17	Camshaft rear cover	66	Bolt
18	Bolt	67	Timing chain cover
19	Plug	68	Timing chain
20	Clamp	69	Crankshaft sprocket
21	Coolant hose	70	Woodruff key
22	Bolt	71	Crankshaft
23	Coolant inlet	72	Gasket
24	Gasket	73	Water pump
25	Plug	74	Pulley
26	Engine block	75	Bolt
27	Connecting rod nut	76	Bolt
28	Crankshaft bearing	77	Timing chain tensioner bolt
29	Crankshaft rear main oil seal	78	Timing chain tensioner
30	Bolt	79	Bolt
31	Flywheel retainer	80	Washer
32	Flywheel	81	Camshaft sprocket
33	Bolt	82	Bolt
34	Lock washer	83	Camshaft thrust plate
35	Pressure plate cover	84	Pin
36	Clutch plate	85	Camshaft bearing
37	Sealant	86	Camshaft
38	Main bearing cap bolt	87	Fuel pump switch
39	Main bearing cap	88	Oil filter by-pass valve
40	Sealant	89	Oil filter
41	Bolt	90	Oil filter adapter connector
42	Oil pump drive	91	Oil filter adapter
43	Oil pump shaft	92	Gasket
44	Retainer	93	Lifter
45	Oil pump	94	Pushrod
46	Bolt	95	Ignition coil/module
47	Stud	96	Bolt
48	Oil pan rear seal	97	Stud
49	Oil pan	98	Crankshaft sensor

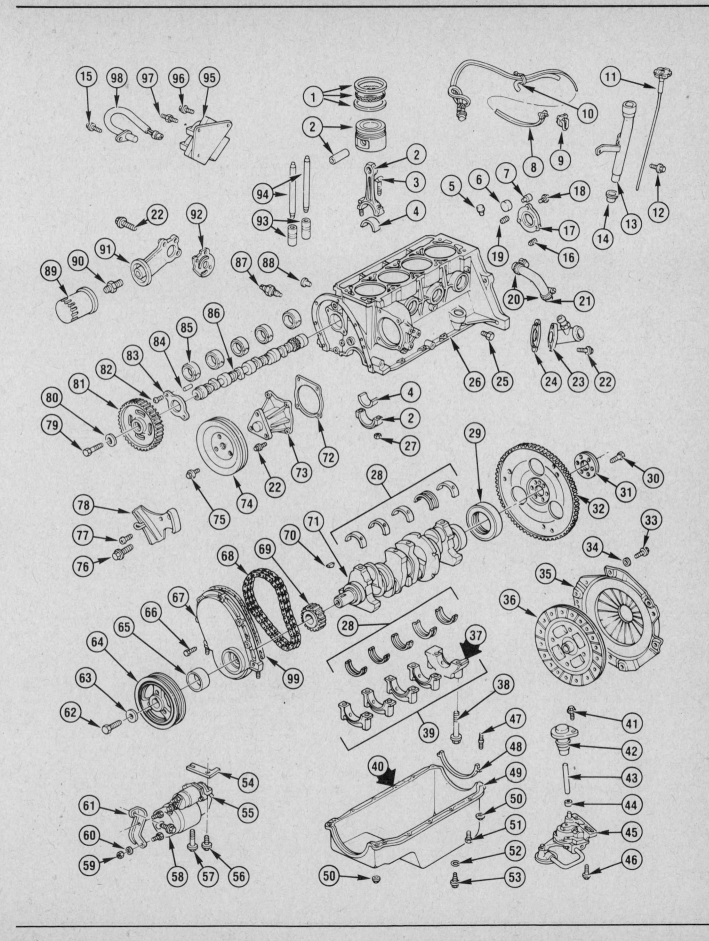

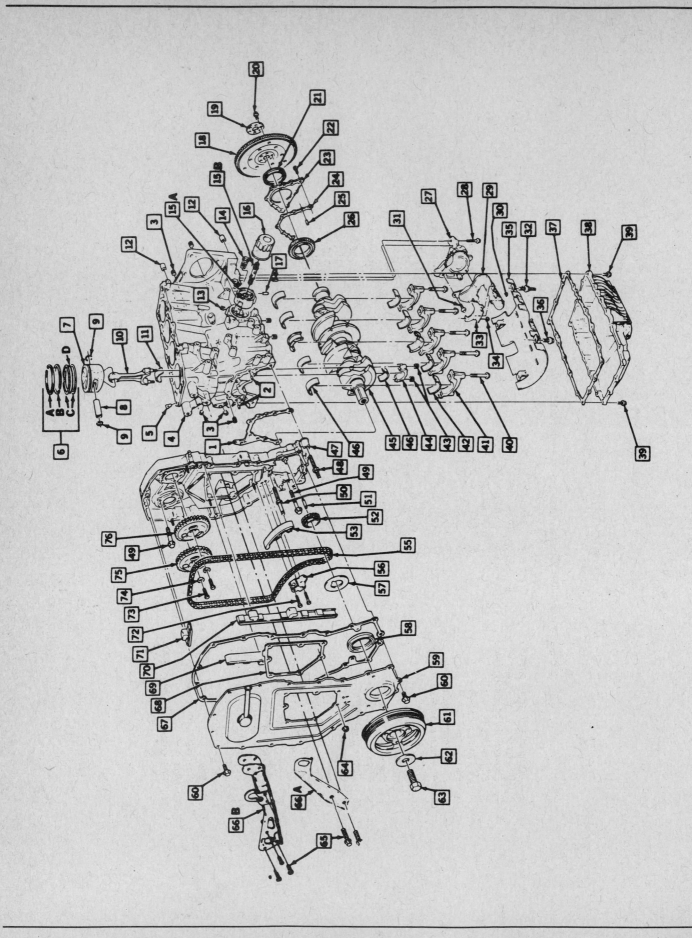

8.3c   2.3 liter four-cylinder (Quad-4) engine block and related components – exploded view

1   Timing chain housing gasket
2   Dowel pin
3   Engine block oil passage plug
4   Engine block
5   Oil flow check valve
6   Piston rings
    A   Top compression ring
    B   Lower compression ring
    C   Oil ring (2)
    D   Spacer
7   Piston
8   Piston pin
9   Piston pin retainer
10 Connecting rod
11 Connecting rod bearing
12 Dowel pin
13 Oil filter bypass plug
14 Oil filter bypass valve
15 Oil filter-to-block connector
15A Oil cooler adapter
15B Oil cooler connector
16 Oil filter
17 Dowel pin
18 Flywheel
19 Driveplate retainer
20 Bolt
21 Rear crankshaft oil seal
22 Bolt
23 Rear crankshaft seal housing

24 Gasket
25 Dowel pin
26 Oil pump drive gear
27 Oil pump
28 Bolt
29 Screen
30 Bolt
31 Bolt
32 Stud
33 Oil pump-to-block brace
34 Nut
35 Oil pan baffle
36 Bolt
37 Oil pan gasket
38 Oil pan
39 Oil pan bolt
    A   to timing chain housing
    B   to block
    C   to seal housing
40 Main bearing cap bolt
41 Main bearing cap
42 Main bearing
43 Connecting rod cap nut
44 Connecting rod cap
45 Crankshaft
46 Main bearing (upper)
47 Timing chain housing
48 Stud bolt

49 Bolt
50 Stud
51 Woodruff key
52 Crankshaft sprocket
53 Timing chain tensioner shoe
54 Timing chain tensioner shoe retainer
55 Timing chain
56 Timing chain tensioner
57 Crankshaft oil slinger
58 Crankshaft front oil seal
59 Timing chain housing cover
60 Bolt
61 Vibration damper
62 Washer
63 Bolt
64 Nut
65 Nut
66 Bracket
67 Gasket
68 Gasket
69 Timing chain guide (RH)
70 Timing chain guide (LH)
71 Timing chain guide (upper)
72 Bolt
73 Camshaft sprocket bolt
74 Washer
75 Exhaust camshaft sprocket
76 Intake camshaft sprocket

2D

8.3d   2.3 liter four-cylinder (Quad-4) engine cylinder head and related components – exploded view

73	Camshaft sprocket bolt		94	Plug
74	Washer		95	Exhaust camshaft cover
75	Exhaust camshaft sprocket		96	Bolt
76	Intake camshaft sprocket		97	Gasket
77	Gasket		98	Cylinder head
78	Gasket		99	Stud (2)
79	Ignition coil and module		100	Gasket
80	Bolts		101	Not used
81	Seal		102	Not used
82A	Camshaft housing-to-cylinder head bolts		103	Intake manifold
			104	Bolt (5)
82B	Camshaft housing cover bolts		105	Nut (2)
83	Camshaft housing cover (intake shown)		106	Pin (2)
84	Camshaft (intake shown)		107	Gasket
85	Intake camshaft housing seal		108	Intake valve (8)
86	Power steering pump drive pulley		109	Plug
87	Valve lifters (16 – 8 per camshaft housing)		110	Stud
			111	Cylinder head bolt (2)
88	Dowel pin		112	Rotator (16)
89	Camshaft housing oil galley plug		113	Valve stem seal (16)
90	Camshaft housing (intake shown)		114	Valve spring (16)
91	Camshaft housing-to-cylinder head gasket		115	Retainer (16)
			116	Keepers (32)
92	Spark plug		117	Dowel pin
93	Cylinder head bolt (8)		118	Dowel pin

8.3e   V6 engine – front

8.3f   V6 engine – drivebelt end

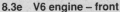

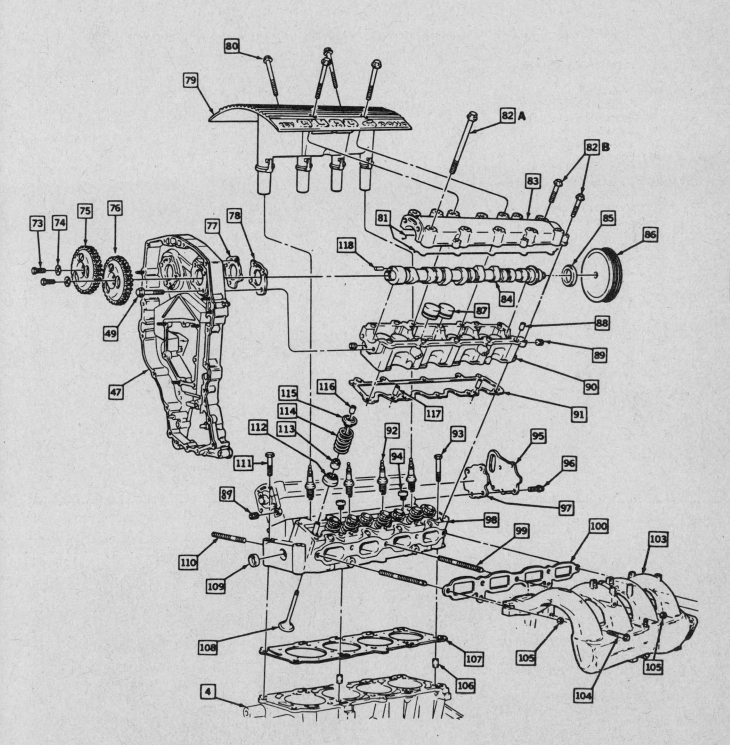

8.3g   V6 engine – rear

9.2   Have several plastic bags ready (one for each valve) before you start disassembling the head – label each bag and put the entire contents of each valve assembly in one bag as shown

9   Cylinder head – disassembly

Refer to illustrations 9.2, 9.3 and 9.4

Note: *New and rebuilt cylinder heads are commonly available for most engines at dealerships and auto parts stores. Due to the fact that some specialized tools are necessary for the disassembly and inspection procedures, and replacement parts aren't always readily available, it may be more practical and economical for the home mechanic to purchase replacement head(s) rather than taking the time to disassemble, inspect and recondition the original(s).*

1   Cylinder head disassembly involves removal of the intake and exhaust valves and related components. If you're working on a Quad-4 engine, the camshafts and housings must be removed before beginning the cylinder head disassembly procedure (see Part B of this Chapter). If you're working on a 2.0/2.2 liter four-cylinder engine or a V6 engine, remove the rocker arm nuts, pivot balls and rocker arms from the cylinder head studs. Label the parts or store them separately so they can be reinstalled in their original locations.

2   Before the valves are removed, arrange to label and store them, along with their related components, so they can be kept separate and reinstalled in their original locations **(see illustration)**.

3   Compress the springs on the first valve with a spring compressor and remove the keepers **(see illustration)**. Carefully release the valve spring compressor and remove the retainer, the spring and the spring seat (if used). Note that valve rotators are installed under the springs on the Quad-4 engine.

4   Pull the valve out of the head, then remove the oil seal from the guide. If the valve binds in the guide (won't pull through), push it back into the head and deburr the area around the keeper groove with a fine file or whetstone **(see illustration)**.

9.3   Use a valve spring compressor to compress the springs, then remove the keepers from the valve stem with a magnet or small needle-nose pliers

9.4   If you can't pull the valve through the guide, deburr the edge of the stem end and the area around the top of the keeper groove with a file or whetstone

10.12 Check the cylinder head gasket surface for warpage by trying to slip a feeler gauge under the straightedge (see this Chapter's Specifications for the maximum warpage allowed and use a feeler gauge of that thickness)

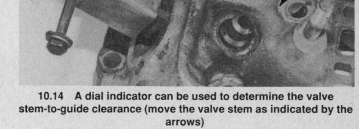

10.14 A dial indicator can be used to determine the valve stem-to-guide clearance (move the valve stem as indicated by the arrows)

2D

5   Repeat the procedure for the remaining valves. Remember to keep all the parts for each valve together so they can be reinstalled in the same locations.

6   Once the valves and related components have been removed and stored in an organized manner, the head should be thoroughly cleaned and inspected. If a complete engine overhaul is being done, finish the engine disassembly procedures before beginning the cylinder head cleaning and inspection process.

10   Cylinder head – cleaning and inspection

1   Thorough cleaning of the cylinder head(s) and related valve train components, followed by a detailed inspection, will enable you to decide how much valve service work must be done during the engine overhaul. **Note:** *If the engine was severely overheated, the cylinder head is probably warped (see Step 12).*

Cleaning

2   Scrape all traces of old gasket material and sealant off the head gasket, intake manifold and exhaust manifold mating surfaces. Be very careful not to gouge the cylinder head. Special gasket removal solvents that soften gaskets and make removal much easier are available at auto parts stores.

3   Remove all built up scale from the coolant passages.

4   Run a stiff wire brush through the various holes to remove deposits that may have formed in them.

5   Run an appropriate size tap into each of the threaded holes to remove corrosion and thread sealant that may be present. If compressed air is available, use it to clear the holes of debris produced by this operation. **Warning:** *Wear eye protection when using compressed air!*

6   Clean the rocker arm pivot stud threads with a wire brush (except Quad-4 engine).

7   Clean the cylinder head with solvent and dry it thoroughly. Compressed air will speed the drying process and ensure that all holes and recessed areas are clean. **Note:** *Decarbonizing chemicals are available and may prove very useful when cleaning cylinder heads and valve train components. They're very caustic and should be used with caution. Be sure to follow the instructions on the container.*

8   Clean the rocker arms, pivot balls, nuts and pushrods (except Quad-4 engine) with solvent and dry them thoroughly (don't mix them up during the

cleaning process). Compressed air will speed the drying process and can be used to clean out the oil passages.

9   Clean all the valve springs, spring seats, rotators (where applicable), keepers and retainers with solvent and dry them thoroughly. Do the components from one valve at a time to avoid mixing up the parts.

10   Scrape off any heavy deposits that may have formed on the valves, then use a motorized wire brush to remove deposits from the valve heads and stems. Again, make sure the valves don't get mixed up.

Inspection

Refer to illustrations 10.12, 10.14, 10.15a, 10.15b, 10.16, 10.17 and 10.18
Note: *Be sure to perform all of the following inspection procedures before concluding machine shop work is required. Make a list of the items that need attention.*

Cylinder head

11   Inspect the head very carefully for cracks, evidence of coolant leakage and other damage. If cracks are found, check with an automotive machine shop concerning repair. If repair isn't possible, a new cylinder head should be obtained.

12   Using a straightedge and feeler gauge, check the head gasket mating surface for warpage **(see illustration)**. If the warpage exceeds the limit in this Chapter's Specifications, it can be resurfaced at an automotive machine shop. **Note:** *If the V6 engine heads are resurfaced, the intake manifold flanges will also require machining.*

13   Examine the valve seats in each of the combustion chambers. If they're pitted, cracked or burned, the head will require valve service that's beyond the scope of the home mechanic.

14   Check the valve stem-to-guide clearance by measuring the lateral movement of the valve stem with a dial indicator attached securely to the head **(see illustration)**. The valve must be in the guide and approximately 1/16-inch off the seat. The total valve stem movement indicated by the gauge needle must be divided by two to obtain the actual clearance. After this is done, if there's still some doubt regarding the condition of the valve guides, they should be checked by an automotive machine shop (the cost should be minimal).

Valves

15   Carefully inspect each valve face for uneven wear, deformation, cracks, pits and burned areas. Check the valve stem for scuffing and galling and the neck for cracks. Rotate the valve and check for any obvious indication that it's bent. Look for pits and excessive wear on the end of the

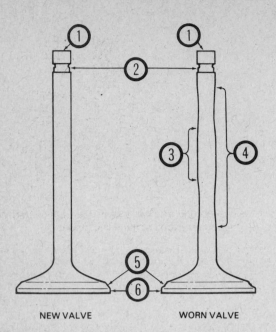

10.15a   Check for valve wear at the points shown here

1	Valve tip	4	Stem (most worn area)
2	Keeper groove	5	Valve face
3	Stem (least worn area)	6	Margin

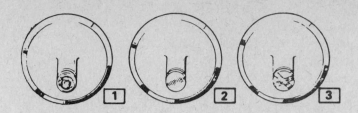

10.15b   Valve stem tip wear patterns (Quad-4 engine)

1   *Proper tip pattern (rotator functioning properly)*
2   *No rotation pattern (replace rotator and check rotation)*
3   *Partial rotation pattern (replace rotator and check rotation)*

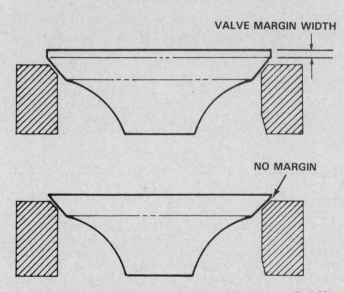

10.16   The margin width on each valve must be as specified (if no margin exists, the valve cannot be reused)

10.17   Measure the free length of each valve spring with a dial or vernier caliper

stem. The presence of any of these conditions (**see illustrations**) indicates the need for valve service by an automotive machine shop.
16   Measure the margin width on each valve (**see illustration**). Any valve with a margin narrower than specified in this Chapter will have to be replaced with a new one.

Valve components

17   Check each valve spring for wear (on the ends) and pits. Measure the free length and compare it to this Chapter's Specifications (**see illustration**). Any springs that are shorter than specified have sagged and shouldn't be reused. The tension of all springs should be checked with a special fixture before deciding they're suitable for use in a rebuilt engine (take the springs to an automotive machine shop for this check).

18   Stand each spring on a flat surface and check it for squareness (**see illustration**). If any of the springs are distorted or sagged, replace all of them with new parts.
19   Check the spring retainers and keepers for obvious wear and cracks. Any questionable parts should be replaced with new ones, as extensive damage will occur if they fail during engine operation. Make sure the rotators (Quad-4 engine only) operate smoothly with no binding or excessive play.

Rocker arm components (overhead valve engines only)

20   Check the rocker arm faces (the areas that contact the pushrod ends and valve stems) for pits, wear, galling, score marks and rough spots. Check the rocker arm pivot contact areas and pivot balls as well. Look for cracks in each rocker arm and nut.
21   Inspect the pushrod ends for scuffing and excessive wear. Roll each pushrod on a flat surface, like a piece of plate glass, to determine if it's bent.
22   Check the rocker arm studs in the cylinder heads for damaged threads and secure installation.
23   Any damaged or excessively worn parts must be replaced with new ones.

Camshafts, lifters and housings (Quad-4 engine only)

24   Refer to Part B for the inspection procedures for these components.

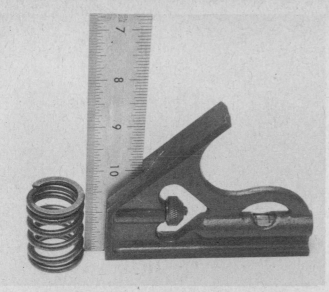

10.18 Check each valve spring for squareness

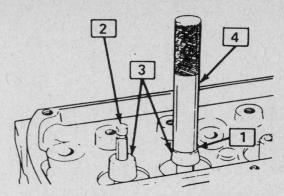

12.4 Make sure the new valve stem seals are seated against the tops of the valve guides

| 1 | Valve seal seated in tool | 3 | Seal |
| 2 | Deburr the end of the valve stem before installing the seal | 4 | Valve seal installation tool |

2D

All components

25 If the inspection process indicates the valve components are in generally poor condition and worn beyond the limits specified, which is usually the case in an engine that's being overhauled, reassemble the valves in the cylinder head and refer to Section 11 for valve servicing recommendations.

11 Valves – servicing

1 Because of the complex nature of the job and the special tools and equipment needed, servicing of the valves, the valve seats and the valve guides, commonly known as a valve job, should be done by a professional.

2 The home mechanic can remove and disassemble the head, do the initial cleaning and inspection, then reassemble and deliver it to a dealer service department or an automotive machine shop for the actual service work. Doing the inspection will enable you to see what condition the head and valvetrain components are in and will ensure that you know what work and new parts are required when dealing with an automotive machine shop.

3 The dealer service department, or automotive machine shop, will remove the valves and springs, recondition or replace the valves and valve seats, recondition the valve guides, check and replace the valve springs, rotators, spring retainers and keepers (as necessary), replace the valve seals with new ones, reassemble the valve components and make sure the installed spring height is correct. The cylinder head gasket surface will also be resurfaced if it's warped.

4 After the valve job has been performed by a professional, the head will be in like new condition. When the head is returned, be sure to clean it again before installation on the engine to remove any metal particles and abrasive grit that may still be present from the valve service or head resurfacing operations. Use compressed air, if available, to blow out all the oil holes and passages.

12 Cylinder head – reassembly

Refer to illustrations 12.4 and 12.6

1 Regardless of whether or not the head was sent to an automotive repair shop for valve servicing, make sure it's clean before beginning reassembly.

2 If the head was sent out for valve servicing, the valves and related components will already be in place. Begin the reassembly procedure with Step 8.

12.6 Apply a small dab of grease to each keeper as shown here before installation – it'll hold them in place on the valve stem as the spring is released

3 Install the spring seats or valve rotators (if equipped) before the valve seals.

4 Install new seals on each of the valve guides. Using a hammer and a deep socket or seal installation tool, gently tap each seal into place until it's completely seated on the guide **(see illustration)**. Don't twist or cock the seals during installation or they won't seal properly on the valve stems.

5 Beginning at one end of the head, lubricate and install the first valve. Apply moly-base grease or clean engine oil to the valve stem.

6 Position the valve springs (and shims, if used) over the valves. Compress the springs with a valve spring compressor and carefully install the keepers in the groove, then slowly release the compressor and make sure the keepers seat properly. Apply a small dab of grease to each keeper to hold it in place if necessary **(see illustration)**.

7 Repeat the procedure for the remaining valves. Be sure to return the components to their original locations – don't mix them up!

8 Check the installed valve spring height with a ruler graduated in 1/32-inch increments or a dial caliper. If the head was sent out for service work, the installed height should be correct (but don't automatically assume it is). The measurement is taken from the top of each spring seat, rotator or top shim to the bottom of the retainer. If the height is greater than specified in this Chapter, shims can be added under the springs to correct

13.3   When checking the camshaft lobe lift, the dial indicator plunger must be positioned directly above and in line with the pushrod

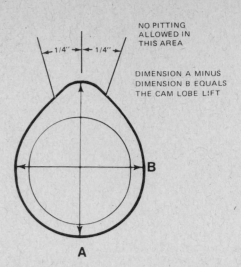

13.9   To verify camshaft lobe lift, measure the major (A) and minor (B) diameters of each lobe with a micrometer or vernier caliper – subtract each minor diameter from the major diameter to arrive at the lobe lift

it. **Caution:** *Do not, under any circumstances, shim the springs to the point where the installed height is less than specified.*

9   Apply moly-base grease to the rocker arm faces and the pivot balls, then install the rocker arms and pivots on the cylinder head studs (except Quad-4 engine – see part A or C).

10   If you're working on a Quad-4 engine, refer to Part B and install the camshafts, lifters and housings on the head.

---

13   Camshaft and bearings – removal and inspection

Note: *This procedure applies to the 2.0/2.2 liter four-cylinder overhead valve engines and all V6 engines. Since there isn't enough room to remove the camshaft with the engine in the vehicle, the engine must be out of the vehicle and mounted on a stand for this procedure.*

Camshaft lobe lift check

With cylinder head installed
Refer to illustration 13.3

1   In order to determine the extent of cam lobe wear, the lobe lift should be checked prior to camshaft removal. Refer to Part A or C and remove the rocker arm cover(s).

2   Position the number one piston at TDC on the compression stroke (see Section 4).

3   Beginning with the number one cylinder valves, mount a dial indicator on the engine and position the plunger against the top surface of the first rocker arm. The plunger should be directly above and in line with the push-rod **(see illustration)**.

4   Zero the dial indicator, then very slowly turn the crankshaft in the normal direction of rotation (clockwise) until the indicator needle stops and begins to move in the opposite direction. The point at which it stops indicates maximum cam lobe lift.

5   Record this figure for future reference, then reposition the piston at TDC on the compression stroke.

6   Move the dial indicator to the remaining number one cylinder rocker arm and repeat the check. Be sure to record the results for each valve.

7   Repeat the check for the remaining valves. Since each piston must be at TDC on the compression stroke for this procedure, work from cylinder-to-cylinder following the firing order sequence.

8   After the check is complete, compare the results to this Chapter's Specifications. If camshaft lobe lift is less than specified, cam lobe wear has occurred and a new camshaft should be installed.

With cylinder head removed
Refer to illustration 13.9

9   If the cylinder head(s) have already been removed, an alternate method of lobe measurement can be used. Remove the camshaft as described below. Using a micrometer, measure the lobe at its highest point. Then measure the base circle perpendicular (90-degrees) to the lobe **(see illustration)**. Do this for each lobe and record the results.

10   Subtract the base circle measurement from the lobe height. The difference is the lobe lift. See Step 8 above.

Removal
Refer to illustrations 13.12a, 13.12b, 13.12c, 13.12d, 13.14 and 13.15

11   Refer to the appropriate Sections in Part A or C and remove the timing chain and sprockets, lifters and pushrods.

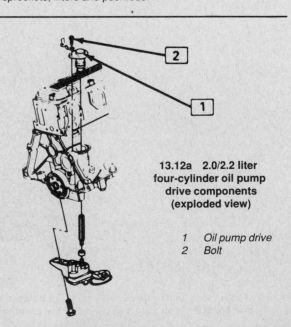

13.12a   2.0/2.2 liter four-cylinder oil pump drive components (exploded view)

1   *Oil pump drive*
2   *Bolt*

13.12b   The V6 engine oil pump drive (arrow) is located at the transaxle-end of the block

13.12c   If the oil pump drive is stuck, remove the pump and push the drive out with a long socket extension (V6 engine shown)

12   Remove the oil pump drive. If it's stuck, remove the oil pump and push the drive out with a long socket extension. Be sure to replace the O-ring before reassembly **(see illustrations)**.

13   On four-cylinder engines, remove the bolts and detach the camshaft thrust plate from the engine block (item 83 in illustration 8.3b).

14   Thread long bolts into the camshaft sprocket bolt holes to use as a handle when removing the camshaft from the block **(see illustration)**.

15   Carefully pull the camshaft out. Support the cam near the block so the lobes don't nick or gouge the bearings as it's withdrawn **(see illustration)**.

Inspection

Refer to illustration 13.17

16   After the camshaft has been removed from the engine, cleaned with solvent and dried, inspect the bearing journals for uneven wear, pitting and evidence of seizure. If the journals are damaged, the bearing inserts in the block are probably damaged as well. Both the camshaft and bearings will have to be replaced.

13.12d   Be sure to replace the O-ring (arrow)

13.14   Thread long bolts into the sprocket bolt holes to use as a handle when removing and installing the camshaft

13.15   Support the camshaft near the block to avoid damaging the bearings

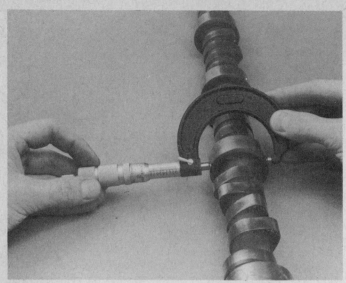

13.17　The camshaft bearing journal diameters are checked to pinpoint excessive wear and out-of-round conditions

14.1　A ridge reamer is required to remove the ridge from the top of each cylinder – do this before removing the pistons!

17　Measure the bearing journals with a micrometer **(see illustration)** to determine if they're excessively worn or out-of-round.

18　Check the camshaft lobes and oil pump drive and driven gears for heat discoloration, score marks, chipped areas, pitting and uneven wear. If the lobes and gears are in good condition and if the lobe lift measurements are as specified, the components can be reused.

19　Check the bearings in the block for wear and damage. Look for galling, pitting and discolored areas.

20　The inside diameter of each bearing can be determined with a small hole gauge and outside micrometer or an inside micrometer. Subtract the camshaft bearing journal diameter(s) from the corresponding bearing inside diameter(s) to obtain the bearing oil clearance. If it's excessive, new bearings will be required regardless of the condition of the originals.

21　Camshaft bearing replacement requires special tools and expertise that place it outside the scope of the home mechanic. Take the block to an automotive machine shop to ensure the job is done correctly.

14　Pistons and connecting rods – removal

Refer to illustrations 14.1, 14.3 and 14.6

Note: *Prior to removing the piston/connecting rod assemblies, remove the cylinder head(s), the oil pan and the oil pump by referring to the appropriate Sections in Parts A, B or C of Chapter 2.*

1　Use your fingernail to feel if a ridge has formed at the upper limit of ring travel (about 1/4-inch down from the top of each cylinder). If carbon deposits or cylinder wear have produced ridges, they must be completely removed with a special tool **(see illustration)**. Follow the manufacturer's instructions provided with the tool. Failure to remove the ridges before attempting to remove the piston/connecting rod assemblies may result in piston breakage.

2　After the cylinder ridges have been removed, turn the engine upside-down so the crankshaft is facing up.

3　Before the connecting rods are removed, check the endplay with feeler gauges. Slide them between the first connecting rod and the crankshaft throw until the play is removed **(see illustration)**. The endplay is equal to the thickness of the feeler gauge(s). If the endplay exceeds the service limit, new connecting rods will be required. If new rods (or a new crankshaft) are installed, the endplay may fall under the minimum specified in this Chapter (if it does, the rods will have to be machined to restore it – consult an automotive machine shop for advice if necessary). Repeat the procedure for the remaining connecting rods.

4　Check the connecting rods and caps for identification marks. If they aren't plainly marked, use a small center punch to make the appropriate

number of indentations on each rod and cap (1, 2, 3, etc., depending on the engine type and cylinder they're associated with).

5　Loosen each of the connecting rod cap nuts 1/2-turn at a time until they can be removed by hand. Remove the number one connecting rod cap and bearing insert. Don't drop the bearing insert out of the cap.

6　Slip a short length of plastic or rubber hose over each connecting rod cap bolt to protect the crankshaft journal and cylinder wall as the piston is removed **(see illustration)**.

7　Remove the bearing insert and push the connecting rod/piston assembly out through the top of the engine. Use a wooden or plastic hammer handle to push on the upper bearing surface in the connecting rod. If resistance is felt, double-check to make sure all of the ridge was removed from the cylinder.

8　Repeat the procedure for the remaining cylinders.

9　After removal, reassemble the connecting rod caps and bearing inserts in their respective connecting rods and install the cap nuts finger tight. Leaving the old bearing inserts in place until reassembly will help prevent the connecting rod bearing surfaces from being accidentally nicked or gouged.

14.3　Check the connecting rod side clearance with a feeler gauge as shown

14.6 To prevent damage to the crankshaft journals and cylinder walls, slip sections of rubber or plastic hose over the rod bolts before removing the pistons

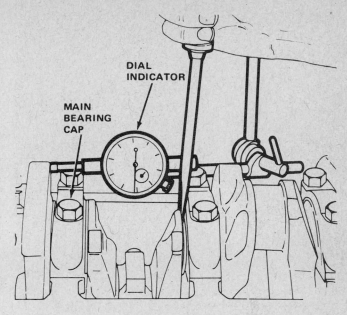

15.1 Check crankshaft endplay with a dial indicator . . .

10 Don't separate the pistons from the connecting rods (see Section 19 for additional information).

15 Crankshaft – removal

Refer to illustrations 15.1, 15.3, 15.4a, 15.4b and 15.4c

Note: *The crankshaft can be removed only after the engine has been removed from the vehicle. It's assumed the flywheel or driveplate, crankshaft balancer/vibration damper, timing chain, oil pan, oil pump and piston/connecting rod assemblies have already been removed. The rear main oil seal housing (Quad-4 only) must be unbolted and separated from the block before proceeding with crankshaft removal.*

1 Before the crankshaft is removed, check the endplay. Mount a dial in-

dicator with the stem in line with the crankshaft and just touching one of the crank throws **(see illustration)**.

2 Push the crankshaft all the way to the rear and zero the dial indicator. Next, pry the crankshaft to the front as far as possible and check the reading on the dial indicator. The distance it moves is the endplay. If it's greater than specified in this Chapter, check the crankshaft thrust surfaces for wear. If no wear is evident, new main bearings should correct the endplay.

3 If a dial indicator isn't available, feeler gauges can be used. Gently pry or push the crankshaft all the way to the front of the engine. Slip feeler gauges between the crankshaft and the front face of the thrust main bearing to determine the clearance **(see illustration)**.

4 Check the main bearing caps to see if they're marked to indicate their locations. They should be numbered consecutively from the front of the engine to the rear. If they aren't, mark them with number stamping dies or a center punch **(see illustrations)**. Main bearing caps generally have a

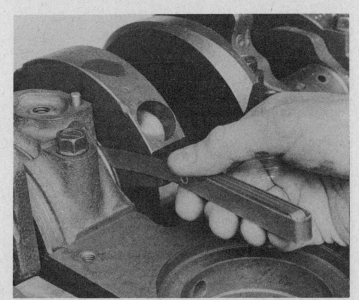

15.3 . . . or slip feeler gauges between the crankshaft and main bearing thrust surfaces – the endplay is equal to the feeler gauge thickness

15.4a Use a center punch or number stamping dies to mark the main bearing caps to ensure installation in their original locations on the block – make the punch marks near one of the bolt heads

15.4b   Mark the caps in order from the front of the engine to the rear (one mark for the front cap, two for the second one and so on)

15.4c   The arrow on the main bearing cap indicates the front of the engine

cast-in arrow, which points to the front of the engine **(see illustration)**. Loosen the main bearing cap bolts 1/4-turn at a time each, until they can be removed by hand. Note if any stud bolts are used and make sure they're returned to their original locations when the crankshaft is reinstalled.

5   Gently tap the caps with a soft-face hammer, then separate them from the engine block. If necessary, use the bolts as levers to remove the caps. Try not to drop the bearing inserts if they come out with the caps.

6   Carefully lift the crankshaft out of the engine. It may be a good idea to have an assistant available, since the crankshaft is quite heavy. With the bearing inserts in place in the engine block and main bearing caps, return the caps to their respective locations on the engine block and tighten the bolts finger tight.

16   Engine block – cleaning

Refer to illustrations 16.3, 16.4, 16.8 and 16.10

1   Remove the main bearing caps and separate the bearing inserts from the caps and the engine block. Tag the bearings, indicating which cylinder they were removed from and whether they were in the cap or the block, then set them aside.

2   Using a gasket scraper, remove all traces of gasket material from the engine block. Be very careful not to nick or gouge the gasket sealing surfaces.

3   Remove all of the covers and threaded oil gallery plugs from the block **(see illustration)**. The plugs are usually very tight – they may have to be

16.3   Remove all covers and plugs from the engine block (rear of V6 engine shown)

1   Camshaft rear cover   *3   Core plug*
2   Threaded oil passage plug

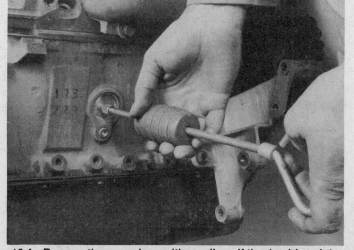

16.4   Remove the core plugs with a puller – if they're driven into the block, they may be impossible to retrieve

**16.8 Clean and restore all threaded holes in the block –
especially the main bearing cap and head bolt holes – with a tap
(be sure to remove debris from the holes when you're done)**

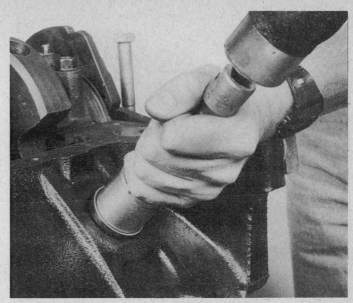

**16.10 A large socket on an extension can be used to drive the
new core plugs into the bores**

2D

drilled out and the holes retapped. Use new plugs when the engine is reassembled.

4 Drill a small hole in the center of each core plug and pull them out with an auto body type dent puller **(see illustration)**. **Caution:** *The core plugs (also known as freeze or soft plugs) may be difficult or impossible to retrieve if they're driven into the block coolant passages.*

5 If the engine is extremely dirty, it should be taken to an automotive machine shop to be steam cleaned or hot tanked.

6 After the block is returned, clean all oil holes and oil galleries one more time. Brushes specifically designed for this purpose are available at most auto parts stores. Flush the passages with warm water until the water runs clear, dry the block thoroughly and wipe all machined surfaces with a light, rust preventive oil. If you have access to compressed air, use it to speed the drying process and blow out all the oil holes and galleries. **Warning:** *Wear eye protection when using compressed air!*

7 If the block isn't extremely dirty or sludged up, you can do an adequate cleaning job with hot soapy water and a stiff brush. Take plenty of time and do a thorough job. Regardless of the cleaning method used, be sure to clean all oil holes and galleries very thoroughly, dry the block completely and coat all machined surfaces with light oil.

8 The threaded holes in the block must be clean to ensure accurate torque readings during reassembly. Run the proper size tap into each of the holes to remove rust, corrosion, thread sealant or sludge and restore damaged threads **(see illustration)**. If possible, use compressed air to clear the holes of debris produced by this operation. Now is a good time to clean the threads on the head bolts and the main bearing cap bolts as well.

9 Reinstall the main bearing caps and tighten the bolts finger tight.

10 After coating the sealing surfaces of the new core plugs with Permatex no. 2 sealant, install them in the engine block **(see illustration)**. Make sure they're driven in straight and seated properly or leakage could result. Special tools are available for this purpose, but a large socket, with an outside diameter that will just slip into the core plug, a 1/2-inch drive extension and a hammer will work just as well.

11 Apply non-hardening sealant (such as Permatex no. 2 or Teflon pipe sealant) to the new oil gallery plugs and thread them into the holes in the block. Make sure they're tightened securely.

12 If the engine isn't going to be reassembled right away, cover it with a large plastic trash bag to keep it clean.

17 Engine block – inspection

Refer to illustrations 17.4a, 17.4b and 17.4c

Note: *The manufacturer recommends checking the block deck and trans-axle mounting bolt hole bosses for warpage and the main bearing bore concentricity and alignment. Since special measuring tools are needed, the checks should be done by an automotive machine shop. Also, if you're working on a Quad-4 engine, it may be a good idea to verify the condition of the oil flow check valve located in the oil passage in the right front corner of the block deck (item 5 in illustration 8.3c).*

1 Before the block is inspected, it should be cleaned as described in Section 16.

2 Visually check the block for cracks, rust and corrosion. Look for stripped threads in the threaded holes. It's also a good idea to have the block checked for hidden cracks by an automotive machine shop that has the special equipment to do this type of work. If defects are found, have the block repaired, if possible, or replaced.

3 Check the cylinder bores for scuffing and scoring.

4 Measure the diameter of each cylinder at the top (just under the ridge area), center and bottom of the cylinder bore, parallel to the crankshaft axis **(see illustrations)**. **Note:** *These measurements should not be made*

**17.4a Measure the diameter of each cylinder just under the wear
ridge (A), at the center (B) and at the bottom (C)**

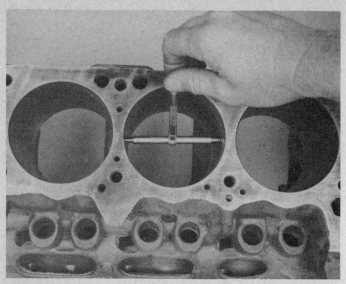

17.4b   The ability to "feel" when the telescoping gauge is at the correct point will be developed over time, so work slowly and repeat the check until you're satisfied the bore measurement is accurate

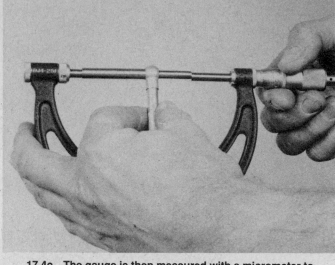

17.4c   The gauge is then measured with a micrometer to determine the bore size

with the bare block mounted on an engine stand – the cylinders will be distorted and the measurements will be inaccurate.

5   Next, measure each cylinder's diameter at the same three locations across the crankshaft axis. Compare the results to this Chapter's Specifications.

6   If the required precision measuring tools aren't available, the piston-to-cylinder clearances can be obtained, though not quite as accurately, using feeler gauge stock. Feeler gauge stock comes in 12-inch lengths and various thicknesses and is generally available at auto parts stores.

7   To check the clearance, select a feeler gauge and slip it into the cylinder along with the matching piston. The piston must be positioned exactly as it normally would be. The feeler gauge must be between the piston and cylinder on one of the thrust faces (90-degrees to the piston pin bore).

8   The piston should slip through the cylinder (with the feeler gauge in place) with moderate pressure.

9   If it falls through or slides through easily, the clearance is excessive and a new piston will be required. If the piston binds at the lower end of the cylinder and is loose toward the top, the cylinder is tapered. If tight spots are encountered as the piston/feeler gauge is rotated in the cylinder, the cylinder is out-of-round.

10   Repeat the procedure for the remaining pistons and cylinders.

11   If the cylinder walls are badly scuffed or scored, or if they're out-of-round or tapered beyond the limits given in this Chapter's Specifications, have the engine block rebored and honed at an automotive machine shop. If a rebore is done, oversize pistons and rings will be required.

12   If the cylinders are in reasonably good condition and not worn to the outside of the limits, and if the piston-to-cylinder clearances can be maintained properly, they don't have to be rebored. Honing is all that's necessary (see Section 18).

18.3a   If this is the first time you've ever honed cylinders, you'll get better results with a "bottle brush" hone than you will with a traditional spring-loaded hone

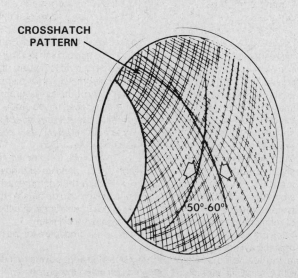

CROSSHATCH PATTERN

50°-60°

18.3b   The cylinder hone should leave a smooth, crosshatch pattern with the lines intersecting at approximately a 60-degree angle

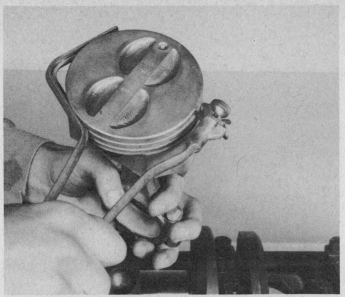

19.4a   The piston ring grooves can be cleaned with a special tool, as shown here, . . .

19.4b   . . . or a piece of broken piston ring

2D

18   Cylinder honing

Refer to illustrations 18.3a and 18.3b

1   Prior to engine reassembly, the cylinder bores must be honed so the new piston rings will seat correctly and provide the best possible combustion chamber seal. **Note:** If *you don't have the tools or don't want to tackle the honing operation, most automotive machine shops will do it for a reasonable fee.*

2   Before honing the cylinders, install the main bearing caps and tighten the bolts to the specified torque.

3   Two types of cylinder hones are commonly available – the flex hone or "bottle brush" type and the more traditional surfacing hone with spring-loaded stones. Both will do the job, but for the less experienced mechanic the "bottle brush" hone will probably be easier to use. You'll also need some honing oil (kerosene will work if honing oil isn't available), rags and an electric drill motor. Proceed as follows:

   a) Mount the hone in the drill motor, compress the stones and slip it into the first cylinder **(see illustration)**. Be sure to wear safety goggles or a face shield!

   b) Lubricate the cylinder with plenty of honing oil, turn on the drill and move the hone up-and-down in the cylinder at a pace that will produce a fine crosshatch pattern on the cylinder walls. Ideally, the crosshatch lines should intersect at approximately a 60-degree angle **(see illustration)**. Be sure to use plenty of lubricant and don't take off any more material than is absolutely necessary to produce the desired finish. **Note:** *Piston ring manufacturers may specify a smaller crosshatch angle than the traditional 60-degrees – read and follow any instructions included with the new rings.*

   c) Don't withdraw the hone from the cylinder while it's running. Instead, shut off the drill and continue moving the hone up-and-down in the cylinder until it comes to a complete stop, then compress the stones and withdraw the hone. If you're using a "bottle brush" type hone, stop the drill motor, then turn the chuck in the normal direction of rotation while withdrawing the hone from the cylinder.

   d) Wipe the oil out of the cylinder and repeat the procedure for the remaining cylinders.

4   After the honing job is complete, chamfer the top edges of the cylinder bores with a small file so the rings won't catch when the pistons are installed. Be very careful not to nick the cylinder walls with the end of the file.

5   The entire engine block must be washed again very thoroughly with warm, soapy water to remove all traces of the abrasive grit produced during the honing operation. **Note:** *The bores can be considered clean when* a lint-free white cloth – dampened with clean engine oil – used to wipe them out doesn't pick up any more honing residue, which will show up as gray areas on the cloth. Be sure to run a brush through all oil holes and galleries and flush them with running water.

6   After rinsing, dry the block and apply a coat of light rust preventive oil to all machined surfaces. Wrap the block in a plastic trash bag to keep it clean and set it aside until reassembly.

19   Pistons and connecting rods – inspection

Refer to illustrations 19.4a, 19.4b, 19.10 and 19.11

1   Before the inspection process can be carried out, the piston/connecting rod assemblies must be cleaned and the original piston rings removed from the pistons. **Note:** *Always use new piston rings when the engine is reassembled.*

2   Using a piston ring installation tool, carefully remove the rings from the pistons. Be careful not to nick or gouge the pistons in the process.

3   Scrape all traces of carbon from the top of the piston. A hand held wire brush or a piece of fine emery cloth can be used once the majority of the deposits have been scraped away. Do not, under any circumstances, use a wire brush mounted in a drill motor to remove deposits from the pistons. The piston material is soft and may be eroded away by the wire brush.

4   Use a piston ring groove cleaning tool to remove carbon deposits from the ring grooves. If a tool isn't available, a piece broken off the old ring will do the job. Be very careful to remove only the carbon deposits – don't remove any metal and do not nick or scratch the sides of the ring grooves **(see illustrations)**.

5   Once the deposits have been removed, clean the piston/rod assemblies with solvent and dry them with compressed air (if available). **Warning:** *Wear eye protection.* Make sure the oil return holes in the back sides of the ring grooves are clear.

6   If the pistons and cylinder walls aren't damaged or worn excessively, and if the engine block isn't rebored, new pistons won't be necessary. Normal piston wear appears as even vertical wear on the piston thrust surfaces and slight looseness of the top ring in its groove. New piston rings, however, should always be used when an engine is rebuilt.

7   Carefully inspect each piston for cracks around the skirt, at the pin bosses and at the ring lands.

8   Look for scoring and scuffing on the thrust faces of the skirt, holes in the piston crown and burned areas at the edge of the crown. If the skirt is scored or scuffed, the engine may have been suffering from overheating

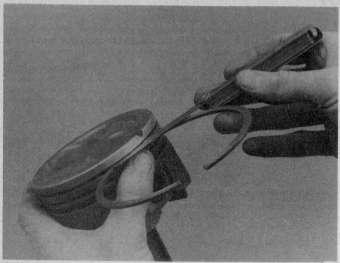

19.10   Check the ring side clearance with a feeler gauge at several points around the groove

19.11   Measure the piston diameter at a 90-degree angle to the piston pin at the specified point on the skirt (see the text)

and/or abnormal combustion, which caused excessively high operating temperatures. The cooling and lubrication systems should be checked thoroughly. A hole in the piston crown is an indication that abnormal combustion (preignition) was occurring. Burned areas at the edge of the piston crown are usually evidence of spark knock (detonation). If any of the above problems exist, the causes must be corrected or the damage will occur again. The causes may include intake air leaks, incorrect fuel/air mixture, low octane fuel, ignition timing and EGR system malfunctions.

9   Corrosion of the piston, in the form of small pits, indicates coolant is leaking into the combustion chamber and/or the crankcase. Again, the cause must be corrected or the problem may persist in the rebuilt engine.

10   Measure the piston ring side clearance by laying a new piston ring in each ring groove and slipping a feeler gauge in beside it **(see illustration)**. Check the clearance at three or four locations around each groove. Be sure to use the correct ring for each groove – they are different. If the side clearance is greater than specified in this Chapter, new pistons will have to be used.

11   Check the piston-to-bore clearance by measuring the bore (see Section 17) and the piston diameter. Make sure the pistons and bores are correctly matched. Measure the piston across the skirt, at a 90-degree angle to the piston pin **(see illustration)**. The measurement must be taken at a specific point, depending on the engine type, to be accurate.

   a) The piston diameter on 2.0/2.2 liter four-cylinder engines is measured directly in line with the piston pin centerline.
   b) If you're working on a Quad-4 engine, measure the piston 0.4724-inch (12.0 mm) up from the lower edge of the skirt.
   c) V6 engine pistons are measured 3/4-inch (19 mm) below the center of the piston pin.

12   Subtract the piston diameter from the bore diameter to obtain the clearance. If it's greater than specified, the block will have to be rebored and new pistons and rings installed.

13   Check the piston-to-rod clearance by twisting the piston and rod in opposite directions. Any noticeable play indicates excessive wear, which must be corrected. The piston/connecting rod assemblies should be taken to an automotive machine shop to have the pistons and rods resized and new pins installed.

14   If the pistons must be removed from the connecting rods for any reason, they should be taken to an automotive machine shop. While they are there have the connecting rods checked for bend and twist, since automotive machine shops have special equipment for this purpose. **Note:** *Unless new pistons and/or connecting rods must be installed, do not disassemble the pistons and connecting rods.*

15   Check the connecting rods for cracks and other damage. Temporarily remove the rod caps, lift out the old bearing inserts, wipe the rod and cap bearing surfaces clean and inspect them for nicks, gouges and scratches.

After checking the rods, replace the old bearings, slip the caps into place and tighten the nuts finger tight. **Note:** *If the engine is being rebuilt because of a connecting rod knock, be sure to install new rods.*

20   Crankshaft – inspection

Refer to illustrations 20.1, 20.3, 20.4, 20.6 and 20.8

1   Remove all burrs from the crankshaft oil holes with a stone, file or scraper **(see illustration)**.
2   Check the main and connecting rod bearing journals for uneven wear, scoring, pits and cracks.

20.1   Clean the crankshaft oil passages with a wire or stiff plastic bristle brush and flush them out with solvent

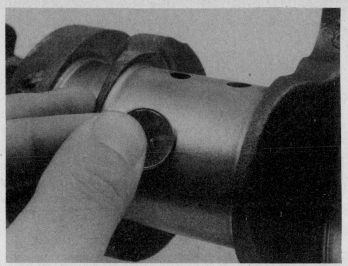

20.3   Rubbing a penny lengthwise on each journal will give you a quick idea of its condition – if copper rubs off the penny and adheres to the crankshaft, the journals should be reground

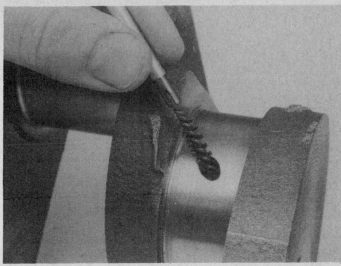

20.4   Chamfer the oil holes to remove sharp edges that might gouge or scratch the new bearings

3   Rub a penny across each journal several times **(see illustration)**. If a journal picks up copper from the penny, it's too rough and must be reground.

4   Clean the crankshaft with solvent and dry it with compressed air (if available). **Warning:** *Wear eye protection when using compressed air.* Be sure to clean the oil holes with a stiff brush **(see illustration)** and flush them with solvent.

5   Check the rest of the crankshaft for cracks and other damage. It should be magnafluxed to reveal hidden cracks – an automotive machine shop will handle the procedure.

6   Using a micrometer, measure the diameter of the main and connecting rod journals and compare the results to this Chapter's Specifications **(see illustration)**. By measuring the diameter at a number of points around each journal's circumference, you'll be able to determine whether or not the journal is out-of-round. Take the measurement at each end of the journal, near the crank throws, to determine if the journal is tapered.

7   If the crankshaft journals are damaged, tapered, out-of-round or worn beyond the limits given in the Specifications, have the crankshaft reground by an automotive machine shop. Be sure to use the correct size bearing inserts if the crankshaft is reconditioned.

8   Check the oil seal journals at each end of the crankshaft for wear and damage. If the seal has worn a groove in the journal, or if it's nicked or scratched **(see illustration)**, the new seal may leak when the engine is reassembled. In some cases, an automotive machine shop may be able to repair the journal by pressing on a thin sleeve. If repair isn't feasible, a new or different crankshaft should be installed.

9   If you're working on a Quad-4 engine, check the oil pump drive gear for wear and damage. If replacement is required, take the crankshaft to a dealer service department or an automotive machine shop. The old gear must be drilled and chiseled off and the new gear must be heated in an oven prior to installation.

10   Refer to Section 21 and examine the main and rod bearing inserts.

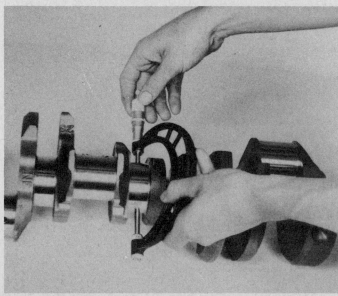

20.6   Measure the diameter of each crankshaft journal at several points to detect taper and out-of-round conditions

20.8   If the seals have worn grooves in the crankshaft journals, or if the seal journals are nicked or scratched, the new seal(s) will leak

21.1 **Typical bearing failures**

21   Main and connecting rod bearings – inspection

Refer to illustration 21.1

1   Even though the main and connecting rod bearings should be replaced with new ones during the engine overhaul, the old bearings should be retained for close examination, as they may reveal valuable information about the condition of the engine **(see illustration)**.

2   Bearing failure occurs because of lack of lubrication, the presence of dirt or other foreign particles, overloading the engine and corrosion. Regardless of the cause of bearing failure, it must be corrected before the engine is reassembled to prevent it from happening again.

3   When examining the bearings, remove them from the engine block, the main bearing caps, the connecting rods and the rod caps and lay them out on a clean surface in the same general position as their location in the engine. This will enable you to match any bearing problems with the corresponding crankshaft journal.

4   Dirt and other foreign particles get into the engine in a variety of ways. It may be left in the engine during assembly, or it may pass through filters or the PCV system. It may get into the oil, and from there into the bearings. Metal chips from machining operations and normal engine wear are often present. Abrasives are sometimes left in engine components after reconditioning, especially when parts aren't thoroughly cleaned using the proper cleaning methods. Whatever the source, these foreign objects often end up embedded in the soft bearing material and are easily recognized. Large particles won't embed in the bearing and will score or gouge the bearing and journal. The best prevention for this cause of bearing failure is to clean all parts thoroughly and keep everything spotlessly clean during engine assembly. Frequent and regular engine oil and filter changes are also recommended.

5   Lack of lubrication (or lubrication breakdown) has a number of interrelated causes. Excessive heat (which thins the oil), overloading (which squeezes the oil from the bearing face) and oil leakage or throw off (from excessive bearing clearances, worn oil pump or high engine speeds) all contribute to lubrication breakdown. Blocked oil passages, which usually are the result of misaligned oil holes in a bearing shell, will also oil starve a bearing and destroy it. When lack of lubrication is the cause of bearing failure, the bearing material is wiped or extruded from the steel backing of the bearing. Temperatures may increase to the point where the steel backing turns blue from overheating.

6   Driving habits can have a definite effect on bearing life. Full throttle, low speed operation (lugging the engine) puts very high loads on bearings, which tends to squeeze out the oil film. These loads cause the bearings to flex, which produces fine cracks in the bearing face (fatigue failure). Eventually the bearing material will loosen in pieces and tear away from the steel backing. Short trip driving leads to corrosion of bearings because insufficient engine heat is produced to drive off the condensed water and corrosive gases. These products collect in the engine oil, forming acid and sludge. As the oil is carried to the engine bearings, the acid attacks and corrodes the bearing material.

7   Incorrect bearing installation during engine assembly will lead to bearing failure as well. Tight fitting bearings leave insufficient oil clearance and will result in oil starvation. Dirt or foreign particles trapped behind a bearing insert result in high spots on the bearing which lead to failure.

22   Engine overhaul – reassembly sequence

1   Before beginning engine reassembly, make sure you have all the necessary new parts, gaskets and seals as well as the following items on hand:

Common hand tools
Torque wrench (1/2-inch drive)
Piston ring installation tool
Piston ring compressor
Vibration damper installation tool
Short lengths of rubber or plastic hose to fit over
    connecting rod bolts
Plastigage
Feeler gauges
Fine-tooth file
New engine oil
Engine assembly lube or moly-base grease
Gasket sealant
Thread locking compound

2   In order to save time and avoid problems, engine reassembly must be done in the following general order:

2.0/2.2 liter four-cylinder engine

New camshaft bearings (must be done by automotive
    machine shop)
Crankshaft and main bearings
Piston/connecting rod assemblies
Oil pump
Camshaft and lifters
Timing chain and sprockets
Timing chain cover
Oil pan
Cylinder head, pushrods and rocker arms
Intake and exhaust manifolds
Rocker arm cover
Engine rear plate
Flywheel/driveplate

2.3 liter four-cylinder (Quad-4) engine

Crankshaft and main bearings
Rear main oil seal housing
Piston/connecting rod assemblies
Oil pump
Oil pan
Cylinder head and camshafts
Timing chain housing
Timing chain and sprockets

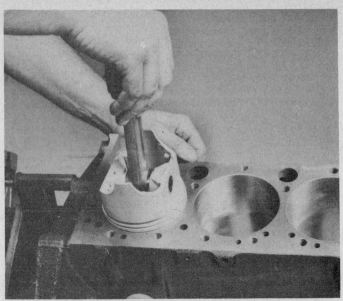

23.3   When checking the piston ring end gap, the ring must be square in the cylinder bore – this is done by pushing the ring down with the top of a piston

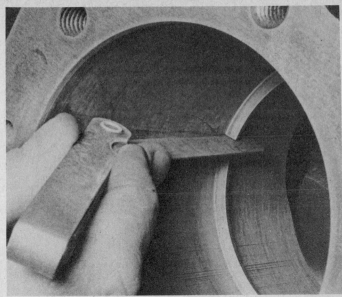

23.4   Once the ring is at the lower limit of travel and square in the cylinder, measure the end gap with a feeler gauge

2D

V6 engines

Crankshaft and main bearings
Rear main oil seal housing
Piston/connecting rod assemblies
Oil pump
Camshaft
Timing chain and sprockets
Timing chain cover
Oil pan
Cylinder heads
Valve lifters
Rocker arms and pushrods
Intake and exhaust manifolds
Rocker arm covers

---

23   Piston rings – installation

Refer to illustrations 23.3, 23.4, 23.5, 23.9a, 23.9b and 23.12

1   Before installing the new piston rings, the ring end gaps must be checked. It's assumed the piston ring side clearance has been checked and verified correct (see Section 19).

2   Lay out the piston/connecting rod assemblies and the new ring sets so the ring sets will be matched with the same piston and cylinder during the end gap measurement and engine assembly.

3   Insert the top (number one) ring into the first cylinder and square it up with the cylinder walls by pushing it in with the top of the piston **(see illustration)**. The ring should be near the bottom of the cylinder, at the lower limit of ring travel.

4   To measure the end gap, slip feeler gauges between the ends of the ring until a gauge equal to the gap width is found **(see illustration)**. The feeler gauge should slide between the ring ends with a slight amount of drag. Compare the measurement to this Chapter's Specifications. If the gap is larger or smaller than specified, double-check to make sure you have the correct rings before proceeding.

5   If the gap is too small, it must be enlarged or the ring ends may come in contact with each other during engine operation, which can cause serious engine damage. The end gap can be increased by filing the ring ends very

carefully with a fine file. Mount the file in a vise equipped with soft jaws, slip the ring over the file with the ends contacting the file teeth and slowly move the ring to remove material from the ends. When performing this operation, file only from the outside in **(see illustration)**.

6   Excess end gap isn't critical unless it's greater than 0.040-inch. Again, double-check to make sure you have the correct rings for the engine.

7   Repeat the procedure for each ring that will be installed in the first cylinder and for each ring in the remaining cylinders. Remember to keep rings, pistons and cylinders matched up.

8   Once the ring end gaps have been checked/corrected, the rings can be installed on the pistons.

9   The oil control ring (lowest one on the piston) is usually installed first. It's composed of three separate components. Slip the spacer/expander

23.5   If the end gap is too small, clamp a file in a vise and file the ring ends (from the outside in only) to enlarge the gap slightly

23.9a   Install the three-piece oil control ring first, one part at a time, beginning with the spacer/expander, . . .

23.9b   . . . followed by the side rails – DO NOT use a piston ring installation tool to install the oil ring side rails

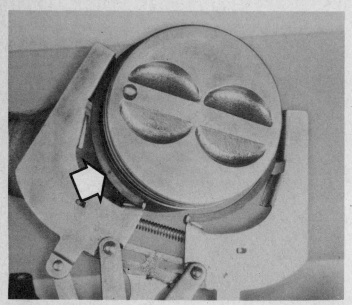

23.12   Install the compression rings with a ring expander – the mark (arrow) must face up

into the groove **(see illustration)**. If an anti-rotation tang is used, make sure it's inserted into the drilled hole in the ring groove. Next, install the lower side rail. Don't use a piston ring installation tool on the oil ring side rails, as they may be damaged. Instead, place one end of the side rail into the groove between the spacer/expander and the ring land, hold it firmly in place and slide a finger around the piston while pushing the rail into the groove **(see illustration)**. Next, install the upper side rail in the same manner.

10   After the three oil ring components have been installed, check to make sure both the upper and lower side rails can be turned smoothly in the ring groove.

11   The number two (middle) ring is installed next. It's usually stamped with a mark, which must face up, toward the top of the piston. **Note:** *Always follow the instructions printed on the ring package or box – different*

manufacturers may require different approaches. Don't mix up the top and middle rings, as they have different cross sections.

12   Use a piston ring installation tool and make sure the identification mark is facing the top of the piston, then slip the ring into the middle groove on the piston **(see illustration)**. Don't expand the ring any more than necessary to slide it over the piston.

13   Install the number one (top) ring in the same manner. Make sure the mark is facing up. Be careful not to confuse the number one and number two rings.

14   Repeat the procedure for the remaining pistons and rings.

---

24   Crankshaft – installation and main bearing oil clearance check

---

Refer to illustrations 24.11 and 24.15

1   Crankshaft installation is the first step in engine reassembly. It's assumed at this point that the engine block and crankshaft have been cleaned, inspected and repaired or reconditioned.

2   Position the engine with the bottom facing up.

3   Remove the main bearing cap bolts and lift out the caps. Lay them out in the proper order to ensure correct installation.

4   If they're still in place, remove the original bearing inserts from the block and the main bearing caps. Wipe the bearing surfaces of the block and caps with a clean, lint-free cloth. They must be kept spotlessly clean.

Main bearing oil clearance check

Note: *Don't touch the faces of the new bearing inserts with your fingers. Oil and acids from your skin can etch the bearings.*

5   Clean the back sides of the new main bearing inserts and lay one in each main bearing saddle in the block. If one of the bearing inserts from each set has a large groove in it, make sure the grooved insert is installed in the block. Lay the other bearing from each set in the corresponding main bearing cap. Make sure the tab on the bearing insert fits into the recess in the block or cap. **Caution:** *The oil holes in the block must line up with the oil holes in the bearing inserts. Do not hammer the bearing into place and don't nick or gouge the bearing faces. No lubrication should be used at this time.*

24.11 Lay the Plastigage strips (arrow) on the main bearing journals, parallel to the crankshaft centerline

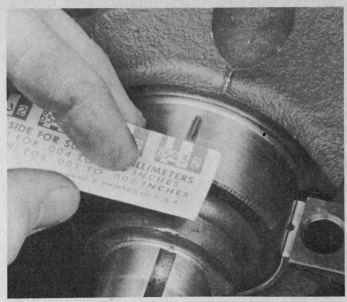

24.15 Compare the width of the crushed Plastigage to the scale on the envelope to determine the main bearing oil clearance (always take the measurement at the widest point of the Plastigage); be sure to use the correct scale – standard and metric ones are included

2D

6   The flanged thrust bearing must be installed in the number four cap and saddle (counting from the front of the engine) on 2.0/2.2 liter four-cylinder engines. On Quad-4 engines, the thrust bearing must be installed in the number three (center) cap and saddle. On V6 engines install it in the number three cap and saddle.

7   Clean the faces of the bearings in the block and the crankshaft main bearing journals with a clean, lint-free cloth.

8   Check or clean the oil holes in the crankshaft, as any dirt here can go only one way – straight through the new bearings.

9   Once you're certain the crankshaft is clean, carefully lay it in position in the main bearings.

10   Before the crankshaft can be permanently installed, the main bearing oil clearance must be checked.

11   Cut several pieces of the appropriate size Plastigage (they should be slightly shorter than the width of the main bearings) and place one piece on each crankshaft main bearing journal, parallel with the journal axis **(see illustration)**.

12   Clean the faces of the bearings in the caps and install the caps in their original locations (don't mix them up) with the arrows pointing toward the front of the engine. Don't disturb the Plastigage.

13   Starting with the center main and working out toward the ends, tighten the main bearing cap bolts, in three steps, to the torque figure listed in this Chapter's Specifications. Don't rotate the crankshaft at any time during this operation.

14   Remove the bolts and carefully lift off the main bearing caps. Keep them in order. Don't disturb the Plastigage or rotate the crankshaft. If any of the main bearing caps are difficult to remove, tap them gently from side-to-side with a soft-face hammer to loosen them.

15   Compare the width of the crushed Plastigage on each journal to the scale printed on the Plastigage envelope to obtain the main bearing oil clearance **(see illustration)**. Check the Specifications to make sure it's correct.

16   If the clearance is not as specified, the bearing inserts may be the wrong size (which means different ones will be required). Before deciding different inserts are needed, make sure no dirt or oil was between the bearing inserts and the caps or block when the clearance was measured. If the Plastigage was wider at one end than the other, the journal may be tapered (refer to Section 20).

17   Carefully scrape all traces of the Plastigage material off the main bearing journals and/or the bearing faces. Use your fingernail or the edge of a credit card – don't nick or scratch the bearing faces.

Final crankshaft installation

18   Carefully lift the crankshaft out of the engine.

19   Clean the bearing faces in the block, then apply a thin, uniform layer of moly-base grease or engine assembly lube to each of the bearing surfaces. Be sure to coat the thrust faces as well as the journal face of the thrust bearing.

20   Make sure the crankshaft journals are clean, then lay the crankshaft back in place in the block.

21   Clean the faces of the bearings in the caps, then apply lubricant to them.

22   Install the caps in their original locations with the arrows pointing toward the front of the engine.

23   Install the bolts.

24   Tighten all except the thrust bearing cap bolts to the specified torque (work from the center out and approach the final torque in three steps).

25   Tighten the thrust bearing cap bolts to 10-to-12 ft-lbs.

26   Tap the ends of the crankshaft forward and backward with a lead or brass hammer to line up the main bearing and crankshaft thrust surfaces.

27   Retighten all main bearing cap bolts to the torque specified in this Chapter, starting with the center main and working out toward the ends.

28   Rotate the crankshaft a number of times by hand to check for any obvious binding.

29   The final step is to check the crankshaft endplay with feeler gauges or a dial indicator as described in Section 15. The endplay should be correct if the crankshaft thrust faces aren't worn or damaged and new bearings have been installed.

30   Refer to Section 26 and install the new rear main oil seal.

---

25   Camshaft – installation

Refer to illustration 25.1
Note: *This procedure applies to 2.0/2.2 liter four-cylinder and V6 engines only.*

25.1   Be sure to prelube the bearing journals and lobes prior to camshaft installation

26.3   Tap around the outer edge of the new oil seal with a hammer and blunt punch to seat it squarely in the bore

1   Lubricate the camshaft bearing journals and cam lobes with moly-base grease or engine assembly lube **(see illustration)**.
2   Slide the camshaft into the engine. Support the cam near the block and be careful not to scrape or nick the bearings. On four-cylinder engines, install the thrust plate and tighten the bolts.
3   Refer to Part A or C to complete the installation of the camshaft, lifters, timing chain and sprockets.

---

26   Rear main oil seal – installation

2.0/2.2 liter four-cylinder and V6 engines

Refer to illustration 26.3

1   Clean the bore in the block/cap and the seal journal on the crankshaft. Check the crankshaft journal for scratches and nicks that could damage the new seal lip and cause oil leaks. If the crankshaft is damaged, the only alternative is a new or different crankshaft.
2   Apply a light coat of engine oil or multi-purpose grease to the outer edge of the new seal. Lubricate the seal lip with moly-base grease or engine assembly lube.
3   Press the new seal into place with the special tool, if available **(see illustration 18.4 in Part A)**. The seal lip must face toward the front of the engine. If the special tool isn't available, carefully work the seal lip over the end of the crankshaft and tap the seal in with a hammer and blunt punch until it's seated in the bore **(see illustration)**.

2.3 liter four-cylinder (Quad-4) engine

4   This engine is equipped with a one-piece seal that fits into a housing attached to the block. The crankshaft must be installed first and the main bearing caps bolted in place, then the new seal should be installed in the housing and the housing bolted to the block **(see illustration 8.3c and Section 15 in Part B)**.
5   Before installing the crankshaft, check the seal journal very carefully for scratches and nicks that could damage the new seal lip and cause oil leaks. If the crankshaft is damaged, the only alternative is a new or different crankshaft.
6   The old seal can be removed from the housing with a hammer and punch by driving it out from the back side (see Section 15 in Part B). Be sure to note how far it's recessed into the housing bore before removing it; the new seal will have to be recessed an equal amount. Be very careful not to scratch or otherwise damage the bore in the housing or oil leaks could develop.

7   Make sure the housing is clean, then apply a thin coat of engine oil to the outer edge of the new seal. The seal must be pressed squarely into the housing bore (see Section 15 in Part B). Work slowly and make sure the seal enters the bore squarely.
8   The seal lips must be lubricated with moly-base grease or engine assembly lube before the seal/housing is slipped over the crankshaft and bolted to the block. Use a new gasket – no sealant is required – and make sure the dowel pins are in place before installing the housing.
9   Tighten the bolts a little at a time until they're all at the torque listed in the Part B Specifications.

---

27   Pistons and connecting rods – installation and rod bearing oil clearance check

---

Refer to illustrations 27.9, 27.11, 27.13 and 27.17

1   Before installing the piston/connecting rod assemblies, the cylinder walls must be perfectly clean, the top edge of each cylinder must be chamfered, and the crankshaft must be in place.
2   Remove the cap from the end of the number one connecting rod (check the marks made during removal). Remove the original bearing inserts and wipe the bearing surfaces of the connecting rod and cap with a clean, lint-free cloth. They must be kept spotlessly clean.

Connecting rod bearing oil clearance check

Note: *Don't touch the faces of the new bearing inserts with your fingers. Oil and acids from your skin can etch the bearings.*

3   Clean the back side of the new upper bearing insert, then lay it in place in the connecting rod. Make sure the tab on the bearing fits into the recess in the rod. Don't hammer the bearing insert into place and be very careful not to nick or gouge the bearing face. Don't lubricate the bearing at this time.
4   Clean the back side of the other bearing insert and install it in the rod cap. Again, make sure the tab on the bearing fits into the recess in the cap, and don't apply any lubricant. It's critically important that the mating surfaces of the bearing and connecting rod are perfectly clean and oil free when they're assembled.
5   Position the piston ring gaps at 120-degree intervals around the piston.
6   Slip a section of plastic or rubber hose over each connecting rod cap bolt.
7   Lubricate the piston and rings with clean engine oil and attach a piston

27.9   The notch or arrow on each piston must face the front (timing chain) end of the engine as the pistons are installed

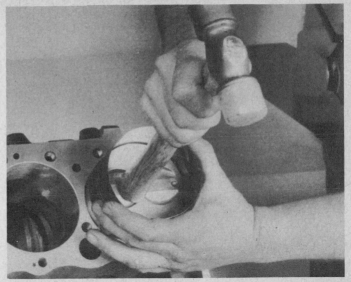

27.11   Drive the piston gently into the cylinder bore with the end of a wooden or plastic hammer handle

ring compressor to the piston. Leave the skirt protruding about 1/4-inch to guide the piston into the cylinder. The rings must be compressed until they're flush with the piston.

8   Rotate the crankshaft until the number one connecting rod journal is at BDC (bottom dead center) and apply a coat of engine oil to the cylinder walls.

9   With the mark or notch on top of the piston **(see illustration)** facing the front of the engine, gently insert the piston/connecting rod assembly into the number one cylinder bore and rest the bottom edge of the ring compressor on the engine block. If you're working on a Quad-4 engine, make sure the oil hole in the lower end of the connecting rod is facing the right (exhaust manifold) side of the engine.

10   Tap the top edge of the ring compressor to make sure it's contacting the block around its entire circumference.

11   Gently tap on the top of the piston with the end of a wooden or plastic hammer handle **(see illustration)** while guiding the end of the connecting rod into place on the crankshaft journal. The piston rings may try to pop out of the ring compressor just before entering the cylinder bore, so keep some downward pressure on the ring compressor. Work slowly, and if any resistance is felt as the piston enters the cylinder, stop immediately. Find out what's hanging up and fix it before proceeding. Do not, for any reason, force the piston into the cylinder – you might break a ring and/or the piston.

12   Once the piston/connecting rod assembly is installed, the connecting rod bearing oil clearance must be checked before the rod cap is permanently bolted in place.

13   Cut a piece of the appropriate size Plastigage slightly shorter than the width of the connecting rod bearing and lay it in place on the number one connecting rod journal, parallel with the journal axis **(see illustration)**.

14   Clean the connecting rod cap bearing face, remove the protective hoses from the connecting rod bolts and install the rod cap. Make sure the mating mark on the cap is on the same side as the mark on the connecting rod.

15   Install the nuts and tighten them to the torque listed in this Chapter's Specifications. Work up to it in three steps. **Note:** *Use a thin-wall socket to avoid erroneous torque readings that can result if the socket is wedged between the rod cap and nut. If the socket tends to wedge itself between the nut and the cap, lift up on it slightly until it no longer contacts the cap. Do not rotate the crankshaft at any time during this operation.*

16   Remove the nuts and detach the rod cap, being very careful not to disturb the Plastigage.

17   Compare the width of the crushed Plastigage to the scale printed on the Plastigage envelope to obtain the oil clearance **(see illustration)**. Compare it to this Chapter's Specifications to make sure the clearance is correct.

27.13   Lay the Plastigage strips on each rod bearing journal, parallel to the crankshaft centerline

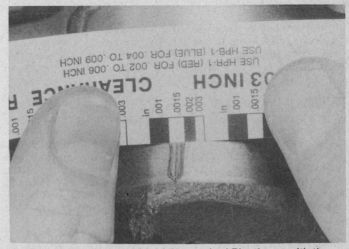

27.17   Measure the width of the crushed Plastigage with the scale on the envelope to determine the rod bearing oil clearance (be sure to use the correct scale – standard and metric ones are included)

18   If the clearance is not as specified, the bearing inserts may be the wrong size (which means different ones will be required). Before deciding different inserts are needed, make sure no dirt or oil was between the bearing inserts and the connecting rod or cap when the clearance was measured. Also, recheck the journal diameter. If the Plastigage was wider at one end than the other, the journal may be tapered (refer to Section 20).

Final connecting rod installation

19   Carefully scrape all traces of the Plastigage material off the rod journal and/or bearing face. Be very careful not to scratch the bearing – use your fingernail or the edge of a credit card.

20   Make sure the bearing faces are perfectly clean, then apply a uniform layer of clean moly-base grease or engine assembly lube to both of them. You'll have to push the piston into the cylinder to expose the face of the bearing insert in the connecting rod – be sure to slip the protective hoses over the rod bolts first.

21   Slide the connecting rod back into place on the journal, remove the protective hoses from the rod cap bolts, install the rod cap and tighten the nuts to the torque specified in this Chapter. Again, work up to the torque in three steps.

22   Repeat the entire procedure for the remaining pistons/connecting rods.

23   The important points to remember are . . .
   a) Keep the back sides of the bearing inserts and the insides of the connecting rods and caps perfectly clean when assembling them.
   b) Make sure you have the correct piston/rod assembly for each cylinder.
   c) The arrow or mark on the piston must face the front (timing chain end) of the engine.
   d) Lubricate the cylinder walls with clean oil.
   e) Lubricate the bearing faces when installing the rod caps after the oil clearance has been checked.

24   After all the piston/connecting rod assemblies have been properly installed, rotate the crankshaft a number of times by hand to check for any obvious binding.

25   As a final step, the connecting rod endplay must be checked. Refer to Section 14 for this procedure.

26   Compare the measured endplay to this Chapter's Specifications to make sure it's correct. If it was correct before disassembly and the original crankshaft and rods were reinstalled, it should still be right. If new rods or a new crankshaft were installed, the endplay may be inadequate. If so, the rods will have to be removed and taken to an automotive machine shop for resizing.

28   Initial start-up and break-in after overhaul

Warning: *Have a fire extinguisher handy when starting the engine for the first time.*

1   Once the engine has been installed in the vehicle, double-check the oil and coolant levels.

2   With the spark plugs out of the engine and the ECM fuse removed, crank the engine until oil pressure registers on the gauge or the light goes out.

3   Install the spark plugs, hook up the plug wires (except Quad-4 engine) and install the ECM fuse.

4   Start the engine. It may take a few moments for the fuel system to build up pressure, but the engine should start without a great deal of effort. **Note:** *If the engine keeps backfiring, recheck the valve timing (and spark plug wires, where applicable).*

5   After the engine starts, it should be allowed to warm up to normal operating temperature. While the engine is warming up, make a thorough check for fuel, oil and coolant leaks.

6   Shut the engine off and recheck the engine oil and coolant levels.

7   Drive the vehicle to an area with minimum traffic, accelerate at full throttle from 30 to 50 mph, then allow the vehicle to slow to 30 mph with the throttle closed. Repeat the procedure 10 or 12 times. This will load the piston rings and cause them to seat properly against the cylinder walls. Check again for oil and coolant leaks.

8   Drive the vehicle gently for the first 500 miles (no sustained high speeds) and keep a constant check on the oil level. It's not unusual for an engine to use oil during the break-in period.

9   At approximately 500 to 600 miles, change the oil and filter.

10   For the next few hundred miles, drive the vehicle normally. Don't pamper it or abuse it.

11   After 2000 miles, change the oil and filter again and consider the engine broken in.

Chapter 3   Cooling, heating and air conditioning systems

Contents

Specifications

General

Cooling system capacity	See Chapter 1
Radiator cap pressure rating	See Chapter 1
Thermostat rating	195 degrees F
Drivebelt tension	See Chapter 1
Refrigerant capacity	
1993 and earlier	2.63 lbs (R-12)
1994 on	2.25 lbs (R-134a)

Torque specifications

Ft-lbs (unless otherwise indicated)

Thermostat cover bolts	
2.0/2.2 liter four-cylinder engines	89 in-lbs
2.3 liter four-cylinder (Quad-4) engine	19
V6 engines	20
Water pump mounting bolts/nuts	
2.0/2.2 liter four-cylinder engines	19
2.3 liter four-cylinder (Quad-4) engine	19
V6 engines	88 in-lbs

1   General information

Note: *On models equipped with the Delco Loc II audio system, be sure the lockout feature is turned off before performing any procedure which requires disconnecting the battery.*

Engine cooling system

All vehicles covered by this manual employ a pressurized engine cooling system with thermostatically controlled coolant circulation. An impeller type water pump mounted on the engine block pumps coolant through the engine and radiator. The coolant flows around each cylinder and back to the radiator. Cast-in coolant passages direct coolant around the intake and exhaust ports, near the spark plug areas and the exhaust valve guides.

A wax pellet type thermostat is located in a housing connected to the upper radiator hose. During warm up the closed thermostat prevents coolant from circulating through the radiator. As the engine nears normal operating temperature, the thermostat opens and allows hot coolant to travel through the radiator, where it's cooled before returning to the engine.

The cooling system is sealed by a pressure-type radiator cap, which raises the boiling point of the coolant and increases the cooling efficiency of the radiator. If the system pressure exceeds the cap pressure relief value, the excess pressure in the system forces the spring-loaded valve inside the cap off its seat and allows the coolant to escape through a hose into a coolant reservoir. When the system cools, the excess coolant is automatically drawn from the reservoir back into the radiator.

The coolant reservoir does double duty as both the point at which fresh coolant is added to the cooling system to maintain the proper level and as a holding tank for expelled coolant.

This type of cooling system is known as a closed design because coolant that escapes past the pressure cap is saved and reused.

Heating system

The heating system consists of a blower fan and heater core located in the heater box, the hoses connecting the heater core to the engine cooling system and the heater/air conditioning control head on the dashboard. Hot engine coolant is circulated through the heater core. When the heater mode is activated, a trap door opens to expose the heater box to the passenger compartment. A fan switch on the control head activates the blower motor, which forces air through the core, heating the air.

Air conditioning system

The air conditioning system consists of a condenser mounted in front of the radiator, an evaporator mounted adjacent to the heater core, a compressor mounted on the engine, a filter-drier (accumulator), which contains a high pressure relief valve, and the hoses and lines connecting all of the above components.

A blower fan forces the warmer air of the passenger compartment through the evaporator core (sort of a radiator-in-reverse), transferring the heat from the air to the refrigerant. The liquid refrigerant boils off into low pressure vapor, taking the heat with it when it leaves the evaporator.

2   Antifreeze – general information

Warning: *Don't allow antifreeze to come in contact with your skin or painted surfaces of the vehicle. Rinse off spills immediately with plenty of water. Never leave antifreeze lying around or in an open container or in a puddle on the driveway or the garage floor. Children and animals are attracted by its sweet smell. Antifreeze is toxic, so use common sense when disposing of it. Some communities maintain toxic material disposal sites and/or offer regular pick-up of hazardous materials. Antifreeze is also combustible, so don't store or use it near open flames.*

The cooling system should be filled with a water/ethylene glycol based antifreeze solution, which will prevent freezing down to at least -20-degrees F, or lower if local climate requires it. It also provides protection against corrosion and increases the coolant boiling point.

The cooling system should be drained, flushed and refilled at the specified intervals (see Chapter 1). Old or contaminated antifreeze solutions are likely to cause damage and encourage the formation of rust and scale in the system. Use distilled water with the antifreeze.

Before adding antifreeze, check all hose connections, because antifreeze tends to search out and leak through very minute openings. Engines don't normally consume coolant, so if the level goes down, find the cause and correct it.

The exact mixture of antifreeze-to-water which you should use depends on the relative weather conditions. The mixture should contain at least 50 percent antifreeze, but should never contain more than 70 percent antifreeze. Consult the mixture ratio chart on the antifreeze container before adding coolant. Hydrometers are available at most auto parts stores to test the coolant. Use antifreeze which meets the vehicle manufacturer's specifications.

3   Thermostat – check and replacement

Warning: *DO NOT remove the radiator cap, drain the coolant or replace the thermostat until the engine has cooled completely.*

Check

1   Before assuming the thermostat is to blame for a cooling system problem, check the coolant level, drivebelt tension (see Chapter 1) and temperature gauge (or light) operation.

2   If the engine seems to be taking a long time to warm up (based on heater output or temperature gauge operation), the thermostat is probably stuck open. Replace the thermostat with a new one.

3   If the engine runs hot, use your hand to check the temperature of the upper radiator hose. If the hose isn't hot, but the engine is, the thermostat is probably stuck closed, preventing the coolant inside the engine from escaping to the radiator. Replace the thermostat. **Caution:** *Don't drive the vehicle without a thermostat. The computer may stay in open loop and emissions and fuel economy will suffer.*

4   If the upper radiator hose is hot, it means the coolant is flowing and the thermostat is open. Consult the Troubleshooting Section at the front of this manual for cooling system diagnosis.

Replacement

Refer to illustrations 3.10a, 3.10b, 3.12, 3.13 and 3.14

5   Disconnect the negative battery cable from the battery and drain the cooling system (see Chapter 1). If the coolant is relatively new or in good condition, save it and reuse it.

6   Remove the air cleaner assembly, if necessary for access (see Chapter 4).

7   Follow the upper radiator hose to the engine to locate the thermostat housing.

8   Loosen the hose clamp, then detach the hose from the fitting. If the hose sticks, grasp it near the end with a pair of adjustable pliers and twist it to break the seal, then pull it off. If the hose is old or deteriorated, cut it off and install a new one. **Note:** *Quad-4 engines have two hoses and a wire harness connected to the thermostat cover – remove all of them.*

9   If the outer surface of the large fitting that mates with the hose is deteriorated (corroded, pitted, etc.) it may be damaged further by hose removal. If it is, the thermostat cover will have to be replaced.

10   Remove the bolts/nuts and detach the thermostat cover **(see illustrations)**. If the cover is stuck, tap it with a soft-face hammer to jar it loose. Be prepared for some coolant to spill as the gasket seal is broken.

11   Note how it's installed (which end is facing up), then remove the thermostat.

12   Remove all traces of old gasket material and sealant from the housing and cover with a gasket scraper **(see illustration)**. Clean the gasket mating surfaces with lacquer thinner or acetone.

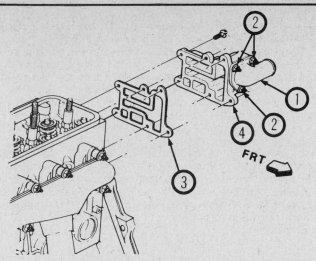

3.10a   2.0/2.2 liter four-cylinder engine thermostat housing components – exploded view

1	*Thermostat cover*	3	*Thermostat housing-to-head*
2	*Thermostat cover nuts*		*gasket*
		4	*Thermostat housing*

3.10b   The V6 thermostat cover is secured by a nut and bolt (arrows)

3.12   Remove all traces of gasket material (Quad-4 engine shown)

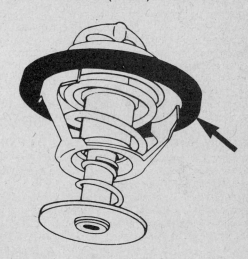

3.13   2.0/2.2 liter four-cylinder and V6 models use a seal (arrow) around the thermostat instead of a gasket

13   On 2.0/2.2 liter four-cylinder and V6 engines, replace the seal on the thermostat **(see illustration)**.

14   Install the new thermostat in the housing. Make sure the correct end faces up – the spring end is normally directed into the engine **(see illustration)**.

15   On Quad-4 engines, apply a thin, uniform layer of RTV sealant to both sides of the new gasket and position it on the housing.

16   Install the cover and bolts/nuts. Tighten them to the torque figure listed in this Chapter's Specifications.

17   The remaining steps are the reverse of removal.

18   Refill the cooling system (see Chapter 1).

19   Start the engine and allow it to reach normal operating temperature, then check for leaks and proper thermostat operation (as described in Steps 2 through 4).

---

4   Engine cooling fan – check and replacement

Check

Refer to illustration 4.1

1   To test the fan motor, unplug the electrical connector at the motor and

3.14   Position the thermostat in the housing as shown here (V6 shown, others similar)

4.1   The motor may be tested by running fused jumper wires directly from the battery to the connector (arrow)

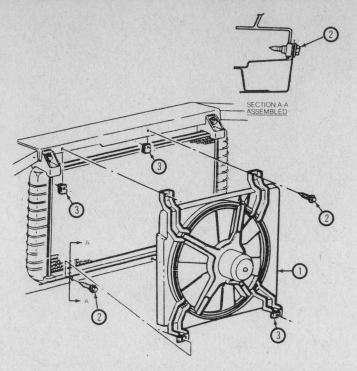

4.6   2.0/2.2 liter four-cylinder and V6 cooling fan mounting details – exploded view

1	Fan	3	Clipnut
2	Bolt		

4.7   Remove the motor shaft nut (arrow) – note the left-hand threads

use jumper wires to connect the fan directly to the battery **(see illustration)**. If the fan still doesn't work, replace the motor.

2   If the motor tested OK, the fault lies in the coolant temperature switch, the relay or the wiring which connects the components. Carefully check all wiring and connections. If no obvious problems are found, further diagnosis should be done by a dealer service department or a repair shop.

Replacement

Refer to illustrations 4.6 and 4.7

3   Disconnect the negative battery cable from the battery.

4   Remove the air cleaner assembly (see Chapter 4).

5   Insert a small screwdriver into the connector to lift the lock tab and unplug the fan wire harness.

6   Unbolt the fan assembly **(see illustration)**, then carefully lift it out of the engine compartment.

7   To detach the fan from the motor, remove the motor shaft nut **(see illustration)**.

8   To remove the fan motor from the bracket, remove the mounting bolts/nuts.

9   Installation is the reverse of removal.

---

5   Radiator – removal and installation

Refer to illustrations 5.4a, 5.4b and 5.7

Warning 1: *Wait until the engine is completely cool before beginning this procedure.*

Warning 2: *On models equipped with airbags, we recommend having a dealer service department or other qualified shop perform this procedure. The impact sensors are located near the radiator, and, if you accidently trip one of these sensors, the airbag will deploy. Airbags are expensive to replace and deployment could cause personal injury. Also, disturbing the impact sensors or their wiring could cause the airbag not to deploy correctly in a collision.*

1   Disconnect the negative battery cable from the battery.

2   Drain the cooling system (see Chapter 1). If the coolant is relatively new or in good condition, save it and reuse it.

3   Remove the air cleaner assembly (see Chapter 4).

4   If the vehicle is equipped with an automatic transaxle, disconnect the cooler lines from the radiator **(see illustrations)**. Use a drip pan to catch spilled fluid.

5   Remove the engine cooling fan assembly (see Section 4).

6   Loosen the hose clamps, then detach the radiator hoses from the fittings. If they're stuck, grasp each hose near the end with a pair of adjustable pliers and twist it to break the seal, then pull it off – be careful not to distort the radiator fittings! If the hoses are old or deteriorated, cut them off and install new ones.

7   Disconnect the reservoir hose from the radiator neck **(see illustration)**.

8   Plug the lines and fittings.

9   Remove the radiator mounting bolts at each upper corner of the radiator.

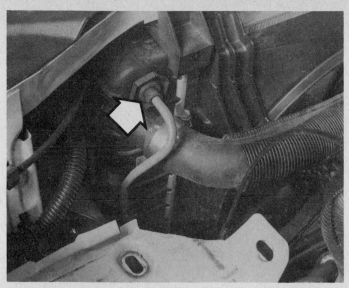

5.4a   The transaxle cooler lines (arrows) are located in the upper . . .

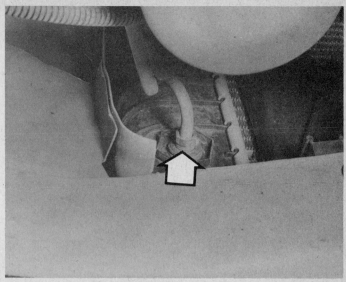

5.4b   . . . and lower corners of the radiator (viewed from below)

10   Remove the four bolts connecting the air conditioner condenser to the radiator.

11   Carefully lift out the radiator. Don't spill coolant on the vehicle or scratch the paint.

12   With the radiator removed, it can be inspected for leaks and damage. If it needs repair, have a radiator shop or dealer service department perform the work as special techniques are required.

13   Bugs and dirt can be removed from the radiator with compressed air and a soft brush. Don't bend the cooling fins as this is done.

14   Check the radiator mounts for deterioration and make sure there's nothing in them when the radiator is installed.

15   Installation is the reverse of the removal procedure.

16   After installation, fill the cooling system with the proper mixture of anti-freeze and water. Refer to Chapter 1 if necessary.

17   Start the engine and check for leaks. Allow the engine to reach normal operating temperature, indicated by the upper radiator hose becoming hot. Recheck the coolant level and add more if required.

18   If you're working on an automatic transaxle equipped vehicle, check and add fluid as needed.

5.7   The coolant reservoir hose (arrow) connects to the right side of the radiator

6   Coolant reservoir – removal and installation

Refer to illustration 6.3

1   Detach the hose from the windshield washer fluid reservoir cap.

2   Disconnect the radiator overflow hose from the top of the radiator.

3   Remove the mounting bolts **(see illustration)** and lift the coolant reservoir from the vehicle.

4   Installation is the reverse of removal.

7   Water pump – check

Refer to illustrations 7.4 and 7.5

1   A failure in the water pump can cause serious engine damage due to overheating.

2   There are three ways to check the operation of the water pump while it's installed on the engine. If the pump is defective, it should be replaced with a new or rebuilt unit.

6.3   Remove the mounting bolts (arrows) to detach the coolant reservoir

7.4   If the pump is leaking, stains will form below the shaft (arrow) – pump removed for clarity

7.5   Rock the pulley back and forth to check for bearing play

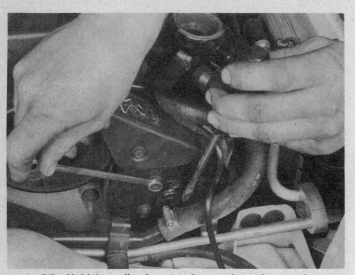

8.3   Hold the pulley from turning as shown here and loosen each bolt

3   With the engine running at normal operating temperature, squeeze the upper radiator hose. If the water pump is working properly, a pressure surge should be felt as the hose is released. **Warning:** *Keep your hands away from the fan blades!*

4   Water pumps are equipped with weep or vent holes. If a failure occurs in the pump seal, coolant will leak from the hole **(see illustration)**. In most cases you'll need a flashlight and mirror to find the hole on the under side of the water pump to check for leaks.

5   If the water pump shaft bearings fail there may be a howling sound coming from the drivebelt area while the engine is running. Shaft wear can be felt if the water pump pulley is rocked up-and-down **(see illustration)**. Don't mistake drivebelt slippage, which causes a squealing sound, for water pump bearing failure.

---

8   Water pump – removal and installation

Warning: *Wait until the engine is completely cool before beginning this procedure.*

1   Disconnect the negative battery cable from the battery.

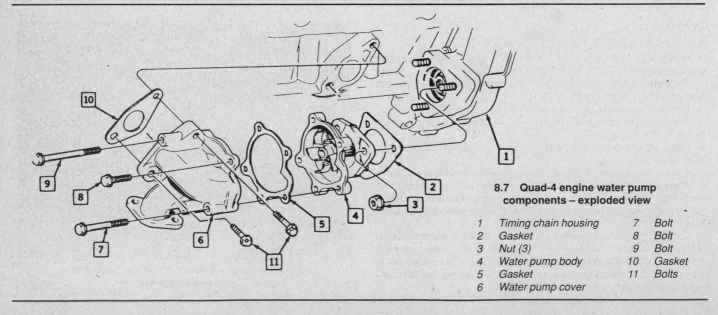

8.7   Quad-4 engine water pump components – exploded view

1	Timing chain housing	7	Bolt
2	Gasket	8	Bolt
3	Nut (3)	9	Bolt
4	Water pump body	10	Gasket
5	Gasket	11	Bolts
6	Water pump cover		

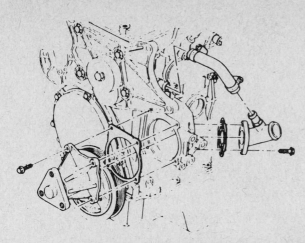

8.8a 2.0/2.2 liter four-cylinder engine water pump – exploded view

NOTE: PUMP MUST ROTATE FREELY AFTER INSTALLATION

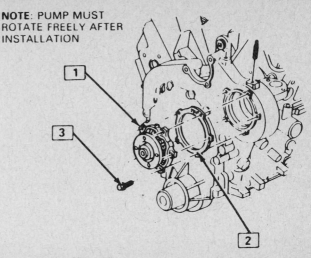

8.8b V6 engine water pump – exploded view

1 Water pump   3 Gasket
2 Bolt

2 Drain the cooling system (see Chapter 1). If the coolant is relatively new or in good condition, save it and reuse it. **Note:** *On Quad-4 models, disconnect the heater hose from the thermostat housing to ensure complete coolant draining.*

All engines except Quad-4
Refer to illustration 8.3

3 Loosen the water pump pulley mounting bolts **(see illustration)**. Remove the drivebelt (see Chapter 1) and then remove the water pump pulley.
4 On 2.0/2.2 liter four-cylinder engines, remove the alternator and brackets (see Chapter 5).

Quad-4 engine only
Refer to illustration 8.7

5 Remove the exhaust manifold (see Chapter 2B).
6 Remove the radiator outlet pipe-to-water pump cover bolts, leaving the lower radiator hose attached. Pull down on the radiator outlet pipe to disengage it from the water pump and detach the pipe from the oil pan and transaxle.
7 Remove the water pump cover-to-block bolts **(see illustration)**.

All models
Refer to illustrations 8.8a, 8.8b, 8.8c, 8.8d and 8.15

8 Remove the bolts/nuts and detach the water pump from the engine **(see illustrations)**.
9 Clean the fastener threads and any threaded holes in the engine to remove corrosion and sealant.
10 Compare the new pump to the old one to make sure they're identical.
11 Remove all traces of old gasket material from the engine with a gasket scraper.
12 Clean the engine and water pump mating surfaces with lacquer thinner or acetone.
13 Apply a thin coat of RTV sealant to the *engine* side of the new gasket.
14 Apply a thin layer of RTV sealant to the gasket mating surface of the new pump, then carefully mate the gasket and the pump. Slip a couple of bolts through the pump mounting holes to hold the gasket in place (except Quad-4).
15 Carefully attach the pump and gasket to the engine and start the bolts/nuts finger tight. **Note:** *On Quad-4 models, lubricate the splines of the water pump drive* **(see illustration)** *with chassis grease (GM no. 1051344 or equivalent) prior to installation. Lubricate the O-ring on the radiator outlet pipe with antifreeze solution before installing.*

8.8c The mounting bolts are located around the perimeter of the pump (arrows) – V6 shown

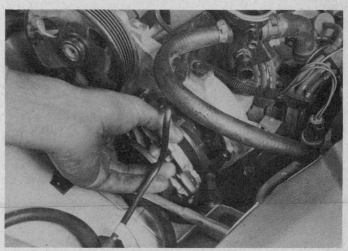

8.8d Pull the pump off – if it's stuck, tap it with a soft-face hammer

3

8.15 4 On Quad-4 models, lubricate the splines (arrow) with grease

16   Tighten the fasteners in 1/4-turn increments to the torque figure listed in this Chapter's Specifications. Don't overtighten them or the pump may be distorted. **Note:** *On Quad-4 models, tighten the fasteners in this order:*

Pump-to-chain housing
Pump cover-to-pump assembly
Cover-to-block, bottom bolt first
Radiator outlet pipe-to-water pump cover

17   Reinstall all parts removed for access to the pump.
18   Refill the cooling system (see Chapter 1). Run the engine and check for leaks.

9   Coolant temperature sending unit – check and replacement

Refer to illustrations 9.1a and 9.1b
Warning: *Wait until the engine is completely cool before beginning this procedure.*

1   The coolant temperature indicator system is composed of a light or temperature gauge mounted in the instrument panel and a coolant temperature sending unit mounted on the engine **(see illustrations)**. Some vehicles have more than one sending unit, but the one used for the indicator system has only one wire.

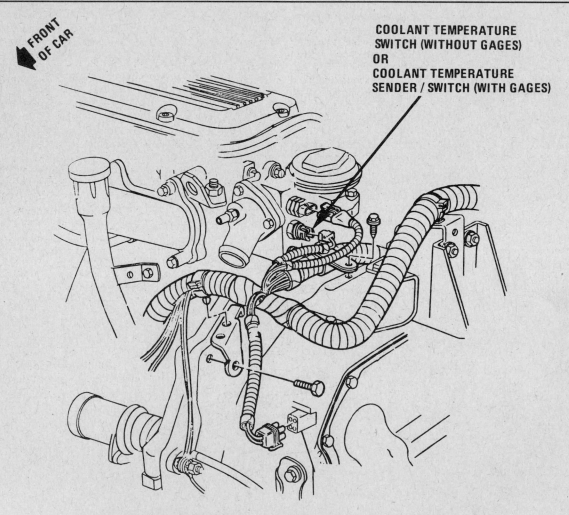

9.1a   Coolant temperature sending unit location – 2.0/2.2 liter four-cylinder engines

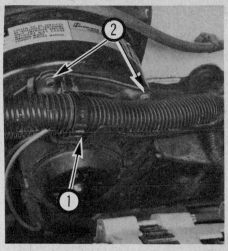

9.1b   On V6 models, the coolant temperature sending unit (arrow) is adjacent to the EGR pipe – follow the wire back to the connector and unplug it (components removed for clarity)

10.2   Remove the central screw (arrow) and lift the firewall covers off

10.3   Detach the wiring harness clip and remove the mounting screws around the perimeter of the blower

1   Wiring harness clip
2   Blower mounting screws

2   If the light or gauge indicates the engine is overheating, check the coolant level in the system and then make sure the wiring between the light or gauge and the sending unit is secure and all fuses are intact.

3   When the ignition switch is turned on and the starter motor is turning, the indicator light (if equipped) should be on (overheated engine indication).

4   If the light isn't on, the bulb may be burned out, the ignition switch may be faulty or the circuit may be open. Test the circuit by grounding the wire to the sending unit while the ignition is on (engine not running for safety). If the gauge deflects full scale or the light comes on, replace the sending unit.

5   As soon as the engine starts, the light should go out and remain out unless the engine overheats. Failure of the light to go out may be due to a grounded wire between the light and the sending unit, a defective sending unit or a faulty ignition switch. Check the coolant to make sure it's the proper type. Plain water may have too low a boiling point to activate the sending unit.

6   If the sending unit must be replaced, simply unscrew it from the engine and install the replacement. Use a light coat of sealant on the threads. Make sure the engine is cool before removing the defective sending unit. There will be some coolant loss as the unit is removed, so be prepared to catch it. Check the level after the replacement has been installed.

10   Heater and air conditioner blower motor – removal and installation

Refer to illustrations 10.2, 10.3, 10.4 and 10.6

1   Disconnect the cable from the negative battery terminal.

2   Working in the engine compartment, remove the plastic firewall covers **(see illustration)**.

3   Disconnect the wires from the blower motor **(see illustration)**.

4   Detach the blower motor cooling tube **(see illustration)**.

5   Remove the blower motor mounting bolts and separate the motor/fan assembly from the housing. **Note:** *On V6 engines, it may be necessary to remove the alternator to improve access (see Chapter 5).*

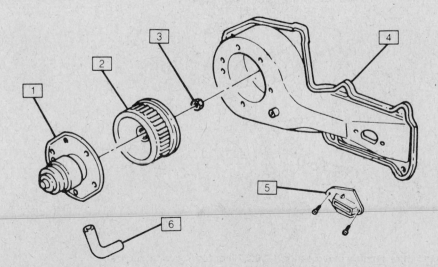

10.4   Blower motor components – exploded view

1   Blower motor
2   Fan
3   Nut
4   Housing
5   Blower motor resistor
6   Motor cooling tube

10.6   Remove the nut (arrow) and slip the fan off the motor shaft (V6 shown)

6   Remove the retaining nut and slide the blower off the motor shaft **(see illustration)**.
7   Installation is the reverse of the removal procedure.

---

11   Heater core – removal and installation

1   Disconnect the battery cables (negative cable first, then the positive one).
2   Raise the front of the vehicle and support it securely on jackstands. Apply the parking brake and block the rear wheels to keep the vehicle from rolling off the jackstands.
3   Drain the cooling system (see Chapter 1).
4   Remove the drain hose from the bottom of the heater case.
5   Working in the engine compartment, disconnect the heater hoses at the firewall.
6   Remove the right and left sound insulators and steering column trim cover.
7   Disassemble the dash as necessary for access (see Chapter 11). Remove the heater outlet duct and glove box.
8   Remove the heater core cover. Pull straight back to avoid breaking the drain tube.
9   Remove the heater core clamps and remove the heater core.
10   Installation is the reverse of removal.

12   Heater and air conditioner control assembly – removal and installation

Refer to illustrations 12.3a and 12.3b

1   Remove the radio assembly (see Chapter 12). **Note:** *On non-air conditioned models, it may be necessary to detach the control cables in order to remove the radio.*
2   Pull the control knobs off the face of the control assembly.
3   Remove the screws on each side of the control assembly **(see illustrations)**.
4   Installation is the reverse of removal.

---

13   Air conditioning system – check and maintenance

Refer to illustration 13.11

Warning: *The air conditioning system is under high pressure. DO NOT loosen any hose or line fittings or remove any components until after the system has been discharged by a dealer service department or service station. Always wear eye protection when disconnecting air conditioning system fittings.*

Check

1   The following maintenance checks should be performed on a regular basis to ensure the air conditioner continues to operate at peak efficiency.
   a) Check the compressor drivebelt. If it's worn or deteriorated, replace it (see Chapter 1).
   b) Check the system hoses. Look for cracks, bubbles, hard spots and deterioration. Inspect the hoses and all fittings for oil bubbles and seepage. If there's any evidence of wear, damage or leaks, replace the hose(s).
   c) Inspect the condenser fins for leaves, bugs and other debris. Use a "fin comb" or compressed air to clean the condenser.
   d) Make sure the system has the correct refrigerant charge.
2   It's a good idea to operate the system for about 10 minutes at least once a month, particularly during the winter. Long term non-use can cause hardening, and subsequent failure, of the seals.
3   Because of the complexity of the air conditioning system and the special equipment necessary to service it, in-depth troubleshooting and repairs are not included in this manual (refer to the Haynes *Automotive Heating & Air Conditioning* manual). However, simple checks and component replacement procedures are provided in this Chapter.
4   The most common cause of poor cooling is simply a low system refrigerant charge. If a noticeable loss of cool air output occurs, one of the following quick checks may help you determine if the refrigerant level is low.
5   Warm the engine up to normal operating temperature.

12.3   Remove the four screws (arrows) . . .

12.3b   . . . and separate the control assembly from the faceplate

6   Place the air conditioning temperature selector at the coldest setting and put the blower at the highest setting. Open the doors (to make sure the air conditioning system doesn't cycle off as soon as it cools the passenger compartment).

7   With the compressor engaged – the compressor clutch will make an audible click and the center of the clutch will rotate – feel the orifice tube located adjacent to the right front frame rail near the radiator.

8   If a significant temperature drop is noticed, the refrigerant level is probably okay. Further inspection of the system is beyond the scope of the home mechanic and should be left to a professional.

9   If the inlet line has frost accumulation or feels cooler than the accumulator surface, the refrigerant charge is low. Add refrigerant.

Adding refrigerant

Caution 1: *1994 and later models use R134a instead of R-12 in the air conditioning system. The two refrigerants are NOT compatible. Even after purging and evacuating an R-12 system, there is enough residual oil and refrigerant in the hoses and components that simply filling the system with R-134a cannot be done. Special fittings and manifold gauge sets are used on the different refrigerant types so that an accidental hook-up of the two systems cannot be made.*

Caution 2: *When replacing entire components, additional refrigerant oil should be added equal to the amount that is removed with the component being replaced. Refrigerant oils, just like refrigerant R-12 vs. R-134a, are not compatible. Be sure to read the can before adding any oil to the system to make sure it is compatible with the type of system being repaired.*

Note: *Because of recent Federal regulations proposed by the Environmental Protection Agency, 14-ounce cans of refrigerant may not be available in your area. If this is the case, it will be necessary to take your vehicle to a licensed air conditioning technician for charging. If you decide to add refrigerant from one of these larger cans, you will need a set of manifold gauges, all the necessary fittings, adapters and hoses to hook everything up and a copy of the Haynes Automotive Heating and Air Conditioning Manual.*

10   Buy an automotive charging kit at an auto parts store (if available). A charging kit includes a 14-ounce can of refrigerant, a tap valve and a short section of hose that can be attached between the tap valve and the system low side service valve. **Note:** *With the change of refrigerant, and their incompatability, has also come a change of necessary equipment to service the system* **(see illustrations)**. Because one can of refrigerant may not be sufficient to bring the system charge up to the proper level, it's a good idea to buy a couple of additional cans. Make sure that one of the cans contains red refrigerant dye. If the system is leaking, the red dye will leak out with the refrigerant and help you pinpoint the location of the leak.

Warning: *Never add more than two cans of refrigerant to the system.*

11   Hook up the charging kit by following the manufacturer's instructions. **Warning:** *DO NOT hook the charging kit hose to the system high side!*

12   Warm up the engine and turn on the air conditioner. Keep the charging kit hose away from the fan and other moving parts.

13   Place a thermometer in the dashboard vent nearest the evaporator **(see illustration)** and add refrigerant until the indicated temperature is around 40 to 45-degrees F.

14   Air conditioner accumulator – removal and installation

Refer to illustrations 14.4 and 14.6

Warning: *The air conditioning system is under high pressure. DO NOT loosen any hose or line fittings or remove any components until after the system has been discharged by a dealer service department or service station. Always wear eye protection when disconnecting air conditioning system fittings.*

1   Have the system discharged (see Warning above).

2   Disconnect the negative battery cable from the battery.

3   Raise the vehicle and support it securely on jackstands.

4   Working from below, disconnect the refrigerant lines from the accumulator **(see illustration)**. Use a back-up wrench to prevent twisting the tubing.

5   Plug the open fittings to prevent entry of dirt and moisture.

6   Loosen the mounting bracket bolts **(see illustration)** and remove the accumulator.

7   If a new accumulator is being installed, remove the Schrader valve and pour the oil out into a measuring cup, noting the amount. Add fresh refrigerant oil to the new accumulator equal to the amount removed from the old unit, plus one ounce.

8   Installation is the reverse of removal.

9   Have the system evacuated, recharged and leak tested by the shop that discharged it.

15   Air conditioner compressor – removal and installation

Refer to illustrations 15.6 and 15.8

Warning: *The air conditioning system is under high pressure. DO NOT loosen any hose or line fittings or remove any components until after the*

13.11   It may be easier to access the accumulator from beneath the vehicle

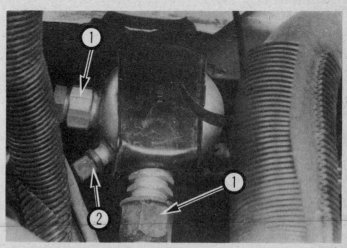

14.4   The accumulator is located in the left front corner of the engine compartment below the battery and air cleaner

1   *Refrigerant line fittings*   2   *Charging port*

14.6   Accumulator and related components – exploded view

1   *Mounting bracket*
2   *Strap*
3   *Accumulator*
4   *Bolt*
5   *Nut*

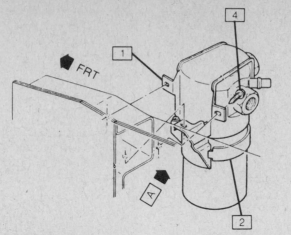

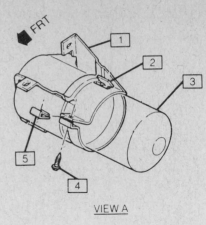

VIEW A

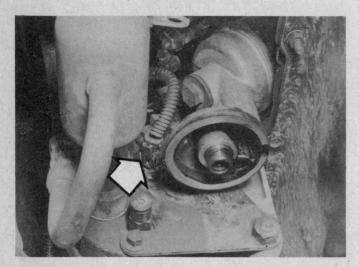

15.6   Disconnect the compressor clutch wiring harness (arrow) – oil filter removed for clarity (V6 shown)

15.8   Air conditioner compressor and related components – exploded view

1   *Bracket assembly*
2   *Bolt/screw*
3   *Bolt/screw*
4   *Bracket – rear*
5   *Compressor assembly*
6   *Bolt/screw*

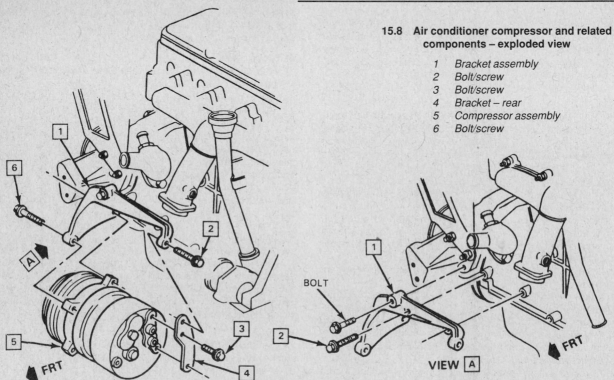

BOLT

VIEW A

system has been discharged by a dealer service department or service station. Always wear eye protection when disconnecting air conditioning system fittings.

Note: *The accumulator (see Section 14) should be replaced whenever the compressor is replaced.*

1   Have the system discharged (see Warning above).
2   Disconnect the negative battery cable from the battery.
3   Set the parking brake and block the rear wheels. Raise the front of the vehicle and support it securely on jackstands.
4   Remove the right lower splash shield.
5   Refer to Chapter 1, then remove the drivebelt (and oil filter, if necessary for clearance).
6   Disconnect the compressor clutch wiring harness **(see illustration)**.
7   Disconnect the refrigerant lines from the rear of the compressor. Plug the open fittings to prevent entry of dirt and moisture.
8   Unbolt the compressor from the mounting brackets and lift it out of the vehicle **(see illustration)**.
9   If a new compressor is being installed, follow the directions with the compressor regarding the draining of excess oil prior to installation.
10   The clutch may have to be transferred from the original to the new compressor.
11   Installation is the reverse of removal. Replace all O-rings with new ones specifically made for A/C system use and lubricate them with refrigerant oil.
12   Have the system evacuated, recharged and leak tested by the shop that discharged it.

---

16   Air conditioner condenser – removal and installation

Refer to illustrations 16.3, 16.5 and 16.12

Warning 1: *The air conditioning system is under high pressure. DO NOT loosen any hose or line fittings or remove any components until after the system has been discharged by a dealer service department or service station. Always wear eye protection when disconnecting air conditioning system fittings.*

Warning 2: *On models equipped with airbags, we recommend having a dealer service department or other qualified shop perform this procedure. The impact sensors are located near the radiator, and, if you accidently trip one of these sensors, the airbag will deploy. Airbags are expensive to replace and deployment could cause personal injury. Also, disturbing the impact sensors or their wiring could cause the airbag not to deploy correctly in a collision.*

Note: *The accumulator (see Section 14) should be replaced whenever the condenser is replaced.*

All models

1   Have the system discharged (see Warning above).
2   Disconnect the negative cable from the battery.
3   Disconnect the refrigerant lines from the condenser **(see illustration)**. Plug the lines to keep dirt and moisture out.
4   Remove the plastic air baffle (splash guard) from above the condenser.
5   Remove the condenser mounting bolts **(see illustration)**.

1987 and 1988 models only

6   Remove the battery (see Chapter 5).
7   Remove the air cleaner assembly and air intake duct (see Chapter 4).
8   Remove the cooling fan (see Section 4).
9   Remove the headlight attaching screws and swing the headlights aside (see Chapter 12).
10   Remove the radiator (see Section 5) and condenser as an assembly.

1989 and later models

11   Remove the grille support brackets (see Chapter 11).
12   Remove the hood latch assembly **(see illustration)**.
13   Lift the condenser out of the vehicle while tilting the driver's side up.

16.3   **Remove the bolt (arrow) to disconnect the refrigerant lines**

16.5   **Remove the condenser mounting bolts (arrow) at the brackets**

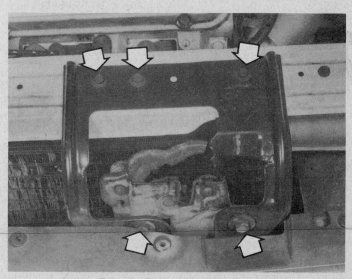

16.12   **Remove the hood latch bolts (arrows)**

All models

14   If the original condenser will be reinstalled, plug the line fittings to prevent oil from draining out.

15   If a new condenser is being installed, pour one ounce of refrigerant oil into it prior to installation.

16   Reinstall the components in the reverse order of removal. Be sure the rubber pads are in place under the condenser.

17   Have the system evacuated, recharged and leak tested by the shop that discharged it.

Chapter 4   Fuel and exhaust systems

Contents

4

Specifications

Fuel pressure

TBI (Throttle Body Injection)	9 to 13 psi
PFI (Port Fuel Injection)	40 to 47 psi

Torque specifications

	Ft-lbs
TBI throttle body mounting bolts	17
PFI throttle body mounting bolts	15
Plenum-to-intake manifold bolts	16

---

1   General information

Note: *On models equipped with the Delco Loc II audio system, be sure the lockout feature is turned off before performing any procedure which requires disconnecting the battery.*

The fuel system consists of a fuel tank, an electric fuel pump, a fuel pump relay, an air cleaner assembly and either a Throttle Body Injection (TBI) system or a Port Fuel Injection (PFI) system. The TBI system is used on the 2.0 and 2.2 liter four-cylinder engines and the PFI system is used on the 2.3 liter (Quad-4) four-cylinder engine, 1992 and later 2.2 liter four-cylinder engines and all V6 engines. The basic difference between throttle body and port fuel injection systems is the number and location of the fuel injectors.

Throttle Body Injection (TBI) system

The throttle body system utilizes one injector, centrally mounted in a carburetor-like housing. The injector is an electrical solenoid, with fuel delivered to the injector at a constant pressure level. To maintain the fuel pressure at a constant level, excess fuel is returned to the fuel tank.

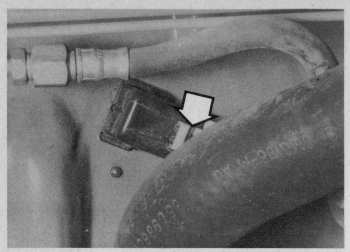

2.4   The fuel tank connector is located behind the fuel filler hose (arrow)

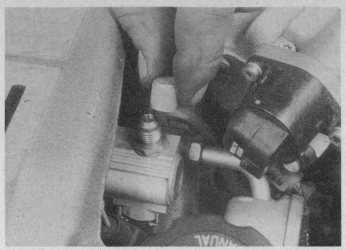

3.5   Remove the cap to gain access to the Schrader valve for connecting a fuel pressure gauge

A signal from the ECM opens the solenoid, allowing fuel to spray through the injector into the throttle body. The amount of time the injector is held open by the ECM determines the fuel/air mixture ratio.

Port Fuel Injection (PFI) system

The port system utilizes four or six injectors of the same type as the throttle body injector and the fuel/air ratio is controlled in the same manner. Instead of a single injector mounted in a centrally located throttle body, one injector is installed above each intake port. The throttle body serves only to control the amount of air passing into the system. Because each cylinder is equipped with an injector mounted immediately adjacent to the intake valve, much better control of the fuel/air mixture ratio is possible.

Fuel pump and lines

Fuel is circulated from the fuel tank to the fuel injection system, and back to the fuel tank, through a pair of metal lines running along the underside of the vehicle. An electric fuel pump is attached to the fuel sending unit inside the fuel tank. A vapor return system routes all vapors and hot fuel back to the fuel tank through a separate return line.

Exhaust system

The exhaust system, which is similar for both four-cylinder and V6 models, includes an exhaust manifold fitted with an exhaust oxygen sensor, a catalytic converter, an exhaust pipe, and a muffler utilizing a "tri-flow" design.

The catalytic converter is an emission control device added to the exhaust system to reduce pollutants. A single-bed converter is used in combination with a three-way (reduction) catalyst. Refer to Chapter 6 for more information regarding the catalytic converter.

2   Fuel pressure relief procedure

Refer to illustration 2.4

Note: *After the fuel pressure has been relieved, it's a good idea to use a shop towel around any fuel connection to absorb the residual fuel that may spray when servicing the fuel system.*

1   Before servicing any fuel system component, you must relieve the fuel pressure to minimize the risk of fire or personal injury.

2   Remove the cap from the gas tank – this will relieve any pressure built up in the tank.

3   On models with TBI injection, there is an internal constant bleed feature which relieves fuel pump system pressure when the engine is turned off. Disconnect the negative battery terminal to avoid any accidental fuel discharge if an attempt is made to start the engine.

4   On models with PFI, disconnect the fuel tank connector **(see illustration)**.

5   Crank the engine over. It will start and run until the fuel supply remaining in the fuel lines is used. When the engine stops, engage the starter again for another three seconds to insure any remaining pressure is dissipated.

6   With the ignition turned to Off, reconnect the fuel tank connector. Disconnect the negative battery cable terminal to avoid any accidental fuel discharge if an attempt is made to start the engine. Unless this procedure is followed before servicing fuel lines or connections, fuel spray (and possible injury) may occur.

7   Reconnect the negative battery cable.

3   Fuel pump/fuel pressure – testing

Warning: *Gasoline is extremely flammable, so extra precautions must be taken when working on any part of the fuel system. Don't smoke or allow open flames or bare light bulbs in or near the work area. Also, don't work in a garage where a natural gas-type appliance with a pilot light is present. Have a fire extinguisher rated for gasoline fires handy and know how to use it!*

Note: *In order to perform the fuel pressure test, you will need to obtain a fuel pressure gauge and adapter set for the fuel injection system being tested.*

Preliminary inspection (all vehicles)

1   Should the fuel system fail to deliver the proper amount of fuel, or any fuel at all, to the fuel injection system, inspect it as follows.

2   Always make certain there is fuel in the tank.

3   With the engine running, inspect for leaks at the threaded fittings at both ends of the fuel line (see Chapter 1). Tighten any loose connections. Inspect all hoses for flattening or kinks which would restrict the flow of fuel.

Pressure check

4   Relieve the fuel system pressure (see Section 2).

Models with port fuel injection (PFI)

Refer to illustration 3.5

5   Install a fuel pressure gauge at the Schrader valve on the fuel rail **(see illustration)**.

6   Turn the ignition switch ON with the air conditioning OFF. The fuel pump should run for about two seconds and note the reading. After the pump stops running the pressure should hold steady. It should be within the specified amount.

7   Start the engine and let it idle at normal operating temperature. The pressure should be lower by 3 – 10 psi. If all the pressure readings are within specifications the system is operating properly.

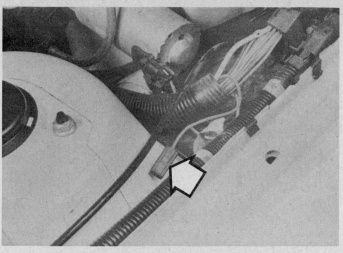

3.14   The fuel pump test lead is located by the left shock tower (arrow)

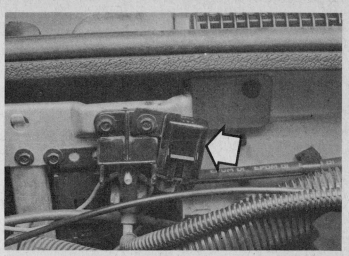

3.22   The fuel pump fuse is in the fuse holder (arrow) located on the firewall

8   If the pressure did not drop by 3 – 10 psi after starting the engine, apply 10 inches of vacuum to the pressure regulator. If the pressure drops, repair the vacuum source to the regulator. If the pressure does not drop, replace the regulator.

9   If the fuel pressure is not within specifications, check the following:
   a) If the pressure is higher than specified, check for a faulty regulator or a pinched or clogged fuel return hose or pipe.
   b) If the pressure is lower than specified:
   c) Inspect the fuel filter – make sure it's not clogged.
   d) Look for a pinched or clogged fuel hose between the fuel tank and the fuel rail.
   e) Check the pressure regulator for a malfunction.
   f) Look for leaks in the fuel line.
   g) Look for a pinched, broken or disconnected regulator vacuum hose.
   h) Check for leaking injectors.
   i) Check the in-tank fuel pump check valve.

10   After the testing is done, relieve the fuel pressure (see Section 2) and remove the fuel pressure gauge.

11   If there are no problems with any of the above-listed components, check the fuel pump (see below).

Models with throttle body injection (TBI)

Refer to illustration 3.14

12   Relieve fuel system pressure (see Section 2).

13   Install a fuel pressure gauge between the fuel feed hose and the inlet fitting of the throttle body.

14   With the ignition OFF, use a fused jumper wire from a 12 volt source, jump the fuel pump test terminal and note the pressure reading **(see illustration)**.

15   If the pressure is within specifications, no further testing is necessary.

16   If the pressure was higher than specified, check for a restricted fuel return line. If the line is OK, then replace the pressure regulator.

17   If the pressure was less than specified, slowly pinch the hose between the gauge and the TBI unit and note the pressure. If the pressure goes above 9 psi, then replace the pressure regulator. If there is not any pressure, then check for a plugged fuel filter, plugged fuel pump inlet filter or a restricted fuel line.

18   After testing is completed, relieve the fuel pressure and remove the fuel gauge tester.

19   If no problems are found with any of the above listed components, check the fuel pump (see below).

Fuel pump check

Refer to illustration 3.22

20   If you suspect a problem with the fuel pump, verify the pump actually runs. Have an assistant turn the ignition switch to On – you should hear a

3.25   The fuel pump relay is located behind the 12 volt junction block and the fuel pump fuse holder (arrow)

brief whirring noise as the pump comes on and pressurizes the system. Have the assistant start the engine. This time you should hear a constant whirring sound from the pump (but it's more difficult to hear with the engine running).

21   If the pump does not come on (makes no sound), proceed to the next step.

22   Check the fuel pump fuse located in the engine compartment **(see illustration)**. If the fuse is good, see fuel pump relay check. If the fuse is blown, replace the fuse and see if the pump works. If the pump still does not work, go to the next step.

23   With the ignition OFF, apply 12 volts to the fuel pump test terminal **(see illustration 3.14)** and listen for the fuel pump running.

24   If the pump runs, then check the fuel pump relay. If the pump does not run, check for an open circuit between the relay and the fuel pump.

Fuel pump relay check

Refer to illustration 3.25

25   To test the fuel pump relay, start the engine and let it idle at normal operating temperature, then disconnect the fuel pump relay **(see illustration)**. If the engine does not continue to run, the oil pressure switch is faulty.

26   If the engine keeps on running, reconnect the relay and turn OFF the ignition. With a test light probe the fuel pump test terminal. If the light does not come on, the fuel pump circuit is OK. If the test light comes on, the oil pressure switch is bad.

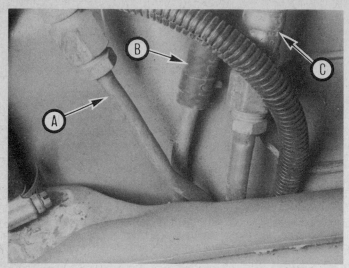

4.13   The fuel return (A), vapor (B) and feed lines (C)

4.19   Typical fuel feed and return line threaded fittings in the left side of the engine compartment

4   Fuel lines and fittings – repair and replacement

Warning: *Gasoline is extremely flammable, so extra precautions must be taken when working on any part of the fuel system. Don't smoke or allow open flames or bare light bulbs in or near the work area. Also, don't work in a garage where a natural gas-type appliance with a pilot light is present. Have a fire extinguisher rated for gasoline fires handy and know how to use it!*

1   Always relieve the fuel pressure before servicing fuel lines or fittings (Section 2).
2   The fuel feed and return lines extend from the in-tank fuel pump to the engine compartment. The lines are secured to the underbody with clip and screw assemblies. Both fuel feed lines must be occasionally inspected for leaks, kinks and dents.
3   If evidence of dirt is found in the system or fuel filter during disassembly, the line should be disconnected and blown out. Check the fuel strainer on the fuel gauge sending unit (see Section 7) for damage and deterioration.

Steel tubing

4   If replacement of a fuel line or emission line is called for, use welded steel tubing meeting GM specification 124-M or its equivalent.
5   Don't use copper or aluminum tubing to replace steel tubing. These materials cannot withstand normal vehicle vibration.
6   Because fuel lines used on fuel injected vehicles are under high pressure, they require special consideration.
7   Most fuel lines have threaded fittings with O-rings. Any time the fittings are loosened to service or replace components:
   a) Use a backup wrench while loosening and tightening the fittings.
   b) Check all O-rings for cuts, cracks and deterioration. Replace any that appear worn or damaged.
   c) If the lines are replaced, always use original equipment parts, or parts that meet the GM standards specified in this Section.

Quick-connect fuel line fittings – removal and installation

8   New quick-connect fuel line fittings were introduced on 1989 and later models. A special tool (GM J-37008 – fuel line separator) is required to disconnect them.
9   To separate the fuel lines, relieve the fuel system pressure (see Section 2), insert the fuel line separator tool into the fitting and pull the lines apart.
10   To reattach quick-connect fittings, push the line into the fitting as far as possible, then pull back on it to verify that the connection is secure. **Warn-**ing: *The line must be pushed in and pulled back to verify proper connector engagement – DO NOT rely on an audible click or visual verification to check the assembly of the quick-connect fittings.*

Rubber hose

11   When rubber hose is used to replace a metal line, use reinforced, fuel resistant hose (GM Specification 6163-M) with the word "Fluoroelastomer" imprinted on it. Hose(s) not clearly marked like this could fail prematurely and could fail to meet Federal emission standards. Hose inside diameter must match line outside diameter.
12   Don't use rubber hose within four inches of any part of the exhaust system or within ten inches of the catalytic converter. Metal lines and rubber hoses must never be allowed to chafe against the frame. A minimum of 1/4-inch clearance must be maintained around a line or hose to prevent contact with the frame.

Removal and installation

Refer to illustrations 4.13, 4.19 and 4.20

Note: *The following procedure and accompanying illustrations are typical for vehicles covered by this manual.*

13   Relieve the fuel pressure and disconnect the fuel feed, return or vapor line at the fuel tank **(see illustration)**.
14   Detach the bracket from the rear crossmember.
15   Detach the bracket from the rear end of the left frame member, just in front of the left rear wheel.
16   Detach the three brackets from the left frame member.
17   Detach the bracket from the left front end of the left frame member, just behind the left front wheel.
18   Detach the bracket from the lower left rear corner of the engine compartment.
19   Detach the threaded fitting(s) that attach the metal lines to the engine compartment fuel hoses **(see illustration)**.
20   Installation is the reverse of removal. Be sure to use new O-rings at the threaded fittings **(see illustration)**.

Repair

21   In repairable areas, cut a piece of fuel hose four inches longer than the portion of the line removed. If more than a six inch length of line is removed, use a combination of steel line and hose so hose lengths won't be more than ten inches. Always follow the same routing as the original line.
22   Cut the ends of the line with a tube cutter. Using the first step of a double flaring tool, form a bead on the end of both line sections. If the line is too corroded to withstand bead operation without damage, the line should be replaced.

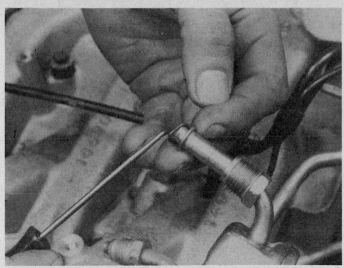

4.20   Always replace fuel line O-rings

23   Use a screw type hose clamp. Slide the clamp onto the line and push the hose on. Tighten the clamps on each side of the repair.
24   Secure the lines properly to the frame to prevent chafing.

5   Fuel tank – removal and installation

Refer to illustration 5.8
Warning: *Gasoline is extremely flammable, so extra precautions must be taken when working on any part of the fuel system. Don't smoke or allow* open flames or bare light bulbs in or near the work area. Also, don't work in a garage where a natural gas-type appliance with a pilot light is present. Have a fire extinguisher rated for gasoline fires handy and know how to use it!

1   If the tank is full or nearly full, drive the vehicle to use up the gas.
2   Relieve the fuel pressure (see Section 2).
3   Detach the cable from the negative terminal of the battery.
4   Raise the vehicle and place it securely on jackstands.
5   Locate the wire harness connector for the electric fuel pump and fuel gauge sending unit **(see illustration 2.4)** in front of the tank, and unplug it. If the vehicle doesn't have a connector, see Step 10 below.
6   Disconnect the fuel feed and return lines, the vapor return line and the filler neck and vent tubes.
7   Support the fuel tank with a floor jack.
8   Disconnect both fuel tank retaining straps **(see illustration)**.
9   Lower the tank enough to disconnect the wires and ground strap from the fuel pump/fuel gauge sending unit, if you haven't already done so.
10   Remove the tank from the vehicle.
11   Installation is the reverse of removal

6   Fuel tank cleaning and repair – general information

1   All repairs to the fuel tank or filler neck should be done by an experienced professional – the job is potentially dangerous! Even after cleaning and flushing of the fuel system, explosive fumes can remain and ignite during repair of the tank.
2   If the fuel tank is removed from the vehicle, it shouldn't be stored in an area where sparks or open flames could ignite the fumes coming out of it. Be especially careful inside a garage where a natural gas-type appliance is located, because the pilot light could cause an explosion.

4

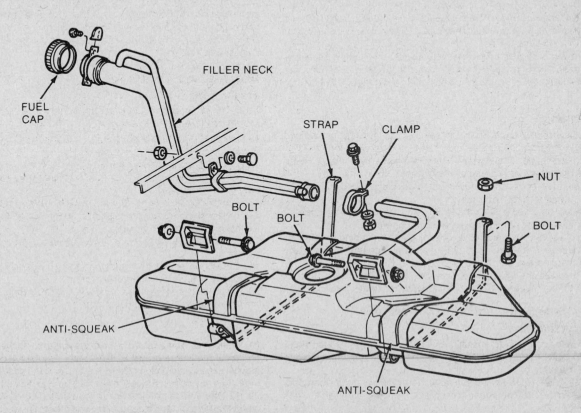

5.8   Typical fuel tank assembly components

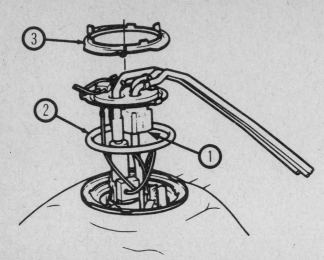

7.5   To remove the fuel gauge sending unit and fuel pump assembly (1) turn the inner cam lockring (3) counterclockwise and pull the pump and O-ring gasket (2) out of the tank – be extremely careful not to bang the float mechanism on the sides of the hole

---

7   Fuel pump – removal and installation

Refer to illustrations 7.5 and 7.8

Warning: *Gasoline is extremely flammable, so extra precautions must be taken when working on any part of the fuel system. Don't smoke or allow open flames or bare light bulbs in or near the work area. Also, don't work in a garage where a natural gas-type appliance with a pilot light is present. Have a fire extinguisher rated for gasoline fires handy and know how to use it!*

Removal

1   Relieve the fuel pressure (Section 2).
2   Remove the cable from the negative battery terminal.
3   Remove the fuel tank (Section 5).
4   The fuel pump/sending unit assembly is located inside the fuel tank. It's held in place by a cam lock ring mechanism consisting of an inner ring with three locking cams and an outer ring with three retaining tangs.
5   To unlock the fuel pump/sending unit assembly, turn the inner ring counterclockwise until the locking cams are free of the retaining tangs **(see illustration). Note:** *If the rings are locked together too tightly to release by hand, tap them gently with a rubber or brass hammer.* **Warning:** *Do not use a steel hammer – a spark could cause an explosion!*
6   Pull the fuel pump/sending unit assembly out of the tank. **Caution:** *The fuel level float and sending unit are delicate. Don't bump them into the lock ring during removal or the accuracy of the sending unit may be affected.*
7   Check the condition of the rubber gasket around the mouth of the lock ring mechanism. If it's dried out, cracked or deteriorated, replace it.
8   Inspect the filter on the lower end of the fuel pump **(see illustration).** If it's dirty, remove it, clean it with solvent and blow it out with compressed air. If it's too dirty to be cleaned, replace it.
9   If you have to separate the fuel pump and sending unit, pull the fuel pump assembly into the rubber connector and slide the pump away from the bottom support. Care should be taken to prevent damage to the rubber insulator and fuel strainer during removal. After the pump assembly is clear of the bottom support, pull the pump assembly out of the rubber connector.

Installation

10   Insert the fuel pump/sending unit assembly into the fuel tank.
11   Turn the inner lock ring counterclockwise until the locking cams are fully engaged by the retaining tangs. **Note:** *If you've installed a new O-ring,*

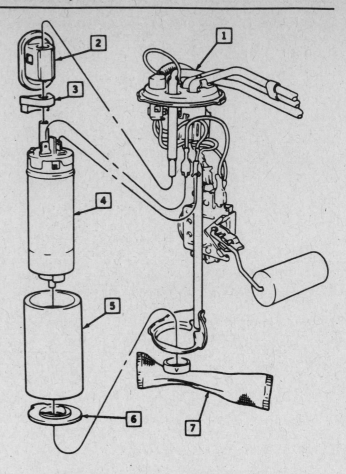

7.8   Exploded view of a typical fuel gauge sending unit and pump assembly

1	Sending unit	4	Fuel pump
2	Pulsator (MPFI equipped vehicle only)	5	Sound isolator sleeve
3	Bumper	6	Sound insulator
		7	Filter

---

it may be necessary to push down on the inner lockring until the locking cams slide under the retaining tangs.
12   Install the fuel tank (Section 5).

---

8   Air cleaner housing assembly – removal and installation

Four-cylinder engines

Refer to illustrations 8.3 and 8.4

1   Detach the cable from the negative terminal of the battery.
2   Remove the air cleaner element (see Chapter 1).
3   On 2.3L engines and 1992 and later 2.2L engines, unclamp the air duct from the housing, remove the crankcase vent tube, remove the housing mounting bolts and lift the housing from the vehicle.
4   On 1990 and 1991 2.2L engines, unclamp the air intake from the air duct, unbolt the air duct from the battery tray and lift the housing from the vehicle **(see illustration)**.
5   On 1987 through 1989 2.0L engines, unclamp the air duct from the throttle body and air cleaner housing, unbolt the housing from the radiator support, then remove the housing from the vehicle.
6   Installation is the reverse of removal.

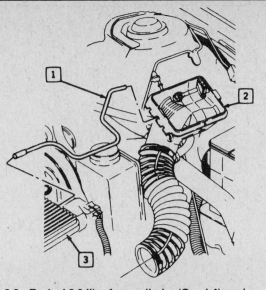

**8.3 Typical 2.3 liter four-cylinder (Quad-4) engine
air cleaner assembly**

1	Tube assembly	3	Engine
2	Air cleaner assembly		

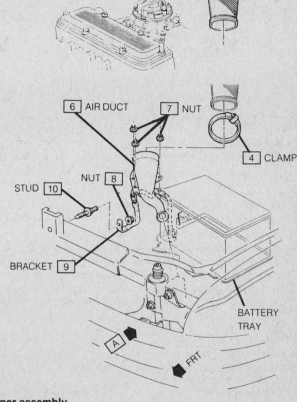

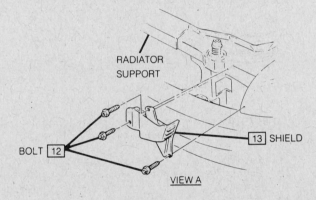

8.4   1990 2.2 liter four-cylinder engine air cleaner assembly

4

V6 engines

Refer to illustrations 8.8, 8.10 and 8.11

7   Detach the cable from the negative terminal, then the positive terminal of the battery. Remove the battery from the vehicle (see Chapter 5).

8   Unplug the electrical connector and unclamp the air duct from the Mass Air Flow (MAF) sensor. Remove the air cleaner housing bracket bolt **(see illustration)**.

9   Remove the air cleaner element (see Chapter 1).

10 On 1990 models, remove the lower air cleaner housing-to-bracket bolt **(see illustration)**.

11 Remove the three bracket-to-battery tray bolts **(see illustration)** and remove the air cleaner housing.

12 Installation is the reverse of removal.

9   Fuel injection system – general information

Electronic fuel injection provides optimum fuel/air mixture ratios at all stages of combustion and offers immediate throttle response characteristics. It also enables the engine to run at the leanest possible fuel/air mixture ratio, reducing exhaust gas emissions.

**8.8   Unplug the electrical connector (1), unclamp the air duct (2)
and remove the bracket bolt (3)**

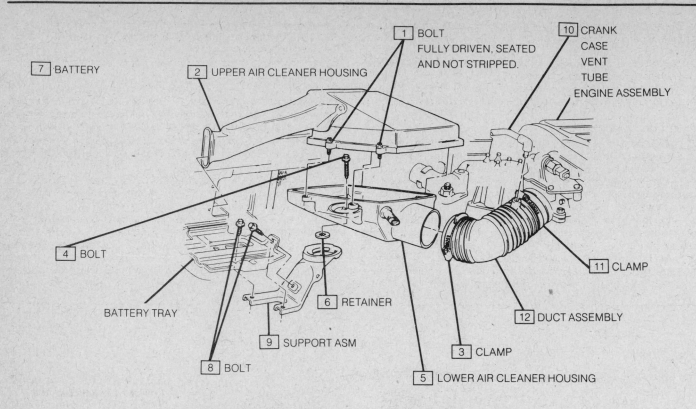

7 BATTERY

2 UPPER AIR CLEANER HOUSING

1 BOLT
FULLY DRIVEN, SEATED
AND NOT STRIPPED.

10 CRANK
CASE
VENT
TUBE
ENGINE ASSEMBLY

4 BOLT

BATTERY TRAY

6 RETAINER

9 SUPPORT ASM

8 BOLT

11 CLAMP

12 DUCT ASSEMBLY

3 CLAMP

5 LOWER AIR CLEANER HOUSING

8.10   Exploded view of 1990 3.1 liter V6 engine air cleaner assembly

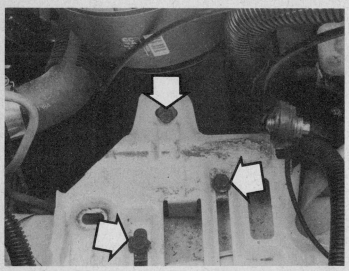

8.11   Remove the bracket-to-battery tray bolts (arrows)

On 2.0L and 2.2L four-cylinder models, a Throttle Body Injection (TBI) unit replaces a conventional carburetor atop the intake manifold. The 2.8L and 3.1L V6 and 2.3L Quad-4 powered vehicles are fitted with a Multi-port Fuel Injection (MFI) system. Both TBI and MFI systems are controlled by an Electronic Control Module (ECM), which monitors engine performance and adjusts the air/fuel mixture accordingly (see Chapter 6 for a complete description of the fuel control system).

An electric fuel pump located in the fuel tank with the fuel gauge sending unit pumps fuel to the fuel injection system through the fuel feed line and an in-line fuel filter. A pressure regulator keeps fuel available at a constant pressure. Fuel in excess of injector needs is returned to the fuel tank by a separate line.

The basic TBI unit is made up of two major casting assemblies – a throttle body with an Idle Air Control (IAC) valve controls air flow and a

Throttle Position Sensor (TPS) monitors throttle angle. The fuel body consists of a fuel meter with a built-in pressure regulator and a fuel injector to supply fuel to the engine.

The fuel injector is a solenoid operated device controlled by the ECM. The ECM turns on the solenoid, which lifts a normally closed ball valve off its seat. The fuel, which is under pressure, is injected in a conical spray pattern at the walls of the throttle body bore above the throttle valve. The fuel which is not used by the injector passes through the pressure regulator before being returned to the fuel tank.

On Port Fuel Injection (PFI) systems, the throttle body has a throttle valve to control the amount of air delivered to the engine. The Throttle Position Sensor (TPS) and Idle Air Control (IAC) valves are located on the throttle body.

The fuel rail is mounted on the top of the engine. It distributes fuel to the individual injectors.

Fuel is delivered to the input end of the rail by the fuel lines, goes through the rail and then to the pressure regulator. The regulator keeps the pressure to the injectors at a constant level.

The remaining fuel is returned to the fuel tank.

10   Fuel injection system – check

Warning: *Gasoline is extremely flammable, so extra precautions must be taken when working on any part of the fuel system. Don't smoke or allow open flames or bare light bulbs in or near the work area. Also, don't work in a garage where a natural gas-type appliance with a pilot light is present. Have a fire extinguisher rated for gasoline fires handy and know how to use it!*

Note: *the following procedure is based on the assumption that the fuel pump and fuel pressure are normal (see Section 3).*

Preliminary checks

1   Check the ground wire connections on the intake manifold for tightness. Check all wiring harness connectors that are related to the system. Loose connectors and poor grounds can cause many problems that resemble more serious malfunctions.

2   Check to see that the battery is fully charged, as the control unit and sensors depend on an accurate supply voltage in order to properly meter the fuel.

3   Check the air filter element – a dirty or partially blocked filter will severely impede performance and economy (see Chapter 1).

4   If a blown fuse is found, replace it and see if it blows again. If it does, search for a grounded wire in the harness to the fuel pump.

Port Fuel Injection only

5   Check the air intake duct from the air mass sensor to the intake manifold for leaks, which will result in an excessively lean mixture. Also check the condition of the vacuum hoses connected to the intake manifold.

6   Remove the air intake duct from the throttle body and check for dirt, carbon or other residue build-up. If it's dirty, clean it with carburetor cleaner and a toothbrush. .

7   With the engine running, place a screwdriver against each injector, one at a time, and listen through the handle for a clicking sound, indicating operation.

8   The remainder of the system checks should be left to a GM service department or other qualified repair shop, as there is a chance that the control unit may be damaged if not performed properly.

11   Throttle body injection (TBI) assembly – removal and installation

Refer to illustration 11.4

Warning: *Gasoline is extremely flammable, so extra precautions must be taken when working on any part of the fuel system. Do not smoke or allow open flames or bare light bulbs near the work area. Also, do not work in a garage if a natural gas-type appliance with a pilot light is present.*

Note: *The fuel injector, pressure regulator, throttle position sensor and the idle air control valve can be replaced without removing the throttle body assembly.*

1   Relieve the fuel system pressure (see Section 2).

2   Disconnect the cable from the negative battery terminal.

3   Remove the air cleaner housing (see Section 8).

4   Unplug the electrical connectors from the idle air control valve, throttle position sensor and fuel injector **(see illustration)**.

5   Remove the wiring harness and insulating grommet from the throttle body.

6   Remove the throttle linkage and return spring, transmission control and cruise control cables (if applicable).

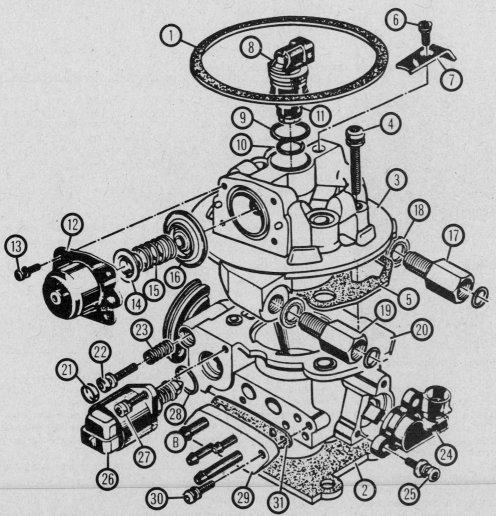

11.4   Exploded view of the model 700 throttle body injection unit

1   Air filter gasket
2   Flange gasket
3   Fuel meter assembly
4   Screw – fuel meter body
5   Fuel meter body-to-throttle body gasket
6   Screw – injector retainer
7   Injector retainer
8   Fuel injector
9   O-ring – fuel injector upper
10 O-ring – fuel injector lower
11 Injector filter
12 Pressure regulator cover assembly
13 Pressure regulator attaching screw
14 Pressure regulator spring seat
15 Pressure regulator spring
16 Pressure regulator diaphragm
17 Nut – fuel inlet
18 Seal – fuel nut
19 Nut – fuel outlet
20 Throttle body assembly
21 Idle stop screw plug
22 Idle stop screw
23 Idle stop screw spring
24 Throttle position sensor (TPS)
25 TPS attaching screw
26 Idle Air Control (IAC) valve
27 IAC attaching screw
28 IAC valve O-ring
29 Tube manifold assembly
30 Manifold attaching screw
31 Tube manifold gasket

7   Using pieces of numbered tape, mark all of the vacuum hoses to the throttle body and disconnect them.
8   Disconnect the fuel inlet and return lines. On 1987 and 1988 models, use a backup wrench on the inlet and return fitting nuts to prevent damage to the throttle body and fuel lines. Remove the fuel line nut O-rings and discard them. 1989 and later models are equipped with quick disconnect fuel lines and a special tool is needed (see Section 4).
9   Remove the TBI assembly mounting bolts and lift the unit from the intake manifold. It is a good idea to stuff a rag into the intake manifold opening to prevent foreign matter from falling in.
10   Installation is the reverse of the removal procedure. Be sure to install a new throttle body-to-intake manifold gasket, new fuel line O-rings and tighten the mounting bolts to the specified torque.
11   Turn the ignition switch on without starting the engine and check for fuel leaks.
12   Check to see if the accelerator pedal is free by depressing the pedal to the floor and releasing it with the ignition switch off.

---

12   Throttle body injection (TBI) – component replacement

Warning: *Gasoline is extremely flammable, so extra precautions must be taken when working on any part of the fuel system. Do not smoke or allow open flames or bare light bulbs near the work area. Also, do not work in garage if a natural gas-type appliance with a pilot light is present.*

Fuel injector

Refer to illustration 12.4

1   Disconnect the negative battery cable
2   Unplug the electrical connector at the injector.
3   Remove the injector retainer screw and the retainer **(see illustration 11.4)**.
4   Using one screwdriver as a fulcrum on the fuel meter body, place another screwdriver tip under the ridge on the fuel injector opposite the electrical connector end and gently pry the injector out **(see illustration)**.
5   If the injector is to be reused, replace the upper and lower O-rings on the injector and in the fuel injector cavity. Install the upper O-ring in the groove on the injector and the lower O-ring flush against the filter element.
6   Install the injector assembly in the fuel meter body by pushing it straight down. Make sure the connector end is facing in the direction of the opening in the fuel meter body for the wire harness grommet.
7   Install the injector retainer and screw. Use a thread locking compound on the retainer screw (GM part no. 10522624 or Loctite 262).

8   Reconnect the negative battery cable. Pressurize the fuel system by turning the ignition key to the On position and inspect the area around the injector for leaks.
9   Plug the electrical connector into the injector and start the engine to check for correct operation.

Pressure regulator assembly

10   Underneath the pressure regulator cover assembly is a large spring which is highly compressed. Repairs to this component should be performed by a dealer service department or repair shop due to the possibility of personal injury.

Idle Air Control valve

Refer to illustrations 12.15a and 12.15b

11   Disconnect the negative battery cable.
12   Remove the air cleaner and unplug the electrical connector from the IAC valve.
13   Remove the two valve retaining screws and pull the valve out of the throttle body.
14   If the same valve is to be reinstalled, be sure to use a new O-ring.
15   Before installing the valve, measure the distance from the end of the pintle to the mounting flange **(see illustration)**. If the distance exceeds 1-1/8 inch (28 mm), reduce that measurement by pushing the pintle into the valve assembly with a slight side-to-side motion **(see illustration)**. If this is not done, the valve will be damaged during installation.
16   Position the valve on the throttle body and install the screws. Plug in the electrical connector to the valve.
17   No adjustment of the IAC valve is necessary, as it is automatically reset by the ECM.

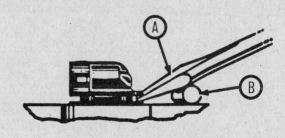

12.4   Pry the injector out of the fuel meter body using one screwdriver as a fulcrum (B) and another as a lever (A)

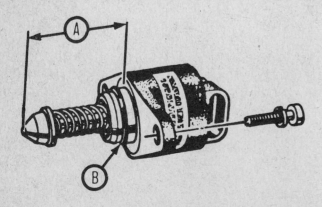

12.15a   The Idle Air Control valve pintle must not extend more than 1-1/8 inch; replace the O-ring if it is cracked or brittle

A   Distance of pintle extension   B   O-ring

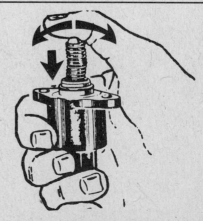

12.15b   To reduce the idle air control valve pintle extension, grasp the valve and depress the pintle using a slight side-to-side motion

12.21   The throttle position sensor mounts to the side of the throttle body and is not adjustable

Throttle Position Sensor (TPS)

Refer to illustration 12.21

18   Disconnect the cable from the negative battery terminal.
19   Remove the air cleaner housing.
20   Unplug the electrical connector from the throttle position sensor.
21   Remove the two sensor mounting screws and pull the sensor from the throttle body **(see illustration)**.
22   To install the TPS, align the slot in the rear of the sensor with the throttle shaft and insert the sensor into the throttle body. Install the mounting crews. This style TPS is not adjustable.
23   The remainder of installation is the reverse of the removal procedure.

---

13   Port fuel injection (PFI) – component removal and installation

Warning: *Before servicing an injector, fuel pump, fuel line, fuel rail or pressure regulator, relieve the pressure in the fuel system to minimize the risk of fire and injury (refer to the fuel pressure relief procedure described in Section 2). After servicing the fuel system, cycle the ignition between On and Off several times (wait 10 seconds between cycles) and check the system for leaks.*

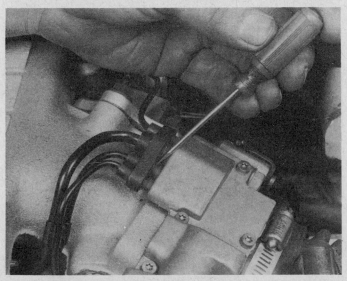

13.3   Using a small screwdriver, remove the vacuum line assembly from the throttle body

Throttle Body

Refer to illustrations 13.2, 13.3 and 13.8

1   Disconnect the cable from the negative terminal of the battery.
2 .   Unplug the Idle Air Control valve (IAC) and the Throttle Position Switch (TPS) connectors **(see illustration)**.
3   Disconnect the vacuum hoses to the throttle body **(see illustration)**.
4   Disconnect the throttle cable (see Section 14).
5   Remove the breather hose.
6   Detach the air inlet duct.
7   Drain the coolant (see Chapter 1) and disconnect the coolant lines.
8   Remove the throttle body bolts and detach the throttle body **(see illustration)**.
9   Install the throttle body and gasket and tighten the bolts to the specified torque.
10   The rest of the procedure is the reverse of removal.

Idle Air Control (IAC) valve

Refer to illustration 13.12

11   Unplug the electrical connector from the Idle Air Control (IAC) valve assembly.

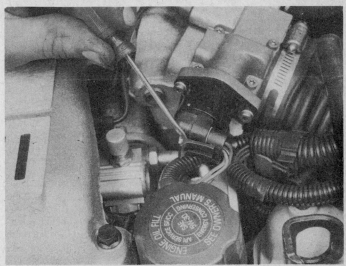

13.2   Using a small screwdriver, release the locking tab and remove the electrical connector

13.8   To detach the throttle body from the plenum, remove these two bolts (arrows) (V6 engine shown)

4

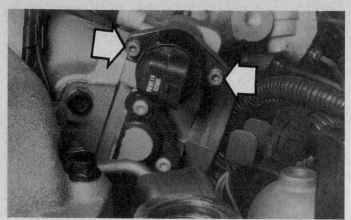

13.12   You'll need a Torx bit or screwdriver to remove the IAC retaining screws (arrows)

13.23   To remove the throttle cable bracket, detach the wiring harness and brake booster vacuum line, then remove the retaining nuts and bolt (arrows)

13.27a   Location of the plenum mounting bolts (arrows)

13.27b   Plenum bolt TIGHTENING sequence (1992 and later 2.2L four-cylinder engines)

16   Measure the distance from the gasket mounting surface of the IAC valve assembly to the tip of the pintle

17   If the distance is greater than 1-1/8 inch, reduce it by applying a firm hand pressure on the pintle to retract it (a slight side-to-side motion may help).

18   Position the new O-ring seal on the IAC valve assembly. Lubricate the O-ring with engine oil.

19   Install the IAC valve in the idle air/vacuum signal housing assembly and tighten it securely.

20   Plug in the electrical connector at the IAC valve assembly. **Note:** *No adjustment is made to the IAC assembly after reinstallation. IAC resetting is controlled by the ECM when the engine is started.*

Throttle position sensor (TPS)

21   Replacement of this component should be performed by a dealer service department or repair shop equipped with a "scan" tool to properly adjust the TPS.

Plenum (V6 and 1992 and later 2.2L engines only)
Refer to illustrations 13.23, 13.27a,, and 13.27b

22   Remove the cable from the negative terminal of the battery.

23   Mark and remove all of the vacuum lines that may interfere, then remove the throttle cable bracket nuts **(see illustration)**.

24   Remove the EGR valve (see Chapter 6).

25   Remove the throttle body (V6 only).

26   Remove the bolts which secure the plastic spark plug wire shield.

27   Remove the plenum bolts **(see illustration)**.

28   Remove the plenum and gaskets. If the plenum sticks, use a block of wood and a hammer (or a soft-face hammer) to dislodge it. Do not pry between the sealing flanges, as this will damage the machined surfaces and vacuum leaks may develop.

29   Remove all traces of old gasket material from the plenum and intake manifold mating surfaces. It is a good idea to stuff rags into the intake manifold openings to prevent debris and old gasket material from falling in.

13.35   Use a backup wrench when disconnecting the fuel lines (V6 engine shown)

12   Remove the two IAC valve attaching screws and withdraw the valve **(see illustration)**.

13   Remove the IAC valve assembly and replace the rubber O-ring.

14   Clean the sealing surface and the bore of the idle air/vacuum signal housing assembly to ensure a good seal. **Caution:** *The IAC valve assembly itself is an electrical component and must not be soaked in any liquid cleaner or solvent or damage may result.*

15   Before installing the IAC valve assembly, the position of the pintle must be checked. If the pintle is extended too far, damage to the assembly may occur.

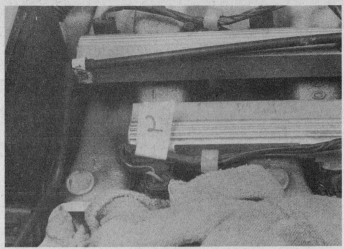

13.38a   Before removing the injector wiring connector, label the connector according to the cylinder number

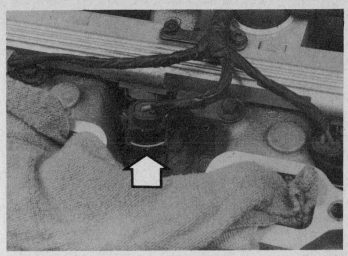

13.38b   To remove the connector, push in the retaining clip and pull up

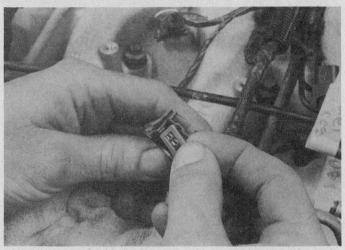

13.38c   Sometimes after removing the connector the insulator will pop out – be sure to reinstall it if it does fall out

13.39   To remove the fuel rail assembly, remove the retaining bolts (arrows)

30   Install the new gaskets and set the plenum into position.
31   Install the plenum bolts and tighten them to the specified torque.
32   The rest of the procedure is the reverse of removal.

Fuel rail and related components

Refer to illustrations 13.35, 13.38a, 13.38b, 13.38c, 13.39 and 13.40

Warning: *Before any work is performed on the fuel lines, fuel rail or injectors, the fuel system pressure must be relieved (refer to the fuel pressure relief procedure in Section 2).*

Note: *An eight digit identification number is stamped on the side of the fuel rail assembly. Refer to this number if servicing or parts replacement is required.*

33   Detach the negative battery cable from the battery.
34   Remove the plenum (if equipped).
35   Using a backup wrench, remove the fuel lines at the fuel rail **(see illustration)**.
36   On models with Quad 4 engines, remove the air/oil separator (see Chapter 6).
37   Remove the vacuum line at the regulator.
38   Label and unplug the injector electrical connectors **(see illustrations)**.
39   Remove the fuel rail retaining bolts **(see illustration)**.

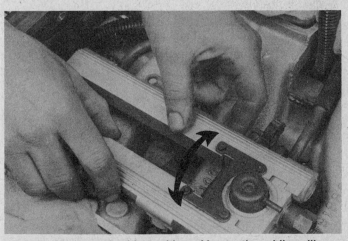

13.40   Use a gentle side-to-side rocking motion while pulling straight up to release the injectors from their bores in the intake manifold

40   Carefully remove the fuel rail with the injectors. **Caution:** *Use care when handling the fuel rail assembly to avoid damaging the injectors* **(see illustration)**.

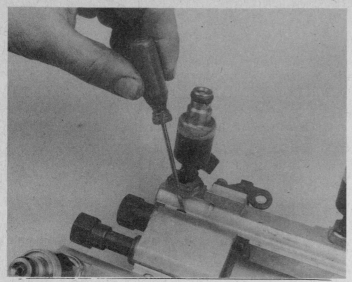

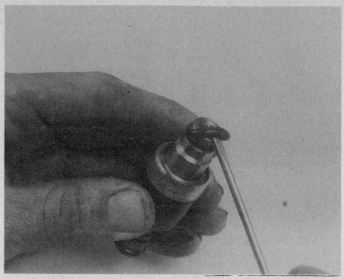

13.41   To remove an injector from the fuel rail assembly, pop off the spring clip with a small screwdriver

13.42   If you plan to reuse the same injector, always replace the O-ring with a new one

Fuel injectors

Refer to illustrations 13.41 and 13.42

Caution: *To prevent dirt from entering the engine, the area around the injectors should be cleaned before servicing.*

41   To remove the fuel injectors, spread open the end of the injector clip slightly and remove it from the fuel rail, then extract the injector **(see illustration)**. On the 2.2L engine, remove the injector retainer and pull the injector(s) from the manifold.

42   Inspect the injector O-ring seal(s). Replace if damaged **(see illustration)**.

43   Install the new O-ring seal(s), as required, on the injector(s) and lubricate them with engine oil.

44   Install the injectors on the fuel rail.

45   Secure the injectors with the retainer clips.

Fuel pressure regulator

Refer to illustrations 13.47, 13.48a, 13.48b and 13.49

46   On 1987 and later V6 models, to remove the fuel pressure regulator from the fuel rail, remove the two fuel line fittings and gaskets.

47   On models with a four-cylinder engine, detach the fuel return line, remove the pressure regulator mounting bracket screws and detach from the fuel rail **(see illustration)**.

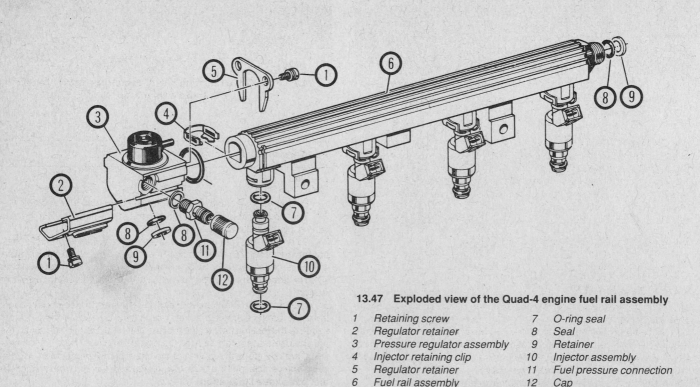

13.47   Exploded view of the Quad-4 engine fuel rail assembly

1	*Retaining screw*	7	*O-ring seal*
2	*Regulator retainer*	8	*Seal*
3	*Pressure regulator assembly*	9	*Retainer*
4	*Injector retaining clip*	10	*Injector assembly*
5	*Regulator retainer*	11	*Fuel pressure connection*
6	*Fuel rail assembly*	12	*Cap*

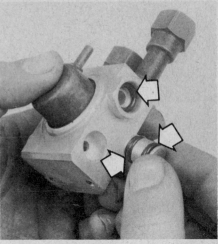

13.48a   A Torx bit or screwdriver is needed to remove the pressure regulator mounting bolts (arrows)

13.48b   Separate the fuel rail(s) from the regulator

13.49   Always replace all O-rings when installing the regulator

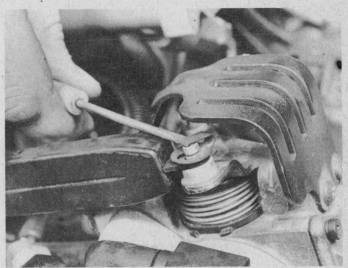

13.52   Location of the MAF sensor mounting bolt

14.3   Pop off the retaining clip to detach the cable from the throttle lever arm

48   On models with a V6 engine, detach the pressure regulator mounting screws **(see illustration)** and separate the two fuel rails from the pressure regulator assembly **(see illustration)**.

49   Reassembly is the reverse of disassembly. Be sure to replace all gaskets and seals **(see illustration)**, otherwise a dangerous fuel leak may develop.

50   Before installing the fuel rail, lubricate all injector O-ring seals with engine oil.

51   Energize the fuel system and check for leaks.

Mass Air Flow (MAF) sensor

Refer to illustration 13.52

52   Remove the mounting screw and disconnect the electrical connector **(see illustration)**.

53   Disconnect the air duct from the MAF sensor. Remove the clamp attaching the MAF sensor to the air cleaner housing and lift the MAF sensor out of the vehicle. **Caution:** *The MAF sensor is delicate – if you plan to reinstall the existing unit, handle it carefully.*

54   Installation is the reverse of the removal procedure.

14   Throttle cable – removal and installation

Refer to illustrations 14.3, 14.4 and 14.6

1   Disconnect the cable from the negative terminal of the battery.

2   The throttle cable will be retained to the throttle linkage by either a retaining clip or a plastic cable retainer.

3   To remove the retaining clip use a small screwdriver to pop it off the post on the throttle lever arm and remove the cable end **(see illustration)**.

4   To remove the plastic cable retainer, push the cable end forward and lift up to detach the cable from the post on the throttle lever arm **(see illustration)**.

5   To detach the throttle cable and, if equipped, cruise control cables from the cable support bracket, use a pair of needle-nose pliers to squeeze the locking tabs on the top and bottom of the cable retainer, then pull the cable assembly through the bracket.

6   Carefully study the routing of the cable before proceeding. Working inside the vehicle, pull the cable toward you and detach it from the accelerator pedal **(see illustration)**.

4

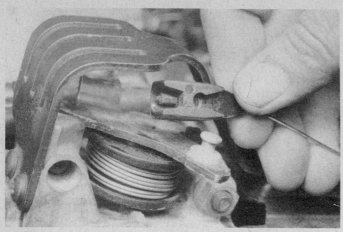

14.4   Push the cable end forward and lift up to detach the cable from the post on the throttle lever arm

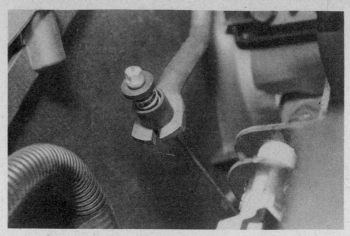

14.6   The throttle cable at the pedal – once the cable is detached at the throttle body end, pull this end toward you and slide it out of the slot in the pedal lever assembly

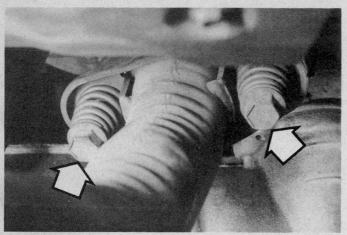

15.3   The exhaust pipe-to-exhaust manifold flange bolts – make sure you don't lose the springs when removing these bolts

15.4   To detach this rubber block type hanger from the exhaust pipe, remove the bolt

7   Follow the cable with your hand until you locate the locking cable retainer on the passenger compartment side of the firewall. Again, with a pair of needle-nose pliers, squeeze the locking tabs of the retainer together and push the retainer through the firewall.
8   Remove the accelerator cable assembly.
9   Installation is the reverse of removal.

15   Exhaust system – removal and installation

Refer to illustrations 15.3 and 15.4
Caution: *DO NOT attempt to work on any part of the exhaust system until the entire system has completely cooled. Be especially careful around the catalytic converter, where the highest temperatures are generated.*

1   Disconnect the cable from the negative terminal of the battery.
2   Raise the vehicle and support it securely on jackstands.
3   Disconnect the exhaust pipe from the exhaust manifold flange by removing the two bolts **(see illustration)**.
4   Remove the bolt from the rubber exhaust pipe hanger just in front of the fuel tank **(see illustration)**.
5   Remove the bolt and detach the hanger from the forward end of the muffler.
6   Remove the bolt and detach the hanger from the rear end of the muffler.
7   Remove the exhaust pipe, catalytic converter and muffler as an assembly. **Note:** *These components cannot be separated without a cutting torch. If you need to replace any of these parts, take the entire assembly to a dealer service department, service station or muffler shop for further service.*

Chapter 5 Engine electrical systems

Contents

5

Specifications

General

Cylinder numbers . . . .   See Chapter 2

Firing order . . . .   See Chapter 2

Charging system

Alternator charging output . . . .   13 to 14.5 volts

---

1   Ignition system – general information

Note: *On models equipped with the Delco Loc II audio system, be sure the lockout feature is turned off before performing any procedure which requires disconnecting the battery.*

The engines covered by this manual are equipped with either a distributorless Direct Ignition System (DIS) or an Integrated Direct Ignition system (IDI).

The DIS and IDI ignition systems use a "waste spark" method of spark distribution. Each cylinder is paired with its opposing cylinder in the firing order (1-4, 2-3 on a four, 1-4, 2-5, 3-6 on a V6) so one cylinder under compression fires simultaneously with its opposing cylinder, where the piston is on the exhaust stroke. Since the cylinder on exhaust requires very little of the available voltage to fire its plug, most of the voltage is used to fire the cylinder on compression.

The DIS system includes a coil pack, an ignition module, a crankshaft reluctor ring, a magnetic sensor, spark plug wires, and the ECM. The IDI system is the same except it does not have spark plug wires. The ignition module is located under the coil pack and is connected to the ECM.

The magnetic crankshaft sensor is mounted on the bottom of the engine block, just above the oil pan rail. The reluctor ring is a special disc cast into the crankshaft, which acts as a signal generator for the ignition timing.

The system uses Electronic Spark Timing (EST) and control wires from the ECM, just like conventional distributor systems. The ECM controls timing based on crankshaft position, engine rpm, engine temperature, manifold absolute pressure (MAP), and on Quad-4 engines only, the manifold air temperature (MAT).

---

2   Battery – removal and installation

Refer to illustration 2.3

Warning: *Hydrogen gas is produced by the battery, so keep open flames and lighted cigarettes away from it at all times. Always wear eye protection when working around a battery. Rinse off spilled electrolyte immediately with large amounts of water.*

1   The battery is located at the left or right front corner of the engine compartment.

Removal

2   **Caution:** *Always disconnect the negative cable first and hook it up last or the battery may be shorted by the tool being used to loosen the cable clamps.* Disconnect both cables from the battery terminals.
3   Remove the hold-down clamp **(see illustration)** from the battery carrier.
4   Carefully lift the battery out of the carrier. **Warning:** *Always keep the battery in an upright position to reduce the possibility of electrolyte spills. If you spill electrolyte on yourself or the vehicle, rinse it off immediately with plenty of water.*
5   If you're installing a new battery, make sure you get one that's identical (same dimensions, amperage rating, cold cranking rating, etc.).

Installation

Note: *The battery carrier and hold-down clamp should be clean and free from corrosion before installing the battery.*
6   Set the battery in position in the carrier. Don't tilt it.
7   Install the hold-down clamp and bolt. The bolt should be snug, but overtightening it may damage the battery case.
8   Install both battery cables – positive first, then negative. **Note:** *The battery terminals and cable ends should be cleaned if necessary (see Chapter 1).*

---

3   Battery – emergency jump starting

Refer to the *Booster battery (jump) starting* procedure at the front of this manual.

---

4   Battery cables – check and replacement

1   Periodically inspect the entire length of each battery cable for damage, cracked or burned insulation and corrosion. Poor battery cable connections can cause starting problems and decreased engine performance.
2   Check the cable-to-terminal connections at the ends of the cables for cracks, loose wire strands and corrosion. The presence of white, fluffy deposits under the insulation at the cable terminal connection is a sign the cable is corroded and should be replaced. Check the terminals for distortion, missing mounting bolts or nuts and corrosion.

3   When removing the cables, always disconnect the negative cable first and hook it up last or the battery may be shorted by the tool used to loosen the cable clamps. Even if only the positive cable is being replaced, be sure to disconnect the negative cable from the battery first (see Chapter 1 for additional information related to battery cable removal).
4   Disconnect the old cables from the battery, then trace each of them to their opposite ends and detach them from the starter solenoid and ground terminals. Note the routing of each cable to ensure correct installation.
5   If you're replacing either or both cables, take the old ones with you when buying the new ones – the replacements must be identical. Cables have characteristics that make them easy to identify: Positive cables are normally red, larger in diameter and have a larger diameter battery post and clamp; ground cables are normally black, smaller in diameter and have a slightly smaller battery post and clamp.
6   Clean the threads of the solenoid or ground connection with a wire brush to remove rust and corrosion. Apply a light coat of petroleum jelly to the threads to prevent future corrosion.
7   Attach the cable to the solenoid or ground connection and tighten the mounting nut/bolt securely.
8   Before connecting a new cable to the battery, make sure it reaches the battery post without having to be stretched.
9   Connect the positive cable first, followed by the negative cable.

---

5   Ignition system – check

Refer to illustration 5.3
Warning: *Because of the very high voltage generated by the ignition system, extreme care should be taken whenever an operation is performed involving ignition components. This not only includes the coils, control module and spark plug wires, but related items connected to the system as well, such as the plug connections, tachometer and any test equipment.*

1   With the ignition switch turned to the On position, a "service engine soon" light is a basic check for ignition and battery supply to the ECM.
2   Check all ignition wiring connections for tightness, cuts, corrosion or any other signs of a bad connection.
3   Use a spark tester to verify adequate available secondary voltage (25,000 volts) at the spark plug **(see illustration)**. On IDI systems it is necessary to install spark plug jumper wires (J-26792) to perform this test. A faulty or poor connection at that plug could also result in a misfire. Also check for carbon deposits inside the spark plug boot.

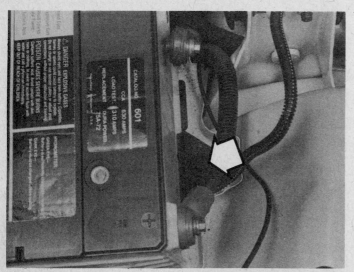

2.3   **Remove the battery hold-down clamp bolt (arrow) from the battery carrier**

5.3   **To use a calibrated ignition tester, simply disconnect a spark plug wire, clip the tester to a convenient ground (like a rocker arm cover bolt) and operate the starter – if there's enough power to fire the plug, sparks will be visible between the electrode tip and the tester body**

4   Check for carbon tracking on the coil. If carbon tracking is evident, replace the coil and be sure the plug wires relating to that coil are clean and tight. Excessive wire resistance or faulty connections could cause damage to the coil.

5   Using an ohmmeter, check the resistance between the coil terminals. If an open is found, replace the coil.

6   On DIS systems, using an ohmmeter, check the resistance of the spark plug wires. Each wire should measure less than 30,000 ohms.

7   Additional checks should be performed by a dealer service department or an automotive repair shop.

6   Ignition coil and module – removal and installation

Note: *A 5.5 mm socket is required to remove the coil pack-to-module screws.*

Direct ignition system (DIS)

Refer to illustrations 6.5, 6.6a, 6.6b, 6.7 and 6.9

1   Refer to the previous Section for checking procedures.
2   Detach the cable from the negative terminal of the battery.
3   On models with a V6 engine, it may be necessary to remove the cooling fan to gain access to the coil/module assembly (see Chapter 3).
4   Unplug the electrical connectors from the module.
5   If the plug wires are not numbered, label them and detach the plug wires at the coil assembly **(see illustration)**.

6   Remove the module/coil assembly mounting bolts and lift the assembly from the vehicle **(see illustrations)**.
7   Remove the bolts attaching the coils to the module and separate them **(see illustration)**.
8   Installation is the reverse of removal.
9   When installing the coils, make sure they are connected properly **(see illustration)**.

6.5   Coils and plug wires will have numbers the same as the cylinder number (arrows)

6.6a   Mounting bolt locations (arrows) for module/coil assemblies for a V6 engine

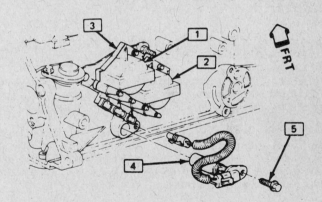

6.6b   Mounting details of typical four-cylinder module/coil assembly

1	2-3 coil	4	Crank sensor
2	1-4 coil	5	Bolt
3	Module		

6.7   A 5.5 mm socket is required to remove the coil mounting bolts (arrows)

6.9   When installing a coil, make sure that it plugs into the module completely

5

Integrated direct ignition (IDI) (Quad-4 engine)

Refer to illustrations 6.12 and 6.14

10   Detach the cable from the negative terminal of the battery.

11   Disconnect the IDI harness connector.

12   Remove the ignition system assembly-to-camshaft housing bolts **(see illustration)**.

13   Lift the ignition system assembly from the engine.

14   Detach the housing-to-cover screws and remove the housing from the cover **(see illustration)**.

15   Detach the coil harness connectors.

16   Remove the coils.

17   Remove the module-to-cover screws and detach the module from the cover.

18   Installation is the reverse of removal.

---

7   Charging system – general information and precautions

The charging system consists of a belt-driven alternator with an integral voltage regulator and the battery. These components work together to supply electrical power for the ignition system, the lights and all accessories.

All models are equipped with the CS type alternator. There are two types of CS alternators in use: The CS-130 and the CS-144. All types have a conventional pulley and fan.

All CS models have special bolts or rivets instead of screws. CS alternators are rebuildable once the rivets are drilled out. However, we don't recommend this practice. For all intents and purposes, CS types should be considered non-serviceable and, if defective, exchanged as cores for new or rebuilt units.

The purpose of the voltage regulator is to limit the alternator's voltage to a preset value. This prevents power surges, circuit overloads, etc., during peak voltage output. On all models with which this manual is concerned, the voltage regulator is mounted inside the alternator housing.

The charging system doesn't ordinarily require periodic maintenance. However, the drivebelt, battery and wires and connections should be inspected at the intervals outlined in Chapter 1.

The dashboard warning light should come on when the ignition key is turned to Start, then go off immediately. If it stays on or comes on when

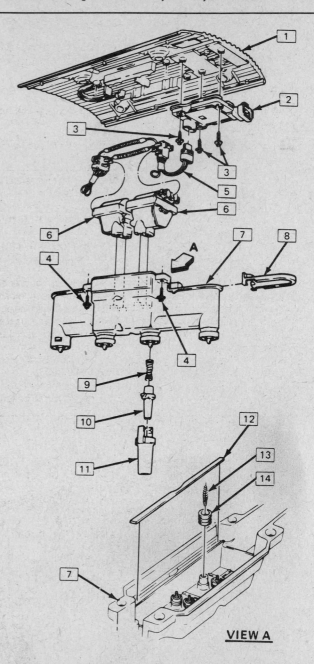

6.14   Exploded view of the IDI ignition system

1	Ignition module cover	8	Cover
2	Module assembly	9	Connector
3	Bolt	10	Boot
4	Bolt	11	Retainer
5	Module wiring harness	12	Spacer
6	Coil assembly	13	Contact
7	Housing assembly	14	Seal

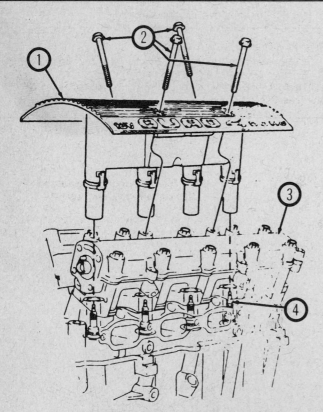

6.12   IDI ignition coil and module assembly

1	Ignition coil and	3	Camshaft housing cover
	module assembly	4	Spark plug
2	Bolts		

the engine is running, a charging system problem has occurred (see Section 8).

Be very careful when making electrical circuit connections to a vehicle equipped with an alternator and note the following:

a) When reconnecting wires to the alternator from the battery, be sure to note the polarity.
b) Before using arc welding equipment to repair any part of the vehicle, disconnect the wires from the alternator and the battery terminals.
c) Never start the engine with a battery charger connected.
d) Always disconnect both battery leads before using a battery charger.
e) The alternator is turned by an engine drivebelt which could cause serious injury if your hands, hair or clothes become entangled in it with the engine running.
f) Because the alternator is connected directly to the battery, it could arc or cause a fire if overloaded or shorted out.
g) Wrap a plastic bag over the alternator and secure it with rubber bands before steam cleaning the engine.

8 Charging system – check

1   If a malfunction occurs in the charging circuit, don't automatically assume the alternator is causing the problem. First check the following items:

a) Check the drivebelt tension and condition (Chapter 1). Replace it if it's worn or deteriorated.
b) Make sure the alternator mounting and adjustment bolts are tight.
c) Inspect the alternator wiring harness and the connectors at the alternator. They must be in good condition and tight.
d) Check the fusible link (if equipped) located between the starter solenoid and alternator. If it's burned, determine the cause, repair the circuit and replace the link (the engine won't start and/or the accessories won't work if the fusible link blows). Sometimes a fusible link may look good, but still be bad. If in doubt, remove it and check it for continuity.
e) Start the engine and check the alternator for abnormal noises (a shrieking or squealing sound indicates a bad bearing).
f) Check the specific gravity of the battery electrolyte. If it's low, charge the battery (doesn't apply to maintenance-free batteries).

g) Make sure the battery is fully charged (one bad cell in a battery can cause overcharging by the alternator).
h) Disconnect the battery cables (negative first, then positive). Inspect the battery posts and the cable clamps for corrosion. Clean them thoroughly if necessary (see Chapter 1). Reconnect the cable to the positive terminal.
i) With the key off, connect a test light between the negative battery post and the disconnected negative cable clamp.
   1) If the test light doesn't come on, reattach the clamp and proceed to the next Step.
   2) If the test light comes on, there's a short (drain) in the electrical system of the vehicle. The short must be repaired before the charging system can be checked.
   3) Disconnect the alternator wiring harness.
      (a) If the light goes out, the alternator is bad.
      (b) If the light stays on, pull each fuse until the light goes out (this will tell you which component is shorted).

2   Using a voltmeter, check the battery voltage with the engine off. If should be approximately 12-volts.

3   Start the engine and check the battery voltage again. It should now be as listed in this Chapter's Specifications.

4   Further testing of this type of alternator must be done by a service station, dealer service department or auto electric shop.

5   If the voltmeter indicates low battery voltage, the alternator is faulty and should be replaced with a new one or there is an open circuit between the alternator and the battery.

6   If the voltage reading is 15-volts or higher and a no charge condition exists, the regulator or field circuit is the problem. Remove the alternator (Section 9) and have it checked by a service station, dealer service department or auto electric shop.

9 Alternator – removal and installation

Refer to illustrations 9.3a and 9.3b

1   Detach the cable from the negative terminal of the battery.
2   Remove the drivebelt (see Chapter 1).
3   Remove the mounting bolts and separate the alternator from the engine **(see illustrations)**.

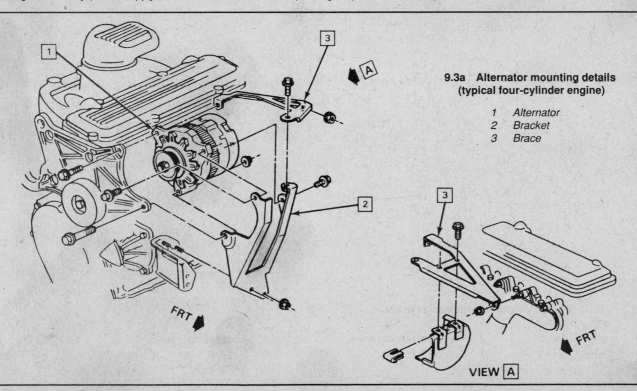

9.3a Alternator mounting details (typical four-cylinder engine)

1   Alternator
2   Bracket
3   Brace

FRT

VIEW A

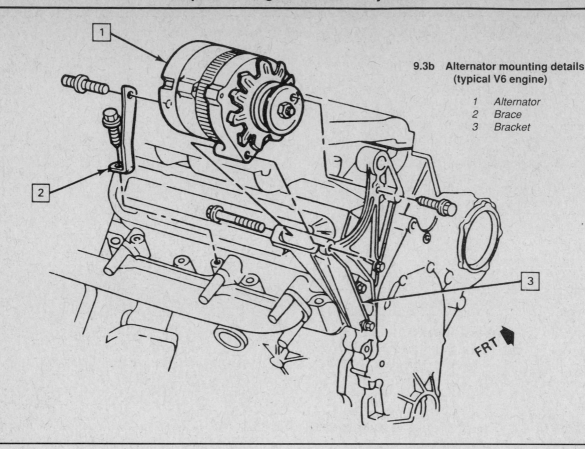

9.3b   Alternator mounting details (typical V6 engine)

1   Alternator
2   Brace
3   Bracket

4   Label and detach the wires from the alternator.
5   If you're replacing the alternator, take the old one with you when purchasing the new one. Make sure the new/rebuilt unit is identical to the old alternator. Look at the terminals – they should be the same in number, size and location as the terminals on the old alternator. Finally, look at the identification numbers – they'll be stamped into the housing or printed on a tag attached to the housing. Make sure the numbers are the same on both alternators.
6   Many new/rebuilt alternators DO NOT have a pulley installed, so you may have to switch the pulley from the old one to the new/rebuilt one.
7   Installation is the reverse of removal.
8   Check the charging voltage to verify proper operation of the alternator (see Section 8).

10   Starting system – general information and precautions

The sole function of the starting system is to turn over the engine quickly enough to allow it to start.
The starting system consists of the battery, the starter motor, the starter solenoid and the wires connecting them. The solenoid is mounted directly on the starter motor. The solenoid/starter motor assembly is installed on the lower part of the engine, next to the transmission bellhousing.
When the ignition key is turned to the Start position, the starter solenoid is actuated through the starter control circuit. The starter solenoid then connects the battery to the starter. The battery supplies the electrical energy to the starter motor, which does the actual work of cranking the engine.
The starter motor on a vehicle equipped with a manual transaxle can only be operated when the clutch pedal is depressed; the starter on a vehicle equipped with an automatic transaxle can only be operated when the selector lever is in Park or Neutral.

Always observe the following precautions when working on the starting system:
a)   Excessive cranking of the starter motor can overheat it and cause serious damage. Never operate the starter motor for more than 30 seconds at a time without pausing to allow it to cool for at least two minutes.
b)   The starter is connected directly to the battery and could arc or cause a fire if mishandled, overloaded or shorted out.
c)   Always detach the cable from the negative terminal of the battery before working on the starting system.

11   Starter motor – testing in vehicle

Note: *Before diagnosing starter problems, make sure the battery is fully charged.*
1   If the starter motor doesn't turn at all when the switch is operated, make sure the shift lever is in Neutral or Park (automatic transaxle) or the clutch pedal is depressed (manual transaxle).
2   Make sure the battery is charged and all cables, both at the battery and starter solenoid terminals, are clean and secure.
3   If the starter motor spins but the engine isn't cranking, the overrunning clutch in the starter motor is slipping and the starter motor must be replaced.
4   If, when the switch is actuated, the starter motor doesn't operate at all but the solenoid clicks, then the problem lies with either the battery, the main solenoid contacts or the starter motor itself (or the engine is seized).
5   If the solenoid plunger can't be heard when the switch is actuated, the battery is bad, the fusible link is burned (the circuit is open) or the solenoid itself is defective.
6   To check the solenoid, connect a jumper lead between the battery (+) and the ignition switch wire terminal (the small terminal) on the solenoid. If the starter motor now operates, the solenoid is okay and the problem is in the ignition switch, neutral start switch or the wiring.

7   If the starter motor still doesn't operate, remove the starter/solenoid assembly for disassembly, testing and repair.

8   If the starter motor cranks the engine at an abnormally slow speed, first make sure the battery is charged and all terminal connections are clean and tight. If the engine is partially seized, or has the wrong viscosity oil in it, it may crank slowly as well.

9   Run the engine until normal operating temperature is reached, then disable the ignition system by removing the ignition fuse.

10   Connect a voltmeter positive lead to the positive battery post and connect the negative lead to the negative post.

11   Crank the engine and take the voltmeter readings as soon as a steady figure is indicated. DO NOT allow the starter motor to turn for more than 30 seconds at a time. A reading of 9-volts or more, with the starter motor turning at normal cranking speed, is normal. If the reading is 9-volts or more but the cranking speed is slow, the motor is faulty. If the reading is less than 9-volts and the cranking speed is slow, the solenoid contacts are probably burned, the starter motor is bad, the battery is discharged or there's a bad connection.

12   Starter motor – removal and installation

Refer to illustrations 12.3a, 12.3b, 12.3c and 12.4

Note: *On some vehicles, it may be necessary to remove the exhaust pipe(s) or frame crossmember to gain access to the starter motor. In extreme cases it may even be necessary to unbolt the mounts and raise the engine slightly to get the starter out.*

1   Detach the cable from the negative terminal of the battery.

2   Raise the front of the vehicle and support it securely on jackstands. Apply the parking brake and block the rear wheels to keep the vehicle from rolling off the jackstands.

3   Remove the mounting bolts and detach the starter. Note the locations of the spacer shims (if used) – they must be reinstalled in the same positions **(see illustrations)**.

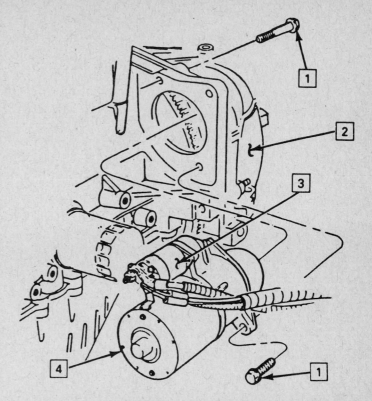

12.3b   Typical starter motor installation on a 2.3 liter four-cylinder (Quad-4) engine

1   Bolt
2   Engine
3   Solenoid
4   Starter motor

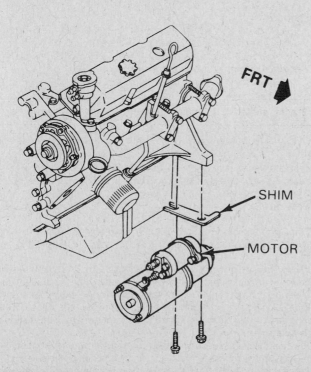

12.3a   Typical starter motor installation on V6 engines

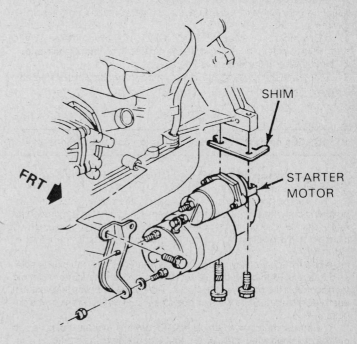

12.3c   Typical starter motor installation on a 2.0 liter four-cylinder engine

12.4   There are three terminals on the end of a typical starter solenoid

A   Battery terminal   C   Motor terminal (M)
B   Switch terminal (S)

4   Working under the vehicle, clearly label, then disconnect the wires from the terminals on the starter motor and solenoid **(see illustration)**.
5   Installation is the reverse of removal.

13.5   To remove the solenoid housing from the starter motor, remove the screws and turn it clockwise

13   Starter solenoid – removal and installation

Refer to illustration 13.5
1   Disconnect the cable from the negative terminal of the battery.
2   Remove the starter motor (Section 12).
3   Disconnect the strap from the solenoid to the starter motor terminal.
4   Remove the screws that secure the solenoid to the starter motor.
5   Twist the solenoid in a clockwise direction to disengage the flange from the starter body **(see illustration)**.
6   Installation is the reverse of removal.

Chapter 6 Emissions control systems

Contents

1 General information

Refer to illustration 1.6

To prevent pollution of the atmosphere from incompletely burned and evaporating gases, and to maintain good driveability and fuel economy, a number of emission control devices are incorporated. They include the:

Fuel control system
Electronic Spark Timing (EST)
Electronic Spark Control (ESC) system
Exhaust Gas Recirculation (EGR) system
Evaporative Emission Control System (EECS)
Positive Crankcase Ventilation (PCV) system
Transaxle Converter Clutch (TCC)
Catalytic converter

All of these systems are linked, directly or indirectly, to the Computer Command Control (CCC or C3) system.

The Sections in this Chapter include general descriptions, checking procedures within the scope of the home mechanic and component replacement procedures (when possible) for each of the systems listed above.

Before assuming an emissions control system is malfunctioning, check the fuel and ignition systems carefully. The diagnosis of some emission control devices requires specialized tools, equipment and training. If checking and servicing become too difficult or if a procedure is beyond the scope of your skills, consult a dealer service department.

This doesn't mean, however, that emission control systems are particularly difficult to maintain and repair. You can quickly and easily perform many checks and do most (if not all) of the regular maintenance at home with common tune-up and hand tools. **Note:** *The most frequent cause of emissions problems is simply a loose or broken vacuum hose or wiring connection, so always check the hose and wiring connections first.*

Pay close attention to any special precautions outlined in this Chapter. It should be noted that the illustrations of the various systems may not exactly match the system installed on your vehicle because of changes made by the manufacturer during production or from year-to-year.

A Vehicle Emissions Control Information label is located in the engine compartment **(see illustration)**. This label contains important emissions specifications and ignition timing procedures, as well as a vacuum hose schematic and emissions components identification guide. When servicing the engine or emissions systems, the VECI label in your particular vehicle should always be checked for up-to-date information. **Note:** *Because of a federally mandated extended warranty which covers the emission control system components (and any components which has a primary purpose other than emission control but have significant effects on emissions), check with your dealer about warranty coverage before working on any emission related systems.* Once the warranty has expired, you may wish to perform some of the components checks and/or replacement procedures in this Chapter to save money.

Note: *On models equipped with the Delco Loc II audio system, be sure the lockout feature is turned off before performing any procedure which requires disconnecting the battery.*

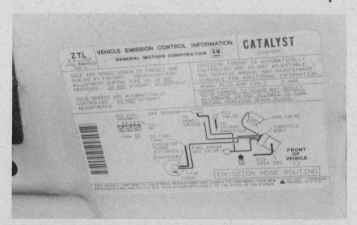

1.6 Look for the VECI label in the engine compartment

2 Computer Command Control (CCC) system and trouble codes

Refer to illustrations 2.1a, 2.1b, 2.1c and 2.5

The Computer Command Control (CCC) system consists of an Electronic Control Module (ECM) and information sensors which monitor various engine functions and send data back to the ECM **(see illustrations)**.

6

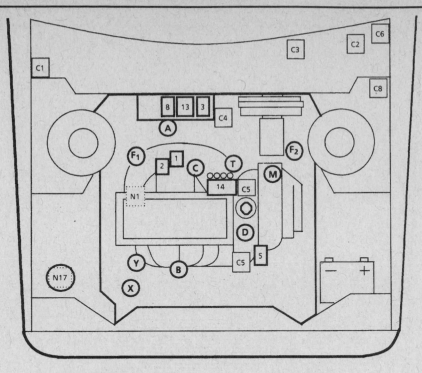

2.1a   Emission control component locations – 2.0/2.2 liter four-cylinder engines through 1991

COMPUTER HARNESS
C1   Electronic Control Module (ECM)
C2   ALDL Diagnostic Connector
C3   "Service Engine Soon" light
C4   ECM Power Fuse
C5   ECM Harness Grounds
C6   Fuse Panel
C8   Fuel Pump Test Connector

NOT ECM CONNECTED
N1   Crankcase Vent Valve (PCV)
N17   Fuel Vapor Canister

CONTROLLED DEVICES
1   Fuel Injector
2   Idle Air Control (IAC) Valve
3   Fuel Pump Relay
5   TCC Solenoid
8   Cooling Fan Relay
13   A/C Compressor Relay
14   Direct Ignition System (DIS) Assembly

INFORMATION SENSORS
A   Manifold Absolute Pressure (MAP) Sensor
B   Oxygen (O$_2$) Sensor
C   Throttle Position Sensor (TPS)

D   Coolant Temperature Sensor (CTS)
F$_1$ Vehicle Speed (Auto Trans.)
F$_2$ Vehicle Speed (Manual Trans.)
M   Park/Neutral (P/N) Switch
T   Manifold Air Temperature (MAT) Sensor (In Air Cleaner Assembly)

X   A/C High Pressure Switch
Y   A/C Low Pressure Switch

   Exhaust Gas Recirculation (EGR) Valve

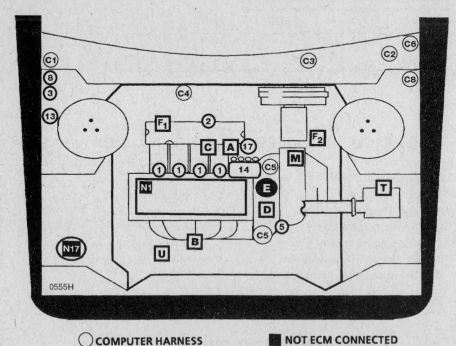

2.1b   1992 Emission control component locations – 2.2 liter four-cylinder engines

INFORMATION SENSORS
A   Manifold Absolute Pressure (MAP) Sensor
B   Oxygen (O$_2$) Sensor
C   Throttle Position Sensor (TPS)
D   Coolant Temperature Sensor (CTS)
F$_1$ Vehicle Speed (Auto Trans.)
F$_2$ Vehicle Speed (Manual Trans.)
M   Park/Neutral (P/N) Switch
T   Intake Air Temperature (IAT) Sensor (On Air Cleaner Assembly)
U   A/C Pressure Sensor

COMPUTER HARNESS
C1   Electronic Control Module (ECM)
C2   ALDL Diagnostic Connector
C3   "Service Engine Soon" Light
C4   Fuel Pump/ECM Power Fuse (Sealed Connector)
C5   ECM Harness Grounds
C6   Fuse Panel
C8   Fuel Pump Test Connector

NOT ECM CONNECTED
N1   Crankcase Vent Valve (PCV)
N17   Fuel Vapor Canister (Beneath Coolant Reservoir)

E   Exhaust Gas Recirculation (EGR) Valve

CONTROLLED DEVICES
1   Fuel Injector
2   Idle Air Control (IAC) Valve
3   Fuel Pump Relay*
5   Torque Converter Clutch (TCC) Solenoid
8   Cooling Fan Relay*
13   A/C Compressor Relay*
14   Direct Ignition System (DIS) Assembly (under intake manifold)
17   Exhaust Gas Recirculation (EGR) Solenoid (Beneath MAP Sensor)

0555H

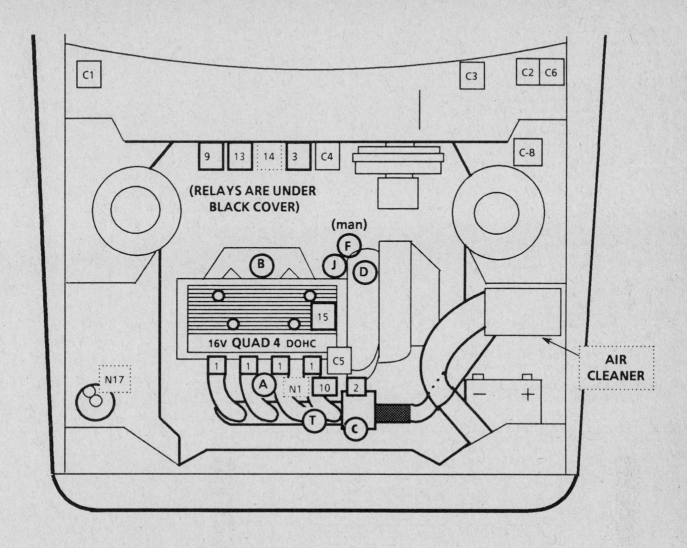

COMPUTER HARNESS

C1 Electronic Control Module (ECM)
C2 ALDL diagnostic connector
C3 "SERVICE ENGINE SOON" light
C4 ECM power (2)
C5 ECM harness ground
C6 Fuse panel
C8 Fuel pump test connector

NOT ECM CONNECTED

N1 Crankcase vent oil/air separator
N17 Fuel vapor canister
N14 A/C High speed fan relay

CONTROLLED DEVICES

1   Fuel injector
2   Idle air control valve
*3   Fuel pump relay
*9   Engine coolant fan relay
10   Canister purge solenoid
*13 A/C compressor relay
*14 A/C High speed fan relay
15   IDI module (under IDI cover)

* Exact order of relays may vary

INFORMATION SENSORS

A Manifold pressure (M.A.P.)
B Exhaust oxygen
C Throttle position
D Coolant temperature
F Vehicle speed
J ESC knock (below manifold)
T Manifold air temperature

2.1c   Emission control component locations – 2.3 liter four-cylinder (Quad-4) engine – on
later models, relays may be located near the right shock tower

2.1d   Typical emission control component locations – V6 engines – note that relays on 1992 models are near the right shock tower

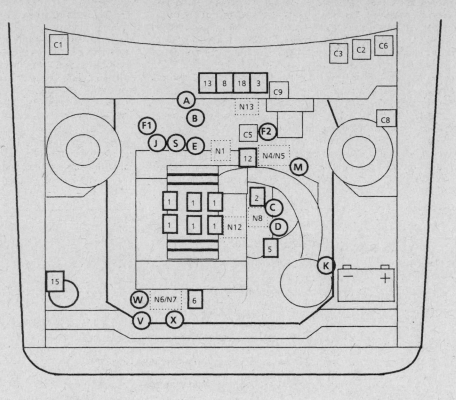

■ COMPUTER HARNESS

- C1   Electronic Control Module (ECM)
- C2   ALDL diagnostic connector
- C3   "SERVICE ENGINE SOON" light
- C5   ECM harness ground
- C6   Fuse panel
- C8   Fuel pump test connector
- C9   Fuel pump / ECM fuse

▦ NOT ECM CONNECTED

- N1   Crankcase vent valve (PCV)
- N4   Engine temp. switch (telltale)
- N5   Engine temp. sensor (gage)
- N6   Oil press. switch (telltale)
- N7   Oil press. sensor (gage)
- N8   Oil press. switch (fuel pump)
- N12   Fuel pressure connector
- N13   12 Volt junction block

■ CONTROLLED DEVICES

- 1   Fuel injector
- 2   Idle air control motor
- 3   Fuel pump relay
- 5   Trans. Converter Clutch connector
- 6   Direct Ignition System (DIS)
- 8   Engine fan relay
- 12   Exhaust Gas Recirc. valve
- 13   A/C compressor relay
- 15   Fuel vapor canister solenoid
- 18   A/C high blower relay

◯ INFORMATION SENSORS

- A   Manifold Pressure (MAP)
- B   Exhaust oxygen
- C   Throttle position
- D   Coolant temperature
- E   Crankshaft Sensor
- F1 Vehicle speed - A/T
- F2 Vehicle speed - M/T
- J   Knock (ESC)
- K   MAT Sensor
- M   P/N switch
- S   P/S pressure switch
- V   A/C Low Press. sw. mounted in Compressor
- W   A/C Hi Press cutout sw.
- X   A/C engine fan control switch

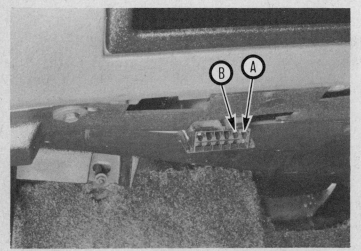

2.5   To use the Assembly Line Communications Link (ALCL), push one end of the jumper wire into the diagnostic terminal (B) and the other end into the ground terminal (A)

The CCC system is analogous to the central nervous system in the human body. The sensors (nerve endings) constantly relay information to the ECM (brain), which processes the data and, if necessary, sends out a command to change the operating parameters of the engine (body).

Here's a specific example of how one portion of this system operates: An oxygen sensor, located in the exhaust manifold, constantly monitors the oxygen content of the exhaust gas. If the percentage of oxygen in the exhaust gas is incorrect, an electrical signal is sent to the ECM. The ECM takes this information, processes it and then sends a command to the fuel injection system, telling it to change the fuel/air mixture. This happens in a fraction of a second and it goes on continuously when the engine is running. The end result is a fuel/air mixture ratio which is constantly maintained at a predetermined ratio, regardless of driving conditions.

One might think that a system which uses an on-board computer and electrical sensors would be difficult to diagnose. This is not necessarily the case. The CCC system has a built-in diagnostic feature which indicates a problem by flashing a Service Engine Soon light on the instrument panel. When this light comes on during normal vehicle operation, a fault in one of the information sensor circuits or the ECM itself has been detected. More importantly, the source of the malfunction is stored in the ECM's memory.

To retrieve this information from the ECM memory, you must use a short jumper wire to ground a diagnostic terminal. This terminal is part of a wiring connector known as the Assembly Line Communications Link (ALCL) **(see illustration)**. The ALCL is located underneath the dashboard, just below the instrument panel and to the left of the center console. To use the ALCL, remove the plastic cover by sliding it toward you. With the connector exposed, push one end of the jumper wire into the diagnostic terminal and the other end into the ground terminal.

When the diagnostic terminal is grounded with the ignition on and the engine stopped, the system will enter the Diagnostic Mode. In this mode the ECM will display a "Code 12" by flashing the Service Engine soon light, indicating the system is operating. A code 12 is simply one flash, followed by a brief pause, then two flashes in quick succession. This code will be flashed three times. If no other codes are stored, Code 12 will continue to flash until the diagnostic terminal ground is removed.

After flashing Code 12 three times, the ECM will display any stored trouble codes. Each code will be flashed three times, then Code 12 will be flashed again, indicating the display of stored trouble codes has been completed.

When the ECM sets a trouble code, the Service Engine Soon light will come on and a trouble code will be stored in memory. If the problem is intermittent, the light will go out after 10-seconds, when the fault goes away. However, the trouble code will stay in the ECM memory until the battery voltage to the ECM is interrupted. Removing battery voltage for 30-seconds will clear all stored trouble codes. Trouble codes should always be cleared after repairs have been completed. **Caution:** *To prevent damage to the ECM, the ignition switch must be off when disconnecting power to the ECM.*

Following is a list of the typical trouble codes which may be encountered while diagnosing the Computer Command Control System. Also included are simplified troubleshooting procedures. If the problem persists after these checks have been made, more detailed service procedures will have to be done by a dealer service department.

Code   Probable cause

Note: *Not all codes will set the MIL (Malfunction Indicator Light)*

Code	Probable cause
12	Diagnostic mode (normal)
13	Oxygen sensor or circuit
14	Coolant sensor or circuit/high temperature indicated
15	Coolant sensor or circuit/low temperature indicated
16	System voltage low (low battery voltage)
16	DIS (Distributorless Ignition System) missing reference circuit (Quad-4)
17	Canshaft Position Sensor or circuit (shorted) or faulty ECM
21	Throttle Position Sensor (TPS) circuit or plunger
22	Throttle Position Sensor (TPS) out of adjustment
21/22 at the same time	Grounded wide-open-throttle (WOT) circuit
23	Manifold Absolute Temperature (MAT) sensor or circuit (fuel-injected models) (low temperature indicated)
24	Vehicle Speed Sensor (VSS) or circuit
25	Manifold Air Temperature (MAT) sensor or circuit (high temperature indicated)
26	Quad Driver Circuit (dealer serviced)
27	Quad Driver Circuit – 2.2L engine (dealer serviced)
27	Gear Switch Diagnosis (dealer serviced)
28	Quad Driver Circuit – 2.2L engine (dealer serviced)
28	Transmission Range Switch Error
32	Digital EGR circuit (3.1L)
33	Manifold Absolute Pressure (MAP) sensor or circuit (low vacuum)
33	MAF (Mass Air Flow) sensor or circuit
33	Manifold Absolute Pressure (MAP) sensor signal voltage high
34	Manifold Absolute Pressure (MAP) sensor signal voltage low
34	MAF (Mass Air Flow) sensor or circuit
35	Idle Speed Control (ISC) switch or circuit (shorted)
36	Distributorless Ignition System (DIS) (Quad-4)

6

Code	Probable cause
36	Ignition Control 24X Signal Circuit Error – possible faulty crankshaft position sensor or circuit
37	Brake switch stuck on
41	Cylinder select error
41	Quad 4 engine 1X reference – check ignition module/ECM wiring
41	Electronic Spark Timing (EST) circuit
42	Electronic Spark Timing (EST) bypass circuit
43	Electronic Spark Control unit (ESC) or knock sensor error
44	Oxygen sensor or circuit – lean exhaust
45	Oxygen sensor or circuit – rich exhaust
46	Vehicle Anti-Theft System (VATS)
51	PROM, MEM-CAL or ECM problem (3.1L)
52	CALPAK or ECM problem (3.1L)
53	System over-voltage (ECM over 17.7 volts)
53	Alternator voltage out of range
54	Fuel pump circuit (3.1L)
58	Transmission code – high temperature (sensor or signal wire grounded)
59	Transmission code – low temperature (sensor or signal wire open)
61	Oxygen sensor signal faulty
62	Transaxle gear switch signal circuits (3.1L V6/Quad-4 engines)
63	MAP sensor voltage high
64	MAP sensor voltage low
65	Fuel Injection Circuit (Quad-4 engines)
66	Air conditioning pressure sensor circuit (Low Pressure)
70	A/C refrigerant pressure sensor circuit (High Pressure)
72	Transmission code – Vehicle Speed Sensor (VSS) signal loss (4L60-E)
75	Digital EGR #1 Solenoid (error)
76	Digital EGR #2 Solenoid (error)
77	Digital EGR #3 Solenoid (error)
79	Transmission fluid temperature high (4L60-E)
80	Transmission component error
82	Ignition control 3X signal error – possible faulty ignition module, crank sensor, camshaft sensor or circuit
85	PROM error (faulty or incorrect calibration)
86	Analog/Digital PCM error
87	Electronically Erasable Programmable Read Only Memory (EEPROM) Error
90	Torque Converter Clutch (TCC) error
96	Transmission System Voltage Low
98	Invalid PCM Program
99	Invalid PCM Program

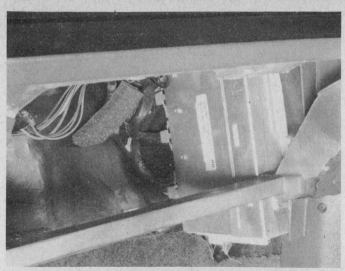

3.4   To remove the Electronic Control Module (ECM) from the vehicle, remove the glove box to gain access to the mounting bolts

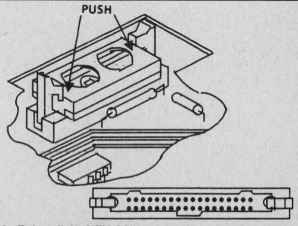

3.7   A typical electronic control module (ECM)

1	ECM assembly	3	MEM-CAL access cover
2	MEM-CAL unit		

---

3   Electronic Control Module (ECM)/MEM-CAL

ECM replacement

Refer to illustration 3.4

Caution: *The ignition switch must be turned off when pulling out or plugging in the connectors to prevent damage to the ECM.*

1   The Electronic Control Module (ECM) is located under the instrument panel.

2   Disconnect the negative battery cable from the battery.

3   Remove the glove box to gain access to the ECM.

4   Remove the retaining bolts **(see illustration)** and carefully slide the ECM out far enough to unplug the electrical connector.

5   Unplug both electrical connectors from the ECM.

6   Installation is the reverse of removal.

MEM-CAL replacement

Refer to illustrations 3.7, 3.9 and 3.12

7   To allow one model of ECM to be used for many different vehicles, a device called a MEM-CAL (Memory and calibration) is used **(see illustration)**. The MEM-CAL is located inside the ECM and contains information

on the vehicle's weight, engine, transaxle, axle ratio, etc. One ECM part number can be used by many GM vehicles but the MEM-CAL is very specific and must be used only in the vehicle for which it was designed. For this reason, it's essential to check the latest parts book and Service Bulletin information for the correct part number when replacing a MEM-CAL. An ECM purchased at a dealer doesn't come with a MEM-CAL. The MEM-CAL from the old ECM must be carefully removed and installed in the new ECM.

8   Remove the MEM-CAL access cover.

9   Using two fingers, push both retaining clips back away from the MEM-CAL **(see illustration)**. At the same time, grasp the MEM-CAL at both ends and lift it up out of the socket. Don't remove the MEM-CAL cover itself. **Caution:** *Use of unapproved removal or installation methods may damage the MEM-CAL or socket.*

10   Verify that the numbers on the old ECM and new ECM match up (or that the numbers of the old and new MEM-CALs match up, depending on the component[s] being replaced).

11   To install the MEM-CAL, press only on the ends.

12   The small notches in the MEM-CAL must be aligned with the small notches in the MEM-CAL socket. Press on the ends of the MEM-CAL until the retaining clips snap into the ends of the MEM-CAL. Don't press on the middle of the MEM-CAL – press only on the ends **(see illustration)**.

6

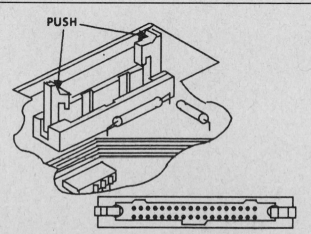

3.9   Using two fingers, push the retaining clips (arrows) away from the MEM-CAL and simultaneously grasp it at both ends and lift it up, out of the socket

3.12   To install the MEM-CAL, press only on the ends (arrows) until the retaining clips snap into the ends of the MEM-CAL – make sure the notches in the MEM-CAL are aligned with the small notches in the socket

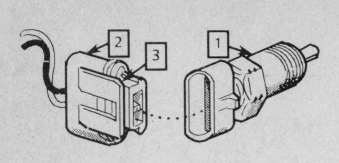

4.2   A typical engine coolant temperature sensor (1) harness connector (2) has a locking tab (3) that must be released to unplug the connector

4.3   To prevent coolant leakage, be sure to wrap the temperature sensor threads with Teflon tape before installation

13   The remainder of the installation is the reverse of removal.
14   Once the new MEM-CAL is installed in the old ECM (or the old MEM-CAL is installed in the new ECM), check the installation to verify its been installed properly by doing the following test:
   a) Turn the ignition switch on.
   b) Enter the diagnostics mode at the ALCL (see Section 2).
   c) Allow Code 12 to flash four times to verify that no other codes are present. This indicates the MEM-CAL is installed properly and the ECM is functioning properly.
15   If trouble codes 41, 42, 43, 51 or 52 occur, or if the Service Engine soon light is on constantly but isn't flashing any codes, the MEM-CAL is either not completely seated or it's defective. If it's not seated, press firmly on the ends of the MEM-CAL. If it's necessary to remove the MEM-CAL, follow the above Steps again.

---

4   Information sensors

Refer to illustrations 4.2, 4.3, 4.5, 4.7, 4.10, 4.12 and 4.24
Note: See the component location illustrations in Section 2 for the location of the following information sensors.

Engine coolant temperature sensor

1   The coolant sensor is a thermistor (a resistor which varies the value of

its voltage output in accordance with temperature changes). A failure in the coolant sensor circuit should set either a Code 14 or a Code 15. These codes indicate a failure in the coolant temperature circuit, so the appropriate solution to the problem will be either repair of a wire or replacement of the sensor.
2   To remove the sensor, release the locking tab **(see illustration)**, unplug the electrical connector, then carefully unscrew the sensor. **Caution:** *Handle the coolant sensor with care. Damage to this sensor will affect the operation of the entire fuel injection system.*
3   Before installing the new sensor, wrap the threads with Teflon sealing tape to prevent leakage and thread corrosion **(see illustration)**.
4   Installation is the reverse of removal.

Manifold Absolute Pressure (MAP) sensor

5   The Manifold Absolute Pressure (MAP) sensor **(see illustration)** monitors the intake manifold pressure changes resulting from changes in engine load and speed and converts the information into a voltage output. The ECM uses the MAP sensor to control fuel delivery and ignition timing.
6   A failure in the MAP sensor circuit should set a Code 33,34,63 or 64.
7   Other than checking for loose hoses and electrical connections, the only service possible is unit replacement if diagnosis indicates it's faulty **(see illustration)**.

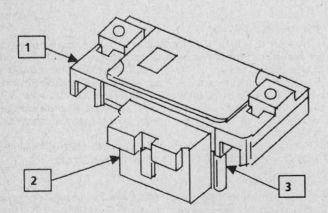

4.5   Typical Manifold Absolute Pressure (MAP) sensor

  1   Sensor assembly   *3   Manifold vacuum tube*
  2   Electrical connector

4.7   Typical MAP sensor installation

  1   MAP sensor assembly   *3   MAP sensor vacuum line*
  2   Mounting screws   *4   MAP sensor electrical connector*

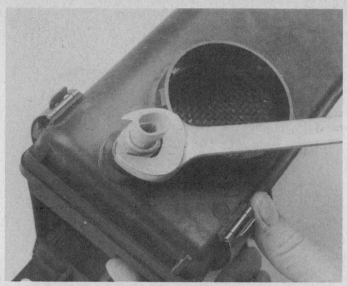

4.10 Removing a MAT sensor from the air cleaner housing (air cleaner housing removed from engine for clarity)

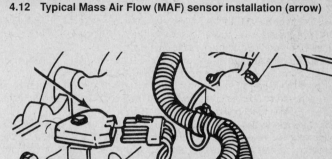

4.12 Typical Mass Air Flow (MAF) sensor installation (arrow)

Manifold Air Temperature (MAT) sensor

8   The Manifold Air Temperature (MAT) sensor, located in the air cleaner housing or air duct, is a thermistor (a resistor which changes the value of its voltage output as the temperature changes). The ECM uses the MAT sensor signal to delay EGR until the manifold air temperature reaches 40-degrees F.

9   A failure in the MAT sensor circuit should set either a Code 23 or a Code 25.

10   To remove a MAT sensor, unplug the electrical connector and remove the sensor with a wrench **(see illustration)**.

11   Installation is the reverse of removal.

Mass Air Flow (MAF) sensor

12   The Mass Air Flow (MAF) sensor, which is located in a housing between the air cleaner housing and the intake duct **(see illustration)**, measures the amount of air entering the engine. The ECM uses this information to control fuel delivery. A large quantity of air indicates acceleration, while a small quantity indicates deceleration or idle.

13   If the sensor fails at a high frequency, a Code 33 should set and if it fails at a low frequency or power is lost to the sensor, a Code 34 should set. A code 44 or 45 may also result if the MAF sensor is faulty.

14   To replace the MAF sensor, unplug the electrical connector, remove the clamps and carefully lift from the vehicle.

15   Installation is the reverse of removal.

Oxygen sensor

16   The oxygen sensor is mounted in the exhaust system where it can monitor the oxygen content of the exhaust gas stream.

17   By monitoring the voltage output of the oxygen sensor, the ECM will know what fuel mixture command to give the injector.

18   An open in the oxygen sensor circuit should set a Code 13. A low voltage in the circuit should set a Code 44. A high voltage in the circuit should set a Code 45. Codes 44 and 45 may also be set as a result of fuel system problems.

19   See Section 5 for the oxygen sensor replacement procedure.

Throttle Position Sensor (TPS)

20   The Throttle Position Sensor (TPS) is located on the TBI unit or on the lower end of the throttle shaft.

21   By monitoring the output voltage from the TPS, the ECM can determine fuel delivery based on throttle valve angle (driver demand). A broken or loose TPS can cause intermittent bursts of fuel from the injector and an unstable idle because the ECM thinks the throttle is moving.

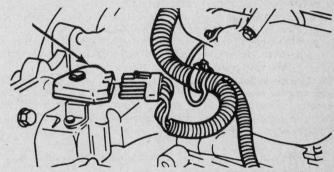

4.24 The Park/Neutral switch (arrow) is located on the upper rear part of the automatic transaxle

6

22   A problem in any of the TPS circuits will set either a Code 21 or 22. Once a trouble code is set, the ECM will use an artificial default value for TPS and some vehicle performance will return.

23   If the TPS must be replaced, the complete procedure is contained in Chapter 4.

Park/Neutral switch

24   The Park/Neutral (P/N) switch, located on the rear upper part of the automatic transaxle **(see illustration)**, indicates to the ECM when the transaxle is in Park or Neutral. This information is used for Transaxle Converter Clutch (TCC), Exhaust Gas Recirculation (EGR) and Idle Air Control (IAC) valve operation. **Caution:** *The vehicle should not be driven with the Park/Neutral switch disconnected because idle quality will be adversely affected and a false Code 24 (failure in the Vehicle Speed Sensor circuit) may be set.*

25   For more information regarding the P/N switch, which is part of the Neutral/start and back-up light switch assembly, see Chapter 7.

A/C On signal

26   This signal tells the ECM the A/C selector switch is in the On position and the high side low pressure switch is closed. The ECM uses this information to turn on the A/C and adjust the idle speed when the air conditioning system is working. If this signal isn't available to the ECM, idle may be rough, especially when the A/C compressor cycles.

27   Diagnosis of the circuit between the A/C On signal and the ECM should be left to a dealer service department.

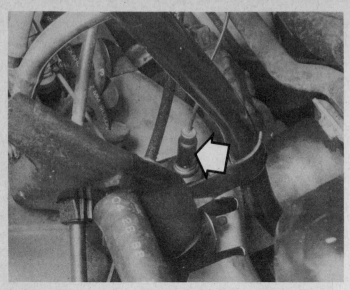

5.1   The oxygen sensor is located in the exhaust manifold

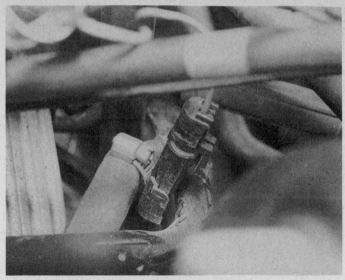

5.10   Typical electrical connector for an oxygen sensor pigtail lead – if you have trouble finding the connector, locate the sensor first, then trace the pigtail lead to the connector

Vehicle Speed Sensor (VSS)

28   The Vehicle Speed Sensor (VSS) sends a pulsing voltage signal to the ECM, which the ECM converts to miles per hour. This sensor controls the operation of the TCC system.

Crankshaft Sensor

29   The crankshaft sensor sends a signal to the ECM to tell it both engine rpm and crankshaft position. See Electronic Spark Timing (Section 6), for further information.

5   Oxygen sensor

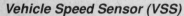

Refer to illustrations 5.1 and 5.10

General description

1   The oxygen sensor, which is located in the exhaust manifold **(see illustration)**, monitors the oxygen content of the exhaust gas stream. The oxygen content in the exhaust reacts with the oxygen sensor to produce a voltage output which varies from 0.1-volt (high oxygen, lean mixture) to 0.9-volt (low oxygen, rich mixture). The ECM constantly monitors this variable voltage output to determine the ratio of oxygen to fuel in the mixture. The ECM alters the fuel/air mixture ratio by controlling the pulse width (open time) of the fuel injectors. A mixture ratio of 14.7 parts air to 1 part fuel is the ideal mixture ratio for minimizing exhaust emissions, thus allowing the catalytic converter to operate at maximum efficiency. It's this ratio of 14.7 to 1 which the ECM and the oxygen sensor attempt to maintain at all times.

2   The oxygen sensor produces no voltage when it's below its normal operating temperature of about 600-degrees F. During this initial period before warm-up, the ECM operates in open loop mode.

3   If the engine reaches normal operating temperature and/or has been running for two or more minutes, and if the oxygen sensor is producing a steady signal voltage between 0.35 and 0.55-volt, even though the TPS indicates the engine isn't at idle, the ECM will set a Code 13.

4   A delay of two minutes or more between engine start-up and normal operation of the sensor, followed by a low voltage signal or a short in the sensor circuit, will cause the ECM to set a Code 44. If a high voltage signal occurs, the ECM will set a Code 45.

5   When any of the above codes occur, the ECM operates in the open loop mode – that is it controls fuel delivery in accordance with a programmed default value instead of feedback information from the oxygen sensor.

6   The proper operation of the oxygen sensor depends on four conditions:

a)   Electrical – The low voltages generated by the sensor depend upon good, clean connections which should be checked whenever a malfunction of the sensor is suspected or indicated.

b)   Outside air supply – The sensor is designed to allow air circulation to its internal areas. Whenever the sensor is removed and installed or replaced, make sure the air passages aren't restricted.

c)   Proper operating temperature – The ECM will not react to the sensor signal until the sensor reaches approximately 600-degrees F. This factor must be taken into consideration when evaluating the performance of the sensor.

d)   Unleaded fuel – The use of unleaded fuel is essential for proper operation of the sensor. Make sure the fuel you're using is this type.

7   In addition to observing the above conditions, special care must be taken whenever the sensor is serviced.

a)   The oxygen sensor has a permanently attached pigtail and connector which should not be removed from the sensor. Damage or removal of the pigtail or connector can adversely affect operation of the sensor.

b)   Grease, dirt and other contaminants should be kept away from the electrical connector and the louvered end of the sensor.

c)   Don't use cleaning solvents of any kind on the oxygen sensor.

d)   Don't drop or handle the sensor roughly.

e)   The silicone boot must be installed in the correct position to prevent the boot from being melted and allow the sensor to operate properly.

Replacement

Note: *Because it's installed in the exhaust manifold or pipe, which contracts when cool, the oxygen sensor may be very difficult to loosen when the engine is cold. Rather than risk damage to the sensor (assuming you're planning to reuse it in another manifold or pipe), start and run the engine for a minute or two, then shut it off. Be careful not to burn yourself during the following procedure.*

8   Disconnect the cable from the negative terminal of the battery.

9   Raise the vehicle and support it securely on jackstands.

10   Carefully disconnect the electrical connector **(see illustration)**.

11   Note the position of the silicone boot, if equipped, and carefully unscrew the sensor from the exhaust manifold. **Caution:** *Excessive force may damage the threads.*

12   Anti-seize compound must be used on the threads of the sensor to facilitate future removal. The threads of a new sensor will already be

6.2   The crankshaft sensor is located on the engine block near the oil pan

7.3   The Electronic Spark Control (ESC) knock sensor (arrow) is located on the engine block

coated with it, but if an old sensor is removed and reinstalled, recoat the threads.

13   Install the sensor and tighten it securely.

14   Reconnect the electrical connector of the pigtail lead to the main engine wiring harness.

15   Lower the vehicle and reconnect the cable to the negative terminal of the battery.

---

6   Electronic Spark Timing (EST)

Refer to illustration 6.2

1   To provide improved engine performance, fuel economy and control of exhaust emissions, the Electronic Control Module (ECM) controls spark advance (ignition timing) with the Electronic Spark Timing (EST) system.

2   The ECM receives a reference pulse from the crankshaft sensor **(see illustration)**, which indicates both engine rpm and crankshaft position. The ECM then determines the proper spark advance for the engine operating conditions and sends an EST pulse to the DIS module. A fault in the EST system will usually set a trouble code 42.

---

7   Electronic Spark Control (ESC) system

Refer to illustration 7.3

General description

1   Irregular octane levels in modern gasoline can cause detonation in an engine. Detonation is sometimes referred to as "spark knock."

2   The Electronic Spark Control (ESC) system is designed to retard spark timing up to 20-degrees to reduce spark knock in the engine. This allows the engine to use maximum spark advance to improve driveability and fuel economy.

3   The ESC knock sensor, which is located on the engine block **(see illustration)**, sends a voltage signal of 8 to 10-volts to the ECM when no spark knock is occurring and the ECM provides normal advance. When the knock sensor detects abnormal vibration (spark knock), the ESC module turns off the circuit to the ECM and the voltage at ECM drops to zero volts. The ECM then retards the timing until spark knock is eliminated.

4   Failure of the ESC knock sensor signal or loss of ground at the ESC module will cause the signal to the ECM to remain high. This condition will result in the ECM controlling the EST as if no spark knock is occurring.

Therefore, no retard will occur and spark knock may become severe under heavy engine load conditions. At this point, the ECM will set a Code 43.

5   Loss of the ESC signal to the ECM will cause the ECM to constantly retard EST. This will result in sluggish performance and cause the ECM to set a Code 43.

ESC sensor replacement

6   Detach the cable from the negative terminal of the battery.

7   Disconnect the wiring harness connector from the ESC sensor.

8   Remove the ESC sensor from the block.

9   Installation is the reverse of the removal procedure.

---

8   Exhaust Gas Recirculation (EGR) system

Refer to illustrations 8.5, 8.11, 8.22a, 8.22b and 8.22c

General description

1   The Exhaust Gas Recirculation (EGR) system is used to lower NOx (oxides of nitrogen) emission levels caused by high combustion temperatures. It does this by decreasing combustion temperature. The main element of the system is the EGR valve, which feeds small amounts of exhaust gas back into the combustion chamber.

2   The EGR valve is usually open during warm engine operation and anytime the engine is running above idle speed. The amount of gas recirculated is controlled by variations in vacuum and exhaust back pressure.

3   There are three types of EGR valves. Their names refer to the means by which they are controlled:

Digital EGR valve
Negative backpressure EGR valve
Integrated Electronic EGR valve

Digital EGR valve

4   The digital EGR valve feeds small amounts of exhaust gas back into the intake manifold and then into the combustion chamber.

5   The digital EGR valve is designed to accurately supply EGR to an engine, independent of intake manifold vacuum. The valve controls EGR flow from the exhaust to the intake manifold through three orifices, which increment in size, to produce seven combinations. When a solenoid is energized, the armature, with attached shaft and swivel pintle, is lifted, opening the orifice. The flow accuracy is dependent on metering orifice size only, which results in improved control **(see illustration)**.

6   The digital EGR valve is opened by the ECM, grounding each solenoid circuit. this activates the solenoid, raises the pintle, and allows ex-

6

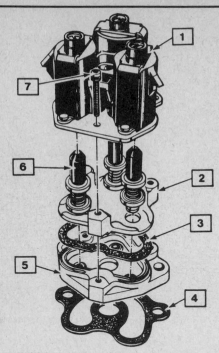

8.5   Exploded view of a typical digital EGR valve

1	Solenoid and mounting plate assembly	4	Insulator gasket
2	EGR base plate	5	EGR base
3	EGR base gasket	6	Armature assembly
		7	Screw

8.11   To check an EGR valve diaphragm for proper operation, warm up the engine and, using a rag to protect your fingers, push up on the diaphragm – the engine should stumble or stall

haust gas flow into the intake manifold. The exhaust gas then moves with the air/fuel mixture into the combustion chamber.

Negative backpressure EGR valve

7   On the negative back pressure EGR valve, the diaphragm on this valve has an internal vacuum bleed hole which is held closed by a small spring when there is no exhaust back pressure. Engine vacuum opens the EGR valve against the pressure of a large spring. When manifold vacuum combines with negative exhaust backpressure, the vacuum bleed hole opens and the EGR valve closes.

Integrated electronic EGR valve

8   The integrated electronic EGR valve functions like a port valve with a remote vacuum regulator, except the regulator and a pintle position sensor are sealed in the black plastic cover. The regulator and the position sensor are not serviceable.

9   This valve has a vacuum regulator, to which the ECM provides variable current. This variable current produces the desired EGR flow using inputs from the mass air flow (MAF) sensor, coolant temperature sensor and engine rpm.

Checking

Negative backpressure EGR valve

10   Hold the top of the EGR valve and try to rotate it back-and-forth. If play is felt, replace the valve.

11   If no play is felt, place the transaxle in Neutral (manual) or Park (automatic), run the engine at idle until it warms up to at least 195-degrees F and push up on the underside of the EGR valve diaphragm **(see illustration)**.

12   The rpm should drop. If there's no change in rpm, clean the EGR passages. If there's still no change in rpm, replace the valve.

13   If the rpm drops, check for movement of the EGR valve diaphragm as the rpm is changed from approximately 2000 rpm to idle. If the diaphragm moves, there is no problem.

14   If the diaphragm doesn't move, check the vacuum signal at the EGR valve as the engine rpm is changed from approximately 2000 rpm to idle.

15   If the vacuum is over six inches, replace the EGR valve. If it's under six inches, check the vacuum hoses for restrictions, leaks and poor connections.

Integrated electronic EGR valve

16   With the ignition off, install a vacuum pump, apply vacuum and the valve should not move. Repeat the test with the ignition switch on. The valve should not move.

17   Ground the diagnostic terminal (see Section 3) and repeat the test. The valve should move and should be able to hold vacuum.

18   Start the engine and lift the EGR diaphragm using a rag to protect your fingers. The idle should roughen. The EGR assembly is okay.

19   Due to the complexity and the interrelationship with ECM, any further checks should be left to a dealer service department.

Digital EGR valve

20   A special "scan" tool is needed to check this valve and should be left to a dealer service department.

Component replacement

EGR valve

21   Disconnect the vacuum hose from the EGR valve and disconnect the electrical connector, if equipped.

22   Remove the nuts or bolts which secure the valve to the intake manifold or adapter **(see illustrations)**.

23   Separate the EGR valve from the engine.

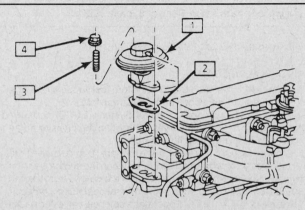

8.22a   The EGR valve assembly on a 2.0/2.2 liter four-cylinder engine

1	EGR valve	3	Stud
2	Gasket	4	Nut

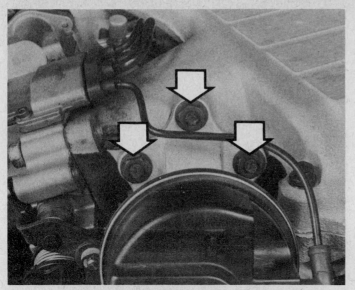

8.22b   On a 2.8 liter V6, remove the retaining bolts (arrows), then . . .

8.22c   . . . disconnect the EGR pipe from the exhaust manifold

EGR valve cleaning

24   Inspect the valve pintle for deposits.
25   Depress the valve diaphragm and check for deposits around the valve seat area.
26   Use a wire brush to carefully clean deposits from the pintle.
27   Remove any deposits from the valve outlet with a screwdriver.
28   If EGR passages in the intake manifold have an excessive build-up of deposits, the passages should be cleaned. Care should be taken to ensure that all loose particles are completely removed to prevent them from clogging the EGR valve or from being ingested into the engine. **Note:** *It's a good idea to place a rag in the passage opening to keep debris from entering while cleaning the manifold.*
29   Using a wire wheel, buff the exhaust deposits off the mounting surface.
30   Clean the mounting surfaces of the EGR valve. Remove all traces of old gasket material.
31   Install the new EGR valve, with a new gasket, on the intake manifold or adapter.
32   Installation is the reverse of removal.

---

9   Evaporative Emission Control System (EECS)

Refer to illustrations 9.2a, 9.2b, 9.2c, 9.10 and 9.13

General description

1   This system is designed to trap and store fuel vapors that evaporate from the fuel tank, throttle body and intake manifold.
2   The Evaporative Emission Control System (EECS) consists of a charcoal-filled canister and the lines connecting the canister to the fuel tank and ported vacuum **(see illustrations)**.
3   Fuel vapors are transferred from the fuel tank, throttle body and intake manifold to a canister where they're stored when the engine isn't running. When the engine is running, the fuel vapors are purged from the canister by intake air flow and consumed in the normal combustion process.
4   On some engines, the ECM operates a solenoid valve (located on top of the canister) which controls vacuum to the purge valve in the charcoal canister. Under cold engine or idle conditions, the solenoid is turned on by the ECM, which closes the valve and blocks vacuum to the canister purge valve. The ECM turns off the solenoid valve and allows purge when the engine is warm.

6

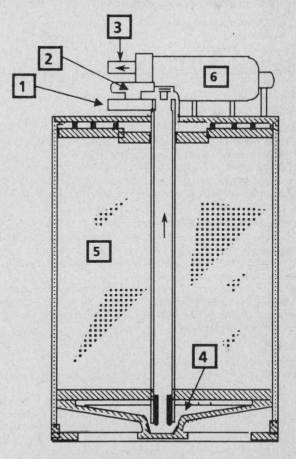

9.2a   Typical evaporative canister – V6 engine

 1   Tank tube
 2   Inlet air
 3   Purge tube
 4   Liquid fuel area
 5   Vapor storage area
 6   Purge solenoid

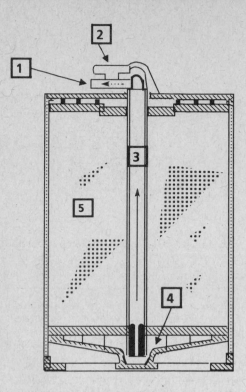

9.2b   Typical evaporative canister – 2.0 liter four-cylinder engine

1   Purge tube
2   Vent
3   Purge vapors
4   Liquid fuel area
5   Vapor storage area

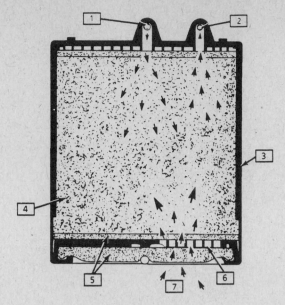

9.2c   Typical evaporative canister – 2.2 and 2.3 liter four-cylinder engines

1	Vapor from fuel tank	5	Filter
2	Canister purge vacuum	6	Grid
3	Canister body	7	Air flow
4	Carbon		during purge

Checking

5   Poor idle, stalling and poor driveability can be caused by an inopera-tive purge valve, a damaged canister, split or cracked hoses or hoses connected to the wrong tubes.

6   Evidence of fuel loss or fuel odor can be caused by liquid fuel leaking from fuel lines or the TBI, a cracked or damaged canister, an inoperative purge valve, disconnected, misrouted, kinked, deteriorated or damaged vapor or control hoses or an improperly seated air cleaner or air cleaner gasket.

7   Inspect each hose attached to the canister for kinks, leaks and cracks along its entire length. Repair or replace as necessary.

8   Inspect the canister. If it's cracked or damaged, replace it.

9   Look for fuel leaking from the bottom of the canister. If fuel is leaking, replace the canister and check the hoses and hose routing.

10   On models so equipped, check the filter at the bottom of the canister and replace if it's dirty, plugged or damaged **(see illustration)**.

11   Any further testing should be left to a dealer service department.

Component replacement

12   Detach the cable from the negative terminal of the battery.

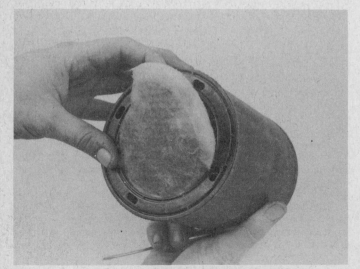

9.10   To replace the filter, simply remove it and install another one

9.13   Overhead view of the evaporative canister showing the solenoid electrical connector and the canister retaining bolt

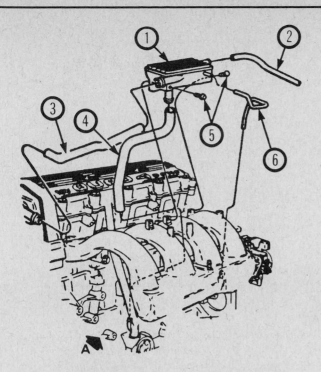

10.5 Typical Quad-4 engine oil/air separator

1   *Oil/air separator*
2   *Intake duct to air cleaner hose*
3   *Chain housing to separator hose*
4   *Fill tube to separator hose*
5   *Retaining bolts*
6   *Intake to separator hose*

13   Unplug the solenoid electrical connectors, if equipped **(see illustration)**.
14   Clearly label, then detach the vacuum hoses from the canister.
15   Installation is the reverse of removal.

10   Positive Crankcase Ventilation (PCV) system

General description

All models except Quad-4 engine

1   The Positive Crankcase Ventilation (PCV) system reduces hydrocarbon emissions by scavenging crankcase vapors. It does this by circulating fresh air from the air cleaner through the crankcase, where it mixes with blow-by gases and is then rerouted through a PCV valve to the intake manifold.
2   The main components of the PCV system are the PCV valve, a fresh air filtered inlet and the vacuum hoses connecting these two components with the engine.
3   To maintain idle quality, the PCV valve restricts the flow when the intake manifold vacuum is high. If abnormal operating conditions arise, the system is designed to allow excessive amounts of blow-by gases to flow back through the crankcase vent tube into the air cleaner to be consumed by normal combustion.
4   Checking and replacement of the PCV valve and filter is covered in Chapter 1.

Quad-4 engine only

Refer to illustration 10.5

5   The Quad-4 engine uses a crankcase ventilation (CV) system to provide scavenging of crankcase vapors. Blow-by gases are passed through a crankcase ventilation oil/air separator into the intake manifold **(see illustration)**.

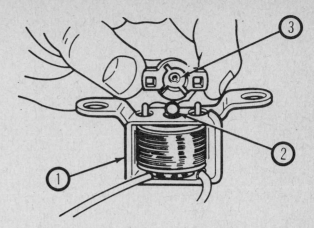

11.2 Typical Transaxle Converter Clutch (TCC) device

1   *TCC solenoid*   3   *Check ball seat*
2   *Check ball*

6   The oil/air separator causes oil, which may be suspended in the blow-by gases, to be separated and allows it to drain back to the crankcase through a hose.
7   If the CV system becomes plugged, it must be replaced as a unit.

Oil/air separator replacement

8   Label and remove all hoses from the oil/air separator.
9   Remove the mounting bolts and detach it from the vehicle.
10   Installation is the reverse of removal.

11   Transaxle Converter Clutch (TCC)

Refer to illustration 11.2

General description

1   The Transaxle Converter Clutch (TCC) uses a solenoid-operated valve in the automatic transaxle to mechanically couple the engine flywheel to the output shaft of the transmission through the torque converter. This reduces the slippage losses in the converter, reducing emissions because engine rpm at any given speed is reduced. It also increases fuel economy.
2   For the converter clutch to operate properly, two conditions must be met:
   a) The engine must be warmed up before the clutch can apply. The engine coolant temperature sensor (see Section 4) tells the ECM when the engine is at operating temperature.
   b) The vehicle must be traveling at the necessary minimum speed to raise the pressure to the level necessary to apply the valve. If the hydraulic pressure is correct, the ECM signals the solenoid to apply the converter clutch **(see illustration)**.
3   After the converter clutch applies, the ECM uses the information from the TPS to release the clutch when the vehicle is accelerating or decelerating at a certain rate.
4   Another switch used in the TCC circuit is a brake switch, which opens the power supply to the TCC solenoid when the brake is applied.
5   A Third gear switch is placed in series on the battery side of the TCC solenoid to prevent TCC application until the transmission is in Third gear.

Checking

6   If the converter clutch is applied at all times, the engine will stall immediately, just like a manual transaxle with the clutch applied.
7   If the converter clutch doesn't apply, fuel economy may be lower than expected. If the Vehicle Speed Sensor (VSS) (see Section 4) fails, the TCC will not apply.
8   A TCC-equipped transaxle has different operating characteristics than an automatic transaxle without TCC. If you detect a "chuggle" or "surge" condition, perform the following check.

6

9   Install a tachometer.
10   Drive the vehicle until normal operating temperature is reached, then maintain a 50 to 55 mph speed.
11   Lightly touch the brake pedal and check it for a slight bumpy sensation, indicating the TCC is releasing. A slight increase in rpm should also be noted.
12   Release the brake and check for reapplication of the converter clutch and a slight decrease in engine rpm.
13   If the TCC fails to perform satisfactorily during this test, take the vehicle to a dealer service department to have the TCC serviced.

12   Catalytic converter

Refer to illustrations 12.1a and 12.1b

General description

1   The catalytic converter is an emission control device added to the exhaust system to reduce pollutants from the exhaust gas stream. There are two types of converters used. One converter contains pellets coated with the three way catalysts while the monolith converter contains a honeycomb mesh which is also coated with three catalysts. The coating on the three way catalyst contains platinum rhodium, which lowers the levels of oxides of nitrogen (NOx) as well as hydrocarbons (HC) and carbon monoxide (CO) **(see illustrations)**.

Checking

2   The test equipment for a catalytic converter is expensive and highly sophisticated. If you suspect the converter is malfunctioning, take it to a dealer service department or authorized emissions inspection facility for diagnosis and repair.
3   Whenever the vehicle is raised for servicing of underbody components, check the converter for leaks, corrosion and other damage. If damage is discovered, the converter should be replaced.
4   Because the converter is welded to the exhaust system, converter replacement requires removal of the exhaust pipe assembly (see Chapter 4). Take the vehicle, or the exhaust system, to a dealer service department or a muffler shop.

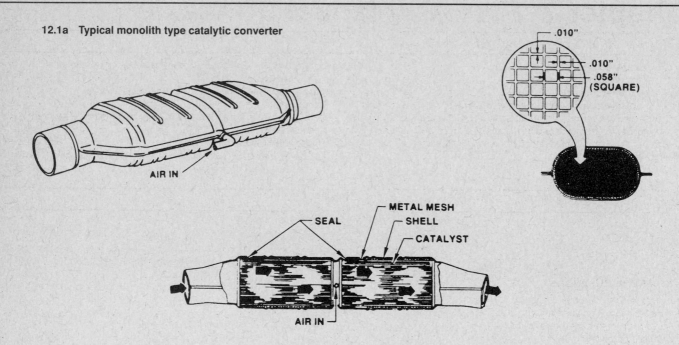

12.1a   Typical monolith type catalytic converter

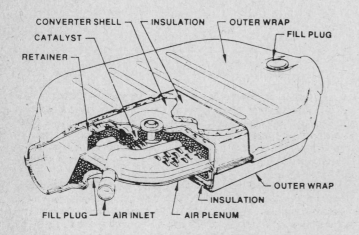

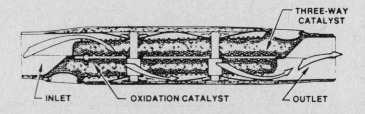

12.1b   Typical pellet type catalytic converter

Chapter 7 Part A   Manual transaxle

Contents

Specifications

General
Lubricant type . . . .   See Chapter 1

Torque specifications   Ft-lbs
Clutch housing cover bolts   10
Muncie transaxle shift shaft nut   61
Transaxle mount through-bolt and nut   80
Transaxle mount-to-frame
  Bolt   40
  Nut   29
Transaxle strut
  Bracket-to-transaxle bracket bolt   38
  Bracket nut   40
  Strut-to-frame bracket through-bolt   50
  Strut-to-transaxle bracket through-bolt   40
Transaxle-to-engine bolts   55

7A

1   General information

Note: *On models equipped with the Delco Loc II audio system, be sure the lockout feature is turned off before performing any procedure which requires disconnecting the battery.*

The vehicles covered by this manual are equipped with either a 5-speed manual or 3-speed automatic transaxle. Information on the manual transaxle is included in this Part of Chapter 7. Information on the automatic transaxle is in Part B.

The 5-speed manual transaxle is essentially a transmission coupled together with a differential in one assembly. Models with a manual transmission are equipped with either an Isuzu or a Muncie unit. Though they're slightly different, they're basically very similar in design and operation.

Because the transaxle is complex, requires special tools and replacement parts aren't readily available, overhauling it is beyond the scope of the average home mechanic. The information contained in this manual is limited to general diagnosis, external adjustments and removal and installation.

Depending on the cost of a transaxle overhaul, it may be a good idea to consider replacing the unit with either a new or rebuilt one. Your local dealer or transmission shop should be able to supply information concerning cost, availability and exchange policy. Regardless of how you decide to remedy a transaxle problem, however, you can still save money by removing and installing it yourself.

**2   Manual transaxle shift cables
(Muncie transaxle) – removal and installation**

Refer to illustration 2.2

Removal

1   Disconnect the negative cable from the battery.
2   Remove the nuts retaining the selector and shift cables to the transaxle levers **(see illustration)**.
3   Remove the console (see Chapter 11).
4   Use a small screwdriver to pry the cable free of the shift control ball sockets.
5   Remove the screws from the carpeting sill plate in the right front corner of the passenger compartment, remove the plate and then pull the carpet back for access to the cables.
6   Remove the cable retainer and grommet screws at the floor pan and pry the two retaining tabs up.
7   Pull the cables through into the passenger compartment and remove them from the vehicle.

Installation

8   Push the cable assembly through the opening from the passenger compartment into the engine compartment.
9   Install the grommet and cable retainer screws and bend the two retaining tabs down.
10   Install the carpet and sill plate.
11   Connect the cable ends to the shifter.
12   Install the console.
13   Connect the cable assembly to the transaxle bracket and shift levers.

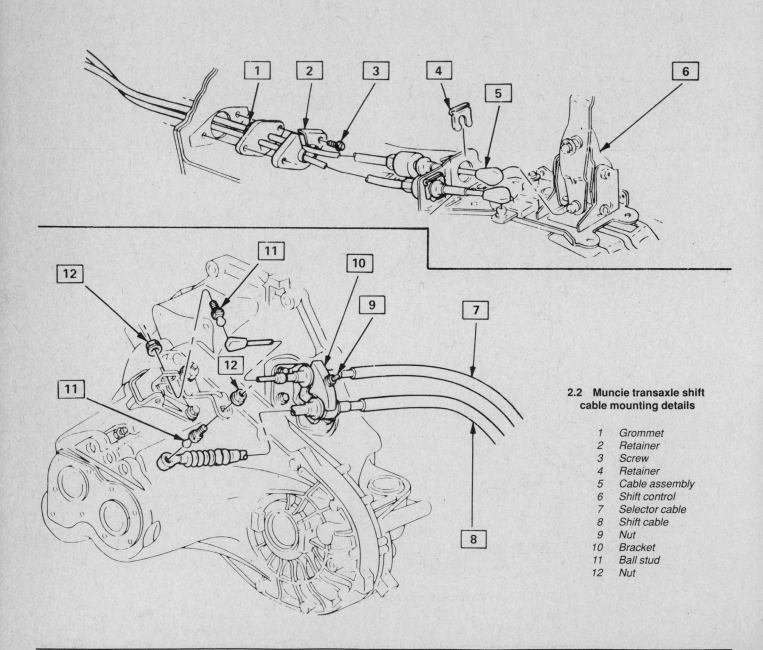

2.2   **Muncie transaxle shift
cable mounting details**

1   Grommet
2   Retainer
3   Screw
4   Retainer
5   Cable assembly
6   Shift control
7   Selector cable
8   Shift cable
9   Nut
10   Bracket
11   Ball stud
12   Nut

3   Manual transaxle shifter shaft seal (Muncie transaxle) – removal and installation

Refer to illustration 3.3

1   Disconnect the negative cable from the battery.
2   Disconnect the shift cables from the shift lever.
3   Remove the shift lever nut, making sure the shift lever itself doesn't move while the nut is loosened **(see illustration)**.
4   Remove the shift lever assembly, keeping all of the components in order.
5   Pry out the old seal with a screwdriver.
6   Install the new seal in the bore and tap it into place with a large socket or piece of pipe and a hammer.
7   Installation of the remaining components is the reverse of removal.

4   Manual transaxle shift cables (Isuzu transaxle) – removal and installation

Refer to illustration 4.2

Removal

1   Disconnect the negative cable from the battery.
2   Working in the engine compartment, remove the clamps and nuts retaining the cables to the shift lever **(see illustration)**.
3   Working in the passenger compartment, remove the shift knob, console and boot (Chapter 11).
4   Disconnect the shift cables from the shifter by prying the cable ends loose from the shifter ball studs with a screwdriver.

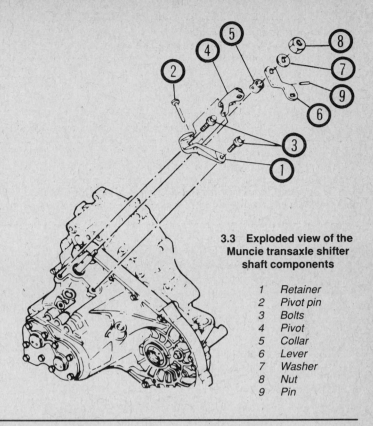

3.3 Exploded view of the Muncie transaxle shifter shaft components

1	Retainer
2	Pivot pin
3	Bolts
4	Pivot
5	Collar
6	Lever
7	Washer
8	Nut
9	Pin

7A

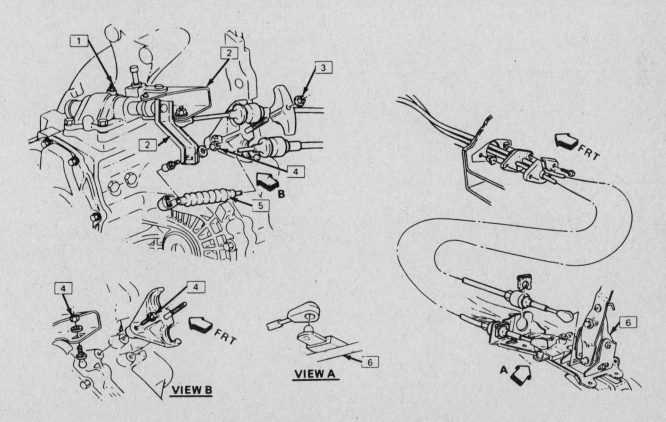

4.2 Shift cable mounting details (Isuzu transaxle)

1	Locking pin	3	Nut	5	Shift cable assembly
2	Transaxle shift lever	4	Nut	6	Shift control assembly

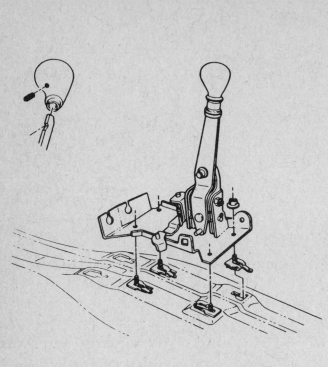

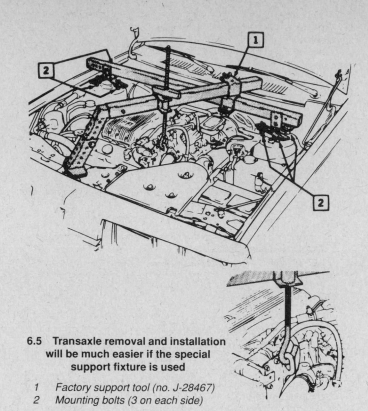

5.5   Shift control assembly mounting details

6.5   Transaxle removal and installation will be much easier if the special support fixture is used

1   Factory support tool (no. J-28467)
2   Mounting bolts (3 on each side)

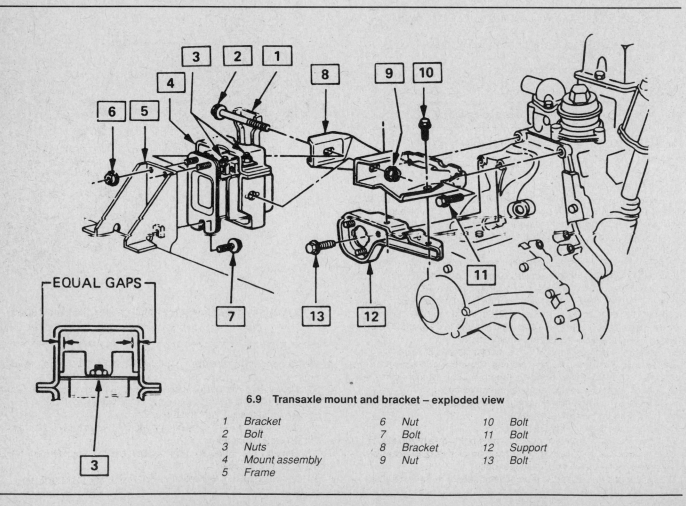

6.9   Transaxle mount and bracket – exploded view

1	Bracket	6	Nut	10	Bolt
2	Bolt	7	Bolt	11	Bolt
3	Nuts	8	Bracket	12	Support
4	Mount assembly	9	Nut	13	Bolt
5	Frame				

5   Remove the spring clips retaining the cables to the shifter.
6   Remove the right front floor carpet sill and carpet for access to the shift cables.
7   Remove the cable grommet screws, lift off the cover, pull the cable assembly through and remove it from the vehicle.

Installation

8   Insert the cable assembly through the floor and install the cable grommet cover.
9   Connect the shift cables to the shifter by placing them in position and popping them onto the ball studs.
10   Install the cable retainer spring clips.
11   Install the carpet and sill cover.
12   Install the console, shift knob and boot.
13   Working in the engine compartment, connect the cables to the shift lever. Reconnect the negative battery cable.

---

5   Manual transaxle shift control (all models) – removal and installation

Refer to illustration 5.5

Removal

1   Disconnect the negative cable from the battery.
2   Remove the console, shift boot and knob (Chapter 11).
3   Disconnect the shift cables from the shifter.
4   Remove the shift cable retaining clips.
5   Remove the retaining nuts and lift the shift control assembly out of the vehicle **(see illustration)**.

Installation

6   Place the shift control assembly in position and install the retaining nuts.
7   Connect the shift cables to the shift control assembly.
8   Install the console.
9   Connect the negative battery cable.

---

6   Manual transaxle – removal and installation

Refer to illustrations 6.5, 6.9, 6.10, 6.18a and 6.18b

Removal

1   Disconnect the negative cable from the battery.
2   Working in the passenger compartment, remove the left hush panel.
3   Disconnect the master cylinder pushrod from the clutch pedal. Unbolt the slave cylinder from the transaxle bracket and move it out of the way.
4   Disconnect the ground cable, shift cables and clamp from the transaxle.
5   The engine must be supported during transaxle removal – this can be accomplished using factory engine support tool J-28467 or equivalent **(see illustration)**. Install a 1/4-inch diameter by two-inch long bolt in the hole in the right front motor mount to maintain driveline alignment if the support tool is used. If this tool isn't available, support the engine with a hoist that can hold it high enough to allow the transaxle to be lowered from the engine compartment with the vehicle raised.
6   Install the engine support or connect a hoist and raise the engine enough to take the weight off the mounts. Raise the vehicle as necessary to allow the transaxle to be removed (approximately 28-inches), support it securely on jackstands and remove the front wheels.
7   Remove the left front brake caliper, hang it out of the way on a piece of wire and remove the disc (Chapter 9).
8   Drain the transaxle fluid (Chapter 1).
9   Remove the transaxle mount-to-frame bolts **(see illustration)**.
10   Remove the front transaxle strut and bracket **(see illustration)**.
11   Remove the clutch housing cover bolts.
12   Disconnect the speedometer cable or sensor at the transaxle.

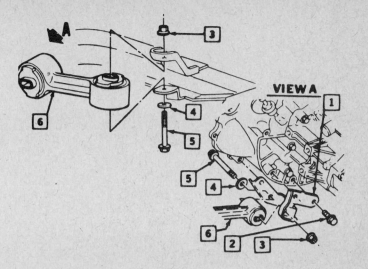

6.10   Transaxle strut and bracket – exploded view

1	Bracket	4	Washer
2	Bolt	5	Bolt
3	Nut	6	Strut

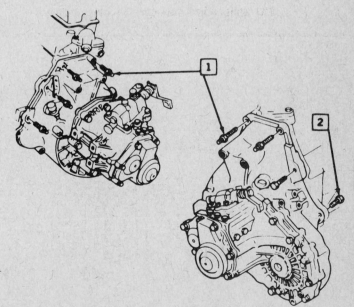

6.18a   Transaxle-to-engine bolt locations (Isuzu transaxle)

1	Bolt	2 Bolt (installed from engine side)

13   Disconnect the stabilizer bar at the control arm and suspension support.
14   Disconnect the balljoint and remove the left suspension support, complete with the lower suspension arm (Chapter 10).
15   Remove the left front fender liner.
16   Disconnect the right side driveaxle from the transaxle and remove the left driveaxle (Chapter 8).
17   Support the transaxle with a jack, preferably a transmission jack made for this purpose.
18   Remove the bellhousing-to-engine bolts **(see illustrations)**.

7A

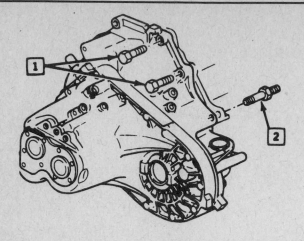

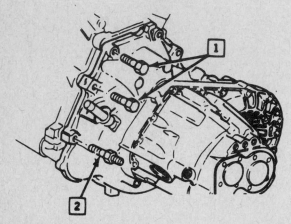

6.18b   Transaxle-to-engine bolt locations (Muncie transaxle)

| 1 | Bolt | 2 | Stud |

---

19   Make a final check that all wiring, cables, etc. are disconnected from the transaxle.

20   Separate the transaxle from the engine by carefully prying the bell-housing away from the engine.

21   Lower the transaxle and remove it from the left side of the engine compartment.

22   The clutch components can now be inspected (Chapter 8). In most cases, new clutch components should be installed as a matter of course when the transaxle is removed.

Installation

23   With the clutch components installed and properly aligned (see Chapter 8), carefully raise the transaxle into place, guide the right side driveaxle into the transaxle and slide the input shaft into place in the clutch hub splines.

24   Install the transaxle-to-engine bolts **(see illustrations 6.18a and 6.18b)**. Tighten the bolts to the specified torque.

25   Install the left driveaxle.

26   Install the suspension support (Chapter 10).

27   Connect the speedometer cable or sensor.

28   Install the clutch housing cover.

29   Install the front strut bracket and strut. Tighten the bolts to the specified torque.

30   Install the transaxle mount bolts. Tighten the bolts to the specified torque.

31   Install the front fender liner (Chapter 11).

32   Install the brake caliper (Chapter 9).

33   Install the wheels and lower the vehicle.

34   Connect the ground cable.

35   Install the slave cylinder and connect the clutch pushrod to the pedal.

36   Connect the shift linkage.

37   Remove the engine support.

38   Fill the transaxle with the specified lubricant (Chapter 1).

39   Connect the negative battery cable.

---

7   Manual transaxle overhaul – general information

Refer to illustrations 7.4a, 7.4b, 7.4c and 7.4d

Overhauling a manual transaxle is a difficult job for the do-it-yourselfer. It involves the disassembly and reassembly of many small parts. Numerous clearances must be precisely measured and, if necessary, changed with select fit spacers and snap-rings. As a result, if transaxle problems arise, it can be removed and installed by a competent do-it-yourselfer, but overhaul should be left to a transmission repair shop. Rebuilt transaxles may be available – check with your dealer parts department and auto parts stores. At any rate, the time and money involved in an overhaul is almost sure to exceed the cost of a rebuilt unit.

Nevertheless, it's not impossible for an inexperienced mechanic to rebuild a transaxle if the special tools are available and the job is done in a deliberate, step-by-step manner so nothing is overlooked.

The tools necessary for an overhaul include internal and external snap-ring pliers, a bearing puller, a slide hammer, a set of pin punches, a dial indicator and possibly a hydraulic press. In addition, a large, sturdy workbench and a vise or transaxle stand will be required.

During disassembly of the transaxle, make careful notes of how each piece comes off, where it fits in relation to other pieces and what holds it in place. Exploded views are included **(see illustrations)** to show where the parts go – but actually noting how they are installed when you remove the parts will make it much easier to get the transaxle back together.

Before taking the transaxle apart for repair, it will help if you have some idea what area of the transaxle is malfunctioning. Certain problems can be closely tied to specific areas in the transaxle, which can make component examination and replacement easier. Refer to the *Troubleshooting* section at the front of this manual for information regarding possible sources of trouble.

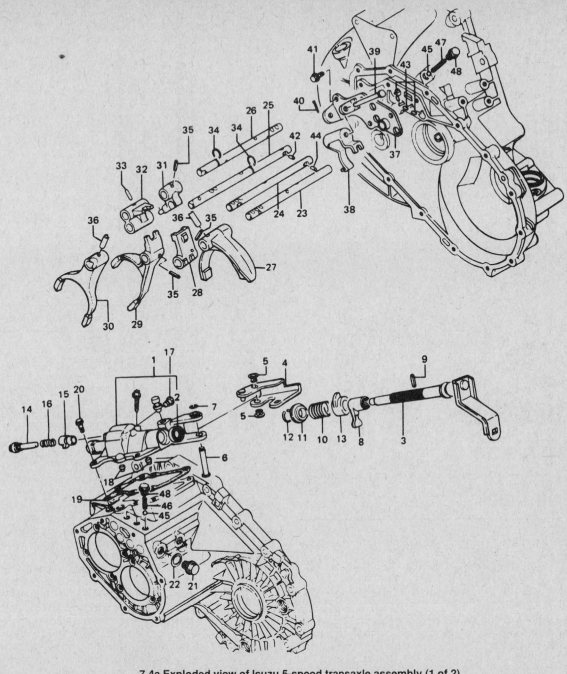

7.4a Exploded view of Isuzu 5-speed transaxle assembly (1 of 2)

1	Shift control box sub-assembly	17	Bolt	33	Lock pin
2	Oil seal	18	Pin	34	Snap–ring
3	Shift lever assembly (external)	19	Gasket	35	Roll pin
4	Select lever assembly (external)	20	Bolt	36	Roll pin
5	Bushing	21	Plug	37	Bracket
6	Pin	22	Gasket	38	Reverse shift lever
7	Snap–ring	23	Gear shift shaft arm – 1st/2nd	39	Pin
8	Shift lever (internal)	24	Gear shift shaft arm – 3rd/4th	40	Cotter pin
9	Roll pin	25	Gear shift shaft arm – 5th	41	Bolt
10	Spring	26	Gear shift shaft arm – Reverse	42	Lock pin
11	Spring seat	27	Shift fork – 1st/2nd	43	Interlock pin
12	Snap–ring	28	Shift block – 1st/2nd	44	Lock pin
13	Stopper (reverse inhibitor)	29	Shift fork – 3rd/4th	45	Detent ball
14	Bolt	30	Shift fork – 5th	46	Spring
15	Stopper cam (reverse inhibitor)	31	Reverse shift lever	47	Spring
16	Spring (stopper cam)	32	Reverse/5th shift block	48	Plug

7A

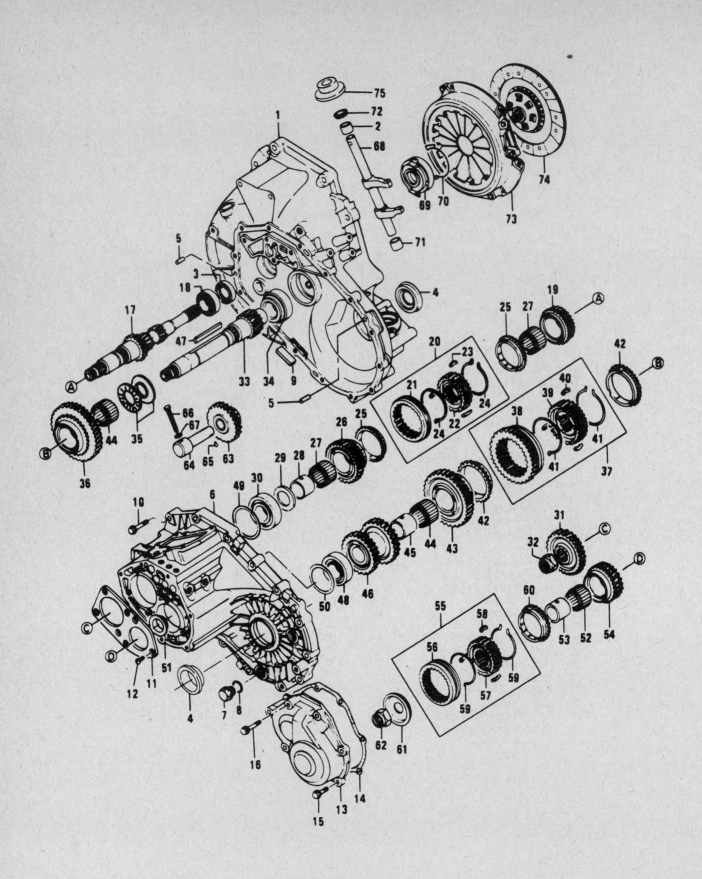

7.4b Exploded view of Isuzu 5-speed transaxle assembly (2 of 2)

1	Housing		39	Synchro hub (reverse)
2	Bushing		40	Insert (1st/2nd)
3	Oil seal		41	Spring
4	Oil seal		42	Blocking ring (1st/2nd)
5	Pin		43	Gear (2nd output)
6	Transaxle case		44	Bearing (1st/2nd)
7	Drain plug		45	Collar
8	O–ring		46	Gear (3rd/4th output)
9	Magnet		47	Key
10	Bolt		48	Bearing
11	Bearing retainer		49	Shim
12	Screw		50	Shim
13	Cover		51	Thrust washer
14	Packing		52	Bearing
15	Bolt		53	Collar
16	Bolt		54	Gear (5th output)
17	Input shaft		55	Synchronizer (5th)
18	Bearing (input shaft – front)		56	Synchro sleeve
19	Gear (3rd input)		57	Synchro hub
20	Synchronizer (3rd/4th)		58	Insert
21	Synchro sleeve (3rd/4th)		59	Spring
22	Synchro hub (3rd/4th)		60	Blocking ring (5th)
23	Insert (3rd/4th)		61	Stopper plate insert
24	Spring		62	Nut
25	Blocking ring (3rd/4th)		63	Gear (idler/reverse)
26	Gear (4th input)		64	Shaft
27	Needle bearing (3rd/4th)		65	Pin
28	Collar (4th gear)		66	Bolt
29	Thrust washer		67	Gasket
30	Bearing		68	Clutch fork shaft
31	Gear (5th input)		69	Clutch release bearing
32	Nut		70	Spring
33	Output shaft		71	Bushing
34	Bearing (output shaft – front)		72	Seal
35	Bearing (1st – with thrust washer)		73	Pressure plate
36	Gear (1st/2nd)		74	Clutch plate
37	Synchronizer (1st/2nd)		75	Cap
38	Synchro gear and sleeve			

7A

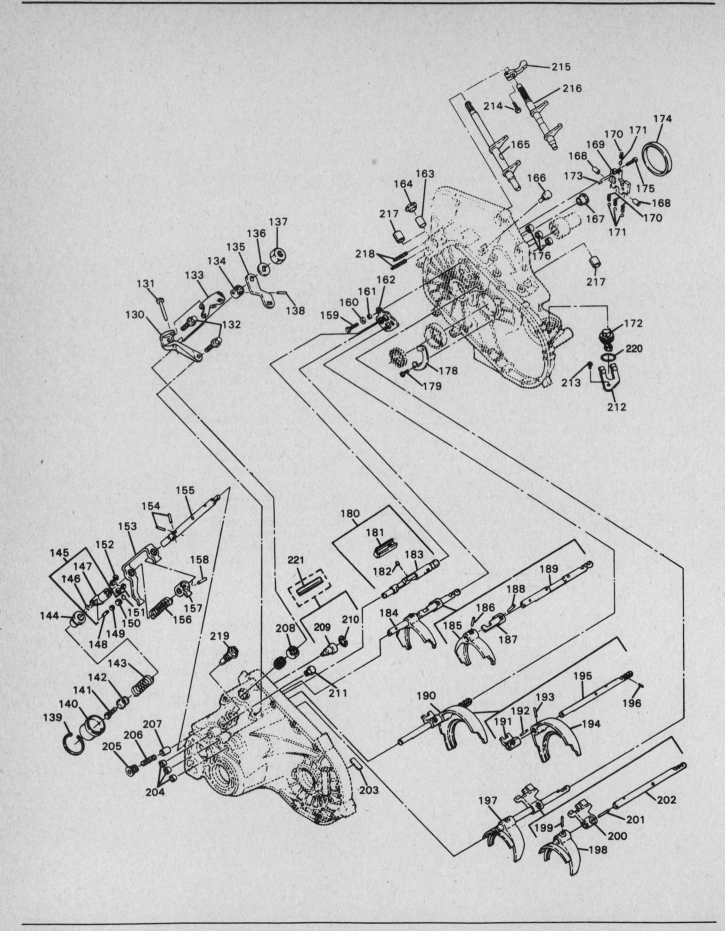

7.4c   Exploded view of Muncie 5-speed transaxle assembly (1 of 2)

130	Retainer		177	Not used
131	Pin		178	Retainer
132	Bolt (2)		179	Bolt/screw (2)
133	Selector lever		180	Reverse shift rail
134	Collar		181	Shift gate (5th/reverse)
135	Shift lever		182	Roller
136	Washer		183	Reverse shift shaft
137	Nut		184	3rd/4th shift rail
138	Roll pin		185	3rd/4th shift fork
139	Snap–ring		186	Pin
140	Cover		187	3rd/4th select lever
141	Bolt/screw		188	Pin
142	Spring seat		189	3rd/4th shift shaft
143	Spring		190	1st/2nd shift rail
144	Spring seat		191	1st/2nd select lever
145	Detent assembly lever		192	Pin
146	Retainer		193	Pin
147	Detent lever		194	1st/2nd shift fork
148	Pin		195	1st/2nd shift shaft
149	Spacer		196	Pin
150	Roller		197	5th shift rail
151	Retainer		198	5th shift fork
152	Roller		199	Pin
153	Reverse lever		200	5th shift lever
154	Pin		201	Pin
155	Shift shaft		202	5th shift shaft
156	Spring		203	Magnet
157	Shift lever		204	Plug (3)
158	Roll pin		205	Bolt/screw
159	Bolt/screw (3)		206	Spring
160	Washer (3)		207	Sleeve
161	Spacer (3)		208	Seal
162	Plate		209	Plug
163	Bushing		210	Snap–ring
164	Seal		211	Stud
165	Shaft		212	Speedo signal assembly retainer
166	Breather assembly		213	Bolt
167	Bushing		214	Bolt
168	Pin (2)		215	Clutch release lever
169	Holder		216	Clutch fork shaft
170	Spring (4)		217	Bearing
171	Ball (4)		218	Stud (2)
172	Speedo signal assembly		219	Back–up light switch
173	Roll pin		220	Seal
174	Cover		221	Roll pin (some models)
175	Bolt/screw (2)			
176	Bushing (3)			

7A

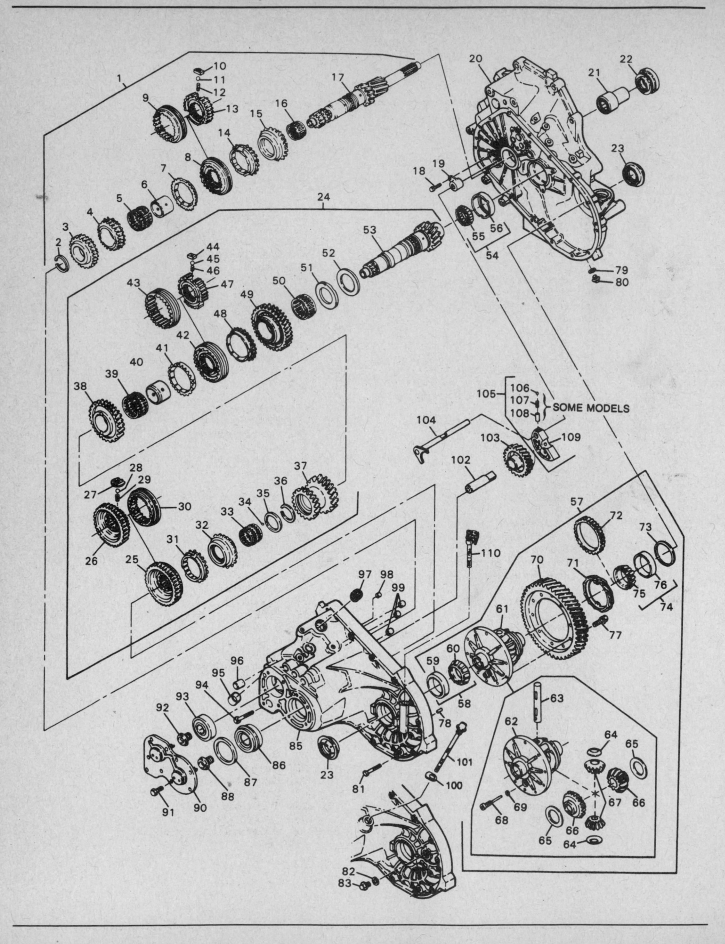

7.4d   Exploded view of Muncie 5-speed transaxle assembly (2 of 2)

1	Input shaft/gear assembly		55	Bearing
2	Snap–ring		56	Race
3	Gear (5th input)		57	Gear and differential assembly
4	Gear (4th input)		58	Bearing assembly (differential)
5	Bearing		59	Race
6	Race		60	Bearing
7	Blocker ring (4th)		61	Case (differential assembly)
8	Synchronizer (3rd/4th)		62	Case (differential)
9	Synchro sleeve		63	Pin
10	Key (3)		64	Thrust washer
11	Ball (3)		65	Thrust washer
12	Spring (3)		66	Side gear
13	Synchro hub		67	Pinion gear
14	Blocker ring		68	Bolt/screw
15	Gear (3rd input)		69	Lock washer
16	Bearing (2)		70	Differential ring gear
17	Input shaft		71	Speedo output gear (mechanical)
18	Bolt/screw		72	Speedo output gear (electronic)
19	Guide (reverse shift rail)		73	Shim
20	Housing (clutch and differential)		74	Bearing assembly
21	Bearing/sleeve assembly (input shaft)		75	Bearing
22	Clutch release bearing assembly		76	Race
23	Seal		77	Bolt/screw (10)
24	Output shaft/gear assembly		78	Pin (2)
25	Gear (reverse output/5th synchronizer assemby)		79	Oil drain plug
26	Gear (reverse)		80	Washer
27	Key (3)		81	Bolt/screw (15)
28	Ball (3)		82	Washer
29	Ball (3)		83	Plug
30	Sleeve		84	Not used
31	Blocker ring		85	Case (transmission)
32	Gear (5th output)		86	Bearing
33	Bearing		87	Shim
34	Ball		88	Retainer
35	Thrust washer		89	Not used
36	Snap–ring		90	End plate
37	Gear (3rd/4th)		91	Bolt/screw (9)
38	Gear (2nd output)		92	Retainer
39	Bearing		93	Bearing
40	Race		94	Bolt/screw
41	Blocker ring		95	Bushing
42	Synchronizer (1st/2nd)		96	Bushing
43	Sleeve (3)		97	Needle roller bearing
44	Key (3)		98	Bushing
45	Ball (3)		99	Bushing (3)
46	Spring (3)		100	Washer
47	Synchro hub		101	Fluid level indicator
48	Blocker ring		102	Reverse idler shaft
49	Gear (1st output)		103	Reverse idler gear
50	Bearing		104	Reverse idler gear shift rail
51	Thrust bearing		105	Bracket
52	Thrust washer		106	Ball (some models)
53	Output shaft		107	Spring (some models)
54	Bearing		108	Sleeve (some models)
			109	Bracket
			110	Transmission fluid level dipstick

7A

Chapter 7 Part B   Automatic transaxle

Contents

Specifications

General

Fluid type and capacity . . . .   See Chapter 1

Torque specifications   **Ft-lbs**

Shift control assembly nuts   17
Transaxle-to-engine bolts   55
Torque converter-to-driveplate bolts
   Through 1989   35
   1990 and later   46
Torque converter cover bolts   10
Transaxle mounting strut through-bolt
   Through 1990   31
   1991   40
   1992   44
Transaxle mount
Bracket-to-engine bolt   31
Bracket-to-transaxle   38
Through-bolt   38
TV cable-to-transaxle case bolt   6

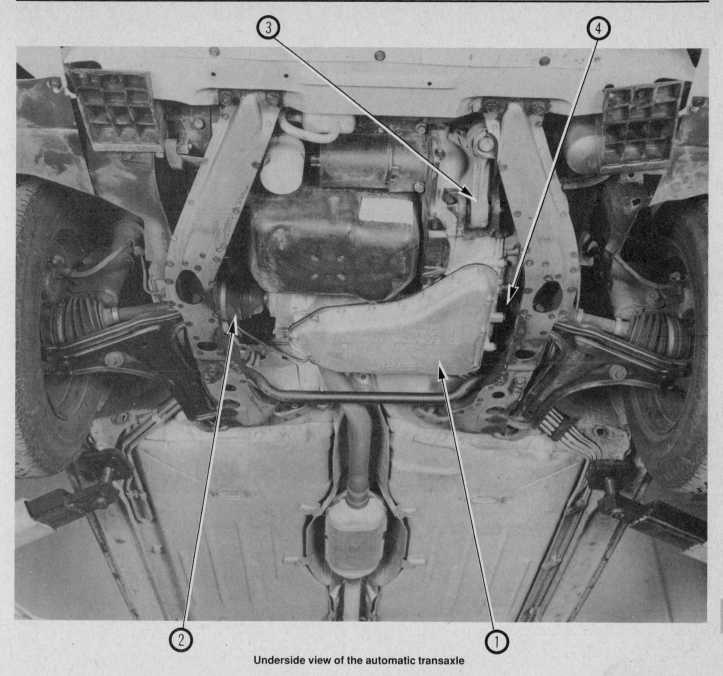

Underside view of the automatic transaxle

1	Transaxle pan	3	Mounting strut
2	Right driveaxle	4	Left driveaxle

7B

1   General information

Due to the complexity of the clutches and the hydraulic control system, and because of the special tools and expertise required to perform an automatic transaxle overhaul, it should not be undertaken by the home mechanic. Therefore, the procedures in this Chapter are limited to general diagnosis, routine maintenance, adjustment and transaxle removal and installation.

If the transaxle requires major repair work, it should be left to a dealer service department or an automotive or transmission repair shop. You can, however, remove and install the transaxle yourself and save the expense, even if the repair work is done by a transmission shop.

Replacement and adjustment procedures the home mechanic can perform include those involving the throttle valve (TV) cable and the shift linkage. **Caution:** *Never tow a disabled vehicle with an automatic transaxle at speeds greater than 35 mph or distances over 50 miles.*

Note: *On models equipped with the Delco Loc II audio system, be sure the lockout feature is turned off before performing any procedure which requires disconnecting the battery.*

2   Diagnosis – general

1   Automatic transaxle malfunctions may be caused by a number of conditions, such as poor engine performance, improper adjustments, hydraulic malfunctions trand mechanical problems.

3.1   Remove the knob (arrow), then detach both halves of the molded plastic firewall cover

3.2   To detach the TV cable from the throttle lever pin, grasp it firmly with needle-nose pliers, move it forward and lift up

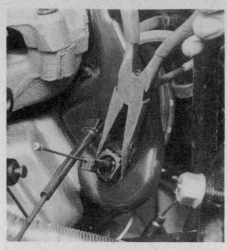

3.3   Use needle-nose pliers to compress the TV cable tangs, then push the housing back through the bracket

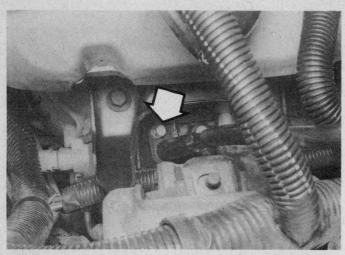

3.5   Remove the TV cable bolt (arrow) and pull up on the cable until it's out of the transmission

3.6   Hold the transaxle TV link with needle-nose pliers and slide the cable link off the pin

3.9a   To adjust the TV cable, press down on the re-adjust tab, move the slider back against the fitting until it stops, release the re-adjust tab and rotate the throttle lever toward the wide open position until you hear an audible click

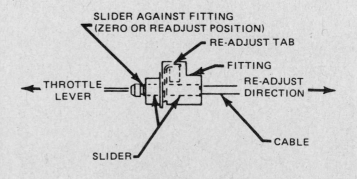

3.9b   TV cable adjuster details

2   The first check should be of the transaxle fluid level and condition. Refer to Chapter 1 for more information. Unless the fluid and filter have been recently changed, drain the fluid and replace the filter (also in Chapter 1).

3   Road test the vehicle and drive in all the various selective ranges, noting discrepancies in operation.

4   Verify that the engine isn't at fault. If the engine hasn't had a tune-up recently, refer to Chapter 1 and make sure all engine components are functioning properly.

5   Check the adjustment of the throttle valve (TV) cable (Section 3).

6   Check the condition of all vacuum and electrical lines and fittings at the transaxle, or leading to it.

7   Check for proper adjustment of the shift control cable (Section 5).

8   If at this point a problem remains, there is one final check before the transaxle is removed for overhaul. The vehicle should be taken to a shop for a line pressure check.

---

3   Throttle valve (TV) cable – replacement and adjustment

Replacement

Refer to illustrations 3.1, 3.2, 3.3, 3.5 and 3.6

1   Unscrew the knob at the center of the firewall **(see illustration)** and remove the two-piece plastic firewall cover.

2   Disconnect the TV cable from the throttle lever by grasping the connector, pulling it forward to disconnect it and then lifting up and off the lever pin **(see illustration)**.

3   Disconnect the TV cable housing from the bracket by compressing the tangs and pushing the housing back through the bracket **(see illustration)**.

4   Disconnect any clips or straps retaining the cable to the transaxle.

5   Remove the bolt retaining the cable to the transaxle **(see illustration)**.

6   Pull up on the cover until the end of the cable can be seen, then disconnect it from the transaxle TV link **(see illustration)**. Remove the cable from the vehicle.

7   To install the cable, connect it to the transaxle TV link and install the bolt. Tighten the bolt to the specified torque and push the cover securely over the cable. Route the cable to the top of the engine, push the housing through the bracket until it clicks into place, place the connector over the throttle lever pin and pull back to lock it. Secure the cable with any retaining clips or straps.

Adjustment

Refer to illustrations 3.9a and 3.9b

8   The engine MUST NOT be running during this adjustment.

9   Depress the re-adjust tab and push the slider through the fitting (away from the throttle lever) as far as it will go **(see illustrations)**.

10   Release the re-adjust tab.

11   Manually turn the throttle lever to the "wide open throttle" position until the re-adjust tab makes an audible click, then release the throttle lever. The cable is now adjusted. **Note:** *Don't use excessive force at the throttle lever to adjust the TV cable. If great effort is required to adjust the cable, disconnect the cable at the transaxle end and check for free operation. If it's still difficult, replace the cable. If it's now free, suspect a bent TV link in the transaxle or a problem with the throttle lever.*

---

4   Starter safety switch – replacement and adjustment

Replacement

Refer to illustrations 4.3, 4.4 and 4.5

1   Disconnect the negative cable from the battery.

2   Shift the transaxle into Neutral.

3   Disconnect the shift linkage **(see illustration)**.

4   Trace the wire harness from the starter safety switch to the connector **(see illustration)** and unplug it.

5   Remove the bolts **(see illustration)** and detach the switch.

4.3   Detach the cable from the starter safety switch by prying it off with a screwdriver

4.4   Trace the wires from the starter safety switch to the connector (arrow) and unplug it

4.5   Remove the starter safety switch bolts (arrows)

7B

6   To install the switch, line up the flats on the shift shaft with the flats in the switch and lower the switch onto the shaft.

7   Install the bolts. If the switch is new and the shaft hasn't been moved, tighten the bolts. If the switch requires adjustment, leave the bolts loose and follow the adjustment procedure below. The remainder of installation is the reverse of removal.

Adjustment

Refer to illustration 4.8

8   Insert a 3/32-inch drill bit into the switch gauge hole **(see illustration)**.

9   Rotate the switch until the drill bit can be felt dropping into the switch,

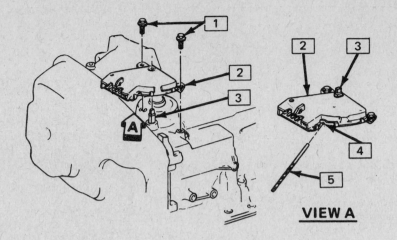

4.8   Starter safety switch installation details

1   *Bolts*
2   *Switch*
3   *Transaxle shifter shaft*
4   *Adjustment hole*
5   *3/32-inch drill bit used for adjustment*

VIEW A

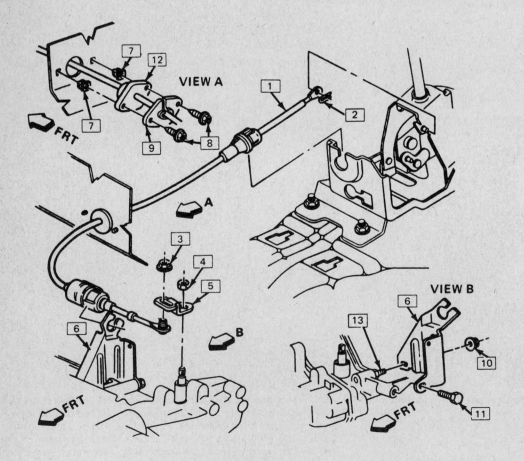

5.2   Floor shift control cable assembly

1   *Shift cable*
2   *Retainer*
3   *Nut*
4   *Nut*
5   *Transaxle lever*
6   *Transaxle bracket*
7   *Nut*
8   *Screws*
9   *Grommet retainer*
10   *Nut*
11   *Bolt**
12   *Grommet*
13   *Stud*

* Note: *Tighten bolt (11) after nut (10)*

VIEW A

FRT

VIEW B

FRT

indicating that it's now in the Neutral position. Tighten the switch bolts.

10   Connect the negative battery cable and verify that the engine will start only in Neutral or Park.

5   Automatic transaxle shift cable – replacement and adjustment

1   Disconnect the negative cable from the battery.

Replacement

Floor shift

Refer to illustrations 5.2, 5.4a, 5.4b and 5.6

2   Working in the engine compartment, disconnect the shift cable from the transaxle lever **(see illustration)**.

3   Remove the console between the seats (see Chapter 11).

4   Disconnect the shift cable from the floor shift lever and bracket **(see illustrations)**.

5   Remove the right and left side sound insulators from the under dash portion of the console, then pull back the carpet for access to the cable (see Chapter 11).

6   Working in the engine compartment, detach the cable from the transaxle bracket **(see illustration)**.

7   Trace the cable up to the firewall grommet. Remove the screws from the grommet retainer, detach the grommet and retainer from the firewall and pull the cable assembly through the firewall.

8   Installation is the reverse of removal. After installation, adjust the cable as described below.

Column shift

Refer to illustration 5.9

9   Working in the engine compartment, disconnect the cable from the transaxle lever and bracket **(see illustration)**.

10   Working in the passenger compartment, remove the left sound insulator located under the dash.

11   Disconnect the cable bracket on the steering column and detach the cable from the column shift lever.

12   Dislodge the grommet in the firewall and withdraw the cable from the vehicle.

13   Installation is the reverse of removal. After installation, adjust the cable as described below.

Adjustment

14   Place the shift lever and the transaxle lever in Neutral, then push the locking tab on the shift cable to automatically adjust the cable **(see illustrations 5.2 and 5.9)**.

15   Reconnect the negative battery cable.

5.4a   To disconnect the cable at the shift control assembly, pull off the clip with needle-nose pliers . . .

5.4b   . . . and pry the cable off the lever pin with a screwdriver

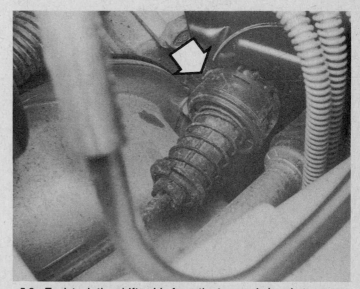

5.6   To detach the shift cable from the transaxle bracket, grasp the housing (arrow) firmly, cock it to one side and pull (though you can't see them in this photo, there's a tang on each side of the housing – the two tangs locate the housing in a square hole in the bracket, so when you rock the housing to one side, one of the tangs comes free)

7B

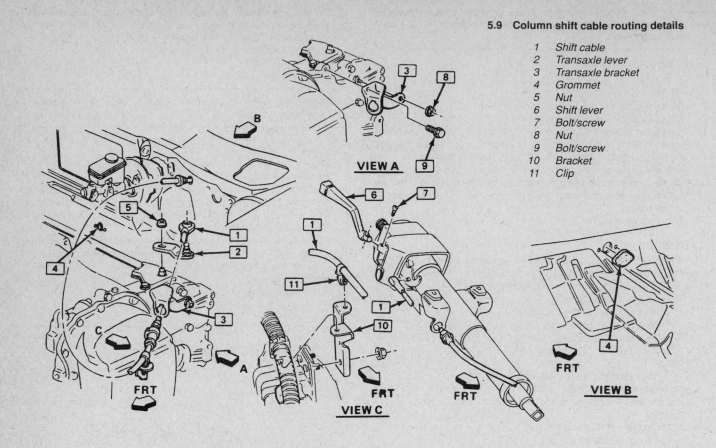

5.9 Column shift cable routing details

1   Shift cable
2   Transaxle lever
3   Transaxle bracket
4   Grommet
5   Nut
6   Shift lever
7   Bolt/screw
8   Nut
9   Bolt/screw
10 Bracket
11 Clip

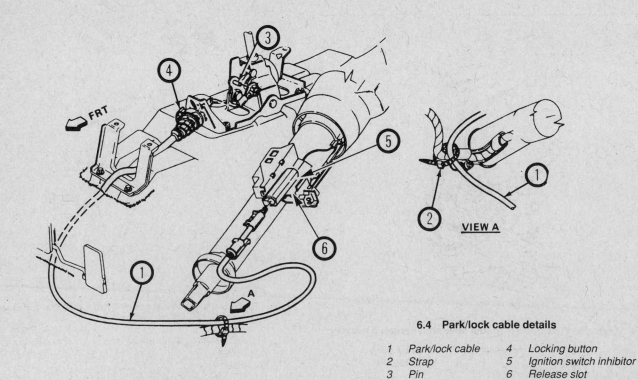

6.4 Park/lock cable details

1   Park/lock cable   4   Locking button
2   Strap   5   Ignition switch inhibitor
3   Pin   6   Release slot

6 Automatic transaxle park/lock cable – removal and installation

Refer to illustration 6.4

Removal

1   Disconnect the negative cable from the battery.
2   Remove the console (Chapter 11).
3   Place the shift lever in Park and the ignition switch in the Run position.
4   Insert a screwdriver blade into the slot in the ignition switch inhibitor, depress the cable latch and detach the cable **(see illustration)**.
5   Push the cable connector lock button (located at the shift control base) to the up position and detach the cable from the park lock lever pin. Depress the two cable connector latches and remove the cable from the shift control base.
6   Remove the cable clips.

Installation

7   Make sure the cable lock button is in the up position and the shift lever is in Park. Snap the cable connector into the shift control base.
8   With the ignition key in the Run position (this is very important), snap the cable into the inhibitor housing.
9   Turn the ignition key to the Lock position.
10   Snap the end of the cable onto the shifter park/lock pin.
11   Push the nose of the cable connector forward to remove the slack.
12   With no load on the connector nose, snap the cable connector lock button on.
13   Check the operation of the park/lock cable as follows.
   a) With the shift lever in Park and the key in Lock, make sure the shift lever cannot be moved to another position and the key can be removed.
   b) With the key in Run and the shift lever in Neutral, make sure the key cannot be turned to Lock.
14   If it operates as described above, the park/lock cable system is properly adjusted. Proceed to Step 16.
15   If the park/lock system doesn't operate as described, return the cable connector lock to the up position and repeat the adjustment procedure. Push the cable connector down and recheck the operation.

16   If the key cannot be removed in the Park position, snap the lock button to the up position and move the nose of the cable connector to the rear until the key can be removed from the ignition switch.
17   Install the cable in the retaining clips.

7 Automatic transaxle floor shift control assembly – removal and installation

Refer to illustrations 7.5a and 7.5b

1   Disconnect the negative cable from the battery.
2   Remove the console (see Chapter 11).
3   Disconnect the shift cable from the gear shift lever (see Section 5).
4   Disconnect the park/lock cable from the gear shift lever (Section 6).
5   Remove the retaining nuts and lift the floor shift control assembly out of the vehicle **(see illustrations)**.
6   Place the floor shift control assembly in position on the mounting studs and install the nuts. Tighten the nuts to the specified torque.
7   Connect the shift cables.
8   Install the console.
9   Reconnect the negative battery cable.

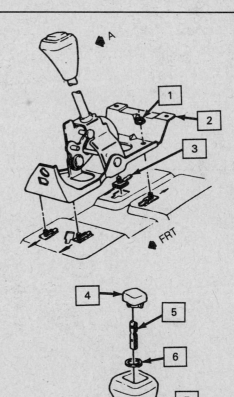

VIEW A

7.5b Exploded view of later model floor shift control assembly

1	*Nut*	5	*Retainer*
2	*Floor shift control assembly*	6	*Snap-ring*
3	*Bolt*	7	*Knob*
4	*Button*		

7B

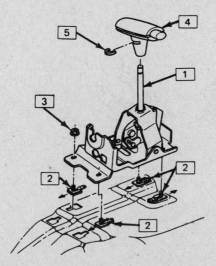

7.5a Exploded view of early model floor shift control assembly

1	*Floor shift control assembly*	4	*Handle*
2	*Stud*	5	*Retainer*
3	*Nut*		

8.3   The rubber-type differential seal (arrow) can be pried out of the housing with a screwdriver – be careful not to damage the splines on the shaft (transaxle removed for clarity)

8.4   Dislodge the metal-type differential seal by working around the outer edge with a chisel and hammer

8   Transaxle differential seals – replacement

Refer to illustrations 8.3 and 8.4

1   Raise the vehicle and support it securely on jackstands.
2   Remove the driveaxle(s) (see Chapter 8).
3   If a rubber-type seal is involved, use a seal remover or a long screwdriver to pry it out of the transaxle. Be careful not to damage the splines on the output shaft **(see illustration)**.
4   If a metal-type seal is involved, use a hammer and chisel to pry up the outer lip of the seal to dislodge it so it can be pried out of the housing **(see illustration)**.
5   Compare the new seal to the old one to make sure they're the same.
6   Coat the lips of the new seal with transmission fluid.
7   Place the new seal in position and tap it into the bore with a hammer and a large socket or a piece of pipe that's the same diameter as the outside edge of the seal.
8   Reinstall the various components in the reverse order of removal.

9   Automatic transaxle – removal and installation

Removal

Refer to illustrations 9.9, 9.10a, 9.10b, 9.10c, 9.10d, 9.17, 9.18, 9.19, 9.26, 9.28, 9.29, 9.30 and 9.35

1   Disconnect the negative cable from the battery, then drain the transaxle fluid (see Chapter 1).
2   Remove the air cleaner assembly, mounting bracket, MAF sensor (V6 engine) and air intake duct (see Chapter 4).
3   If the vehicle has a V6 engine, remove the exhaust crossover bolts at the rear manifold and the front exhaust manifold bolts (see Chapter 4). Raise the front manifold/crossover assembly and support it out of the way.
4   Detach the vent hose.
5   Remove the nut securing the wire harness to the transaxle.
6   Unplug the electrical connectors from the speed sensor, the TCC, the starter safety switch and the Park/Neutral/back-up light switch.
7   Disconnect the TV cable from the throttle lever and transaxle (see Section 3).
8   Detach the shift cable from the transaxle lever and bracket (see Section 5).

9   Remove the bolt and detach the dipstick tube **(see illustration)**.
10   Install engine support fixture J 28467 and adapter J 35953 **(see illustrations)**. If the tool isn't available, support the engine with a hoist from above **(see illustration)** or a jack and a block of wood (to spread the load) under the oil pan . Whatever you use must hold the engine high enough to allow the transaxle to be lowered from the engine compartment after the vehicle is raised. The best way to ensure adequate clearance is to measure the height you've got to work with **(see illustration)**.
11   Remove the two uppermost transaxle-to-engine bolts.
12   Remove the rest of the upper engine-to-transaxle bolts.
13   Loosen the front wheel lug nuts.
14   Raise the vehicle and support it securely on jackstands.
15   Remove both front wheels.
16   Remove the left splash shield.
17   Remove the transaxle strut **(see illustration)**.

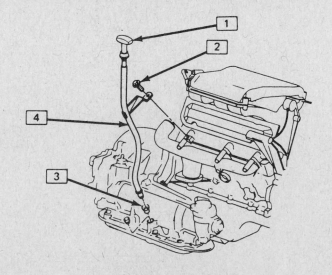

9.9   Dipstick tube assembly

1	*Dipstick*	*3*	*Seal*
2	*Bolt*	*4*	*Tube*

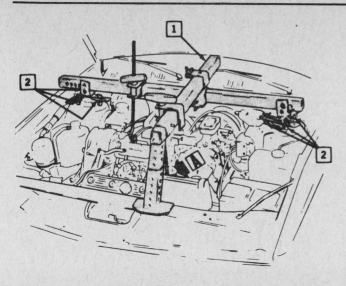

9.10a Typical four-cylinder engine support tool

1 *Support tool (no. J-28467)*
2 *Mounting nuts*
3 *Engine hook*

VIEW A

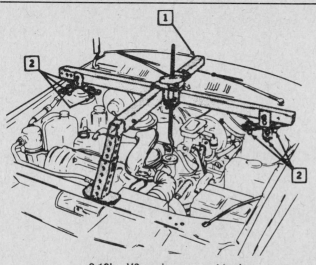

9.10b V6 engine support tool

1 *Support tool (no. J-28467)*   2 *Mounting nuts*

9.10c If an engine support tool isn't available, connect a chain to the lifting eyes and raise the weight off the engine mounts with a hoist

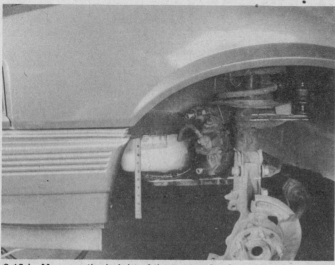

9.10d Measure the height of the transaxle, then raise the vehicle enough to allow room for the transaxle to be removed from under the vehicle

9.17 Transaxle strut through-bolts (arrows)

7B

18   If the vehicle has a V6 engine, remove the lateral strut, if equipped **(see illustration)**.

19   If the vehicle has a V6 engine, remove the transaxle brace bolts **(see illustration)**.

20   Install driveaxle seal protectors (see Chapter 8).

21   Disengage both driveaxles (see Chapter 8).

22   Detach both driveaxles (see Chapter 8).

23   Remove the left stabilizer bar link pin bolt (see Chapter 10).

24   Remove the left stabilizer bar bushing clamp nuts at the support (see Chapter 10).

25   Remove the left frame support bolts and swing the support aside.

26   Remove the torque converter cover **(see illustration)**.

27   Mark the torque converter and one of the drive studs with white paint to ensure correct alignment when reinstalled.

28   Remove the torque converter-to-driveplate bolts. Turn the crankshaft for access to each bolt **(see illustration)**.

29   Disconnect the transaxle cooler lines **(see illustration)** and plug them to prevent leakage.

30   Remove the transaxle-to-engine support bracket **(see illustration)**.

31   Support the transaxle with a jack - preferably a special jack made for this purpose. Safety chains will help steady the transaxle on the jack.

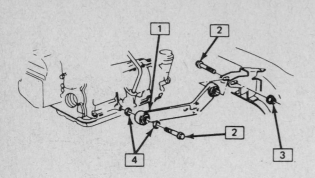

9.18   Transaxle lateral strut assembly details (some V6 models)

1	Lateral strut	3	Nut
2	Bolt	4	Washer

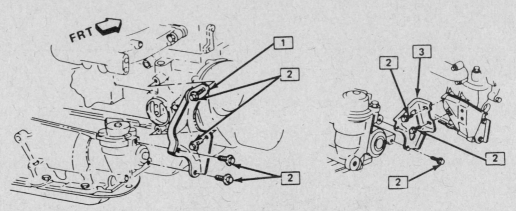

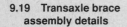

9.19   Transaxle brace assembly details

1   Brace (four-cylinder models)
2   Bolt
3   Brace (V6 models)

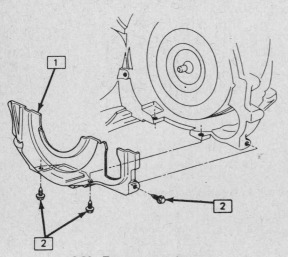

9.26   Torque converter cover

1   Cover   2   Bolt

9.28   Lock the driveplate starter ring gear teeth with a screwdriver and remove the torque converter-to-driveplate bolts

32   Remove any other chassis or suspension components which will interfere with transaxle removal.

33   Remove the remaining engine-to-transaxle bolts.

34   Make a final check that all wiring, cables, etc. which could interfere with transaxle removal are disconnected or moved out of the way.

35   To separate the transaxle from the engine, pry the bellhousing away very carefully with a large screwdriver or pry bar **(see illustration)**. Make sure the torque converter is detached from the driveplate. Secure the torque converter to the transaxle so it won't fall out of the bellhousing during removal.

36   Lower the transaxle and remove it from the left side of the engine compartment.

Installation

Refer to illustration 9.41

37   Inspect the driveplate for missing weights, cracks, corrosion and damaged or broken starter gear teeth. Refer to Chapter 2 if the driveplate must be replaced.

38   If the engine rear main oil seal is leaking, refer to Chapter 2 for the replacement procedure.

39   Inspect all hoses, cables and wires that connect to the transaxle for damage and repair or replace them as necessary.

40   Whenever the transaxle is removed for overhaul or replacement of the torque converter, pump or case, make sure you flush the transaxle oil cooler lines with General Motors J-35944, or its equivalent prior to installation.

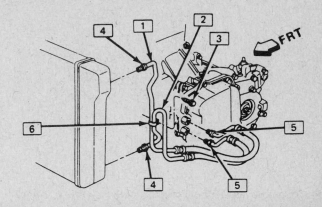

9.29   Oil cooler line details

1	Upper line	4	Fitting
2	Lower line	5	Fitting
3	Bolt	6	Clip

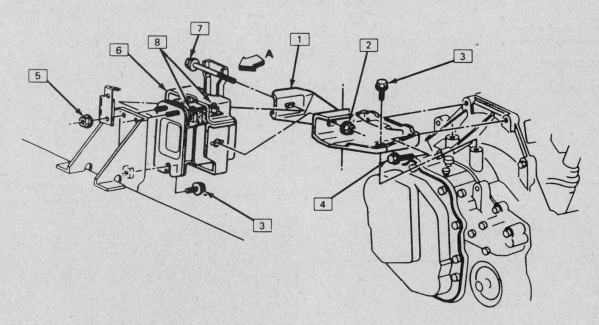

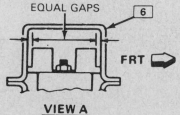

VIEW A

9.30   Transaxle-to-engine mount assembly

1	Bracket	5	Nut
2	Nut	6	Mount
3	Bolt	7	bolt
4	Bolt	8	Nut

7B

9.35   Pry the transaxle bellhousing away from the engine with a large screwdriver or pry bar

9.41   Lubricate the torque converter hub with grease

41   Lubricate the torque converter hub with a light coat of chassis grease **(see illustration)**.

42   Make sure the torque converter hub is fully engaged in the oil pump.

43   With the transaxle secured to the jack, raise it into position. Be sure to keep it level so the torque converter doesn't slide out. As the transaxle is being raised, guide the right driveaxle into the transaxle. The right driveaxle can't be installed after the transaxle is bolted to the engine.

44   Carefully move the transaxle forward until the dowel pins and the torque converter are engaged.

45   Install the lower transaxle-to-engine bolts. Tighten them securely.

46   Remove the transaxle jack.

47   Install the transaxle-to-engine support bracket.

48   Rotate the torque converter until the holes are aligned with the holes in the driveplate. Make sure the marks you made on the torque converter and driveplate during removal are aligned.

49   Install the torque converter-to-driveplate bolts. Tighten the bolts to the specified torque.

50   Install the torque converter cover.

51   Attach the transaxle cooler lines.

52   Install the left driveaxle (see Chapter 8).

53   Install the left frame support assembly.

54   Install the left stabilizer bar frame bushing bolts.

55   Install the stabilizer bar link pin bolt.

56   Install the transaxle strut.

57   On V6 models, install the lateral strut, if equipped.

58   Install any other suspension and chassis components which were detached or removed.

59   Seat the driveaxles in the transaxle.

60   Remove the driveaxle seal protectors.

61   Install the splash shield.

62   Attach the shift linkage bracket to the transaxle.

63   Install both front wheels.

64   Remove the jacks supporting the transaxle and the engine.

65   Lower the vehicle.

66   Install the upper engine-to-transaxle bolts.

67   Attach the shift cable to the transaxle lever and bracket.

68   Attach the wiring connectors to the speed sensor, TCC, starter safety switch and Park/Neutral/back-up light switch. Secure the wire harness to the transaxle.

69   Remove the engine support fixture, lifting hoist or jack from the engine.

70   Install the dipstick and tube.

71   Attach the TV cable to the transaxle and throttle lever.

72   Install the rubber transaxle vent hose.

73   If the vehicle has a V6 engine, install the front exhaust manifold and crossover pipe.

74   Install the air cleaner assembly and air intake duct.

75   Attach the cable to the negative battery terminal.

76   Fill the transaxle with fresh transaxle fluid.

Chapter 8   Clutch and driveaxles

Contents

Specifications

Clutch

Fluid type	See Chapter 1
Disc runout	0.020 in maximum
Slave cylinder pushrod travel	0.433 in minimum

Torque specifications
Ft-lbs (unless otherwise indicated)

Release lever bolt	30 to 45
Pedal-to-mounting bracket bolt	
Through 1991	20 to 25
1992	16
Pressure plate-to-flywheel bolts	
Through 1990	14 to 18
1991	
2.2L and 3.1L engines	18
2.3L engine	22
1992	
2.2L and 3.1L engines	18 plus an additional 30-degrees rotation
2.3L engine	15 plus an additional 30-degrees rotation
Master cylinder mounting nuts	15 to 25
Release cylinder mounting nuts	14 to 20

Driveaxles

Collapsed CV joint boot dimension	5-1/16 in

Torque specifications
Ft-lbs

Hub nut	
Initial	74
Final	191
Intermediate shaft mounting bolts	35
Wheel lug nuts	See Chapter 1

8

1   General information

The information in this Chapter deals with the components from the rear of the engine to the drive wheels, except for the transaxle, which is covered in the previous Chapter. For the purposes of this Chapter, these components are grouped into two categories: Clutch and driveaxles. Separate Sections within this Chapter cover components in both groups.

Warning: *Since many of the procedures covered in this Chapter involve working under the vehicle, make sure it's securely supported on sturdy jackstands or on a hoist where the vehicle can easily be raised and lowered.*

Note: *On models equipped with the Delco Loc II audio system, be sure the lockout feature is turned off before performing any procedure which requires disconnecting the battery.*

2   Clutch – description and check

Refer to illustration 2.1

1   All vehicles with a manual transaxle use a single dry plate, diaphragm spring-type clutch **(see illustration)**. The clutch disc has a splined hub which allows it to slide along the splines of the transaxle input shaft. The clutch and pressure plate are held in contact by spring pressure exerted by the diaphragm in the pressure plate.

2   The clutch release system is operated by hydraulic pressure. The hydraulic release system consists of the clutch pedal, a master cylinder, the hydraulic line, a slave cylinder which actuates the clutch release lever and the clutch release (or throwout) bearing.

3   When pressure is applied to the clutch pedal to release the clutch, hydraulic pressure is exerted against the outer end of the clutch release lever. As the lever pivots, the shaft fingers push against the release bearing. The bearing pushes against the fingers of the diaphragm spring in the pressure plate assembly, which in turn releases the clutch plate.

4   Terminology can be a problem when discussing the clutch components because common names are in some cases different from those used by the manufacturer. For example, the driven plate is also called the clutch plate or disc, the clutch release bearing is sometimes called a throwout bearing and the slave cylinder is often called an operating or release cylinder.

5   Other than to replace components with obvious damage, some preliminary checks should be performed to diagnose clutch problems.

   a) The first check should be of the fluid level in the clutch master cylinder. If the fluid level is low, add fluid as necessary and inspect the hydraulic system for leaks. If the master cylinder reservoir has run dry, bleed the system as described in Section 4 and recheck the clutch operation.

   b) To check "clutch spin down time," run the engine at normal idle speed with the transaxle in Neutral (clutch pedal up – engaged). Disengage the clutch (pedal down), wait nine seconds and shift the transaxle into Reverse. No grinding noise should be heard. A grinding noise would most likely indicate a problem in the pressure plate or the clutch disc.

   c) To check for complete clutch release, run the engine (with the parking brake on to prevent vehicle movement) and hold the clutch pedal approximately 1/2-inch from the floor. Shift the transaxle between First gear and Reverse several times. If the shift isn't smooth, component failure is indicated. Measure the slave cylinder pushrod travel. With the clutch pedal depressed completely the pushrod should extend the amount indicated in this Chapter's Specifications. If it doesn't, check the fluid level in the clutch master cylinder.

   d) Visually inspect the clutch pedal bushing at the top of the clutch pedal to make sure it's not sticking or worn excessively.

3   Hydraulic clutch components – removal and installation

Note: *The hydraulic clutch release system is serviced as a complete unit and has been bled (to remove air) at the factory. Individual components are not available separately. Other than replacing the entire system, bleeding the system is the only service procedure that may be necessary. There are no provisions for adjustment of clutch pedal height or freeplay.*

Removal

Refer to illustration 3.4

1   Disconnect the cable from the negative battery terminal.

2   On vehicles with a V6 engine, remove the air cleaner, mass air flow sensor and air intake duct as an assembly (see Chapter 4).

3   Remove the left side under-dash hush panel.

4   Remove the clutch master cylinder pushrod retaining clip and slide the pushrod off the pedal pin **(see illustration)**.

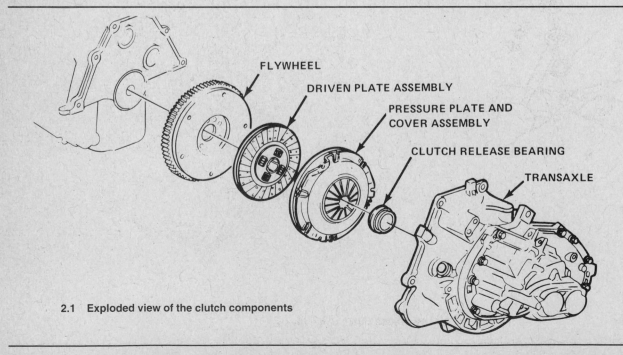

2.1   Exploded view of the clutch components

FLYWHEEL

DRIVEN PLATE ASSEMBLY

PRESSURE PLATE AND COVER ASSEMBLY

CLUTCH RELEASE BEARING

TRANSAXLE

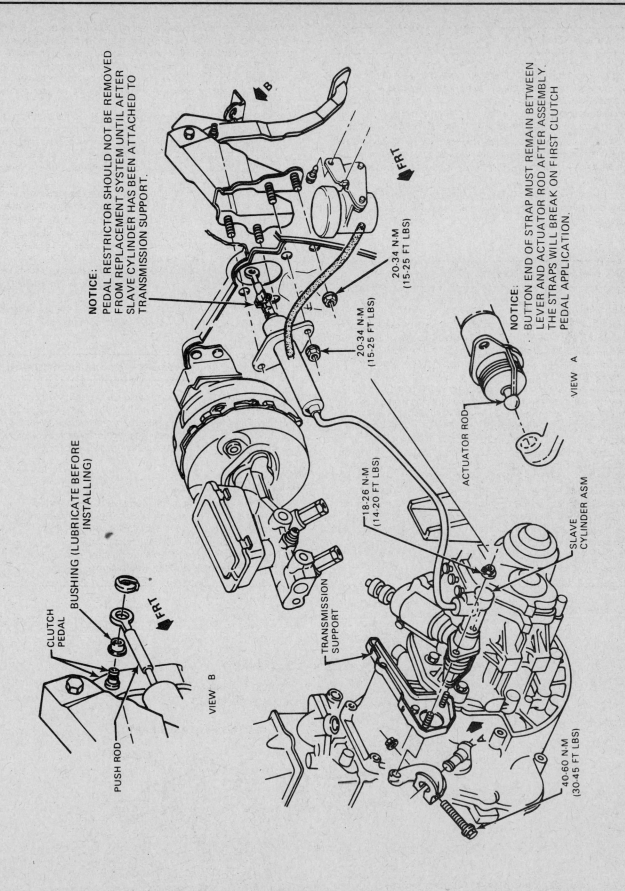

NOTICE:
PEDAL RESTRICTOR SHOULD NOT BE REMOVED FROM REPLACEMENT SYSTEM UNTIL AFTER SLAVE CYLINDER HAS BEEN ATTACHED TO TRANSMISSION SUPPORT.

B

FRT

20-34 N·M
(15-25 FT LBS)

20-34 N·M
(15-25 FT LBS)

NOTICE:
BUTTON END OF STRAP MUST REMAIN BETWEEN LEVER AND ACTUATOR ROD AFTER ASSEMBLY. THE STRAPS WILL BREAK ON FIRST CLUTCH PEDAL APPLICATION.

ACTUATOR ROD

VIEW   A

BUSHING (LUBRICATE BEFORE INSTALLING)

CLUTCH PEDAL

FRT

PUSH ROD

VIEW   B

18-26 N·M
(14-20 FT LBS)

SLAVE CYLINDER ASM

TRANSMISSION SUPPORT

40-60 N·M
(30-45 FT LBS)

3.4 Hydraulic clutch components

5   Remove the trim cover from the front of the dash.
6   Remove the clutch master cylinder mounting nuts at the front of the dash and the remote reservoir mounting screws.
7   Remove the release cylinder mounting nuts at the transaxle.
8   Remove the hydraulic system as a unit from the vehicle.

Installation

9   Guiding the pushrod into the pocket on the clutch release lever, attach the slave cylinder to the transmission support bracket. To avoid warping the slave cylinder, tighten the nuts in 1/4-turn increments to the specified torque. **Caution:** *Don't remove the plastic pushrod retainer from the slave cylinder – the straps will break during the first clutch pedal application.*
10   Install the clutch master cylinder on the firewall. To avoid warping the master cylinder, tighten the nuts in 1/4-turn increments to the specified torque. Install the reservoir and the mounting screws. Tighten the screws securely.
11   Install the trim cover at the front of the dash.
12   Remove the pedal restrictor from the pushrod. Lubricate the pushrod bushing on the clutch pedal. If the bushing is cracked or worn, replace it with a new one. Connect the pushrod to the clutch pedal.
13   If the vehicle is equipped with cruise control, have the switch adjustment at the clutch pedal bracket checked by a dealer service department.
14   Install the hush panel.
15   Press the clutch pedal down several times. This will break the plastic retaining straps on the slave cylinder pushrod. Don't remove the plastic button on the end of the pushrod.
16   Connect the cable to the negative battery terminal.

---

4   Hydraulic clutch system – bleeding

---

1   If you have to bleed the hydraulic clutch system, clean and remove the reservoir cap and fill the reservoir with the recommended fluid (see Chapter 1).
2   Open the bleed screw on the slave cylinder body and allow the fluid to drip into a container (DO NOT depress the clutch pedal). When it's apparent there are no more bubbles at the bleed screw opening and a steady stream of fluid is flowing out, close the bleed screw.
3   Recheck the fluid level – add more if necessary. The system should now be free of air.
4   To confirm this, measure the slave cylinder pushrod travel as described in Section 2.

---

5   Clutch release bearing and lever – removal and installation

---

Removal

Refer to illustration 5.5
1   Disconnect the negative cable from the battery.
2   Remove the under-dash panel.
3   Disconnect the clutch master cylinder pushrod from the clutch pedal pin.
4   Remove the transaxle (see Chapter 7, Part B).
5   Remove the clutch release bearing from the clutch fork. Make a mark on the release bearing pad and the release fork so the bearing can be returned to its original position if it's reused **(see illustration)**. Remove the bearing retaining spring from the release fork holes and detach the bearing.
6   Hold the center of the bearing and turn the outer race. If the bearing doesn't turn smoothly or if it's noisy, replace it with a new one. Wipe the bearing with a clean rag and inspect it for damage, wear and cracks. Don't immerse the bearing in solvent – it's sealed and would be ruined by the solvent.

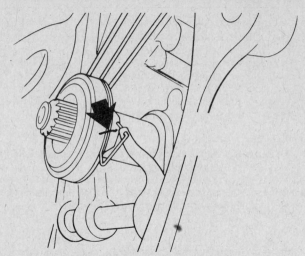

5.5   Before removing the release bearing from the transaxle, mark the bearing pad and the clutch release fork (arrow)

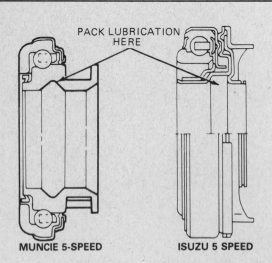

PACK LUBRICATION HERE

MUNCIE 5-SPEED   ISUZU 5 SPEED

5.7   Fill the groove in the release bearing bore with multi–purpose grease

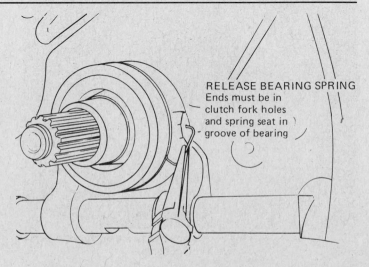

RELEASE BEARING SPRING
Ends must be in clutch fork holes and spring seat in groove of bearing

5.8   When installing the release bearing, make sure the retaining spring is seated in the bearing groove and the spring ends are located in the clutch release fork holes

Installation

Refer to illustrations 5.7 and 5.8

7   Lightly lubricate the clutch fork ends, where they contact the bearing, with white lithium-base grease. Pack the inner groove of the bearing with grease as well **(see illustration)**.

8   Install the release bearing on the transaxle retainer so both of the fork tangs fit into the outer diameter of the bearing groove. Be sure the bearing pads are resting on the fork ends with the previously inscribed marks aligned, then install the retaining spring. The spring must be fully seated in the retaining groove and both ends secured in the clutch fork holes **(see illustration)**.

9   Install the transaxle (see Chapter 7, Part B). Make sure the clutch release lever doesn't move toward the flywheel until the transaxle is bolted to the engine.

10   Reconnect the clutch master cylinder pushrod.

11   Install the under-dash cover.

12   Attach the cable to the negative battery terminal.

13   Check the clutch operation.

---

6   Clutch components – removal, inspection and installation

Refer to illustrations 6.5, 6.9, 6.11 and 6.13

Warning: *Dust produced by clutch wear and deposited on clutch components contains asbestos, which is hazardous to your health. DO NOT blow it out with compressed air or inhale it. DO NOT use gasoline or petroleum-based solvents to remove the dust. Brake system cleaner should be used to flush it into a drain pan. After the clutch components are wiped clean with a rag, dispose of the contaminated rags and cleaner in a sealed, marked container.*

Removal

1   Access to the clutch components is normally accomplished by removing the transaxle, leaving the engine in the vehicle. If the engine is being removed for major overhaul, then check the clutch for wear and replace worn components as necessary. The following procedures are based on the assumption the engine will stay in place.

2   Remove the left side under-dash hush panel and disconnect the clutch master cylinder pushrod from the clutch pedal (see Section 3).

3   Referring to Chapter 7, Part A, remove the transaxle from the vehicle. Remove the release bearing (see Section 5).

4   To support the clutch disc during removal, install a clutch alignment tool through the splined hole.

5   Check the pressure plate and flywheel for indexing marks. They're usually an X, an O or some other white letter. If no marks are visible, make some with a scribe or center punch and hammer to ensure installation of the components in the same relationship to each other **(see illustration)**.

6   Loosen the pressure plate-to-flywheel bolts in 1/4-turn increments until they can be removed by hand. Follow a criss-cross pattern to avoid warping the pressure plate assembly. Support the pressure plate and completely remove the bolts, then detach the pressure plate and clutch disc.

Inspection

7   Ordinarily, when a problem develops with the clutch, it can be attributed to wear of the clutch driven plate assembly (clutch disc). However, all components should be inspected at this time. **Note:** *If the clutch components are contaminated with oil, there will be shiny, black glazed spots on the clutch disc lining, which will cause the clutch to slip. Replacing clutch components won't completely cure the problem – be sure to check the rear crankshaft oil seal and the transaxle input shaft seal for leaks. If it looks like a seal is leaking, be sure to install a new one to avoid the same problem with a new clutch.*

8   Inspect the flywheel for cracks, heat checking, grooves and other obvious defects. If the imperfections are slight, a machine shop can machine the surface flat and smooth, which is highly recommended regardless of the surface appearance. Refer to Chapter 2 for the flywheel removal and installation procedure.

9   Inspect the lining on the clutch disc. There should be at least 1/16-inch of lining above the rivet heads. Check for loose rivets, distortion, cracks, broken springs and other obvious damage **(see illustration)**. As mentioned above, ordinarily the clutch disc is routinely replaced, so if in doubt about its condition, replace it with a new one.

10   Ordinarily, the release bearing is also replaced along with the clutch disc (see Section 5).

6.5   After removal of the transmission, this will be the view of the clutch components

| 1 | Pressure plate assembly (clutch disc inside) | 2 | Flywheel |

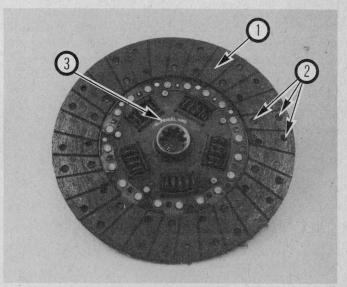

6.9   The clutch disc

1   Lining – this will wear down in use
2   Rivets – these secure the lining and will damage the flywheel or pressure plate if allowed to contact the surfaces
3   Index marks – "Flywheel side" or something similar

11   Check the diaphragm spring fingers and the machined surfaces of the pressure plate **(see illustration)**. If the surface is grooved or otherwise damaged, take it to a machine shop for possible machining or replacement. Also check for obvious damage, distortion, cracks, etc. Light glazing can be removed with medium grit emery cloth. If a new pressure plate is required, new and factory-rebuilt units are available.

Installation

12   Before installation, clean the flywheel and pressure plate machined surfaces with lacquer thinner or acetone. It's important that no oil or grease is on these surfaces or the lining of the clutch disc. Handle the parts only with clean hands.

6.11   The machined face of the pressure plate (arrow) must be inspected for scoring and other damage – if damage is slight, a machine shop can make the surface smooth again

13   Position the clutch disc and pressure plate against the flywheel with the clutch plate held in place with an alignment tool **(see illustration)**. Make sure it's installed properly (most replacement clutch plates will be marked "flywheel side" or something similar – if it's not marked, install it with the damper springs toward the transaxle).
14   Tighten the pressure plate-to-flywheel bolts only finger tight, working around the pressure plate.
15   Center the clutch disc by inserting the alignment tool through the splined hub and into the bore in the crankshaft. Wiggle the alignment tool up, down or from side-to-side as needed to center the clutch. Tighten the pressure plate-to-flywheel bolts a little at a time, working in a criss-cross pattern to prevent distorting the cover. After all the bolts are snug, tighten them to the specified torque. Remove the alignment tool.
16   Using high-temperature grease, lubricate the inner groove of the release bearing (refer to Section 5). Also place grease on the fork fingers.
17   Install the clutch release bearing as described in Section 5.
18   Install the transaxle, slave cylinder and all components that were removed previously.
19   Adjust the shift linkage as outlined in Chapter 7 Part A.

---

7   Clutch pedal – removal and installation

Removal

Refer to illustration 7.4

1   Disconnect the negative battery cable from the battery.
2   Remove the left-side hush panel from under the dash.
3   Remove the clutch master cylinder pushrod retaining clip and slide the pushrod off the pedal pin (see Section 3).
4   Remove the clutch pedal pivot bolt and pull the pedal off the mounting bracket **(see illustration)**. Extract the bushings and spacer and inspect them for wear. Replace them with new ones as necessary.

Installation

5   Lubricate the spacer and bushings with multi-purpose grease and install them on the clutch pedal. Position the pedal in the bracket and install the pivot bolt.

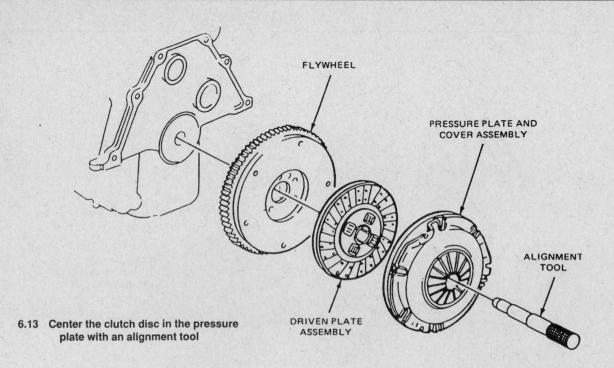

6.13   Center the clutch disc in the pressure plate with an alignment tool

FLYWHEEL

PRESSURE PLATE AND COVER ASSEMBLY

ALIGNMENT TOOL

DRIVEN PLATE ASSEMBLY

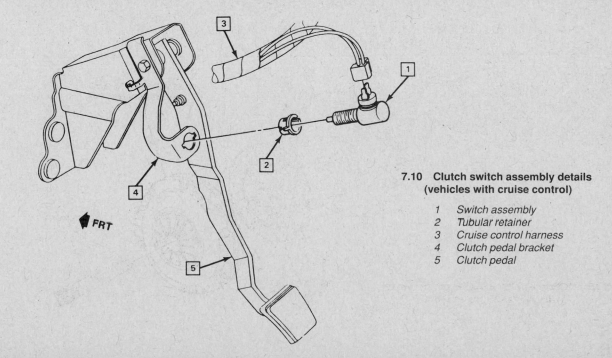

7.4   Clutch pedal assembly mounting details

1	Clutch pedal	4	Spacer
2	Pivot bolt nut	5	Pivot bolt
3	Bushing		

6   Lubricate the master cylinder pushrod bushing with multi-purpose grease, slide it onto the pedal pin and install the retaining clip.

7   Install and adjust the starter safety switch (refer to Section 8).

8   If the vehicle is equipped with cruise control, adjust the clutch switch (see below).

9   Install the under-dash panel.

Clutch switch adjustment (cruise control-equipped vehicles)

Refer to illustration 7.10

10   Insert the tubular retainer into the clutch pedal **(see illustration)**.

11   Depress the clutch pedal and insert the switch into the retainer until the switch is completely seated. Listen to the audible clicks made by the threaded portion of the switch as it's pushed through the retainer toward the clutch pedal.

12   Pull the clutch pedal all the way up (against the pedal stop) until the clicking sound ceases.

13   Release the clutch pedal and repeat the previous Step to verify that the switch doesn't click.

8   Starter safety switch – check and replacement

1   The starter safety switch is mounted on the clutch pedal support and allows the engine to be started only with the clutch pedal fully depressed. Refer to Chapter 1 for the checking procedure.

2   Disconnect the negative cable from the battery.

3   Remove the left side under-dash panel to gain access to the top of the clutch pedal.

4   At the top of the clutch pedal is a small rod which passes through the pedal. Remove the clip from the end of this rod.

5   Remove the screw which secures the starter safety switch to the clutch pedal support bracket.

6   Disconnect the electrical lead and remove the switch.

7   Install the new switch by reversing the removal procedure. Check to make sure the engine can be started only when the clutch pedal is fully depressed. Be sure to perform this test with the transaxle in Neutral.

9   Driveaxles – general information

Refer to illustrations 9.1a, 9.1b and 9.1c·

Power is transmitted from the transaxle to the front wheels by two driveaxles, which consist of splined solid axles with constant velocity (CV) joints at each end. There are two types of inner CV joints used. On certain models a double-offset design using ball bearings with an inner and outer race is used to allow angular movement. The other CV joint used is a tri-pot design, with a spider bearing assembly and tripot housing to allow angular movement **(see illustrations)**. To determine which CV joint is used on your vehicle, look at the housing while it's still installed on the vehicle and compare it to the accompanying illustrations, noting that the tri-pot housing will have three major indentations in it and a very thin retaining clamp holding the boot in position **(see illustration)**. All outer CV joints are the double-offset type.

7.10   Clutch switch assembly details (vehicles with cruise control)

1   Switch assembly
2   Tubular retainer
3   Cruise control harness
4   Clutch pedal bracket
5   Clutch pedal

8

9.1a   Driveaxle and CV joint component layout
(double offset design)

1   Deflector ring
2   Outer bearing race
3   Bearing cage
4   Inner bearing race
5   Ball bearings
6   Race retaining ring
7   Boot retaining clamp
8   Outer driveaxle boot
9   Boot retaining clamp
10   Driveaxle
11   Inner driveaxle boot
12   Ball bearing retaining ring
13   Inner race
14   Bearing cage
15   Outer race
16   Retaining ring

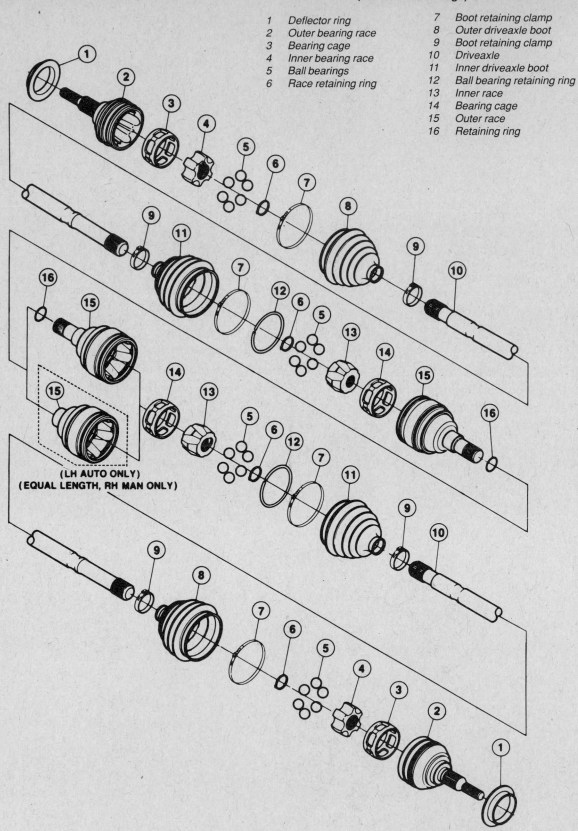

(LH AUTO ONLY)
(EQUAL LENGTH, RH MAN ONLY)

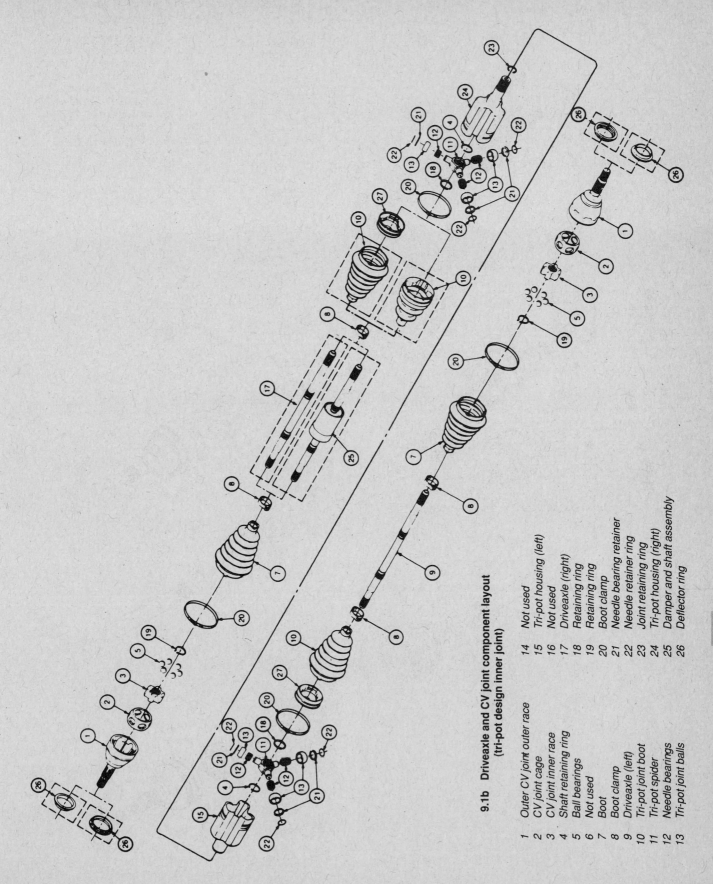

9.1b Driveaxle and CV joint component layout (tri-pot design inner joint)

1   Outer CV joint outer race
2   CV joint cage
3   CV joint inner race
4   Shaft retaining ring
5   Ball bearings
6   Not used
7   Boot
8   Boot clamp
9   Driveaxle (left)
10 Tri-pot joint boot
11 Tri-pot joint spider
12 Needle bearings
13 Tri-pot joint balls
14 Not used
15 Tri-pot housing (left)
16 Not used
17 Driveaxle (right)
18 Retaining ring
19 Retaining ring
20 Boot clamp
21 Needle bearing retainer
22 Needle retainer ring
23 Joint retaining ring
24 Tri-pot housing (right)
25 Damper and shaft assembly
26 Deflector ring

8

The CV joints are protected by rubber boots, which are retained by clamps so the joints are protected from water and dirt. The boots should be inspected periodically (see Chapter 1). The inner boots have very small breather holes which may leak a small amount of lubricant under some circumstances, such as when the joint is compressed during removal. Damaged CV joint boots must be replaced immediately or the joints can be damaged. Boot replacement involves removing the driveaxles (Section 10). It's a good idea to disassemble, clean, inspect and repack the CV joint whenever replacing a CV joint boot to make sure the joint isn't contaminated with moisture or dirt, which would cause premature failure of the CV joint.

The most common symptom of worn or damaged CV joints, besides lubricant leaks, are a clicking noise in turns, a clunk when accelerating from a coasting condition or vibration at highway speeds.

10 Driveaxles – removal and installation

Refer to illustrations 10.2, 10.5a, 10.5b, 10.6 and 10.8

Removal

1   Remove the wheel cover and loosen the hub nut. Loosen the wheel lug nuts, raise the front of the vehicle and support it securely on jackstands. Apply the parking brake and block the rear wheels to keep the vehicle from rolling off the jackstands. Remove the front wheel.
2   Remove the driveaxle hub nut. To prevent the hub from turning, insert a screwdriver through the caliper and into a rotor cooling vane, then remove the nut **(see illustration)**.
3   Remove the brake caliper and disc and support the caliper out of the way with a piece of wire (see Chapter 9).
4   Remove the control arm-to-steering knuckle balljoint stud nut and separate the lower arm from the steering knuckle (see Chapter 10 if necessary).
5   Push the driveaxle out of the hub with a puller, then support the outer end of the driveaxle with a piece of wire to prevent damage to the inner CV joint **(see illustrations)**.

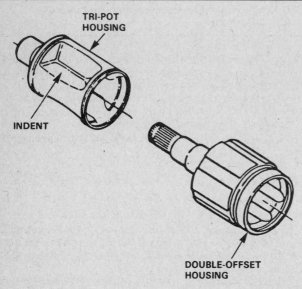

9.1c   Two types of inner CV joint housings – note the indents on the tri-pot housing

10.2   A screwdriver inserted through the caliper and into a disc cooling vane will hold the hub stationary while loosening the hub nut

10.5a   A two-jaw puller works well for pushing the stub axle out of the hub

10.5b   Support the driveaxle with a piece of wire after it's been freed from the hub – don't let it hang unsupported or the CV joint could be damaged

6   Carefully pry the inner end of the driveaxle out of the transaxle, using a large pry bar positioned between the transaxle housing and the CV joint housing **(see illustration)**. On some models, the right driveaxle connects to an intermediate shaft (see Section 12) rather than the transaxle. Removal of the driveaxle is the same, except there's no need to pry it out of the transaxle.

7   Support the CV joints and carefully remove the driveaxle from the vehicle.

Installation

8   Lubricate the differential seal with multi-purpose grease, raise the driveaxle into position while supporting the CV joints and insert the splined end of the inner CV joint into the differential side gear. Seat the shaft in the side gear by positioning the end of a screwdriver in the groove in the CV joint and tapping it into position with a hammer **(see illustration)**. On models with an intermediate shaft, slide the driveaxle inner CV joint onto the end of the intermediate shaft.

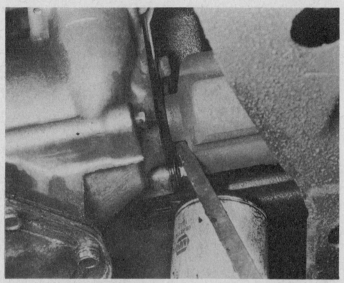

10.6   Use a large pry bar positioned as shown to "pop" the inner CV joint out of the transaxle – it may be necessary to tap the pry bar with a hammer if the driveaxle is stuck

10.8   A large punch or screwdriver, positioned in the groove on the CV joint housing, can be used to seat the joint in the transaxle

9   Apply a light coat of multi-purpose grease to the outer CV joint splines, pull out on the strut/steering knuckle assembly and install the stub axle in the hub.

10   Insert the control arm balljoint stud into the steering knuckle and tighten the nut. Be sure to use a new cotter pin (refer to Chapter 10).

11   Install the brake disc and caliper (see Chapter 9 if necessary).

12   Install the hub nut. Lock the disc so it can't turn, using a screwdriver or punch inserted through the caliper into a disc cooling vane, and tighten the hub nut to the initial specified torque.

13   Grasp the inner CV joint housing (not the driveaxle) and pull out to make sure the axle has seated securely in the transaxle.

14   Install the wheel and lower the vehicle.

15   Tighten the hub nut to the final specified torque and install the wheel cover.

---

11   Driveaxle boot replacement and constant velocity (CV) joint overhaul

---

Note: *If the CV joints exhibit wear indicating the need for an overhaul (usually due to torn boots), explore all options before beginning the job. Complete rebuilt driveaxles are available on an exchange basis, which eliminates a lot of time and work. Whatever is decided, check on the cost and availability of parts before disassembling the vehicle.*

1   Remove the driveaxle (see Section 10).

2   Place the driveaxle in a vise lined with rags to avoid damage to the shaft.

Inner CV joint

Tri-pot design

Refer to illustrations 11.4, 11.5, 11.10, 11.11 and 11.13

3   Cut off the boot seal retaining clamps and slide the boot towards the center of the driveaxle. Mark the tri-pot housing and driveaxle so they can be reinstalled in the same relative positions, then slide the housing off the spider assembly.

4   Remove the spider assembly from the axle by first removing the inner retaining ring and sliding the spider assembly back to expose the front retaining ring. Remove the front retaining ring and slide the joint off the driveaxle **(see illustration)**.

11.4   Snap-ring pliers should be used to remove both the inner and outer retaining rings

8

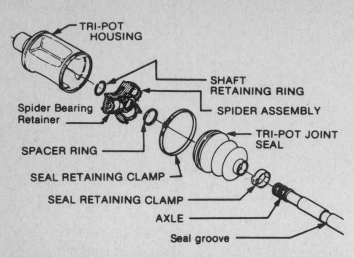

11.5   Boot installation layout for a tri-pot inner CV joint – note the tape around the spider assembly to prevent it from coming apart

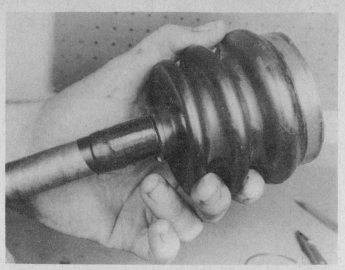

11.10   Before installing the CV joint boot, wrap the axle splines with tape to prevent damage to the boot

11.11   When installing the spider assembly on the driveaxle, make sure the recess in the counterbore (arrow) is facing the end of the driveaxle

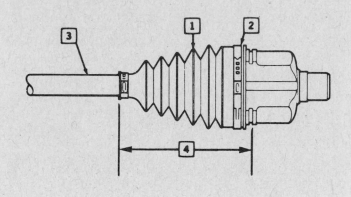

11.13   The collapsed dimension of all inner CV joints must be adjusted before the large boot clamp is tightened

1	Boot	4	Adjust the collapsed length of the joint,
2	Clamp		from the small end of the boot to the
3	Axleshaft		groove in the outer race, to 5-1/16 inches

5   Use tape or a cloth wrapped around the spider bearing assembly to retain the bearings during removal and installation **(see illustration)**.

6   Remove the spider assembly from the axle.

7   Slide the boot off the axle.

8   Clean all of the old grease out of the housing and spider assembly. Carefully disassemble each section of the spider assembly, one at a time, and clean the needle bearings with solvent. Inspect the rollers, spider cross, bearings and housing for scoring, pitting and other signs of abnormal wear. Apply a coat of CV joint grease to the inner bearing surfaces to hold the needle bearings in place when reassembling the spider assembly.

9   Pack the housing with half of the grease furnished with the new boot and place the remainder in the boot.

10   Wrap the driveaxle splines with tape to avoid damaging the boot, then slide the boot onto the axle **(see illustration)**.

11   Install the spider bearing with the recess in the counterbore facing the end of the driveaxle **(see illustration)**.

12   Install the tri-pot housing.

13   Seat the boot in the housing and axle seal grooves, then adjust the collapsed dimension of the joint **(see illustration)**. Install the retaining clamps, then install the driveaxle as described in Section 10.

Double offset design

Refer to illustrations 11.14a and 11.14b

14   Refer to the procedure outlined in Steps 15 through 33, but note that the cage and inner race assembly is retained in the outer race by a ball retaining ring, which is removed after the driveaxle is withdrawn from the CV joint **(see illustration)**. Also, the inner race and cage must be marked in relation to each other, as the cage is not symmetrical **(see illustration)**. Refer to Step 13 when adjusting the CV joint collapsed dimension.

Outer CV joint

Refer to illustrations 11.15, 11.17, 11.20, 11.21, 11.22, 11.23, 11.24a, 11.24b, 11.27, 11.28 and 11.32

15   Tap lightly around the outer circumference of the seal retainer with a hammer and punch to dislodge and remove it. Be very careful not to de-

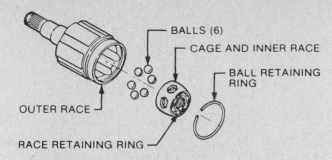

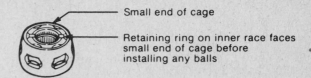

11.14a   After the driveaxle has been removed from the joint assembly, remove the ball retaining ring and slide the inner race and cage out of the outer race

11.14b   The inner race must be assembled as shown, as the cage is not symmetrical – when installing the inner race and cage in the outer race, the large diameter side of the cage goes in first

11.15   Carefully tap around the circumference of the retaining ring to remove it from the housing

11.17   Use snap-ring pliers to remove the inner retaining ring

11.20   Gently tap the inner race with a brass punch to tilt it enough to allow ball bearing removal

11.21   Using a dull screwdriver, carefully pry the balls out of the cage

form the retainer, or it won't seal properly **(see illustration)**.

16   Cut off the band retaining the boot to the shaft.

17   Remove the snap-ring and slide the joint assembly off **(see illustration)**.

18   Slide the old boot off the driveaxle.

19   Place marks on the inner race and cage so they both can be installed facing out when reassembling the joint.

20   Press down on the inner race far enough to allow a ball bearing to be removed. If it's difficult to tilt, tap the inner race with a brass punch and hammer **(see illustration)**.

21   Pry the balls out of the cage, one at a time, with a blunt screwdriver or wooden tool **(see illustration)**.

22   With all of the balls removed from the cage and the cage/inner race assembly tilted 90-degrees, align the cage windows with the outer race

8

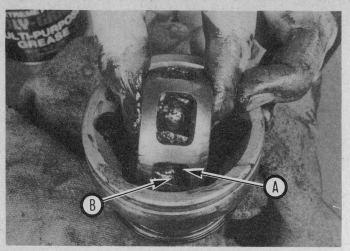

11.22   Tilt the inner race and cage 90-degrees, then align the windows in the cage (A) with the lands (B) and rotate the inner race up and out of the outer race

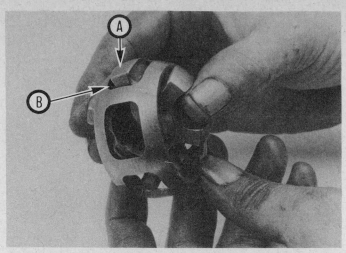

11.23   Align the inner race lands (A) with the cage windows (B) and rotate the inner race out of the cage

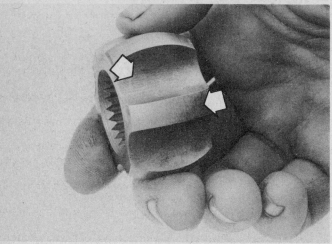

11.24a   Check the inner race lands and grooves for pitting and score marks

11.24b   Check the cage for cracks, pitting and score marks – shiny spots are normal and don't affect operation

11.27   Align the cage windows and the inner and outer race grooves, then tilt the cage and inner race to insert the balls

11.28   Apply grease through the splined hole, then insert a wooden dowel (approximately 15/16-inch diameter) through the splined hole and push down – the dowel will force the grease into the joint

11.32   Carefully tap around the circumference of the retaining ring to install it on the housing

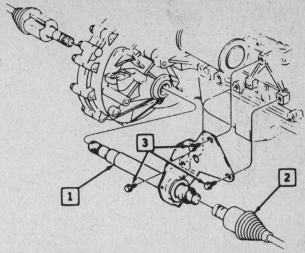

12.7   Intermediate shaft installation details

1   Intermediate shaft   3   Bracket bolts
2   Right driveaxle

lands and remove the assembly from the outer race **(see illustration)**.

23   Remove the inner race from the cage by turning the inner race 90-degrees in the cage, aligning the inner lands with the cage windows and rotating the inner race out of the cage **(see illustration)**.

24   Clean the components with solvent to remove all traces of grease. Inspect the cage and races for pitting, score marks, cracks and other signs of wear and damage. Shiny, polished spots are normal and won't adversely affect CV joint operation **(see illustrations)**.

25   Install the inner race in the cage by reversing the technique described in Step 22.

26   Install the inner race and cage assembly in the outer race by reversing the procedure in Step 21. The marks that were previously applied to the inner race and cage must both be visible after the assembly is installed in the outer race.

27   Press the balls into the cage windows **(see illustration)**.

28   Pack the CV joint assembly with lubricant through the inner splined hole. Force the grease into the bearing by inserting a wooden dowel through the splined hole and pushing it to the bottom of the joint. Repeat this procedure until the bearing is completely packed **(see illustration)**.

29   Install the boot on the driveaxle as described in Step 10. Apply a liberal amount of grease to the inside of the axle boot.

30   Position the CV joint assembly on the driveaxle, aligning the splines. Using a soft-face hammer, drive the CV joint onto the driveaxle until the retaining ring is seated in the groove.

31   Seat the inner end of the boot in the seal groove and install the retaining clamp.

32   Install the seal retainer securely by tapping evenly around the outer circumference with a hammer and punch **(see illustration)**.

33   Install the driveaxle as described in Section 10.

---

12   Intermediate axleshaft – removal and installation

Refer to illustration 12.7

Removal

1   Loosen the right front wheel lug nuts, raise the front of the vehicle and support it securely on jackstands. Apply the parking brake and block the rear wheels to keep the vehicle from rolling off the jackstands. Remove the wheel.

2   Disconnect the stabilizer bar from the right control arm (refer to Chapter 10 if necessary).

3   Remove the balljoint stud nut and separate the control arm from the steering knuckle (refer to Chapter 10).

4   Pull the inner end of the right driveaxle out of the intermediate shaft and support it with a piece of wire. Don't let it hang, or damage to the outer CV joint may occur.

5   Disconnect the detonation (knock) sensor electrical connector and remove the sensor (refer to Chapter 6).

6   Remove the power steering pump brace (see Chapter 10 if necessary).

7   Remove the intermediate shaft bracket bolts and pull the shaft out of the transaxle **(see illustration)**.

Installation

8   Lubricate the lips of the differential seal with multi-purpose grease and slide the intermediate shaft into the transaxle. Install the bolts and tighten them to the specified torque.

9   Install the power steering pump brace.

10   Install the detonation sensor and reconnect the electrical connector.

11   Apply multi-purpose grease to the intermediate shaft splines and install the driveaxle in the shaft.

12   Insert the balljoint stud into the steering knuckle and tighten the nut. Be sure to use a new cotter pin.

13   Install the stabilizer bar-to-control arm bolt (refer to Chapter 10 if necessary).

14   Install the wheel and tire and tighten the lug nuts to the specified torque.

8

Chapter 9 Brakes

Contents

Specifications

General

Brake fluid type	See Chapter 1

Disc brakes

Brake pad lining minimum thickness	See Chapter 1
Rotor thickness	
Standard	
Through 1991	0.885 in
1992 on	0.806 in
Discard thickness	Refer to the dimension cast into the rotor
Rotor runout	
Through 1991	0.004 in
1992 on	0.003 in
Rotor thickness variation limit	0.0005 in
Caliper-to-bracket stop clearance	0.005 to 0.012 in

Drum brakes

Brake shoe lining minimum thickness	See Chapter 1
Drum diameter	
Standard	7.879 in
Service limit	7.899 in
Discard diameter*	7.929 in
Drum out-of-round limit	0.006 in

Refer to the marks cast into the drum (they supersede information printed here)

Torque Specifications

	Ft-lbs
Caliper mounting bolts	38
Brake hose-to-caliper bolt	33
Master cylinder-to-booster nuts	20
Proportioner valve caps	20
Booster-to-pedal bracket nuts	
Through 1990	15
1991 on	20
Wheel lug nuts	See Chapter 1

---

1 General information

Conventional (non–ABS) system

All vehicles covered by this manual are equipped with hydraulically operated front and rear brake systems. The front brakes are disc type, and the rear brakes are drum type.

All brakes are self-adjusting. The front disc brakes automatically compensate for pad wear, while the rear drum brakes incorporate an adjustment mechanism which is activated as the brakes are applied when the vehicle is driven in reverse.

The hydraulic system consists of separate front and rear circuits. The master cylinder has separate reservoirs for the two circuits; in the event of a leak or failure in one hydraulic circuit, the other circuit will remain operative. A visual warning of circuit failure, air in the system, or other pressure differential conditions in the brake system is given by a warning light activated by a failure warning switch in the master cylinder.

The proportioner valves are designed to provide better front to rear braking balance with heavy brake application. These valves allow more presure to be applied to the front brakes (under certain braking operations) due to the fact the rear of the vehicle is lighter and does not require as much braking force.

The parking brake mechanically operates the rear brakes only. It's activated by a pull-handle in the center console between the front seats.

The power brake booster, located in the engine compartment on the firewall, uses engine manifold vacuum and atmospheric pressure to provide assistance to the hydraulically operated brakes.

After completing any operation involving the disassembly of any part of the brake system, always test drive the vehicle to check for proper braking performance before resuming normal driving. Test the brakes while driving on a clean, dry, flat surface. Conditions other than these can lead to inaccurate test results. Test the brakes at various speeds with both light and heavy pedal pressure. The vehicle should stop evenly without pulling to one side or the other. Avoid locking the brakes because this slides the tires and diminishes braking efficiency and control.

Tires, vehicle load and front end alignment are factors which also affect braking performance.

Anti-lock Brake System (ABS)

This system is available as an option. It is designed to reduce lost traction while braking. The system is similar to the non-ABS system except for the controller (computer) and related wiring, speed sensors and the hydraulic pump which replaces the master cylinder and power brake booster.

Anti-lock braking occurs only when a wheel is about to lock up (lose traction). Input signals from the wheel speed sensors to the computer are used to determine when a wheel is about to lose traction during braking. Hydraulic pressure will be reduced for the wheel about to loose traction. Diagnosis of this system is beyond the scope of the home mechanic. **Note:** *The ABS system is equipped with a self-diagnosis system similar to the engine codes. However, it is necessary to use a Tech 1 Diagnostic Computer (#94–00101 A) linked into the ALDL for access to these codes. Any failures in the ABS system should be repaired by a dealer service department or other repair shop.*

---

2   Disc brake pads – replacement

Refer to illustrations 2.5 and 2.6a through 2.6k

Warning: *Disc brake pads must be replaced on both front wheels at the same time – never replace the pads on only one wheel. Also, the dust created by the brake system may contain asbestos, which is harmful to your health. Never blow it out with compressed air and don't inhale any of it. An approved filtering mask should be worn when working on the brakes. Do not, under any circumstances, use petroleum-based solvents to clean brake parts. Use brake system cleaner or denatured alcohol only.*

Note: *When servicing the disc brakes, use only high-quality, nationally-recognized, brand name parts.*

1   Remove the cover from the brake fluid reservoir, siphon off about two-thirds of the fluid into a container and discard it.

2   Loosen the wheel lug nuts, raise the front of the vehicle and support it securely on jackstands. Apply the parking brake and block the rear wheels to keep the vehicle from rolling off the jackstands.

3   Remove the front wheel, then reinstall two lug nuts (flat side toward the rotor) to hold the rotor in place. Work on one brake assembly at a time, using the assembled brake for reference if necessary.

4   Inspect the rotor carefully as outlined in Section 4. If machining is necessary, follow the information in that Section to remove the rotor, at which time the pads can be removed from the calipers as well.

5   Push the piston back into the bore. If necessary, a C-clamp can be used, but a pry bar will usually do the job **(see illustration)**. As the piston is depressed to the bottom of the caliper bore, the fluid in the master cylinder will rise. Make sure it doesn't overflow. If necessary, siphon off more of the fluid as directed in Step 1.

2.5   A large C-clamp can be used to compress the piston into the caliper for removal

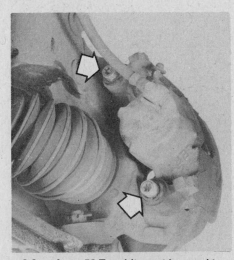

2.6a   A no. 50 Torx bit must be used to remove the two caliper mounting bolts (arrows) – don't attempt to loosen them with an Allen wrench, because the bolt heads could be damaged

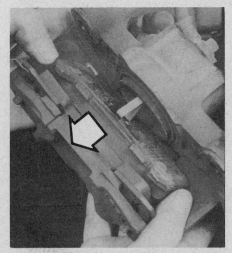

2.6b   Remove the inner pad by snapping it out of the piston in the direction shown (arrow)

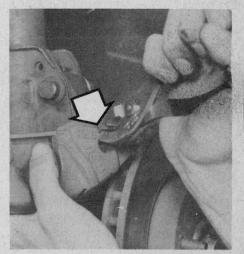

2.6c   Remove the outer pad by bending the tabs (arrow) straight out with a pair of pliers

9

2.6d   After bending the tabs straight, the outer pad can be removed by dislodging it from the caliper with a hammer

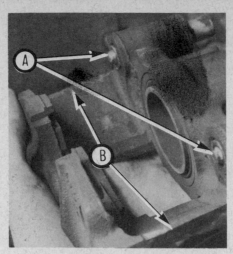

2.6e   Inspect the caliper bolts and bushings (A) for damage and the contact surfaces (B) for corrosion

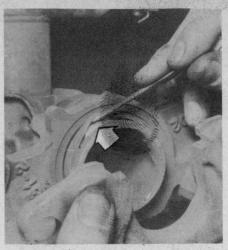

2.6f   Carefully peel back the edge of the piston boot and check for corrosion and leaking fluid

2.6g   Snap the inner pad retainer spring into the new pad in the direction shown (arrow)

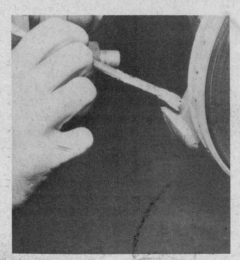

2.6h   Lubricate the lower steering knuckle contact surface with a small amount of white lithium-base grease

2.6i   Apply a light coat of white lithium-base grease to the upper steering knuckle-to-caliper contact surface

2.6j   Place the pads in position and snap the inner pad into place in the piston

2.6k   After installing the caliper, insert a large screwdriver between the outer pad flange and the disc hat to seat the pad, then bend the tabs over with a hammer

6   Follow the accompanying illustrations, beginning with 2.6a, for the actual pad replacement procedure. Be sure to stay in order and read the caption under each photograph.

7   When reinstalling the caliper, be sure to tighten the mounting bolts to the torque listed in this Chapter's Specifications. After the job has been completed, firmly depress the brake pedal a few times to bring the pads into contact with the rotor.

---

3   Disc brake caliper – removal, overhaul and installation

Refer to illustrations 3.9, 3.10, 3.11, 3.12, 3.15, 3.16, 3.17, 3.18, 3.20 and 3.23

Warning 1: *This procedure should not be undertaken on vehicles equipped with ABS (Anti-lock brake system), since special tools are needed to properly bleed the brakes. Take the vehicle to a dealer service department or other repair shop that has the proper tools.*

Warning 2: *Dust created by the brake system contains asbestos, which is harmful to your health. Never blow it out with compressed air and don't inhale any of it. An approved filtering mask should be worn when working on the brakes. Do not, under any circumstances, use petroleum-based solvents to clean brake parts. Use brake system cleaner or denatured alcohol only.*

Note: *If an overhaul is indicated (usually because of fluid leakage) explore all options before beginning the job. New and factory rebuilt calipers are available on an exchange basis, which makes this job quite easy. If you decide to rebuild the calipers, make sure rebuild kits are available before proceeding.*

Removal

1   Remove the cover from the brake fluid reservoir, siphon off two-thirds of the fluid into a container and discard it.

2   Loosen the wheel lug nuts, raise the front of the vehicle and support it securely on jackstands. Apply the parking brake and block the rear wheels to keep the vehicle from rolling off the jackstands. Remove the front wheels.

3   Reinstall two lug nuts on each rotor, flat side against the rotor, to hold them in place.

4   Bottom the piston in the caliper bore. This is accomplished by pushing on the caliper, although it may be necessary to carefully use a flat pry bar or a large C-clamp.

5   Remove the brake hose inlet fitting bolt and disconnect the fitting. Have a rag handy to catch spilled fluid and wrap a plastic bag tightly around the end of the hose to prevent fluid loss and contamination.

6   Using a no. 50 Torx bit, remove the two mounting bolts and detach the caliper from the vehicle (refer to Section 2 if necessary).

Overhaul

7   Refer to Section 2 and remove the brake pads from the caliper.

8   Clean the exterior of the caliper with brake cleaner or denatured alcohol. **Warning:** *DO NOT use gasoline, kerosene or petroleum-based cleaning solvents.* Place the caliper on a clean workbench.

9   Position a wood block or several shop rags in the caliper as a cushion, then use compressed air to remove the piston from the bore **(see illustration)**. Use only enough air pressure to ease the piston out. If it's blown out, even with the cushion in place, it may be damaged. **Warning:** *Never place your fingers in front of the piston in an attempt to catch or protect it when applying compressed air – serious injury could result.*

10   Carefully pry the dust boot out of the caliper bore **(see illustration)**.

11   Using a wood or plastic tool, remove the piston seal from the groove in the caliper bore **(see illustration)**. Metal tools may damage the bore.

3.9   With the caliper padded to catch the piston, use compressed air to force the piston out of the bore – DO NOT position your hands or fingers between the piston and caliper!

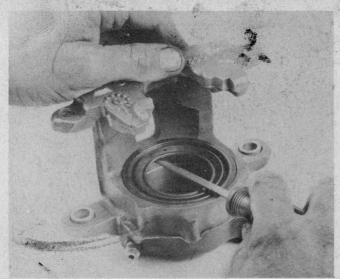

3.10   Carefully pry the dust boot out of the housing, taking care not to scratch the bore surface

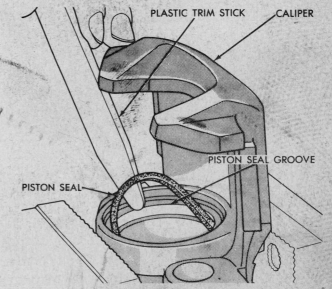

PLASTIC TRIM STICK   CALIPER

PISTON SEAL GROOVE

PISTON SEAL

3.11   To avoid damage to the caliper bore or seal groove, remove the seal with a plastic or wooden tool (a pencil will do the job)

9

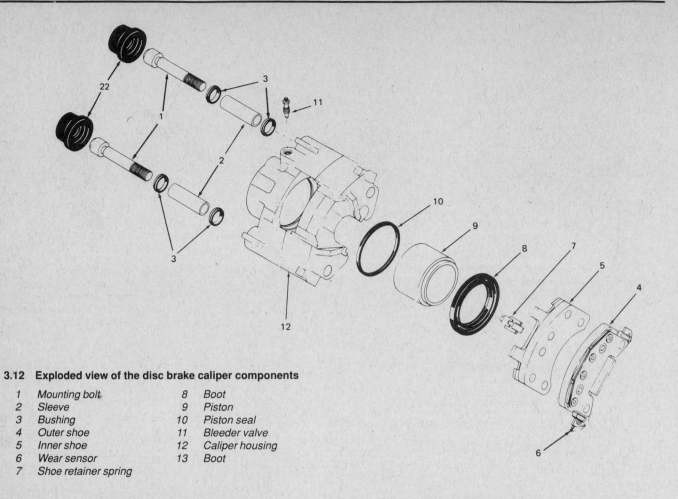

3.12   Exploded view of the disc brake caliper components

1	Mounting bolt	8	Boot
2	Sleeve	9	Piston
3	Bushing	10	Piston seal
4	Outer shoe	11	Bleeder valve
5	Inner shoe	12	Caliper housing
6	Wear sensor	13	Boot
7	Shoe retainer spring		

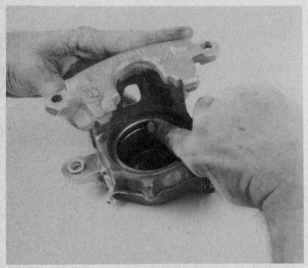

**3.15   Position the seal in the caliper bore – make sure
it isn't twisted**

12   Remove the caliper bleeder valve, then remove and discard the sleeves and bushings from the caliper ears. Discard all rubber parts **(see illustration)**.
13   Clean the remaining parts with brake cleaner or denatured alcohol, then blow them dry with compressed air.
14   Carefully examine the piston for scratches, nicks, burrs and loss of plating. If surface defects are noted, a new piston will be needed. Check

the caliper bore in a similar way. Light polishing with crocus cloth is permissible to remove light corrosion and stains. Discard the mounting bolts if they're corroded or damaged.
15   When reassembling the caliper, lubricate the piston bore and seal with clean brake fluid. Position the seal in the caliper bore groove **(see illustration)**.
16   Lubricate the piston with clean brake fluid, then install a new boot in the piston groove with the fold toward the open end of the piston **(see illustration)**.
17   Insert the piston squarely into the caliper bore, then apply force to bottom the piston in the bore **(see illustration)**.
18   Position the dust boot in the caliper counterbore, then use a punch to drive it into position **(see illustration)**. Make sure the boot is evenly installed below the caliper face.
19   Install the bleeder valve.
20   Install new bushings in the mounting bolt holes and fill the area between the bushings with silicone grease (supplied with the rebuild kit) **(see illustration)**. Push the sleeves into the mounting bolt holes.

Installation

21   Inspect the mounting bolts for corrosion. Use new ones if the originals are pitted.
22   Place the caliper in position over the rotor and mounting bracket, install the bolts and tighten them to the torque figure listed in this Chapter's Specifications.
23   Check to make sure the clearance between the caliper and the bracket stops is between 0.005 and 0.012-inch **(see illustration)**.
24   Install the brake hose-to-caliper bolt, using new copper washers, then tighten the bolt to the torque listed in this Chapter's Specifications. Bleed the brakes (Section 9).

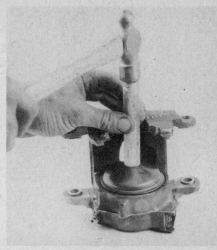

3.16   Install the new dust boot in the piston groove with the folds toward the open end of the piston

3.17   Push the piston squarely into the caliper bore

3.18   Use a seal driver to seat the boot in the caliper housing counterbore – if a seal driver isn't available, carefully tap around the outer edge of the boot with a punch until it's seated

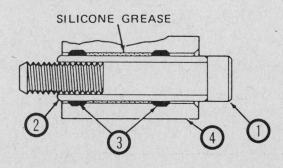

3.20   Pack the area between the mounting bolt sleeve bushings with silicone grease

1	Mounting bolt	3	Bushing
2	Sleeve	4	Caliper housing

3.23   Measure the clearance between the caliper and bracket stops at the points indicated

25   Install the wheels and lower the vehicle..

26   After the job has been completed, firmly depress the brake pedal a few times to bring the pads into contact·with the rotor.

4   Brake rotor (disc) – inspection, removal and installation

Refer to illustrations 4.2, 4.3, 4.4a, 4.4b, 4.5a and 4.5b

Inspection

1   Loosen the wheel lug nuts, raise the front of the vehicle and support it securely on jackstands. Apply the parking brake and block the rear wheels to keep the vehicle from rolling off the jackstands. Remove the wheel and install two lug nuts to hold the rotor in place.

2   Remove the brake caliper as outlined in Section 3. You don't have to disconnect the brake hose. After removing the caliper bolts, suspend the caliper out of the way with a piece of wire – DO NOT let it hang by the hose **(see illustration)**.

3   Visually inspect the rotor surface for score marks and other damage. Light scratches and shallow grooves are normal and may not be detrimental to brake operation, but deep score marks – over 0.015-inch (0.38 mm) deep – require rotor removal and refinishing by an automotive machine

4.2   Suspend the caliper with a piece of wire whenever it's necessary to reposition it – DO NOT let it hang by the brake hose!

4.3   The brake pads on this vehicle were obviously neglected as they wore down completely and cut deep grooves into the rotor – wear this severe will require replacement of the rotor

4.4a   Check for runout with a dial indicator – mount it with the indicator needle about 1/2-inch from the outer edge

4.4b   If you don't have the rotors machined, at the very least be sure to break the glaze on the rotor surface with emery cloth

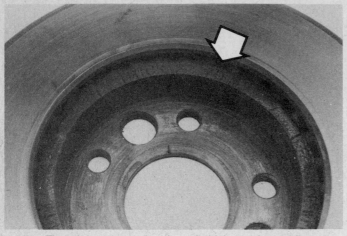

4.5a   The minimum wear (or discard) thickness (arrow) is cast into the inside of the rotor

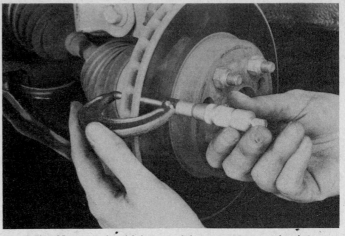

4.5b   Measure the thickness of the rotor at several points with a micrometer

shop. Be sure to check both sides of the rotor **(see illustration)**. If pulsating has been felt during application of the brakes, suspect excessive rotor runout.

4   To check rotor runout, mount a dial indicator with the stem resting at a point about 1/2-inch from the outer edge of the rotor **(see illustration)**. Set the indicator to zero and turn the rotor. The indicator reading should not exceed the specified allowable runout limit. If it does, the rotor should be refinished by an automotive machine shop. **Note:** *The rotors should be resurfaced, regardless of the dial indicator reading, to impart a smooth finish and ensure perfectly flat brake pad surfaces (which will eliminate pedal pulsations. At the very least, if you don't have the rotors resurfaced, remove the glaze with medium-grit emery cloth using a swirling motion* **(see illustration)**.

5   Never machine the rotor to a thickness less than the specified minimum allowable refinish thickness. The minimum wear (or discard) thickness is cast into the inside of the rotor **(see illustration)**. This shouldn't be confused with the minimum refinish thickness. The rotor thickness can be checked with a micrometer **(see illustration)**.

Removal

6   Remove the two lug nuts that were put on to hold the rotor in place and remove the rotor from the hub.

Installation

7   Place the rotor in position over the threaded studs.

8   Install the caliper and brake pad assembly over the rotor and position it on the steering knuckle (refer to Section 3 for the caliper installation procedure, if necessary). Tighten the caliper bolts to the torque listed in this Chapter's Specifications.

9   Install the wheel, then lower the vehicle to the ground. Depress the brake pedal a few times to bring the brake pads into contact with the rotor. Bleeding of the system won't be necessary unless the brake hose was disconnected from the caliper. Check the operation of the brakes carefully before driving the vehicle in traffic.

5   Rear brake shoes – inspection and replacement

Warning: *Drum brake shoes must be replaced on both rear wheels at the same time – never replace the shoes on only one wheel. Also, the dust created by the brake system contains asbestos, which is harmful to your health. Never blow it out with compressed air and don't inhale any of it. An approved filtering mask should be worn when working on the brakes. Do not, under any circumstances, use petroleum-based solvents to clean brake parts. Use brake cleaner or denatured alcohol only!*

Caution: *Whenever the brake shoes are replaced, the return and hold-down springs should also be replaced. Due to the continuous heating/cooling cycle the springs are subjected to, they lose tension over a period of time and may allow the shoes to drag on the drum and wear at a much*

5.4a   If the brake drum won't come off, it may be necessary to remove the plug with a hammer and chisel, then turn the adjuster screw to move the brake shoes away from the drum

5.4b   Before removing anything, clean the brake assembly with brake system cleaner or denatured alcohol – DO NOT use compressed air to blow the dust out of the brake assembly!

5.4c   Anchor plate (duo-servo) type drum brake components – exploded view

1	Return spring	15	Pivot nut
2	Return spring	16	Adjusting screw
3	Hold-down spring	17	Retaining ring
4	Lever pivot	18	Pin
5	Hold-down pin	19	Parking brake lever
6	Actuator link	20	Bleeder valve
7	Actuator lever	21	Cylinder retainer
8	Lever return spring	22	Boot
9	Parking brake strut	23	Piston
10	Strut spring	24	Seal
11	Primary shoe	25	Spring assembly
12	Secondary shoe	26	Wheel cylinder
13	Adjusting screw spring	27	Backing plate
14	Socket		

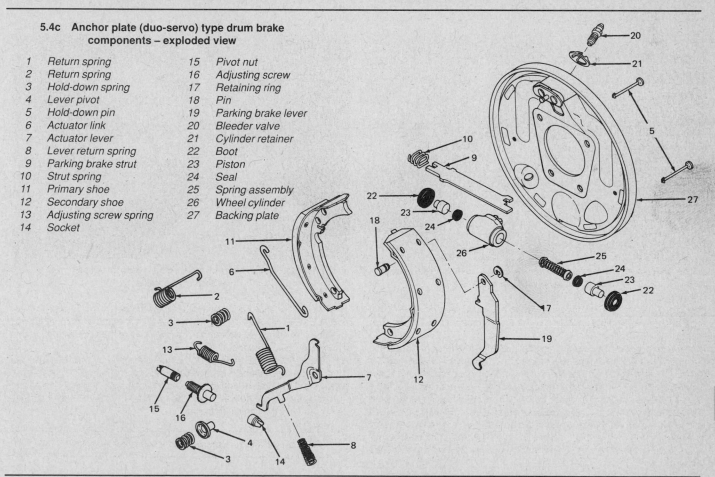

9

faster rate than normal. When replacing the rear brake shoes, use only high-quality, nationally-recognized brand name parts.

1   Loosen the wheel lug nuts, raise the rear of the vehicle and support it securely on jackstands. Block the front wheels to keep the vehicle from rolling off the jackstands.

2   Release the parking brake.

3   Remove the wheel. **Note:** *All four rear shoes must be replaced at the same time, but to avoid mixing up parts, work on only one brake assembly at a time.*

Anchor plate (duo-servo) type

Refer to illustrations 5.4a through 5.4z

4   Remove the brake drum. Refer to the accompanying photographs and perform the brake shoe inspection and, if necessary, the replacement procedure. Start with illustration 5.4a and be sure to read each caption. **Note:** *If the brake drum is stuck, make sure the parking brake is completely released, then apply some penetrating oil to the hub-to-brake drum joint. Allow the oil to soak in, then try to pull the drum off. If the drum still won't come off, the brake shoes will have to be retracted. This is done by remov-*

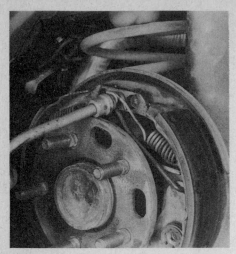

5.4d Remove the return springs with a brake spring tool

5.4e Remove the hold-down springs and pins by pushing in with pliers and turning them (arrows)

5.4f Lift up on the actuator lever and remove the actuating link from the anchor pin pivot along with the actuator lever and return spring (arrows)

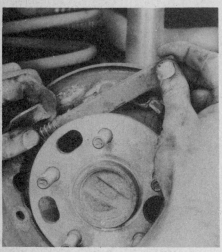

5.4g Spread the shoes apart at the top and remove the parking brake strut

5.4h With the shoe assembly spread to clear the hub flange, lift it away from the backing plate

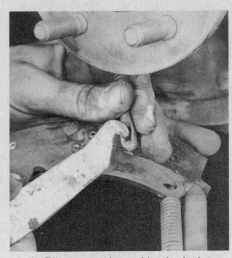

5.4i Disconnect the parking brake lever from the cable and remove the shoe assembly

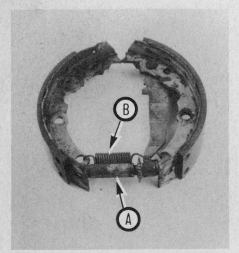

5.4j Remove the adjusting screw (A) and spring (B) from the shoe assembly – be sure to note how they're positioned

5.4k Remove the parking brake lever by prying off the C-clip

5.4l Install the parking brake lever on the new brake shoe and press the C-clip into place with needle-nose pliers

5.4m   Lubricate the contact surfaces of the backing plate with high-temperature brake grease

5.4n   Lubricate the adjuster screw with white lithium-base grease prior to installation

5.4o   Connect the parking brake lever to the cable

5.4p   Spread the brake assembly apart sufficiently to clear the hub flange and raise it into position

5.4q   Install the parking brake strut and spring

5.4r   Make sure the parking brake strut is positioned in the shoes properly (arrows)

5.4s   Install the primary brake shoe hold-down pin and spring

5.4t   Attach the actuator link and lever to the secondary brake shoe

5.4u   Install the actuator lever return spring

9

5.4v   Install the secondary brake shoe hold-down pin and spring

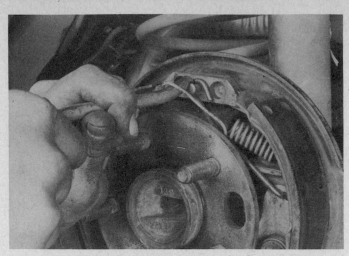

5.4w   Install the return springs

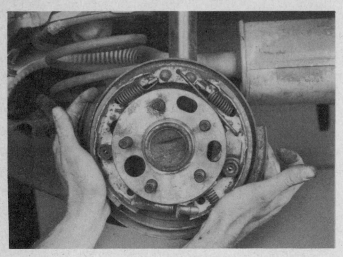

5.4x   Center the brake shoe assembly so the drum will slide over it

5.4y   Turn the adjusting screw so the drum fits snugly over the shoes

5.4z   Remove the glaze from the drum with emery cloth – use a swirling motion

ing the plug from the brake drum with a hammer and chisel **(see illustration 5.4a)**. *With the plug removed, pull the lever off the adjusting star wheel with one small screwdriver while turning the star wheel with another small screwdriver, moving the shoes away from the drum. The drum should now come off.*

Leading/trailing type

Refer to illustrations 5.5a, 5.5b, 5.18 and 5.25

5   Remove the brake drum. If it's difficult to remove, back off the parking brake cable, remove the access hole plug from the backing plate **(see illustration)**, insert a screwdriver through the hole and press in to push the parking brake lever off its stop **(see illustration)**. This will allow the brake shoes to retract slightly. Insert a punch through the hole at the bottom of the splash shield and tap gently on the punch to loosen the drum. Use a rubber mallet to tap gently on the outer rim of the drum and/or around the inner drum diameter by the spindle. Avoid using excessive force.

6   Remove the actuator spring with pliers.

7   Remove the upper return spring.

8   Remove the spring connecting link, adjuster actuator and spring washer.

9   Remove the hold-down springs and pins with pliers.

10   Remove the brake shoes after disconnecting the parking brake cable.

11   Remove the adjusting screw assembly and the lower return spring.

5.5a Leading/trailing type rear drum brake components – exploded view

1	Actuator spring	15	Retaining ring
2	Upper return spring	16	Pin
3	Spring connecting link	17	Spring washer
4	Adjuster actuator	18	Parking brake lever
5	Spring washer	19	Screw and lock washer
6	Lower return spring	20	Boot
7	Hold-down spring assembly	21	Piston
8	Hold-down pin	22	Seal
9	Adjuster brake shoe	23	Spring assembly
10	Brake shoe	24	Bleeder valve
11	Adjuster socket	25	Wheel cylinder
12	Spring clip	26	Bleeder valve cap
13	Adjuster nut	27	Backing plate assembly
14	Adjuster screw	28	Access hole plug
		29	Adjuster pin

12 Remove the retaining ring, pin, spring washer and parking brake lever from the brake shoe.

13 If any of the parts appear questionable in strength or quality because of discoloration from heat, overstress or wear, replace them.

14 Inspect the wheel cylinder dust boots for damage. If the wheel cylinder is leaking, see Section 6.

15 Attach the parking brake lever to the brake shoe with the spring washer, pin and retaining ring. **Note:** *Install the spring washer with the concave side against the parking brake lever.*

16 Install the adjuster pin in the brake shoe so the pin projects 0.275 to 0.283 inches from the side of the shoe web where the adjuster actuator is installed.

17 Clean the adjusting screw assembly with denatured alcohol and check the threads for smooth rotation over their full length.

18 Apply brake lubricant to the adjuster screw threads, the inside diameter of the socket and the socket face **(see illustration)**. Lubrication is adequate when there's a continuous bead of lubricant at the open end of the adjuster nut and socket with the threads fully engaged.

19 Install the spring clip in the same position it was in when removed.

20 Install the lower return spring. **Caution:** *Don't over-stretch the lower return spring. It will be damaged if its extended length is greater than 3.88 inches.*

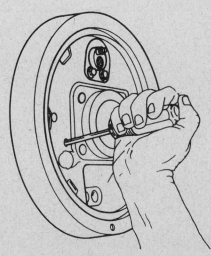

5.5b If you have trouble removing the drum, remove the access hole plug, insert a screwdriver through the hole and press in to push the parking brake lever off its stop – this will allow the brake shoes to retract slightly

9

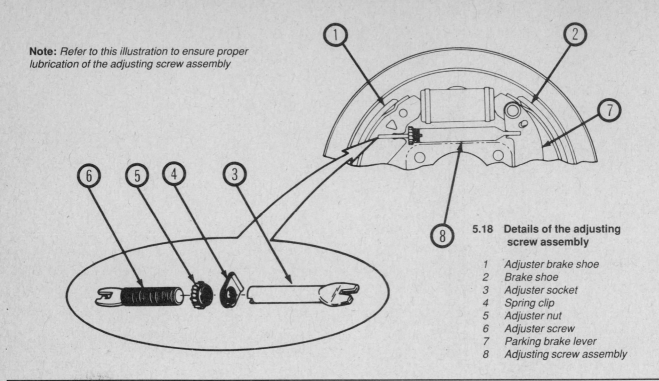

Note: *Refer to this illustration to ensure proper lubrication of the adjusting screw assembly*

5.18   **Details of the adjusting screw assembly**

1   *Adjuster brake shoe*
2   *Brake shoe*
3   *Adjuster socket*
4   *Spring clip*
5   *Adjuster nut*
6   *Adjuster screw*
7   *Parking brake lever*
8   *Adjusting screw assembly*

21   Install the brake shoes (after connecting the parking brake cable) with the hold-down pins and springs. The lower return spring should be positioned under the anchor plate. **Note:** *The "adjuster brake shoe" faces to the front of the vehicle on the left brake assembly and to the rear of the vehicle on the right brake assembly.*

22   Adjust the parking brake cable (see Section 10).

23   Install the adjusting screw assembly between the brake shoes on the backing plate. **Note:** *The adjuster screw should be installed so the engaging notch in the brake shoe and the spring clip point towards the backing plate.*

24   Install the spring washer with the concave side against the web of the adjuster shoe and lining.

25   Install the adjuster actuator so the top leg engages the notch in the adjuster screw **(see illustration – view C).**

26   Install the spring connecting link and hold it in place.

27   Insert the angled hook end of the upper return spring through the parking brake lever and the shoe **(see illustration 5.25 – view A).** Grasp the long, straight section of the spring with pliers. Pull the spring straight across and then down to hook into the crook on the spring connecting link. **Caution:** *Don't overstretch the upper return spring. It will be damaged if the extended length is greater than 5.49 inches.*

28   Install the actuator spring with pliers **(see illustration 5.25 – view B).** **Caution:** *Don't overstretch the actuator spring. It will be damaged if the extended length is greater than 3.27 inches.*

29   Make sure the parking brake lever is on its stop and the brake shoes are properly centered on the wheel cylinder pistons.

Both types

Refer to illustration 5.30

30   Before reinstalling the drum, check it for cracks, score marks, deep scratches and hard spots, which will appear as blue discolored areas. If the hard spots can't be removed with fine emery cloth or if any of the other conditions listed above exist, the drum must be taken to an automotive machine shop to have it turned. **Note:** *The drums should be resurfaced, regardless of the surface appearance, to impart a smooth finish and ensure a perfectly round drum (which will eliminate brake pedal pulsations related to out-of-round drums). At the very least, if you don't have the*

drums resurfaced, remove the glaze from the surface with medium-grit emery cloth using a swirling motion. If the drum won't "clean up" before the maximum service limit is reached in the machining operation, install a new one. The maximum wear diameter is cast into each brake drum **(see illustration).** This shouldn't be confused with the service limit (the dimension that requires the drum to be thrown away).

31   Install the brake drum on the axle flange.

32   Mount the wheel, install the lug nuts, then lower the vehicle.

33   If the vehicle is equipped with anchor plate type brakes, make a number of forward and reverse stops to adjust the brakes until satisfactory pedal feel is obtained. If it's equipped with leading/trailing type brakes, apply and release the brake pedal 30 to 35 times using normal pedal force. Pause about one second between pedal applications. After adjustment, make sure that both wheels turn freely.

5.30   **The drum has a maximum permissible diameter cast into it (arrow) which is a wear dimension, not a refinish dimension**

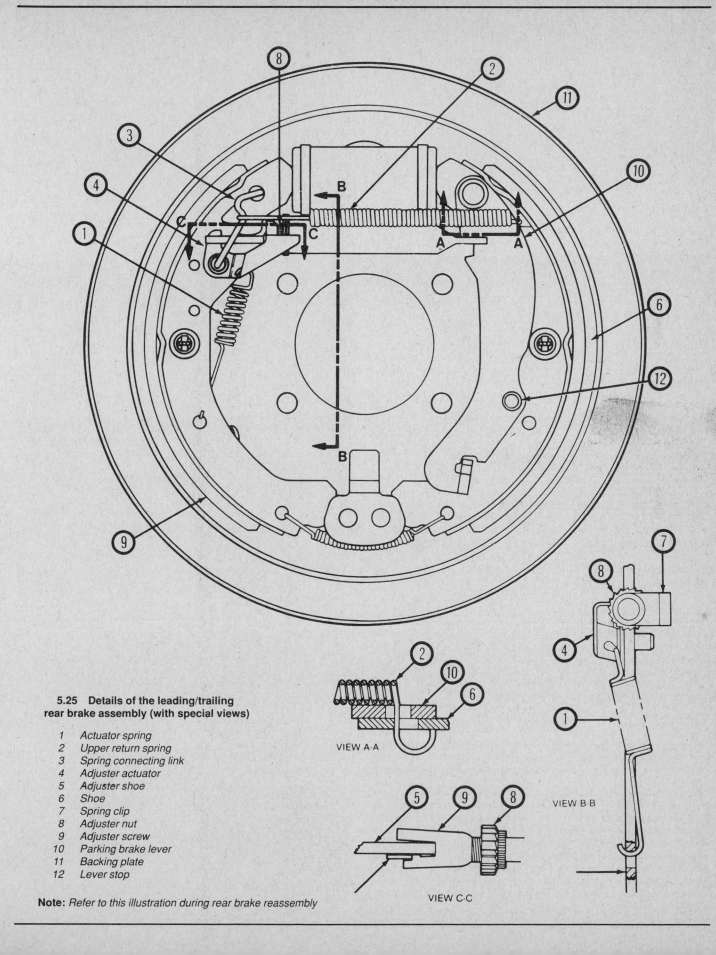

5.25   Details of the leading/trailing rear brake assembly (with special views)

1   Actuator spring
2   Upper return spring
3   Spring connecting link
4   Adjuster actuator
5   Adjuster shoe
6   Shoe
7   Spring clip
8   Adjuster nut
9   Adjuster screw
10   Parking brake lever
11   Backing plate
12   Lever stop

VIEW A-A

VIEW B-B

VIEW C-C

Note: *Refer to this illustration during rear brake reassembly*

9

6.4   A flare nut wrench should be used to disconnect the brake line (arrow)

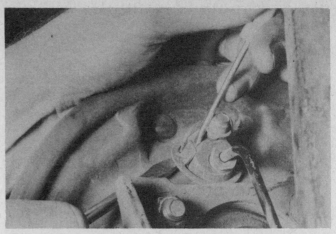

6.5   Two screwdrivers are used to remove the wheel cylinder retainer

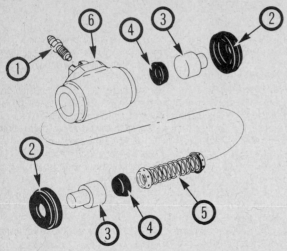

6.7   Wheel cylinder components – exploded view

1	Bleeder valve	4	Seal
2	Boot	5	Spring assembly
3	Piston	6	Wheel cylinder body

---

6   Rear wheel cylinder – removal, overhaul and installation

Refer to illustrations 6.4, 6.5, 6.7 and 6.13

Warning: *This procedure should not be undertaken on vehicles equipped with ABS (Anti-lock brake system), since special tools are needed to properly bleed the brakes. Take the vehicle to a dealer service department or other repair shop that has the proper tools.*

Note: *If an overhaul is indicated (usually because of fluid leakage or sticking brakes) explore all options before beginning the job. New wheel cylinders are available, which makes this job quite easy. If you do rebuild the wheel cylinder, make sure rebuild kits are available before proceeding.*

Removal

1   Raise the rear of the vehicle and support it securely on jackstands. Block the front wheels to keep the vehicle from rolling off the jackstands.
2   Remove the brake shoe assembly (Section 5).
3   Carefully clean the area around the wheel cylinder on both sides of the backing plate.
4   Unscrew the brake line fitting **(see illustration)**, but don't pull the line away from the wheel cylinder.
5   Remove the wheel cylinder retainer with two screwdrivers **(see illustration)**.

6.13   A wood block (arrow) should be used to hold the wheel cylinder in position

6   Remove the wheel cylinder from the brake backing plate and place it on a clean workbench. Immediately plug the brake line to prevent fluid loss and contamination.

Overhaul

7   Remove the bleeder valve, seals, pistons, boots and spring assembly from the wheel cylinder body **(see illustration)**.
8   Clean the wheel cylinder with brake fluid, denatured alcohol or brake system cleaner. **Warning:** *Do not, under any circumstances, use petroleum-based solvents to clean brake parts.*
9   Use compressed air to dry the wheel cylinder and blow out the passages.
10   Check the bore for corrosion and score marks. Crocus cloth may be used to remove light corrosion and stains, but the cylinder must be replaced with a new one if the defects can't be removed easily, or if the bore is scored.
11   Lubricate the new seals with brake fluid.
12   Assemble the brake cylinder components, making sure the boots are properly seated.

Installation

13   Place the wheel cylinder in position and wedge a wood block between the axle flange and the wheel cylinder body to hold it in place **(see illustration)**.
14   Install the retainer over the wheel cylinder (use a 1-1/8 inch 12-point socket to press it into place).
15   Connect the brake line and install the brake shoe assembly.
16   Bleed the brakes.

7.2   Unplug the fluid level sensor connector (arrow) and unscrew the brake line fittings (arrows)

7.6   Remove the master cylinder mounting nuts (arrows)

7   Master cylinder – removal, overhaul and installation

Refer to illustrations 7.2, 7.6, 7.9, 7.11, 7.12, 7.16, 7.18, 7.19a, 7.19b, 7.19c, 7.19d, 7.19e, 7.19f, 7.20 and 7.32

Warning: *This procedure should not be undertaken on vehicles equipped with ABS (Anti-lock brake system), since special tools are needed to properly bleed the brakes. Take the vehicle to a dealer service department or other repair shop that has the proper tools.*

Note: *Before deciding to overhaul the master cylinder, check on the availability and cost of a new or factory-rebuilt unit and the availability of a rebuild kit.*

Removal

1   Detach the cable from the negative battery terminal.
2   Unplug the fluid level sensor switch connector **(see illustration)**.
3   Place rags under the line fittings and prepare caps or plastic bags to cover the ends of the lines once they're disconnected. **Caution:** *Brake fluid will damage paint. Cover all painted parts and be careful not to spill fluid during this procedure.*
4   Loosen the fittings at the ends of the brake lines where they enter the master cylinder. To prevent rounding off the flats on the fittings, use a flare-nut wrench, which wraps around the hex.
5   Pull the brake lines away from the master cylinder and plug the ends to prevent contamination.
6   Remove the two mounting nuts **(see illustration)** and detach the master cylinder from the vehicle.
7   Remove the reservoir cover and reservoir diaphragm, then discard any remaining fluid in the reservoir.
8   Mount the master cylinder in a vise. Be sure to line the vise jaws with blocks of wood to prevent damage to the cylinder body.
9   Drive out the roll pins **(see illustration)** with a 1/8-inch punch. Pull straight up on the reservoir assembly and separate it from the master cylinder body. Remove and discard the two O-rings.
10   Using needle-nose pliers, remove the proportioner valve cap assemblies, the O-rings, the springs and the proportioner valve pistons. Make sure you don't scratch or otherwise damage the piston stems. Set each proportioner valve assembly aside.
11   Remove the primary piston lock ring by depressing the piston and prying the ring out with a screwdriver **(see illustration)**.
12   Remove the primary piston assembly from the bore **(see illustration)**.
13   Remove the secondary piston assembly from the bore. It may be necessary to remove the master cylinder from the vise and invert it, carefully tapping it against a block of wood to expel the piston.

Overhaul

14   Clean the master cylinder body, the primary and secondary piston as-

semblies, the proportioner valve assemblies and the reservoir in denatured alcohol and dry them off with unlubricated compressed air or a clean (lint-free) shop rag. **Warning:** *DO NOT, under any circumstances, use petroleum-based solvents to clean brake parts.*
15   Inspect the master cylinder piston bore for corrosion and score marks. If any corrosion or damage in the bore is evident, replace the master cylinder body – don't use abrasives to try to clean it up.
16   Remove the old seals from the secondary piston assembly and install the new seals with the cup lips facing out **(see illustration)**.
17   Attach the spring retainer to the secondary piston assembly.
18   Lubricate the cylinder bore with clean brake fluid and install the spring and secondary piston assembly **(see illustration)**.
19   Disassemble the primary piston assembly, noting the locations of the parts, then lubricate the new seals with clean brake fluid and install them on the piston **(see illustrations)**.
20   Install the primary piston assembly in the cylinder bore **(see illustration)**, depress it and install the lock ring.
21   Inspect the proportioner valves for corrosion and score marks. Replace them if necessary.
22   Lubricate the new O-rings and proportioner valve seals with the silicone grease supplied with the rebuild kit. Also lubricate the stem of the proportioner valve pistons.
23   Install the new seals on the proportioner valve pistons with the seal lips facing toward the cap assembly.
24   Install the proportioner valve pistons and seals in the master cylinder body.
25   Install the springs in the master cylinder body.
26   Install the new O-rings in their respective grooves in the proportioner valve cap assemblies.
27   Install the proportioner valve caps in the master cylinder and tighten them to the specified torque.
28   Inspect the reservoir for cracks and distortion. If any damage is evident, replace it.
29   Lubricate the new reservoir O-rings with clean brake fluid and press them into their respective grooves in the master cylinder body. Make sure they're properly seated.
30   Lubricate the reservoir fittings with clean brake fluid and install the reservoir on the master cylinder body by pressing it straight down.
31   Drive in the reservoir retaining (roll) pins. Make sure you don't damage the reservoir or master cylinder body.
32   Inspect the reservoir diaphragm and cover for cracks and deformation. Replace any damaged parts with new ones and attach the diaphragm to the cover **(see illustration)**. **Note:** *Whenever the master cylinder is removed, the complete hydraulic system must be bled. The time required to bleed the system can be reduced if the master cylinder is filled with fluid and bench bled (refer to Steps 33 through 36) before it's installed on the vehicle.*

9

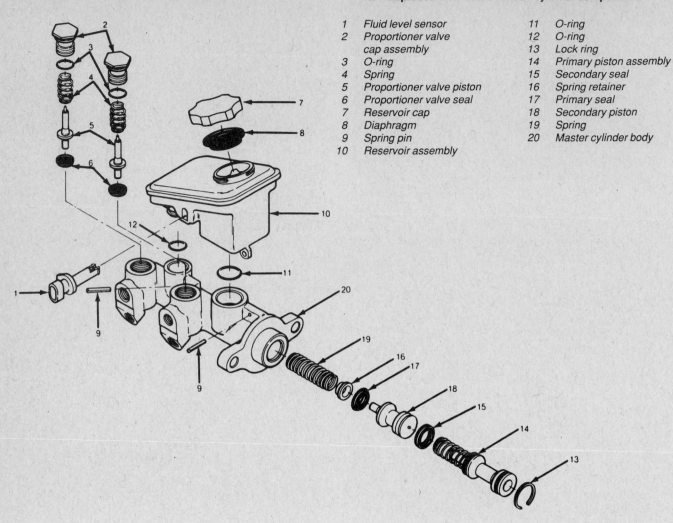

7.9   Exploded view of the master cylinder components

1	Fluid level sensor	11	O-ring
2	Proportioner valve	12	O-ring
	cap assembly	13	Lock ring
3	O-ring	14	Primary piston assembly
4	Spring	15	Secondary seal
5	Proportioner valve piston	16	Spring retainer
6	Proportioner valve seal	17	Primary seal
7	Reservoir cap	18	Secondary piston
8	Diaphragm	19	Spring
9	Spring pin	20	Master cylinder body
10	Reservoir assembly		

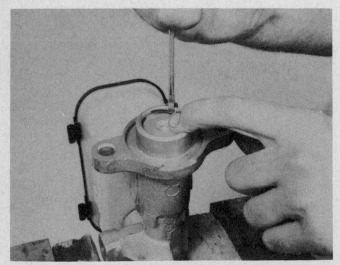

7.11   Press down on the piston and remove the primary piston lock ring

7.12   Remove the primary piston assembly

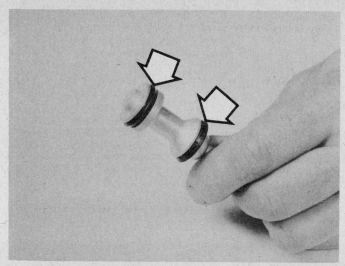

7.16 The secondary piston seals must be installed with the lips facing out as shown

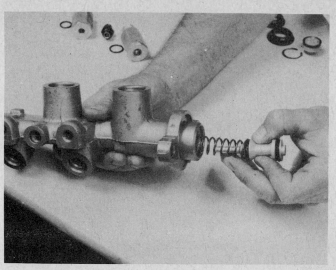

7.18 Install the secondary piston assembly

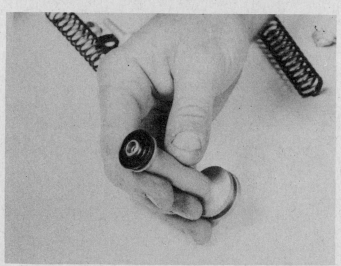

7.19a The primary piston seal must be installed with the lip facing away from the piston

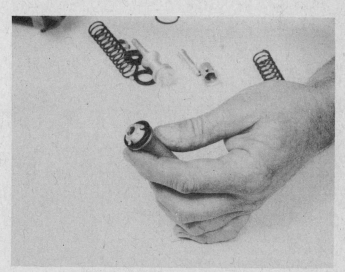

7.19b Install the seal guard over the seal

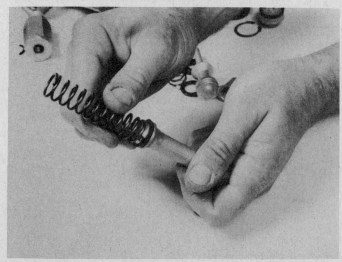

7.19c Place the primary piston spring in position

7.19d Insert the spring retainer into the spring

9

7.19e   Insert the spring retaining bolt through the retainer and spring and thread it into the piston

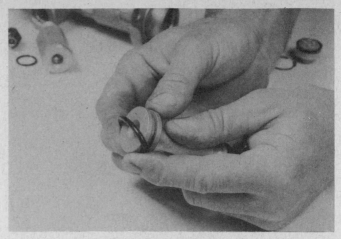

7.19f   Install the O-ring on the piston

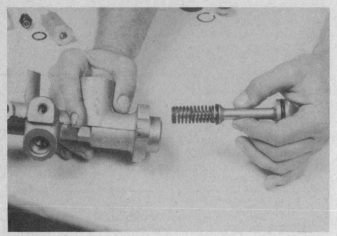

7.20   Insert the primary piston assembly into the body

7.32   Install the reservoir diaphragm in the cover

33   Insert threaded plugs of the correct size into the brake line outlet holes and fill the reservoirs with brake fluid. The master cylinder should be supported so brake fluid won't spill during the bench bleeding procedure.

34   Loosen one plug at a time and push the piston assembly into the bore to force air from the master cylinder. To prevent air from being drawn back in, the appropriate plug must be replaced before allowing the piston to return to its original position.

35   Stroke the piston three or four times for each outlet to ensure that all air has been expelled.

36   Since high pressure isn't involved in the bench bleeding procedure, there is an alternative to the removal and replacement of the plugs with each stroke of the piston assembly. Before pushing in on the piston assembly, remove one of the plugs completely. Before releasing the piston, however, instead of replacing the plug, simply put your finger tightly over the hole to keep air from being drawn back into the master cylinder. Wait several seconds for the brake fluid to be drawn from the reservoir into the piston bore, then repeat the procedure. When you push down on the piston it'll force your finger off the hole, allowing the air inside to be expelled. When only brake fluid is being ejected from the hole, replace the plug and go on to the other port.

37   Refill the master cylinder reservoirs and install the diaphragm and cover assembly. **Note:** *The reservoirs should only be filled to the top of the reservoir divider to prevent overflowing when the cover is installed.*

Installation

38   Carefully install the master cylinder by reversing the removal steps, then bleed the brakes at each wheel (see Section 9).

8   Brake hoses and lines – inspection and replacement

Refer to illustration 8.2

Inspection

1   About every six months, raise the vehicle and support it securely on jackstands, then check the flexible hoses that connect the steel brake lines to the front and rear brake assemblies. Look for cracks, chafing of the outer cover, leaks, blisters and other damage. The hoses are important and vulnerable parts of the brake system and the inspection should be thorough. A light and mirror will be helpful to see into restricted areas. If a hose exhibits any of the above conditions, replace it with a new one.

Replacement

Warning: *This procedure should not be undertaken on vehicles equipped with ABS (Anti-lock brake system), since special tools are needed to properly bleed the brakes. Take the vehicle to a dealer service department or other repair shop that has the proper tools.*

Front brake hose

2   Using a back-up wrench, disconnect the brake line from the hose fitting, being careful not to bend the frame bracket or brake line **(see illustration)**.

3   Use pliers to remove the U-clip from the female fitting at the bracket, then remove the hose from the bracket.

4   At the caliper end of the hose, remove the bolt from the fitting block, then remove the hose and the copper gaskets on either side of the fitting block.

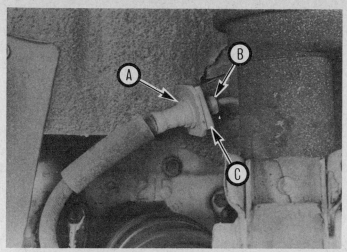

8.2   Using a back-up wrench on the flexible hose side of the fitting (A), loosen the tube nut (B) with a flare nut wrench and remove the U-clip (C) from the hose fitting

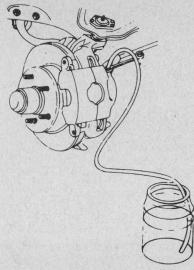

9.8   When bleeding the brakes, a hose is connected to the bleeder valve at the caliper (or wheel cylinder) and then submerged in brake fluid – air will be seen as bubbles in the container or in the tube (all air must be expelled before continuing to the next wheel)

5   When installing the hose, always use new copper gaskets on either side of the fitting block and lubricate all bolt threads with clean brake fluid before installation.
6   With the fitting flange engaged with the caliper locating ledge, attach the hose to the caliper.
7   Without twisting the hose, install the female fitting in the hose bracket. It'll fit the bracket in only one position.
8   Install the U-clip retaining the female fitting to the frame bracket.
9   Using a back-up wrench, attach the brake line to the hose fitting.
10   When the brake hose installation is complete, there shouldn't be any kinks in the hose. Make sure the hose doesn't contact any part of the suspension. Check it by turning the wheels to the extreme left and right positions. If the hose makes contact, remove the hose and correct the installation as necessary.

Rear brake hose

11   Using a back-up wrench, disconnect the hose at both ends, being careful not to bend the bracket or steel lines (refer to illustration 8.2 if necessary).
12   Remove the two U-clips with pliers and separate the female fittings from the brackets.
13   Unbolt the hose retaining clip and remove the hose.
14   Without twisting the hose, install the female ends in the frame brackets. It'll fit the bracket in only one position.
15   Install the U-clips retaining the female end to the bracket.
16   Using a back-up wrench, attach the steel line fittings to the female fittings. Again, be careful not to bend the bracket or steel line.
17   Make sure the hose installation didn't loosen the frame bracket. Tighten the bracket if necessary.
18   Fill the master cylinder reservoir and bleed the system (refer to Section 9).

Metal brake lines

19   When replacing brake lines, be sure to buy the correct replacement parts. Don't use copper or any other tubing for brake lines.
20   Prefabricated brake lines, with the ends already flared and fittings installed, are available at auto parts stores and dealer service departments. The lines are also bent to the proper shapes if necessary.
21   If prefabricated lines aren't available, obtain the recommended steel tubing and fittings to match the line to be replaced. Determine the correct length by measuring the old brake line (a piece of string can usually be used for this) and cut the new tubing to length, allowing about 1/2-inch extra for flaring the ends.
22   Install the fittings on the cut tubing and flare the ends of the line with an ISO flaring tool.
23   If necessary, carefully bend the line to the proper shape. A tube bender is recommended for this. **Caution:** *Don't crimp or damage the line.*

24   When installing the new line, make sure it's securely supported in the brackets with plenty of clearance between moving or hot components.
25   After installation, check the master cylinder fluid level and add fluid as necessary. Bleed the brake system as outlined in the next Section and test the brakes carefully before driving the vehicle in traffic.

9   Brake system bleeding

Refer to illustration 9.8
Warning 1: *This procedure should not be undertaken on vehicles equipped with ABS (Anti-lock brake system), since special tools are needed to properly bleed the brakes. Take the vehicle to a dealer service department or other repair shop that has the proper tools.*
Warning 2: *Wear eye protection when bleeding the brake system. If you get fluid in your eyes, rinse them immediately with water and seek medical attention.*
Note: *Bleeding the brakes is necessary to remove air that manages to find its way into the system when its been opened during removal and installation of a hose, line, caliper or master cylinder.*
1   It'll probably be necessary to bleed the system at all four brakes if air has entered the system due to low fluid level, or if the brake lines have been disconnected at the master cylinder.
2   If a brake line was disconnected at only one wheel, then only that caliper or wheel cylinder must be bled.
3   If a brake line is disconnected at a fitting located between the master cylinder and any of the brakes, that part of the system served by the disconnected line must be bled.
4   Remove any residual vacuum from the power brake booster by applying the brake several times with the engine off.
5   Remove the master cylinder reservoir cover and fill the reservoir with brake fluid. Reinstall the cover. **Note:** *Check the fluid level often during the bleeding procedure and add fluid as necessary to prevent the level from falling low enough to allow air bubbles into the master cylinder.*
6   Have an assistant on hand, as well as a supply of new brake fluid, an empty, clear plastic container, a length of 3/16-inch plastic, rubber or vinyl tubing to fit over the bleeder valve and a wrench to open and close the bleeder valve.
7   Beginning at the right rear wheel, loosen the bleeder valve slightly, then tighten it to a point where it's snug but can still be loosened quickly and easily.
8   Place one end of the tubing over the bleeder valve and submerge the other end in brake fluid in the container **(see illustration)**.

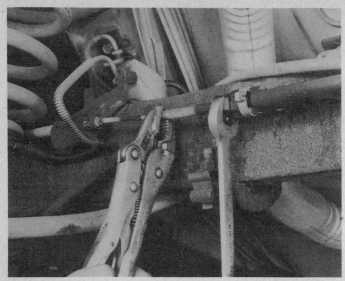

10.4   With a pair of locking pliers clamped to the end of the threaded rod to hold it still, turn the adjusting nut until the right rear wheel can just barely be turned backwards but not forward

9   Have your assistant pump the brakes slowly a few times to get pressure in the system, then hold the pedal down firmly.
10   While the pedal is held down, open the bleeder valve just enough to allow fluid to flow out of the valve. Watch for air bubbles to exit the submerged end of the tube. When the fluid slows after a couple of seconds, close the valve and have your assistant release the pedal.
11   Repeat Steps 9 and 10 until no more air is seen leaving the tube, then tighten the bleeder valve and proceed to the left rear wheel, the right front wheel and the left front wheel, in that order, and perform the same procedure. Be sure to check the fluid in the master cylinder reservoir frequently.
12   Never use old brake fluid. It contains moisture which will deteriorate the brake system components.
13   Refill the master cylinder with fluid at the end of the operation.
14   Check the operation of the brakes. The pedal should feel firm when depressed. If necessary, repeat the entire procedure. **Warning:** *Don't operate the vehicle if you're in doubt about the effectiveness of the brake system.*

---

10   Parking brake – adjustment

Vehicles with anchor plate (duo-servo) type rear brakes

Refer to illustration 10.4

1   Apply the parking brake lever exactly three ratchet clicks.
2   Raise the vehicle and support it securely on jackstands.
3   Before adjusting the parking brake, make sure the equalizer nut groove is lubricated with multi-purpose grease.
4   Tighten the adjusting nut **(see illustration)** until the right rear wheel can barely be turned backwards with two hands, but locks when turned forward.
5   Release the parking brake lever and check to make sure the rear wheels turn freely in both directions.
6   Lower the vehicle.

Vehicles with leading/trailing type rear brakes

Refer to illustration 10.12

7   Apply and release the parking brake six times to ten ratchet clicks.
8   Check the parking brake pedal assembly for full release by turning the ignition to On and noting whether the Brake warning light is off. If it's on even though the brake appears to be released, operate the pedal release

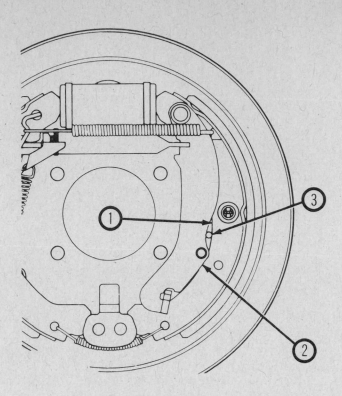

10.12   Parking brake adjustment details (leading/trailing type rear brakes)

1   *Brake shoe*   3   *Drill bit*
2   *Parking brake lever*

---

lever and pull down on the front parking brake cable to remove slack from the assembly. Check both rear wheels to make sure they still turn freely.
9   Apply the parking brake to four clicks.
10   Raise the vehicle and place it securely on jackstands.
11   Remove the access hole plug.
12   Adjust the parking brake cable until you can insert a 1/8-inch drill bit – but not a 1/4-inch bit – through the access hole into the space between the shoe web and the parking brake **(see illustration)**. **Note:** *The drill bit must be perpendicular (at a right angle) to the backing plate.*
13   Release the parking brake and verify that both wheels rotate freely.
14   Replace the access hole plug.
15   Lower the vehicle.

---

11   Parking brake cables – removal and installation

Refer to illustrations 11.4 and 11.12

Front cable

1   Remove the rear console trim to gain access to the parking brake handle mechanism (refer to Chapter 11).
2   Remove the cable nut from the cable at the handbrake lever and push the cable and housing assembly through the floorpan.
3   Raise the rear of the vehicle and support it securely on jackstands.
4   Pull the cable housing out of the L-shaped guide just above the rear of the exhaust pipe heat shield **(see illustration)**.
5   Maneuver the cable out of the wire bracket at the left rear suspension pivot.
6   Slide the cable housing out of the equalizer and disconnect the cable from the cable joiner.

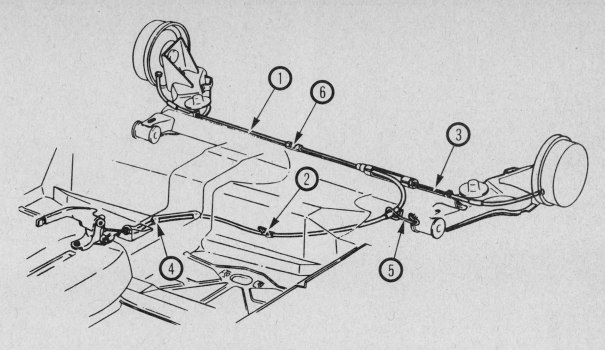

11.4   Parking brake cable routing diagram

1	Right rear cable	3	Left rear cable	5	Bracket
2	Clip	4	Guide	6	Cable joiner

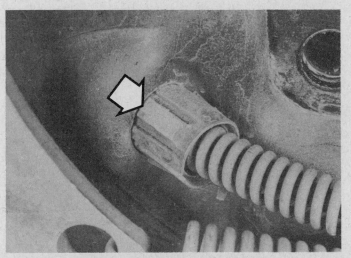

11.12   Depress the tangs on the cable housing retainer and push it through the backing plate

7   Installation is the reverse of the removal procedure. Refer to Section 10 for the cable adjustment procedure.

Left cable

8   Raise the vehicle and support it securely on jackstands.
9   Loosen the equalizer adjusting screw and disconnect the left cable from the equalizer.
10   Disconnect the cable housing at the frame mounting bracket by depressing the tangs on the retainer with a pair of pliers.
11   Remove the brake drum and brake shoes as described in Section 5. Disconnect the parking brake cable from the parking brake lever.
12   Using a pair of pliers, depress the tangs on the cable housing retainer and push the cable and housing out through the backing plate **(see illustration)**.
13   Installation is the reverse of the removal procedure. Be sure to adjust the cable as described in Section 10.

Right cable

14   Raise the rear of the vehicle and support it securely on jackstands.
15   Remove enough tension at the equalizer to enable the cable to be removed from the cable joiner.
16   Disconnect the cable housing at the frame mounting bracket by depressing the tangs on the retainer with a pair of pliers.
17   Remove the brake drum and brake shoes as described in Section 5. Disconnect the parking brake cable from the parking brake lever.
18   Using a pair of pliers, depress the tangs on the cable housing retainer and push the cable and housing out through the backing plate **(see illustration 11.12)**.
19   Installation is the reverse of the removal procedure. Be sure to adjust the cable as described in Section 10.

12   Power brake booster – inspection, removal and installation

Refer to illustration 12.6
Warning: *Do not attempt this procedure on models equipped with ABS (anti-lock brakes). Take the vehicle to a dealer service department or other qualified shop.*

1   The power brake booster unit requires no special maintenance apart from periodic inspection of the vacuum hose and the case. Early models have an in-line filter which should be inspected periodically and replaced if clogged or damaged.
2   Dismantling of the power unit requires special tools and is not ordinarily done by the home mechanic. If a problem develops, install a new or factory rebuilt unit.
3   Remove the nuts attaching the master cylinder to the booster and carefully pull the master cylinder forward until it clears the mounting studs. Be careful to avoid bending or kinking the brake lines.
4   Disconnect the vacuum hose where it attaches to the power brake booster.
5   From the passenger compartment, disconnect the power brake push-rod from the top of the brake pedal.

9

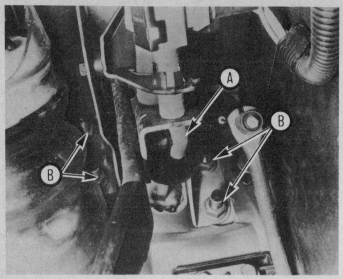

12.6   Remove the retaining clip and slide the power brake pushrod (A) off the brake pedal pin, then remove the booster-to-firewall nuts (B)

6   Also from this location, remove the nuts attaching the booster to the firewall **(see illustration)**.
7   Carefully lift the booster unit away from the firewall and out of the engine compartment.
8   To install the booster, place it in position and tighten the mounting nuts. Reconnect the brake pedal.
9   Install the master cylinder and vacuum hose.
10   Carefully test the operation of the brakes before driving the vehicle in traffic.

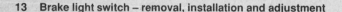

13   Brake light switch – removal, installation and adjustment

Refer to illustration 13.3

Removal

1   The brake light switch is located on a bracket at the top of the brake pedal. The switch activates the brake lights at the rear of the vehicle when the pedal is depressed.
2   Remove the under dash cover and disconnect the wiring to the courtesy light in the panel.

13.3   The brake light switch (arrow) is located to the right of the steering column at the end of the mounting bracket

3   Locate the switch at the top of the brake pedal **(see illustration)**. If the vehicle is equipped with cruise control, there will be another switch very similar in appearance. The brake light switch is the one towards the end of the bracket.
4   Disconnect the negative battery cable from the battery.
5   Detach the wiring connectors at the brake light switch.
6   Depress the brake pedal and pull the switch out of the clip. The switch appears to be threaded, but it's designed to be pushed into and out of the clip, not turned.

Installation and adjustment

7   With the brake pedal depressed, push the new switch into the clip. Note that audible clicks will be heard as this is done.
8   Pull the brake pedal all the way to the rear, against the pedal stop until the clicking sounds can no longer be heard. This action will automatically move the switch the proper amount and no further adjustment will be required. **Caution:** *Don't apply excessive force during this adjustment procedure, as power booster damage may result.*
9   Connect the wiring at the switch and the battery. Make sure the brake lights are functioning properly.

Chapter 10
Suspension and steering systems

Contents

Specifications

Torque specifications

Ft-lbs (unless otherwise indicated)

Front suspension

Control arm pivot bolts

1994 and earlier	63
1995 on	
Front bushing	89
Rear vertical bushing	111
Suspension support (in the following order)	
Center bolts	66
Front bolts	66
Rear bolts	66
Balljoint-to-steering knuckle nut	
Through 1990	55
1991	26 plus an additional 60-degrees rotation
1992	41 to 50
1993 on	55 plus an additional 60-degrees rotation
Stabilizer bar-to-control arm	
Non-GTZ models	14
GTZ models	70
Stabilizer bar bushing clamp nuts	
Through 1991	18
1992 on	16
Front hub and wheel bearing assembly bolts	70
Strut-to-steering knuckle nuts	133
Strut-to-body nuts	18
Strut damper shaft nut	
Through 1990	59
1991 and later	65
Hub nut	
Initial	74
Final	
1991 and earlier	191
1992 on	185

Rear suspension

Rear hub and wheel bearing assembly bolts

1992 and earlier	38
1993 on	44
Rear axle assembly pivot bolts	
Through 1990	66
1991 through 1993	52 plus an additional 120-degrees rotation
1994 on	59 plus an additional 120-degrees rotation

Torque specifications (continued)   Ft-lbs

Steering

	Ft-lbs
Steering gear-to-firewall clamp nuts	
1991 and earlier	28
1992 on	22
Coupling-to-steering column bolt	
Through 1990	34
1991 and later	30
Coupling-to-stub shaft bolt	
Through 1990*	37
1991 and later	30
Power steering pump mounting bolts	
2.0/2.2 liter four-cylinder engines	22*
2.3 liter four-cylinder (Quad-4) engine	19
V6 engine	18
Inner tie-rod-to-steering rack bolts	65
Tie-rod end-to-steering arm	
1992 and earlier	35
1993 on	44
Steering wheel hub nut	30
Wheel lug nuts	See Chapter 1

See illustration 18.5a for the specific bolt tightening sequence.

1   General information

Refer to illustrations 1.1 and 1.2

Warning: *Whenever any of the suspension or steering fasteners are loosened or removed, they must be inspected and, if necessary, replaced with new ones of the same part number or of original equipment quality and design. Torque specifications must be followed for proper reassembly and component retention. Never attempt to heat or straighten any suspension or steering components. Instead, replace any bent or damaged part with a new one.*

The front suspension is a MacPherson strut design. The steering knuckles are located by lower control arms which are mounted to longitudinally positioned, removable frame members. The control arms are connected by a stabilizer bar, which reduces body lean during cornering **(see illustration)**.

The rear suspension is semi-independent with a cross-beam axle with integrated trailing arms, two coil springs and insulator assemblies, two shock absorbers and a stabilizer bar. The axle assembly attaches to the vehicle at two points, one on each side rail **(see illustration)**.

The rack-and-pinion steering gear is located behind the engine/transaxle assembly on the firewall and actuates the steering arms which pro-

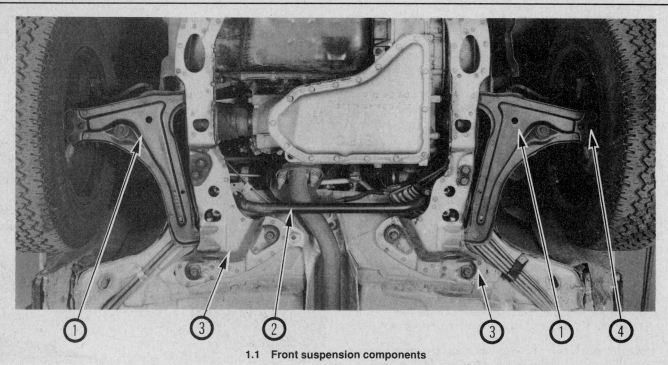

1.1   Front suspension components

1	Control arm	3	Suspension support
2	Stabilizer bar	4	Balljoint

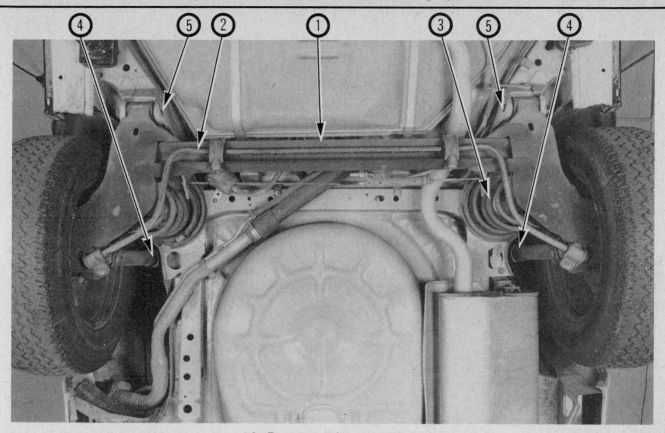

1.2   Rear suspension components

1	Rear axle assembly	3	Coil spring	5	Rear axle-to-underbody
2	Stabilizer bar	4	Shock absorber		bracket mounting point

trude from the strut housings. Most vehicles are equipped with power steering. The steering column is connected to the steering gear through an insulated coupler. The steering column is designed to collapse in the event of an accident.

Note 1: *These vehicles have a combination of standard and metric fasteners on the various suspension and steering components, so it would be a good idea to have both types of tools available when beginning work.*

Note 2: *On models equipped with the Delco Loc II audio system, be sure the lockout feature is turned off before performing any procedure which requires disconnecting the battery.*

2   Front stabilizer bar and bushings – removal and installation

Refer to illustrations 2.2, 2.4a, 2.4b, 2.5, 2.6 and 2.7

Removal

1   Loosen the lug nuts on both front wheels, raise the front of the vehicle and support it securely on jackstands. Apply the parking brake and block the rear wheels to keep the vehicle from rolling off the jackstands. Remove the front wheels.

2   Remove the stabilizer bar-to-control arm bolts. Note how the link bushings, spacers and washers are arranged **(see illustration)**. **Note:** *Beretta GTZ models have a slightly different link arrangement. They bolt to the stabilizer bar ends and brackets on the strut assembly rather than the control arms.*

3   Remove the stabilizer bar bushing clamp nuts through the access holes in the suspension supports **(see illustration 2.4a)**.

4   Working on one side at a time, place a jack under the suspension support, then remove the two rear and the two center mounting bolts from the

suspension support. Slowly lower the jack and allow the support to drop down. You may have to loosen the two front support mounting bolts on each side to provide adequate clearance for stabilizer bar removal **(see illustrations)**.

5   Push up on the stabilizer bar while pulling down on the suspension support to separate the bushing clamp from the support **(see illustration)**.

2.2   The stabilizer bar link has washers, rubber bushings and spacers to connect the stabilizer bar to the control arm

10

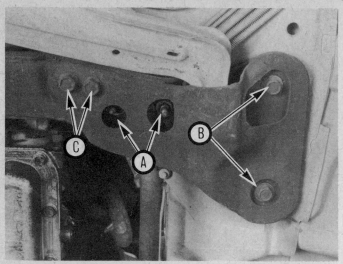

2.4a   After removing the stabilizer bar bushing clamp nuts (A), place a jack under the suspension support and remove the rear (B) and center (C) mounting bolts

2.4b   If the suspension support doesn't hang down far enough to allow stabilizer bar removal, loosen the two front mounting bolts (arrows) on each suspension support

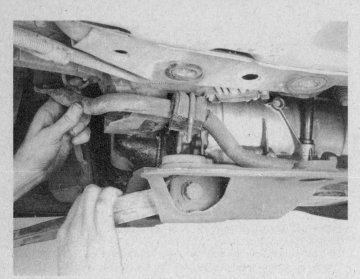

2.5   Separate the stabilizer bar from the suspension support

2.6   Guide the stabilizer bar out through the wheel well

2.7   Pry the stabilizer bar bushing clamp off the bushing

6   Remove the stabilizer bar through the wheel well **(see illustration)**.
7   Inspect the bushings for wear and damage and replace them if necessary. To remove them, pry the bushing clamp off with a screwdriver **(see illustration)** and pull the bushings off the bar. To ease installation, spray the inside and outside of the bushings with a silicone-based lubricant. Do not use petroleum-based lubricants on any rubber suspension part!

Installation

8   Assemble the shaft bushings and clamps on the bar, guide the bar through the wheel well, over the suspension supports and into position.
9   Insert the clamp studs through the suspension support and install the nuts finger tight.
10   Raise the suspension supports (one at a time) and install the bolts loosely.
11   Center the bar in the vehicle and install the stabilizer bar-to-control arm bolts, spacers, bushings and washers. Tighten all of the fasteners to the torque figures listed in this Chapter's Specifications at this time.
12   Install the wheels and lower the vehicle. Tighten the lug nuts to the torque specified in Chapter 1.

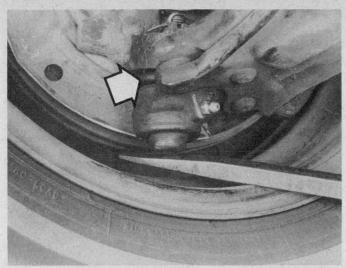

3.3a   Check for movement between the balljoint and steering knuckle (arrow) when prying up

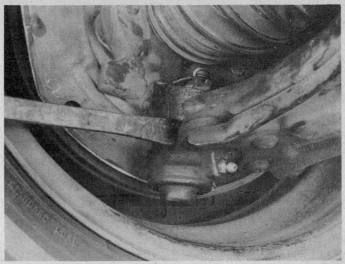

3.3b   With the pry bar positioned between the steering knuckle boss and the balljoint, pry down and check for play in the balljoint – if there's any play, replace the balljoint

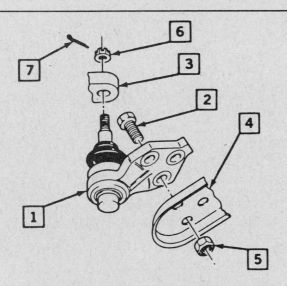

3.11   Replacement balljoint installation details (typical) – be sure to tighten the bolts to the torque specified on the instruction sheet

1	Replacement balljoint	5	Nut
2	Bolt	6	Castellated nut
3	Steering knuckle	7	Cotter pin
4	Control arm		

3   Balljoint – check and replacement

Refer to illustrations 3.3a, 3.3b and 3.11

Check

1   Raise the front of the vehicle and support it securely on jackstands. Apply the parking brake and block the rear wheels to keep the vehicle from rolling off the jackstands.

2   Visually inspect the rubber seal for damage, deterioration and leaking grease. If any of these conditions are noticed, the balljoint should be replaced.

3   Place a large pry bar under the balljoint and attempt to push the balljoint up. Next, position the pry bar between the steering knuckle and control arm and pry down **(see illustrations)**. If any movement is seen or felt during either of these checks, a worn out balljoint is indicated.

4   Have an assistant grasp the tire at the top and bottom and move the top of the tire in-and-out. Touch the balljoint stud castellated nut. If any looseness is felt, suspect a worn out balljoint stud or a widened hole in the steering knuckle boss. If the latter problem exists, the steering knuckle should be replaced as well as the balljoint.

5   Separate the control arm from the steering knuckle (Section 4). Using your fingers (don't use pliers), try to twist the stud in the socket. If the stud turns, replace the balljoint.

Replacement

6   Loosen the wheel lug nuts, raise the front of the vehicle and support it securely on jackstands. Apply the parking brake and block the rear wheels to keep the vehicle from rolling off the jackstands. Remove the wheel.

7   Separate the control arm from the steering knuckle (Section 4). Temporarily insert the balljoint stud back into the steering knuckle (loosely). This will ease balljoint removal after Step 9 has been performed, as well as hold the assembly stationary while drilling out the rivets.

8   Using a 1/8-inch drill bit, drill a pilot hole into the center of each balljoint-to-control arm rivet. Be careful not to damage the CV joint boot in the process.

9   Using a 1/2-inch drill bit, drill the head off each rivet. Work slowly and carefully to avoid deforming the holes in the control arm.

10   Loosen (but don't remove) the stabilizer bar-to-control arm nut. Pull the control arm and balljoint down to remove the balljoint stud from the steering knuckle, then dislodge the balljoint from the control arm.

11   Position the new balljoint on the control arm and install the bolts (supplied in the balljoint kit) from the top of the control arm **(see illustration)**. Tighten the bolts to the torque specified in the new balljoint instruction sheet.

12   Insert the balljoint into the steering knuckle, install the castellated nut, tighten it to the torque listed in this Chapter's Specifications and install a new cotter pin. It may be necessary to tighten the nut some to align the cotter pin hole with an opening in the nut, which is acceptable. Never loosen the castellated nut to allow cotter pin insertion.

13   Tighten the stabilizer bar-to-control arm nut to the torque listed in this Chapter's Specifications.

14   Install the wheel, lower the vehicle and tighten the lug nuts to the specified torque. It's a good idea to take the vehicle to a dealer service department or service station to have the front end alignment checked and, if necessary, adjusted.

10

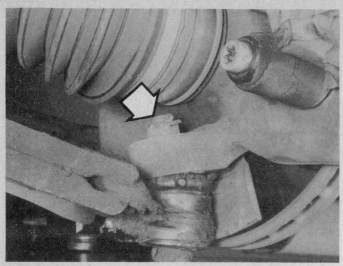

4.3   Remove the cotter pin and castellated nut (arrow) from the balljoint stud

4.4   Pry the balljoint out of the steering knuckle – if it's stubborn and won't come out, strike the steering knuckle boss on both sides (arrow) simultaneously with two hammers, then try again

4.5a   The control arm mounting bolts are accessible through the reliefs in the suspension support

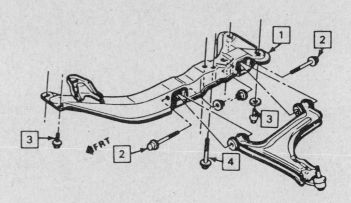

4.5b   Control arm and suspension support installation details

1	*Suspension support assembly*	*3*	*Front and rear suspension*
2	*Control arm pivot bolts*		*support bolts*
		4	*Center suspension support bolts*

4   Control arm – removal and installation

Refer to illustrations 4.3, 4.4, 4.5a and 4.5b

Removal

1   Loosen the wheel lug nuts, raise the front of the vehicle and support it securely on jackstands. Apply the parking brake and block the rear wheels to keep the vehicle from rolling off the jackstands. Remove the wheel.

2   If only one control arm is being removed, disconnect only that end of the stabilizer bar. If both control arms are being removed, disconnect both ends (see Section 2 if necessary).

3   Remove the balljoint stud-to-steering knuckle castellated nut and cotter pin **(see illustration)**.

4   Using a large pry bar positioned between the control arm and steering knuckle, "pop" the balljoint out of the knuckle **(see illustration)**. **Caution:** *When removing the balljoint from the knuckle, be careful not to overextend the inner CV joint or it may be damaged.*

5   Remove the two control arm pivot bolts and detach the control arm **(see illustrations)**.

6   The control arm bushings are replaceable, but special tools and expertise are necessary to do the job. Carefully inspect the bushings for hardening, excessive wear and cracks. If they appear to be worn or deteriorated, take the control arm to a dealer service department or repair shop.

7   The suspension support may also be removed if desired. Refer to illustrations 2.4a and 2.4b and remove the mounting bolts and support assembly.

Installation

8   Position the control arm in the suspension support and install the pivot bolts. Do not tighten them completely at this time.

9   Insert the balljoint stud into the steering knuckle boss, install the castellated nut and tighten it to the torque listed in this Chapter's Specifications. If necessary, tighten the nut a little more if the cotter pin hole doesn't line up with an opening on the nut. Install a new cotter pin.

10 Install the stabilizer bar-to-control arm bolt, spacer, bushings and washers and tighten the nut to the torque listed in this Chapter's Specifications.

11 Install the wheel and lower the vehicle. Tighten the lug nuts to the specified torque.

5.2   Mark the strut-to-steering knuckle relationship and draw a line around the nuts with paint or a scribe

5.4   Remove the strut-to-knuckle nuts and bolts – the bolts are splined and must be driven out with a brass, lead or plastic hammer

5.5   Push in on the strut while pulling out on the top of the brake rotor to separate the knuckle and strut

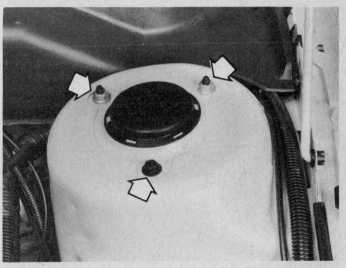

5.6   Remove the three strut-to-shock tower nuts (arrows) while supporting the strut assembly

12   With the weight of the vehicle on the suspension, tighten the control arm pivot bolts to the torque listed in this Chapter's Specifications. **Caution:** *If the bolts aren't tightened with the weight of the vehicle on the suspension, control arm bushing damage may occur.*

13   Drive the vehicle to a dealer service department or an alignment shop to have the front wheel alignment checked and, if necessary, adjusted.

5   Front strut and spring assembly – removal, inspection and installation

Refer to illustrations 5.2, 5.4, 5.5 and 5.6

Removal

1   Loosen the wheel lug nuts, raise the front of the vehicle and support it securely on jackstands. Apply the parking brake and block the rear wheels to keep the vehicle from rolling off the jackstands. Remove the wheel.

2   Using white paint or a scribe, mark the strut-to-steering knuckle relationship and make a line around the strut-to-steering knuckle nuts **(see illustration)**.

3   Separate the tie-rod end from the steering arm as described in Section 15.

4   Remove the strut-to-knuckle nuts **(see illustration)** and knock the bolts out with a brass, lead or plastic hammer.

5   Separate the strut from the steering knuckle **(see illustration)**. Be careful not to overextend the inner CV joint or stretch the brake hose.

6   Support the strut and spring assembly with one hand and remove the three strut-to-shock tower nuts **(see illustration)**. Remove the assembly out through the fender well.

Inspection

7   Check the strut body for leaking fluid, dents, cracks and other obvious damage which would warrant repair or replacement.

8   Check the coil spring for chips and cracks in the spring coating (this will cause premature spring failure due to corrosion). Inspect the spring seat for hardening, cracks and general deterioration.

9   If wear or damage is evident, proceed to Section 6 for the strut disassembly procedure.

Installation

10   Verify that the flat in the upper spring seat is in line with the steering knuckle flange. Guide the strut assembly up into the fender well and insert

10

6.4   After the spring has been compressed, remove the damper shaft nut

6.5a   Remove the bearing cap . . .

6.5b   . . . and the upper spring seat and insulator from the damper shaft

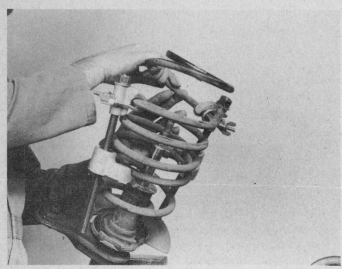

6.6   Remove the compressed spring assembly – be EXTREMELY CAREFUL when handling the spring!

6.7   Using a tubing cutter, cut the end cap off the strut body at the groove (arrow)

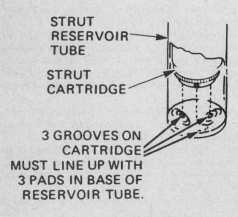

STRUT RESERVOIR TUBE

STRUT CARTRIDGE

3 GROOVES ON CARTRIDGE MUST LINE UP WITH 3 PADS IN BASE OF RESERVOIR TUBE.

6.11   Turn the cartridge until it seats in the depressions at the bottom of the tube

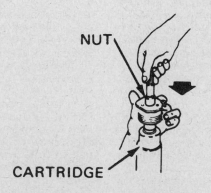

NUT

CARTRIDGE

6.12   Install the cartridge retaining nut – be careful not to cross-thread it

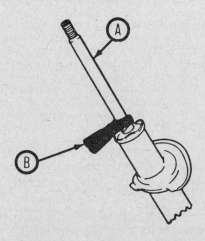

A

B

6.14   Extend the damper shaft (A) and hold it in place with a clothes pin (B)

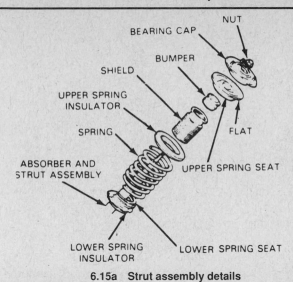

6.15a   Strut assembly details

NUT
BEARING CAP
BUMPER
SHIELD
UPPER SPRING INSULATOR
SPRING
FLAT
ABSORBER AND STRUT ASSEMBLY
UPPER SPRING SEAT
LOWER SPRING INSULATOR
LOWER SPRING SEAT

6.15b   Install the upper spring seat with the flat (arrow) facing the steering knuckle flange

the three upper mounting studs through the holes in the shock tower. Once the three studs protrude from the shock tower, install the nuts so the strut won't fall back through. This may require an assistant, since the strut is quite heavy and awkward.

11   Slide the steering knuckle into the strut flange and insert the two bolts. They should be positioned with the flats situated horizontally. Install the nuts, align the marks and tighten the nuts to the torque listed in this Chapter's Specifications.

12   Install the tie-rod end in the steering arm and tighten the castellated nut to the specified torque. Install a new cotter pin. If the cotter pin won't pass through, tighten the nut a little more, but just enough to align the hole in the stud with a castellation on the nut (don't loosen the nut).

13   Install the wheel, lower the vehicle and tighten the lug nuts to the torque listed in the Chapter 1 Specifications.

14   Tighten the three upper mounting nuts to the specified torque.

6   Strut cartridge – replacement

Refer to illustrations 6.4, 6.5a, 6.5b, 6.6, 6.7, 6.11, 6.12, 6.14, 6.15a, 6.15b and 6.15c

1   If the struts exhibit the telltale signs of wear (leaking fluid, loss of dampening capability) explore all options before beginning any work. The strut cartridges can be replaced. However, rebuilt strut assemblies (some complete with springs) are available on an exchange basis which eliminates much time and work. Whichever route you choose to take, check on the cost and availability of parts before disassembling anything. **Warning:** *Disassembling a strut is a dangerous job. Be very careful and follow the instructions to the letter or serious injury may result. Use only a high quality spring compressor and carefully follow the manufacturer's instructions furnished with the tool. After removing the coil spring from the strut assembly, set it aside in a safe, isolated area (a steel cabinet is preferred).*

2   Remove the strut and spring assembly following the procedure described in Section 5. Mount the strut assembly in a vise. Cushion the vise jaws with rags or blocks of wood.

3   Following the tool manufacturer's instructions, install the spring compressor (which can be obtained at most auto parts stores or equipment yards on a daily rental basis) on the spring and compress it sufficiently to relieve all pressure from the spring seat. This can be verified by wiggling the spring seat.

4   Loosen the damper shaft nut while using a socket wrench on the shaft hex to prevent it from turning **(see illustration)**.

5   Lift the bearing cap, upper spring seat and upper insulator off the damper shaft **(see illustrations)**. Inspect the bearing in the spring seat for smooth operation and replace it if necessary.

6   Carefully remove the compressed spring assembly **(see illustration)** and set it in a safe place, such as inside a steel cabinet. **Warning:** *Don't*

6.15c   The bearing cap must also be positioned with the flat (arrow) facing the knuckle flange

position your head near the end of the spring!

7   Locate the groove cut in the strut reservoir tube, 3/4-inch from the top of the tube **(see illustration)**. Using a tubing cutter, cut around the groove until the reservoir tube is severed. Lift out the piston rod assembly with the cylinder and end cap. Discard these items.

8   Remove the strut reservoir tube from the vise and pour the damper fluid into an approved oil container.

9   Place the strut back in the vise and lightly file around the inner edge of the opening to eliminate any burrs that may have resulted from the cutting operation. Be careful not to damage the internal threads in the strut body.

10   Thread the cartridge retaining nut into the reservoir tube, as straight as possible, to establish a clean path in the existing threads. Remove the nut.

11   Insert the replacement strut cartridge into the reservoir tube and turn it until you feel the pads on the bottom of the cartridge seat in the depressions at the bottom of the reservoir tube **(see illustration)**.

12   Slide the nut over the cartridge and thread it into the tube **(see illustration)**, tightening it to the torque specified in the kit instructions.

13   Stroke the damper shaft up-and-down a few times to verify proper operation.

14   Extend the damper shaft all the way and hold it in place with a clothes pin at the bottom of the rod **(see illustration)**.

15   Assemble the strut beginning with the lower spring insulator and spring, then the upper spring insulator, spring seat and bearing cap. Position the spring seat and bearing cap with the flats facing the steering knuckle flange **(see illustrations)**.

10

7.6   A no. 55 Torx bit is required to remove the hub bolts – DO NOT use an Allen wrench or the bolts will be damaged

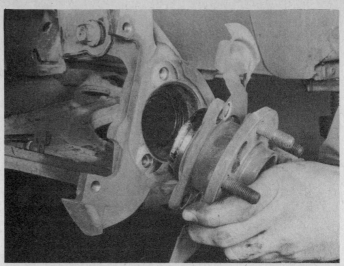

7.7   Pull the hub and bearing assembly and the rotor shield out of the steering knuckle

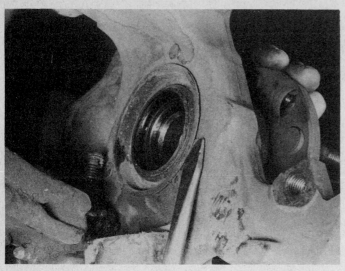

7.8   Pry the seal out of the knuckle with a screwdriver

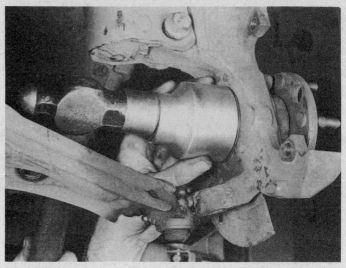

7.9   Using a large socket, drive the new seal into place

16   Install the damper shaft nut and tighten it to the specified torque. Remove the clothes pin from the damper shaft.

17   Install the strut and spring assembly as outlined in Section 5.

7   Front hub and wheel bearing assembly – removal and installation

Refer to illustrations 7.6, 7.7, 7.8, 7.9 and 7.10

Note: *The front hub and wheel bearing assembly is sealed-for-life and must be replaced as a unit.*

1   Loosen the wheel lug nuts, raise the front of the vehicle and support it securely on jackstands. Apply the parking brake and block the rear wheels to keep the vehicle from rolling off the jackstands. Remove the wheel.

2   Disconnect the stabilizer bar from the control arm (see Section 2 if necessary).

3   Remove the balljoint-to-steering knuckle nut and separate the control arm from the knuckle (see Section 4).

4   Remove the caliper from the steering knuckle and hang it out of the way with a piece of wire (see Chapter 9).

5   Pull the rotor off the hub and remove the driveaxle (see Chapter 8 if necessary).

6   Using a no. 55 Torx bit, remove the three hub retaining bolts through the opening in the flange **(see illustration)**.

7   Wiggle the hub and bearing assembly back-and-forth and pull it out of the steering knuckle, along with the rotor shield **(see illustration)**.

8   If the hub and bearing assembly is being replaced with a new one, it's a good idea to replace the dust seal in the back of the steering knuckle. Pry it out of the knuckle with a screwdriver **(see illustration)**.

9   Drive the new dust seal into the knuckle with a large socket or a seal driver and a hammer **(see illustration)**. Try not to cock the seal in the bore.

10   Install a new O-ring around the rear of the bearing and push it up against the bearing flange **(see illustration)**.

11   Clean the mating surfaces on the steering knuckle, bearing flange and knuckle bore. Lubricate the outside diameter of the bearing and the seal lips with high-temperature grease and insert the hub and bearing into the steering knuckle. Position the rotor shield and install the three bolts. Tightening them to the torque listed in this Chapter's Specifications.

12   Install the driveaxle (see Chapter 8).

13   Attach the control arm to the steering knuckle (see Section 4).

14   Reconnect the stabilizer bar to the control arm (see Section 2).

15   Install the brake rotor and caliper (see Chapter 9).

16   Install the hub nut and tighten it to the initial torque to seat the driveaxle in the hub. Prevent the axle from turning by inserting a screwdriver

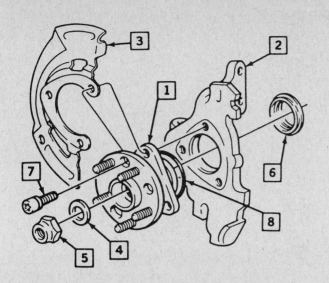

7.10   Hub and bearing installation details

1	Hub and bearing assembly	5	Hub nut
2	Steering knuckle	6	Seal
3	Rotor shield	7	Hub and bearing retaining bolt
4	Washer	8	O-ring

through the caliper and into a rotor cooling vane (see Chapter 8 if necessary).

17   Install the wheel, lower the vehicle and tighten the lug nuts to the specified torque.

18   Tighten the hub nut to the final specified torque.

---

8   Steering knuckle and hub – removal and installation

Removal

1   Loosen the wheel lug nuts, raise the front of the vehicle and support it securely on jackstands. Apply the parking brake and block the rear wheels to keep the vehicle from rolling off the jackstands. Remove the wheel.

2   Remove the hub nut. Insert a screwdriver through the caliper and into a rotor cooling vane to prevent the driveaxle from turning.

3   Remove the caliper and suspend it out of the way with a piece of wire. Lift the rotor off the hub.

4   Mark the position of the two strut-to-knuckle nuts and remove them **(see illustration 5.2)**. Don't drive out the bolts at this time.

5   Separate the control arm balljoint from the steering knuckle (see Section 4 if necessary).

6   Attach a puller to the hub flange and push the driveaxle out of the hub (see Chapter 8). Hang the driveaxle with a piece of wire to prevent damage to the inner CV joint.

7   Support the knuckle and drive out the two strut-to-knuckle bolts with a soft-face hammer. Remove the steering knuckle assembly from the strut.

Installation

8   Position the knuckle in the strut and insert the two splined bolts, with the flats on the bolt heads in the horizontal position. Tap the bolts into place and install the nuts, but don't tighten them at this time.

9   Install the driveaxle in the hub.

10   Connect the control arm to the steering knuckle and tighten the castellated nut to the torque listed in this Chapter's Specifications. Install a new cotter pin.

11   Align the strut-to-knuckle nuts with the previously applied marks and tighten them to the specified torque.

12   Install the brake rotor and caliper.

13   Tighten the hub nut to the initial specified torque to seat the driveaxle in the hub.

14   Install the wheel, lower the vehicle and tighten the lug nuts to the specified torque.

15   Tighten the hub nut to the final specified torque.

---

9   Rear stabilizer bar – removal and installation

Refer to illustrations 9.2 and 9.3

1   Raise the rear of the vehicle and support it securely on jackstands. Block the front wheels to keep the vehicle from rolling off the jackstands.

2   Remove the outer stabilizer bar bushing bracket nuts and bolts and detach the brackets from the trailing arms **(see illustration)**.

3   Remove the two inner stabilizer bushing clamp bolts and nuts **(see illustration)** and detach the stabilizer bar.

4   Inspect the bushings for cracks, hardening and wear. Replace them if necessary.

5   Installation is the reverse of the removal procedure. Before tightening the bolts, make sure the stabilizer bar is centered from side-to-side in the rear axle assembly.

10

9.2   Remove the outer stabilizer bar brackets, . . .

9.3   . . . then disconnect the inner bushing clamps and remove the stabilizer bar

10.2   Remove the lower shock mounting bolt (arrow) – be sure to support the trailing arm with a jack

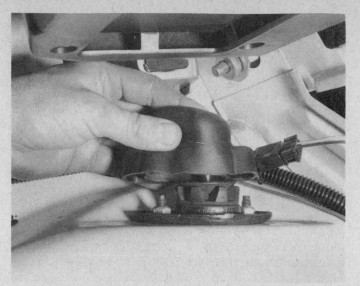

10.3   Locate the upper shock mount behind the trunk compartment side panel trim and remove the upper mount cover

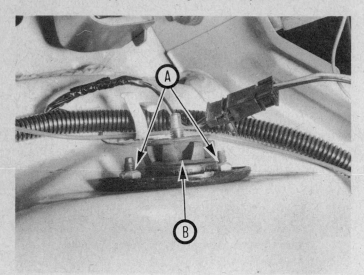

10.4   Hold the damper shaft with an open-end wrench on the flats, then remove the shaft-to-upper mount nut (A) – the upper mount is held in place by two nuts (B)

10   Rear shock absorber – removal and installation

Refer to illustrations 10.2, 10.3 and 10.4

Caution: *Don't remove both shock absorbers at the same time. They limit the movement of the rear suspension and damage to the brake hoses and lines may occur if the suspension is allowed to hang.*

1   Loosen the wheel lug nuts, raise the rear of the vehicle and support it securely on jackstands. Block the front wheels to keep the vehicle from rolling off the jackstands. Remove the wheel.

2   Support the trailing arm with a jack and remove the lower shock absorber mounting bolt **(see illustration)**.

3   Open the trunk and peel back the side trim panel to expose the upper shock mount. Pull the plastic cap off the mount **(see illustration)**.

4   Remove the damper shaft-to-upper mount nut and detach the shock absorber from the vehicle. Inspect the upper mount for cracks, hardening, separation and other damage. If any of these conditions are noted, unscrew the two mounting nuts and remove the mount from the fender well **(see illustration)**.

5   Installation is the reverse of the removal procedure.

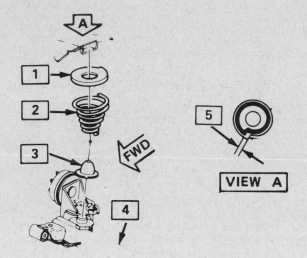

11.5   Rear spring installation details

1	Spring insulator	5 The end of the upper coil
2	Spring	spring must be within
3	Compression bumper	19/32-inch (15 mm) of the
4	Axle assembly	spring stop in the spring seat

11   Rear springs and insulators – removal and installation

Refer to illustration 11.5

Removal

1   Loosen the wheel lug nuts, raise the rear of the vehicle and support it securely on jackstands. Block the front wheels to keep the vehicle from rolling off the jackstands. Remove both rear wheels.

2   Locate the right and left brake line brackets and unbolt them from the frame, allowing the lines to hang freely.

3   Place a floor jack under the center of the axle beam to support it. Remove both lower shock mounting bolts and slowly lower the jack until the coil spring is fully extended. Keep an eye on the brake hoses to make sure they don't get hung-up on anything.

12.3   Remove the four hub and bearing assembly bolts with a no. 55 Torx bit

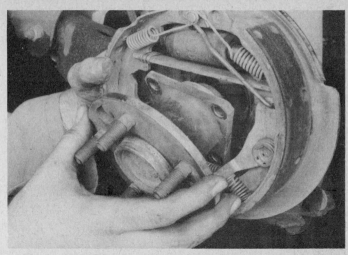

12.4a   Angle the hub and bearing assembly out through the brake assembly

12.4b   Temporarily reinstall two bolts (arrows) to retain the brake assembly to the trailing arm, rather than let it hang by the brake line

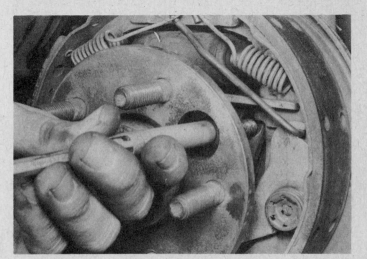

12.5   A magnet is useful for installing the bolts

4   Remove the coil spring, compression bumper and upper spring insulator. Inspect the rubber components for cracks, hardening and general deterioration and replace them if necessary.

Installation

5   Position the compression bumpers on the lower spring pockets and place the coil springs on the axle assembly. Install the upper spring insulators on top of the springs **(see illustration)** and raise the axle, guiding the springs into place. An assistant may be necessary to accomplish this.
6   If difficulty is encountered in keeping the upper spring insulators in place, glue them to the contact area on the body with spray adhesive.
7   Install the lower shock absorber mounting bolts.
8   Attach the brake line brackets to the frame.
9   Install the wheels, lower the vehicle and tighten the wheel lug nuts to the specified torque.

12   Rear hub and wheel bearing assembly – removal and installation

Refer to illustrations 12.3, 12.4a, 12.4b and 12.5
Note: *The rear hub and wheel bearing assembly is sealed-for-life and must be replaced as a unit.*

Removal

1   Loosen the wheel lug nuts, raise the rear of the vehicle and support it securely on jackstands. Block the front wheels to keep the vehicle from rolling off the jackstands. Remove the wheel.
2   Pull the brake drum off the hub. If difficulty is encountered, refer to Chapter 9 for the removal procedure.
3   Using a no. 55 Torx bit, remove the four hub-to-trailing arm bolts, accessible by turning the hub flange so the circular cutout exposes each bolt **(see illustration)**. Save the upper rear bolt for last, because there isn't much clearance between the bolt and the parking brake strut.
4   Remove the hub and bearing assembly, maneuvering it out through the brake assembly. Reinstall two bolts through the brake backing plate into the trailing arm to avoid hanging the brake assembly by the hydraulic line **(see illustrations)**.

Installation

5   Position the hub and bearing assembly on the trailing arm and align the holes in the backing plate. Install the bolts, beginning with the upper rear bolt. A magnet is useful for guiding the bolts through the hub flange and into position **(see illustration)**. After all four bolts have been installed, tighten them to the torque listed in this Chapter's Specifications.
6   Install the brake drum and wheel. Lower the vehicle and tighten the wheel lug nuts to the specified torque.

10

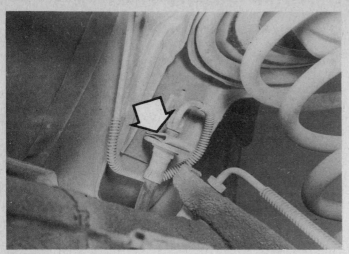

13.6   Loosen the brake line fittings and remove the hose retaining clips

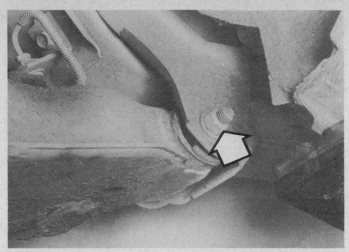

13.7   Remove the rear axle assembly pivot bolt (arrow) and carefully lower the axle to the ground

13   Rear axle assembly – removal and installation

Refer to illustrations 13.6 and 13.7

Removal

1   Loosen the wheel lug nuts, raise the rear of the vehicle and support it securely on jackstands. Block the front wheels to keep the vehicle from rolling off the jackstands. Remove the wheels.

2   If the axle assembly is being replaced, remove the stabilizer bar as outlined in Section 9.

3   Remove the brake drums from the hubs. See Chapter 9 if difficulty is encountered.

4   Remove the coil springs (see Section 11).

5   Disconnect the parking brake cable at the equalizer (Chapter 9).

6   Loosen the brake line fittings and remove the brake hose retaining clips, disconnecting the brake lines from the rear axle assembly **(see illustration)**.

7   With a floor jack supporting the axle assembly, unbolt the axle from the vehicle at the pivot points on the underbody side rails **(see illustration)**. Lower the axle assembly to the ground.

Installation

8   If a new axle assembly is being installed, transfer the hub and bearing assemblies, the brake assemblies, the parking brake cables and the hydraulic lines to the new axle.

9   Place the new axle on the jack and raise it into position. Install the pivot bolts, but don't tighten them completely yet.

10   Install the coil springs and insulators and connect the shock absorbers (see Section 11).

11   Reconnect the brake lines.

12   Reconnect the parking brake cable to the equalizer and position it in the cable guide.

13   Install the stabilizer bar.

14   Install the brake drums.

15   Bleed the brake system following the procedure described in Chapter 9.

16   Install the wheels, lower the vehicle and tighten the lug nuts to the specified torque.

17   With the vehicle standing at normal ride height, tighten the axle pivot bolts to the specified torque.

14   Steering system – general information

Warning: *Whenever any of the steering fasteners are removed, they must be inspected and, if necessary, replaced with new ones of the same part number or of original equipment quality and design. Torque specifications must be followed for proper reassembly and component retention. Never attempt to heat or straighten any suspension or steering components. Instead, replace any bent or damaged part with a new one.*

All vehicles covered by this manual have power rack-and-pinion steering systems. The components making up the system are the steering wheel, steering column, rack and pinion assembly, tie-rods and tie-rod ends. The power steering system has a belt-driven pump to provide hydraulic pressure.

In the power steering system, the motion of turning the steering wheel is transferred through the column to the pinion shaft in the rack-and-pinion assembly. Teeth on the pinion shaft are meshed with teeth on the rack, so when the shaft is turned, the rack is moved left or right in the housing. A rotary control valve in the rack-and-pinion unit directs hydraulic fluid under pressure from the power steering pump to either side of the integral rack piston, which is connected to the rack, thereby reducing manual steering force. Depending on which side of the piston this hydraulic pressure is applied to, the rack will be forced either left or right, which moves the tie-rods, etc. If the power steering system loses hydraulic pressure it will still function manually, though with increased effort.

The steering column is a collapsible, energy-absorbing type, designed to compress in the event of a front end collision to minimize injury to the driver. The column also houses the ignition switch lock, key warning buzzer, turn signal controls, headlight dimmer control and windshield wiper controls. The ignition and steering wheel can both be locked while the vehicle is parked.

Due to the column's collapsible design, it's important that only the specified screws, bolts and nuts be used as designated and that they're tightened to the specified torque. Other precautions particular to this design are noted in appropriate Sections.

In addition to the standard steering column, optional tilt and key release versions are also offered. The tilt model can be set in five different positions, while with the key release model the ignition key is locked in the column until a lever is depressed to extract it.

Because disassembly of the steering column is more often performed to repair a switch or other electrical part than to correct a problem in the steering, the upper steering column disassembly and reassembly procedure is included in Chapter 12.

15   Tie-rod ends – removal and installation

Refer to illustrations 15.2, 15.3 and 15.4

Removal

1   Loosen the wheel lug nuts, raise the front of the vehicle and support it securely on jackstands. Apply the parking brake and block the rear wheels to keep the vehicle from rolling off the jackstands. Remove the wheel.

15.2   Before disconnecting the tie-rod end from the steering arm, loosen the pinch bolt (arrow)

15.3   A two-jaw puller works well for separating the tie-rod end from the steering arm – DO NOT pound on the stud!

15.4   Using white paint, mark the relationship of the tie-rod end and the threaded adjuster

16.3   Remove the upper steering coupler pinch bolt (arrow)

2   Loosen the tie-rod end pinch bolt **(see illustration)**.
3   Disconnect the tie-rod from the steering arm with a puller **(see illustration)**.
4   Mark the relationship of the tie-rod end to the threaded adjuster **(see illustration)**. This will ensure the toe-in setting is restored when reassembled.
5   Unscrew the tie-rod end from the tie-rod.

Installation

6   Thread the tie-rod end onto the tie-rod to the marked position and connect the tie-rod end to the steering arm. Install the castellated nut and tighten it to the torque listed in this Chapter's Specifications. Install a new cotter pin.
7   Tighten the pinch bolt securely and install the wheel. Lower the vehicle and tighten the lug nuts to the specified torque.
8   Have the front end steering geometry checked by a dealer service department or an alignment shop.

---

16   Steering gear – removal and installation

Refer to illustrations 16.3 and 16.4
Warning: *If the vehicle is equipped with an airbag, DO NOT allow the steering wheel to turn after the steering gear has been removed.*

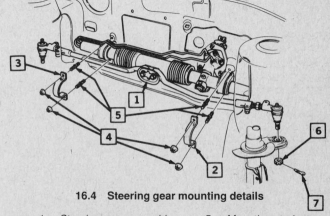

16.4   Steering gear mounting details

1	Steering gear assembly	5	Mounting stud
2	Clamp (left)	6	Castellated nut
3	Clamp (right)	7	Cotter pin
4	Nut		

Removal

1   Disconnect the cable from the negative battery terminal.
2   Remove the left side under-dash panel.
3   Roll back the boot at the bottom of the steering column to expose the flange and steering coupler assembly. Mark the coupler and steering column shaft and remove the upper pinch bolt **(see illustration)**.
4   Remove the two left side steering gear-to-firewall clamp nuts and the right upper clamp nut **(see illustration)**.
5   Remove the pressure hose retainer from the support bracket at the center of the rack.
6   Place a drain pan or tray under the vehicle, positioned beneath the left side of the steering gear. Using a flare-nut wrench, disconnect the pressure and return lines from the steering gear (the two lines closest to the firewall, angled toward the left side of the vehicle). Plug the lines to prevent excessive fluid loss.
7   Loosen the front wheel lug nuts, raise the front of the vehicle and support it securely on jackstands. Apply the parking brake and block the rear wheels to keep the vehicle from rolling off the jackstands. Remove both front wheels.
8   Remove the lower right side clamp nut.
9   Separate the tie-rod ends from the steering arms (see Section 15).
10   Move the steering gear forward and remove the lower pinch bolt from the coupler. Slide the coupler off the pinion shaft.

10

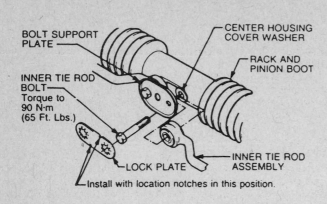

17.2   Tie-rod installation details

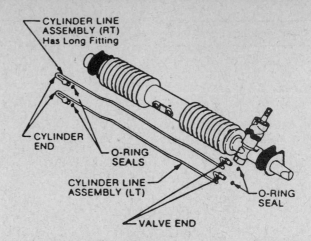

17.3   Power steering hydraulic line installation details – be sure to use new O-ring seals when reinstalling them

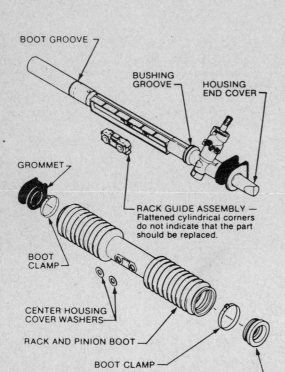

17.4   Steering gear boot installation details

11   Support the steering gear and carefully maneuver the entire assembly out through the left side wheel opening.

12   If any of the mounting studs came out with the clamps, apply thread locking compound to the firewall side of the threads and install them snugly in the firewall.

Installation

13   Pass the steering gear assembly through the left wheel opening into its approximate position.

14   Install the coupler and tighten the lower pinch bolt securely.

15   Center the steering gear, and make sure the dash seal is installed properly. Have an assistant guide the coupler onto the steering column shaft, with the previously applied marks aligned. Position the right side

clamp and install the lower clamp nut, tightening it to the torque listed in this Chapter's Specifications.

16   Install the tie-rod ends in the steering arms and tighten the nuts to the specified torque. Install new cotter pins.

17   Install the front wheels, lower the vehicle and tighten the lug nuts to the specified torque.

18   Attach the pressure and return lines to the steering gear. Connect the line retainer to the support bracket.

19   Install the left side clamp and nuts and the upper right side clamp nut. Tighten them to the torque listed in this Chapter's Specifications.

20   Install the upper pinch bolt in the coupler and tighten it to the specified torque.

21   Install the under-dash panel.

22   Reconnect the negative battery cable.

23   Fill the power steering pump with the recommended fluid, bleed the system (see Section 19) and recheck the fluid level. Check for leaks.

24   Have the front end checked by a dealer service department or an alignment shop.

17   Steering gear boots – replacement

Refer to illustrations 17.2, 17.3 and 17.4

1   Remove the steering gear from the vehicle (see Section 16).

2   Remove the tie-rods from the steering gear **(see illustration)**.

3   Using a flare-nut wrench, detach the lines from the steering gear assembly **(see illustration)**.

4   Remove the right mounting grommet from the rack housing **(see illustration)**.

5   Cut off both boot clamps and discard them.

6   Slide the cylinder end (right end) of the boot toward the center of the steering gear, enough to expose the boot groove. Place a rubber band in the groove to occupy the space, then slide the boot off the steering gear.

7   Install a new clamp on the left end of the boot and insert the boot retaining bushing into the end of the boot. Apply multi-purpose grease to the inside of the bushing and slide the boot onto the steering gear housing.

8   Press the washers into the center housing cover.

9   Align the center housing bolt holes with the rack guide assembly and install the two tie-rod bolts. This will ensure proper alignment of the center housing, rack and rack guide.

10   Tighten the left side boot clamp.

11   Slide the right end of the boot onto the housing, remove the rubber band and seat the boot in the groove. Install the clamp and tighten it.

12   Install the hydraulic lines.

13   Install the tie-rods **(see illustration 17.2)** and tighten the bolts to the torque listed in this Chapter's Specifications.

14   Install the mounting grommet.

15   Install the steering gear assembly.

18   Power steering pump – removal and installation

Refer to illustrations 18.3, 18.5a, 18.5b and 18.5c

Removal

1   Disconnect the cable from the negative battery terminal. **Note:** *If*

18.3   Loosen the return line hose clamp and separate the line from the pump (V6 engine shown)

you're working on a Quad-4 engine, refer to illustration 18.5c and remove the parts in the order indicated by the numbers next to each part.

2   Remove the pump drivebelt.
3   Position a drain pan under the vehicle. Remove as much fluid as possible with a suction gun, then remove the return line from the pump **(see illustration)**.
4   Using a flare-nut wrench and a back-up wrench, disconnect the pressure hose from the pump **(see illustration 18.3)**.
5   Remove the pump mounting bolts and detach the pump from the engine, being careful not to spill the remaining fluid **(see illustrations)**.

Installation

6   Position the pump on the mounting bracket and install the bolts.
7   Connect the pressure and return lines to the pump. If the vehicle is equipped with a 2.0 or 2.2 liter four-cylinder engine, note that the pump mounting bolts have a specific tightening sequence **(see illustration 18.5a)**.
8   Fill the reservoir with the recommended fluid and bleed the system, following the procedure described in the next Section.

19   Power steering system – bleeding

1   Following any operation in which the power steering fluid lines have been disconnected, the power steering system must be bled to remove air and obtain proper steering performance.

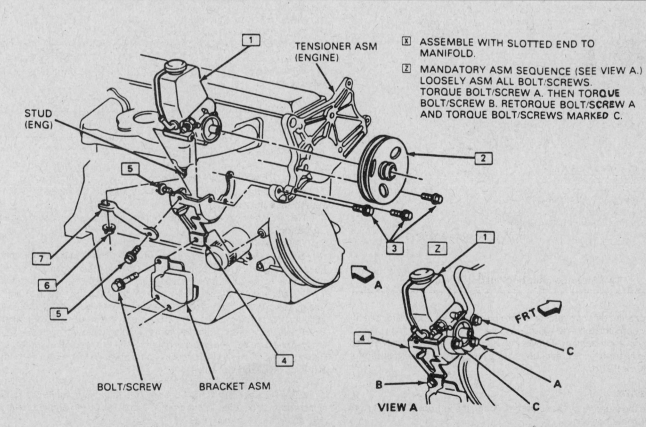

18.5a   Power steering pump mounting details and bolt tightening sequence (2.0/2.2 liter four-cylinder engines)

1	*Power steering pump*	*3*	*Bolt/screw*	*5*	*Bolt/screw*	*7*	*Brace*
2	*Pulley*	*4*	*Bracket*	*6*	*Nut*		

10

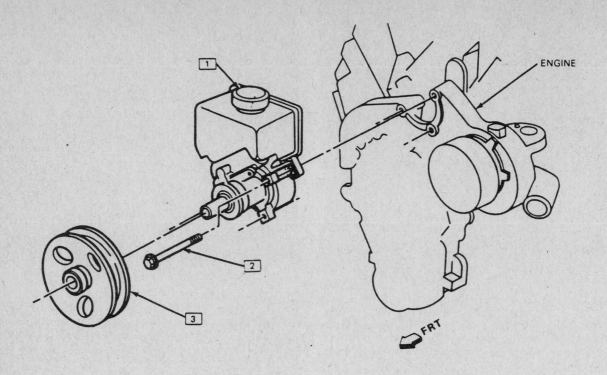

18.5b   Power steering pump mounting details (V6 engine)

1   *Power steering pump*   3   *Pulley*
2   *Bolt/screw*

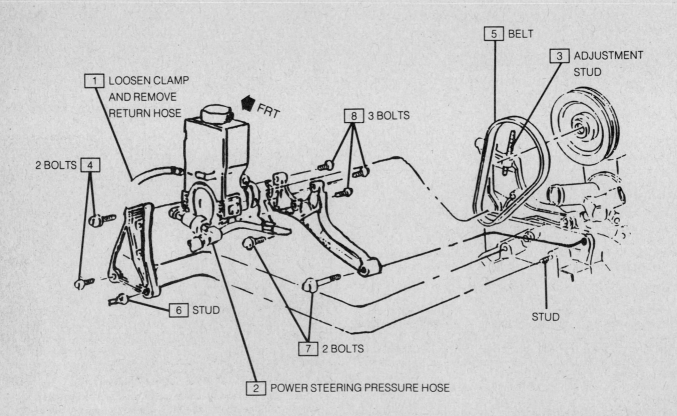

18.5c   Power steering pump mounting details (Quad-4 engine) – remove the parts in the numerical sequence to detach the pump

20.3   Remove the safety clip with a pair of snap-ring pliers

20.4   Remove the horn contact and spring

2   With the front wheels turned all the way to the left, check the power steering fluid level and, if low, add fluid until it reaches the Cold mark on the dipstick.

3   Start the engine and allow it to run at fast idle. Recheck the fluid level and add more if necessary to reach the Cold mark on the dipstick.

4   Bleed the system by turning the wheels from side-to-side, without hitting the stops. This will work the air out of the system. Don't allow the reservoir to run out of fluid.

5   When the air is worked out of the system, return the wheels to the straight ahead position and leave the engine running for several minutes before shutting it off. Recheck the fluid level.

6   Road test the vehicle to be sure the steering system is functioning normally with no noise.

7   Recheck the fluid level to be sure it's up to the Hot mark on the dipstick while the engine is at normal operating temperature. Add fluid if necessary.

20.5   Make alignment marks on the steering wheel hub and shaft

20   Steering wheel – removal and installation

Refer to illustrations 20.3, 20.4, 20.5 and 20.6

Warning: *Do not attempt this procedure on airbag-equipped vehicles. Take the vehicle to a dealer service department that has the special tools and expertise to perform this procedure. Attempting this procedure at home could result in the airbag deploying accidently, possibly causing personal injury, or an airbag that does not deploy correctly in a collision.*

1   Disconnect the cable from the negative battery terminal.

2   Pull the horn pad off the steering wheel.

3   Remove the safety clip from the steering shaft **(see illustration)**.

4   Push down on the horn contact and twist it to allow removal **(see illustration)**.

5   Remove the steering wheel retaining nut, then mark the relationship of the steering shaft and hub to simplify installation and ensure steering wheel alignment **(see illustration)**.

6   Use a puller to disconnect the steering wheel from the shaft **(see illustration)**.

7   To install the wheel, align the mark on the steering wheel hub with the mark made on the shaft during removal and slip the wheel onto the shaft.

20.6   Use a steering wheel puller to separate the steering wheel from the shaft – DO NOT attempt to remove the wheel with a hammer!

10

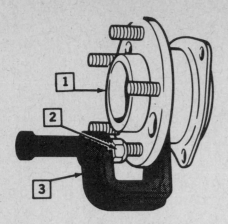

21.3 Use GM tool no. J-6627-A or equivalent to push the stud out of the flange

1 Hub	3 Tool
2 Lug nut on stud	

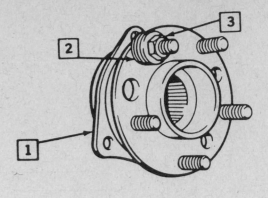

21.4 Install four washers and a lug nut on the stud, then tighten the nut to draw the stud into place

1 Hub and wheel bearing assembly	2 Washers installed on stud 3 Lug nut

Install the hub nut and tighten it to the torque listed in this Chapter's Specifications. Install the safety clip.

8   Install the horn contact and press the horn pad into place on the steering wheel.

9   Connect the negative battery cable.

21   Wheel studs – replacement

Refer to illustrations 21.3 and 21.4

Note: *This procedure applies to both the front and rear wheel studs.*

1   Remove the hub and wheel bearing assembly (see Sections 7 or 12).

2   Install a lug nut part way onto the stud being replaced.

3   Push the stud out of the hub flange with GM tool no. J-6627-A or equivalent **(see illustration)**.

4   Insert the new stud into the hub flange from the back side and install four flat washers and a lug nut on the stud **(see illustration)**.

5   Tighten the lug nut until the stud is seated in the flange.

6   Reinstall the hub and wheel bearing assembly.

22   Wheels and tires – general information

Refer to illustration 22.1

All vehicles covered by this manual are equipped with metric-size fiberglass or steel belted radial tires **(see illustration)**. The use of other size or type tires may affect the ride and handling of the vehicle. Don't mix different types of tires, such as radials and bias belted, on the same vehicle, since handling may be seriously affected. Tires should be replaced in pairs on the same axle, but if only one tire is being replaced, be sure it's the same size, structure and tread design as the other.

Because tire pressure affects handling and wear, the tire pressures should be checked at least once a month or before any extended trips (see Chapter 1).

Wheels must be replaced if they're bent, dented, leak air, have elongated bolt holes, are heavily rusted, out of vertical symmetry or if the lug nuts won't stay tight. Wheel repairs by welding or peening aren't recommended.

Tire and wheel balance is important to the overall handling, braking and performance of the vehicle. Unbalanced wheels can adversely affect handling and ride characteristics as well as tire life. Whenever a tire is installed on a wheel, the tire and wheel should be balanced by a shop with the proper equipment.

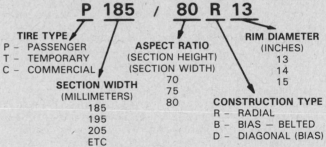

METRIC TIRE SIZES

P 185 / 80 R 13

TIRE TYPE	ASPECT RATIO	RIM DIAMETER
P – PASSENGER	(SECTION HEIGHT)	(INCHES)
T – TEMPORARY	(SECTION WIDTH)	13
C – COMMERCIAL		14
	70	15
SECTION WIDTH	75	
(MILLIMETERS)	80	**CONSTRUCTION TYPE**
185		R – RADIAL
195		B – BIAS – BELTED
205		D – DIAGONAL (BIAS)
ETC		

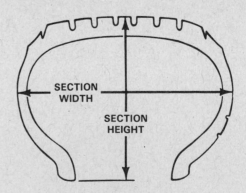

22.1 Metric tire size code

23   Front end alignment – general information

Refer to illustration 23.1

A front end alignment refers to the adjustments made to the front wheels so they're in proper angular relationship to the suspension and the ground. Front wheels that are out of proper alignment not only affect steering control, but also increase tire wear. The only front end adjustment normally required is the toe-in adjustment **(see illustration)**. Camber adjustments are also possible, but only after the strut has been modified.

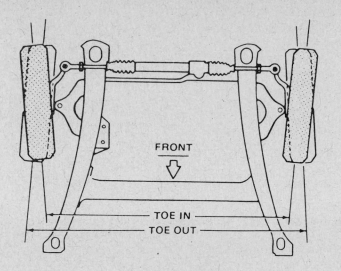
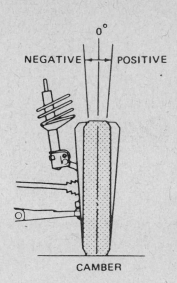

23.1   A front end alignment normally consists of a toe-in adjustment only; however, camber adjustment is possible after strut modification

Getting the proper front wheel alignment is a very exacting process, one in which complicated and expensive machines are necessary to perform the job properly. Because of this, you should have a technician with the proper equipment perform these tasks. We will, however, attempt to give you a basic idea of what's involved with front end alignment so you can better understand the process and deal intelligently with the shop that does the work.

Toe-in is the turning in of the front wheels. The purpose of a toe specification is to ensure parallel rolling of the front wheels. In a vehicle with zero toe-in, the distance between the front edges of the wheels will be the same as the distance between the rear edges of the wheels. The actual amount of toe-in is normally only a fraction of an inch. Toe-in adjustment is controlled by the tie-rod end position on the inner tie-rod. Incorrect toe-in will cause the tires to wear improperly by making them scrub against the road surface.

Camber is the tilting of the front wheels from the vertical when viewed from the front of the vehicle. When the wheels tilt out at the top, the camber is said to be positive (+). When the wheels tilt in at the top the camber is negative (-). The amount of tilt is measured in degrees from the vertical and this measurement is called the camber angle. This angle affects the amount of tire tread which contacts the road and compensates for changes in the suspension geometry when the vehicle is cornering or travelling over an undulating surface.

Caster is the tilting of the top of the front steering axis from the vertical. A tilt toward the rear is positive caster and a tilt toward the front is negative caster. Caster is not adjustable on these vehicles.

10

Chapter 11 Body

Contents

Specifications

Torque specifications

	Ft-lbs (unless otherwise indicated)
Door hinge-to-body pillar nuts and bolts	15 to 20
Trunk lid latch striker	
Bolt (Beretta)	53 in-lbs
Nut (Corsica)	124 in-lbs
Seat track guide-to-floor pan bolt	
Through 1990	10
1991 and later	26
Seat adjuster-to-seat frame nut	
Through 1990	10
1991 and later	21
Door latch striker nut	34 to 46

1 General information

Warning: *Later models are equipped with airbags. Impact sensors for the airbag system are located just above the radiator grille on the right side. The airbag(s) could accidently deploy if these sensors are disturbed, so be extremely careful when working in this area. Airbag system components are also located in the steering wheel, steering column and base of the steering column, so be extremely careful in these areas and don't disturb any airbag system components or wiring. You could easily be injured if an airbag accidently deploys, and the airbag might not deploy correctly in a collision if any components or wiring in the system have been disturbed.*

Note: *On models equipped with the Delco Loc II audio system, be sure the lockout feature is turned off before performing any procedure which requires disconnecting the battery.*

These models are available in two-door coupe (Beretta) and four-door sedan (Corsica) body styles. The vehicle is a "unibody" type, which means the body is designed to provide vehicle rigidity so a separate frame isn't necessary.

Body maintenance is an important part of the retention of the vehicle's market value. It's far less costly to handle small problems before they grow into larger ones.

Major body components which are particularly vulnerable in accidents are removable. These include the hood, front fenders, grille, doors, trunk lid and tail light assembly. It's often cheaper and less time consuming to replace an entire panel than it is to attempt a restoration of the old one. However, this must be decided on a case-by-case basis.

2   Maintenance – body

1   The condition of the body is very important, because the value of the vehicle is dependent on it. It's much more difficult to repair a neglected or damaged body than it is to repair mechanical components. The hidden areas of the body, such as the fender wells and the engine compartment, are equally important, although they obviously don't require as frequent attention as the rest of the body.

2   Once a year, or every 12,000 miles, it's a good idea to have the underside of the body steam cleaned. All traces of dirt and oil will be removed and the underside can then be inspected carefully for rust, damaged brake lines, frayed electrical wiring, damaged cables and other problems. The front suspension components should be greased after completion of this job.

3   At the same time, clean the engine and the engine compartment with a water soluble degreaser.

4   The fender wells should be given particular attention, as undercoating can peel away and stones and dirt thrown up by the tires can cause the paint to chip and flake, allowing rust to set in. If rust is found, clean down to the bare metal and apply an anti-rust paint.

5   The body should be washed as needed. Wet the vehicle thoroughly to soften the dirt, then wash it down with a soft sponge and plenty of clean soapy water. If the surplus dirt isn't washed off very carefully, it will in time wear down the paint.

6   Spots of tar or asphalt coating thrown up from the road should be removed with a cloth soaked in solvent.

7   Once every six months, wax the body thoroughly. If a chrome cleaner is used to remove rust from any of the vehicle's plated parts, remember that the cleaner also removes part of the chrome, so use it sparingly.

3   Maintenance – upholstery and carpets

1   Every three months remove the carpets or mats and clean the interior of the vehicle (more frequently if necessary). Vacuum the upholstery and carpets to remove loose dirt and dust.

2   If the upholstery is soiled, apply upholstery cleaner with a damp sponge and wipe it off with a clean, dry cloth.

4   Vinyl trim – maintenance

Vinyl trim should not be cleaned with detergents, caustic soaps or petroleum-based cleaners. Plain soap and water or a mild vinyl cleaner is best for stains. Test a small area for color fastness. Bubbles under the vinyl can be eliminated by piercing them with a pin and then working the air out.

5   Body repair – minor damage

See photo sequence

Repair of minor scratches

1   If the scratch is superficial and does not penetrate to the metal of the body, repair is very simple. Lightly rub the scratched area with a fine rubbing compound to remove loose paint and built up wax. Rinse the area with clean water.

2   Apply touch-up paint to the scratch, using a small brush. Continue to apply thin layers of paint until the surface of the paint in the scratch is level with the surrounding paint. Allow the new paint at least two weeks to harden, then blend it into the surrounding paint by rubbing with a very fine rubbing compound. Finally, apply a coat of wax to the scratch area.

3   If the scratch has penetrated the paint and exposed the metal of the body, causing the metal to rust, a different repair technique is required. Remove all loose rust from the bottom of the scratch with a pocket knife, then apply rust inhibiting paint to prevent the formation of rust in the future. Us-

ing a rubber or nylon applicator, coat the scratched area with glaze-type filler. If required, the filler can be mixed with thinner to provide a very thin paste, which is ideal for filling narrow scratches. Before the glaze filler in the scratch hardens, wrap a piece of smooth cotton cloth around the tip of a finger. Dip the cloth in thinner and then quickly wipe it along the surface of the scratch. This will ensure that the surface of the filler is slightly hollow. The scratch can now be painted over as described earlier in this section.

Repair of dents

4   When repairing dents, the first job is to pull the dent out until the affected area is as close as possible to its original shape. There is no point in trying to restore the original shape completely as the metal in the damaged area will have stretched on impact and cannot be restored to its original contours. It is better to bring the level of the dent up to a point which is about 1/8-inch below the level of the surrounding metal. In cases where the dent is very shallow, it is not worth trying to pull it out at all.

5   If the back side of the dent is accessible, it can be hammered out gently from behind using a soft-face hammer. While doing this, hold a block of wood firmly against the opposite side of the metal to absorb the hammer blows and prevent the metal from being stretched.

6   If the dent is in a section of the body which has double layers, or some other factor makes it inaccessible from behind, a different technique is required. Drill several small holes through the metal inside the damaged area, particularly in the deeper sections. Screw long, self tapping screws into the holes just enough for them to get a good grip in the metal. Now the dent can be pulled out by pulling on the protruding heads of the screws with locking pliers.

7   The next stage of repair is the removal of paint from the damaged area and from an inch or so of the surrounding metal. This is easily done with a wire brush or sanding disk in a drill motor, although it can be done just as effectively by hand with sandpaper. To complete the preparation for filling, score the surface of the bare metal with a screwdriver or the tang of a file or drill small holes in the affected area. This will provide a good grip for the filler material. To complete the repair, see the Section on filling and painting.

Repair of rust holes or gashes

8   Remove all paint from the affected area and from an inch or so of the surrounding metal using a sanding disk or wire brush mounted in a drill motor. If these are not available, a few sheets of sandpaper will do the job just as effectively.

9   With the paint removed, you will be able to determine the severity of the corrosion and decide whether to replace the whole panel, if possible, or repair the affected area. New body panels are not as expensive as most people think and it is often quicker to install a new panel than to repair large areas of rust.

10   Remove all trim pieces from the affected area except those which will act as a guide to the original shape of the damaged body, such as headlight shells, etc. Using metal snips or a hacksaw blade, remove all loose metal and any other metal that is badly affected by rust. Hammer the edges of the hole inward to create a slight depression for the filler material.

11   Wire brush the affected area to remove the powdery rust from the surface of the metal. If the back of the rusted area is accessible, treat it with rust-inhibiting paint.

12   Before filling is done, block the hole in some way. This can be done with sheet metal riveted or screwed into place, or by stuffing the hole with wire mesh.

13   Once the hole is blocked off, the affected area can be filled and painted. See the following sub-section on filling and painting.

Filling and painting

14   Many types of body fillers are available, but generally speaking, body repair kits which contain filler paste and a tube of resin hardener are best for this type of repair work. A wide, flexible plastic or nylon applicator will be necessary for imparting a smooth and contoured finish to the surface of the filler material. Mix up a small amount of filler on a clean piece of wood or cardboard (use the hardener springly). Follow the manufacturer's instructions on the package, otherwise the filler will set incorrectly.

11

15   Using the applicator, apply the filler paste to the prepared area. Draw the applicator across the surface of the filler to achieve the desired contour and to level the filler surface. As soon as a contour that approximates the original one is achieved, stop working the paste. If you continue, the paste will begin to stick to the applicator. Continue to add thin layers of paste at 20-minute intervals until the level of the filler is just above the surrounding metal.

16   Once the filler has hardened, the excess can be removed with a body file. From then on, progressively finer grades of sandpaper should be used, starting with a 180-grit paper and finishing with 600-grit wet-or-dry paper. Always wrap the sandpaper around a flat rubber or wooden block, otherwise the surface of the filler will not be completely flat. During the sanding of the filler surface, the wet-or-dry paper should be periodically rinsed in water. This will ensure that a very smooth finish is produced in the final stage.

17   At this point, the repair area should be surrounded by a ring of bare metal, which in turn should be encircled by the finely feathered edge of good paint. Rinse the repair area with clean water until all of the dust produced by the sanding operation is gone.

18   Spray the entire area with a light coat of primer. This will reveal any imperfections in the surface of the filler. Repair the imperfections with fresh filler paste or glaze filler and once more smooth the surface with sandpaper. Repeat this spray-and-repair procedure until you are satisfied that the surface of the filler and the feathered edge of the paint are perfect. Rinse the area with clean water and allow it to dry completely.

19   The repair area is now ready for painting. Spray painting must be carried out in a warm, dry, windless and dust free atmosphere. These conditions can be created if you have access to a large indoor work area, but if you are forced to work in the open, you will have to pick the day very carefully. If you are working indoors, dousing the floor in the work area with water will help settle the dust which would otherwise be in the air. If the repair area is confined to one body panel, mask off the surrounding panels. This will help minimize the effects of a slight mismatch in paint color. Trim pieces such as chrome strips, door handles, etc., will also need to be masked off or removed. Use masking tape and several thicknesses of newspaper for the masking operations.

20   Before spraying, shake the paint can thoroughly, then spray a test area until the spray painting technique is mastered. Cover the repair area with a thick coat of primer. The thickness should be built up using several thin layers of primer rather than one thick one. Using 600-grit wet-or-dry sandpaper, rub down the surface of the primer until it is very smooth. While doing this, the work area should be thoroughly rinsed with water and the wet-or-dry sandpaper periodically rinsed as well. Allow the primer to dry before spraying additional coats.

21   Spray on the top coat, again building up the thickness by using several thin layers of paint. Begin spraying in the center of the repair area and then, using a circular motion, work out until the whole repair area and about two inches of the surrounding original paint is covered. Remove all masking material 10 to 15 minutes after spraying on the final coat of paint. Allow the new paint at least two weeks to harden, then use a very fine rubbing compound to blend the edges of the new paint into the existing paint. Finally, apply a coat of wax.

6   Body repair – major damage

1   Major damage must be repaired by an auto body/frame repair shop with the necessary welding and hydraulic straightening equipment.

2   If the damage has been serious, it is vital that the structure be checked for proper alignment or the vehicle's handling characteristics may be adversely affected. Other problems, such as excessive tire wear and wear in the driveline and steering may occur.

3   Due to the fact that all of the major body components (hood, fenders, etc.) are separate and replaceable units, any seriously damaged components should be replaced rather than repaired. Sometimes these components can be found in a wrecking yard that specializes in used vehicle components, often at considerable savings over the cost of new parts.

9.1   Pad the back corners of the hood with rags so the windshield won't be damaged if the hood accidentally swings to the rear

7   Maintenance – hinges and locks

Every 3000 miles or three months, the door, hood and trunk lid hinges should be lubricated with a few drops of oil. The door striker plates should also be given a thin coat of white lithium-base grease to reduce wear and ensure free movement.

8   Windshield and fixed glass – replacement

1   Replacement of the windshield and fixed glass requires the use of special fast-setting adhesive/caulk materials. These operations should be left to a dealer or a shop specializing in glass work.

2   Windshield-mounted rear view mirror support removal is also best left to experts, as the bond to the glass also requires special tools and adhesives.

9   Hood – removal and installation

Refer to illustrations 9.1 and 9.2

1   Use rags or pads to protect the windshield from the rear of the hood **(see illustration)**.

2   Scribe or draw alignment marks around the hinge bolts **(see illustration)**.

3   On models so equipped, detach the assist strut.

4   Remove the bolts and, with the help of an assistant, detach the hood from the vehicle.

5   Installation is the reverse of removal.

10   Hood latch cable – replacement

Refer to illustrations 10.1, 10.2, 10.3 and 10.4

1   In the passenger compartment, remove the trim panel **(see illustration)**.

2   Remove the latch handle retaining screws and detach the handle **(see illustration)**.

9.2   Use a scribe or a felt-tip pen to mark the hood bolt positions

10.1   Pull the trim panel down for access to the two screws behind the hood latch handle

10.2   Remove the two screws with a Phillips screwdriver

10.3   Pry the hood latch cable up (arrow) to detach it from the clip

3   In the engine compartment, pry the cable grommet out of the clip **(see illustration)**.

4   Spread the clip with a screwdriver and detach the end of the cable from the latch **(see illustration)**.

5   Connect a piece of string or thin wire of suitable length to the end of the wire to the cable and pull the cable through into the passenger compartment.

6   Connect the string or wire to the new cable and pull it back into the engine compartment.

7   Connect the cable and install the latch screws and trim panel.

11   Front fender liner – removal and installation

Refer to illustrations 11.2, 11.4 and 11.6

1   Raise the vehicle, support it securely on jackstands and remove the front wheel.

2   The fender liner is held in place with special plastic retainers. Use wire cutters or a similar tool to pry the heads of the retainers out of the retainer

10.4   Pry the clip back and lift the cable up to detach it (arrows)

11

11.2   Pry the head out of the retainer body – do not cut the head off

11.4   Grasp the fender liner and pull the ends in to detach it from the fender well

bodies to release them **(see illustration)**. Pry the heads out, do not cut them off to remove them.

3   Once all of the retainers are released, remove them from the fender liner.

4   Detach the liner and remove it from the vehicle **(see illustration)**.

5   To install, place the liner in position and align the retainer holes.

6   Install the retainers and push the heads in to securely lock them in place **(see illustration)**.

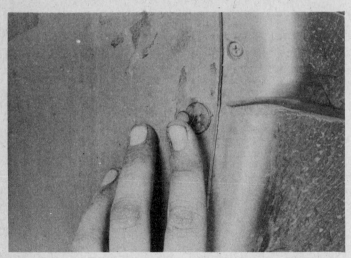

11.6   Push the head of the retainer into the body until it locks in place

---

12   Front fender – removal and installation

Refer to illustration 12.3a and 12.3b

1   Raise the front of the vehicle, support it securely on jackstands and remove the front wheel.

2   Remove the front fender liner (Section 11).

3   Remove the retaining bolts and detach the fender from the vehicle **(see illustrations)**.

4   To install, place the fender in place and install the retaining nuts. Tighten the nuts securely.

5   The remainder of installation is the reverse of removal.

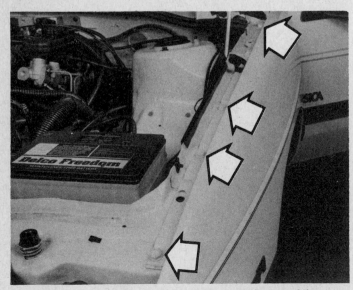

12.3a   Remove the mounting bolts along the top of the fender (arrows)

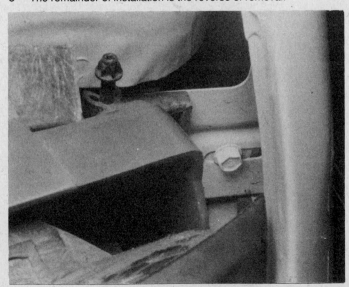

12.3b   Remove the inner fender mounting bolt

13.2   Remove the trim panel retaining screws (arrows)

13.3   Use a socket to remove the front grille retaining screws (arrow)

13   Radiator grille – removal and installation

Refer to illustrations 13.2 and 13.3

Warning: *We do not recommend attempting this procedure on airbag-equipped models. The impact sensor for the airbag system is located just above the grille on the right side tie bar. If this sensor is disturbed, the airbag could deploy, possibly resulting in personal injury. Also, disturbing this sensor or its wiring could cause the airbag not to deploy properly in a collision.*

1   Open the hood.
2   Remove the trim panel retaining screws directly over the front grille (see illustration) and lift the trim panels up.
3   Remove the front grille retaining screws **(see illustration)**.
4   Rotate the top of the grille out and lift it from the vehicle.
5   Installation is the reverse of removal.

14   Door trim panel – removal and installation

Refer to illustrations 14.1a, 14.1b, 14.3 and 14.4

1   Remove door glass regulator handle (if equipped) (Section 17), and the visible door panel screws from the door trim panel **(see illustrations)**.

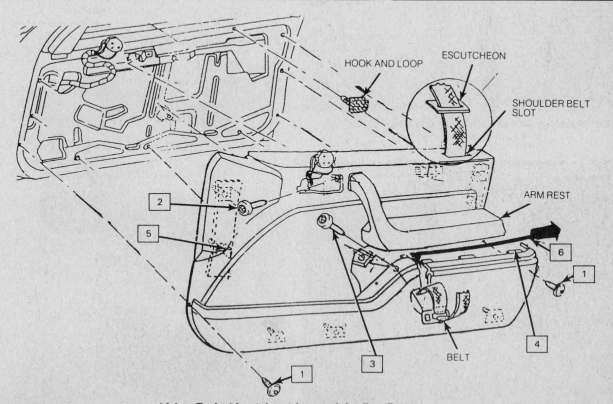

14.1a   Typical front door trim panel details – Beretta

1 Two lower panel screws to door	3 Lower panel screw (front)	5 Seven clips and hook
2 Arm rest upper screw – remove inside handle	4 Three tabs that press into arm rest clips to retain lower to armrest	6 Slide belt in opening during removal and installation of trim panel

11

These photos illustrate a method of repairing simple dents. They are intended to supplement *Body repair - minor damage* in this Chapter and should not be used as the sole instructions for body repair on these vehicles.

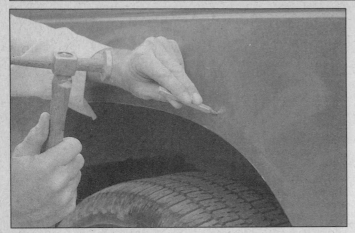

1   If you can't access the backside of the body panel to hammer out the dent, pull it out with a slide-hammer-type dent puller. In the deepest portion of the dent or along the crease line, drill or punch hole(s) at least one inch apart . . .

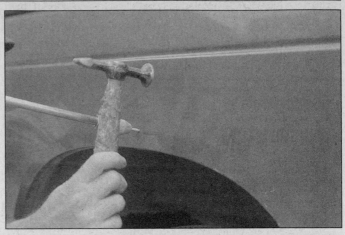

2   . . . then screw the slide-hammer into the hole and operate it. Tap with a hammer near the edge of the dent to help 'pop' the metal back to its original shape. When you're finished, the dent area should be close to its original contour and about 1/8-inch below the surface of the surrounding metal

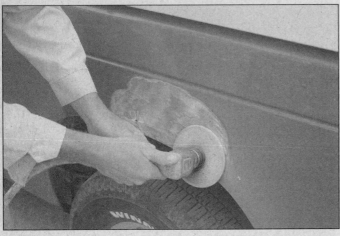

3   Using coarse-grit sandpaper, remove the paint down to the bare metal. Hand sanding works fine, but the disc sander shown here makes the job faster. Use finer (about 320-grit) sandpaper to feather-edge the paint at least one inch around the dent area

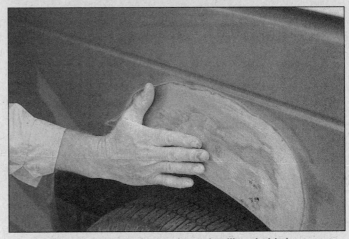

4   When the paint is removed, touch will probably be more helpful than sight for telling if the metal is straight. Hammer down the high spots or raise the low spots as necessary. Clean the repair area with wax/silicone remover

5   Following label instructions, mix up a batch of plastic filler and hardener. The ratio of filler to hardener is critical, and, if you mix it incorrectly, it will either not cure properly or cure too quickly (you won't have time to file and sand it into shape)

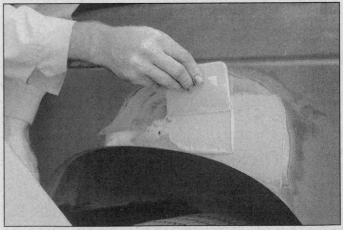

6   Working quickly so the filler doesn't harden, use a plastic applicator to press the body filler firmly into the metal, assuring it bonds completely. Work the filler until it matches the original contour and is slightly above the surrounding metal

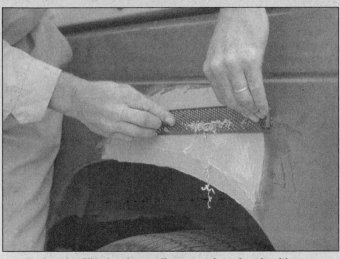

7   Let the filler harden until you can just dent it with your fingernail. Use a body file or Surform tool (shown here) to rough-shape the filler

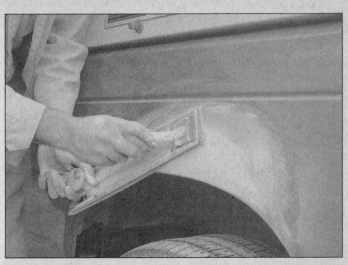

8   Use coarse-grit sandpaper and a sanding board or block to work the filler down until it's smooth and even. Work down to finer grits of sandpaper - always using a board or block - ending up with 360 or 400 grit

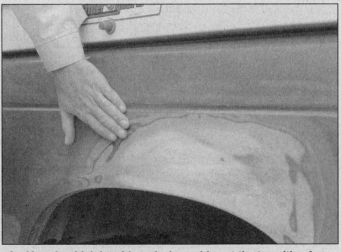

9   You shouldn't be able to feel any ridge at the transition from the filler to the bare metal or from the bare metal to the old paint. As soon as the repair is flat and uniform, remove the dust and mask off the adjacent panels or trim pieces

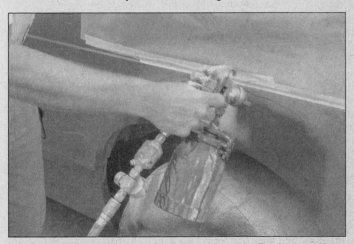

10   Apply several layers of primer to the area. Don't spray the primer on too heavy, so it sags or runs, and make sure each coat is dry before you spray on the next one. A professional-type spray gun is being used here, but aerosol spray primer is available inexpensively from auto parts stores

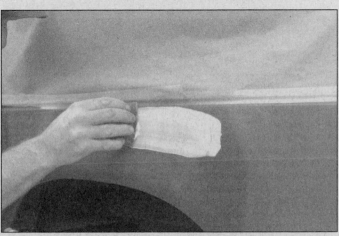

11   The primer will help reveal imperfections or scratches. Fill these with glazing compound. Follow the label instructions and sand it with 360 or 400-grit sandpaper until it's smooth. Repeat the glazing, sanding and respraying until the primer reveals a perfectly smooth surface

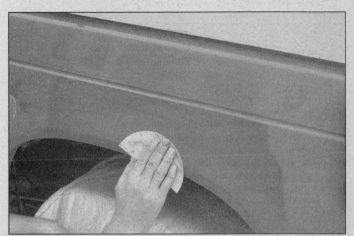

12   Finish sand the primer with very fine sandpaper (400 or 600-grit) to remove the primer overspray. Clean the area with water and allow it to dry. Use a tack rag to remove any dust, then apply the finish coat. Don't attempt to rub out or wax the repair area until the paint has dried completely (at least two weeks)

14.1b   On the Corsica, remove the door glass regulator handle with a special upholstery tool.

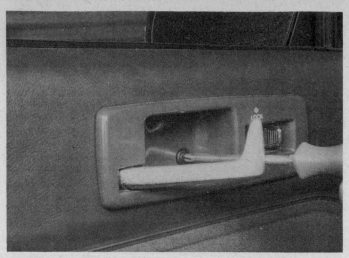

14.3   Corsica handle cover assembly

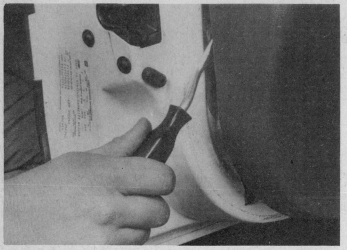

14.4   Pry around the door panel with an upholstery tool or a large screwdriver

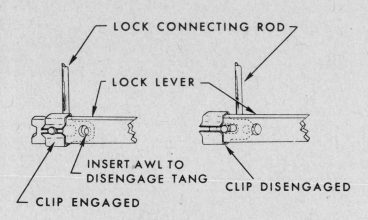

15.2a   Door lever rod spring clip installation details

2   Remove the screws from the arm rest (if equipped).
3   Remove the door handle cover assembly by removing the screws **(see illustration)**.
4   Pry around the outer circumference of the door panel with a pry bar or large screwdriver to disengage the clips **(see illustration)**.
5   Grasp the door trim panel securely and lift up to disengage it from the door upper edge.
6   Unplug any electrical switches and lift the door trim panel from the vehicle.
7   Carefully peel the water shield from the door for access to the inner door components. Take care not to tear the water shield as it must be reinstalled.
8   Installation is the reverse of removal.

---

15   Door lock assembly – removal and installation

Refer to illustrations 15.2a, 15.2b and 15.2c

1   With the window glass in the full up position, remove the door trim panel and water shield (Section 14).
2   Disconnect spring clips from the remote control connecting rods at the lock assembly **(see illustrations)**.

3   Remove the lock assembly-to-door screws and lift the assembly from the door.
4   To install, place the assembly in position and install the retaining screws.
5   Connect the lock rods.
6   Install the water shield and door trim panel.

---

16   Door window glass – removal and installation

---

1   With the window glass in the full up position, remove the door trim panel and water shield (Section 14).

Front door

Refer to illustration 16.3

2   Remove the outside mirror (Section 28).
3   Remove the rubber stop bumper, screws and front run channel **(see illustration)**.
4   Lower the glass to the bottom of the door, slide the window regulator guide block off the sash channel and tilt the glass inboard of the door frame to remove it.
5   To install, insert the glass into the door and engage the regulator guide block to the sash channel. Engage the rear guide clip on the glass to the rear run channel weatherstrip.

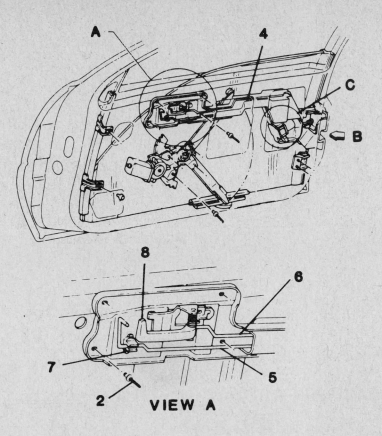

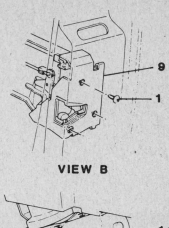

VIEW B

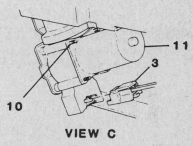

VIEW C

VIEW A

15.2b Door lock module – Beretta

1	Screws	7	Retainer
2	Rivets	8	Handle
3	Connector	9	Lock assembly
4	Lock module assembly	10	Screws
5	Rod	11 ·	Actuator
6	Rod		

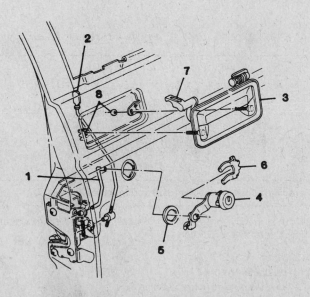

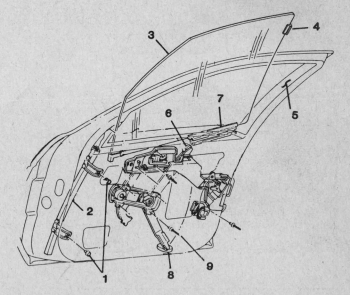

15.2c Front door outside handle – Corsica

1	Lock cylinder to lock rod	5	Gasket
2	Outside handle to lock rod	6	Retainer
3	Handle	7	Slot in lever of handle
4	Lock cylinder	8	Nuts

16.3 Typical front door glass details

1	Screws	6	Regulator arm roller
2	Front run channel retainer	7	Glass sash channel
3	Glass assembly	8	Stop bumper
4	Rear guide	9	Rivets
5	Rear run channel		

11

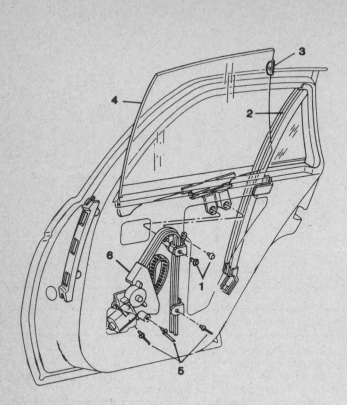

16.10   Rear door glass details

1	Screws	4	Glass assembly
2	Division channel	5	Rivets
3	Rear guide on glass	6	Regulator

6   Raise the glass to the half way up position and install the front run channel bolts finger tight.

7   Engage the front clip on the glass in the front run channel and tighten the bolts securely.

8   Install the rubber stop bumper.

9   The remainder of installation is the reverse of removal.

Rear door

Refer to illustration 16.10

10   Remove the bolts retaining the regulator block to the window glass **(see illustration)**.

11   Disengage the glass and lower it to the bottom of the door.

12   Remove the run channel from the door frame at the front and rear of the glass division channel.

13   Lift the glass from the door.

14   To install, insert the glass into the door and connect the division channel, making sure to engage the glass guide securely to the channel.

15   Connect the regulator guide block to the glass sash channel and install the bolts. Tighten the bolts securely.

16   The remainder of installation is the reverse of removal.

17   Door glass regulator – removal and installation

Refer to illustrations 17.2a and 17.2b

Removal

1   On power window equipped models, disconnect the negative cable at the battery. Place the cable out of the way so it cannot accidentally come in

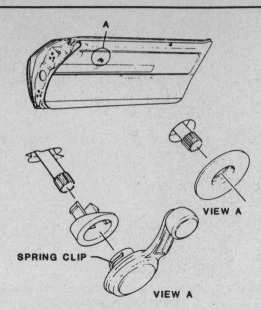

17.2a   Disengage the manual door glass regulator handle spring clip and withdraw the assembly from the door

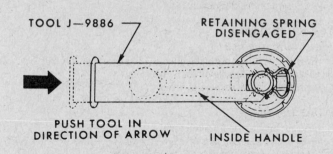

17.2b   A special tool can be used to disengage the spring clip

contact with the negative terminal of the battery, as this would once again allow power into the electrical system of the vehicle.

2   On manual window glass regulator equipped models, remove the handle by pressing the bearing plate and door trim panel in and, with a piece of hooked wire, pulling off the spring clip **(see illustration)**. A special tool is available for this purpose **(see illustration)** but its use is not essential. With the clip removed, take off the handle and the bearing plate.

3   With the window glass in the full up position, remove the door trim panel and water shield (Section 14).

4   Secure the window glass in the up position with strong adhesive tape fastened to the glass and wrapped over the door frame.

5   Punch out the center pins of the rivets that secure the window regulator and drill the rivets out with a 1/4-inch drill bit.

6   On power window equipped models, unplug the electrical connector.

7   Remove the retaining bolts and move the regulator until it is disengaged from the sash channel. Lift the regulator from the door.

Installation

8   Place the regulator in position in the door and engage it in the sash channel.

9   Secure the regulator to the door using 3/16-inch rivets and a rivet tool.

10   Install the bolts and tighten them securely.

11   Plug in the electrical connector (if equipped).

12   Install the water shield, door trim panel and window regulator handle. Connect the negative battery cable.

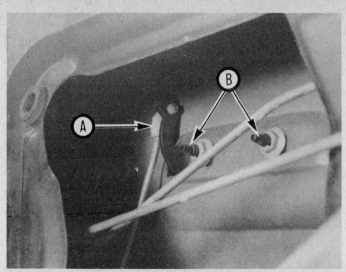

18.2 Push the outside handle rod clip (A) off and remove the two handle retaining nuts (B)

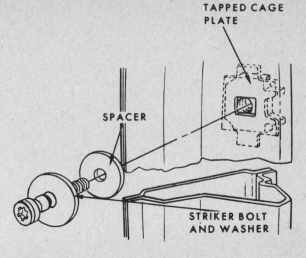

20.2 Door lock striker details

18 Door handles – removal and installation

1   With the window glass in the full up position, remove the door trim panel and water shield (Section 14).

Outside handle

Refer to illustration 18.2

2   Pry the remote rod out of the handle with a small screwdriver, remove the nuts and lift the handle off **(see illustration)**.
3   Installation is the reverse of removal.

Inside handle

4   Disconnect the rod from the handle.
5   Punch out the center pins of the rivets that secure the window regulator and drill the rivets out with a 3/16-inch drill bit.
6   Lift the handle from the door.
7   To install, place the handle in position and secure it to the door, using 3/16-inch rivets and a rivet tool.
8   The remainder of installation is the reverse of removal.

19 Door lock cylinder – removal and installation

1   With the window glass in the full up position, remove the door trim panel and water shield (Section 14).
2   Disconnect the rod from the lock cylinder.
3   Use a screwdriver to pry the retainer off and withdraw the lock cylinder from the door.
4   Installation is the reverse of removal.

20 Door lock striker – removal and installation

Refer to illustration 20.2

1   Mark the position of the striker bolt on the door pillar with a pencil.
2   It will be necessary to use a special tool to fit the star-shaped recess in the striker bolt head (tool J-23457 or BT-7107). Unscrew the bolt and remove it **(see illustration)**.
3   To install, screw the lock striker bolt into the tapped cage plate in the door pillar and tighten it finger tight at the marked position. Tighten the bolt securely.

21 Door – removal and installation

1   Remove the door trim panel and water shield.
2   Unplug any wiring connectors.
3   Open the door all the way and support it on jacks or blocks covered with cloth or pads to prevent damage to the paint.
4   Scribe around the hinges to ensure correct realignment during installation.
5   Remove the bolts and nuts retaining the hinges to the door and with the help of an assistant lift the door away.
6   Install the door by reversing the removal procedure. Tighten the nuts and bolts securely.

22 Trunk lid – removal and installation

Refer to illustration 22.2

1   Open the trunk lid and unplug any electrical connectors and disconnect the solenoid (if equipped).
2   Scribe or mark around the heads of the retaining bolts to mark their locations for ease of reinstallation **(see illustration)**.

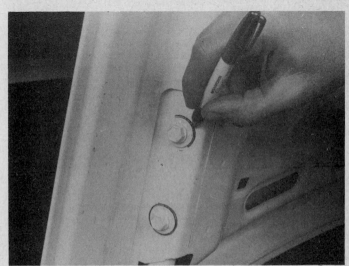

22.2 Mark the position of the trunk lid bolts with a scribe or a felt-tip pen before removing them

11

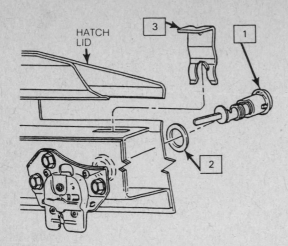

23.2a   Trunk lock cylinder details – Corsica hatchback

1   *Lock cylinder*
2   *Gasket*
3   *Retainer*

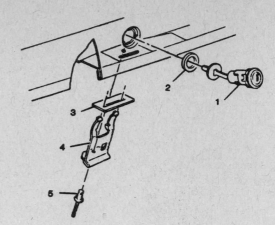

23.2b   Trunk lock cylinder details – Corsica sedan

1   *Lock cylinder*   4   *Retainer*
2   *Gasket*   5   *Rivet*
3   *Gasket*

3   With an assistant supporting the trunk lid, remove the bolts. Lift the trunk lid from the vehicle.
4   Installation is the reverse of removal.

23   Trunk lock cylinder – removal and installation

Refer to illustrations 23.2a and 23.2b
1   Open the trunk lid.
2   Pry the retaining clip off and withdraw the lock cylinder from the vehicle (see illustration). Some retaining clips will be secured with a rivet which must be drilled out with a 5/32-inch drill bit (see illustration).
3   To install, place the lock cylinder in place and secure it with the retaining clip.

24   Trunk latch and striker – removal and installation

Refer to illustrations 24.2a, 24.2b, 24.4a, 24.4b and 24.4c
1   Disconnect the negative cable from the battery. Place the cable out of the way so it cannot accidentally come in contact with the negative terminal of the battery, as this would once again allow power into the electrical system of the vehicle.
2   On models so equipped, disconnect the trunk lock cylinder cable by inserting a small screwdriver into the connector to hold the release tab down and then pull the cable out of the solenoid (see illustrations).
3   Remove the electronic solenoid (if equipped) and unbolt and remove the latch and (if equipped) the ajar switch.
4   Remove the retaining nut and lift off the striker (see illustrations).
5   Installation is the reverse of removal.

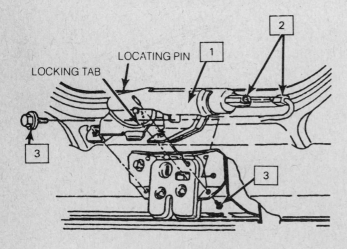

24.2a   Lock release solenoid – Corsica

1   *Solenoid*   3   *Screw*
2   *Connector*

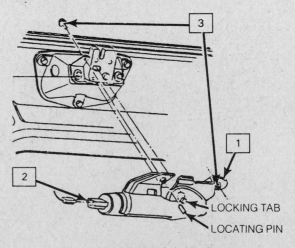

24.2b   Lock release solenoid – Beretta

1   *Solenoid*   3   *Screw*
2   *Connector*

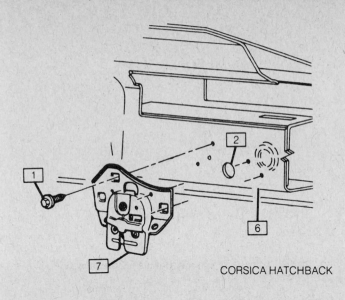

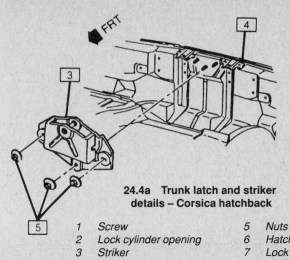

24.4a Trunk latch and striker details – Corsica hatchback

1	Screw	5	Nuts
2	Lock cylinder opening	6	Hatchback lid
3	Striker	7	Lock
4	Body end panel		

CORSICA HATCHBACK

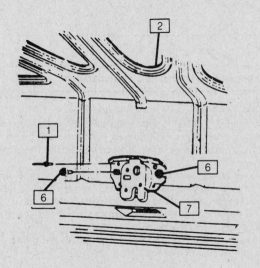

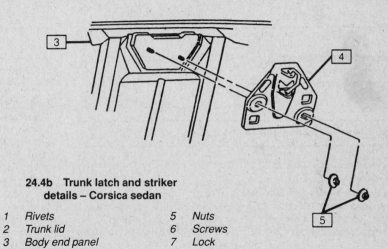

24.4b Trunk latch and striker details – Corsica sedan

1	Rivets	5	Nuts
2	Trunk lid	6	Screws
3	Body end panel	7	Lock
4	Striker		

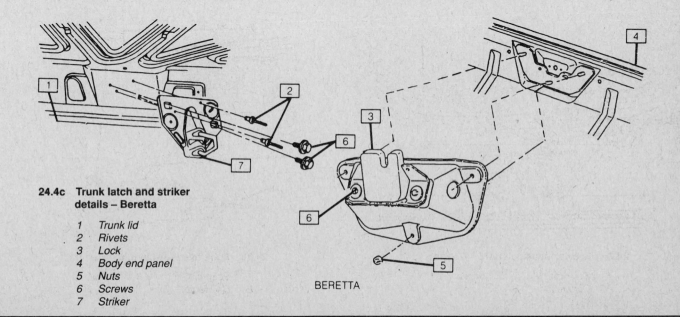

24.4c Trunk latch and striker details – Beretta

1	Trunk lid
2	Rivets
3	Lock
4	Body end panel
5	Nuts
6	Screws
7	Striker

BERETTA

11

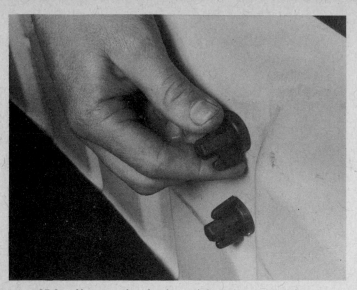

25.3a   Unscrew the plastic retaining wing nuts and . . .

25.3b   . . . remove the lens assembly from the body of the vehicle

25   Rear lens assembly – removal and installation

Refer to illustrations 25.3a and 25.3b

1   Disconnect the negative cable at the battery. Place the cable out of the way so it cannot accidentally come in contact with the negative terminal of the battery, as this would once again allow power into the electrical system of the vehicle.
2   Open the trunk lid.
3   Unscrew the plastic wing nuts, pull the lens assembly out and lean it back **(see illustrations)**. Disconnect the bulb holders (Chapter 12) and lift the assembly from the vehicle.
4   Installation is the reverse of removal.

26   Console – removal and installation

Refer to illustrations 26.6, 26.8a and 26.8b

1   Disconnect the negative cable at the battery. Place the cable out of the way so it cannot accidentally come in contact with the negative terminal of the battery, as this would once again allow power into the electrical system of the vehicle:
2   Remove the ash receptacle and cigarette lighter.
3   Remove the retaining screw at the base of the parking brake handle.
4   Use a 10 mm Torx drive to remove the retaining screw out of the automatic transaxle shift handle and manual transaxle shift handles. Pull the handle or knob off the shift lever.

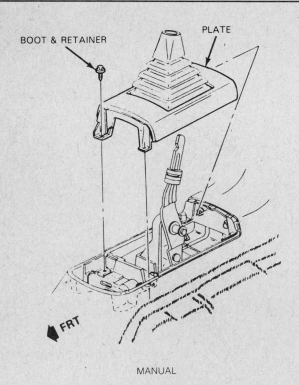

BOOT & RETAINER

PLATE

FRT

MANUAL

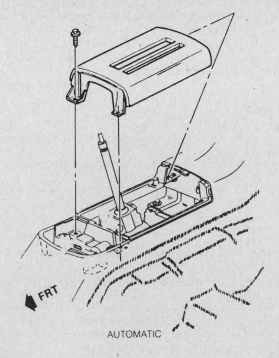

FRT

AUTOMATIC

26.6   Trim plate details

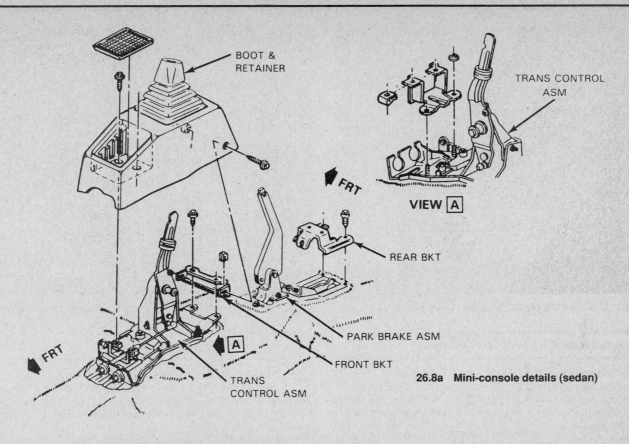

26.8a   Mini-console details (sedan)

5   Unsnap the cover and pull the parking brake handle off.
6   Remove the console trim plates **(see illustration)**.
7   Remove the front inserts on full size consoles.
8   Remove the bolts, rubber liner and the trunk release switch (if equipped) and then pull the console up **(see illustrations)**.
9   Lift the console up for access and unplug the electrical connectors.
10   Some or all of the retaining clips will probably come out during removal, so be sure to reinstall them prior to console installation.
11   Installation is the reverse of removal.

27   Seats – removal and installation

Front seat

1   Move the seat all the way forward.
2   Remove the seat track covers and pull the carpet away from the adjuster and retaining nuts.
3   Remove the seat adjuster-to-floor panel retaining nuts.
4   Move the seat all the way to the rear.
5   Remove the front seat retaining nuts. On power seats, unplug the electrical connector. Lift the seat from the vehicle.
6   Installation is the reverse of removal.

Rear seat

7   Remove the seat cushion retaining bolts, detach the seat cushion and remove it from the vehicle .
8   Installation is the reverse of removal.

28   Outside mirror – removal and installation

Refer to illustrations 28.2a, 28.2b, 28.3 and 28.6
1   Remove the door trim panel (Section 14).

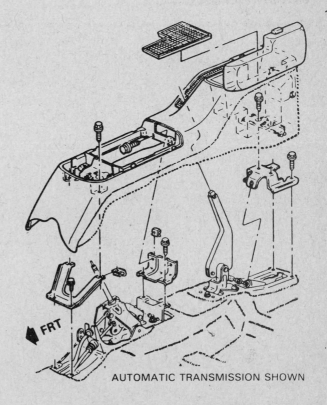

AUTOMATIC TRANSMISSION SHOWN

26.8b   Full size console details

11

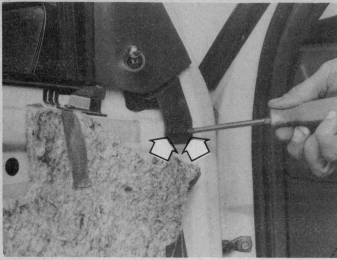

28.2a   The mirror escutcheon is held in place by two Phillips head screws (arrows)

28.2b   Pull the escutcheon down and away from the door to release it from the clip

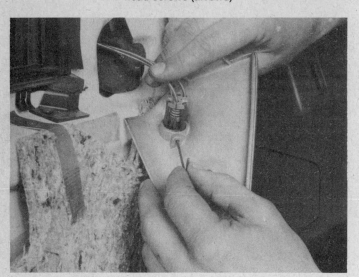

28.3   This Allen head screw must be removed to release the control cable from the escutcheon

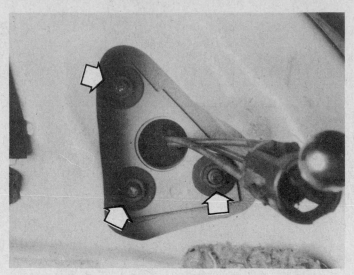

28.6   Remove the mirror retaining nuts (arrows)

2   Remove retaining screws **(see illustrations)** and pull the escutcheon down and away from the door frame.
3   On manual mirrors, loosen the Allen screw holding the control on the escutcheon **(see illustration)**.
4   On power mirrors, unplug the electrical connector.

5   Remove the escutcheon.
6   Remove the three nuts and lift off the mirror assembly **(see illustration)**.
7   Installation is the reverse of removal.

Chapter 12   Chassis electrical system

Contents

1   General information

The electrical system is a 12-volt, negative ground type. Power for the lights and all electrical accessories is supplied by a lead/acid-type battery which is charged by the alternator.

This Chapter covers repair and service procedures for the various electrical components not associated with the engine. Information on the battery, alternator, ignition system and starter motor can be found in Chapter 5.

It should be noted that when portions of the electrical system are serviced, the negative battery cable should be disconnected from the battery to prevent electrical shorts and/or fires. **Note:** *On models equipped with the Delco Loc II audio system, be sure the lockout feature is turned off before performing any procedure which requires disconnecting the battery.*

2   Electrical troubleshooting – general information

A typical electrical circuit consists of an electrical component, any switches, relays, motors, fuses, fusible links or circuit breakers related to

that component and the wiring and connectors that link the component to both the battery and the chassis. To help you pinpoint an electrical circuit problem, wiring diagrams are included at the end of this book.

Before tackling any troublesome electrical circuit, first study the appropriate wiring diagrams to get a complete understanding of what makes up that individual circuit. Trouble spots, for instance, can often be narrowed down by noting if other components related to the circuit are operating properly. If several components or circuits fail at one time, chances are the problem is in a fuse or ground connection, because several circuits are often routed through the same fuse and ground connections.

Electrical problems usually stem from simple causes, such as loose or corroded connections, a blown fuse, a melted fusible link or a bad relay. Visually inspect the condition of all fuses, wires and connections in a problem circuit before troubleshooting it.

If testing instruments are going to be utilized, use the diagrams to plan ahead of time where you will make the necessary connections in order to accurately pinpoint the trouble spot.

The basic tools needed for electrical troubleshooting include a circuit tester or voltmeter (a 12-volt bulb with a set of test leads can also be used), a continuity tester, which includes a bulb, battery and set of test leads, and a jumper wire, preferably with a circuit breaker incorporated, which can be

12

used to bypass electrical components. Before attempting to locate a problem with test instruments, use the wiring diagram(s) to decide where to make the connections.

Voltage checks

Voltage checks should be performed if a circuit is not functioning properly. Connect one lead of a circuit tester to either the negative battery terminal or a known good ground. Connect the other lead to a connector in the circuit being tested, preferably nearest to the battery or fuse. If the bulb of the tester lights, voltage is present, which means that the part of the circuit between the connector and the battery is problem free. Continue checking the rest of the circuit in the same fashion. When you reach a point at which no voltage is present, the problem lies between that point and the last test point with voltage. Most of the time the problem can be traced to a loose connection. **Note:** *Keep in mind that some circuits receive voltage only when the ignition key is in the Accessory or Run position.*

Finding a short

One method of finding shorts in a circuit is to remove the fuse and connect a test light or voltmeter in its place to the fuse terminals. There should be no voltage present in the circuit. Move the wiring harness from side-to-side while watching the test light.

If the bulb goes on, there is a short to ground somewhere in that area, probably where the insulation has rubbed through. The same test can be performed on each component in the circuit, even a switch.

Ground check

Perform a ground test to check whether a component is properly grounded. Disconnect the battery and connect one lead of a selfpowered test light, known as a continuity tester, to a known good ground. Connect the other lead to the wire or ground connection being tested. If the bulb goes on, the ground is good. If the bulb does not go on, the ground is not good.

Continuity check

A continuity check is done to determine if there are any breaks in a circuit – if it is passing electricity properly. With the circuit off (no power in the circuit), a self-powered continuity tester can be used to check the circuit. Connect the test leads to both ends of the circuit (or to the "power" end and a good ground), and if the test light comes on the circuit is passing current properly. If the light doesn't come on, there is a break somewhere in the circuit. The same procedure can be used to test a switch, by con-

necting the continuity tester to the switch terminals. With the switch turned On, the test light should come on.

Finding an open circuit

When diagnosing for possible open circuits, it is often difficult to locate them by sight because oxidation or terminal misalignment are hidden by the connectors. Merely wiggling a connector on a sensor or in the wiring harness may correct the open circuit condition. Remember this when an open circuit is indicated when troubleshooting a circuit. Intermittent problems may also be caused by oxidized or loose connections.

Electrical troubleshooting is simple if you keep in mind that all electrical circuits are basically electricity running from the battery, through the wires, switches, relays, fuses and fusible links to each electrical component (light bulb, motor, etc.) and to ground, from which it is passed back to the battery. Any electrical problem is an interruption in the flow of electricity to and from the battery.

---

3   Fuses – general information

Refer to illustrations 3.1 and 3.3

The electrical circuits of the vehicle are protected by a combination of fuses, circuit breakers and fusible links. The fuse block is located under the instrument panel on the left side of the dashboard **(see illustration)**.

Each of the fuses is designed to protect a specific circuit, and the various circuits are identified on the fuse panel itself.

Miniaturized fuses are employed in the fuse block. These compact fuses, with blade terminal design, allow fingertip removal and replacement. If an electrical component fails, always check the fuse first. A blown fuse is easily identified through the clear plastic body. Visually inspect the element for evidence of damage **(see illustration)**. If a continuity check is called for, the blade terminal tips are exposed in the fuse body.

Be sure to replace blown fuses with the correct type. Fuses of different ratings are physically interchangeable, but only fuses of the proper rating should be used. Replacing a fuse with one of a higher or lower value than specified is not recommended. Each electrical circuit needs a specific amount of protection. The amperage value of each fuse is molded into the fuse body.

If the replacement fuse immediately fails, don't replace it again until the cause of the problem is isolated and corrected. In most cases, the cause will be a short circuit in the wiring caused by a broken or deteriorated wire.

3.1   The fuse box is located in the left side of the dashboard behind a small protective panel

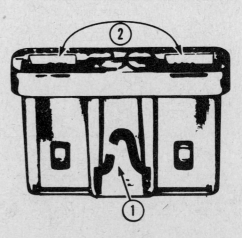

3.3   To check for a blown fuse, pull it out and inspect it visually for an open (1), then, with the circuit activated, use a test light across the points shown (2)

6.2   These relays (arrows) on the firewall are typical of the relays you'll find throughout this vehicle

4   Fusible links – general information

Some circuits are protected by fusible links. The links are used in circuits which are not ordinarily fused, such as the ignition circuit.

Although the fusible links appear to be a heavier gauge than the wire they are protecting, the appearance is due to the thick insulation. All fusible links are four wire gauges smaller than the wire they are designed to protect.

Fusible links cannot be repaired, but a new link of the same size wire can be put in its place. The procedure is as follows:
a) Disconnect the negative cable from the battery.
b) Disconnect the fusible link from the wiring harness.
c) Cut the damaged fusible link out of the wiring just behind the connector.
d) Strip the insulation back approximately 1/2-inch.
e) Position the connector on the new fusible link and crimp it into place.
f) Use rosin core solder at each end of the new link to obtain a good solder joint.
g) Use plenty of electrical tape around the soldered joint. No wires should be exposed.

h) Connect the battery ground cable. Test the circuit for proper operation.

5   Circuit breakers – general information

Circuit breakers protect components such as power windows, power door locks and headlights. Some circuit breakers are located in the fuse box.

On some models the circuit breaker resets itself automatically, so an electrical overload in a circuit breaker protected system will cause the circuit to fail momentarily, then come back on. If the circuit doesn't come back on, check it immediately. Once the condition is corrected, the circuit breaker will resume its normal function. Some circuit breakers must be reset manually.

6   Relays – general information

Refer to illustration 6.2

Several electrical accessories in the vehicle use relays to transmit the electrical signal to the component. If the relay is defective, that component will not operate properly.

The various relays are grouped together in several locations **(see illustration)**.

If a faulty relay is suspected, it can be removed and tested by a dealer service department or a repair shop. Defective relays must be replaced as a unit.

7   Hazard flasher, horn relay, seat belt-ignition key-headlight buzzer and signal flasher – replacement

Note: *The hazard flasher, horn relay, signal flasher and seat belt-ignition key-headlight buzzer are mounted on the "convenience center," which – depending on the model – is either a fixed or a swing down junction block.*

Fixed convenience center

Refer to illustrations 7.2, 7.3 and 7.4
1   Detach the cable from the negative terminal of the battery.
2   Remove the insulator panel from under the left side of the dash **(see illustration)**.
3   Locate the convenience center in the upper left corner of the cavity under the dash **(see illustration)**.

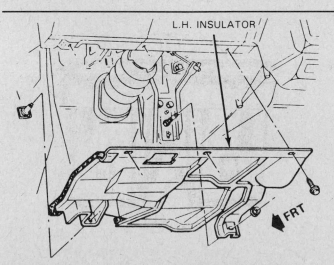

7.2   To gain access to the fixed type convenience center (or the connectors for most instrument panel-related electrical devices), remove this under-dash panel

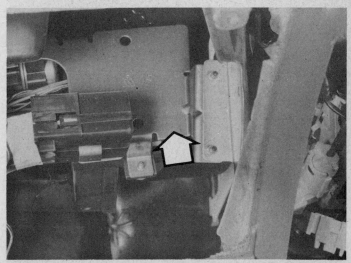

7.3   The fixed type convenience center (arrow) is located in the upper left corner of the cavity ahead of the dash – unfortunately, the convenience center on some models faces forward, so the flashers, relays and buzzer are difficult to remove and install

12

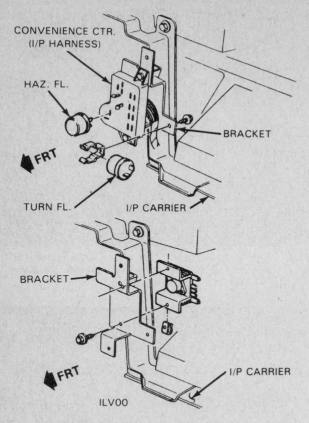

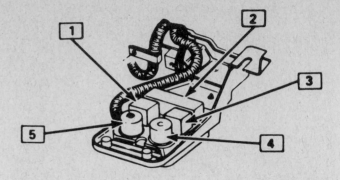

7.6   Typical swing-down type convenience center

1   *Horn relay*
2   *Seat belt-ignition key-headlight buzzer*
3   *Choke relay (not used on vehicles covered in this manual)*
4   *Hazard flasher*
5   *Signal flasher*

7.4   Exploded view of a typical fixed type convenience center – note that the number and purpose of the flashers, relays and buzzers on the convenience center varies from one model to another

Swing-down convenience center

Refer to illustration 7.6

6   On some models, the convenience center is a swing down unit **(see illustration)** located on the underside of the dash, near the steering column. To replace a hazard flasher, horn relay, seat belt-ignition key-headlight buzzer or signal flasher, simply swing down the convenience center and replace the defective unit.

4   Remove the defective unit **(see illustration)**. **Note:** *Because the various buzzers, flashers and relays face forward (toward the firewall), they're difficult to see, so it's easy to confuse them. Make sure you replace the correct one.*

5   Installation is the reverse of removal.

8   Turn signal switch assembly – replacement

Refer to illustrations 8.3, 8.4, 8.5a, 8.5b, 8.6, 8.8, 8.9, 8.10 and 8.11

1   Detach the cable from the negative battery terminal.
2   Remove the steering wheel (see Chapter 10).
3   Remove the cancel cam assembly **(see illustration)**.
4   Remove the hazard warning knob **(see illustration)**.

8.3   Remove the cancel cam assembly (arrow)

8.4   Remove the hazard warning knob screw (arrow) and the knob

8.5a Remove the column housing cover screw (arrow) . . .

8.5b . . . then remove the turn signal arm screw (arrow) and detach the turn signal arm and the column housing cover at the same time

8.6 Remove the column housing cover plastic spacer (arrow) – don't forget this piece when reassembling the column housing

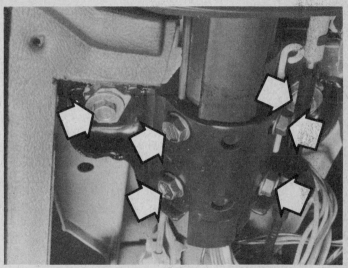

8.8 Remove the steering column bracket bolts (arrows)

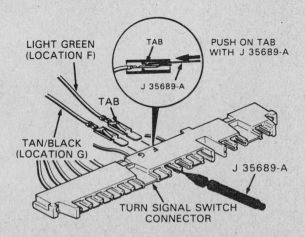

8.9 The turn signal switch electrical connector is located under the dash near the steering column. Use a tool as shown, or a length of stiff wire, to release the wiring tabs

8.10 Remove the two screws (arrows) . . .

12

8.11 . . . and detach the turn signal switch assembly

5   Remove the column housing cover screw **(see illustration)**. Remove the turn signal lever mounting screw **(see illustration)** and remove the lever and the housing.
6   Remove the plastic spacer in the lower left corner of the housing **(see illustration)**. Don't forget this spacer during reassembly.
7   Remove the under-dash panel below the steering column **(see illustration 7.2)**.
8   Remove the steering column bracket bolts **(see illustration)** and lower the steering column from the dash.
9   Locate the turn signal switch electrical connector. Detach the wires to the buzzer switch assembly (tan and black wire and light green wire) from the back of the connector **(see illustration)**.
10   Remove the turn signal switch assembly mounting screws **(see illustration)**.
11   Pull the electrical lead and connector up through the steering column and remove the switch assembly **(see illustration)**.
12   Installation is the reverse of removal.

---

9   Ignition switch key lock cylinder – replacement

Fixed steering column

1   Detach the cable from the negative battery terminal.

2   Remove the steering wheel (see Chapter 10).
3   Remove the turn signal switch assembly (see Section 8).
4   Place the lock cylinder in the Run position.
5   Remove the turn signal switch housing screws.
6   Remove the turn signal switch housing and steering shaft assembly as a complete unit.
7   Using a screwdriver, lift the switch tab, then pull gently on the buzzer switch wires and remove the buzzer switch.
8   Place the lock cylinder in the Accessory position.
9   Remove the lock cylinder retaining screw.
10   Remove the lock cylinder.
11   Installation is the reverse of removal.

Tilt steering column

12   Take the vehicle to a dealer. A special tool is needed to remove the pivot pins in the steering column housing on tilt steering columns, making key lock cylinder replacement impossible for the home mechanic.

---

10   Headlight switch – replacement

Refer to illustrations 10.2 and 10.3

1   Detach the cable from the negative terminal of the battery.
2   Pop out the headlight switch assembly with a small screwdriver **(see illustration)** and pull it out from the dash.
3   Unplug the electrical connector **(see illustration)** and remove the headlight switch assembly.
4   Installation is the reverse of removal.

---

11   Headlight – removal and installation

Refer to illustrations 11.2, 11.3a, 11.3b, 11.4, 11.5a and 11.5b

1   Detach the cable from the negative terminal of the battery.
2   Twist the plastic cover screws **(see illustration)** and remove the plastic cover over the headlight.
3   Remove the two plastic lock screws **(see illustrations)** and tilt the headlight assembly forward.
4   Unplug the electrical connector **(see illustration)**.
5   Twist the bulb lock ring counterclockwise **(see illustration)** and pull the bulb holder assembly out of the headlight **(see illustration)**.
6   Installation is the reverse of removal.

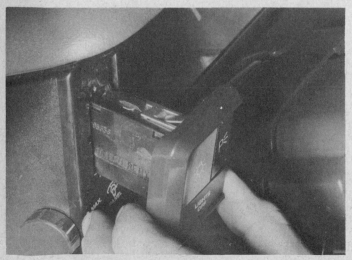

10.2   To remove the headlight switch, simply pop it out with a screwdriver

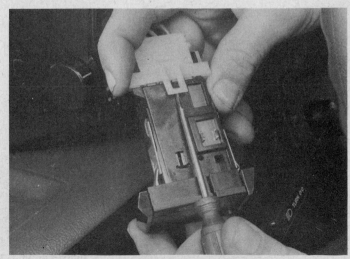

10.3   Unplug the electrical connector from the back of the headlight switch

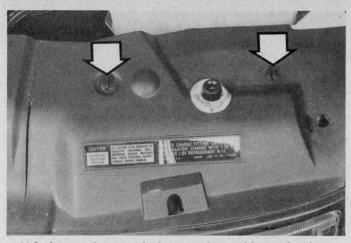

11.2   Loosen these two lock screws (arrows) by turning them counterclockwise and flip open the plastic headlight cover

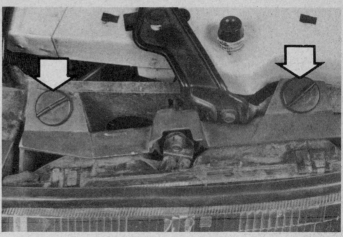

11.3a   Typical headlight assembly (sedan) – to separate it from the body, simply loosen the two lock screws and tilt it out

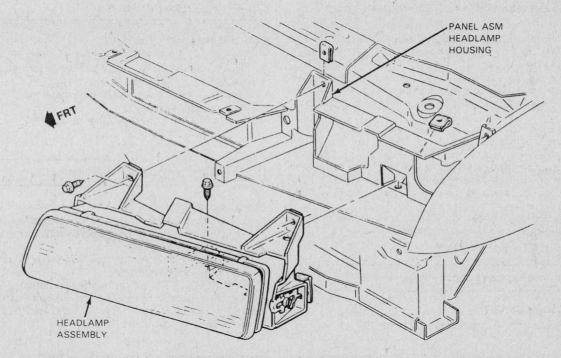

PANEL ASM HEADLAMP HOUSING

FRT

HEADLAMP ASSEMBLY

11.3b   Typical headlight assembly (coupe) – to detach it from the body, simply remove the fasteners

11.4   Unplug the headlight electrical connector

11.5a   To remove the headlight bulb holder, turn it counterclockwise . . .

11.5b   . . . and pull it out of the headlight assembly (don't try to pull the bulb out of the holder – they're sold as a single unit)

12

12.1a　Vertical headlight adjustment screw (arrow)

12.1b　Horizontal headlight adjustment screw (arrow)

12　Headlights – adjustment

Refer to illustrations 12.1a and 12.1b

Note: *The headlights must be aimed correctly. If adjusted incorrectly they could blind the driver of an oncoming vehicle and cause a serious accident or seriously reduce your ability to see the road. The headlights should be checked for proper aim every 12 months and any time a new headlight is installed or front end body work is performed. It should be emphasized that the following procedure is only an interim step which will provide temporary adjustment until the headlights can be adjusted by a properly equipped shop.*

1　Headlights have two spring loaded adjusting screws, one on the top controlling up-and-down movement and one on the side controlling left-and-right movement **(see illustrations)**.

2　There are several methods of adjusting the headlights. The simplest method requires a blank wall 25-feet in front of the vehicle and a level floor.

3　Position masking tape vertically on the wall in reference to the vehicle centerline and the centerlines of both headlights.

4　Position a horizontal tape line in reference to the centerline of all the headlights. **Note:** *It may be easier to position the tape on the wall with the vehicle parked only a few inches away.*

5　Adjustment should be made with the vehicle sitting level, the gas tank half-full and no unusually heavy load in the vehicle.

6　Starting with the low beam adjustment, position the high intensity zone so it's two inches below the horizontal line and two inches to the right of the headlight vertical line. Adjustment is made by turning the top adjusting screw clockwise to raise the beam and counterclockwise to lower the beam. The adjusting screw on the side should be used in the same manner to move the beam left or right.

7　With the high beams on, the high intensity zone should be vertically centered with the exact center just below the horizontal line. **Note:** *It may not be possible to position the headlight aim exactly for both high and low beams. If a compromise must be made, keep in mind that the low beams are the most used and have the greatest effect on driver safety.*

8　Have the headlights adjusted by a dealer service department or service station at the earliest opportunity.

13　Bulb replacement

Refer to illustrations 13.1 and 13.3a thru 13.3e

1　The lenses of many lights are held in place by screws, which makes it a simple procedure to gain access to the bulbs **(see illustration)**.

2　On some lights, the lenses are held in place by tabs. Simply pop them off with your fingers or pry them off with a small screwdriver.

3　Several types of bulbs are used **(see illustrations)**. Some are removed by pushing in and turning them counterclockwise; others can simply be pulled straight out of the socket.

4　To gain access to the instrument panel lights, the instrument cluster will have to be removed first (see Section 16).

14　Radio and speakers – removal and installation

Note: *Detach the cable from the negative terminal of the battery prior to removing the radio or speakers.*

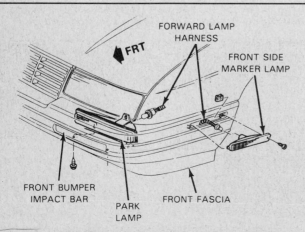

13.1　Exploded view of typical park and side marker lights

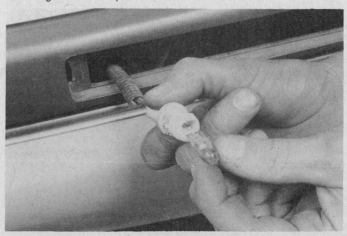

13.3a　To replace a front side marker light, remove the lens screw, pull off the lens and pull the bulb straight out

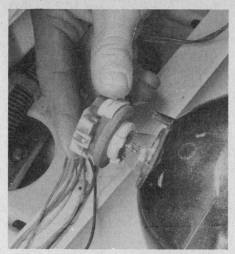

13.3b   To remove the holder for the rear brake/turn signal bulb from the tail light lens assembly, turn the holder counterclockwise and pull it out . . .

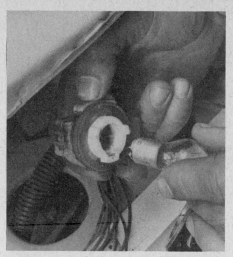

13.3c   . . . then push down on the bulb, turn it counterclockwise and remove it from the holder

13.3d   To replace the dome light, simply pop off the plastic lens with a small screwdriver, then pull the bulb straight down

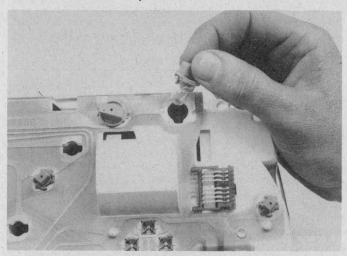

13.3e   To replace an instrument cluster bulb, remove the instrument cluster (see Section 16), then twist the holder counterclockwise, pull it out of the cluster and pull the bulb straight out of the holder

Delco Loc II general information

1   Some audio systems in the models covered by this manual feature the Delco Loc II anti–theft feature. In this system, the owner can program an access code into the radio, which will automatically scramble if the radio is deprived of battery power, rendering it inoperative.
2   Before beginning any procedure which requires the battery to be disconnected or the radio to be removed, make sure you know the access code stored in the radio. It must be entered after the battery is reconnected.
3   The radio can also be unlocked before battery power is disconnected by entering the access code, at which time the display on the radio will momentarily indicate "–" then the clock will be displayed.
4   If you don't know your access code or encounter difficulty in reactivating the radio, consult your dealer service department.

Radio removal and installation

Refer to illustrations 14.7 and 14.10

5   Carefully pry off the radio trim plate.
6   Remove the knobs and heater control switches.
7   Remove the radio mounting screws **(see illustration)**.
8   Pull the radio out from the dash.

14.7   Remove the radio/heater and air conditioner control assembly mounting screws (arrows)

9   Remove the ash tray assembly from underneath the radio and heater control assembly.
10   Reach up behind the radio and unplug the antenna, speaker, power and ground connectors from the radio **(see illustration)**. Unplug the connectors from the heater and air conditioner control assembly.

14.10   Pull the radio/heater and air conditioner control assembly out from the dash and unplug the antenna and all electrical connectors

12

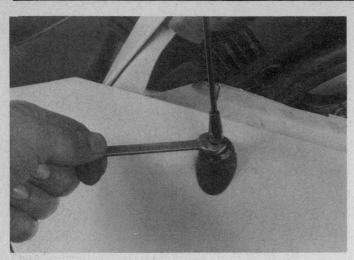

15.1   To remove the antenna, simply unscrew it

11   Remove the radio and the heater and air conditioner control assembly as a single unit.
12   Detach the radio from the heater and air conditioner control assembly.
13   Installation is the reverse of removal.

Speaker removal and installation

Dashboard speakers
14   Pry off the speaker cover.
15   Remove the speaker mounting screws.
16   Lift the speaker out of its enclosure, unplug the electrical connector and remove the speaker.
17   Installation is the reverse of removal.

Rear speakers
18   Open the trunk lid and locate the speakers – they're affixed to the underside of the package tray.

19   Remove the speaker enclosure retaining clip and lower the enclosure to the trunk floor.
20   Remove the speaker mounting screws and remove the speaker from the enclosure.
21   Unplug the speaker electrical connector.
22   Installation is the reverse of removal.

15   Radio antenna – removal and installation

Refer to illustration 15.1
    Simply unscrew the antenna from the base **(see illustration)** and screw on a new antenna.

16   Instrument panel – removal and installation

Refer to illustrations 16.4a, 16.4b, 16.5a, 16.5b and 16.6
Warning: *We do not recommend attempting this procedure on airbag-equipped models, which have airbag system components located in this area. Disturbing any of these components could cause the airbag to accidently deploy, resulting in personal injury. Also, disturbing these components could cause the airbag not to deploy properly in a collision.*
1   Detach the cable from the negative battery terminal.
2   Remove the under-dash panel.
3   Remove the steering column bracket bolts and lower the steering column.
4   Remove the instrument panel bezel (analog gauges) or trim plate (digital gauges) screws **(see illustrations)**.
5   Pull out the instrument panel bezel far enough to unplug the connectors for the headlight and windshield wiper switches **(see illustrations)**. On models with digital gauges, the trim plate is separate from the switch assemblies, so it can be removed by itself.
6   Remove the instrument cluster retaining screws **(see illustration)**.
7   Pull the instrument cluster from its cavity in the dashboard, unplug the electrical connectors and remove it.
8   Installation is the reverse of removal.

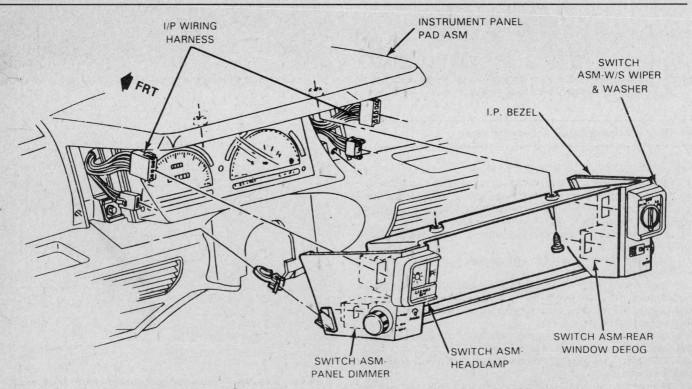

16.4a   Exploded view of the instrument panel bezel used on models with an analog gauge cluster

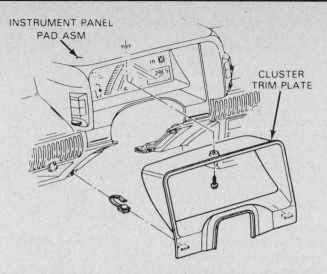

16.4b   Exploded view of the cluster trim plate used on models with a digital gauge cluster

16.5a   Pull out the instrument panel bezel . . .

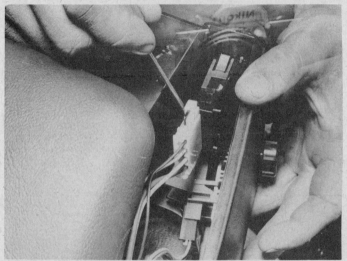

16.5b   . . . and unplug all switch connectors (analog bezel shown, digital trim plate similar)

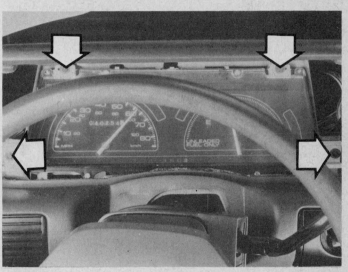

16.6   Remove the instrument cluster mounting screws (arrows)

17   Rear window defogger – check and repair

Refer to illustrations 17.5a, 17.5b and 17.11

1   This option consists of a rear window with a number of horizontal elements baked into the glass surface during the glass forming operation.

2   Small breaks in the element can be successfully repaired without removing the rear window.

3   To test the grids for proper operation, start the engine and turn on the system.

4   Ground one lead of a test light and carefully touch the other lead to each element line.

5   The brilliance of the test light should increase as the lead is moved across the element **(see illustrations)**. If the test light glows brightly at both ends of the lines, check for a loose ground wire. All of the lines should be checked in at least two places.

6   To repair a break in a line, it is recommended that a repair kit specifically for this purpose be purchased from a GM dealer. Included in the repair kit will be a decal, a container of silver plastic and hardener, a mixing stick and instructions.

7   To repair a break, first turn off the system and allow it to de-energize for a few minutes.

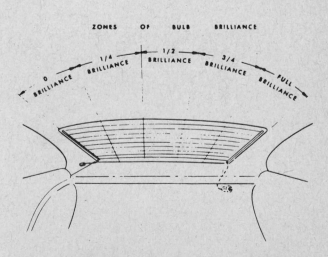

17.5a   The brilliance of a test light should vary in brightness when the rear window defogger is functioning normally

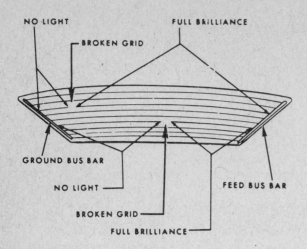

17.5b   When the grid is tested on the ground bus bar side of a break, the light will go out

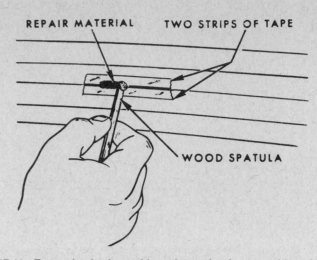

17.11   To repair a broken grid, apply a strip of tape to either side of the grid, then apply the proper mixture of hardener and silver plastic with a small wooden stick or spatula

8   Lightly buff the element area with fine steel wool, then clean it thoroughly with alcohol.

9   Use the decal supplied in the repair kit or apply strips of electrician's tape above and below the area to be repaired. The space between the pieces of tape should be the same width as the existing lines. This can be checked from outside the vehicle. Press the tape tightly against the glass to prevent seepage.

10   Mix the hardener and silver plastic thoroughly.

11   Using the wood spatula, apply the silver plastic mixture between the pieces of tape, overlapping the undamaged area slightly on either end **(see illustration)**.

12   Carefully remove the decal or tape and apply a constant stream of hot air directly to the repaired area. A heat gun set at 500 to 700 degrees Fahrenheit is recommended. Hold the gun one inch from the glass for two minutes.

13   If the new element appears off color, tincture of iodine can be used to clean the repair and bring it back to the proper color. This mixture should not remain on the repair for more than 30 seconds.

14   Although the defogger is now fully operational, the repaired area should not be disturbed for at least 24 hours.

18   Windshield wiper motor, washer pump and switch – removal and installation

Refer to illustrations 18.2, 18.5, 18.6, 18.7, 18.9, 18.12a and 18.12b

1   Detach the cable from the negative terminal of the battery.

Windshield wiper motor/washer pump

2   Unplug the electrical connectors from the motor and the pump **(see illustration)**.

3   Detach the windshield washer fluid hoses from the washer pump.

4   Disconnect the connector for the windshield washer fluid line at the wiper blade.

5   Pop off the windshield wiper blade cap over the nut and remove the nut **(see illustration)**.

18.2   Unplug the electrical connectors from the windshield wiper motor and pump (arrows) and detach the windshield washer fluid hoses from the pump

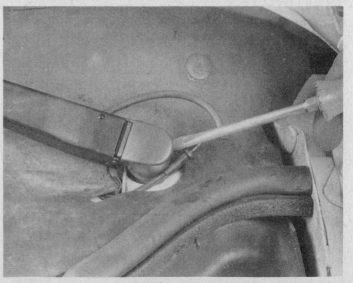

18.5   Pry the windshield wiper arm retaining nut cap loose with a screwdriver

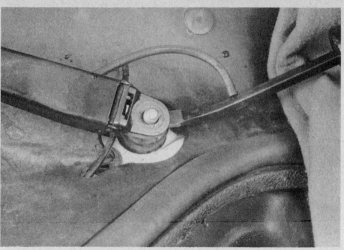

18.6   If you don't have a battery post puller or some other type of small puller, you can pry the windshield wiper arm off with a screwdriver, but be careful

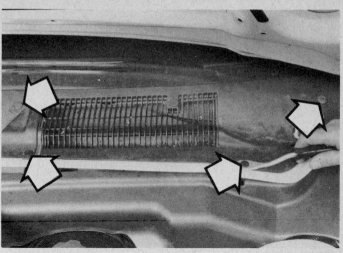

18.7   To get at the windshield wiper motor transmission (linkage), remove the rubber molding along the upper edge of the firewall, pry the four fasteners loose (arrows) and remove the left half of the vent grille

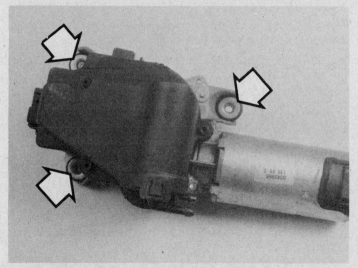

18.9   The windshield wiper motor/washer fluid pump assembly has three mounting bolts (assembly removed from vehicle for clarity)

18.12a   To remove the windshield washer fluid pump from the motor, pop out this retaining clip with a small screwdriver . . .

6   Using a small battery post puller or similar tool, remove the left windshield wiper blade assembly. If you don't have a battery post puller, pry the blade off with a screwdriver **(see illustration)**.

7   Remove the four plastic pop fasteners from the left vent grille and remove the grille **(see illustration)**. Be careful when removing these fasteners – they break easily.

8   Remove the nut that fastens the transmission linkage arm to the motor shaft and detach the linkage from the motor.

9   Remove the motor mounting bolts **(see illustration)** and remove the motor.

10   If you're replacing the motor, be sure to switch the washer pump to the new motor (see Step 12).

11   Installation is the reverse of removal.

12   If you're only replacing the windshield washer pump, remove the small locking clip **(see illustration)** and pull the pump from the bottom of the motor **(see illustration)**.

Switch

13   Pop the windshield wiper switch assembly loose from the dash with with a small screwdriver and pull it out.

18.12b   . . . and pull the pump out of the motor

12

14   Pull the switch from the dash far enough to unplug the electrical connector.
15   Installation is the reverse of removal.

19   Horn – replacement

1   Detach the cable from the negative terminal of the battery.
2   Raise the vehicle and place it securely on jackstands.
3   Remove the protective panel from the underside of the front left corner of the bumper.
4   Remove the horn mounting bracket bolt, lower the horn, unplug the electrical connector and remove the horn.
5   Installation is the reverse of removal.

20   Cruise control system – description and check

The cruise control system maintains vehicle speed with a vacuum actuated servo motor located in the engine compartment, which is connected to the throttle linkage by a cable. The system consists of the servo motor, clutch switch, brake switch, control switches, a relay and associated vacuum hoses.

Because of the complexity of the cruise control system and the special tools and techniques required for diagnosis, repair should be left to a dealer service department or a repair shop. However, it is possible for the home mechanic to make simple checks of the wiring and vacuum connections for minor faults which can be easily repaired. These include:

a) Inspect the cruise control actuating switches for broken wires and loose connections.
b) Check the cruise control fuse.
c) The cruise control system is operated by vacuum so it's critical that all vacuum switches, hoses and connections are secure. Check the hoses in the engine compartment for tight connections, cracks and obvious vacuum leaks.

21   Power window system – description and check

The power window system operates the electric motors mounted in the doors which lower and raise the windows. The system consists of the control switches, the motors (regulators), glass mechanisms and associated wiring.

Because of the complexity of the power window system and the special tools and techniques required for diagnosis, repair should be left to a dealer service department or a repair shop. However, it is possible for the home mechanic to make simple checks of the wiring connections and motors for minor faults which can be easily repaired. These include:

a) Inspect the power window actuating switches for broken wires and loose connections.
b) Check the power window fuse/and or circuit breaker.
c) Remove the door panel(s) and check the power window motor wires to see if they're loose or damaged. Inspect the glass mechanisms for damage which could cause binding.

22   Power door lock system – description and check

The power door lock system operates the door lock actuators mounted in each door. The system consists of the switches, actuators and associated wiring. Since special tools and techniques are required to diagnose the system, it should be left to a dealer service department or a repair shop. However, it is possible for the home mechanic to make simple checks of the wiring connections and actuators for minor faults which can be easily repaired. These include:

a) Check the system fuse and/or circuit breaker.
b) Check the switch wires for damage and loose connections. Check the switches for continuity.
c) Remove the door panel(s) and check the actuator wiring connections to see if they're loose or damaged. Inspect the actuator rods (if equipped) to make sure they aren't bent or damaged. Inspect the actuator wiring for damaged or loose connections. The actuator can be checked by applying battery power momentarily. A discernible click indicates that the solenoid is operating properly.

23   Wiring diagrams – general information

Since it isn't possible to include all wiring diagrams for every year covered by this manual, the following diagrams are those that are typical and most commonly needed.

Prior to troubleshooting any circuits, check the fuse and circuit breakers (if equipped) to make sure they're in good condition. Make sure the battery is properly charged and check the cable connections (Chapter 1).

When checking a circuit, make sure that all connectors are clean, with no broken or loose terminals. When unplugging a connector, do not pull on the wires. Pull only on the connector housings themselves.

Refer to the accompanying table for the wire color codes applicable to your vehicle.

Wiring diagram color codes

BLK	Black	BLU	Blue
BRN	Brown	PPL	Purple
CHK	Check	TR	Tracer
CR	Cross	YEL	Yellow
GRN	Green	//	Parallel
NAT	Natural	WHT	White
SGL	Single	STR	Stripe
ORN	Orange	PNK	Pink
GR	Gray	DK	Dark

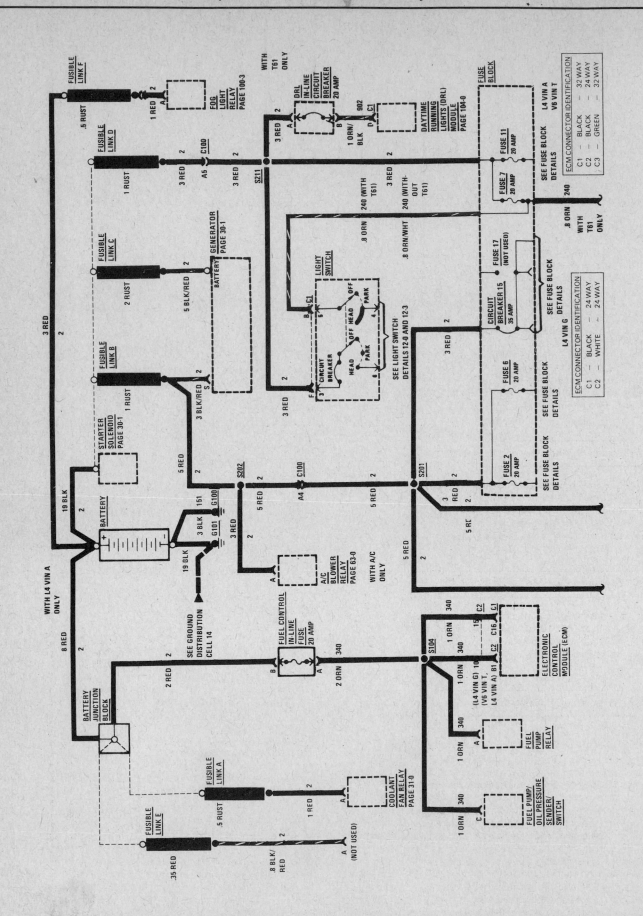

Power distribution

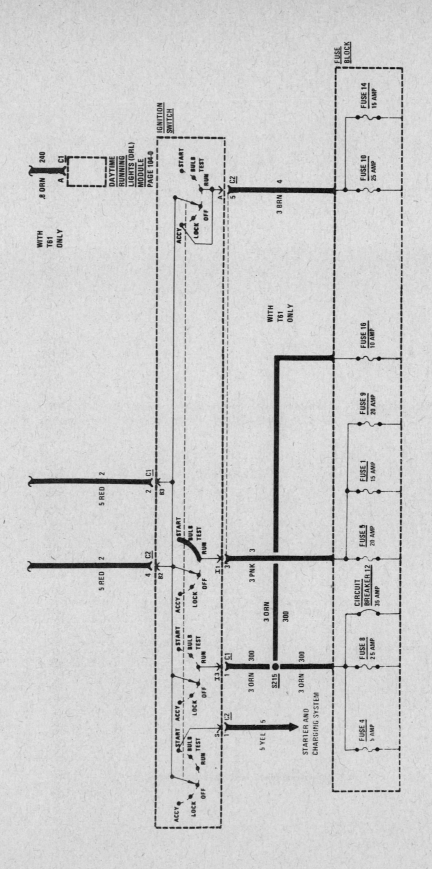

Power distribution (continued)

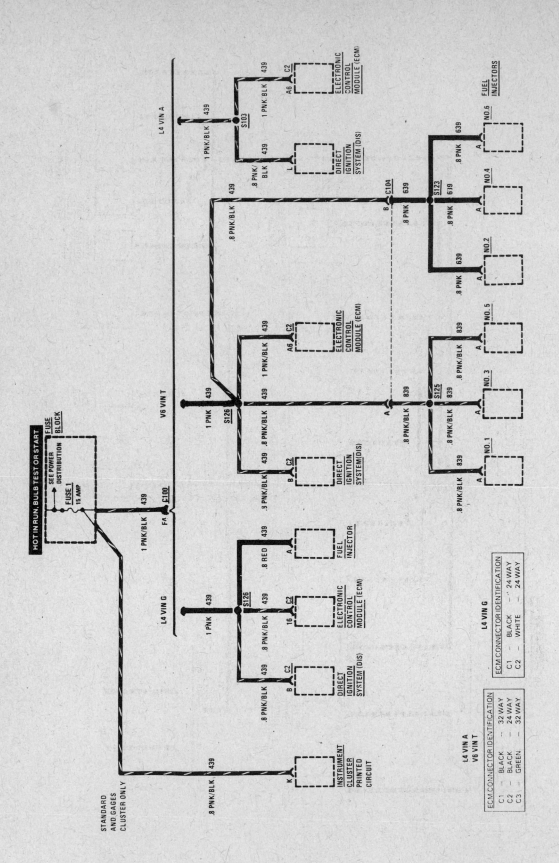

Fuse block details

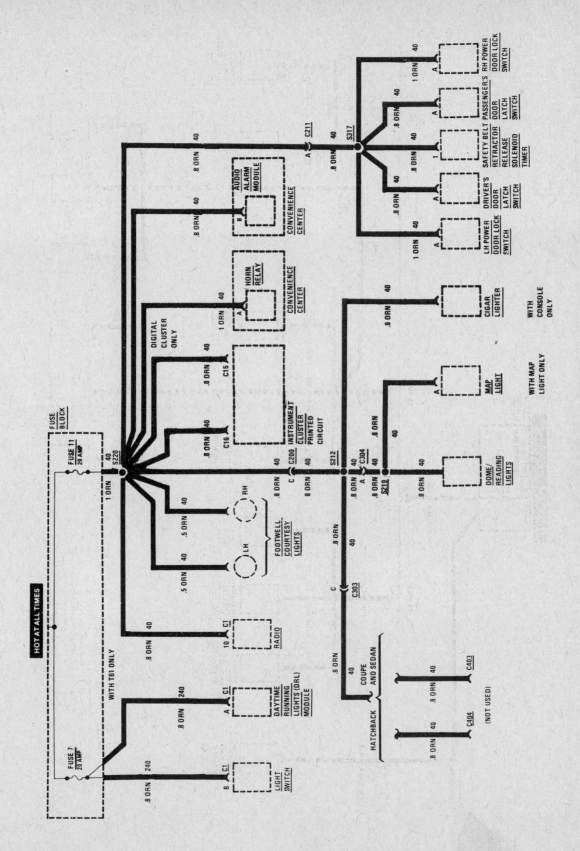

Fuse block details (continued)

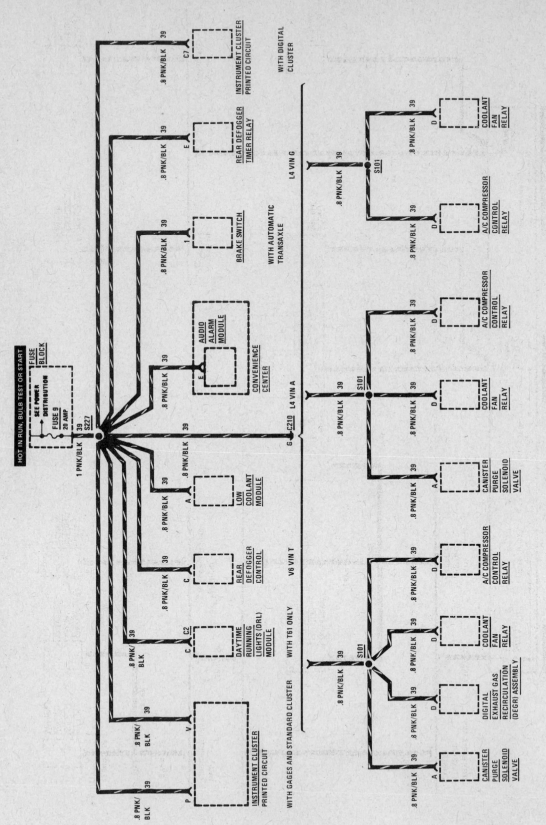

Fuse block details (continued)

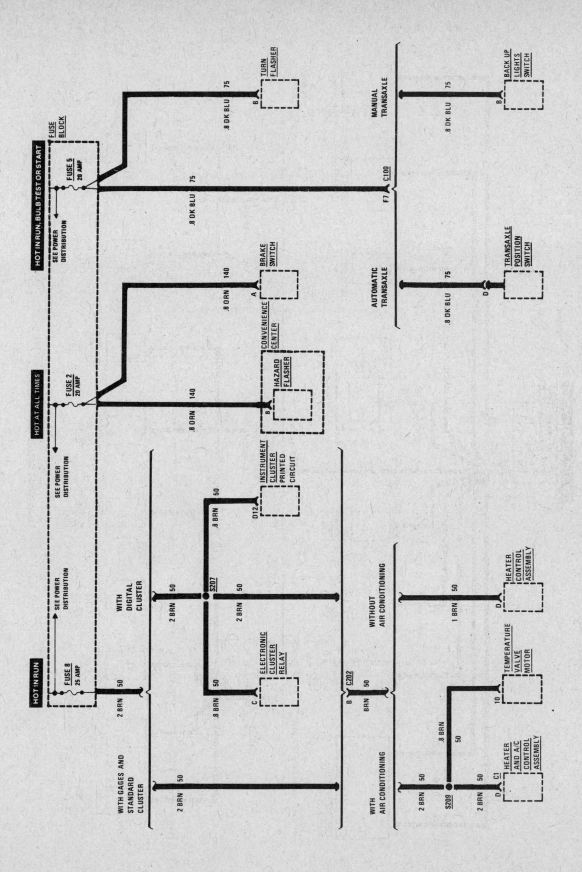

Fuse block details (continued)

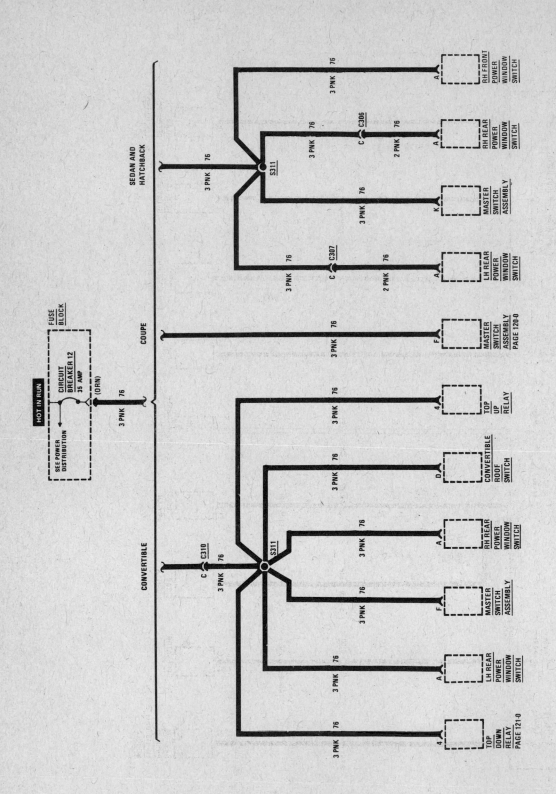

Fuse block details (continued)

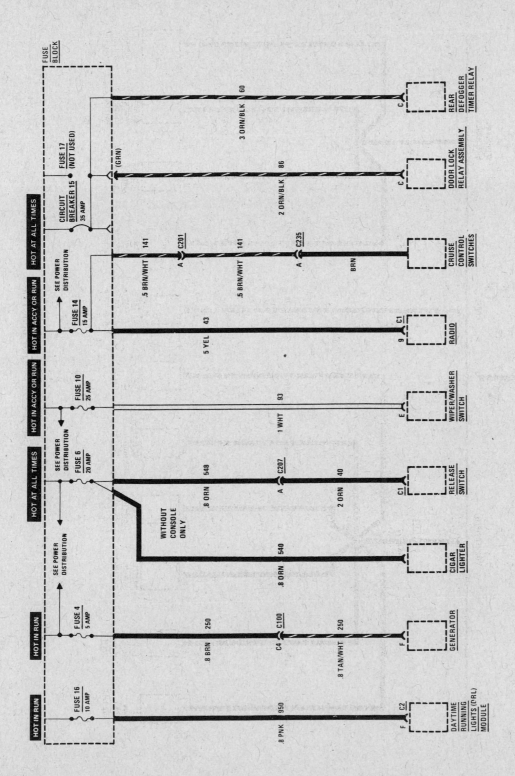

Fuse block details (continued)

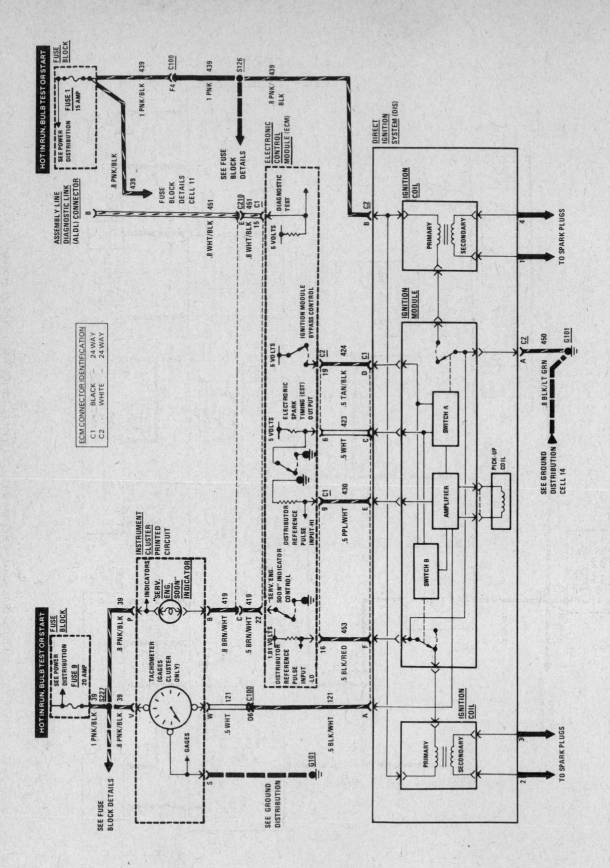

Ignition details (OHV four-cylinder models)

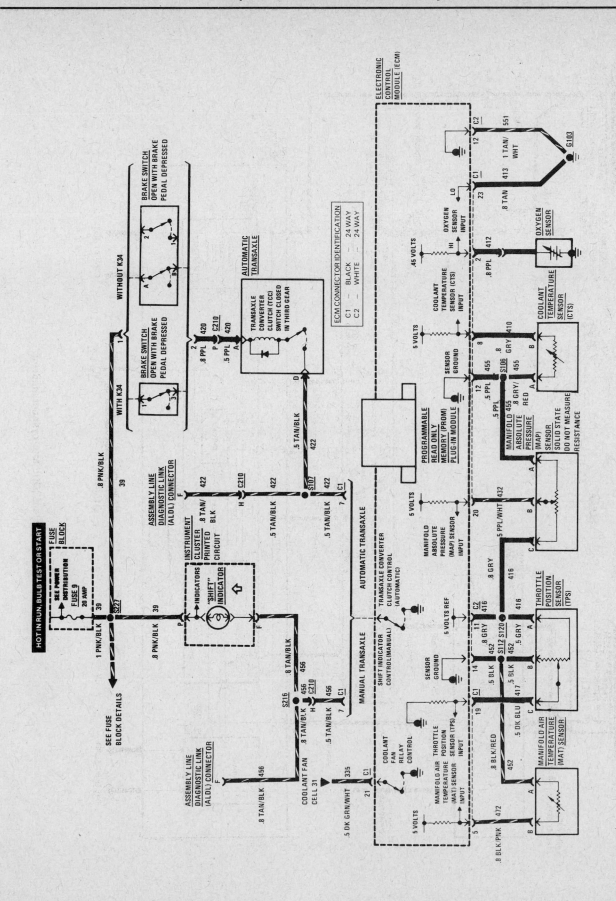

Engine data sensors and transaxle converter clutch (OHV four-cylinder models)

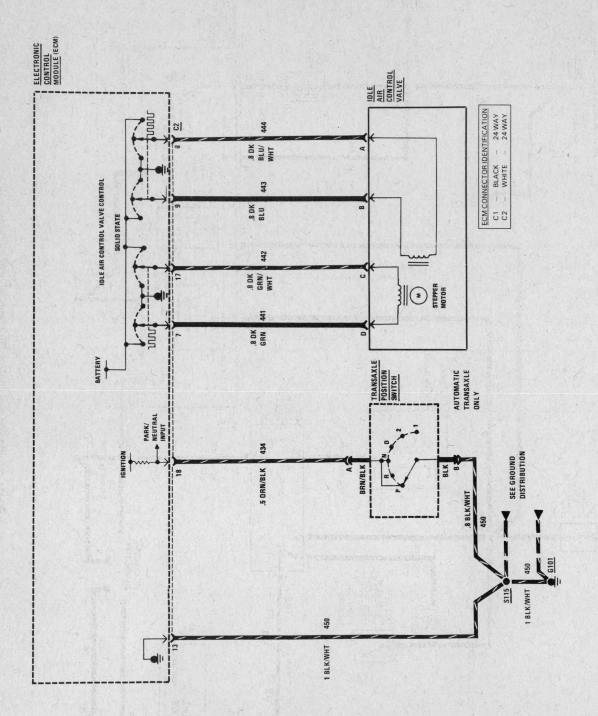

Idle speed control and vehicle data sensors (OHV four-cylinder models)

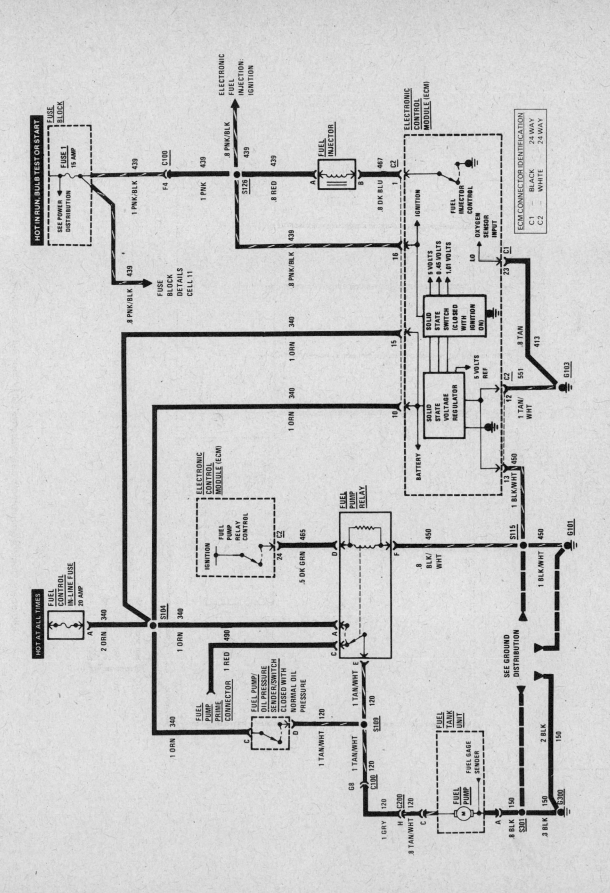

Power, ground and fuel control (OHV four-cylinder models)

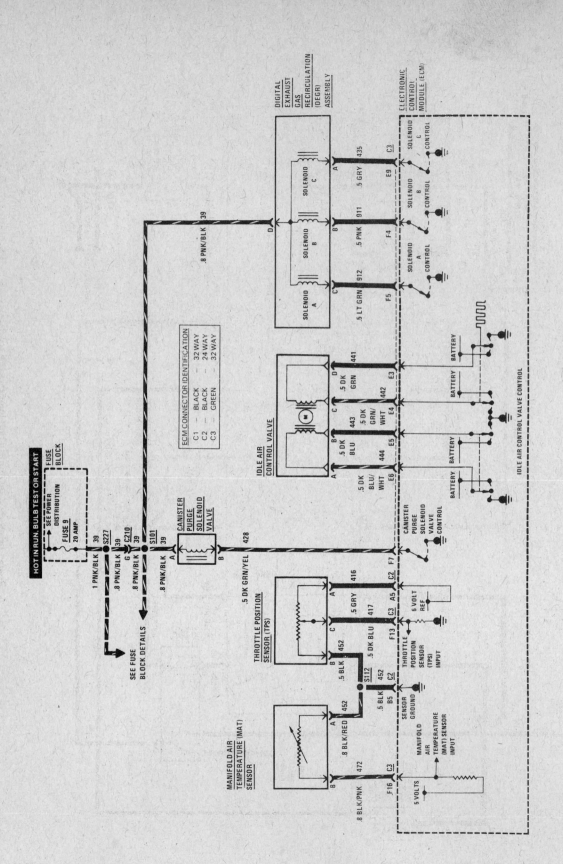

Engine data sensors, emission control and idle air control (V6 models)

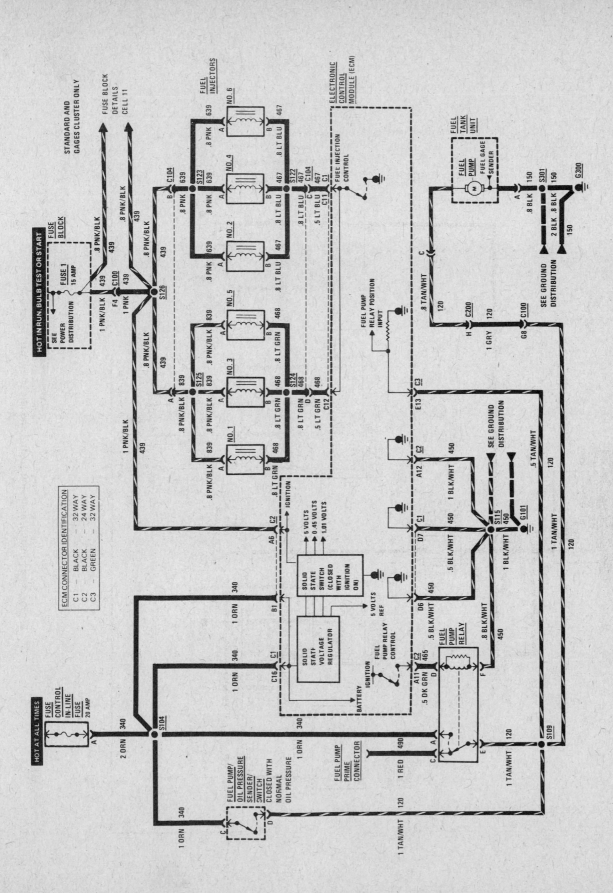

Power, grounds, fuel control and injectors (V6 models)

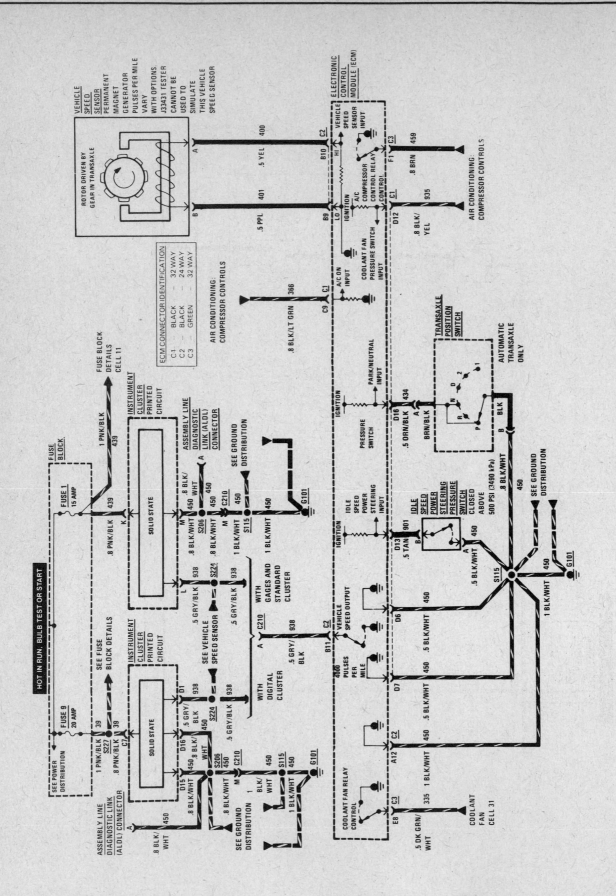

Vehicle data sensors and vehicle speed sensor (V6 models)

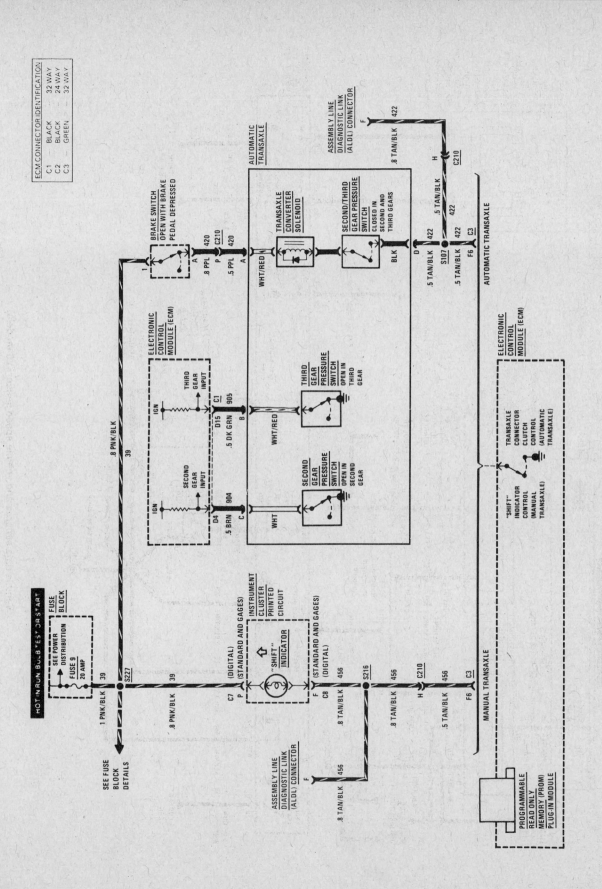

Transaxle Converter Clutch and shift indicator (V6 models)

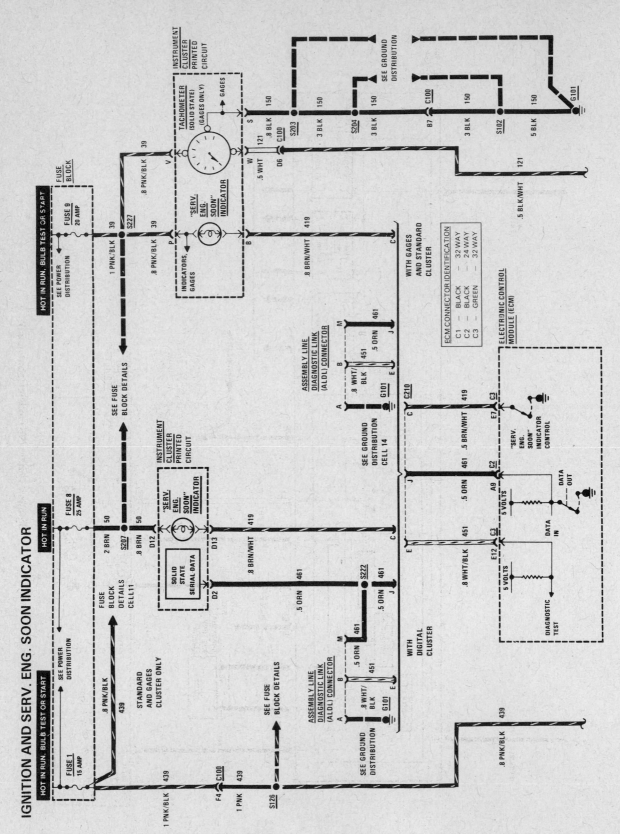

IGNITION AND SERV. ENG. SOON INDICATOR

Ignition system (V6 models)

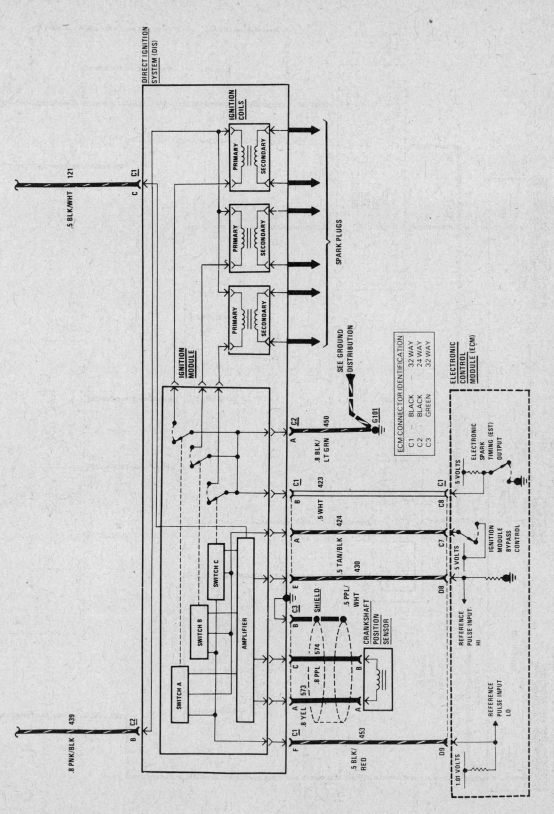

Ignition system (V6 models) (continued)

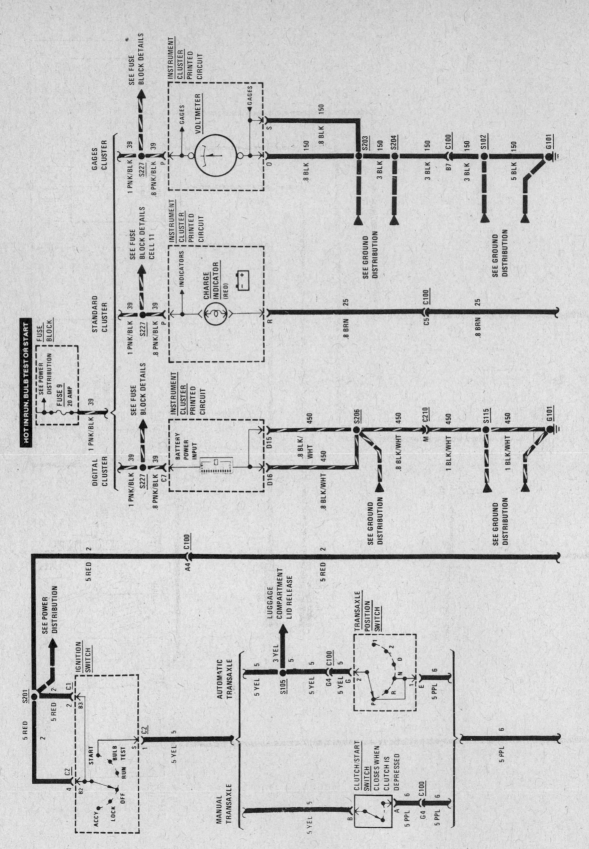

Starter and charging system

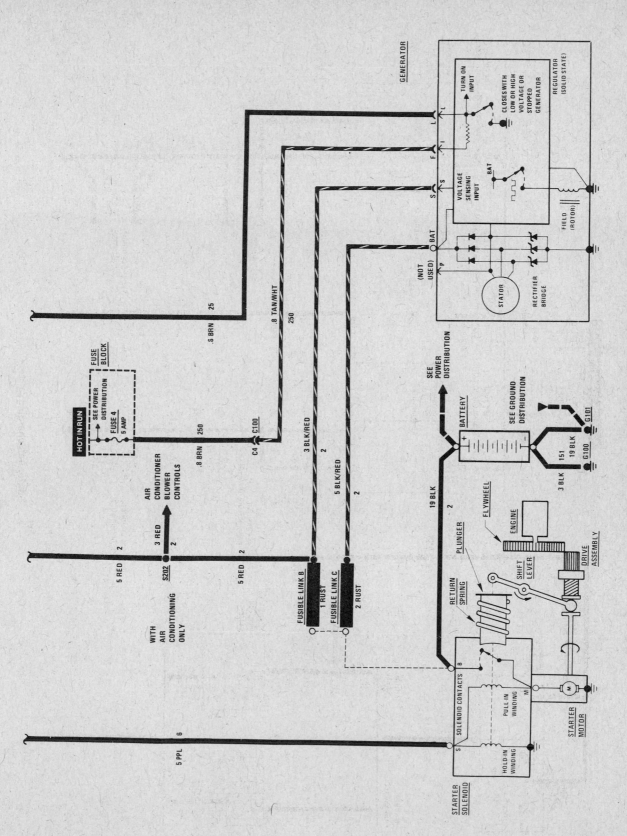

Starter and charging system (continued)

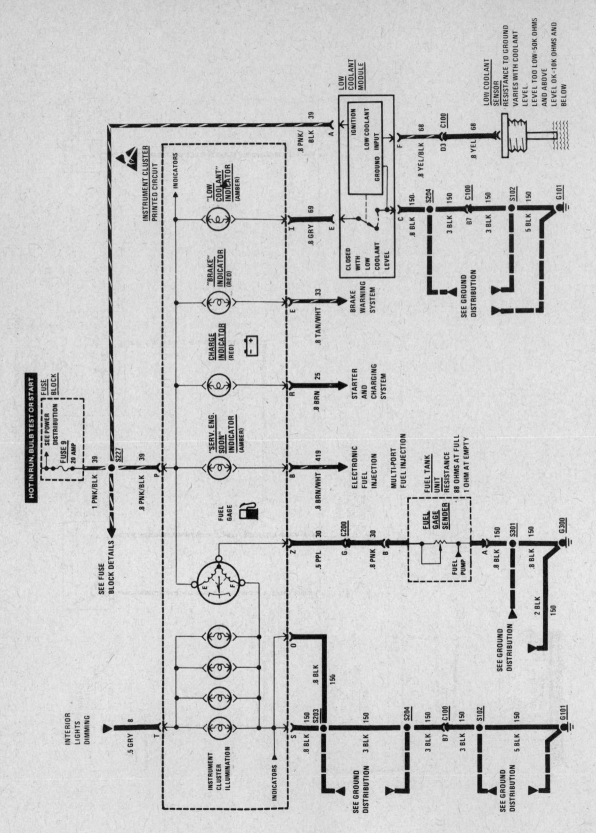

Standard instrument cluster

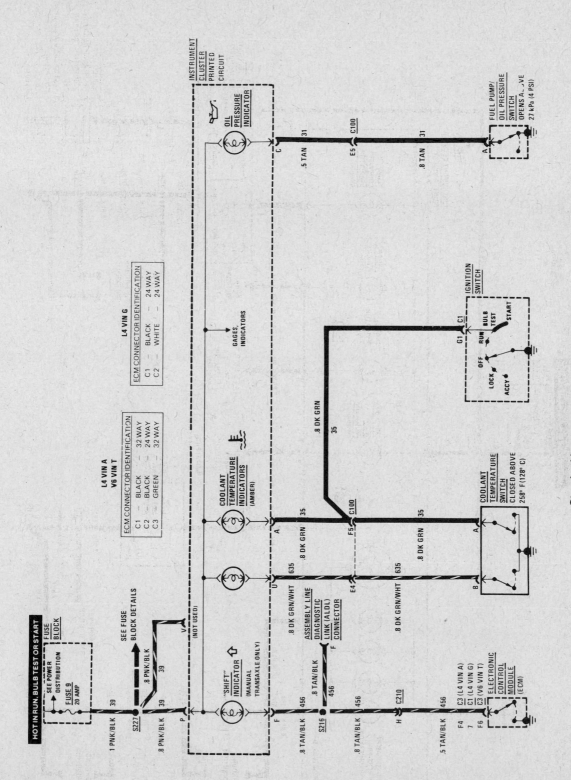

Standard instrument cluster (continued)

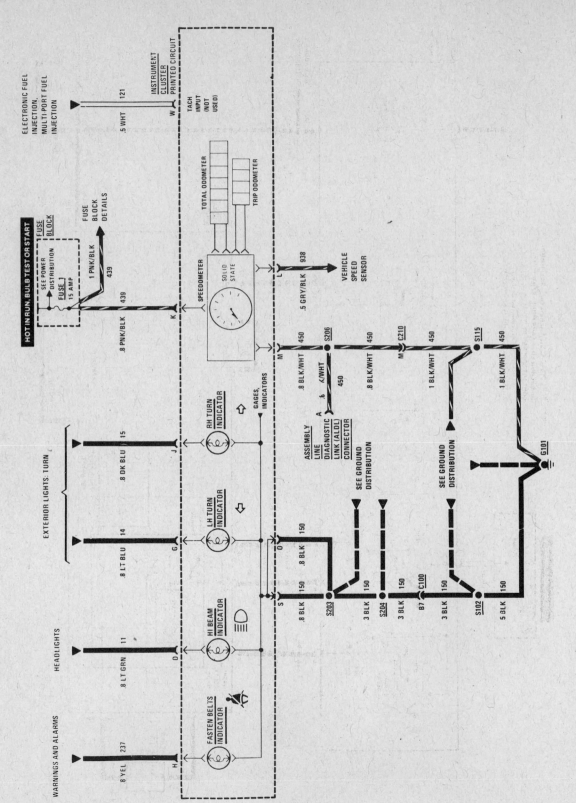

Standard instrument cluster (continued)

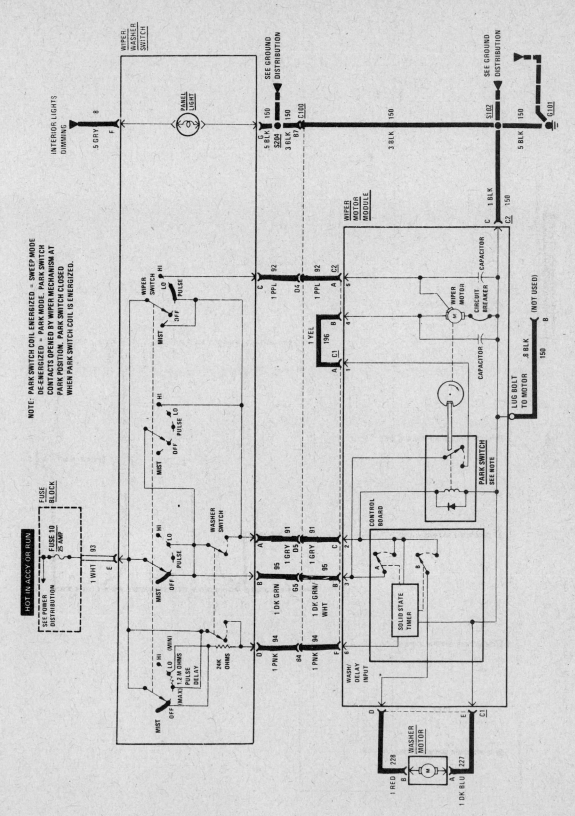

Pulse windshield wiper/washer

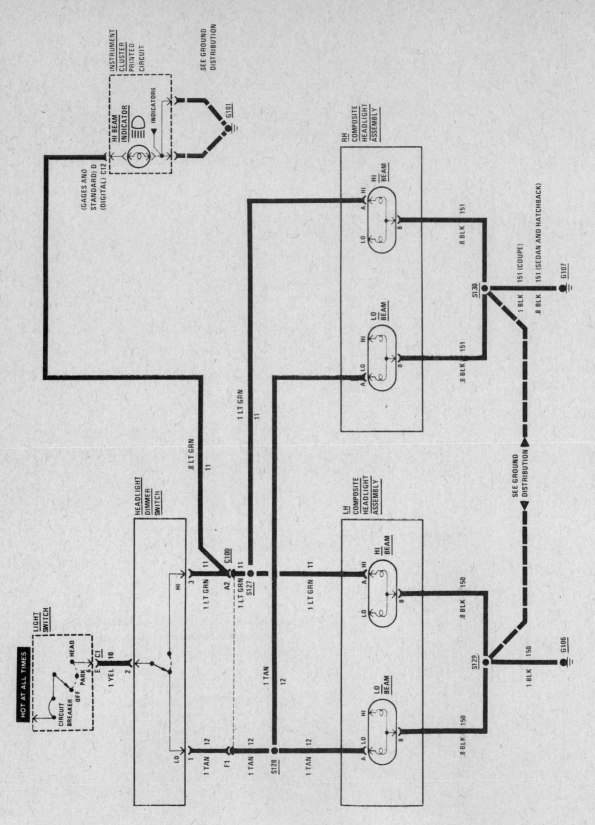

Headlights (without fog lights)

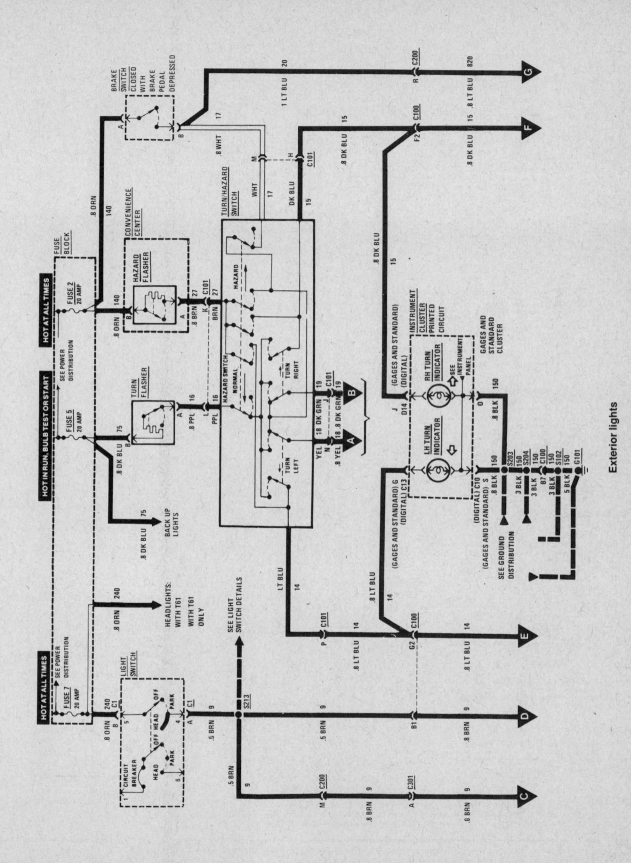

Exterior lights

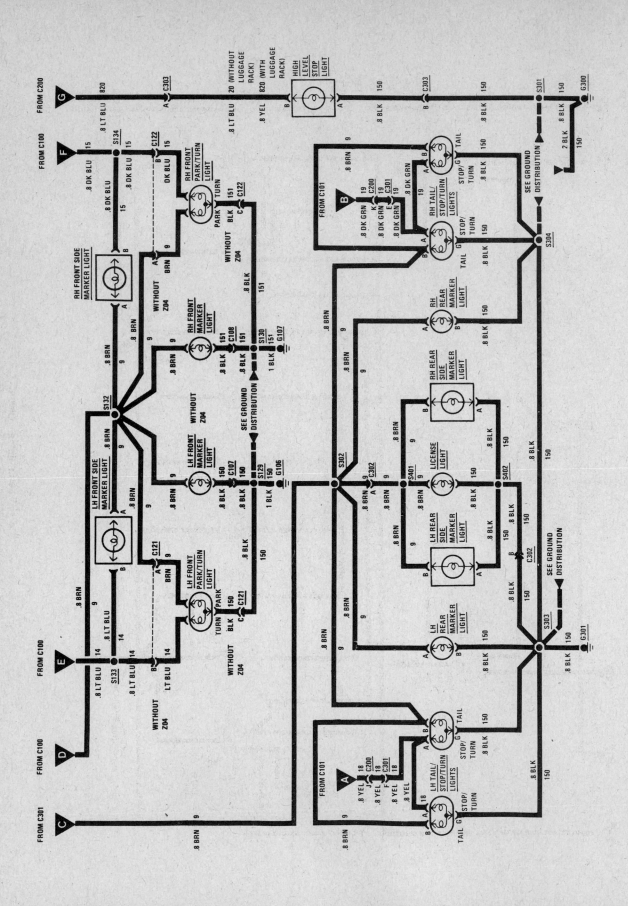

Exterior lights – coupe

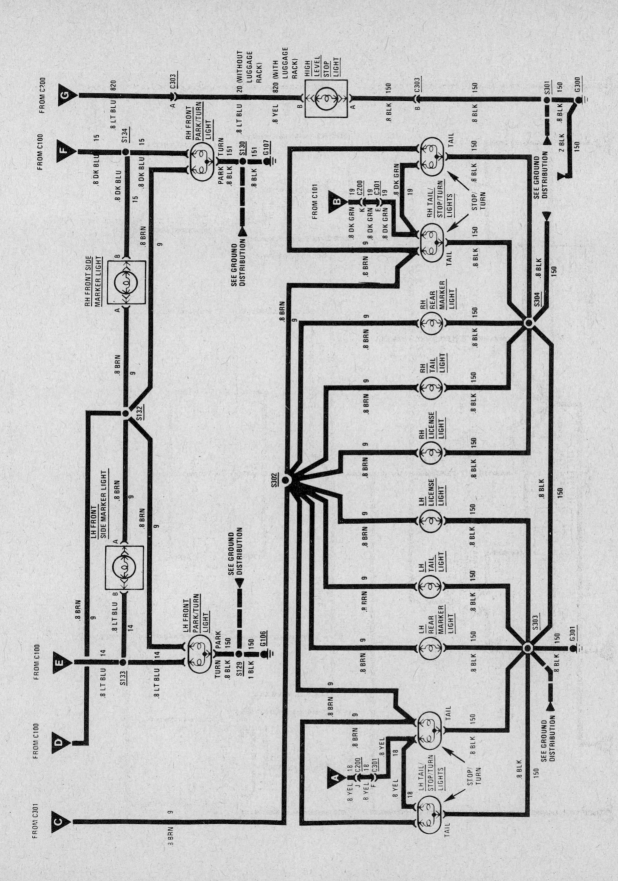

Exterior lights – sedan

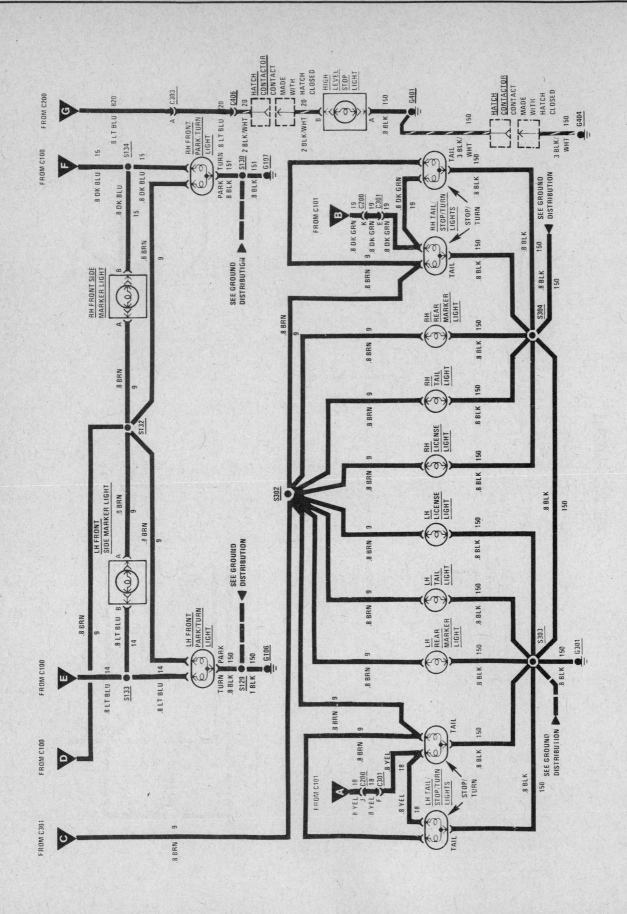

Exterior lights – hatchback

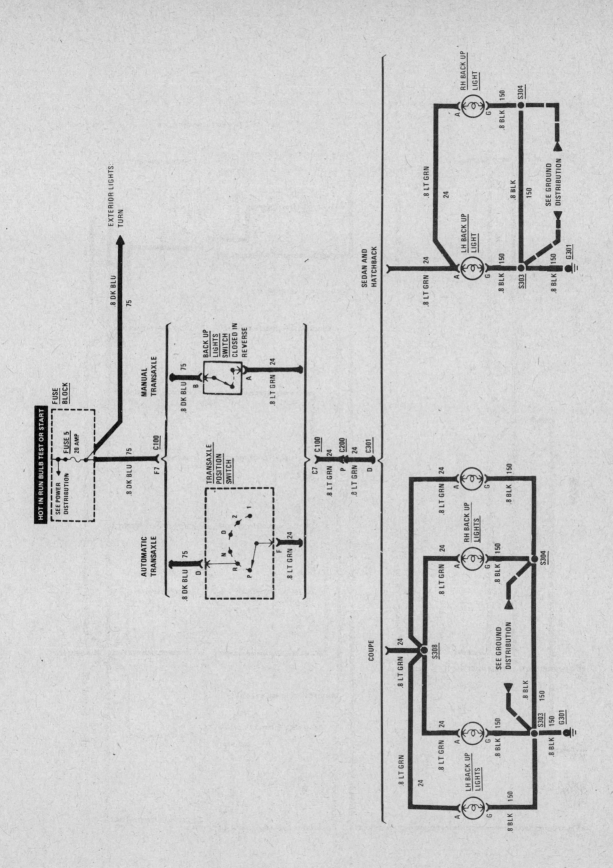

Backup lights

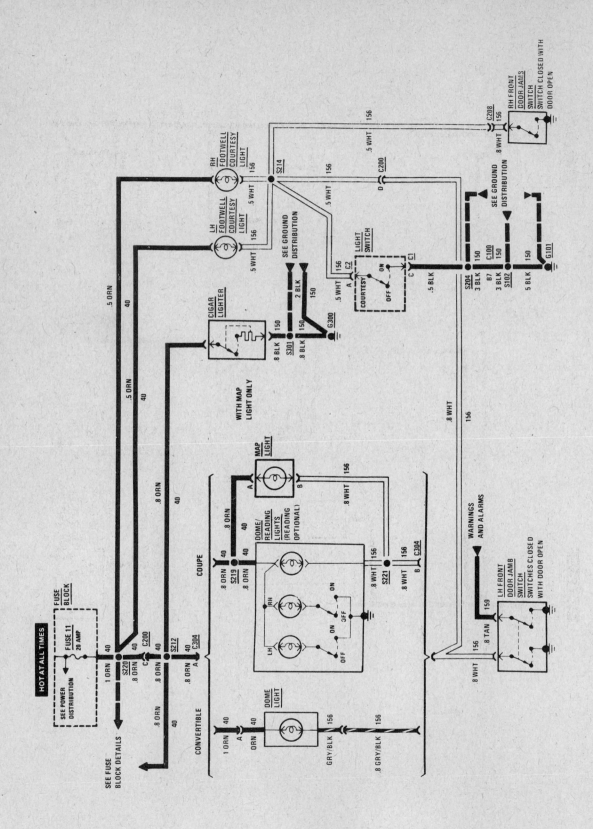

Interior lights – coupe and convertible

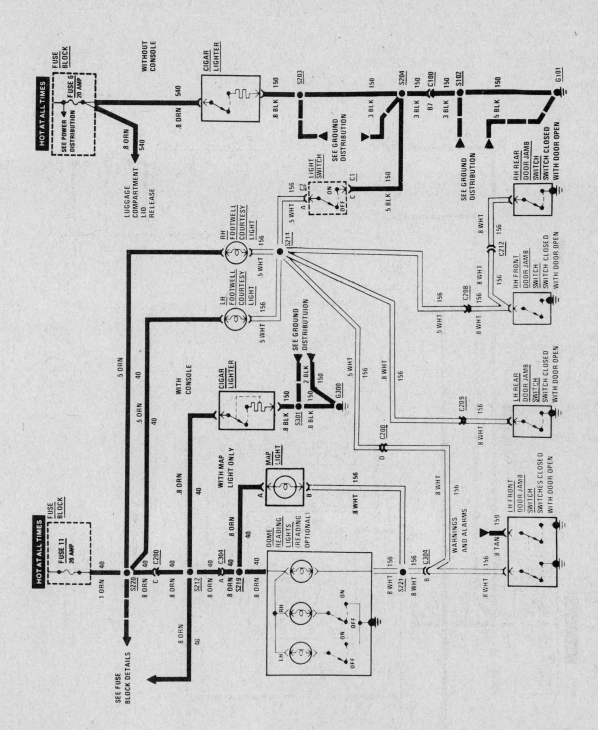

Interior lights – sedan

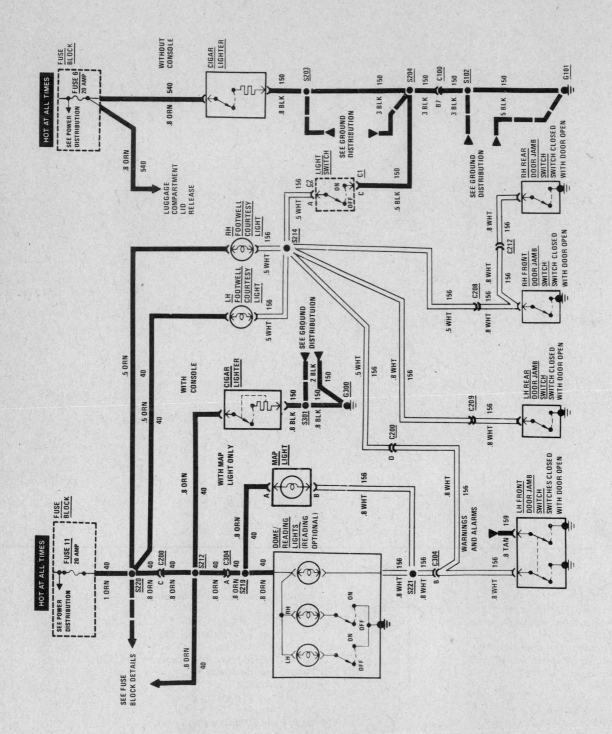

Interior lights – hatchback

Index